THE TIMES

ATLAS
OF THE
WORLD

MINI EDITION

TIMES BOOKS
London

Times Books, 77-85 Fulham Palace Road,
London W6 8JB

The Times is a registered trademark of
Times Newspapers Ltd

First published 1991
Published as The Times Atlas
of the World Mini Edition 1994
Second Edition 1999

Third Edition 2006
Reprinted with changes 2007

Printed and bound in Singapore by Imago

British Library Cataloguing in Publication Data
A catalogue record for this book is available from the British Library

ISBN 978-0-00-720665-0

All mapping in this atlas is generated from Collins Bartholomew™
digital databases. Collins Bartholomew™, the UK's leading
independent geographical information supplier, can provide a
digital, custom, and premium mapping service to a variety of markets.
For further information:
Tel: +44 (0) 141 306 3752
e-mail: collinsbartholomew@harpercollins.co.uk

or visit our website at: www.collinsbartholomew.com

www.harpercollins.co.uk
Visit the book lover's website

Pages	Title	Scale

GEOGRAPHICAL INFORMATION

6–19	**COUNTRIES OF THE WORLD**	
20–21	**OCEANIA PHYSICAL FEATURES**	
22–23	**ASIA PHYSICAL FEATURES**	
24–25	**EUROPE PHYSICAL FEATURES**	
26–27	**AFRICA PHYSICAL FEATURES**	
28–29	**NORTH AMERICA PHYSICAL FEATURES**	
30–31	**SOUTH AMERICA PHYSICAL FEATURES**	
32–33	**OCEANS AND POLES PHYSICAL FEATURES**	
34–35	**CLIMATE**	
36–37	**LAND COVER**	
38–39	**POPULATION**	
40–41	**URBANIZATION**	
42–43	**SYMBOLS AND ABBREVIATIONS**	

WORLD

44–45	**WORLD PHYSICAL FEATURES**	1:170 000 000
46–47	**WORLD COUNTRIES**	1:170 000 000

OCEANIA

48–49	**OCEANIA**	1:70 000 000
50–51	**AUSTRALIA**	1:25 000 000
52–53	**AUSTRALIA SOUTHEAST**	1:10 000 000
54	**NEW ZEALAND**	1:10 000 000

ANTARCTICA

55	**ANTARCTICA**	1:60 000 000

ASIA

56–57	**ASIA**	1:70 000 000
58–59	**SOUTHEAST ASIA**	1:30 000 000
60–61	**MALAYSIA AND INDONESIA WEST**	1:15 000 000
62–63	**CONTINENTAL SOUTHEAST ASIA**	1:15 000 000
64	**PHILIPPINES**	1:15 000 000

4 CONTENTS

Pages	Title	Scale
65	NORTH KOREA AND SOUTH KOREA	1:9 000 000
66–67	JAPAN	1:10 000 000
68–69	CHINA AND MONGOLIA	1:30 000 000
70–71	CHINA Central	1:15 000 000
72–73	SOUTH ASIA	1:20 000 000
74–75	PAKISTAN, INDIA AND BANGLADESH	1:15 000 000
76–77	CENTRAL ASIA	1:20 000 000
78–79	ARABIAN PENINSULA	1:15 000 000
80–81	EAST MEDITERRANEAN	1:15 000 000
82–83	RUSSIAN FEDERATION	1:42 000 000
84–85	**EUROPE**	1:40 000 000
86–87	EUROPEAN RUSSIAN FEDERATION	1:20 000 000
88–89	NORTHEAST EUROPE	1:8 000 000
90–91	UKRAINE AND MOLDOVA	1:8 000 000
92–93	SCANDINAVIA AND ICELAND	1:10 000 000
94–95	BRITISH ISLES	1:8 000 000
96	SCOTLAND	1:4 000 000
97	IRELAND	1:4 000 000
98–99	ENGLAND AND WALES	1:4 000 000
100–101	NORTHWEST EUROPE	1:4 000 000
102–103	CENTRAL EUROPE	1:8 000 000
104–105	FRANCE AND SWITZERLAND	1:8 000 000
106–107	SPAIN AND PORTUGAL	1:8 000 000
108–109	ITALY AND THE BALKANS	1:8 000 000
110–111	GREECE, ROMANIA AND BULGARIA	1:8 000 000
112–113	**AFRICA**	1:60 000 000
114–115	NORTHWEST AFRICA	1:26 000 000

Pages	Title	Scale
116–117	**NORTHEAST AFRICA**	1:26 000 000
118–119	**CENTRAL AFRICA**	1:20 000 000
120–121	**SOUTHERN AFRICA**	1:20 000 000
122–123	**REPUBLIC OF SOUTH AFRICA**	1:10 000 000
124–125	**NORTH AMERICA**	1:70 000 000
126–127	**CANADA**	1:30 000 000
128–129	**CANADA** WEST	1:15 000 000
130–131	**CANADA** EAST	1:15 000 000
132–133	**UNITED STATES OF AMERICA**	1:25 000 000
134–135	**USA** WEST	1:11 000 000
136–137	**USA** NORTH CENTRAL	1:11 000 000
138–139	**USA** SOUTH CENTRAL	1:11 000 000
140–141	**USA** NORTHEAST	1:11 000 000
142–143	**USA** SOUTHEAST	1:11 000 000
144–145	**MEXICO**	1:15 000 000
146–147	**CARIBBEAN**	1:20 000 000
148–149	**SOUTH AMERICA**	1:70 000 000
150–151	**SOUTH AMERICA** NORTH	1:25 000 000
152–153	**SOUTH AMERICA** SOUTH	1:25 000 000
154–155	**BRAZIL** SOUTHEAST	1:10 000 000
	OCEANS	
156–157	**PACIFIC OCEAN**	1:120 000 000
158	**ATLANTIC OCEAN**	1:120 000 000
159	**INDIAN OCEAN**	1:120 000 000
160	**ARCTIC OCEAN**	1:60 000 000
161–256	**INDEX**	

6   COUNTRIES OF THE WORLD

AFGHANISTAN
Islamic State of Afghanistan
Capital Kābul

Area sq km	652 225	Currency	Afghani
Area sq miles	251 825	Languages	Dari, Pushtu,
Population	29 863 000		Uzbek, Turkmen

ALBANIA
Republic of Albania
Capital Tirana (Tiranë)

Area sq km	28 748	Currency	Lek
Area sq miles	11 100	Languages	Albanian, Greek
Population	3 130 000		

ALGERIA
People's Democratic Republic of Algeria
Capital Algiers (Alger)

Area sq km	2 381 741	Currency	Algerian dinar
Area sq miles	919 595	Languages	Arabic, French,
Population	32 854 000		Berber

ANDORRA
Principality of Andorra
Capital Andorra la Vella

Area sq km	465	Currency	Euro
Area sq miles	180	Languages	Spanish,
Population	67 000		Catalan, French

ANGOLA
Republic of Angola
Capital Luanda

Area sq km	1 246 700	Currency	Kwanza
Area sq miles	481 354	Languages	Portuguese,
Population	15 941 000		Bantu, local lang.

ANTIGUA AND BARBUDA
Capital St John's

Area sq km	442	Currency	East Caribbean
Area sq miles	171		dollar
Population	81 000	Languages	English, creole

ARGENTINA
Argentine Republic
Capital Buenos Aires

Area sq km	2 766 889	Currency	Argentinian peso
Area sq miles	1 068 302	Languages	Spanish, Italian,
Population	38 747 000		Amerindian lang.

ARMENIA
Republic of Armenia
Capital Yerevan (Erevan)

Area sq km	29 800	Currency	Dram
Area sq miles	11 506	Languages	Armenian, Azeri
Population	3 016 000		

AUSTRALIA
Commonwealth of Australia
Capital Canberra

Area sq km	7 692 024	Currency	Australian dollar
Area sq miles	2 969 907	Languages	English, Italian,
Population	20 155 000		Greek

AUSTRIA
Republic of Austria
Capital Vienna (Wien)

Area sq km	83 855	Currency	Euro
Area sq miles	32 377	Languages	German,
Population	8 189 000		Croatian, Turkish

AZERBAIJAN
Republic of Azerbaijan
Capital Baku (Bakı)

Area sq km	86 600	Currency	Azerbaijani manat
Area sq miles	33 436	Languages	Azeri, Armenian,
Population	8 411 000		Russian, Lezgian

THE BAHAMAS
Commonwealth of The Bahamas
Capital Nassau

Area sq km	13 939	Currency	Bahamian dollar
Area sq miles	5 382	Languages	English, creole
Population	323 000		

BAHRAIN
Kingdom of Bahrain
Capital Manama (Al Manāmah)

Area sq km	691	Currency	Bahraini dinar
Area sq miles	267	Languages	Arabic, English
Population	727 000		

BANGLADESH
People's Republic of Bangladesh
Capital Dhaka (Dacca)

Area sq km	143 998	Currency	Taka
Area sq miles	55 598	Languages	Bengali, English
Population	141 822 000		

BARBADOS
Capital Bridgetown

Area sq km	430	Currency	Barbados dollar
Area sq miles	166	Languages	English, creole
Population	270 000		

BELARUS
Republic of Belarus
Capital Minsk

Area sq km	207 600	Currency Belarus rouble
Area sq miles	80 155	Languages Belorussian,
Population	9 755 000	Russian

BELGIUM
Kingdom of Belgium
Capital Brussels (Bruxelles)

Area sq km	30 520	Currency Euro
Area sq miles	11 784	Languages Dutch (Flemish),
Population	10 419 000	French (Walloon),
		German

BELIZE
Capital Belmopan

Area sq km	22 965	Currency Belize dollar
Area sq miles	8 867	Languages English, Spanish,
Population	270 000	Mayan, creole

BENIN
Republic of Benin
Capital Porto-Novo

Area sq km	112 620	Currency CFA franc*
Area sq miles	43 483	Languages French, Fon,
Population	8 439 000	Yoruba, Adja,
		local lang.

BHUTAN
Kingdom of Bhutan
Capital Thimphu

Area sq km	46 620	Currency Ngultrum,
Area sq miles	18 000	Indian rupee
Population	2 163 000	Languages Dzongkha,
		Nepali, Assamese

BOLIVIA
Republic of Bolivia
Capital La Paz/Sucre

Area sq km	1 098 581	Currency Boliviano
Area sq miles	424 164	Languages Spanish, Quechua,
Population	9 182 000	Aymara

BOSNIA-HERZEGOVINA
Republic of Bosnia and Herzegovina
Capital Sarajevo

Area sq km	51 130	Currency Marka
Area sq miles	19 741	Languages Bosnian, Serbian,
Population	3 907 000	Croatian

BOTSWANA
Republic of Botswana
Capital Gaborone

Area sq km	581 370	Currency Pula
Area sq miles	224 468	Languages English, Setswana,
Population	1 765 000	Shona, local lang.

BRAZIL
Federative Republic of Brazil
Capital Brasília

Area sq km	8 514 879	Currency Real
Area sq miles	3 287 613	Languages Portuguese
Population	186 405 000	

BRUNEI
State of Brunei Darussalam
Capital Bandar Seri Begawan

Area sq km	5 765	Currency Brunei dollar
Area sq miles	2 226	Languages Malay, English,
Population	374 000	Chinese

BULGARIA
Republic of Bulgaria
Capital Sofia (Sofiya)

Area sq km	110 994	Currency Lev
Area sq miles	42 855	Languages Bulgarian,
Population	7 726 000	Turkish, Romany,
		Macedonian

BURKINA
Democratic Republic of Burkina Faso
Capital Ouagadougou

Area sq km	274 200	Currency CFA franc
Area sq miles	105 869	Languages French, Moore
Population	13 228 000	(Mossi), Fulani,
		local lang.

BURUNDI
Republic of Burundi
Capital Bujumbura

Area sq km	27 835	Currency Burundian franc
Area sq miles	10 747	Languages Kirundi (Hutu,
Population	7 548 000	Tutsi), French

CAMBODIA
Kingdom of Cambodia
Capital Phnom Penh

Area sq km	181 035	Currency Riel
Area sq miles	69 884	Languages Khmer,
Population	14 071 000	Vietnamese

* CFA Communauté Financière Africaine

CAMEROON
Republic of Cameroon
Capital Yaoundé

Area sq km	475 442	**Currency**	CFA franc
Area sq miles	183 569	**Languages**	French, English,
Population	16 322 000		Fang, Bamileke,
			local lang.

CANADA
Capital Ottawa

Area sq km	9 984 670	**Currency**	Canadian dollar
Area sq miles	3 855 103	**Languages**	English, French
Population	32 268 000		

CAPE VERDE
Republic of Cape Verde
Capital Praia

Area sq km	4 033	**Currency**	Cape Verde
Area sq miles	1 557		escudo
Population	507 000	**Languages**	Portuguese, creole

CENTRAL AFRICAN REPUBLIC
Capital Bangui

Area sq km	622 436	**Currency**	CFA franc
Area sq miles	240 324	**Languages**	French, Sango,
Population	4 038 000		Banda, Baya,
			local lang.

CHAD
Republic of Chad
Capital Ndjamena

Area sq km	1 284 000	**Currency**	CFA franc
Area sq miles	495 755	**Languages**	Arabic, French,
Population	9 749 000		Sara, local lang.

CHILE
Republic of Chile
Capital Santiago

Area sq km	756 945	**Currency**	Chilean peso
Area sq miles	292 258	**Languages**	Spanish,
Population	16 295 000		Amerindian lang.

CHINA
People's Republic of China
Capital Beijing (Peking)

Area sq km	9 584 492	**Currency**	Yuan, HK dollar,
Area sq miles	3 700 593		Macau pataca
Population	1 323 345 000	**Languages**	Mandarin, Hsiang,
			Cantonese, Wu,
			regional lang.

COLOMBIA
Republic of Colombia
Capital Bogotá

Area sq km	1 141 748	**Currency**	Colombian peso
Area sq miles	440 831	**Languages**	Spanish,
Population	45 600 000		Amerindian lang.

COMOROS
Union of the Comoros
Capital Moroni

Area sq km	1 862	**Currency**	Comoros franc
Area sq miles	719	**Languages**	Comorian,
Population	798 000		French, Arabic

CONGO
Republic of the Congo
Capital Brazzaville

Area sq km	342 000	**Currency**	CFA franc
Area sq miles	132 047	**Languages**	French, Kongo,
Population	3 999 000		Monokutuba,
			local lang.

**CONGO, DEMOCRATIC
REPUBLIC OF THE**
Capital Kinshasa

Area sq km	2 345 410	**Currency**	Congolese franc
Area sq miles	905 568	**Languages**	French, Lingala,
Population	57 549 000		Swahili, Kongo,
			local lang.

COSTA RICA
Republic of Costa Rica
Capital San José

Area sq km	51 100	**Currency**	Costa Rican colón
Area sq miles	19 730	**Languages**	Spanish
Population	4 327 000		

CÔTE D'IVOIRE
Republic of Côte d'Ivoire
Capital Yamoussoukro

Area sq km	322 463	**Currency**	CFA franc
Area sq miles	124 504	**Languages**	French, creole,
Population	18 154 000		Akan, local lang.

CROATIA
Republic of Croatia
Capital Zagreb

Area sq km	56 538	**Currency**	Kuna
Area sq miles	21 829	**Languages**	Croatian, Serbian
Population	4 551 000		

CUBA
Republic of Cuba
Capital Havana (La Habana)

Area sq km	110 860	**Currency**	Cuban peso
Area sq miles	42 803	**Languages**	Spanish
Population	11 269 000		

CYPRUS
Republic of Cyprus
Capital Nicosia (Lefkosia)

Area sq km	9 251	**Currency**	Cyprus pound
Area sq miles	3 572	**Languages**	Greek, Turkish,
Population	835 000		English

CZECH REPUBLIC
Capital Prague (Praha)

Area sq km	78 864	**Currency**	Czech koruna
Area sq miles	30 450	**Languages**	Czech, Moravian,
Population	10 220 000		Slovak

DENMARK
Kingdom of Denmark
Capital Copenhagen (København)

Area sq km	43 075	**Currency**	Danish krone
Area sq miles	16 631	**Languages**	Danish
Population	5 431 000		

DJIBOUTI
Republic of Djibouti
Capital Djibouti

Area sq km	23 200	**Currency**	Djibouti franc
Area sq miles	8 958	**Languages**	Somali, Afar,
Population	793 000		French, Arabic

DOMINICA
Commonwealth of Dominica
Capital Roseau

Area sq km	750	**Currency**	East Caribbean
Area sq miles	290		dollar
Population	79 000	**Languages**	English, creole

DOMINICAN REPUBLIC
Capital Santo Domingo

Area sq km	48 442	**Currency**	Dominican peso
Area sq miles	18 704	**Languages**	Spanish, creole
Population	8 895 000		

EAST TIMOR
Democratic Republic of Timor-Leste
Capital Dili

Area sq km	14 874	**Currency**	US dollar
Area sq miles	5 743	**Languages**	Portuguese, Tetun,
Population	947 000		English

ECUADOR
Republic of Ecuador
Capital Quito

Area sq km	272 045	**Currency**	US dollar
Area sq miles	105 037	**Languages**	Spanish, Quechua,
Population	13 228 000		and other
			Amerindian lang.

EGYPT
Arab Republic of Egypt
Capital Cairo (Al Qāhirah)

Area sq km	1 000 250	**Currency**	Egyptian pound
Area sq miles	386 199	**Languages**	Arabic
Population	74 033 000		

EL SALVADOR
Republic of El Salvador
Capital San Salvador

Area sq km	21 041	**Currency**	El Salvador colón,
Area sq miles	8 124		US dollar
Population	6 881 000	**Languages**	Spanish

EQUATORIAL GUINEA
Republic of Equatorial Guinea
Capital Malabo

Area sq km	28 051	**Currency**	CFA franc
Area sq miles	10 831	**Languages**	Spanish, French,
Population	504 000		Fang

ERITREA
State of Eritrea
Capital Asmara

Area sq km	117 400	**Currency**	Nakfa
Area sq miles	45 328	**Languages**	Tigrinya, Tigre
Population	4 401 000		

ESTONIA
Republic of Estonia
Capital Tallinn

Area sq km	45 200	**Currency**	Kroon
Area sq miles	17 452	**Languages**	Estonian, Russian
Population	1 330 000		

ETHIOPIA
Federal Democratic Republic of Ethiopia
Capital Addis Ababa (Ādīs Ābeba)

Area sq km	1 133 880	Currency	Birr
Area sq miles	437 794	Languages	Oromo, Amharic,
Population	77 431 000		Tigrinya,
			local lang.

FIJI
Sovereign Democratic Republic of Fiji
Capital Suva

Area sq km	18 330	Currency	Fiji dollar
Area sq miles	7 077	Languages	English, Fijian,
Population	848 000		Hindi

FINLAND
Republic of Finland
Capital Helsinki (Helsingfors)

Area sq km	338 145	Currency	Euro
Area sq miles	130 559	Languages	Finnish, Swedish
Population	5 249 000		

FRANCE
French Republic
Capital Paris

Area sq km	543 965	Currency	Euro
Area sq miles	210 026	Languages	French, Arabic
Population	60 496 000		

GABON
Gabonese Republic
Capital Libreville

Area sq km	267 667	Currency	CFA franc
Area sq miles	103 347	Languages	French, Fang,
Population	1 384 000		local lang.

THE GAMBIA
Republic of The Gambia
Capital Banjul

Area sq km	11 295	Currency	Dalasi
Area sq miles	4 361	Languages	English, Malinke,
Population	1 517 000		Fulani, Wolof

Gaza
semi-autonomous region
Capital Gaza

Area sq km	363	Currency	Israeli shekel
Area sq miles	140	Languages	Arabic
Population	1 406 423		

GEORGIA
Republic of Georgia
Capital T'bilisi

Area sq km	69 700	Currency	Lari
Area sq miles	26 911	Languages	Georgian, Russian,
Population	4 474 000		Armenian, Azeri,
			Ossetian, Abkhaz

GERMANY
Federal Republic of Germany
Capital Berlin

Area sq km	357 022	Currency	Euro
Area sq miles	137 849	Languages	German, Turkish
Population	82 689 000		

GHANA
Republic of Ghana
Capital Accra

Area sq km	238 537	Currency	Cedi
Area sq miles	92 100	Languages	English, Hausa,
Population	22 113 000		Akan, local lang.

GREECE
Hellenic Republic
Capital Athens (Athina)

Area sq km	131 957	Currency	Euro
Area sq miles	50 949	Languages	Greek
Population	11 120 000		

GRENADA
Capital St George's

Area sq km	378	Currency	East Caribbean
Area sq miles	146		dollar
Population	103 000	Languages	English, creole

GUATEMALA
Republic of Guatemala
Capital Guatemala City

Area sq km	108 890	Currency	Quetzal, US dollar
Area sq miles	42 043	Languages	Spanish,
Population	12 599 000		Mayan lang.

GUINEA
Republic of Guinea
Capital Conakry

Area sq km	245 857	Currency	Guinea franc
Area sq miles	94 926	Languages	French, Fulani,
Population	9 402 000		Malinke,
			local lang.

GUINEA-BISSAU
Republic of Guinea-Bissau
Capital Bissau

Area sq km	36 125	Currency	CFA franc
Area sq miles	13 948	Languages	Portuguese,
Population	1 586 000		crioulo, local lang.

GUYANA
Co-operative Republic of Guyana
Capital Georgetown

Area sq km	214 969	Currency	Guyana dollar
Area sq miles	83 000	Languages	English, creole,
Population	751 000		Amerindian lang.

HAITI
Republic of Haiti
Capital Port-au-Prince

Area sq km	27 750	Currency	Gourde
Area sq miles	10 714	Languages	French, creole
Population	8 528 000		

HONDURAS
Republic of Honduras
Capital Tegucigalpa

Area sq km	112 088	Currency	Lempira
Area sq miles	43 277	Languages	Spanish,
Population	7 205 000		Amerindian lang.

HUNGARY
Republic of Hungary
Capital Budapest

Area sq km	93 030	Currency	Forint
Area sq miles	35 919	Languages	Hungarian
Population	10 098 000		

ICELAND
Republic of Iceland
Capital Reykjavík

Area sq km	102 820	Currency	Icelandic króna
Area sq miles	39 699	Languages	Icelandic
Population	295 000		

INDIA
Republic of India
Capital New Delhi

Area sq km	3 064 898	Currency	Indian rupee
Area sq miles	1 183 364	Languages	Hindi, English,
Population	1 103 371 000		many regional
			lang.

INDONESIA
Republic of Indonesia
Capital Jakarta

Area sq km	1 919 445	Currency	Rupiah
Area sq miles	741 102	Languages	Indonesian,
Population	222 781 000		local lang.

IRAN
Islamic Republic of Iran
Capital Tehrān

Area sq km	1 648 000	Currency	Iranian rial
Area sq miles	636 296	Languages	Farsi, Azeri,
Population	69 515 000		Kurdish,
			regional lang.

IRAQ
Republic of Iraq
Capital Baghdād

Area sq km	438 317	Currency	Iraqi dinar
Area sq miles	169 235	Languages	Arabic, Kurdish,
Population	28 807 000		Turkmen

IRELAND
Capital Dublin (Baile Átha Cliath)

Area sq km	70 282	Currency	Euro
Area sq miles	27 136	Languages	English, Irish
Population	4 148 000		

ISRAEL
State of Israel
Capital Jerusalem* (Yerushalayim) (El Quds)

Area sq km	20 770	Currency	Shekel
Area sq miles	8 019	Languages	Hebrew, Arabic
Population	6 725 000		

* De facto capital. Disputed.

ITALY
Italian Republic
Capital Rome (Roma)

Area sq km	301 245	Currency	Euro
Area sq miles	116 311	Languages	Italian
Population	58 093 000		

JAMAICA
Capital Kingston

Area sq km	10 991	Currency	Jamaican dollar
Area sq miles	4 244	Languages	English, creole
Population	2 651 000		

Jammu and Kashmir
Disputed territory (India/Pakistan/China)
Capital Srinagar

Area sq km	222 236		
Area sq miles	85 806		
Population	13 000 000		

JAPAN
Capital Tōkyō

Area sq km	377 727	Currency	Yen
Area sq miles	145 841	Languages	Japanese
Population	128 085 000		

JORDAN
Hashemite Kingdom of Jordan
Capital 'Ammān

Area sq km	89 206	Currency	Jordanian dinar
Area sq miles	34 443	Languages	Arabic
Population	5 703 000		

KAZAKHSTAN
Republic of Kazakhstan
Capital Astana (Akmola)

Area sq km	2 717 300	Currency	Tenge
Area sq miles	1 049 155	Languages	Kazakh, Russian, Ukrainian, German, Uzbek, Tatar
Population	14 825 000		

KENYA
Republic of Kenya
Capital Nairobi

Area sq km	582 646	Currency	Kenyan shilling
Area sq miles	224 961	Languages	Swahili, English, local lang.
Population	34 256 000		

KIRIBATI
Republic of Kiribati
Capital Bairiki

Area sq km	717	Currency	Australian dollar
Area sq miles	277	Languages	Gilbertese, English
Population	99 000		

KUWAIT
State of Kuwait
Capital Kuwait (Al Kuwayt)

Area sq km	17 818	Currency	Kuwaiti dinar
Area sq miles	6 880	Languages	Arabic
Population	2 687 000		

KYRGYZSTAN
Kyrgyz Republic
Capital Bishkek (Frunze)

Area sq km	198 500	Currency	Kyrgyz som
Area sq miles	76 641	Languages	Kyrgyz, Russian, Uzbek
Population	5 264 000		

LAOS
Lao People's Democratic Republic
Capital Vientiane (Viangchan)

Area sq km	236 800	Currency	Kip
Area sq miles	91 429	Languages	Lao, local lang.
Population	5 924 000		

LATVIA
Republic of Latvia
Capital Rīga

Area sq km	63 700	Currency	Lats
Area sq miles	24 595	Languages	Latvian, Russian
Population	2 307 000		

LEBANON
Republic of Lebanon
Capital Beirut (Beyrouth)

Area sq km	10 452	Currency	Lebanese pound
Area sq miles	4 036	Languages	Arabic, Armenian, French
Population	3 577 000		

LESOTHO
Kingdom of Lesotho
Capital Maseru

Area sq km	30 355	Currency	Loti, S. African rand
Area sq miles	11 720	Languages	Sesotho, English, Zulu
Population	1 795 000		

LIBERIA
Republic of Liberia
Capital Monrovia

Area sq km	111 369	Currency	Liberian dollar
Area sq miles	43 000	Languages	English, creole, local lang.
Population	3 283 000		

LIBYA
Great Socialist People's Libyan Arab Jamahiriya
Capital Tripoli (Ṭarābulus)

Area sq km	1 759 540	Currency	Libyan dinar
Area sq miles	679 362	Languages	Arabic, Berber
Population	5 853 000		

LIECHTENSTEIN
Principality of Liechtenstein
Capital Vaduz

Area sq km	160	Currency Swiss franc
Area sq miles	62	Languages German
Population	35 000	

LITHUANIA
Republic of Lithuania
Capital Vilnius

Area sq km	65 200	Currency Litas
Area sq miles	25 174	Languages Lithuanian,
Population	3 431 000	Russian, Polish

LUXEMBOURG
Grand Duchy of Luxembourg
Capital Luxembourg

Area sq km	2 586	Currency Euro
Area sq miles	998	Languages Letzeburgish,
Population	465 000	German, French

MACEDONIA (F.Y.R.O.M.)
Republic of Macedonia
Capital Skopje

Area sq km	25 713	Currency Macedonian denar
Area sq miles	9 928	Languages Macedonian,
Population	2 034 000	Albanian, Turkish

MADAGASCAR
Republic of Madagascar
Capital Antananarivo

Area sq km	587 041	Currency Malagasy ariary,
Area sq miles	226 658	Malagasy franc
Population	18 606 000	Languages Malagasy, French

MALAWI
Republic of Malawi
Capital Lilongwe

Area sq km	118 484	Currency Malawian kwacha
Area sq miles	45 747	Languages Chichewa,
Population	12 884 000	English, local lang.

MALAYSIA
Federation of Malaysia
Capital Kuala Lumpur/Putrajaya

Area sq km	332 965	Currency Ringgit
Area sq miles	128 559	Languages Malay, English,
Population	25 347 000	Chinese, Tamil, local lang.

MALDIVES
Republic of the Maldives
Capital Male

Area sq km	298	Currency Rufiyaa
Area sq miles	115	Languages Divehi
Population	329 000	(Maldivian)

MALI
Republic of Mali
Capital Bamako

Area sq km	1 240 140	Currency CFA franc
Area sq miles	478 821	Languages French, Bambara,
Population	13 518 000	local lang.

MALTA
Republic of Malta
Capital Valletta

Area sq km	316	Currency Maltese lira
Area sq miles	122	Languages Maltese, English
Population	402 000	

MARSHALL ISLANDS
Republic of the Marshall Islands
Capital Delap-Uliga-Djarrit

Area sq km	181	Currency US dollar
Area sq miles	70	Languages English,
Population	62 000	Marshallese

MAURITANIA
Islamic Arab and African Rep. of Mauritania
Capital Nouakchott

Area sq km	1 030 700	Currency Ouguiya
Area sq miles	397 955	Languages Arabic, French,
Population	3 069 000	local lang.

MAURITIUS
Republic of Mauritius
Capital Port Louis

Area sq km	2 040	Currency Mauritius rupee
Area sq miles	788	Languages English, creole,
Population	1 245 000	Hindi, Bhojpurī, French

MEXICO
United Mexican States
Capital Mexico City

Area sq km	1 972 545	Currency Mexican peso
Area sq miles	761 604	Languages Spanish,
Population	107 029 000	Amerindian lang.

MICRONESIA, FEDERATED STATES OF
Capital Palikir

Area sq km	701	Currency	US dollar
Area sq miles	271	Languages	English, Chuukese, Pohnpeian, local lang.
Population	110 000		

MOLDOVA
Republic of Moldova
Capital Chişinău (Kishinev)

Area sq km	33 700	Currency	Moldovan leu
Area sq miles	13 012	Languages	Romanian, Ukrainian, Gagauz, Russian
Population	4 206 000		

MONACO
Principality of Monaco
Capital Monaco-Ville

Area sq km	2	Currency	Euro
Area sq miles	1	Languages	French, Monegasque, Italian
Population	35 000		

MONGOLIA
Capital Ulan Bator (Ulaanbaatar)

Area sq km	1 565 000	Currency	Tugrik (tögrög)
Area sq miles	604 250	Languages	Khalka (Mongolian), Kazakh, local lang.
Population	2 646 000		

MONTENEGRO
Republic of Montenegro
Capital Podgorica

Area sq km	13 812	Currency	Euro
Area sq miles	5 333	Languages	Serbian (Montenegrin), Albanian
Population	620 145		

MOROCCO
Kingdom of Morocco
Capital Rabat

Area sq km	446 550	Currency	Moroccan dirham
Area sq miles	172 414	Languages	Arabic, Berber, French
Population	31 478 000		

MOZAMBIQUE
Republic of Mozambique
Capital Maputo

Area sq km	799 380	Currency	Metical
Area sq miles	308 642	Languages	Portuguese, Makua, Tsonga, local lang.
Population	19 792 000		

MYANMAR
Union of Myanmar
Capital Naypyidaw/Rangoon (Yangôn)

Area sq km	676 577	Currency	Kyat
Area sq miles	261 228	Languages	Burmese, Shan, Karen, local lang.
Population	50 519 000		

NAMIBIA
Republic of Namibia
Capital Windhoek

Area sq km	824 292	Currency	Namibian dollar
Area sq miles	318 261	Languages	English, Afrikaans, German, Ovambo, local lang.
Population	2 031 000		

NAURU
Republic of Nauru
Capital Yaren

Area sq km	21	Currency	Australian dollar
Area sq miles	8	Languages	Nauruan, English
Population	14 000		

NEPAL
Kingdom of Nepal
Capital Kathmandu

Area sq km	147 181	Currency	Nepalese rupee
Area sq miles	56 827	Languages	Nepali, Maithili, Bhojpuri, English, local lang.
Population	27 133 000		

NETHERLANDS
Kingdom of the Netherlands
Capital Amsterdam/The Hague ('s-Gravenhage)

Area sq km	41 526	Currency	Euro
Area sq miles	16 033	Languages	Dutch, Frisian
Population	16 299 000		

NEW ZEALAND
Capital Wellington

Area sq km	270 534	Currency	New Zealand dollar
Area sq miles	104 454	Languages	English, Maori
Population	4 028 000		

NICARAGUA
Republic of Nicaragua
Capital Managua

Area sq km	130 000	Currency	Córdoba
Area sq miles	50 193	Languages	Spanish, Amerindian lang.
Population	5 487 000		

NIGER
Republic of Niger
Capital Niamey

Area sq km	1 267 000	Currency	CFA franc
Area sq miles	489 191	Languages	French, Hausa,
Population	13 957 000		Fulani, local lang.

NIGERIA
Federal Republic of Nigeria
Capital Abuja

Area sq km	923 768	Currency	Naira
Area sq miles	356 669	Languages	English, Hausa,
Population	131 530 000		Yoruba, Ibo,
			Fulani, local lang.

NORTH KOREA
People's Democratic Republic of Korea
Capital P'yŏngyang

Area sq km	120 538	Currency	North Korean won
Area sq miles	46 540	Languages	Korean
Population	22 488 000		

NORWAY
Kingdom of Norway
Capital Oslo

Area sq km	323 878	Currency	Norwegian krone
Area sq miles	125 050	Languages	Norwegian
Population	4 620 000		

OMAN
Sultanate of Oman
Capital Muscat (Masqaṭ)

Area sq km	309 500	Currency	Omani riyal
Area sq miles	119 499	Languages	Arabic, Baluchi,
Population	2 567 000		Indian lang.

PAKISTAN
Islamic Republic of Pakistan
Capital Islamabad

Area sq km	803 940	Currency	Pakistani rupee
Area sq miles	310 403	Languages	Urdu, Punjabi,
Population	157 935 000		Sindhi, Pushtu
			English

PALAU
Republic of Palau
Capital Melekeok

Area sq km	497	Currency	US dollar
Area sq miles	192	Languages	Palauan, English
Population	20 000		

PANAMA
Republic of Panama
Capital Panama City

Area sq km	77 082	Currency	Balboa
Area sq miles	29 762	Languages	Spanish, English,
Population	3 232 000		Amerindian lang.

PAPUA NEW GUINEA
Independent State of Papua New Guinea
Capital Port Moresby

Area sq km	462 840	Currency	Kina
Area sq miles	178 704	Languages	English,
Population	5 887 000		Tok Pisin (creole),
			local lang.

PARAGUAY
Republic of Paraguay
Capital Asunción

Area sq km	406 752	Currency	Guaraní
Area sq miles	157 048	Languages	Spanish, Guaraní
Population	6 158 000		

PERU
Republic of Peru
Capital Lima

Area sq km	1 285 216	Currency	Sol
Area sq miles	496 225	Languages	Spanish, Quechua,
Population	27 968 000		Aymara

PHILIPPINES
Republic of the Philippines
Capital Manila

Area sq km	300 000	Currency	Philippine peso
Area sq miles	115 831	Languages	English, Filipino,
Population	83 054 000		Tagalog, Cebuano,
			local lang.

POLAND
Polish Republic
Capital Warsaw (Warszawa)

Area sq km	312 683	Currency	Złoty
Area sq miles	120 728	Languages	Polish, German
Population	38 530 000		

PORTUGAL
Portuguese Republic
Capital Lisbon (Lisboa)

Area sq km	88 940	Currency	Euro
Area sq miles	34 340	Languages	Portuguese
Population	10 495 000		

QATAR
State of Qatar
Capital Doha (Ad Dawḥah)

Area sq km	11 437	**Currency** Qatari riyal
Area sq miles	4 416	**Languages** Arabic
Population	813 000	

ROMANIA
Capital Bucharest (Bucureşti)

Area sq km	237 500	**Currency** Romanian leu
Area sq miles	91 699	**Languages** Romanian,
Population	21 711 000	Hungarian

RUSSIAN FEDERATION
Capital Moscow (Moskva)

Area sq km	17 075 400	**Currency** Russian rouble
Area sq miles	6 592 849	**Languages** Russian, Tatar,
Population	143 202 000	Ukrainian, local lang.

RWANDA
Republic of Rwanda
Capital Kigali

Area sq km	26 338	**Currency** Rwandan franc
Area sq miles	10 169	**Languages** Kinyarwanda,
Population	9 038 000	French, English

ST KITTS AND NEVIS
Federation of St Kitts and Nevis
Capital Basseterre

Area sq km	261	**Currency** East Caribbean
Area sq miles	101	dollar
Population	43 000	**Languages** English, creole

ST LUCIA
Capital Castries

Area sq km	616	**Currency** East Caribbean
Area sq miles	238	dollar
Population	161 000	**Languages** English, creole

ST VINCENT AND THE GRENADINES
Capital Kingstown

Area sq km	389	**Currency** East Caribbean
Area sq miles	150	dollar
Population	119 000	**Languages** English, creole

SAMOA
Independent State of Samoa
Capital Apia

Area sq km	2 831	**Currency** Tala
Area sq miles	1 093	**Languages** Samoan, English
Population	185 000	

SAN MARINO
Republic of San Marino
Capital San Marino

Area sq km	61	**Currency** Euro
Area sq miles	24	**Languages** Italian
Population	28 000	

SÃO TOMÉ AND PRÍNCIPE
Democratic Rep. of São Tomé and Príncipe
Capital São Tomé

Area sq km	964	**Currency** Dobra
Area sq miles	372	**Languages** Portuguese, creole
Population	157 000	

SAUDI ARABIA
Kingdom of Saudi Arabia
Capital Riyadh (Ar Riyāḍ)

Area sq km	2 200 000	**Currency** Saudi Arabian
Area sq miles	849 425	riyal
Population	24 573 000	**Languages** Arabic

SENEGAL
Republic of Senegal
Capital Dakar

Area sq km	196 720	**Currency** CFA franc
Area sq miles	75 954	**Languages** French, Wolof,
Population	11 658 000	Fulani, local lang.

SERBIA
Republic of Serbia
Capital Belgrade (Beograd)

Area sq km	88 361	**Currency** Serbian dinar,
Area sq miles	34 116	Euro
Population	9 379 437	**Languages** Serbian, Albanian,
		Hungarian

SEYCHELLES
Republic of Seychelles
Capital Victoria

Area sq km	455	**Currency** Seychelles rupee
Area sq miles	176	**Languages** English, French,
Population	81 000	creole

SIERRA LEONE
Republic of Sierra Leone
Capital Freetown

Area sq km	71 740	**Currency** Leone
Area sq miles	27 699	**Languages** English, creole,
Population	5 525 000	Mende, Temne, local lang.

SINGAPORE
Republic of Singapore
Capital Singapore

Area sq km	639	**Currency**	Singapore dollar
Area sq miles	247	**Languages**	Chinese, English,
Population	4 326 000		Malay, Tamil

SLOVAKIA
Slovak Republic
Capital Bratislava

Area sq km	49 035	**Currency**	Slovakian koruna
Area sq miles	18 933	**Languages**	Slovak,
Population	5 401 000		Hungarian, Czech

SLOVENIA
Republic of Slovenia
Capital Ljubljana

Area sq km	20 251	**Currency**	Tólar
Area sq miles	7 819	**Languages**	Slovene, Croatian,
Population	1 967 000		Serbian

SOLOMON ISLANDS
Capital Honiara

Area sq km	28 370	**Currency**	Solomon Islands
Area sq miles	10 954		dollar
Population	478 000	**Languages**	English, creole,
			local lang.

SOMALIA
Somali Democratic Republic
Capital Mogadishu (Muqdisho)

Area sq km	637 657	**Currency**	Somali shilling
Area sq miles	246 201	**Languages**	Somali, Arabic
Population	8 228 000		

SOUTH AFRICA, REPUBLIC OF
Capital Pretoria (Tshwane)/Cape Town

Area sq km	1 219 090	**Currency**	Rand
Area sq miles	470 693	**Languages**	Afrikaans,
Population	47 432 000		English, nine
			official local lang.

SOUTH KOREA
Republic of Korea
Capital Seoul (Sŏul)

Area sq km	99 274	**Currency**	South Korean
Area sq miles	38 330		won
Population	47 817 000	**Languages**	Korean

SPAIN
Kingdom of Spain
Capital Madrid

Area sq km	504 782	**Currency**	Euro
Area sq miles	194 897	**Languages**	Castilian, Catalan,
Population	43 064 000		Galician, Basque

SRI LANKA
Democratic Socialist Republic of Sri Lanka
Capital Sri Jayewardenepura Kotte

Area sq km	65 610	**Currency**	Sri Lankan rupee
Area sq miles	25 332	**Languages**	Sinhalese,
Population	20 743 000		Tamil, English

SUDAN
Republic of the Sudan
Capital Khartoum

Area sq km	2 505 813	**Currency**	Sudanese dinar
Area sq miles	967 500	**Languages**	Arabic, Dinka,
Population	36 233 000		Nubian, Beja,
			Nuer, local lang.

SURINAME
Republic of Suriname
Capital Paramaribo

Area sq km	163 820	**Currency**	Suriname guilder
Area sq miles	63 251	**Languages**	Dutch,
Population	449 000		Surinamese,
			English, Hindi

SWAZILAND
Kingdom of Swaziland
Capital Mbabane

Area sq km	17 364	**Currency**	Emalangeni,
Area sq miles	6 704		South African
Population	1 032 000		rand
		Languages	Swazi, English

SWEDEN
Kingdom of Sweden
Capital Stockholm

Area sq km	449 964	**Currency**	Swedish krona
Area sq miles	173 732	**Languages**	Swedish
Population	9 041 000		

SWITZERLAND
Swiss Confederation
Capital Bern (Berne)

Area sq km	41 293	**Currency**	Swiss franc
Area sq miles	15 943	**Languages**	German, French,
Population	7 252 000		Italian, Romansch

SYRIA
Syrian Arab Republic
Capital Damascus (Dimashq)

Area sq km	185 180	**Currency**	Syrian pound
Area sq miles	71 498	**Languages**	Arabic, Kurdish,
Population	19 043 000		Armenian

TAIWAN
Republic of China
Capital T'aipei

Area sq km	36 179	**Currency**	Taiwan dollar
Area sq miles	13 969	**Languages**	Mandarin, Min,
Population	22 858 000		Hakka, local lang.

TAJIKISTAN
Republic of Tajikistan
Capital Dushanbe

Area sq km	143 100	**Currency**	Somoni
Area sq miles	55 251	**Languages**	Tajik, Uzbek,
Population	6 507 000		Russian

TANZANIA
United Republic of Tanzania
Capital Dodoma

Area sq km	945 087	**Currency**	Tanzanian shilling
Area sq miles	364 900	**Languages**	Swahili, English,
Population	38 329 000		Nyamwezi,
			local lang.

THAILAND
Kingdom of Thailand
Capital Bangkok (Krung Thep)

Area sq km	513 115	**Currency**	Baht
Area sq miles	198 115	**Languages**	Thai, Lao,
Population	64 233 000		Chinese, Malay,
			Mon-Khmer lang.

TOGO
Republic of Togo
Capital Lomé

Area sq km	56 785	**Currency**	CFA franc
Area sq miles	21 925	**Languages**	French, Ewe,
Population	6 145 000		Kabre, local lang.

TONGA
Kingdom of Tonga
Capital Nuku'alofa

Area sq km	748	**Currency**	Pa'anga
Area sq miles	289	**Languages**	Tongan, English
Population	102 000		

TRINIDAD AND TOBAGO
Republic of Trinidad and Tobago
Capital Port of Spain

Area sq km	5 130	**Currency**	Trinidad and
Area sq miles	1 981		Tobago dollar
Population	1 305 000	**Languages**	English, creole,
			Hindi

TUNISIA
Tunisian Republic
Capital Tunis

Area sq km	164 150	**Currency**	Tunisian dinar
Area sq miles	63 379	**Languages**	Arabic, French
Population	10 102 000		

TURKEY
Republic of Turkey
Capital Ankara

Area sq km	779 452	**Currency**	Turkish lira
Area sq miles	300 948	**Languages**	Turkish, Kurdish
Population	73 193 000		

TURKMENISTAN
Republic of Turkmenistan
Capital Aşgabat (Ashkhabad)

Area sq km	488 100	**Currency**	Turkmen manat
Area sq miles	188 456	**Languages**	Turkmen, Uzbek,
Population	4 833 000		Russian

TUVALU
Capital Vaiaku

Area sq km	25	**Currency**	Australian dollar
Area sq miles	10	**Languages**	Tuvaluan, English
Population	10 000		

UGANDA
Republic of Uganda
Capital Kampala

Area sq km	241 038	**Currency**	Ugandan shilling
Area sq miles	93 065	**Languages**	English, Swahili,
Population	28 816 000		Luganda,
			local lang.

UKRAINE
Capital Kiev (Kyiv)

Area sq km	603 700	**Currency**	Hryvnia
Area sq miles	233 090	**Languages**	Ukrainian,
Population	46 481 000		Russian

UNITED ARAB EMIRATES
Federation of Emirates
Capital Abu Dhabi (Abū Ẓabī)

Area sq km	77 700	**Currency** UAE dirham
Area sq miles	30 000	**Languages** Arabic, English
Population	4 496 000	

UNITED KINGDOM
United Kingdom of Great Britain and
Northern Ireland
Capital London

Area sq km	243 609	**Currency** Pound sterling
Area sq miles	94 058	**Languages** English, Welsh,
Population	59 668 000	Gaelic

UNITED STATES OF AMERICA
Capital Washington

Area sq km	9 826 635	**Currency** US dollar
Area sq miles	3 794 085	**Languages** English, Spanish
Population	298 213 000	

URUGUAY
Oriental Republic of Uruguay
Capital Montevideo

Area sq km	176 215	**Currency** Uruguayan peso
Area sq miles	68 037	**Languages** Spanish
Population	3 463 000	

UZBEKISTAN
Republic of Uzbekistan
Capital Toshkent

Area sq km	447 400	**Currency** Uzbek som
Area sq miles	172 742	**Languages** Uzbek, Russian,
Population	26 593 000	Tajik, Kazakh

VANUATU
Republic of Vanuatu
Capital Port Vila

Area sq km	12 190	**Currency** Vatu
Area sq miles	4 707	**Languages** English,
Population	211 000	Bislama (creole),
		French

VATICAN CITY
Vatican City State
Capital Vatican City

Area sq km	0.5	**Currency** Euro
Area sq miles	0.2	**Languages** Italian
Population	552	

VENEZUELA
Republic of Venezuela
Capital Caracas

Area sq km	912 050	**Currency** Bolívar
Area sq miles	352 144	**Languages** Spanish,
Population	26 749 000	Amerindian lang.

VIETNAM
Socialist Republic of Vietnam
Capital Ha Nôi

Area sq km	329 565	**Currency** Dong
Area sq miles	127 246	**Languages** Vietnamese, Thai,
Population	84 238 000	Khmer, Chinese,
		local lang.

West Bank
Disputed territory

Area sq km	5 860	**Currency** Jordanian dinar,
Area sq miles	2 263	Isreali shekel
Population	2 421 491	**Languages** Arabic, Hebrew

Western Sahara
Disputed territory (Morocco)
Capital Laâyoune

Area sq km	266 000	**Currency** Moroccan dirham
Area sq miles	102 703	**Languages** Arabic
Population	341 000	

YEMEN
Republic of Yemen
Capital Şan'â'

Area sq km	527 968	**Currency** Yemeni riyal
Area sq miles	203 850	**Languages** Arabic
Population	20 975 000	

ZAMBIA
Republic of Zambia
Capital Lusaka

Area sq km	752 614	**Currency** Zambian kwacha
Area sq miles	290 586	**Languages** English, Bemba,
Population	11 668 000	Nyanja, Tonga,
		local lang.

ZIMBABWE
Republic of Zimbabwe
Capital Harare

Area sq km	390 759	**Currency** Zimbabwean
Area sq miles	150 873	dollar
Population	13 010 000	**Languages** English, Shona,
		Ndebele

Total Land Area 8 844 516 sq km / 3 414 887 sq miles
(includes New Guinea and Pacific Island nations)

HIGHEST MOUNTAIN
Puncak Jaya
5 030 m / 16 502 feet

Line of cross section

Joseph
Bonaparte Gulf
Melville
Island

Arnhem Land

Cape York
Peninsula

Gulf of
Carpentaria

Great Dividing
Range

Cook Strait

North Island

North Cape

Tasman Sea

Oceania perspective view and cross section

HIGHEST MOUNTAINS	metres	feet	Location	Map page
Puncak Jaya	5 030	16 502	Indonesia	59 D3
Puncak Trikora	4 730	15 518	Indonesia	59 D3
Puncak Mandala	4 700	15 420	Indonesia	59 D3
Puncak Yamin	4 595	15 075	Indonesia	—
Mt Wilhelm	4 509	14 793	Papua New Guinea	59 D3
Mt Kubor	4 359	14 301	Papua New Guinea	—

LARGEST ISLAND
New Guinea
808 510 sq km /
312 167 sq miles

LARGEST ISLANDS	sq km	sq miles	Map page
New Guinea	808 510	312 167	59 D3
South Island, New Zealand	151 215	58 384	54 B2
North Island, New Zealand	115 777	44 702	54 B1
Tasmania	67 800	26 178	51 D4

LONGEST RIVERS	km	miles	Map page
Murray-Darling	3 750	2 330	52 B2
Darling	2 739	1 702	52 B2
Murray	2 589	1 608	52 B3
Murrumbidgee	1 690	1 050	52 B2
Lachlan	1 480	919	53 C2
Macquarie	950	590	53 C2

LARGEST LAKE AND LOWEST POINT
Lake Eyre
0 – 8 900 sq km / 0 – 3 436 sq miles
16 m / 53 feet below sea level

LONGEST RIVER AND
LARGEST DRAINAGE BASIN
Murray-Darling
3 750 km / 2 330 miles
1 058 000 sq km / 408 000 sq miles

LARGEST LAKES	sq km	sq miles	Map page
Lake Eyre	0–8 900	0–3 436	52 A1
Lake Torrens	0–5 780	0–2 232	52 A1

Total Land Area 45 036 492 sq km / 17 388 686 sq miles

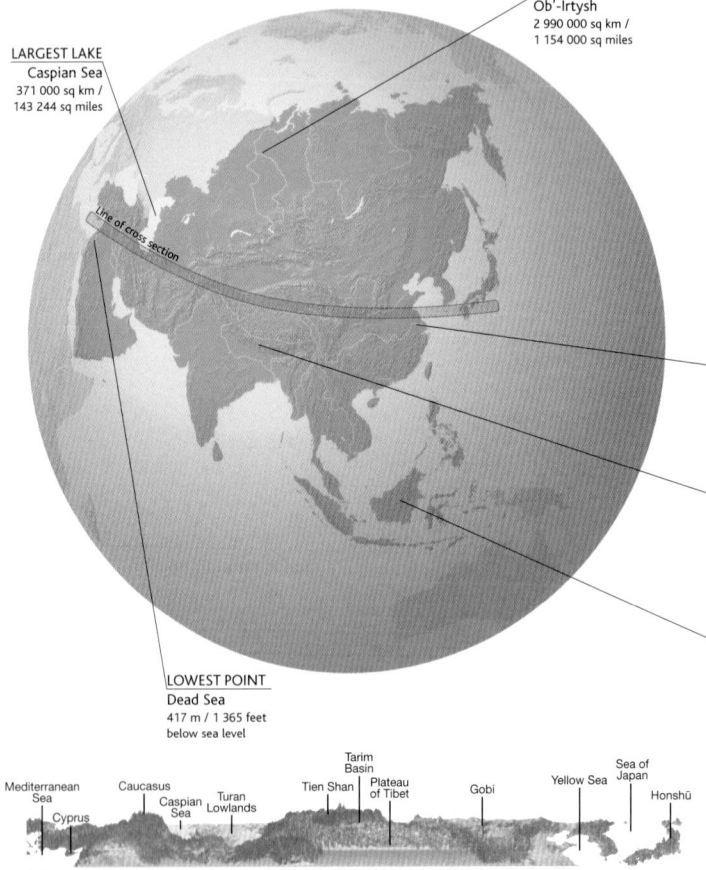

LARGEST DRAINAGE BASIN
Ob'-Irtysh
2 990 000 sq km /
1 154 000 sq miles

LARGEST LAKE
Caspian Sea
371 000 sq km /
143 244 sq miles

Line of cross section

LOWEST POINT
Dead Sea
417 m / 1 365 feet
below sea level

Mediterranean Sea | Cyprus | Caucasus | Caspian Sea | Turan Lowlands | Tien Shan | Tarim Basin | Plateau of Tibet | Gobi | Yellow Sea | Sea of Japan | Honshū

Asia perspective view and cross section

HIGHEST MOUNTAINS	metres	feet	Location	Map page
Mt Everest (Sagarmatha/ Qomolangma Feng)	8 848	29 028	China/Nepal	75 C2
K2 (Qogir Feng)	8 611	28 251	China/Jammu and Kashmir	74 B1
Kangchenjunga	8 586	28 169	India/Nepal	75 C2
Lhotse	8 516	27 939	China/Nepal	—
Makalu	8 463	27 765	China/Nepal	—
Cho Oyu	8 201	26 906	China/Nepal	—

LARGEST ISLANDS	sq km	sq miles	Map page
Borneo	745 561	287 863	61 C1
Sumatra (Sumatera)	473 606	182 860	60 A1
Honshū	227 414	87 805	67 B3
Sulawesi (Celebes)	189 216	73 057	58 C3
Java (Jawa)	132 188	51 038	61 B2
Luzon	104 690	40 421	64 B1

LONGEST RIVER
Yangtze (Chang Jiang)
6 380 km /
3 965 miles

LONGEST RIVERS	km	miles	Map page
Yangtze (Chang Jiang)	6 380	3 965	70 C3
Ob'-Irtysh	5 568	3 460	86 F2
Yenisey-Angara-Selenga	5 550	3 448	83 H3
Huang He (Yellow River)	5 464	3 395	70 B2
Irtysh	4 440	2 759	86 F2
Mekong	4 425	2 749	63 B2

HIGHEST MOUNTAIN
Mt Everest
8 848 m / 29 028 feet

LARGEST ISLAND
Borneo
745 561 sq km /
287 863 sq miles

LARGEST LAKES	sq km	sq miles	Map page
Caspian Sea	371 000	143 244	81 C1
Lake Baikal (Ozero Baykal)	30 500	11 776	69 D1
Lake Balkhash	17 400	6 718	77 D2
Aral Sea (Aral'skoye More)	17 158	6 625	76 B2
Ysyk-Köl	6 200	2 393	77 D2

Total Land Area 9 908 599 sq km / 3 825 731 sq miles

LARGEST ISLAND
Great Britain
218 476 sq km /
84 354 sq miles

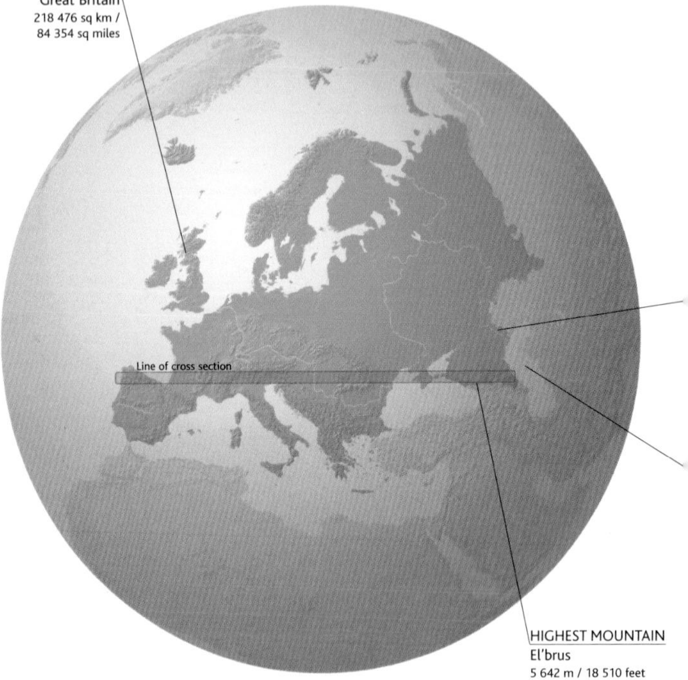

Line of cross section

HIGHEST MOUNTAIN
El'brus
5 642 m / 18 510 feet

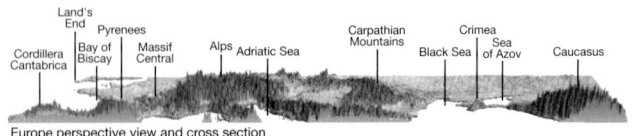

Europe perspective view and cross section

HIGHEST MOUNTAINS	metres	feet	Location	Map pages
El'brus	5 642	18 510	Russian Federation	87 D4
Gora Dykh-Tau	5 204	17 073	Russian Federation	—
Shkhara	5 201	17 063	Georgia/Russian Federation	—
Kazbek	5 047	16 558	Georgia/Russian Federation	76 A2
Mont Blanc	4 808	15 774	France/Italy	105 D2
Dufourspitze	4 634	15 203	Italy/Switzerland	—

LARGEST ISLANDS	sq km	sq miles	Map pages
Great Britain	218 476	84 354	95 C3
Iceland	102 820	39 699	92 A3
Novaya Zemlya	90 650	35 000	86 E1
Ireland	83 045	32 064	97 C2
Spitzbergen	37 814	14 600	82 C1
Sicily (Sicilia)	25 426	9 817	108 B3

LONGEST RIVER AND LARGEST DRAINAGE BASIN
Volga
3 688 km / 2 291 miles
1 380 000 sq km / 533 000 sq miles

LONGEST RIVERS	km	miles	Map pages
Volga	3 688	2 291	89 F2
Danube	2 850	1 770	110 A1
Dnieper	2 285	1 419	91 C2
Kama	2 028	1 260	86 E3
Don	1 931	1 199	89 E3
Pechora	1 802	1 119	86 E2

LARGEST LAKE AND LOWEST POINT
Caspian Sea
371 000 sq km / 143 243 sq miles
28m / 92 feet below sea level

LARGEST LAKES	sq km	sq miles	Map pages
Caspian Sea	371 000	143 243	81 C1
Lake Ladoga (Ladozhskoye Ozero)	18 390	7 100	86 C2
Lake Onega (Onezhskoye Ozero)	9 600	3 706	86 C2
Vänern	5 585	2 156	93 F4
Rybinskoye Vodokhranilishche	5 180	2 000	89 E2

Total Land Area 30 343 578 sq km / 11 715 721 sq miles

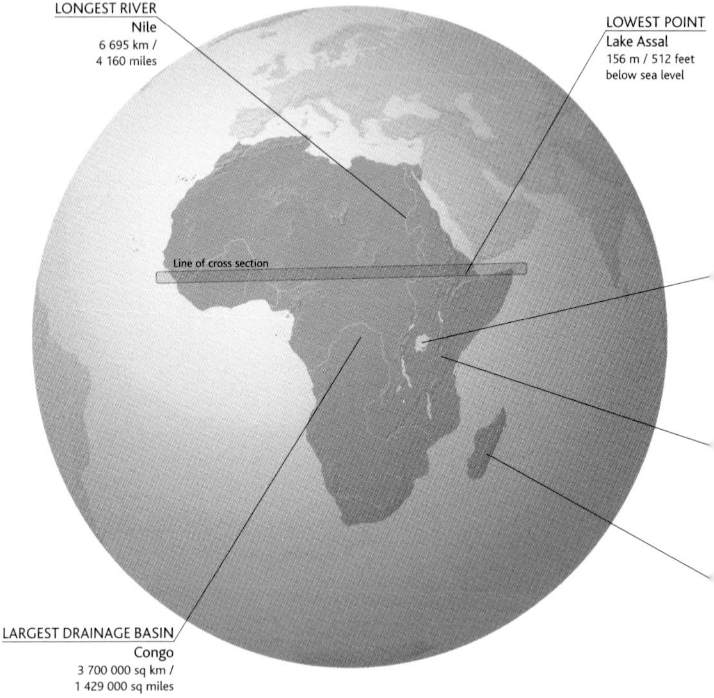

<u>LONGEST RIVER</u>
Nile
6 695 km /
4 160 miles

<u>LOWEST POINT</u>
Lake Assal
156 m / 512 feet
below sea level

Line of cross section

<u>LARGEST DRAINAGE BASIN</u>
Congo
3 700 000 sq km /
1 429 000 sq miles

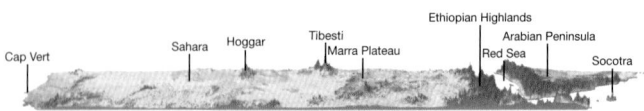

Cap Vert   Sahara   Hoggar   Tibesti   Marra Plateau   Ethiopian Highlands   Arabian Peninsula   Red Sea   Socotra

Africa perspective view and cross section

HIGHEST MOUNTAINS	metres	feet	Location	Map page
Kilimanjaro	5 892	19 331	Tanzania	119 D3
Kirinyaga (Mt Kenya)	5 199	17 057	Kenya	119 D3
Margherita Peak (Mt Stanley)	5 110	16 765	Dem. Rep. Congo/Uganda	119 C2
Meru	4 565	14 977	Tanzania	119 D3
Ras Dejen	4 533	14 872	Ethiopia	117 B3
Mt Karisimbi	4 510	14 796	Rwanda	—

LARGEST LAKE
Lake Victoria
68 800 sq km /
26 564 sq miles

LARGEST ISLANDS	sq km	sq miles	Map page
Madagascar	587 040	226 657	121 D3

LONGEST RIVERS	km	miles	Map page
Nile	6 695	4 160	116 B1
Congo	4 667	2 900	118 B3
Niger	4 184	2 599	115 C4
Zambezi	2 736	1 700	120 C2
Webi Shabeelle	2 490	1 547	117 C4
Ubangi	2 250	1 398	118 B3

HIGHEST MOUNTAIN
Kilimanjaro
5 892 m / 19 331 feet

LARGEST ISLAND
Madagascar
587 040 sq km /
226 657 sq miles

LARGEST LAKES	sq km	sq miles	Map page
Lake Victoria	68 800	26 564	52 B2
Lake Tanganyika	32 900	12 702	119 C3
Lake Nyasa (Lake Malawi)	30 044	11 600	121 C1
Lake Volta	8 485	3 276	114 C4
Lake Turkana	6 475	2 500	119 D2
Lake Albert	5 600	2 162	119 D2

Total Land Area 24 680 331 sq km / 9 529 129 sq miles
(including Hawaiian Islands)

HIGHEST MOUNTAIN
Mt McKinley
6 194 m / 20 321 feet

LARGEST ISLAND
Greenland
2 175 600 sq km /
840 004 sq miles

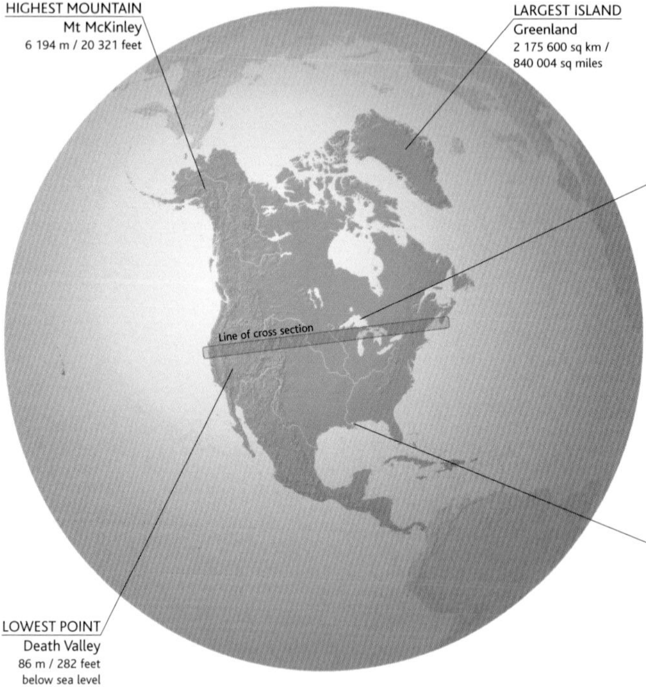

Line of cross section

LOWEST POINT
Death Valley
86 m / 282 feet
below sea level

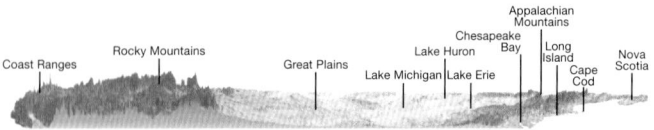

Coast Ranges

Rocky Mountains

Great Plains

Lake Michigan

Lake Huron

Lake Erie

Chesapeake
Bay

Appalachian
Mountains

Long
Island

Cape
Cod

Nova
Scotia

North America perspective view and cross section

HIGHEST MOUNTAINS	metres	feet	Location	Map page
Mt McKinley	6 194	20 321	USA	124 F2
Mt Logan	5 959	19 550	Canada	126 B2
Pico de Orizaba	5 747	18 855	Mexico	145 C3
Mt St Elias	5 489	18 008	USA	126 B2
Volcán Popocatépetl	5 452	17 887	Mexico	145 C3
Mt Foraker	5 303	17 398	USA	—

LARGEST LAKE
Lake Superior
82 100 sq km /
31 699 sq miles

LARGEST ISLANDS	sq km	sq miles	Map page
Greenland	2 175 600	840 004	127 I2
Baffin Island	507 451	195 928	127 G2
Victoria Island	217 291	83 897	126 D2
Ellesmere Island	196 236	75 767	127 F1
Cuba	110 860	42 803	146 B2
Newfoundland	108 860	42 031	131 E2
Hispaniola	76 192	29 418	147 C2

LONGEST RIVERS	km	miles	Map page
Mississippi-Missouri	5 969	3 709	133 D3
Mackenzie-Peace-Finlay	4 241	2 635	126 C2
Missouri	4 086	2 539	137 E3
Mississippi	3 765	2 339	142 C3
Yukon	3 185	1 979	126 A2
Rio Grande (Río Bravo del Norte)	3 057	1 899	144 B1

LONGEST RIVER AND
LARGEST DRAINAGE BASIN
Mississippi-Missouri
5 969 km / 3 709 miles
3 250 000 sq km / 1 255 000 sq miles

LARGEST LAKES	sq km	sq miles	Map page
Lake Superior	82 100	31 699	140 B1
Lake Huron	59 600	23 012	140 C2
Lake Michigan	57 800	22 317	140 B2
Great Bear Lake	31 328	12 095	126 C2
Great Slave Lake	28 568	11 030	128 C1
Lake Erie	25 700	9 922	140 C2
Lake Winnipeg	24 387	9 415	129 E2
Lake Ontario	18 960	7 320	141 D2

Total Land Area 17 815 420 sq km / 6 878 572 sq miles

LARGEST LAKE
Lago Titicaca
8 340 sq km /
3 220 sq miles

Line of cross section

LARGEST ISLAND
Isla Grande de Tierra del Fuego
47 000 sq km / 18 1147 sq miles

Andes

Selvas

Planalto do
Mato Grosso

Bahia de
São Marcos

Cabo de
São Roque

South America perspective view and cross section

HIGHEST MOUNTAINS	metres	feet	Location	Map page
Cerro Aconcagua	6 959	22 831	Argentina	153 B4
Nevado Ojos del Salado	6 908	22 664	Argentina/Chile	152 B3
Cerro Bonete	6 872	22 546	Argentina	—
Cerro Pissis	6 858	22 500	Argentina	—
Cerro Tupungato	6 800	22 309	Argentina/Chile	—
Cerro Mercedario	6 770	22 211	Argentina	—

LONGEST RIVER AND
LARGEST DRAINAGE BASIN
Amazon
8 516 km / 4 049 miles
7 050 000 sq km / 2 722 000 sq miles

LARGEST ISLANDS	sq km	sq miles	Map page
Isla Grande de Tierra del Fuego	47 000	18 147	153 B6
Isla de Chiloé	8 394	3 240	153 A5
East Falkland	6 760	2 610	153 C6
West Falkland	5 413	2 090	153 B6

HIGHEST MOUNTAIN
Cerro Aconcagua
6 959 m / 22 831 feet

LONGEST RIVERS	km	miles	Map page
Amazon	6 516	4 049	150 C1
Río de la Plata-Paraná	4 500	2 796	153 C4
Purus	3 218	1 999	150 B2
Madeira	3 200	1 988	150 C2
São Francisco	2 900	1 802	151 E3
Tocantins	2 750	1 708	151 D2

LOWEST POINT
Península Valdés
40 m / 131 feet below sea level

LARGEST LAKES	sq km	sq miles	Map page
Lago Titicaca	8 340	3 220	152 B2

PACIFIC OCEAN

Total Area
166 241 000 sq km
64 186 000 sq miles

Sea of Okhotsk

Bering Sea

Sea of Japan
(East Sea)

East China Sea
and Yellow Sea

DEEPEST POINT
Challenger Deep
10 920 m / 35 826 feet

South China Sea

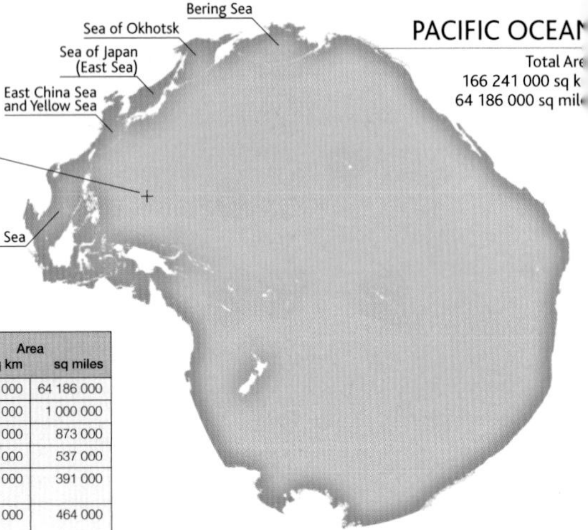

PACIFIC OCEAN	Area	
	sq km	sq miles
Total extent	166 241 000	64 186 000
South China Sea	2 590 000	1 000 000
Bering Sea	2 261 000	873 000
Sea of Okhotsk	1 392 000	537 000
Sea of Japan (East Sea)	1 013 000	391 000
East China Sea and Yellow Sea	1 202 000	464 000

ANTARCTICA

Total Land Area 12 093 000 sq km /
4 669 133 sq miles (excluding ice shelves)

HIGHEST MOUNTAINS	metres	feet
Vinson Massif	4 897	16 066
Mt Tyree	4 852	15 918
Mt Kirkpatrick	4 528	14 855
Mt Markham	4 351	14 275
Mt Jackson	4 190	13 747
Mt Sidley	4 181	13 717

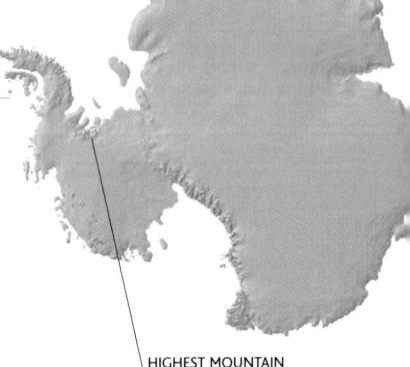

HIGHEST MOUNTAIN
Vinson Massif
4 897m / 16 066 feet

ATLANTIC OCEAN

Arctic Ocean

Total Area
86 557 000 sq km
33 420 000 sq miles

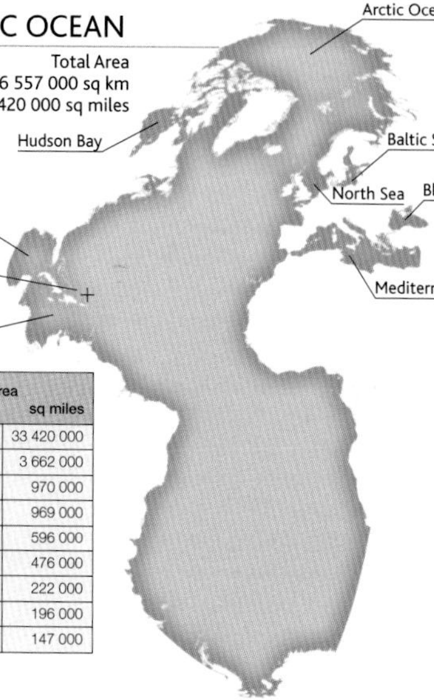

Hudson Bay

Baltic Sea

North Sea   Black Sea

Gulf of Mexico

DEEPEST POINT
Milwaukee Deep
8 605 m / 28 231 feet

Mediterranean Sea

Caribbean Sea

ATLANTIC OCEAN	Area	
	sq km	sq miles
Total extent	86 557 000	33 420 000
Arctic Ocean	9 485 000	3 662 000
Caribbean Sea	2 512 000	970 000
Mediterranean Sea	2 510 000	969 000
Gulf of Mexico	1 544 000	596 000
Hudson Bay	1 233 000	476 000
North Sea	575 000	222 000
Black Sea	508 000	196 000
Baltic Sea	382 000	147 000

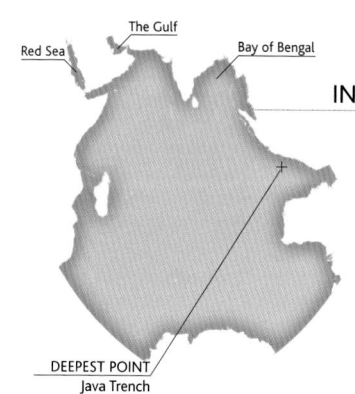

The Gulf

Red Sea   Bay of Bengal

INDIAN OCEAN

Total Area
73 427 000 sq km
28 350 000 sq miles

INDIAN OCEAN	Area	
	sq km	sq miles
Total extent	73 427 000	28 350 000
Bay of Bengal	2 172 000	839 000
Red Sea	453 000	175 000
The Gulf	238 000	92 000

DEEPEST POINT
Java Trench
7 125 m / 23 376 feet

MAJOR CLIMATIC REGIONS AND SUB-TYPES

Köppen classification system

Winkel Tripel Projection
scale 1:200 000 000

Polar

EF	Ice cap
ET	Tundra

Cooler humid

Dc Dd	Subarctic
Db	Continental cool summer
Da	Continental warm summer

Warmer humid

Cb Cc	Temperate
Ca	Humid subtropical
Cs	Mediterranean

Dry

BS	Steppe
BW	Desert

Tropical humid

Aw As	Savanna
Af Am	Rain forest

● Weather extreme location

A   Rainy climate with no winter: coolest month above 18°C (64.4°F).

B   Dry climates; limits are defined by formulae based on rainfall effectiveness:
    BS   Steppe or semi-arid climate.
    BW   Desert or arid climate.

°C   Rainy climates with mild winters: coolest month above 0°C (32°F), but below 18°C (64.4°F); warmest month above 10°C (50°F).

°D   Rainy climates with severe winters: coolest month below 0°C (32°F) warmest month above 10°C (50°F).

E   Polar climates with no warm season: warmest month below 10°C (50°F).
    ET   Tundra climate: warmest month below 10°C (50°F) but above 0°C (32°F).
    EF   Perpetual frost: all months below 0°C (32°F).

a	Warmest month above 22°C (71.6°F).
b	Warmest month below 22°C (71.6°F).
c	Less than four months over 10°C (50°F).
d	As 'c', but with severe cold: coldest month below -38°C (-36.4°F).
f	Constantly moist rainfall throughout the year.
*h	Warmer dry: all months above 0°C (32°F).
*k	Cooler dry: at least one month below 0°C (32°F).
m	Monsoon rain: short dry season, compensated by heavy rains during rest of the year.
f	Frequent fog.
s	Dry season in summer.
w	Dry season in winter.
*	Modification of Köppen definition.

WORLD WEATHER EXTREMES

Highest shade temperature	57.8°C/136°F **Al 'Aziziyah**, Libya (13th September 1922)
Hottest place — Annual mean	34.4°C/93.9°F **Dalol**, Ethiopia
Driest place — Annual mean	0.1 mm/0.004 inches **Atacama Desert**, Chile
Most sunshine — Annual mean	90% **Yuma**, Arizona, USA (over 4 000 hours)
Least sunshine	Nil for 182 days each year, **South Pole**
Lowest screen temperature	-89.2°C/-128.6°F **Vostok Station**, Antarctica (21st July 1983)
Coldest place — Annual mean	-56.6°C/-69.9°F **Plateau Station**, Antarctica
Wettest place — Annual mean	11 873 mm/467.4 inches **Meghalaya**, India
Highest surface wind speed — High altitude	372 km per hour/231 miles per hour **Mount Washington**, New Hampshire, USA, (12th April 1934)
— Low altitude	333 km per hour/207 miles per hour **Qaanaaq (Thule)**, Greenland (8th March 1972)
— Tornado	512 km per hour/318 miles per hour **Oklahoma City**, Oklahoma, USA (3rd May 1999)
Greatest snowfall	31 102 mm/1 224.5 inches **Mount Rainier**, Washington, USA (19th February 1971 — 18th February 1972)

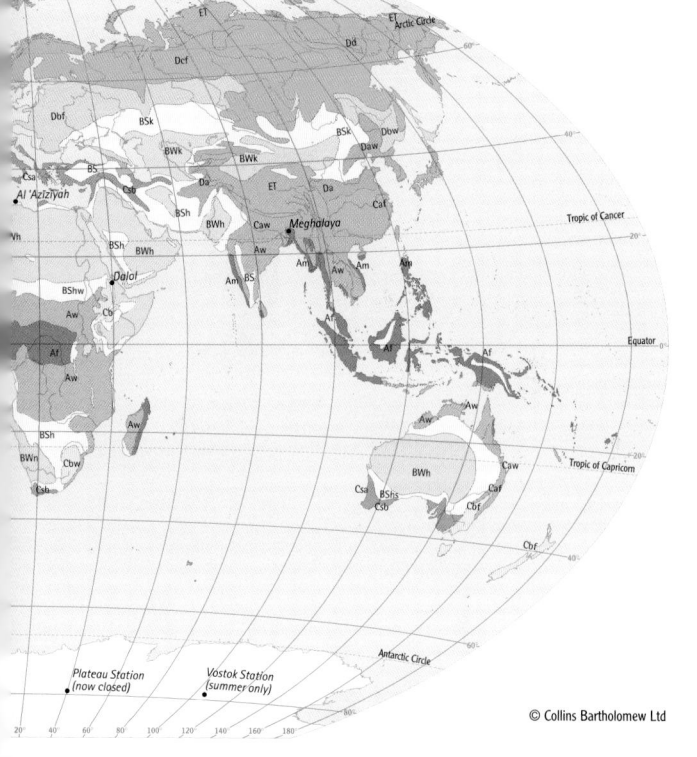

© Collins Bartholomew Ltd

WORLD LAND COVER

Winkel Tripel Projection
scale: 1:190 000 000

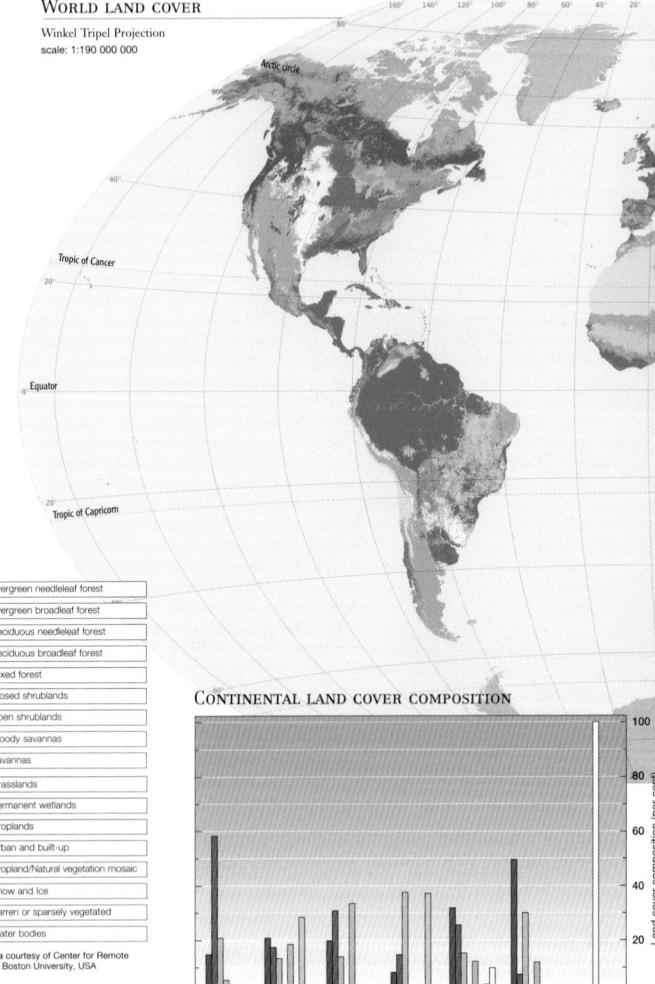

Legend:

- Evergreen needleleaf forest
- Evergreen broadleaf forest
- Deciduous needleleaf forest
- Deciduous broadleaf forest
- Mixed forest
- Closed shrublands
- Open shrublands
- Woody savannas
- Savannas
- Grasslands
- Permanent wetlands
- Croplands
- Urban and built-up
- Cropland/Natural vegetation mosaic
- Snow and ice
- Barren or sparsely vegetated
- Water bodies

Map data courtesy of Center for Remote Sensing, Boston University, USA

CONTINENTAL LAND COVER COMPOSITION

Land cover composition (per cent)

Oceania   Asia   Europe   Africa   North America   South America   Antarctica

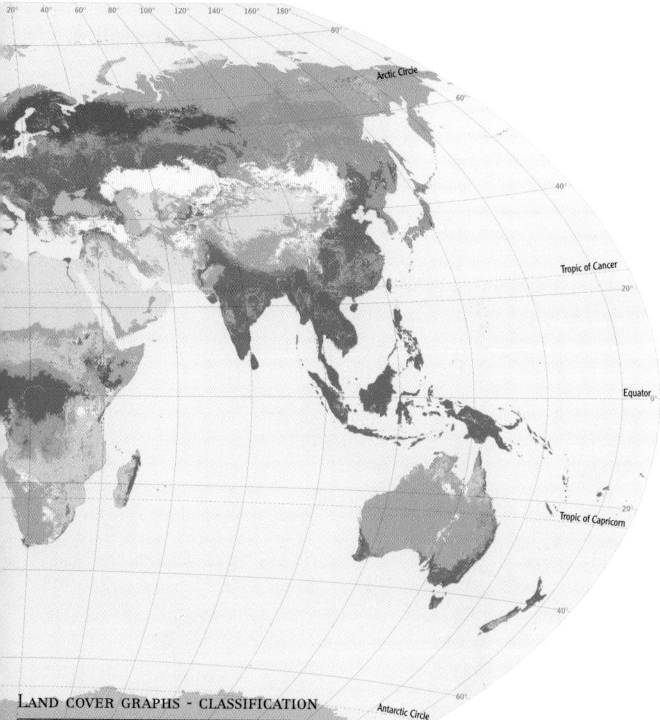

20° 40° 60° 80° 100° 120° 140° 160° 180°

Arctic Circle

Tropic of Cancer

Equator

Tropic of Capricorn

Antarctic Circle

LAND COVER GRAPHS - CLASSIFICATION

Class description	Map classes
Forest/Woodland	Evergreen needleleaf forest
	Evergreen broadleaf forest
	Deciduous needleleaf forest
	Deciduous broadleaf forest
	Mixed forest
Shrubland	Closed shrublands
	Open shrublands
Grass/Savanna	Woody savannas
	Savannas
	Grasslands
Wetland	Permanent wetlands
Crops/Mosaic	Croplands
	Cropland/Natural vegetation mosaic
Urban	Urban and built-up
Snow/Ice	Snow and Ice
Barren	Barren or sparsely vegetated

GLOBAL LAND COVER COMPOSITION

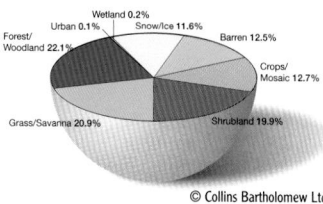

Wetland 0.2%
Urban 0.1%
Snow/Ice 11.6%
Forest/Woodland 22.1%
Barren 12.5%
Crops/Mosaic 12.7%
Shrubland 19.9%
Grass/Savanna 20.9%

© Collins Bartholomew Ltd

TOP TEN COUNTRIES

Rank	Country	Population 2005
1	China	1 323 345 000
2	India	1 103 371 000
3	USA	298 213 000
4	Indonesia	222 781 000
5	Brazil	186 405 000
6	Pakistan	157 935 000
7	Russian Federation	143 202 000
8	Bangladesh	141 822 000
9	Nigeria	131 530 000
10	Japan	128 085 000

WORLD POPULATION DISTRIBUTION

Population Density
Winkel Tripel Projection
scale 1:190 000 000

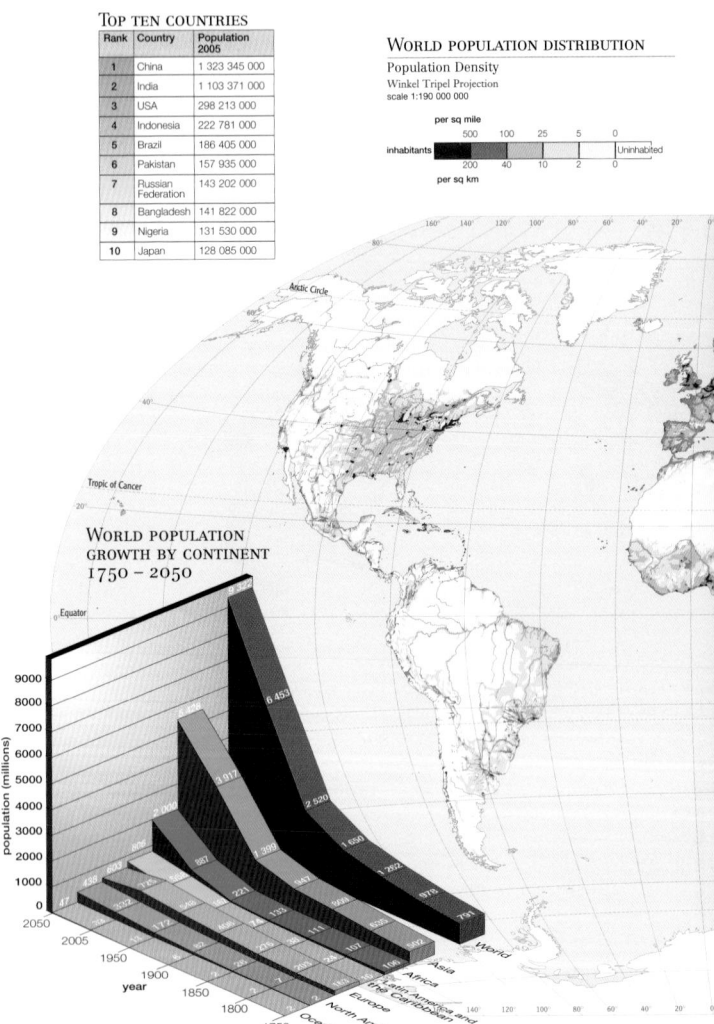

WORLD POPULATION GROWTH BY CONTINENT 1750 – 2050

Key population statistics for major regions

	Population (millions) 2005	Growth (per cent)	Infant mortality rate	Total fertility rate	Life expectancy
World	6 453	1.21	57	2.65	65.4
More developed regions[2]	1 209	0.30	8	1.56	75.6
Less developed regions[2]	5 243	1.43	62	2.90	63.4
Africa	887	2.18	94	4.97	49.1
Asia	3 917	1.21	54	2.47	67.3
Europe[3]	725	0.00	9	1.40	73.7
Latin America and the Caribbean[4]	558	1.42	26	2.55	71.5
North America	332	0.97	7	1.99	77.6
Oceania	33	1.32	29	2.32	74.0

Except for population (2005) the data are annual averages projected for the period 2000–2005.

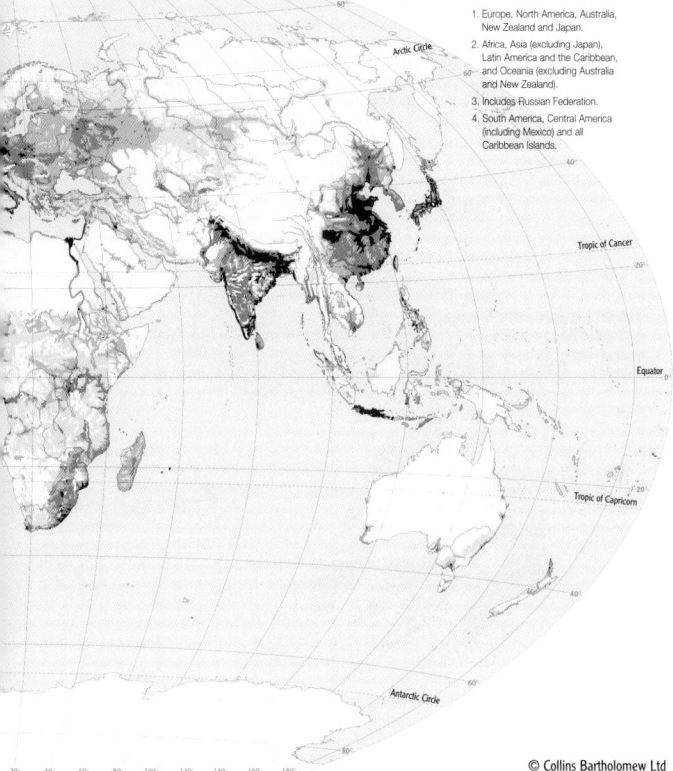

1. Europe, North America, Australia, New Zealand and Japan.

2. Africa, Asia (excluding Japan), Latin America and the Caribbean, and Oceania (excluding Australia and New Zealand).

3. Includes Russian Federation.

4. South America, Central America (including Mexico) and all Caribbean Islands.

© Collins Bartholomew Ltd

THE WORLD'S MAJOR CITIES

Urban agglomerations with over 1 million inhabitants.
Winkel Tripel Projection
scale 1:190 000 000

- over 20 million
- 10 million – 20 million
- 5 million – 10 million
- 2.5 million – 5 million
- 1 million – 2.5 million

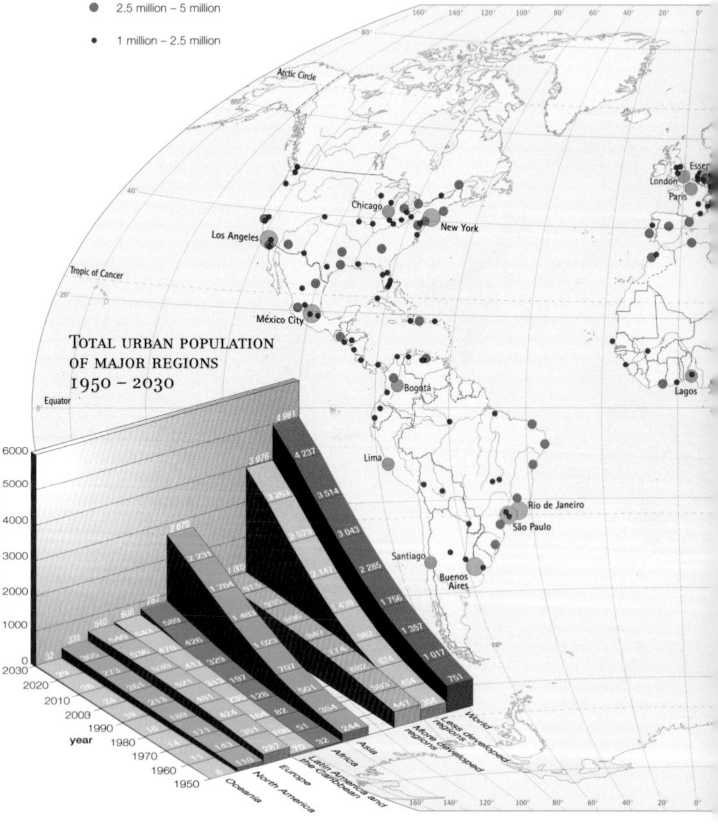

TOTAL URBAN POPULATION OF MAJOR REGIONS 1950 – 2030

urban population (millions)

LEVEL OF URBANIZATION BY MAJOR REGION 1970–2030

Urban population as a percentage of total population

	1970	2003	2030
World	37	48	60
More developed regions[1]	68	75	83
Less developed regions[2]	25	42	56
Africa	23	39	53
Asia	23	39	54
Europe[3]	65	73	81
Latin America and the Caribbean[4]	58	77	84
North America	74	80	85
Oceania	71	73	71

1. Europe, North America, Australia, New Zealand and Japan.
2. Africa, Asia (excluding Japan), Latin America and the Caribbean, and Oceania (excluding Australia and New Zealand).
3. Includes Russian Federation.
4. South America, Central America (including Mexico) and all Caribbean Islands.

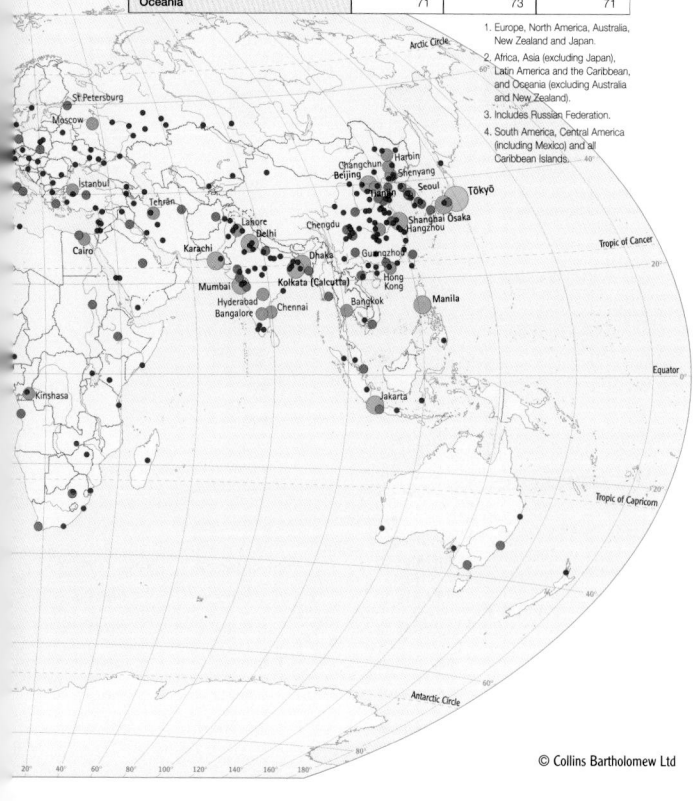

© Collins Bartholomew Ltd

SYMBOLS

Map symbols used on the map pages are explained here. The depiction of relief follows the tradition of layer-colouring, with colours depicting altitude bands. Ocean pages have a different contour interval. Settlements are classified in terms of both population and administrative significance. The abbreviations listed are those used in place names on the map pages and within the index.

LAND AND WATER FEATURES

Lake		River	
Impermanent lake		Impermanent river	
Salt lake or lagoon		Ice cap / Glacier	
Impermanent salt lake		123 Pass height in metres	
Dry salt lake or salt pan		Site of special interest	
		Wall	

RELIEF

Contour intervals used in layer-colouring for land height and sea depth

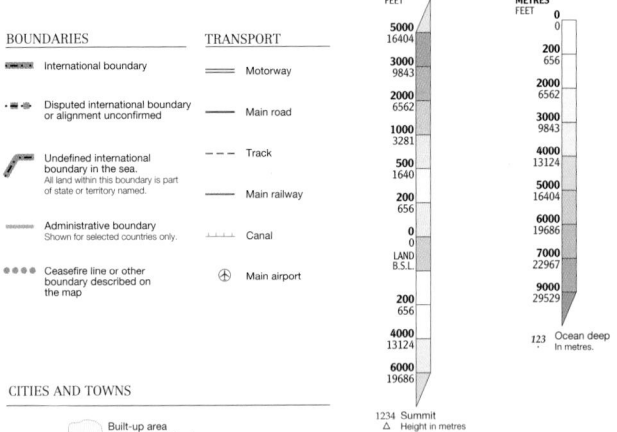

BOUNDARIES

- International boundary
- Disputed international boundary or alignment unconfirmed
- Undefined international boundary in the sea. All land within this boundary is part of state or territory named.
- Administrative boundary Shown for selected countries only.
- Ceasefire line or other boundary described on the map

TRANSPORT

- Motorway
- Main road
- Track
- Main railway
- Canal
- Main airport

CITIES AND TOWNS

Built-up area
Scale 1:4 000 000 only

Population	National Capital	Administrative Capital Shown for selected countries only	Other City or Town
over 10 million	BEIJING ▣	São Paulo ⊙	New York ⊙
5 to 10 million	PARIS ⊡	St Petersburg ⊙	Chicago ⊙
1 to 5 million	KUWAIT ☐	Sydney ○	Seattle ○
500 000 to 1 million	BANGUI ☐	Edmonton ○	Jeddah ○
100 000 to 500 000	WELLINGTON ☐	Edinburgh ○	Apucarana ○
50 000 to 100 000	PORT OF SPAIN ☐	Bismarck ○	Invercargill ○
under 50 000	MALABO ☐	Charlottetown ○	Ceres ○

STYLES OF LETTERING
Cities and towns are explained separately

		Physical features	
Country	**FRANCE**	Island	*Gran Canaria*
Overseas Territory/Dependency	**Guadeloupe**	Lake	*Lake Erie*
Disputed Territory	AKSAI CHIN	Mountain	*Mt Blanc*
Administrative name Shown for selected countries only.	**SCOTLAND**	River	*Thames*
Area name	PATAGONIA	Region	*LAPPLAND*

CONTINENTAL MAPS

BOUNDARIES

——— International boundary

------- Disputed international boundary

········ Ceasefire line

CITIES AND TOWNS

National capital	Other city or town
Kuwait □	Seattle ○

ABBREVIATIONS

Abbr.		Language	Meaning
Arch.	Archipelago		
B.	Bay		
	Bahía, Baia	Portuguese	bay
	Bahía	Spanish	bay
	Baie	French	bay
C.	Cape		
	Cabo	Portuguese, Spanish	cape, headland
	Cap	French	cape, headland
Co	Cerro	Spanish	hill, peak, summit
E.	East, Eastern		
Est.	Estrecho	Spanish	strait
Gt	Great		
I.	Island, Isle		
	Ilha	Portuguese	island
	Islas	Spanish	island
Is	Islands, Isles		
	Islas	Spanish	islands
Khr.	Khrebet	Russian	mountain range
L.	Lake		
	Loch	(Scotland)	lake
	Lough	(Ireland)	lake
	Lac	French	lake
	Lago	Portuguese, Spanish	lake
M.	Mys	Russian	cape, point
Mt	Mount		
	Mont	French	hill, mountain
Mt.	Mountain		
Mte	Monte	Portuguese, Spanish	hill, mountain

Abbr.		Language	Meaning
Mts	Mountains		
	Monts	French	hills, mountains
N.	North, Northern		
O.	Ostrov	Russian	island
Pt	Point		
Pta	Punta	Italian, Spanish	cape, point
R.	River		
	Rio	Portuguese	river
	Río	Spanish	river
	Rivière	French	river
Ra.	Range		
S.	South, Southern		
	Salar, Salina, Salinas	Spanish	salt pan, salt pans
Sa	Serra	Portuguese	mountain range
	Sierra	Spanish	mountain range
Sd	Sound		
S.E.	Southeast, Southeastern		
St	Saint		
	Sankt	German	saint
	Sint	Dutch	saint
Sta	Santa	Italian, Portuguese, Spanish	saint
Ste	Sainte	French	saint
Str.	Strait		
W.	West, Western		
	Wadi, Wādī	Arabic	watercourse

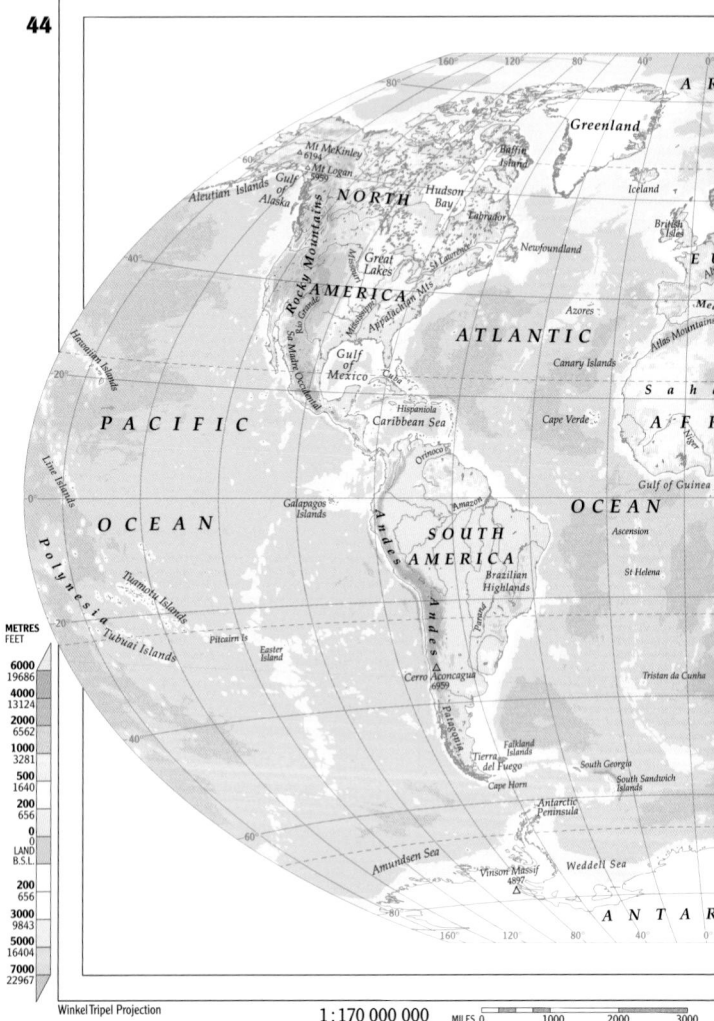

A R

Greenland

Iceland

Baffin Island

Hudson Bay

Labrador

British Isles

E U

Mt McKinley 6194

Mt Logan

Gulf of Alaska

Aleutian Islands

NORTH

Rocky Mountains

Great Lakes

St Lawrence

Newfoundland

AMERICA

Appalachian Mts

Mississippi

Azores

ATLANTIC

Med

Atlas Mountains

Hawaiian Islands

Sierra Madre Occidental

Rio Grande

Gulf of Mexico

Canary Islands

S a h a r a

Hispaniola

Caribbean Sea

Cape Verde

A F R

Niger

PACIFIC

Line Islands

Orinoco

Gulf of Guinea

Galapagos Islands

A n d e s

Amazon

OCEAN

OCEAN

SOUTH

Ascension

P o l y n e s i a

AMERICA

Brazilian Highlands

St Helena

Tuamotu Islands

A n d e s

METRES
FEET

Tubuai Islands

Pitcairn Is

Easter Island

Parana

Tristan da Cunha

6000	19686
4000	13124
2000	6562
1000	3281
500	1640
200	656
0	0
LAND	B.S.L.

P a t a g o n i a

Cerro Aconcagua 6959

Tierra del Fuego

Falkland Islands

South Georgia

Cape Horn

South Sandwich Islands

Antarctic Peninsula

200	656
3000	9843
5000	16404
7000	22967

Amundsen Sea

Vinson Massif 4897 △

Weddell Sea

A N T A R

Winkel Tripel Projection

1:170 000 000

MILES 0   1000   2000   3000

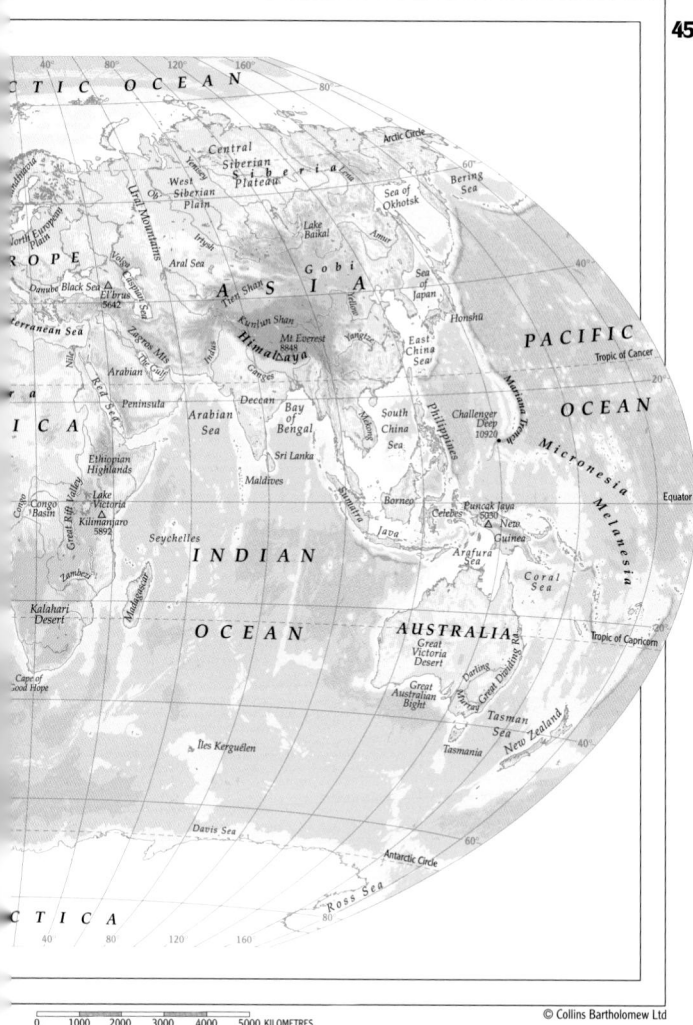

ARCTIC OCEAN

40° 80° 120° 160° 80°

Arctic Circle

Central
Siberian
Plateau
West
Siberian
Plain
Yenisey
Ob
Irtysh
Lena
60°

Bering
Sea

North European
Plain
Ural Mountains
Volga
Caspian Sea
Aral Sea
Lake
Baikal
Amur
Sea of
Okhotsk

EUROPE
Danube
Black Sea
El'brus
5642

A S I A
Tien Shan
Gobi
Sea
of
Japan
40°

Mediterranean Sea
Kunlun Shan
Himalaya
Mt Everest
8848
Yangtze
Honshū

PACIFIC
Tropic of Cancer

Zagros Mts
The Gulf
Ganges
20°

Nile
Red Sea
Arabian
Peninsula
Indus
Deccan
Bay
of
Bengal
Mekong
South
China
Sea
Philippines
Challenger
Deep
10920
Mariana Trench
OCEAN

AFRICA
Arabian
Sea
Sri Lanka
Micronesia

Ethiopian
Highlands
Maldives
Borneo
Sumatra
Puncak Jaya
5030
New
Guinea
Equator

Congo
Congo
Basin
Great Rift Valley
Lake
Victoria
Kilimanjaro
5892
Seychelles
Java
Celebes
Arafura
Sea
Melanesia

Zambezi
Madagascar
I N D I A N
Coral
Sea

Kalahari
Desert
AUSTRALIA
Tropic of Capricorn

Cape of
Good Hope
O C E A N
Great
Victoria
Desert
Darling
Great Dividing Range

Murray
Great
Australian
Bight
Tasman
Sea
New Zealand
40°

Îles Kerguélen
Tasmania

Davis Sea
60°

Antarctic Circle

ANTARCTICA
Ross Sea
80°
40 80 120 160

0 1000 2000 3000 4000 5000 KILOMETRES

© Collins Bartholomew Ltd

46

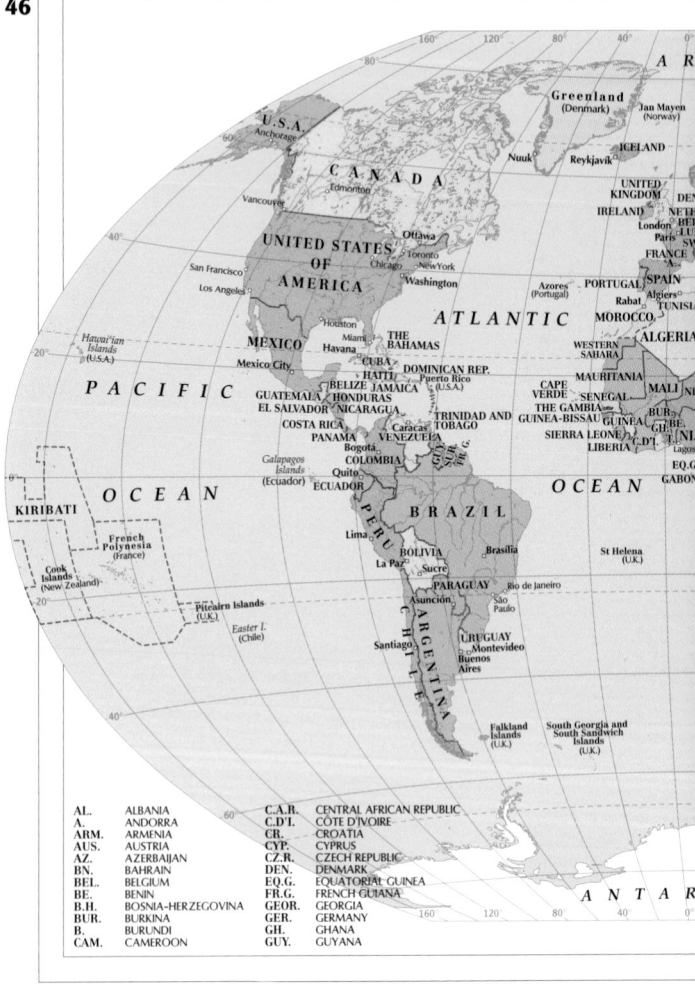

AL. ALBANIA
A. ANDORRA
ARM. ARMENIA
AUS. AUSTRIA
AZ. AZERBAIJAN
BN. BAHRAIN
BEL. BELGIUM
BE. BENIN
B.H. BOSNIA-HERZEGOVINA
BUR. BURKINA
B. BURUNDI
CAM. CAMEROON

C.A.R. CENTRAL AFRICAN REPUBLIC
C.D'I. CÔTE D'IVOIRE
CR. CROATIA
CYP. CYPRUS
CZ.R. CZECH REPUBLIC
DEN. DENMARK
EQ.G. EQUATORIAL GUINEA
FR.G. FRENCH GUIANA
GEOR. GEORGIA
GER. GERMANY
GH. GHANA
GUY. GUYANA

Winkel Tripel Projection

1 : 170 000 000

MILES 0   1000   2000   3000

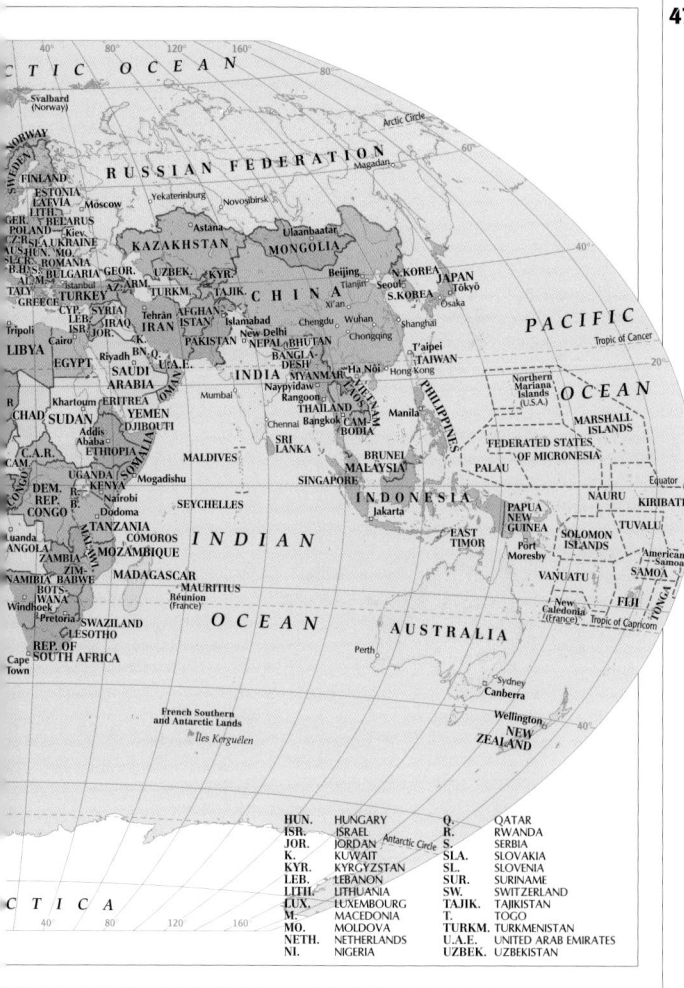

HUN.	HUNGARY	Q.	QATAR
ISR.	ISRAEL	R.	RWANDA
JOR.	JORDAN	S.	SERBIA
K.	KUWAIT	SLA.	SLOVAKIA
KYR.	KYRGYZSTAN	SL.	SLOVENIA
LEB.	LEBANON	SUR.	SURINAME
LITH.	LITHUANIA	SW.	SWITZERLAND
LUX.	LUXEMBOURG	TAJIK.	TAJIKISTAN
M.	MACEDONIA	T.	TOGO
MO.	MOLDOVA	TURKM.	TURKMENISTAN
NETH.	NETHERLANDS	U.A.E.	UNITED ARAB EMIRATES
NI.	NIGERIA	UZBEK.	UZBEKISTAN

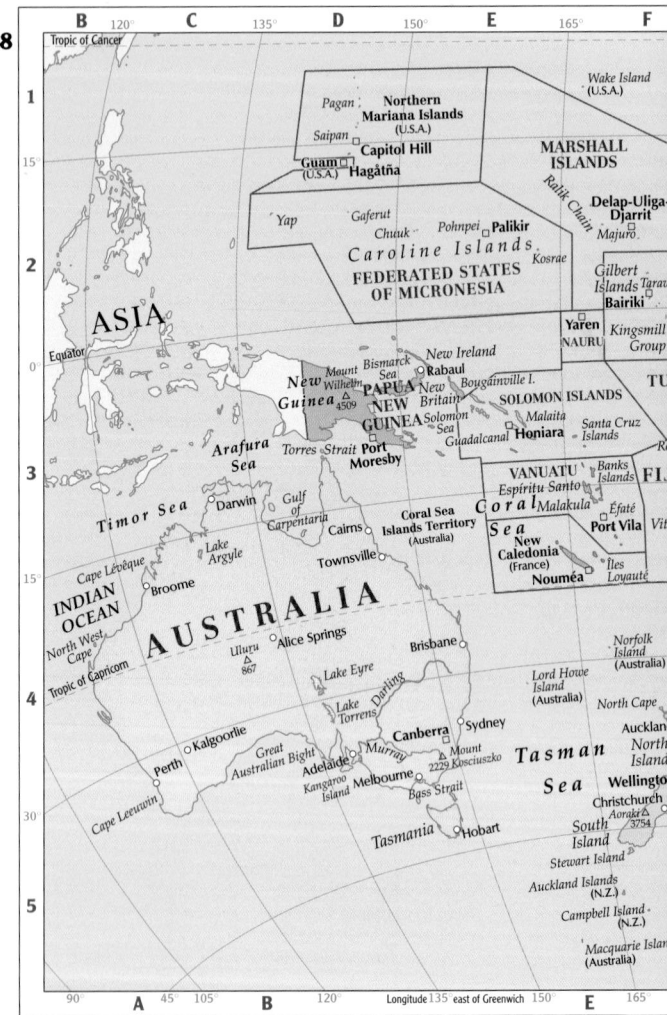

48

| | B | 120° | C | 135° | D | 150° | E | 165° | F |

Tropic of Cancer

Wake Island (U.S.A.)

1

Pagan **Northern Mariana Islands** (U.S.A.)

Saipan **Capitol Hill**

MARSHALL ISLANDS

Guam **Capitol Hill**
(U.S.A.) **Hagåtña**

Ralik Chain

Delap-Uliga-Djarrit
Majuro

Yap *Gaferut*

Chuuk *Pohnpei* **Palikir**

C a r o l i n e I s l a n d s

2

Kosrae

FEDERATED STATES OF MICRONESIA

Gilbert *Tarawa*
Islands
Bairiki

ASIA

Yaren
NAURU *Kingsmill Group*

Equator

New Ireland

TUV

Mount **Rabaul** *Bismarck Sea*

New
Wilhelm **PAPUA** *New* *Bougainville I.*
Guinea 4509 **NEW** *Britain*

SOLOMON ISLANDS

Solomon *Malaita*
GUINEA *Sea* *Guadalcanal* **Honiara** *Santa Cruz Islands*

Rot

Arafura
Sea *Torres Strait* **Port Moresby**

3

VANUATU *Banks Islands*

FIJI

Espíritu Santo

Timor Sea *Darwin*

Gulf of Carpentaria

Coral Sea Islands Territory (Australia)

Malakula *Éfaté*
C o r a l **Port Vila** *Viti*

Sea
New
Caledonia
(France)

Cape Lévêque *Lake Argyle*

Cairns

Townsville

Îles Loyauté

Noumèa

INDIAN OCEAN

Broome

15°

North West Cape

Tropic of Capricorn

Uluru *Alice Springs*
△
867

AUSTRALIA

Brisbane

Norfolk Island (Australia)

Lord Howe Island (Australia)

North Cape

Auckland
North Island

4

Kalgoorlie

Lake Eyre

Lake Torrens *Darling*

Canberra *Sydney*

Tasman

Perth

Great Australian Bight *Murray*
Adelaide *Mount*
Kangaroo **Melbourne** 2229 *Kosciuszko*
Island *Bass Strait*

Sea

Wellington

Christchurch

30°

Cape Leeuwin

Tasmania *Hobart*

South
Island
Aoraki △
3754

Stewart Island

5

Auckland Islands (N.Z.)

Campbell Island (N.Z.)

Macquarie Island (Australia)

| 90° | | | | | | | | | |

A 45° 105° **B** 120° Longitude 135° east of Greenwich 150° **E** 165°

1 : 72 000 000   MILES 0   500   1000

OCEANIA COUNTRIES

Hawai'ian Islands (U.S.A.)

Johnston Atoll (U.S.A.)

PACIFIC OCEAN

Palmyra Atoll (U.S.A.)

Howland Island (U.S.A.)
Baker Island (U.S.A.)

Phoenix Islands

Jarvis Island (U.S.A.)

Kiritimati

Malden Island

K I R I B A T I

Line Islands

Marquesas Islands

ALU

VAIAKU
Funafuti

Tokelau (N.Z.)

American Samoa (U.S.A.)

Penrhyn

Nuku Hiva
Hiva Oa

Wallis-and-Futuna Islands (France)

Matā'utu
Savai'i
SAMOA

Apia
Fagatogo

Vanua Levu

TONGA

Niue (N.Z.)

Cook Islands (N.Z.)

Îles Palliser

Îles du Désappointement

Tuamotu Islands

Suva
vu

Vava'u Group

Alofi

Society Islands

Papeete
Tahiti

French Polynesia

Tofua
Tongatapu Group

Nuku'alofa

Rarotonga

Avarua

Tubuai Islands

Groupe Actéon

Mururoa
Îles Gambier

Kermadec Islands (N.Z.)

Tubuai

Rapa

Adamstown

Pitcairn Island (U.K.)

NEW ZEALAND

Chatham Islands (N.Z.)

Antipodes Islands (N.Z.)

0   500   1000   1500 KILOMETRES

© Collins Bartholomew Ltd

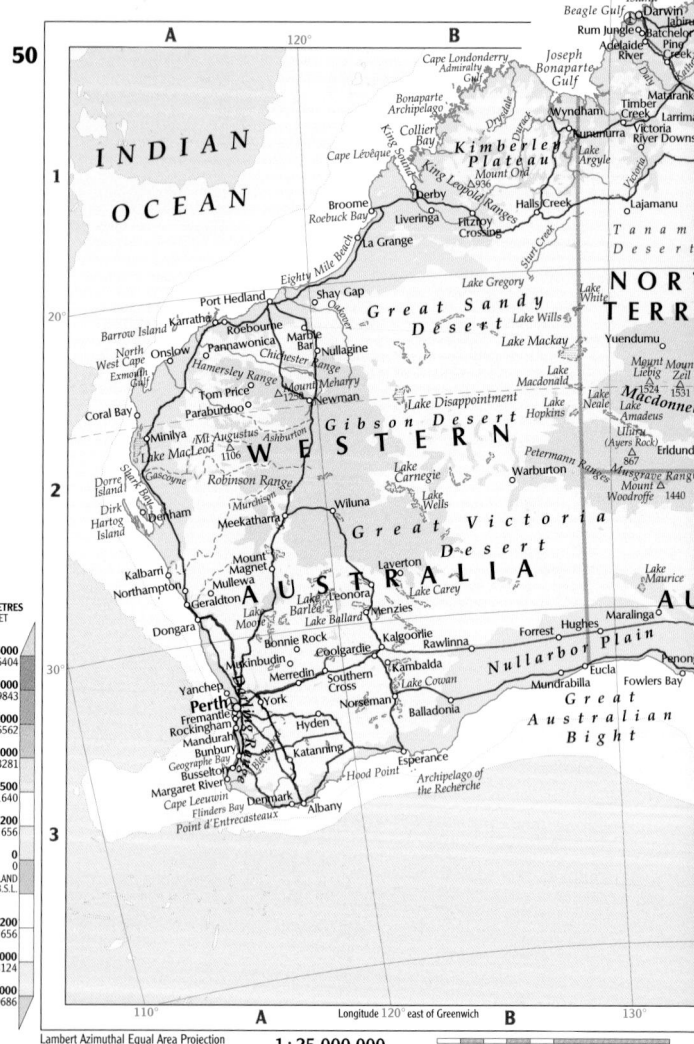

50

INDIAN

OCEAN

A 120° **B**

Bathurst Island
Beagle Gulf
Melville Pen.
Island
Darwin
Jabiru
Rum Jungle
Batchelor
Ping

Joseph
Bonaparte
Gulf
Adelaide
River

Cape Londonderry
Admiralty
Bonaparte
Archipelago
Collier
Bay
Kimberley
Plateau
King Leopold Ranges
Mount Ord
936
Wyndham
Nunamurra
Matarank
Timber
Creek
Larrima
Victoria
River Downs
Lake
Argyle

1

Cape Lévêque

Broome
Roebuck Bay
Derby
Liveringa
Fitzroy
Crossing
Halls Creek
Sturt Creek
Lajamanu

NOR
TERR

Tanami
Desert

La Grange

Eighty Mile Beach

Shay Gap
Port Hedland

Great Sandy
Desert
Lake Gregory
Lake
White
Lake Wills
Lake Mackay
Yuendumu

20°

Barrow Island
Karratha
Roebourne
Pannawonica
Onslow
North
West Cape
Exmouth
Gulf
Marble
Bar
Nullagine
Chichester Range
Hamersley Range
Tom Price
Paraburdoo
Coral Bay
Newman
1226

Lake Disappointment
Lake
Macdonald
Lake
Hopkins
Lake
Neale
Mount
Liebig
1524
Mount
Zeil
1531
Macdonnell
867
Lake
Amadeus
Uluru
(Ayers Rock)
Musgrave Range
Mount
Woodroffe 1440
Erlduna
AU

Minilya
Mt Augustus
1106
Lake MacLeod
Ashburton
Gibson Desert
WESTERN
Robinson Range
Gascoyne
Murchison
Lake
Carnegie
Warburton
Petermann Ranges

2

Dorre
Island
Dirk
Hartog
Island
Denham
Meekatharra
Wiluna
Lake
Wells
Great Victoria
Desert

AUSTRALIA
Kalbarri
Northampton
Mount
Magnet
Mullewa
Geraldton
Lake
Moore
Lake
Barlee
Leonora
Lake Carey
Laverton
Lake
Maurice

Dongara
Bonnie Rock
Lake Ballard
Menzies
Kalgoorlie
Rawlinna
Forrest
Hughes
Maralinga
AU

Mukinbudin
Merredin
Coolgardie
Kambalda
Nullarbor Plain
Mundrabilla
Eucla
Fowlers Bay
Penong

30°

Yanchep
Perth
Fremantle
Rockingham
Mandurah
Bunbury
York
Southern
Cross
Hyden
Lake Cowan
Norseman
Balladonia
Great
Australian
Bight

Geographe Bay
Busselton
Margaret River
Cape Leeuwin
Katanning
Denmark
Albany
Esperance
Hood Point
Archipelago of
the Recherche

Flinders Bay
Point d'Entrecasteaux

3

110°

METRES
FEET

5000
16404
3000
9843
2000
6562
1000
3281
500
1640
200
656
0
0
LAND
B.S.L.
200
656
4000
13124
6000
19686

Lambert Azimuthal Equal Area Projection

1 : 25 000 000

MILES 0   250   500

AUSTRALIA

51

Wessel Is *Cape Wessel*
Buckingham Bay
Nhulunbuy
Cape Arnhem
Arnhem Arnhem Bay
Land
Isle Woodah
Alyangula
Gulf of
Groote
Eylandt Sir Edward
Pellew Group
Carpentaria
Borroloola
Daly
Waters
Barkly Tableland
Lake
Woods
Burketown
Wellesley
Islands
Mornington
Island
Tennant
Creek
Camooweal
Kajabbi
HERN
Mount
TORY
Isa
Cloncurry
Dajarra
Barrow
Creek
Richmond
Alice
Springs
QUEENSLAND
Boulia
Ranges
Longreach
Barcaldine
Simpson
Desert
Cluny
Yaraka
Blackall
Birdsville
Windorah
Alberga
Oodnadatta
Lake Eyre
(North)
Quilpie
Charleville
Coober Pedy
Lake
Blanche
SOUTH
Sturt
Stony
Desert
Hungerford
Cunnamulla
STRALIA
Lake
Eyre (South)
Tibooburra
Dirranbandi
Tarcoola
Lake
Frome
Brewarrina
Lake
Gairdner
Woomera
Broken Hill
Wilcannia
Bourke
Ceduna
Lagoon
Streaky
Bay
Whyalla
Cobar
Anxious
Bay
Eyre
Peninsula
Port Augusta
Port Pirie
Jamestown
Burra
NEW SOUTH WALES
Warren
Dubbo
Port Lincoln
Cape Carnot
Ivanhoe
Cape Jaffa
Gawler
Mildura
ADELAIDE
Murray Bridge
Hay
Griffith
Parkes
Orange
Kangaroo
Island
Swan
Hill
Nhill
Lake Torrens
Horsham
Wagga Wagga
Goulburn
VICTORIA
Mount William
1167
Bendigo
Ballarat
CANBERRA
Geelong
Colac
MELBOURNE
Moe
Sale
Mount Gambier
Warrnambool
Bairnsdale
Portland
Cape Otway
Discovery Bay
Wilson's Promontory
Bass Strait
Currie
King Island
Hunter Islands
Burnie
Devonport
Launceston
Queenstown
Zeehan
TASMANIA
Lake Gordon
HOBART
Port Arthur

Cape York
Bamaga
C. Grenville
Cape
York
Albatross Bay Weipa
C. Duyfken
Princess
Charlotte Bay
Cape
Melville
Peninsula
Laura
Cooktown
Cape
Flattery
Mossman
Cairns
Mount Bartle Frere
Innisfail
Tully
Hinchinbrook
Island
Townsville
Ayr Bowen
Charters
Towers
Proserpine
Whitsunday I.
Mt Dalrymple
1277
Mackay
Clermont
Percy Islands
Arthur Point
Emerald
Rockhampton
Yeppoon
Curtis I. *Tropic of Capricorn*
Moura
Gladstone
Biloela
Bundaberg
Monto
Maryborough
Hervey Bay
Sandy Cape
Fraser Island
Gympie
Buckland
Tableland
Kingaroy
Tewantin
Nambour
Roma
Dalby
Caboolture
Brisbane
St George
Goondiwindi
Toowoomba
Beenleigh
Gold Coast
Moree
Warwick
Byron Bay
Ballina
Mungindi
Narrabri
Glen
Innes
Casino
Grafton
Walgett
Inverell
Moree
Armidale
Macksville
Tamworth
Port Macquarie
Muswellbrook
Taree
Sydney
Newcastle
Botany Bay
Lithgow
Wollongong
Nowra
Mt Kosciuszko
Batemans Bay
Eden
Bega
Cape Howe

CORAL
SEA

GREAT BARRIER REEF

GREAT DIVIDING RANGE

TASMAN
SEA

Gregory
Range
Flinders
Forsayth
Normanton
Winton

Great Dividing Range

Darling

Grey Range

Paroo

Warrego

Condamine

Barwon

Namoi

Macquarie

Lachlan

Murrumbidgee

Murray

140°
150°
D
E
51
1
20°
Tropic of Capricorn
2
30°
3
40°
C
140°
150°
E

0   250   500 KILOMETRES

© Collins Bartholomew Ltd

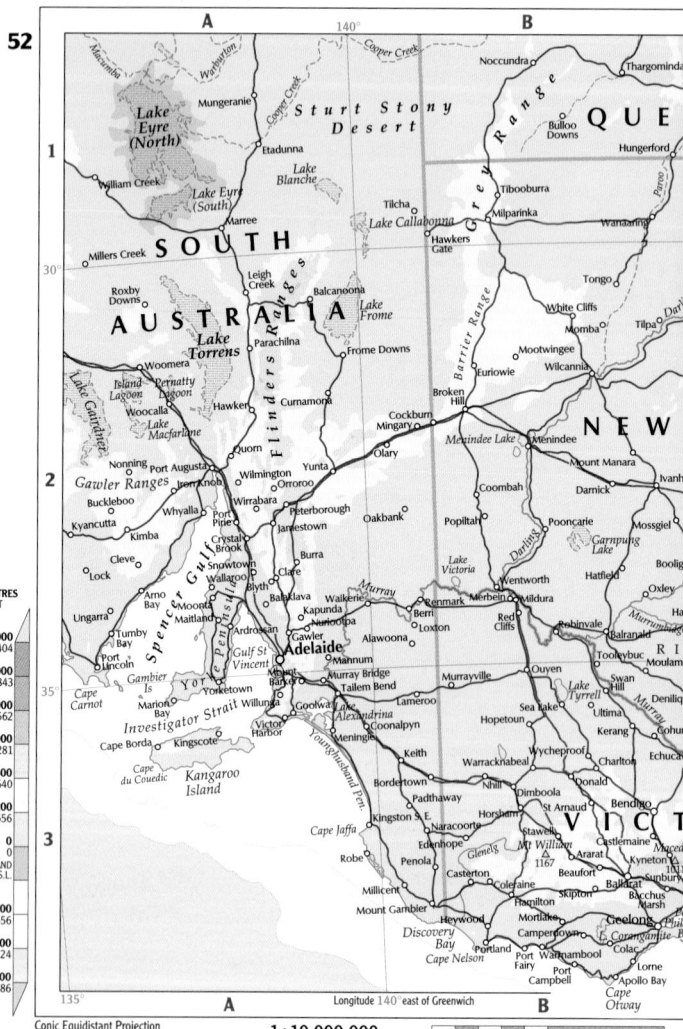

A 140° B

52

Macumba
Warrington Creek
Cooper Creek
Noccundra
Thargomindah

Lake
Eyre
(North)
Mungeranie
S t u r t S t o n y
D e s e r t
Bulloo
Downs
QUEE

William Creek
Etadunna
Lake
Blanche
Hungerford

1

Lake Eyre
(South)
Marree
Tilcha
Lake Callabonna
Tiboobura
Milparinka
Wanaaring

Parroo
Darling

30°
Millers Creek
S O U T H
Leigh
Creek
Balcanoona
Hawkers
Gate
Tongo

Roxby
Downs
Lake
Frome
White Cliffs
Momba
Tilpa

A U S T R A L I A
Woomera
Parachilna
Frome Downs
Euriowie
Wilcannia

Island
Lagoon
Pernatty
Lagoon
Hawker
Curnamona
Cockburn
Mingary
Broken
Hill
Menindee
Menindee Lake

Woocalla
Lake
Torrens
Quorn
Olary
Mount Manara

Lake
Gairdner
Nonning
Port Augusta
Wilmington
Yunta
Coombah
Darnick
Ivanhoe

2
Gawler Ranges
Buckleboo
Iron Knob
Orroroo
Peterborough
Popiltah
Pooncarie
Garnpung
Lake
Mossgiel

Kyancutta
Kimba
Whyalla
Port
Pirie
Jamestown
Oakbank
Darling
Booligal

Cleve
Lock
Crystal
Brook
Burra
Lake
Victoria
Wentworth
Hatfield
Oxley

Ungarra
Arno
Bay
Moonta
Wallaroo
Snowtown
Blyth
Clare
Walkerie
Murray
Renmark
Merbein
Mildura
Robinvale
Murrumbidgee
Hay

Tumby
Bay
Maitland
Balaklava
Kapunda
Berri
Loxton
Red
Cliffs
Tooleybuc
Moulamein
R I

Port
Lincoln
Ardrossan
Gawler
Alawoona
Swan
Hill
Balranald
Deniliquin

Cape
Carnot
Gambier Is
Yor
Adelaide
Mount
Barker
Nuriootpa
Murray Bridge
Murrayville
Ouyen
Lake
Tyrrell
Ultima
Kerang
Gohuna

Marion
Bay
Yorketown
Tailem Bend
Lameroo
Sea Lake
Echuca

Port
Lincoln
Investigator Strait
Willunga
Victor
Harbor
Goolwa
Lake
Alexandrina
Coonalpyn
Hopetoun
Wycheproof
Charlton
V I C T

Cape Borda
Kingscote
Youngbunbun Pen.
Meningie
Keith
Warracknabeal
Donald
Bendigo

Cape
du Couedic
Kangaroo
Island
Bordertown
Padthaway
Nhill
Dimboola
St Arnaud
Castlemaine
Macedon

3
Cape Jaffa
Kingston S.E.
Naracoorte
Horsham
Stawell
Mt William
1167
Ararat
Beaufort
Kyneton
Sunbury

Robe
Penola
Edenhope
Glenelg
Skipton
Ballarat
Bacchus
Marsh

Millicent
Casterton
Coleraine
Hamilton
Geelong
Colac
Corangamite Bay

Mount Gambier
Heywood
Mortlake
Camperdown
Bacchus
Port Phillip

Discovery
Bay
Cape Nelson
Portland
Port
Fairy
Warrnambool
Port
Campbell
Apollo Bay
Cape
Otway

135°
Longitude 140° east of Greenwich
B

METRES
FEET

5000
16404

3000
9843

2000
6562

1000
3281

500
1640

200
656

0
LAND
B.S.L.

200
656

4000
13124

6000
19686

1 : 10 000 000
MILES 0   100   200

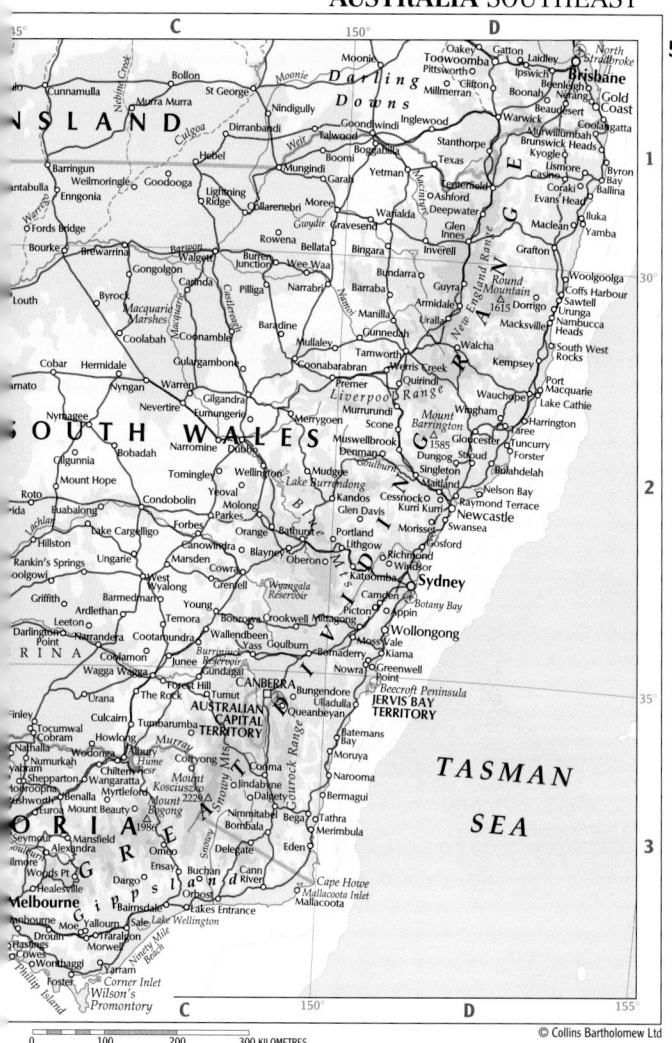

QUEENSLAND

Cunnamulla
Bollon
Moonie
Oakey Gatton Laidley
Toowoomba
Pittsworth Clifton
Millmerran
Inglewood

Brisbane
Beenleigh
Beaudesert
Gold
Coast
Coolangatta

Murra Murra
St George
Nindigully
Goondiwindi
Warwick
Boonah

Nabina Creek
Darling
Downs

Barringun
Weilmoringle
Goodooga
Hebel
Talwood
Boggabilla
Texas
Stanthorpe
Tenterfield
Ashford
Deepwater

Murwillumbah
Kyogle
Brunswick Heads
Lismore
Casino
Coraki
Evans Head
Byron
Bay
Ballina

Enngonia
Lightning
Ridge
Collarenebri
Moree
Wallala
Glen
Innes
Maclean
Iluka
Yamba

O Fords Bridge
Bourke
Brewarrina
Walgett
Burren
Junction
Rowena
Bellata
Bingara
Inverell
Grafton

Louth
Gongolgon
Byrock
Carinda
Pilliga
Narrabri
Barraba
Guyra

Round
Mountain
1615
Dorrigo
Woolgoolga
Coffs Harbour
Sawtell
Urunga
Nambucca
Heads

Macquarie
Marshes
Coonamble
Baradine
Manilla
Armidale
Uralla
Macksville
South West
Rocks

Cobar
Hermidale
Nyngan
Warren
Gulargambone
Mullaley
Gunnedah
Walcha
Kempsey
Port
Macquarie

Nymagee
Gilgandra
Coonabarabran
Premer
Werris Creek
Quirindi
Wauchope
Lake Cathie

NEW SOUTH WALES

Nevertire
Eumungerie
Merrygoen
Liverpool
Range
Wingham
Taree
Harrington
Tuncurry
Forster

Bobadah
Narromine
Dubbo
Wellington
Muswellbrook
Scone
Mount
Barrington
1585
Gloucester
Stroud

Mount Hope
Condobolin
Yeoval
Molong
Mudgee
Kandos
Glen Davis
Denman
Singleton
Dungog
Buladelah

Roto
Euabalong
Parkes
Forbes
Orange
Bathurst
Portland
Lithgow
Cessnock
Kurri Kurri
Maitland
Raymond Terrace
Newcastle

Hillston
Ungarie
Marsden
Canowindra
Blayney
Oberon
Katoomba
Richmond
Windsor
Morisset
Swansea
Gosford

Rankin's Springs
West
Wyalong
Grenfell
Cowra
Wyangala
Reservoir
Richmond
Sydney

Griffith
Ardlethan
Barmedman
Young
Boorowa
Crookwell
Goulburn
Camden
Picton
Appin
Botany Bay

Leeton
Temora
Cootamundra
Wallendbeen
Yass
Moss
Vale
Wollongong
Kiama

Darlington
Point
Narrandera
Junee
Gundagai
Bungendore
Berrima
Nowra
Greenwell
Point

Coleambally
Wagga Wagga
Forest Hill
Tumut
Canberra
Queanbeyan
Ulladulla

The Rock
Tumbarumba
AUSTRALIAN
CAPITAL
TERRITORY
JERVIS BAY
TERRITORY

Culcairn
Cooma
Batemans
Bay

VICTORIA

Tocumwal
Howlong
Albury
Corryong
Jindabyne
Nimmitabel
Moruya

Nathalia
Cobram
Wodonga
Chiltern
Mount
Kosciuszko
2229
Dalgety
Narooma

Shepparton
Wangaratta
Myrtleford
Mount Bogong
1986
Bombala
Bega
Merimbula

Euroa
Mount Beauty
Omeo
Delegate
Eden

Seymour
Mansfield
Ensay
Buchan
Cann
River

Alexandra
Dargo
Bairnsdale
Orbost
Mallacoota
Mallacoota Inlet

Healesville
Lakes Entrance

Melbourne
Moe
Yallourn
Sale
Lake Wellington

Traralgon
Morwell
Ninety Mile
Beach

Drouin
Foster
Corner Inlet
Wilson's
Promontory

Phillip
Island

TASMAN SEA

SCALE

0   100   200   300 KILOMETRES

NEW ZEALAND

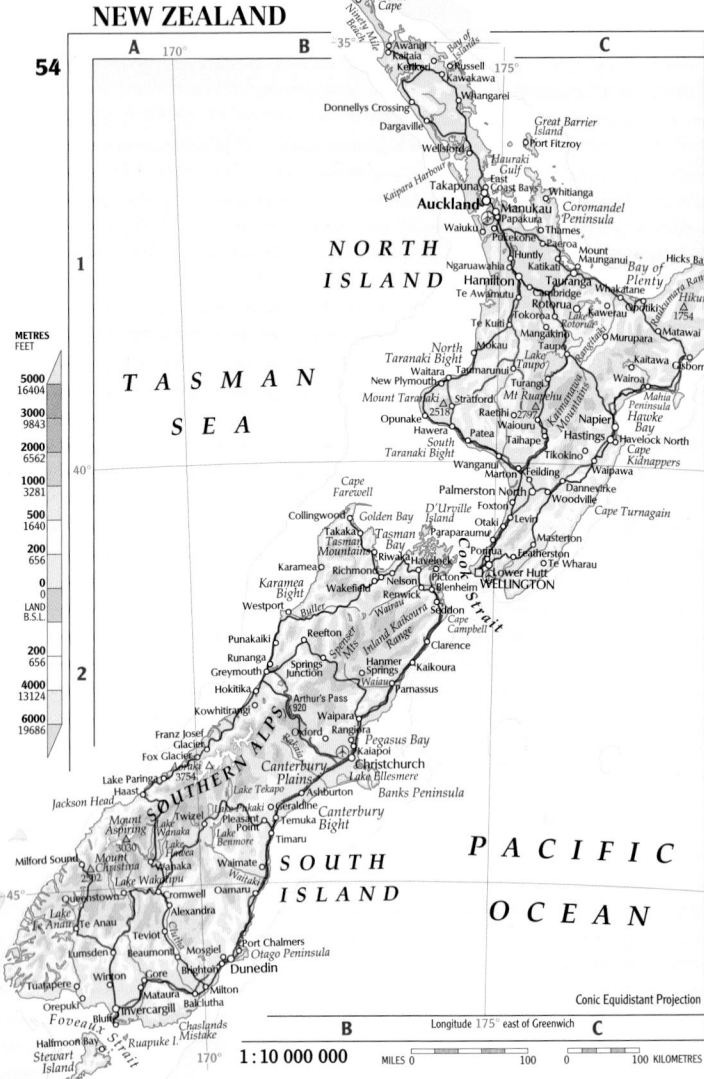

54

| | A | 170° | B | 35 | | C | 175° |

NORTH ISLAND

Te Paki
North Cape
North Cape
Reinga
Ninety Mile Beach
Te Paki
Awanui
Kaitaia
Kerikeri
Bay of Islands
Russell
Kawakawa
Whangarei
Donnellys Crossing
Dargaville
Wellsford
Great Barrier Island
Port Fitzroy
Kaipara Harbour
Takapuna
Coast Bays
Whitianga
Coromandel Peninsula
Auckland
Manukau
Papakura
Hicks Bay
Waiuku
Pukekohe
Thames
Paeroa
Mount Maunganui
Ngaruawahia
Huntly
Katikati
Tauranga
Bay of Plenty
Hamilton
Te Awamutu
Cambridge
Whakatane
Rotorua
Kawerau
Hikurangi 1754
Te Kuiti
Tokoroa
Lake Rotorua
Matawai
Mokau
Taupo
Murupara
Kaitaia
North Taranaki Bight
Lake Taupo
Gisborne
Waitara
Taumarunui
Turangi
Wairoa
New Plymouth
Mount Taranaki 2518
Stratford
Mt Ruapehu 2797
Napier
Mahia Peninsula
Hawke Bay
Opunake
Raetihi
Waiouru
Hastings
Havelock North
Hawera
Patea
Taihape
Tikokino
Cape Kidnappers
Wanganui
Marton
Feilding
Waipawa
Palmerston North
Dannevirke
Woodville
Cape Turnagain
Foxton
Otaki
Levin
Masterton
Paraparaumu
Porirua
Featherston
Te Wharau
Lower Hutt
WELLINGTON

SOUTH ISLAND

Cape Farewell
Collingwood
Golden Bay
D'Urville Island
Takaka
Tasman Mountains
Tasman Bay
Karamea
Richmond
Nelson
Picton
Karamea Bight
Riwaka
Havelock
Blenheim
Wakefield
Renwick
Westport
Buller
Reefton
Warau
Seddon
Cape Campbell
Punakaiki
Inland Kaikoura Range
Runanga
Springs Junction
Hanmer Springs
Clarence
Greymouth
Kaikoura
Hokitika
Arthur's Pass 920
Waiau
Parnassus
Kowhitirangi
Waipara
SOUTHERN ALPS
Oxford
Rangiora
Franz Josef Glacier
Pegasus Bay
Fox Glacier
Pleasant Point
Canterbury Plains
Christchurch
Lake Paringa
Haast
Lake Ellesmere
Jackson Head
Lake Tekapo
Geraldine
Banks Peninsula
Ashburton
Mount Aspiring 3030
Twizel
Temuka
Canterbury Bight
Lake Hawea
Wanaka
Timaru
Milford Sound
Lake Pukaki
Waimate
Mount Christina 2912
Lake Wakatipu
Waitaki
Queenstown
Cromwell
SOUTH ISLAND
Lake Te Anau
Alexandra
Lumsden
Teviot
Clutha
Winton
Beaumont
Mosgiel
Port Chalmers
Gore
Brighton
Otago Peninsula
Tuatapere
Mataura
Milton
Dunedin
Orepuki
Balclutha
Foveaux Strait
Riverton
Invercargill
Chaslands Mistake
Bluff
Ruapuke I.
Halfmoon Bay
Stewart Island

TASMAN SEA

METRES FEET

METRES	FEET
5000	16404
3000	9843
2000	6562
1000	3281
500	1640
200	656
0	0
LAND	B.S.L.
200	656
4000	13124
6000	19686

PACIFIC OCEAN

Cook Strait

Conic Equidistant Projection

| | B | Longitude 175° east of Greenwich | C |

1 : 10 000 000

MILES 0 — 100

0 — 100 KILOMETRES

ANTARCTICA

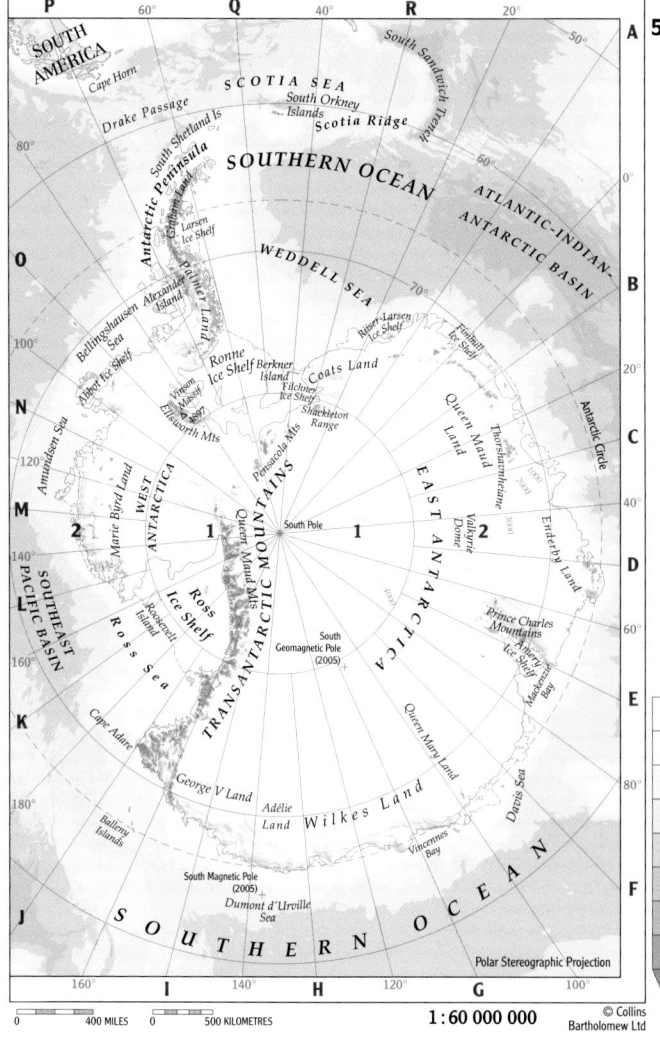

SOUTH AMERICA

Cape Horn

SCOTIA SEA

South Orkney Islands

South Sandwich Trench

Drake Passage

Scotia Ridge

South Shetland Is

SOUTHERN OCEAN

Antarctic Peninsula

ATLANTIC-INDIAN-

Graham Land

ANTARCTIC BASIN

Larsen Ice Shelf

WEDDELL SEA

Bellingshausen Sea

Alexander Island

Palmer Land

Riiser-Larsen Ice Shelf

Fimbul Ice Shelf

Abbot Ice Shelf

Ronne Ice Shelf

Berkner Island

Coats Land

Queen Maud Land

Thorshavnheiane

Antarctic Circle

Amundsen Sea

Vinson Massif

Filchner Ice Shelf

Shackleton Range

Ellsworth Mts

Pensacola Mts

Enderby Land

WEST ANTARCTICA

Marie Byrd Land

Queen Maud Mts

South Pole

EAST ANTARCTICA

Valkyrie Dome

SOUTHEAST PACIFIC BASIN

Ross Ice Shelf

Roosevelt Island

TRANSANTARCTIC MOUNTAINS

South Geomagnetic Pole (2005)

Prince Charles Mountains

Amery Ice Shelf

Mackenzie Bay

Ross Sea

Cape Adare

Queen Mary Land

Davis Sea

George V Land

Adélie Land

Wilkes Land

Balleny Islands

South Magnetic Pole (2005)

Vincennes Bay

Dumont d'Urville Sea

SOUTHERN OCEAN

Polar Stereographic Projection

METRES / FEET

0	0
200	656
2000	6562
3000	9843
4000	13124
5000	16404
6000	19686
7000	22967
9000	29529

0   400 MILES

0   500 KILOMETRES

1:60 000 000

© Collins Bartholomew Ltd

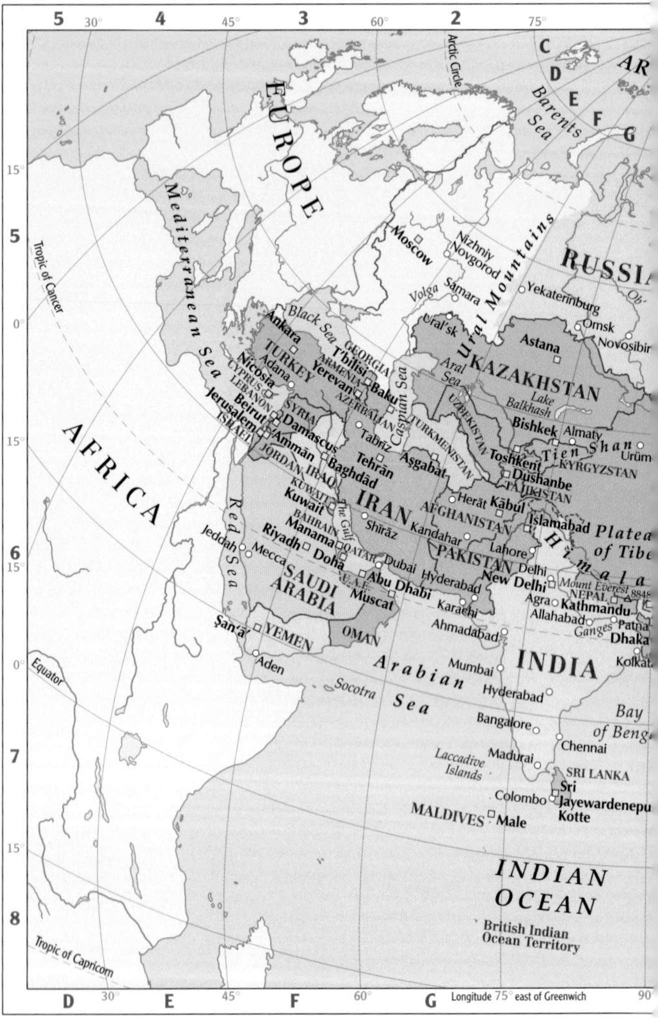

5 30° 4 45° 3 60° 75° 2

EUROPE

Arctic Circle

C
D
AR
E
F
Barents
G
Sea

RUSSIA

15°

Tropic of Cancer

5

Moscow
Nizhniy
Novgorod
Yekaterinburg

Volga
Samara

0°

Ural'sk
Omsk
Novosibir
Astana

Black Sea

Ankara
GEORGIA
Tbilisi
ARMENIA
Baku
Aral
Sea
KAZAKHSTAN

TURKEY
Yerevan
AZERBAIJAN
Caspian Sea
Lake
Balkhash

Nicosia
Adana
CYPRUS
SYRIA
Tabriz
TURKMENISTAN
Bishkek
Almaty

15°
Beirut
Damascus
UZBEKISTAN
Toshkent
Tian Shan
Urüm
LEBANON
Amman
Baghdad
Tehran
Aşgabat
Dushanbe
KYRGYZSTAN

Jerusalem
ISRAEL
JORDAN
IRAQ
TAJIKISTAN

AFRICA
KUWAIT
IRAN
Herät
Käbul
Islamabad
Platea

Kuwait
Shiräz
AFGHANISTAN
of Tibe

BAHRAIN
Kandahar
Lahore
Mount Everest 8848
Himala

Riyadh
Manama
QATAR
Dubai
PAKISTAN
Delhi
NEPAL

6
15°
Doha
U.A.E.
Hyderabad
New Delhi
Kathmandu

Mecca
Abu Dhabi
Muscat
Karachi
Agra
Allahabad
Ganges
Patna
Dhaka

Jeddah
SAUDI
ARABIA
OMAN
Ahmadabad

San'a
YEMEN
Mumbai
Hyderabad
INDIA

0°
Equator
Aden
Arabian
Sea
Socotra

Bangalore
Bay
of Beng

Laccadive
Islands
Madurai
Chennai

SRI LANKA
Sri
MALDIVES
Male
Colombo
Jayewardenepu
Kotte

15°

INDIAN
OCEAN

8
British Indian
Ocean Territory

Tropic of Capricorn

D 30° E 45° F 60° G Longitude 75° east of Greenwich 90°

1 : 86 000 000

MILES 0 500 1000 1500

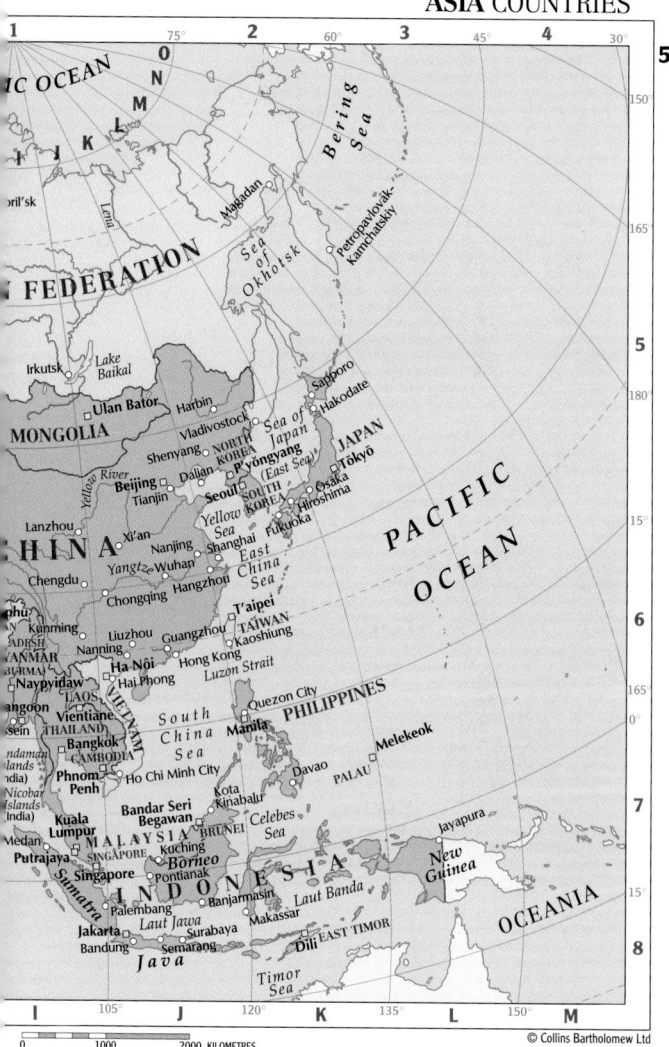

ARCTIC OCEAN

Bering Sea

RUSSIAN FEDERATION

Noril'sk

Lena

Magadan

Sea of Okhotsk

Petropavlovsk-Kamchatskiy

Irkutsk
Lake Baikal

MONGOLIA
Ulan Bator

Harbin

Vladivostock
Sapporo
Hakodate

Sea of Japan (East Sea)

JAPAN

Shenyang
NORTH KOREA
P'yŏngyang
Dalian

Yellow River
Beijing
Tianjin
Seoul
SOUTH KOREA
Hiroshima
Ōsaka
Tōkyō
Fukuoka

Lanzhou
Xi'an
Yellow Sea

CHINA
Nanjing
Shanghai
East China Sea

Chengdu
Yangtze
Wuhan

Chongqing
Hangzhou

PACIFIC OCEAN

Kunming
T'aipei

Liuzhou
Guangzhou
TAIWAN
Kaoshiung

Nanning

Ha Nôi
Hai Phong
Hong Kong
Luzon Strait

MYANMAR
(BURMA)
Naypyidaw

VIETNAM

Quezon City

Yangon
LAOS
Vientiane
THAILAND

South China Sea

Manila
PHILIPPINES

Bangkok
CAMBODIA

Melekeok

Andaman Islands
(India)

Phnom Penh
Ho Chi Minh City

Davao
PALAU

Nicobar Islands
(India)

Bandar Seri Begawan
Kota Kinabalu

Celebes Sea

Jayapura

Medan
Kuala Lumpur
MALAYSIA
BRUNEI
Kuching

New Guinea

Putrajaya
SINGAPORE
Borneo
Pontianak

INDONESIA

OCEANIA

Sumatra
Palembang
Banjarmasin
Laut Banda
Makassar

Jakarta
Laut Jawa
Surabaya

Bandung
Semarang
Dili
EAST TIMOR

Java

Timor Sea

0   1000   2000 KILOMETRES

© Collins Bartholomew Ltd

A · 105° · B · 120°

1

Pyinmana
Taung-ngu Phayao
Chiang Rai
Chiang Mai
Lampang
Phrae
Mawlamyaing
Thaton
Pegu
Uttaradit
Khon Kaen
Pak-sane

Louangphabang
Nam Đinh
Xuwen Haikou
Gulf of Chenpang Wenchang
Xiangkhoang
Tongking Dongfang Wanning
Thanh Hoa
Vinh
Ha Tinh
Đong Hoi
Hainan
(China)

Luzon
Batan Islands
Strait
Babuyan Islands
Laoag Apar
Tuguegar
Bontoc Ilag
Vigan
San Fernando Dagupan Luzo

VIENTIANE
(Viangchan)
Savannakhet
Salavan

Huê
Đa Nang

Quang Ngai

Quezon City
Lucena MANILA
Batangas
Mindoro
Calamian
Group Romblo
Cuyo
Islands

THAILAND
Tak
Lampang
Nakhon
Ratchasima
Lop Buri
Ayutthaya
Ubon
Ratchathani

Quy Nhon

Buôn Mê Thuôt
Nha Trang

Tavoy
Tenasserim
Prachuap
Khiri Khan
Myeik
Palaw

BANGKOK
(Krung Thep)
Pattaya
CAMBODIA
PHNOM PENH
Takêv
Battambang

Đa Lat
Biên
Hoa
Phan Thiêt

SOUTH
CHINA
SEA

Pana
Ilo Tatay'c
Negre

Gulf of
Thailand
Sihanoukville

Long Xuyên
Can
Tho
Ho Chi Minh City
(Saigon)

Puerto
Princesa Palawan
Sulu
Sea

2

Chumphon
Ranong
Takua Pa
Phuket
Krabi Phatthalung

Rach Gia
Ca Mau
Bac
Liêu
Mui Ca Mau

Brooke's Balabac Strait
Point

Zamboang
Isabela
Basilar
Jol

Banda
Aceh
Sigli
Bireun
Langsa
Hat Yai
Songkhla
Yala Kota
Alor Setar Bharu
Pasir Putih
George Town Pasir Putih
Taiping Kuala Terengganu
Kuala Lipis
Ipoh

MALAYSIA

Kudat
Gunung Kinabalu
Kota Kinabalu Sandakan
BANDAR SERI Banggi
BEGAWAN
BRUNEI
Miri Lahad Datu
Sempori
Tawau

Su
Archipela

Pangkalansusu
Medan
Simeulue
Sibolga
Labuhanbilik

Kuala Lumpur

Natuna Besar
Kepulauan
Anambas
Kepulauan
Natuna

Bintulu
Igan
Mukan
Sibu
Tanjungselor
Tanjungredeb
Tarakan

Gunungsitoli
Payakumbuh
Padang

PUTRAJAYA
KUALA
LUMPUR
Melaka
Kluang
Muar
Johor Bahru
SINGAPORE

Singkawang
Kuching
Debak
Lubok Antu
Sambas
Serian
Sangkulirang

Semenanju
Tolit
Moutong
Donggala

3

Sijunjung
Jambi
Pagai
Utara
Bangko

Kepulauan
Riau
Kepulauan
Lingga
Belinyu
Pontianak

Sukadana
Ketapang

Samarinda
Balikpapan

Palu
Teluk
Tomin

CELEBES
(SULAWES

Bengkulu
Palembang
Lahat
Muaraenim
Toboali
Kepulauan
Bangka

BORNEO

Kendawangan
Sampit
Pangkalanbuun
Banjarmasin
Kotabaru
Amuntai
Martapura

Parepare
Watampone
Makassar
Makale

METRES / FEET
5000 / 16404
3000 / 9843
2000 / 6562
1000 / 3281
500 / 1640
200 / 656
0 / 0
LAND / B.S.L.
200 / 656
4000 / 13124
6000 / 19686

Bintuhan
Krui
Bandar
Lampung

Pangkalpinang

Tg Selatan
Laut
(Java Sea)

Makassar Strait
(Macassar Str.)

Bulukumb
Bontosunggu
Bente
Salay

INDIAN

OCEAN

Sukabumi
Tk Palabuhanratu
Bandung
Cilacap

JAKARTA
Cirebon
Semarang
Surakarta
Surabaya
Malang
Jember

JAVA
(JAWA)
Denpasar
Bali
Mataram
Lombok
Praya
Selat Lombok

Madura
Kepulauan
Kangean
Laut Bali

Sumbawa
Laut Flores
Raba
Flor
Ende

Tanahjampe
Kep. Bonerat
Waikabubak
Sumba

Waingar

Christmas I.
(Australia)

Timo

A Longitude 105° east of Greenwich B 120°

Albers Equal Area Conic Projection   1:30 000 000   MILES 0   200   400   600

C · 135° · D

1

PHILIPPINE

SEA

PACIFIC

OCEAN

Northern

Mariana

Islands

(U.S.A.)

Pagan

CAPITOL HILL ⊙ Saipan

Tinian

15°

PHILIPPINES

Guam

(U.S.A.) ⊕ HAGÅTÑA

Rota

Catanduanes

⊙Sorsogon

Catarman

Samar

⊙Catbalogan

⊙Tacloban

Bacolod

Cebu

Tagbilaran

⊙Surigao

Butuan

⊙Cagayan de Oro

⊙Iloilo

Bohol Sea

Ulithi · Fais

⊕ Yap

FEDERATED STATES

Ngulu

OF MICRONESIA

Sorol

Eauripik

Caroline

Islands

2

Roquieta

⊙Pagadian Mindanao

PALAU

⊙Cotabato Davao

⊙Mati

MELEKEOK

Gulf

⊙General Santos

Equator

0°

Pelileluhu Is

Hermit Is

Kepulauan

Talaud

Celebes

Kepulauan

a Sangir

Morotai

⊙Manado

Tondano

Gorontalo

Tobelo

Ternate Halmahera

Sao-sio

Waigeo

Ppulauan

wuk

⊙Peleng

Taliabu Mangole

Bangai Sula

Kwoka

Tanjung d'Urville

Kepulauan G Dampir Jazirah

Misool Doberai

Sorong Ransiki

Manokwari Biak

Numfoor Yapen

Teluk

Berau

Salawati

Biak

Yapen

Sarmi

Jayapura Vanimo

Aitape

Schouten Islands

Manam Long

Wewak

Umboi

Bacan Obi

uaan Kepulauan

nggai Sula

Manui

Peng

SI A

Seram

Amboina

Kaimana

Fafanlap Inanwatan

Babo

Namlea

Buru Saparua

Laut Seram

(Seram Sea)

Ambon Kepulauan

Banda

Nabire

Teluk

Cenderawasih

Pegunungan Van Rees

Taritatu

Idenburg

3000

5030

Mamberamo

Taritatu

4509

Central Ra

4000

PAPUA Madang

Mount

Hagen Goroka

Lae

Wowoni

aha

Buton

Kepulauan

Tukangbesi

Laut Banda

(Banda Sea)

Kepulauan Kai

Tual Dobo

Kai Besar

Adi

Amamapare

NEW GUINEA

4700

Mendi

Kikori

NEW GUINEA

Wabag

Huon

Peninsula

Victoria 4073

Mi

Wau

ubau

Kalabahi

Alor

Kepulauan Barat Daya

Pulau Romang

Kepulauan Leti

Damar

Wetar

Kalwatu

Benjina

Sia Kobroör

Trangan

Larat

Kepulauan Tanimbar

Saumlaki

Seru

Tg Deyong

Pk Dolak

Wokam

Watubela

Kerema

Bereina

Morehead

Gulf

of

Papua

PORT

MORESBY

Kepulauan

Kalabahi

OCUSSI

⊙DILI

Kelamenanu

Kupang

EAST

TIMOR

2960

Wuliaru

Sermata

Selaru

Tg Vals

Daru

Balimo

Merauke

Arafura Sea

C. Wessel

Wessel Is

AUSTRALIA C. Wessel

Bamaga

Weipa

Rote

Timor

Sea

Melville

Island

Bathurst Beagle Gulf

Island

Croker I.

Van Diemen

Gulf

Darwin Jabiru

Nhulunbuy

C. Arnhem

Gulf

of

Carpentaria

C. York

Coen

C · 135° · D

0 · 500 · 1000 KILOMETRES

© Collins Bartholomew Ltd

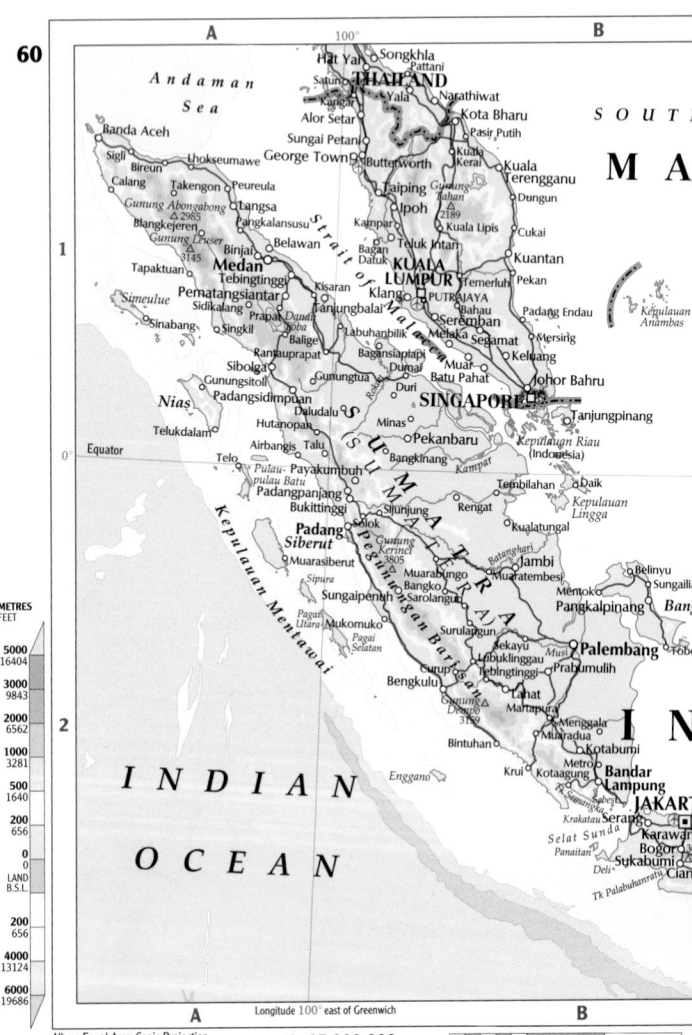

A   100°   B

Andaman
Sea

Hat Yai · Songkhla
Pattani
Satun · **THAILAND** · Yala · Narathiwat
Kangar · Alor Setar · Kota Bharu
Banda Aceh · Sigli · Bireun
Sungai Petani · Pasir Putih
Lhokseumawe · George Town · Butterworth
Kuala Kerai · Kuala Terengganu
Calang · Takengon · Peureula · Langsa
Dungun
Taiping · *Gunung Tahan* · Kuala Lipis
Gunung Abongabong △2985 · Pangkalansusu
Blangkejeren · Ipoh △2189 · Cukai
Gunung L Euser · Belawan · Binjai · Kampar
Kuantan
3145 · Belawan · Binjai · Teluk Intan
Tapaktuan · **Medan** · Bagan · Datuk
Tebingtinggi · **KUALA**
Simeulue · Pematangsiantar · Kisaran · **LUMPUR** · Klang · **PUTRAJAYA** · Temerluh · Pekan
Sidikalang · Tanjungbalai
Sinabang · Singkil · Balige · *Danau* · Labuhanbilik · Seremban · Padang Endau
Prapat · *Toba* · Bagansiapiapi · Melaka · Segamat · Mersing
Sibolga · Rantauprapat · Dumai · Muar · Keluang
Nias · Gunungsitoli · Gunungtua · Duri · Batu Pahat
Padangsidimpuan · Daludalu · **SINGAPORE** · Johor Bahru
Telukdalam · Hutanopan · Minas · Tanjungpinang

Equator · Airbangis · Talu · Pekanbaru · *Kepulauan Riau (Indonesia)*
Telo · Bangkinang
Pulau-pulau Batu · Payakumbuh · *Kampar* · Tembilahan · *Kepulauan Lingga*
Bukittinggi · Rengat · Kualatungal · Daik
Padang · *Padangpanjang* · Solok · Sijunjung
Siberut · *Gunung Kerinci* · △ · *Batanghari*
Muarasiberut · 3805 · Muarabungo · Jambi
Sungaipenuh · Bangko · Muaratembesi · Belinyu · Sungailiat
Sipura · Sarolangun · Mentok · **Pangkalpinang** · *Bang*
Pagai Utara · Mukomuko · Surulangun · Sekayu · *Musi* · **Palembang** · Toboa
Pagai Selatan · Curup · Tebingtinggi · Prabumulih
Bengkulu · Lubuklinggau
Gunung Dempo △ · Lahat · **IN**
3159 · Martapura
Menggala
Bintuhan · Muaradua
Kotabumi
Enggano · Krui · Kotaagung · **Bandar**
Lampung
JAKART
Krakatau · Serang · Karawan
Bogor
Panaitan · Sukabumi · Cianju
Deli
Tk Palabuhanratu

Strait of Malacca
Pesisir pulau
Kepulauan Mentawai
SUMATRA

SOUTH
MA

Kepulauan Anambas

IN

INDIAN
OCEAN

A   Longitude 100° east of Greenwich   B

Albers Equal Area Conic Projection   1:15 000 000   MILES 0   100   200   300

CHINA SEA

LAYSIA

Natuna Besar

Kepulauan
Natuna

Panarik

Kudat □ *Banggi*

Kota Belud

Gunung
Kinabalu
4095
Kota
Kinabalu

SULU
SEA

Sandakan

Beaufort

Labuan □

BANDAR SERI
BEGAWAN

BRUNEI
Kuala Belait
Lutong
Miri

Seria

Ranau

Lamag

Lahad
Datu

Kuamut

Pensiangan

SABAH

Lumbis

Tawau

Tumindao

CELEBES

Semporna

Bintulu

Igan Mukah

Sibu

Sarikei

Liku

Sematan

Kuching

Kota
Saratok
Samarahan
Debak
Sri Aman
Serian
Lubok
Antu

Bengkayang

Sambas

Pemangkat

ngkawang

Kepulauan
ambelan

Mempawah

Ngabang

Pontianak

Pulau-pulau
Karimata

Sukadana

Ketapang

Kendawangan

Tanjungpandan

Manggar

Belitung

Selat K a r i m a t a

Balaiberkuak

Telukbatang

Nangatayap

Sukaraja

Pangkalanbuun

Kualapembuang

Long
Akah

Belaga

Kapit

S A R A W A K

Datadian

2988

Putusibau

Pegunungan Muller

Semitau

Sintang

Nangahpinoh

Kapuas

Sanggau

Barito

B O R N E O

Bintik

Kubuang

Tarakan

Tanjungselor

Tanjungredeb

Sepinang

Sangkulirang

Bontang

Muaralaung

Muarateweh

K A L I M A N T A N

Rantaupanjang

Pegunungan Schwaner

Palangkaraya

Mahakam

Longiram

Samarinda

Tenggarong

Balikpapan

Tanahgrogot

S a m b a l i u n g

Sepinang

Selat Makassar
(Macassar Strait)

Babana

Mamuju

Gandadiwata
3074

Polewali

0°

Sampit

Seruyan

Amuntai

Kandangan

Kahayan

Kotabaru

Banjarmasin

Martapura

Pagatan

Tanjung
Sambar

Tanjung
Puting

Tanjung
Selatan

Laut

Majene

1

D O N E S I A

LAUT JAWA
(JAVA SEA)

Kepulauan
Laut Kecil

urwakarta

irebon

Bandung

Garut

iamis

Cilacap

Temanggung

Kebumen

Tegal

Pekalongan

Semarang

Kudus

Yogyakarta

Madiun

Surakarta

Pati

Tuban

Jombang

Bangkalan

Surabaya

Pasuruan

Tanjung
Indramayu

Pulau-pulau
Karimunjawa

Bawean

Kemujan

Tanjung
Bugel

Madura

Sumenep

Kepulauan
Kangean

Sabalana

JAVA
(JAWA)

3428
G. Raung
3332

Lumajang

Malang

Jember

Situbondo

Banyuwangi

Singaraja

Gilimanuk

Denpasar

Bali

Barung

Selat Lombok

Raas

Laut Bali
(Bali Sea)

Kepulauan
Tengah

Sumbawa

Alas

Dompu

Raba

Mataram

Sumbawabesar

Taliwang

Praya

Lombok

3142

Selat Madura

G. Semeru
3676

2

0   250   500 KILOMETRES

© Collins Bartholomew Ltd

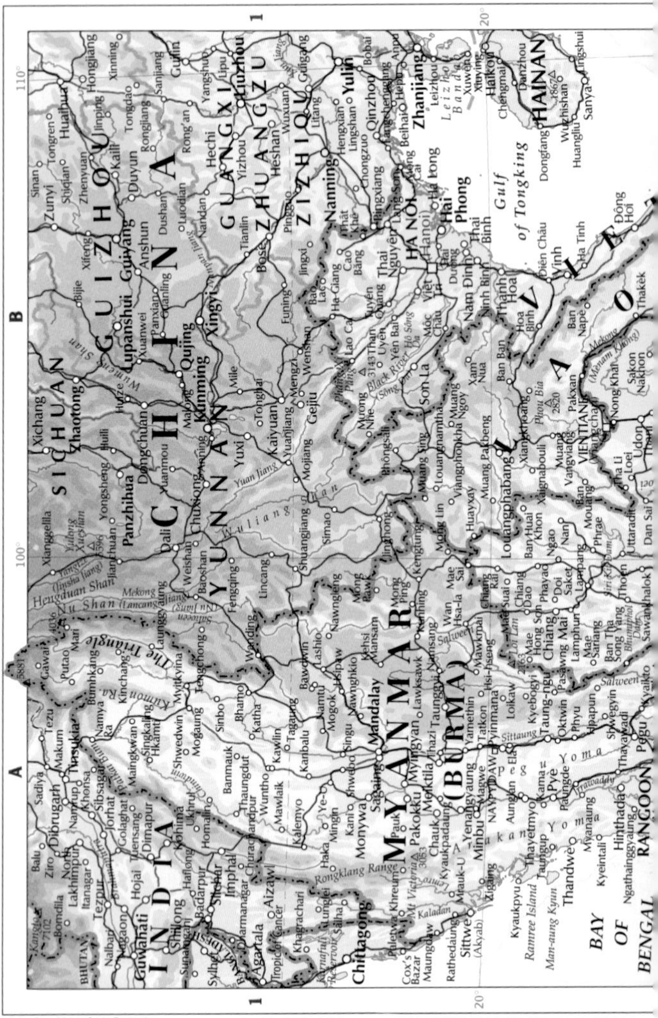

METRES
FEET

5000	16404
3000	9843
2000	6562
1000	3281
500	1640
200	656
0	0
LAND	B.S.L.
200	656
4000	13124
6000	19686

Albers Equal Area Conic Projection

1:15 000 000

MILES 0   100   200   300

CONTINENTAL SOUTHEAST ASIA

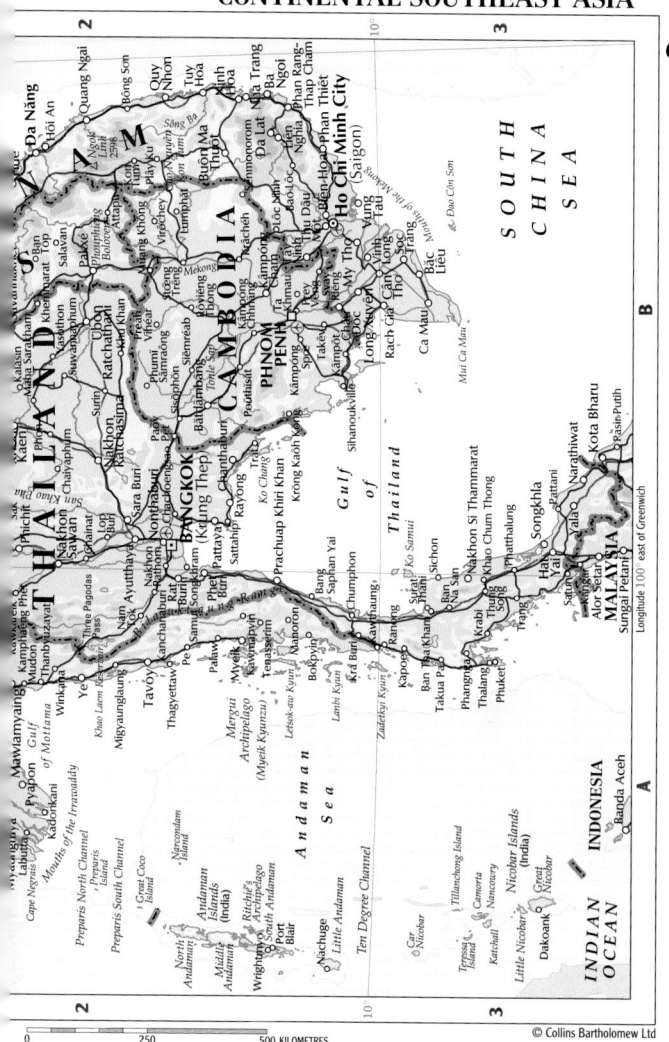

Quang Ngai
Da Năng
Hôi An
Bông Son
Quy Nhon
Tuy Hòa
Nha Trang
Phan Rang-Thap Cham
Phan Thiêt
Đà Lạt
Buôn Ma Thuột
Mnong
Ho Chi Minh City
(Saigon)
Vung Tau
Attapu
Salavan
Pakxé
Champasak
Savan
Khemmarat
Kompong Cham
Phnom Penh
CAMBODIA
Battambang
Poipet
Siemreab
Paôy Pêt
Krong Kaôh Kong
Sihanoukville
Gulf of Thailand
THAILAND
BANGKOK (Krung Thep)
Chanthaburi
Rayong
Pattaya
Sattahip
Prachuap Khiri Khan
Chumphon
Ranong
Surat Thani
Ko Samui
Nakhon Si Thammarat
Khao Chum Thong
Phatthalung
Songkhla
Trang
Hat Yai
Pattani
Narathiwat
Kota Bharu
MALAYSIA
Alor Setar
Pasir Putih
Sungai Petani
Phuket
Krabi
Phangnga
Takua Pa
INDONESIA
Banda Aceh

SOUTH CHINA SEA

Andaman Sea

INDIAN OCEAN

PHILIPPINES

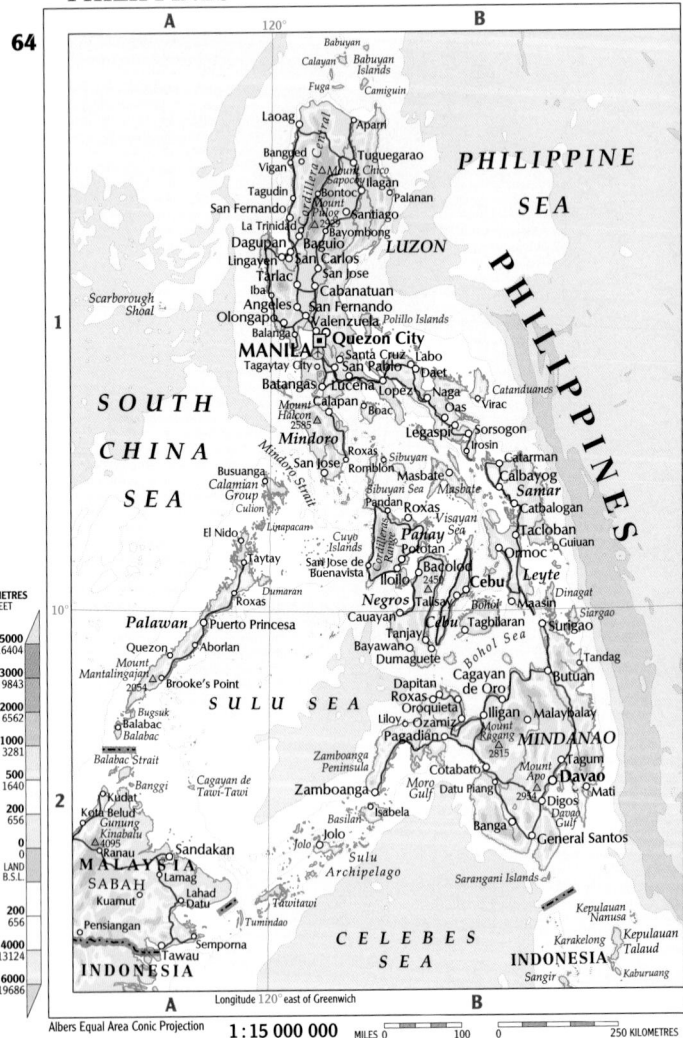

Babuyan
Calayan *Babuyan Islands*
Fuga Camiguin

Laoag
Bangued Aparri
Vigan Tuguegarao
Tagudin *Mount Chico* Ilagan Palanan
San Fernando Bontoc Santiago
La Trinidad *Mount Pulog*
Dagupan Baguio Bayombong
Lingayen San Carlos **LUZON**
Tarlac San Jose
Ibac Cabanatuan
Angeles San Fernando *Polillo Islands*
Olongapo Valenzuela
Balanga □ **Quezon City**
MANILA Santa Cruz Labo
Tagaytay City San Pablo Daet
Batangas Lucena Naga *Catanduanes*
Mount Halcon Calapan Lopez Oas Virac
2285 Boac Legaspi Sorsogon
Mindoro Irosin Catarman
San Jose Roxas *Sibuyan*
Romblon Masbate Calbayog
Busuanga *Sibuyan Sea* **Samar**
Calamian Pandan *Masbate* Catbalogan
Group Roxas Tacloban
Culion *Visayan* Guiuan
El Nido *Cuyo* *Panay* Ormoc
Linapacam *Islands* Pototan **Leyte**
Taytay San Jose de Iloilo Bacolod Cebu
Buenavista *2459* Maasin
Roxas *Dumaran* **Negros** Talisay **Cebu** Dinagat
Palawan Puerto Princesa Cauayan *Bohol* Tagbilaran Surigao
Quezon Tanjay Bayawan Siargao
Mount Dumaguete *Bohol Sea* Tandag
Mantalingajan Dapitan Cagayan
2054 Brooke's Point Roxas de Oro Butuan
Bugsuk **SULU SEA** Oroquieta Iligan Malaybalay
Balabac Liloy Ozamiz **MINDANAO**
Balabac Pagadian *Mount Ragang*
Balabac Strait *Zamboanga* *2815*
Peninsula Cotabato *Mount Apo* **Davao**
Zamboanga *Moro* Datu Piang *2954* Digos
Kudat Isabela *Gulf* Banga *Davao* Mati
Kota Belud *Banggi* Jolo *Gulf*
Gunung Kinabalu *Cagayan de* *Sulu* General Santos
4095 *Tawi-Tawi* *Jolo* *Archipelago*
Ranau Sandakan *Basilan* *Sarangani Islands* *Kepulauan*
MALAYSIA *Nanusa*
SABAH Lamag *Tawitawi* *Tumindao* *Kepulauan*
Kuamut Lahad Datu **CELEBES** *Karakelong* *Talaud*
Pensiangan **SEA** *Kaburung*
Semporna **INDONESIA** **INDONESIA**
Tawau *Sangir*

Scarborough Shoal

SOUTH

CHINA

SEA

Mindoro Strait

PHILIPPINE

SEA

PHILIPPINES

METRES / FEET

METRES	FEET
5000	16404
3000	9843
2000	6562
1000	3281
500	1640
200	656
0	0
LAND	B.S.L.
200	656
4000	13124
6000	19686

Longitude 120° east of Greenwich

Albers Equal Area Conic Projection   1:15 000 000   MILES 0   100   0   250 KILOMETRES

NORTH KOREA AND SOUTH KOREA

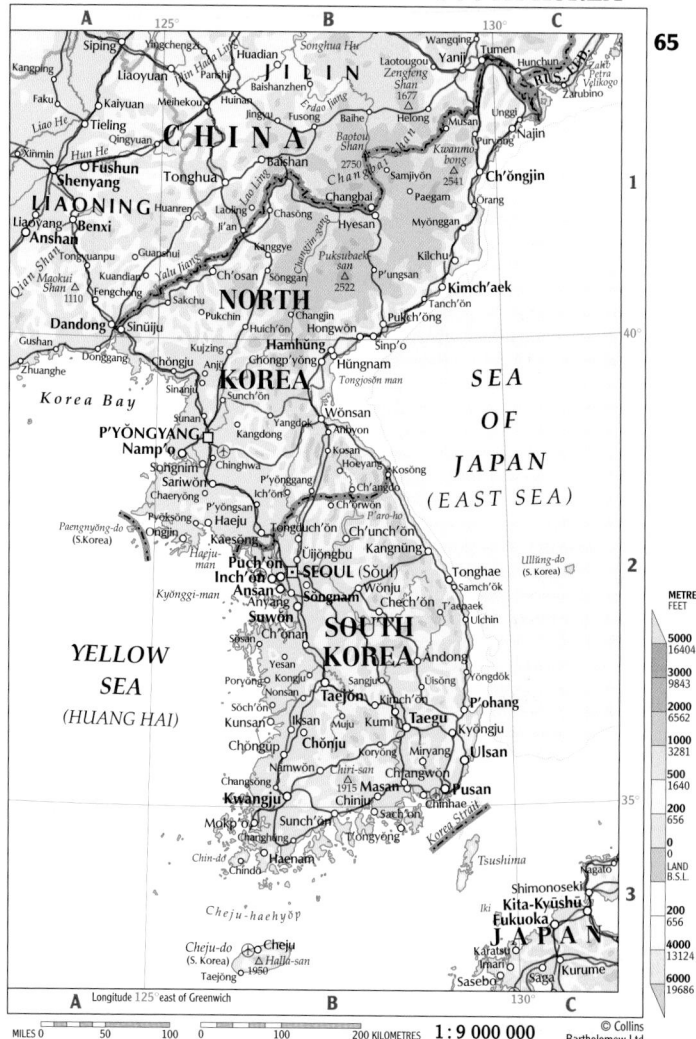

METRES
FEET

5000
16404

3000
9843

2000
6562

1000
3281

500
1640

200
656

0
0

LAND
B.S.L.

200
656

4000
13124

6000
19686

MILES 0   50   100

0   100   200 KILOMETRES

1 : 9 000 000

© Collins
Bartholomew Ltd

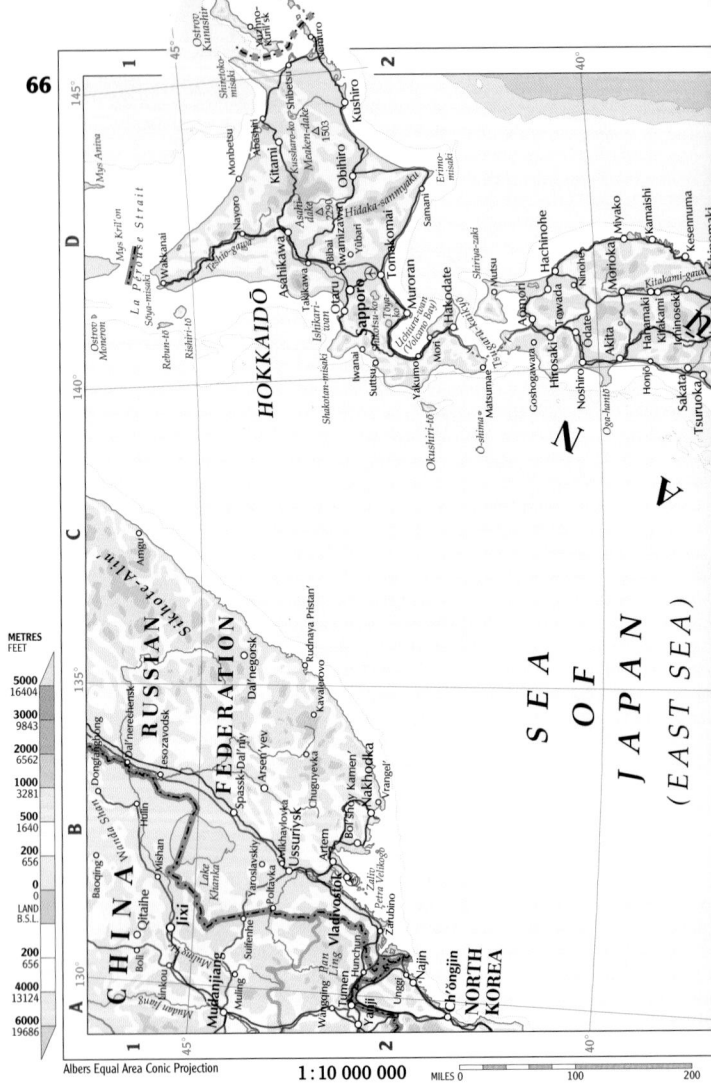

Ostrov Kunashir

Yuzhno-Kuril'sk

Kushiro

1

45°

145°

40°

2

Mys Anma

Mys Krll'on

Shiretoko-misaki

La Pérouse Strait

Monbetsu

Abashiri

Kushiro-dake

Kitami

Kussharo-ko

Meaken-dake
1503

Obihiro

Erimo-misaki

D

Ostrov
Moneron

Rebun-tō

Rishiri-tō

Sōya-misaki

Wakkanai

Shakotan-misaki

Iwanai

Suttsu

Okushiri-tō

HOKKAIDŌ

Teshio

Nayoro

Asahikawa

Asahi-dake
2290

Takikawa

Ishikari-wan

Otaru

SAPPORO

Biei

Iburi

Yūbari

Iwamizawa

Tomakomai

Muroran

Uchiura-wan
(Volcano Bay)

Hidaka-sanmyaku

Samani

Muta

Usu

Mori

Hakodate

Esan-misaki

Shiriya-zaki

Mutsu

O-shima

Matsumae

Tsugaru-kaikyo

Tappi-zaki

Aomori

Towada

Ōwani

Hirosaki

Goshogawara

Noshiro

Oga-hantō

Akita

Hachinohe

Towada

Odate

Hanamaki

Morioka

Miyako

Kamaishi

Ofunato

Ōfunato

Kesennuma

Ninohe

Ichinoseki

Kitakami-gawa

Honjō

Sakata

Tsuruoka

140°

N

H

O

N

S

E

A

O

F

J

A

P

A

N

(EAST SEA)

C

Sikhote-Alin'

Amgu

RUSSIAN

Dal'nerechensk

Rudnaya Pristan'

135°

Dal'negorsk

Kavalerovo

Arsen'yev

FEDERATION

Spassk-Dal'niy

Chuguyevka

Bol'shoy Kamen'

Nakhodka

Oranges

B

Wanda Shan

Dong'ning

Boli

Qitaihe

Baoqing

Hulin

Mishan

Lake
Khanka

Yaroslavskiy

Dmitriyevka

Ussuriysk

Artem

Zaliv
Petra Velikogo

VLADIVOSTOK

CHINA

Jixi

Mudanjiang

Suifenhe

Muling

Wangqing

Hunchun

Tumen

Yanji

Zarubino

Najin

Unggi

Chōngjin

A

Mudan Jiang

Songhua Jiang

Linkou

Zhang Guang Cai Ling

Tumen

NORTH KOREA

1

45°

130°

2

40°

METRES
FEET

5000
16404

3000
9843

2000
6562

1000
3281

500
1640

200
656

0
0

LAND
B.S.L.

200
656

4000
13124

6000
19686

Albers Equal Area Conic Projection

1 : 10 000 000

MILES 0   100   200

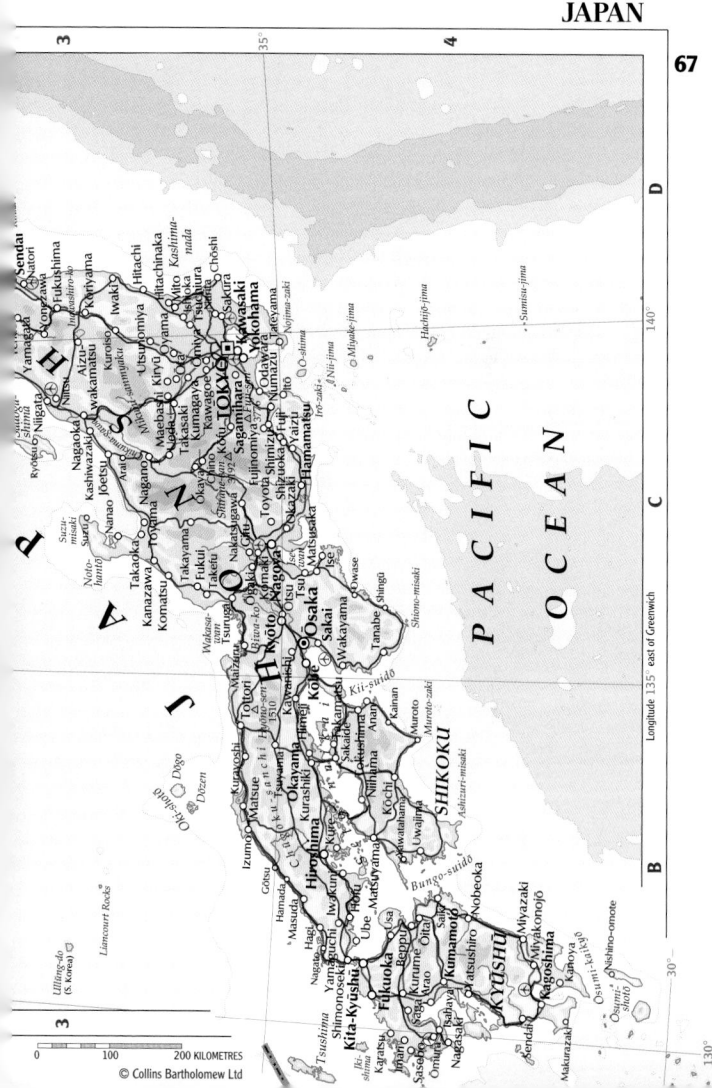

PACIFIC

OCEAN

Longitude 135° east of Greenwich

HONSHU

SHIKOKU

KYUSHU

Kii-suidō

Bungo-suidō

TOKYO
Yokohama
Kawasaki

Sendai
Yamagata
Fukushima
Niigata

Kyōto
Osaka
Kōbe
Sakai
Nagoya

Fukuoka
Kita-Kyūshū
Kumamoto
Kagoshima
Miyazaki

0   100   200 KILOMETRES

© Collins Bartholomew Ltd

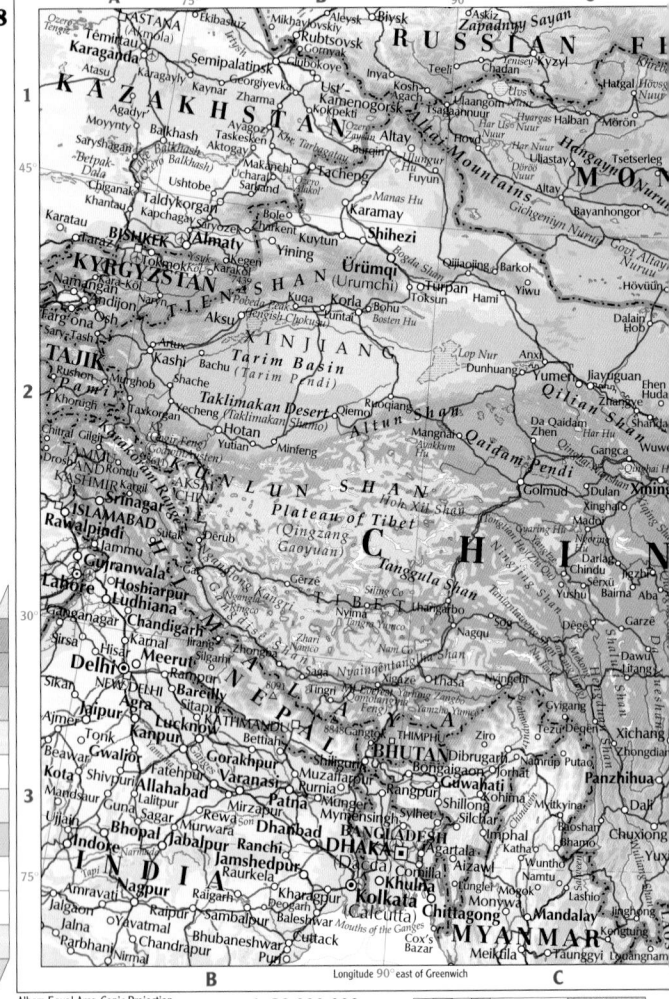

METRES
FEET

5000
16404

3000
9843

2000
6562

1000
3281

500
1640

200
656

0
0

LAND
B.S.L.

200
656

4000
13124

6000
19686

Albers Equal Area Conic Projection

1 : 30 000 000

MILES 0   200   400   600

Longitude 90° east of Greenwich

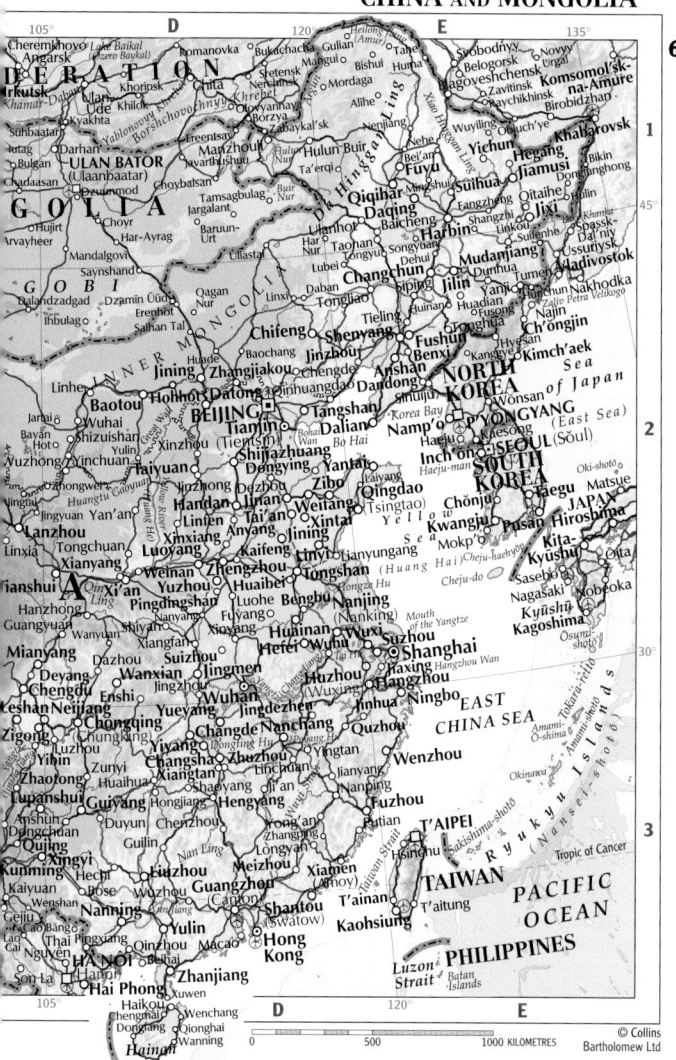

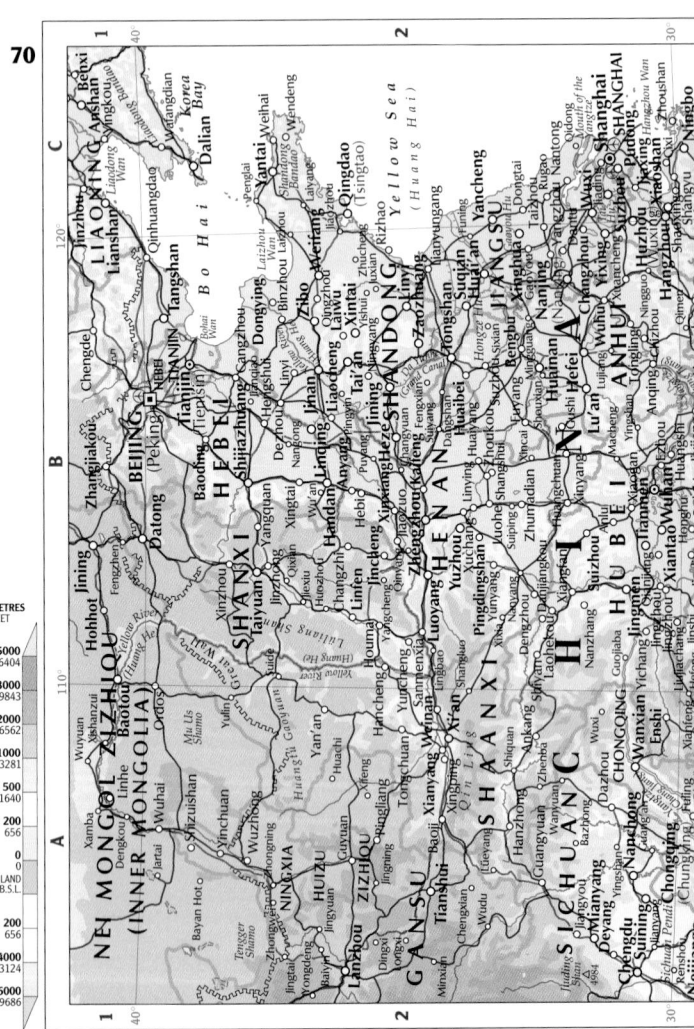

METRES
FEET

5000 16404
3000 9843
2000 6562
1000 3281
500 1640
200 656
0 0
LAND B.S.L.
200 656
4000 13124
6000 19686

Albers Equal Area Conic Projection

1 : 15 000 000

MILES 0   100   200   300

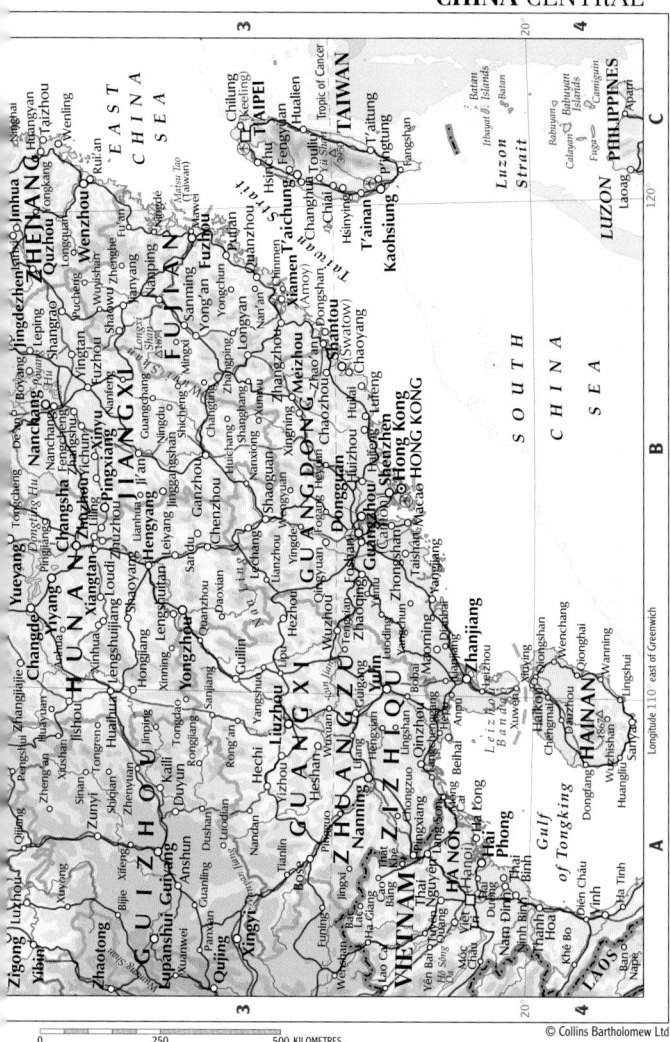

0   250   500 KILOMETRES

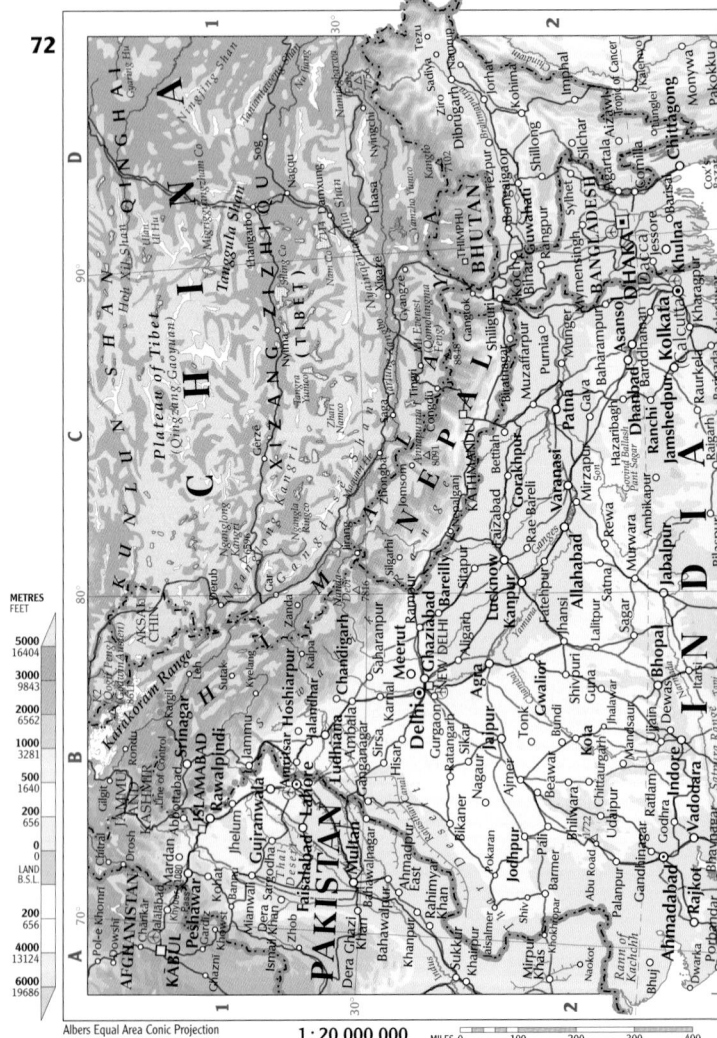

METRES
FEET

5000	16404
3000	9843
2000	6562
1000	3281
500	1640
200	656
0	0
LAND	B.S.L.
200	656
4000	13124
6000	19686

Albers Equal Area Conic Projection

1 : 20 000 000

MILES 0   100   200   300   400

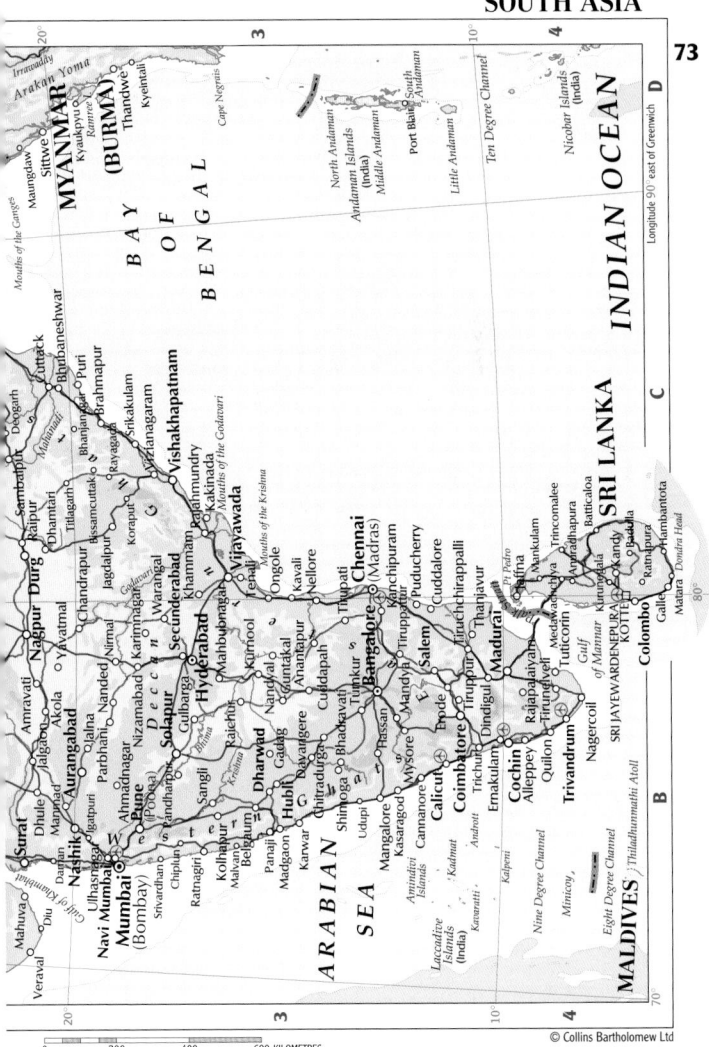

MYANMAR (BURMA)

Irrawaddy
Arakan Yoma
Mouths of the Ganges

Maungdaw
Sittwe
Kyaukpyu
Ramree
Thandwe
Kyeintali
Cape Negrais

North Andaman
Andaman Islands (India)
Middle Andaman
South Andaman
Port Blair
Little Andaman
Ten Degree Channel

Nicobar Islands (India)

INDIAN OCEAN

Longitude 90° east of Greenwich

B A Y O F B E N G A L

Cuttack
Deogarh
Puri
Bhubaneshwar
Brahmapur
Raipur
Dhamtari
Sambalpur
Bhanjanagar
Kesarncuttak
Ravangala
Srikakulam
Vizianagaram
Vishakhapatnam
Kakinada
Rajahmundry
Mouths of the Godavari
Eluru
Vijayawada
Mouths of the Krishna
Machilipatnam
Ongole
Kavali
Nellore

Durg
Nagpur
Amravati
Akola
Jalgaon
Chandrapur
Ayyatmal
Nirmal
Nizamabad
Karimnagar
Warangal
Khammam
Hyderabad
Secunderabad
Mahbubnagar
Nalgonda
Kurnool
Anantapur
Cuddapah
Tirupati
Kanchipuram
Chennai (Madras)
Puducherry
Cuddalore

Deccan
Godavari
Krishna

Surat
Daman
Diu
Mahuva
Veraval
Gulf of Khambhat
Navsari
Dhule
Nashik
Malegaon
Dhulia
Jalgaon
Aurangabad
Jalna
Parbhani
Nanded
Ahmadnagar
Pune (Poona)
Solapur
Gulbarga
Raichur
Bidar
Bijapur
Bagalkot
Gadag
Bellary
Hospet
Chitradurga
Tumkur
Bangalore
Kolar
Salem
Erode
Karur
Tiruchchirappalli
Thanjavur
Pudukkottai
Madurai
Dindigul

Sangli
Kolhapur
Ratnagiri
Chiplun
Savdardhan
Malvan
Panaji
Madgaon
Karwar
Dharwad
Hubli
Belgaum
Shimoga
Udupi
Mangalore
Hassan
Mandya
Mysore
Kasaragod
Cannanore
Calicut
Trichur
Coimbatore
Tiruppur
Palaiyankottai
Tirunelveli
Tuticorin
Rajapalaiyam
Kochi (Cochin)
Ernakulam
Alleppey
Quilon
Trivandrum
Nagercoil

ARABIAN SEA

Mumbai (Bombay)
Navi Mumbai
Ulhasnagar

Gulf of Kachchh

Laccadive Islands (India)
Amindivi Islands
Kadmat
Androth
Kavaratti
Kalpeni
Minicoy
Nine Degree Channel
Eight Degree Channel
Thiladhunmathi Atoll

MALDIVES

SRI LANKA

Jaffna
Pt Pedro
Mannar
Gulf of Mannar
Medawachchiya
Mankulam
Mullaittivu
Trincomalee
Anuradhapura
Batticaloa
Kurunegala
Kandy
Negombo
Kotte
Colombo
SRI JAYEWARDENEPURA KOTTE
Ratnapura
Galle
Matara
Dondra Head
Hambantota

80°
70°
20°
10°

© Collins Bartholomew Ltd

0   200   400   600 KILOMETRES

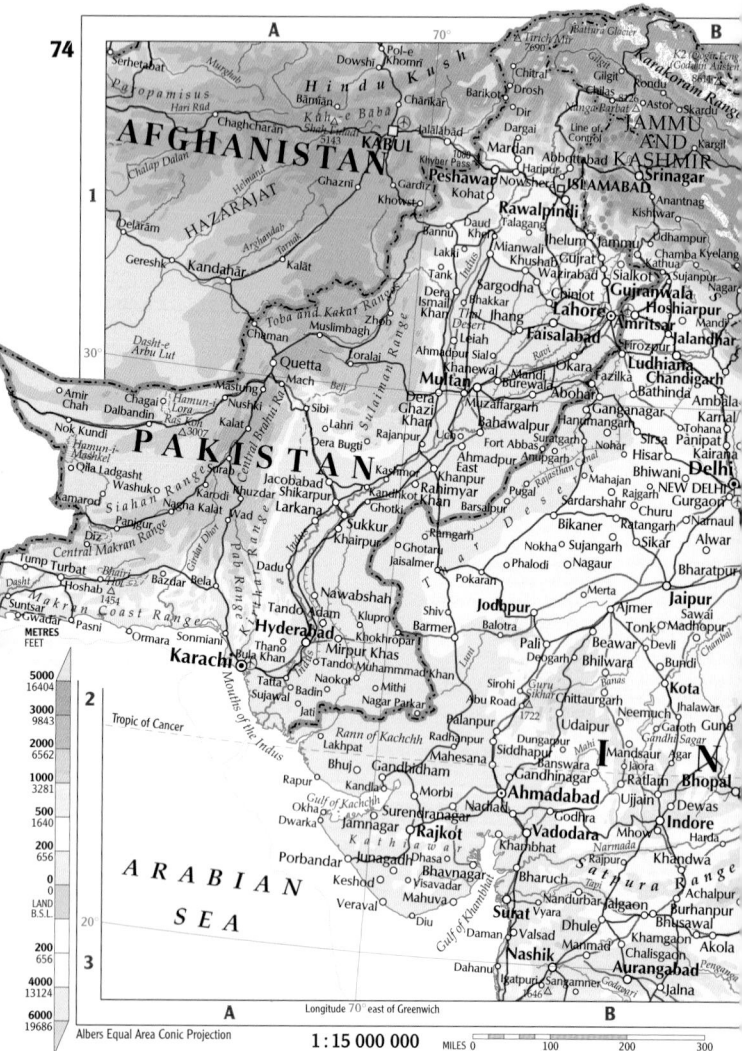

A 70° B

Serhetabad
Dowshi
Pol-e Khomri
Tirich Mir 7690
Rattaia Glacier
K2 (Qogir Feng Godwin Austen) 8611
Karakoram Range
Mary
Maymana
Chaghcharan
Hari Rud
Bamian
Kah-e Baba 5143
Charikan
Barikot
Chitral
Drosh
Gilgit
Nanga Parbat
Astor
Skardu
Roudu

Hindu Kush

AFGHANISTAN
Chalap Dalan
Delaram
Ghazni
Gardiz
Khowst

HAZARAJAT
Helmand
Arghandab
Tarnak

Jalalabad
KABUL
Khyber Pass
Dargai
Mardan
Nowshera
Peshawar
Kohat
Daud Khel
Bannu
Lakki
Haripur
Abbottabad
ISLAMABAD
Rawalpindi
Talagang
Jhelum
Line of Control
JAMMU AND KASHMIR
Srinagar
Anantnag
Kishtwar
Jammu
Udhampur
Chamba
Kyelang
Nagar

Line of Control

1

Gereshk
Kandahar
Kalat

Dasht-e Arbu Lut

Chaman
Muslimbagh
Loralai

Toba and Kakar Ranges

Quetta
Mastung
Mach
Sibi
Lahri
Bejī

Zhob

Central Brahui Range

Sulaiman Range

Dera Ismail Khan
Tank
Mianwali
Khushab
Sargodha
Wazirabad
Sialkot
Gujrat
Gujranwala
Hoshiarpur
Nagar
Sujanpur
Mandi

Bhakkar
Leiah

Thal Desert
Jhang
Faisalabad
Chiniot
Lahore
Amritsar
Jalandhar

30°

Amir Chah
Nok Kundi

Chagai
Dalbandin
Washuk
Nushki

Ras Koh
3007

Kalat
Surab

Dera Ghazi Khan
Rajanpur

Multan
Khanewal
Burewala
Abohar
Fazilka
Ludhiana
Chandigarh
Ambala
Karnal
Panipat
Kaithal

Hamun-i-Lora
Hamun-i-Mashkel
Qila Ladgasht
Kharan

Siahan Range

Panjgur
Karodi
Khuzdar
Jacobabad
Shikarpur
Larkana

Kashmor
Kandhkot
Ghotki
Rahimyar Khan
Ahmadpur East
Khanpur
Barsalpur
Fort Abbas
Anupgarh
Pugal

Sardarshahr
Nohar
Sirsa
Bhiwani
Hisar
Delhi
NEW DELHI
Gurgaon
Rohtak

Kamarod
Diz
Panjgur

Garuk Dhor

Bela
Bazdar

Pab Range
Wad

Nal
Surab

Sukkur
Khairpur
Ghotari
Jaisalmer

Mahajan
Bikaner
Nokha
Ratangarh
Churu
Sikar
Alwar
Narnaul

Tump
Turbat
Hoshab
Bit
1454

Central Makran Range

Dadu
Nawabshah
Kluporo
Shiv

Pokaran
Phalodi
Nagaur
Sujangarh
Raigarh

Jaipur
Sawai
Madhopur

Dasht
Suntsar
Gwadar
Pasni
Ormara

Makran Coast Range

Sonmiani
Thano Bula Khan
Hyderabad
Tando Adam
Mirpur Khas
Tando Muhammad Khan

Barmer
Balotra
Pali
Sirohi
Abu Road
1722

Jodhpur
Merta
Ajmer
Deogarh
Bhilwara

Tonk
Devli
Bundi

Guru Sikhar 1722

Kota
Jhalawar

Karachi
Tatta
Sujawal
Badin
Nagar Parkar
Mithi
Naokot

Radhanpur
Palanpur

Sirohi
Banswara

Chittaurgarh
Udaipur

INDIA
Mandsaur
Agar
Neemuch

Gangrar Guna

2

Tropic of Cancer

Mounts of the Indus
Rann of Kachchh
Lakhpat

Siddhpur
Mahesana

Gandhidham
Bhuj

Gandhinagar
Ahmadabad

Banswara
Ratlam
Mhow
Mandsaur
Indore
Dewas
Ujjain

Bhopal

METRES FEET
5000 16404
3000 9843
2000 6562
1000 3281
500 1640
200 656
0 0
LAND B.S.L.
200 656
4000 13124
6000 19686

Rapur
Kandla
Morbi
Surendranagar
Nadiad
Godhra
Harda

Khandwa
Khargon

Okha
Dwarka
Jamnagar
Rajkot

Kathiawar
Visavadar
Phasa

Kheda
Dhasa
Bhavnagar

Vadodara
Bharuch

Narmada
Rajpipla

Achalpur
Burhanpur

A R A B I A N

Porbandar
Junagadh
Keshod
Veraval
Diu

Gulf of Kachchh

Gulf of Khambhat

Khambhat

Vyara
Daman

Surat
Valsad

Satpura Range

Jalgaon
Bhusawal
Akola

S E A

20°

Dahanu

Nashik
Manmad
Chalisgaon

Aurangabad
Jalna

3

Dhule
Nandurbar

Godavari

Sangamner
1646

A

Longitude 70° east of Greenwich

B

Albers Equal Area Conic Projection

1 : 15 000 000

MILES 0   100   200   300

PLATEAU OF TIBET
(QINGZANG GAOYUAN)

XINJIANG UYGUR ZIZHIQU
(SINKIANG)

Hoh Xil Shan

QINGHAI

C H I N A

AKSAI CHIN
Under Chinese administration
claimed by India

Muztag 7282

Gozha Co

Dogai Coring

Ulan Ul Hu

Leh

Derub

Ladakh Range

Ngangla Ringco

Gar

Ge'gyal

XIZANG ZIZHIQU
(TIBET)

Tanggula Shan

Migriggyangzham 6099

Gangdisê Shan

Ngangong Kangri 6596

Zanda

Kalpa

Shimla

Dehra Dun

Saharanpur
Roorkee

Nanda Devi

Almora

Nagina

Meerut

Ghaziabad

Delhi

Moradabad

Bareilly

Aligarh

Mathura

Agra

Firozabad

Gwalior

Etawah

Kalpi

Jhansi

Shivpuri

Lalitpur

Bina-Etawa

Sagar

Jabalpur

Damoh

Murwara

Shahdol

Itarsi

Betul

Seoni

Mandla

Nagpur

Amravati

Wardha

Durg

Raipur

Gondia

Dhamtari

Yavatmal

Hinganghat

Adilabad

Chandrapur

Gadchiroli

Kondagaon Bhawanipatna

Titlagarh

Baligura

BAY
OF
BENGAL

Bhanjanagar

Puri

Mouths of the Ganges

Cox's Bazar

Chittagong

Barisal

Khulna

Kolkata
(Calcutta)

DHAKA
(Dacca)

BANGLADESH

Rajshahi

Pabna

BHUTAN

THIMPHU

Guwahati

Shillong

Silchar

Tezpur

Nagaon

Bomdila

Nalbari

Goalpara

Rangpur

Jalpaiguri

Darjiling

KATHMANDU

NEPAL

Pokhara

Annapurna 8091

Lhasa

Gyangzê

Xigazê

Nyima

Zhongba

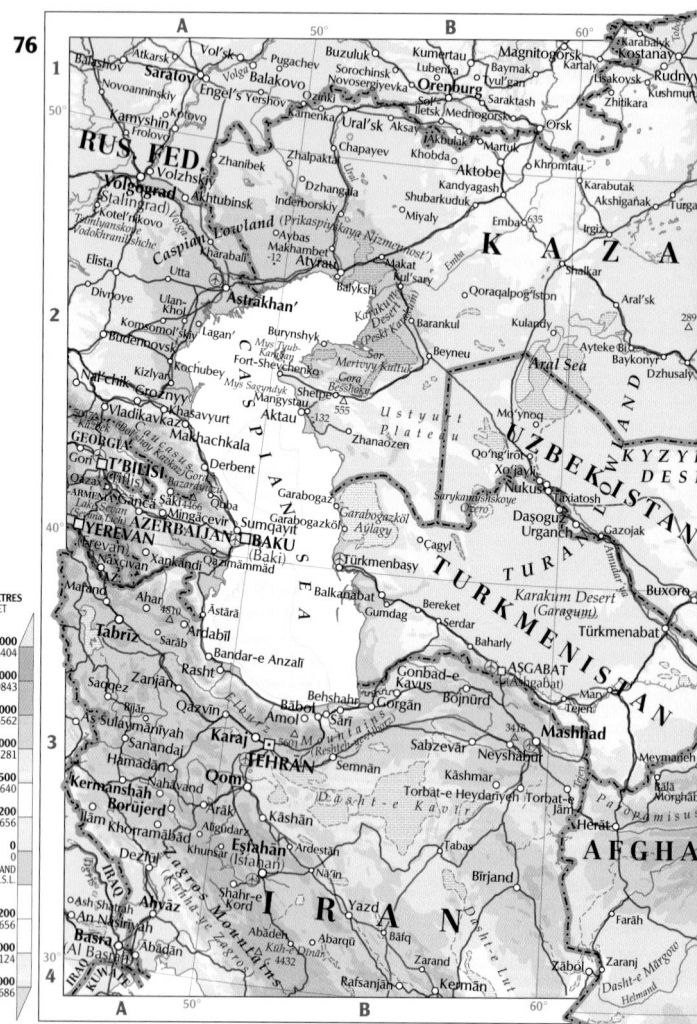

76

A 50° **B** 60°

RUS. FED.

Balashov · Atkarsk · Vol'sk · Pugachevo · Buzuluk · Kumertau · Magnitogorsk · Karabash · Kostanay
Novoanninskiy · Saratov · Balakovo · Sorochinsk · Novosergiyevka · Orenburg · Baymak · Lisakovsk · Rudnyy
Kamyshin · Engel's · Yershov · Ozinki · Kamenka · Ural'sk · Aksay · Akbulak · Mednogorsk · Saraktash · Kartaly · Zhitikara · Kushmurun
Frolovo · Kotovo · Zhanibek · Zhalpaktal · Chapayevo · Khobda · Martuk · Khromtau
Volgograd · Volzhskiy · Aktobe · Karabutak
(Stalingrad) · Akhtubinsk · Inderborskiy · Shubarkuduk · Kandyagash · Akshiganak · Turgay
Kotel'nikovo · Baskunchak · Makhambet · Dossor · Makat · Kul'sary · Emba · 635 · Irgiz · Shalkar
Tormosinskaya · Volgodonsk · Utta · Atyrau · Balykshi · Oporny · Qoraqalpog'iston
Elista · -12 · **K A Z A**
Divnoye · Ulan- · Astrakhan' · Makhambet · Dzhangala
Khol

GEORGIA
T'BILISI
YEREVAN
AZERBAIJAN
BAKU
ARMENIA

UZBEKISTAN
KYZYL
DESE

TURKMENISTAN
Karakum Desert
(Garagum)

IRAN

AFGHA

METRES FEET
5000 16404
3000 9843
2000 6562
1000 3281
500 1640
200 656
0 0
LAND B.S.L.
200 656
4000 13124
6000 19686

Albers Equal Area Conic Projection

1 : 20 000 000

MILES 0 · 100 · 200

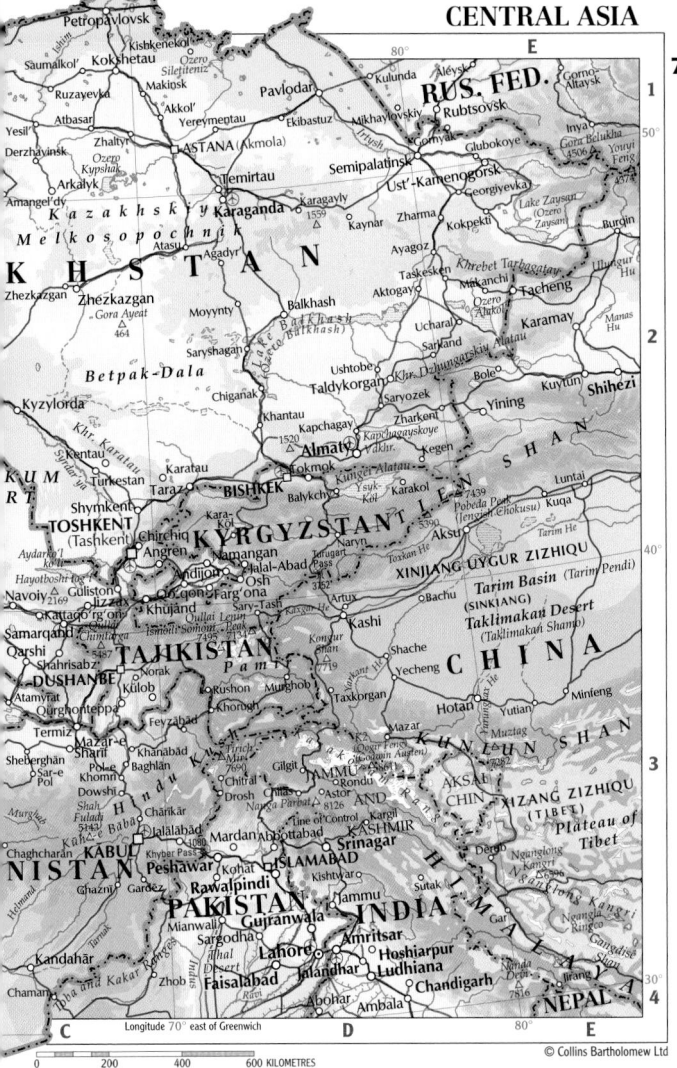

Petropavlovsk
Kishkenekol'
Saumalkol' Kokshetau
Ruzayevka Makinsk Akkol'
Yesil' Zhaltyr Yereymentau
Derzhavinsk Ozero
Arkalyk Kypshak
Amangel'dy Kazakhskiy Karaganda
Melkosopochnik
Zhezkazgan Zhezkazgan
Gora Ayeat
Kyzylorda Kentau Khr. Karatau
Karatau
Shymkent
TOSHKENT BISHKEK
(Tashkent) Chirchiq
Navoiy Guliston Angren
Samarqand Khüjand
Qarshi Shahrisabz
DUSHANBE
Atamyrat Norak
Qurghonteppa
Termiz Mazar-e
Sheberghan Sharif
Sar-e Pol-e
Pol Khomri
Dowshi
Chaghcharan Shah
KABUL
NISTAN
Ghazni Gardez
Kandahār
Chaman

RUS. FED.

Pavlodar
Kulunda Aleysk
Mikhaylovskiy Rubtsovsk
Semipalatinsk
Ust'-Kamenogorsk
Georgiyevka
Kopekti
Lake Zaysan
(Ozero Zaysan)
Khrebet Tarbagatay
Taskesken Aktogay
Ucharal
Sarkand Alatau
Karamay
Shihezi
Yining
TIEN SHAN
CHINA
HIMALAYA
NEPAL

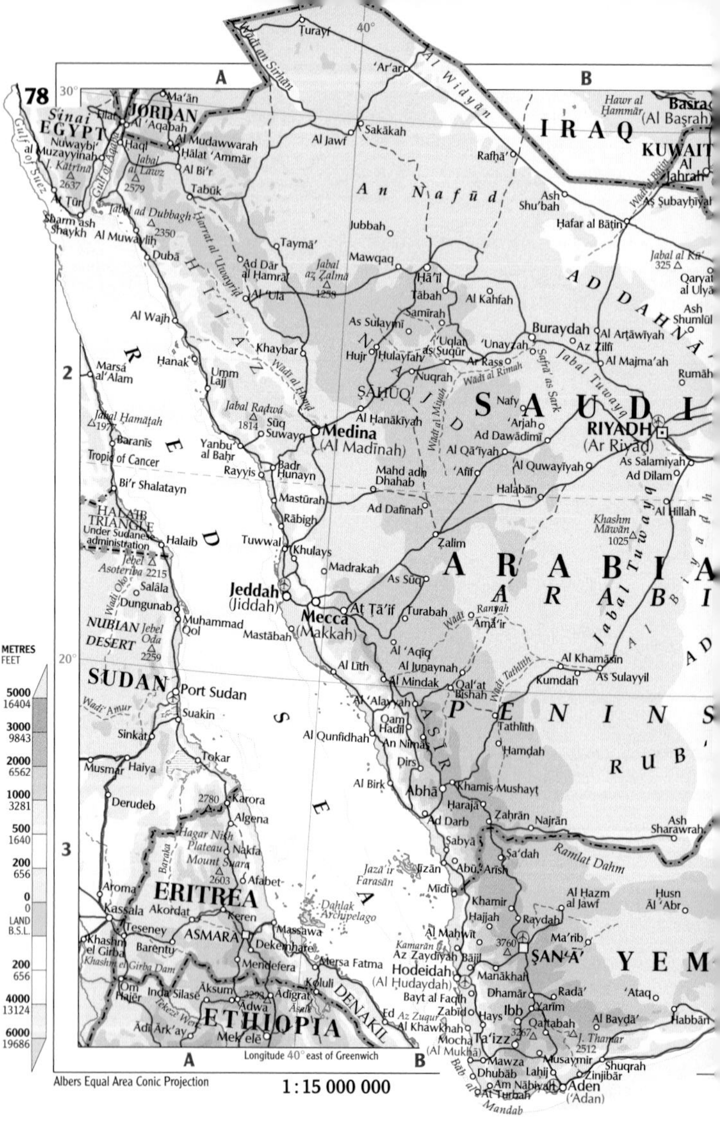
A
B
30°
40°
2
3
20°
JORDAN
EGYPT
Sinai
IRAQ
KUWAIT
SAUDI
ARABIA
ARABIAN
PENINSULA
SUDAN
ERITREA
ETHIOPIA
YEM
RED SEA
HIJAZ
NAJD
ASIR
An Nafud
AD DAHNA'
RUB'
DENAKIL
NUBIAN DESERT
HALAIB TRIANGLE
Under Sudanese administration
Tropic of Cancer
Gulf of Suez
Gulf of Aqaba
Wadi as Sirhān
Al Widyān
Wādī al Bātin
Harrat al 'Uwayrid
Wādī al Ḥamḍ
Wādī al Miyāh
Wādī al Rimah
Safrā' as Sark
Jabal Ṭuwayq
Wādī Tathlīth
Wādī Ranyah
Ramlat Dahm
Bab al Mandab
Wadi Oko
Wādī 'Amur
Baraka
Tekezē Wenz
Ṭurayf
'Ar'ar
Sakākah
Al Jawf
Rafḥā'
Hawr al Ḥammār
Basra
(Al Baṣrah)
Al Jahrah
Ash Shu'bah
Ḥafar al Bāṭin
Aṣ Ṣubayhīyah
Jabal al Ka'
325
Qaryat al Ulyā
Ash Shumlūl
Ma'ān
Eilat
Al 'Aqabah
Al Mudawwarah
Ḥālat 'Ammār
Ḥaql
Nuwaybi'
al Muzayyinah
J. Kātrīnā
2637
Jabal al Lawz
2579
Al Bi'r
Tabūk
Aṭ Ṭūr
Sharm ash Shaykh
Jabal ad Dubbagh
2350
Al Muwaylih
Dubā
Taymā'
Jubbah
Mawqaq
Ad Dār al Ḥamrā'
Jabal az Zalmā
1258
Al 'Ulā
Ḥā'il
Ṭābah
Al Kahfah
Samīrah
As Sulaymī
'Uqlat aṣ Ṣuqūr
Buraydah
Al Arṭāwīyah
Az Zilfī
'Unayzah
Ar Rass
Al Majma'ah
Rumāh
Al Wajh
Khaybar
Hujr
Hulayfah
Nuqrah
Ḥanak
Marsā al 'Alam
Umm Lajj
ṢAḤŪQ
Nafy
'Arjah
Jabal Radwá
1814
Sūq Suwayq
Medina
(Al Madīnah)
Al Ḥanākīyah
Ad Dawādimī
RIYADH
(Ar Riyāḍ)
Jabal Ḥamāṭah
1977
Baranīs
Yanbu' al Baḥr
Badr Ḥunayn
Rayyis
Al Qā'īyah
'Afīf
Al Quwayīyah
As Salamiyah
Ad Dilam
Mahd adh Dhahab
Halabān
Bi'r Shalatayn
Mastūrah
Ad Dafīnah
Al Ḥillah
Khashm Māwān
1025
Rābigh
Halaib
Tuwwal
Khulays
Ẓalim
Jebel Asoteriba
2215
Madrakah
Salâla
As Sūq
Jeddah
(Jiddah)
Dungunab
Mecca
(Makkah)
Aṭ Ṭā'if
Turabah
Amā'ir
Muhammad Qol
Mastābah
Jebel Oda
2259
Al 'Aqīq
Al Junaynah
Al Līth
Al Khamāsīn
As Sulayyil
Kumdah
Al Mindak
Qal'at Bīshah
Port Sudan
Suakin
Al 'Alayyah
Qam Hadil
Tathlīth
Al Qunfidhah
An Nimāṣ
Sinkat
Ḥamḍah
Tokar
Musmar
Haiya
Dirs
Al Birk
Abhā
Khamīs Mushayt
Derudeb
2780
Karora
Ḥarajah
Algena
Ad Darb
Zahrān
Najrān
Ash Sharawrah
Hagar Nish Plateau
Nakfa
Mount Soara
2603
Afabet
Ṣabyā
Ṣa'dah
Jazā'ir Farasān
Jīzān
Abū 'Arīsh
Aroma
Kassala
Akordat
Keren
Dahlak Archipelago
Mīdī
Khamir
Al Ḥazm al Jawf
Ḥusn Āl 'Abr
Teseney
Ḥajjah
Raydah
Khashm el Girba
ASMARA
Massawa
Al Maḥwīt
Ma'rib
Barentu
Dekemhare
Kamarān
3760
Khashm el Girba Dam
Mendefera
Az Zaydīyah
Bājil
ṢAN'Ā'
Mersa Fatma
Hodeidah
(Al Ḥudaydah)
Manākhah
Om Hajer
Inda Silasē
Āksum
3293
Ādigrat
Koluli
Dhamār
Radā'
'Ataq
Ādwa
Āsale
Bayt al Faqīh
Yarīm
Ed
Az Zuqur
Zabīd
Hays
Ibb
Al Bayḍā'
Ḥabbān
Ādī Ārk'ay
Mek'elē
Al Khawkhah
Qa'ṭabah
3267
J. Thamar
2512
Mocha
(Al Mukhā)
Ta'izz
Mawza
Musaymīr
Shuqrah
Dhubāb
Laḥij
Zinjibār
Am Nābiyah
Aden
('Adan)
Al Turbah
METRES
FEET
5000
16404
3000
9843
2000
6562
1000
3281
500
1640
200
656
0
0
LAND B.S.L.
200
656
4000
13124
6000
19686
Longitude 40° east of Greenwich

Albers Equal Area Conic Projection

1:15 000 000

80

Sibiu
Sfântu Gheorghe
Râmnicu Vâlcea
Focşani
Braşov
Artsyz
Odesa
Armyans'k
UKRAINE
Gulf of Taganrog
Yeysk
Staromynska
Primors'ko-
Akhtarsk
Pavlovskaya
Timashevsk
Slatina
Piteşti
Ploieşti
ROMANIA
Galaţi
Bolhrad
Bilhorod-
Dnistrovs'kyy
Skadovs'k
Kamyanets'ka Zatoka
Krasnoperekops'k
Novooleksiyivka
Dzhankoy
Sea
of Azov
Slavyans'k-
na-Kubani
Caracal
Roşiori de Vede
Corabia
Ruse
BUCHAREST
(Bucureşti)
(Dunav)
Călăraşi
Constanţa
Chornomors'ke
Yevpatoriya
Kherson
Simferopol'
Kerch
Feodosiya
Temryuk
Krymsk
Krasnodar
Maykop
Pleven
Lovech
Razgrad
Dobrich
Mangalia
Sevastopol'
Sudak
Novorossiysk
Khadyzhensk
Kazanluk
Shumen
Kavarna
*Roman-
Kosh*
1545
Tuapse
BULGARIA
Sliven
Burgas
Varna
Sochi
Plovdiv
Stara Zagora
Dimitrovgrad
Khaskovo
B L A C K   S E A
1
Smolyan
Edirne
Saray
Silivri
İnce Burun
Xanthi
Komotini
Keşan
Tekirdağ
İstanbul
Kadıköy
Zonguldak
Ereğli
Bartın
İnebolu
Boyabat
Sinop
Bafra
Samsun
Thasos
Gökçeada
İmroz
Çanakkale
Sea of Marmara
Bandırma
Gemlik
Bolu
Karabük
Gerede
Kastamonu
Tosya
Vezirköprü
Amasya
Terme
Ordu
Giresun
Trabzon
Límnos
Ezine
Can
Bursa
Bilecik
Sakarya
Mudurnu
Çankırı
Osmancık
Chíos
Ayvalık
Soma
Susurluk
Balıkesir
İnegöl
Eskişehir
ANKARA
Kırıkkale
Çorum
Sungurlu
Yıldızeli
Sivas
Susehri
Erzincan
Mytilíni
Bergama
Akhisar
Simav
Kütahya
Emirdağ
Yozgat
Akdağmadeni
Zara
Divriği
İzmir
Manisa
Salihli
Uşak
Afyon
Yunak
Kaman
Líke Tuz
(Tuz Gölü)
Kayseri
391
Kangal
GREECE
Kuşadası
Aydın
Denizli
Dinar
Sandıklı
Akşehir
Cihanbeyli
Aksaray
Niğde
Develi
Pınarbaşı
Elazığ
Tunceli
Ikaría
Nazilli
Çivril
2799
Eğridir Gölü
Karapınar
Bor
Dağ
3917
Kahramanmaraş
Malatya
Erganı
Diyarbakır
Sámos
Dodecanese
Dhodhekánisos
Söke
Yatağan
Milas
Muğla
Burdur
Beyşehir Gölü
Bucak
Beyşehir
Konya
Ereğli
Elbistan
Adıyaman
Siverek
Şanlıurfa
Bodrum
Marmaris
Dalaman
Köyceğiz
Korkuteli
Serik
Karaman
Gaziantep
Kilis
Bilecik
Akçakale
Maras
Datça
Fethiye
Elmalı
Antalya
Manavgat
Taurus Mts
Ermenek
Mut
Silifke
Adana
Tarsus
Osmaniye
İskenderun (Alexandretta)
3073
Rhodes
(Ródos)
Alanya
Antalya
Körfezi
Anamur
Cape Apostolos
Andreas
Mersin
Antakya
(Antioch)
(Hatay)
Aleppo
Halab
Euphrates
Fırat
Aegean
Sea
Karpathos
(Scarpanto)
Agios
Nikólaos
Kyrenia
(Keryneia)
NICOSIA (Lefkosía)
Cape Arnauti
Aigialousa
İdlib
Lefke
Lataka
Hamāh
Dayr az Zawr
Euphrates
CRETE
(KRÍTI)
Cape Kormakiti
Evrychou
Paphos (Páfos)
CYPRUS
Larnaca
Limassol
(Lemesós)
Baniyas
SYRIA
Tarṭūs
Ṭarābulus
Tripoli
Al Lādhiqīyah
Latakia
Hamah
Homs
Tadmur
Megísti
2
M E D I T E R R A N E A N
S E A
BEIRUT (Beyrouth)
Sidon (Saïda)
Tyre (Soûr)
Al Qunayṭirah
Zaḥlé
LEBANON
DAMASCUS
(Dimashq)
Sab' Ābār
Al Qaryatayn
Haifa (Ḥefa)
Nazareth
Galilee (L. Tiberias)
Irbid
As Suwaydā'
Ar Ruṭbah
ISRAEL
Jenin
Dar'ā
Syrian Desert
(Bādiyat ash Shām)
Tel Aviv-Yafo
Nāblus
JERUSALEM
WEST
BANK
AMMAN
Az Zarqā'
Turayf
Alexandria
(Al Iskandarīyah)
Al 'Amirīyah
Damanhūr
Balṭīm
Al 'Arīsh
Beersheba
Dead Sea
Al Karak
Wadi as Sirhan
Marsá
Maṭrūḥ
Al Hammam
Mansûra
Ṭanṭā
Bur Sa'īd
Al Ismā'ilīyah
GAZA
3
Qattara
Depression
Munkhafad al Qattārah
Shubrā al Khaymah
Giza (Al Jīzah)
Pyramids of Giza
Az Zaqāzīq
Suez Canal
Qanāt as Suways
Sinai
Ma'ān
Petra
Al 'Aqabah
Sakākah
Al Jawf
SAUDI
EGYPT
CAIRO
(Al Qāhirah)
Memphis
Suez (As Suways)
Al Mudawwarah

METRES
FEET

METRES	FEET
5000	16404
3000	9843
2000	6562
1000	3281
500	1640
200	656
0	0
LAND	B.S.L.
200	656
4000	13124
6000	19686

Albers Equal Area Conic Projection

1 : 15 000 000

MILES 0   100   200   300

Longitude 30° east of Greenwich

Sal'sk *Ozero Manych-Gudilo* Elista Utta
Tikhoretsk Ipatovo Divnoye Ulan-
Kropotkin Stavropol'skaya Komsomol'skiy Khol' Lagan'
RUSSIAN
Armavir *Voznyshemost* Budennovsk
Labinsk Nevinnomyssk Kochubey
Cherkessk Pyatigorsk Prokhladnyy Kizlyar
Kislovodsk Nal'chik Grozny Khasavyurt
FEDERATION
Gagra Vladikavkaz Makhachkala
Sokhumi Buynaksk Izberbash
Zugdidi K'utaisi Telavi Derbent
GEORGIA Samtredia
P'ot'i Bat'umi T'BILISI
Pazar Artvin Ardahan Şəki Bazardüzü
Rize Gyumri Mingəçevir Göyçay Samaxı Sumqayıt
ARMENIA AZERBAIJAN
Erzurum İğdır **YEREVAN** Ağdam **BAKU**
Doğubeyazıt Sisian **(Baki)**
Bingöl Malazgirt Naxçıvan Salyan
Muş Van Xankəndi Lənkəran
Tatvan Lake Van Khoy Marand Aştārā
Siirt Salmas Ahar Bandar-e Anzalī
Batman Başkale Sarab
Mardin Hakkari Maragheh Miāneh Rasht
Al Qāmishlī Zāxū Oshnoviyeh Mahābād **Now** Bābol Sāri
Al Ḥasakah Mosul Arbīl Zanjān shahr Amol Dāmghān
Elburz Mountains
Ash As Sulaymānīyah Bījār Qazvīn
Sharqāt Kirkūk Sanandaj **Karaj**
Tuz Khurmātū Halabja **TEHRĀN** Semnān
Bayjī Tikrīt Ravānsar Hamadān
Al Haditha Sāmarrā' Kermānshāh Malāyer **Qom** Kāshān
Hit Islamabad Nahāvand Arāk
Al Ramādī Ba'qūbah Ghary **IRAN** Ardestān
Buhayrat ath Tharthar **BAGHDAD** Īlām Borūjerd Golpāyegān
Buhayrat ar Razāzah Khorramābād Aligūdarz Khunsār
IRAQ Karbalā' Dezfūl Najafābād **Eşfahān**
Hillah Shahr-e Kord **(Isfahan)**
An Najaf Al Kūt Shūshtar Shahrezā Yazd
Ad Dīwānīyah Masjed
Ash Shatrah Soleymān Ābādeh Abarqū
As Samāwah Süq ash **Ahvāz** Rāmhormoz
An Nāşirīyah Shuyūkh
BASRA Khorramshahr
Ar'ar **ARABIA** (Al Başrah) Ābādān Kāzerūn Zargān Darya-ye Tashk **Shīrāz**
Al Fāw **KUWAIT** Ganāveh

© Collins Bartholomew Ltd

0   250   500 KILOMETRES

METRES
FEET

5000	16404
3000	9843
2000	6562
1000	3281
500	1640
200	656
0	0
LAND	B.S.L.
200	656
4000	13124
6000	19686

Conic Equidistant Projection

1 : 42 000 000

MILES 0   250   500   750

Longitude 75° east of Greenwich

© Collins Bartholomew Ltd

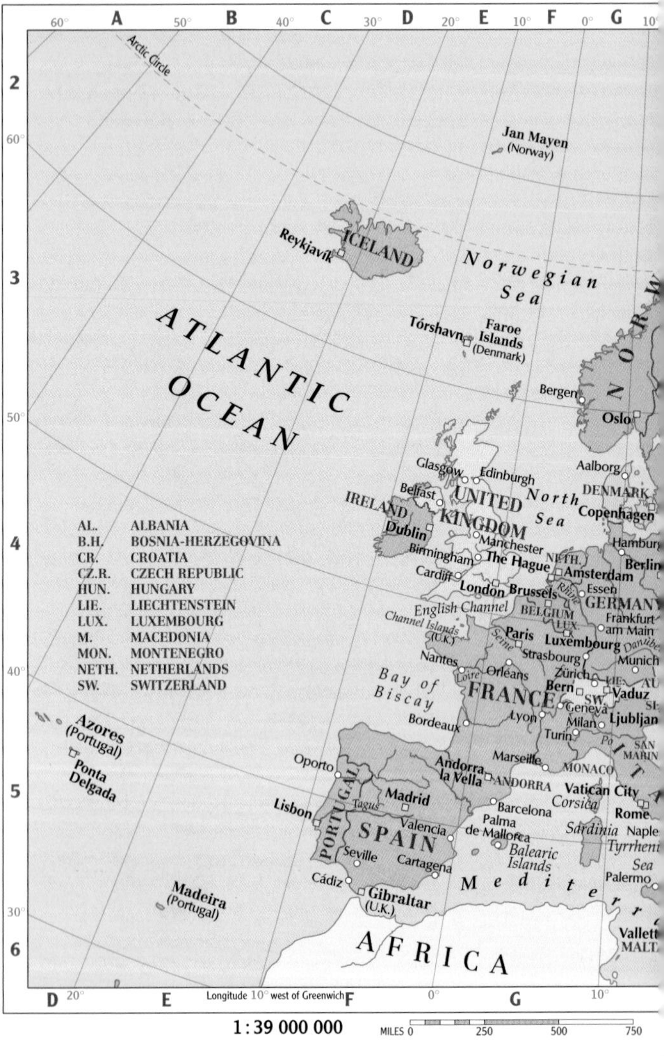

84

AL.	ALBANIA
B.H.	BOSNIA-HERZEGOVINA
CR.	CROATIA
CZ.R.	CZECH REPUBLIC
HUN.	HUNGARY
LIE.	LIECHTENSTEIN
LUX.	LUXEMBOURG
M.	MACEDONIA
MON.	MONTENEGRO
NETH.	NETHERLANDS
SW.	SWITZERLAND

Arctic Circle

Jan Mayen
(Norway)

Reykjavik ICELAND

Norwegian Sea

Tórshavn Faroe Islands
(Denmark)

Bergen

ATLANTIC OCEAN

NORW

Oslo

Glasgow Edinburgh Aalborg

Belfast North Sea DENMARK

IRELAND UNITED KINGDOM Copenhagen

Dublin Manchester Hamburg

Birmingham The Hague Berlin

Cardiff London NETH. Amsterdam Essen

English Channel Brussels GERMANY

Channel Islands BELGIUM Frankfurt
(U.K.) Seine Luxembourg am Main Danube

Paris Strasbourg Munich

Nantes Orleans Zürich LIE. Vaduz

Bay of Biscay FRANCE Bern SW. Geneva Ljubljan

Bordeaux Lyon Milan Turin Po SAN MARIN

Marseille MONACO IT

Oporto Andorra la Vella ANDORRA Vatican City

Madrid Barcelona Corsica Rome

Lisbon Tagus Valencia Palma Sardinia Naple

PORTUGAL de Mallorca Tyrrheni

SPAIN Balearic Sea

Seville Cartagena Islands Palermo

Cádiz Mediter

Gibraltar Vallett
(U.K.) MALT

Azores
(Portugal)

Ponta
Delgada

Madeira
(Portugal)

AFRICA

1 : 39 000 000

MILES 0   250   500   750

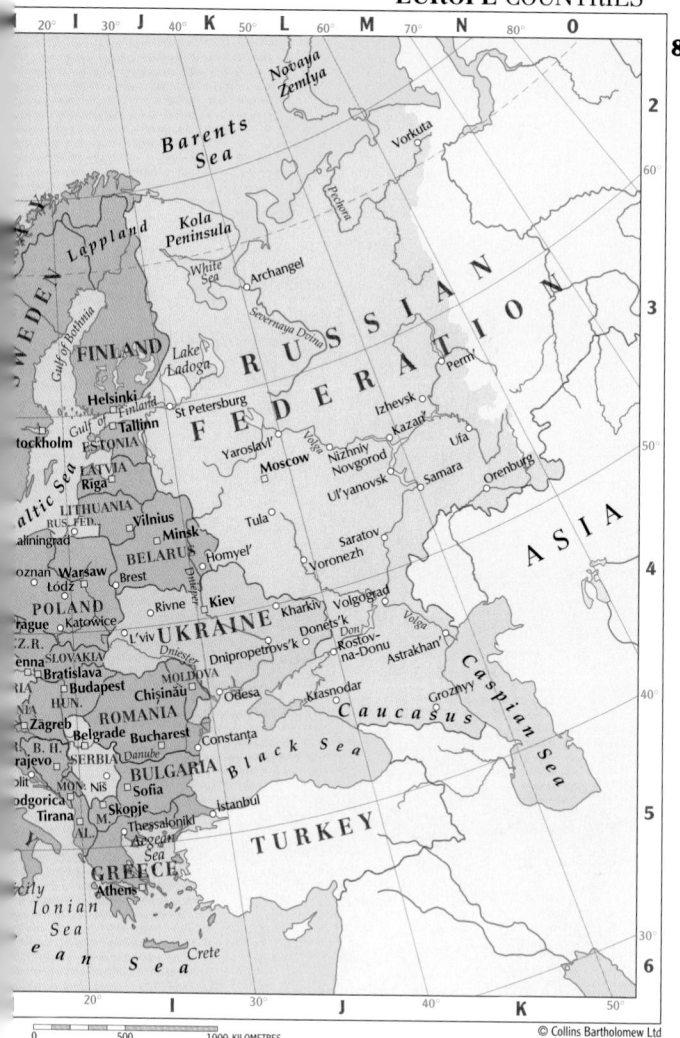

20° I 30° J 40° K 50° L 60° M 70° N 80° O

Novaya Zemlya

Barents Sea

Vorkuta

2

60°

Kola Peninsula

Archangel

White Sea

SWEDEN *Lappland*

Severnaya Dvina

Lake Ladoga

Pechora

3

FINLAND

Helsinki

St Petersburg

Perm

Gulf of Finland

Izhevsk

Tallinn

ESTONIA

Yaroslavl'

Kazan'

50°

Ufa

tockholm

Nizhniy Novgorod

Samara

LATVIA

Riga

Volga

Moscow

Ul'yanovsk

Orenburg

R U S S I A N

F E D E R A T I O N

Gulf of Bothnia

altic Sea

LITHUANIA

Vilnius

RUS. FED.

alingrad

Tula

Saratov

BELARUS

Minsk

A S I A

Homyel'

Voronezh

oznan

Warsaw

Brest

Dnieper

50°

Łódź

POLAND

Rivne

Kiev

Kharkiv

Volgograd

rague

Katowice

UKRAINE

Don

Volga

C.Z.R.

L'viv

Donets'k

Dniester

Dnipropetrovs'k

Rostov-na-Donu

Astrakhan'

enna

SLOVAKIA

Bratislava

Budapest

MOLDOVA

Chişinău

Odesa

Krasnodar

Grozvyy

Caspian Sea

RIA

HUN.

Zagreb

ROMANIA

C a u c a s u s

40°

B.H.

Belgrade

Bucharest

Constanţa

rajevo

SERBIA

Danube

Black Sea

olit

MON. Niš

BULGARIA

odgorica

Skopje

Sofia

İstanbul

5

Tirana

AL.

Thessaloníki

Aegean Sea

erly

GREECE

Athens

TURKEY

Ionian Sea

30°

ean Sea

Crete

6

20° I 30° J 40° K 50°

0 500 1000 KILOMETRES

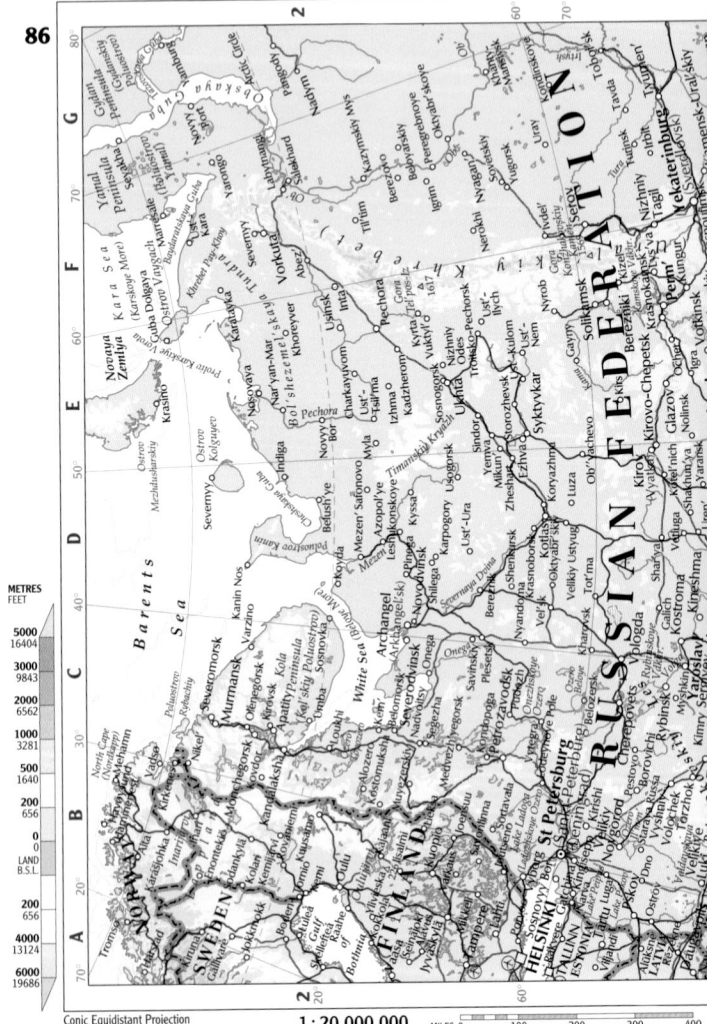

2

60° 70°

80°

G

Cydanskiy
Peninsula
(Gydanskiy
Poluostrov)

Gyda

Obskaya
Guba

Pangody
Nadym

60°

Tazovskiy
Novyy Urengoy

Arctic Circle

Yamal
Peninsula
(Poluostrov Yamal)

Salekhard
Labytnangi

Yar-Sale

70°

F

Novyy Port
Kharasavey
Marresale (Kharasavey)
Ostrov Bely

Kara Sea
(Karskoye More)

Severnyy

Kazymskiy Mys

Berezovo
Igrim
Saranpaul

Muzhi

Nyagan

Khanty-Mansiysk

Surgut

Uray
Sovetskiy

Novaya
Zemlya

Proliv Karskiye Vorota

Khabei Payudyey

Yamburg

Amderma

Vorkuta

Tiľtim

Yekaterinburg

Novaya
Zemlya

Guba Dolgaya

Ostrov Vaygach

Kara

Khalmer-Yu

Intaa
Usinsk

Kotelnich

Pechora

Konecchnyy

Severnyy

Ostrov
Kolguyev

Indiga

Naryan-Mar
Khoreyver

Konin
1617

Sosnogorsk

Vuktyl

Pechora

E

Proliv
Matochkin Shar

Krasino

Severnyy

Bol'shaye
Zemel'skaya Tundra

Nizhniy
Odes

Troitsko-Pechorsk

Izhma

Kirov

Kyrta

Kadzherom

Ukhta

Ust'-
Tsiľma

Barents
Sea

D

Poluostrov Kanin

Kanin Nos

Mezen'

Pinega

Kotlas

Syktyvkar

50°

60°

C

Murmansk

White Sea

Arkhangel'sk

Kola

Onega

Petrozavodsk

40°

B

Norway
Sweden

Finland

Gulf of
Bothnia

St Petersburg

Helsinki

RUSSIAN FEDERATION

A

70°

20°

60°

2

20°

METRES
FEET

5000
16404

3000
9843

2000
6562

1000
3281

500
1640

200
656

0
0
LAND
B.S.L.

200
656

4000
13124

6000
19686

Conic Equidistant Projection

1 : 20 000 000

MILES 0   100   200   300   400

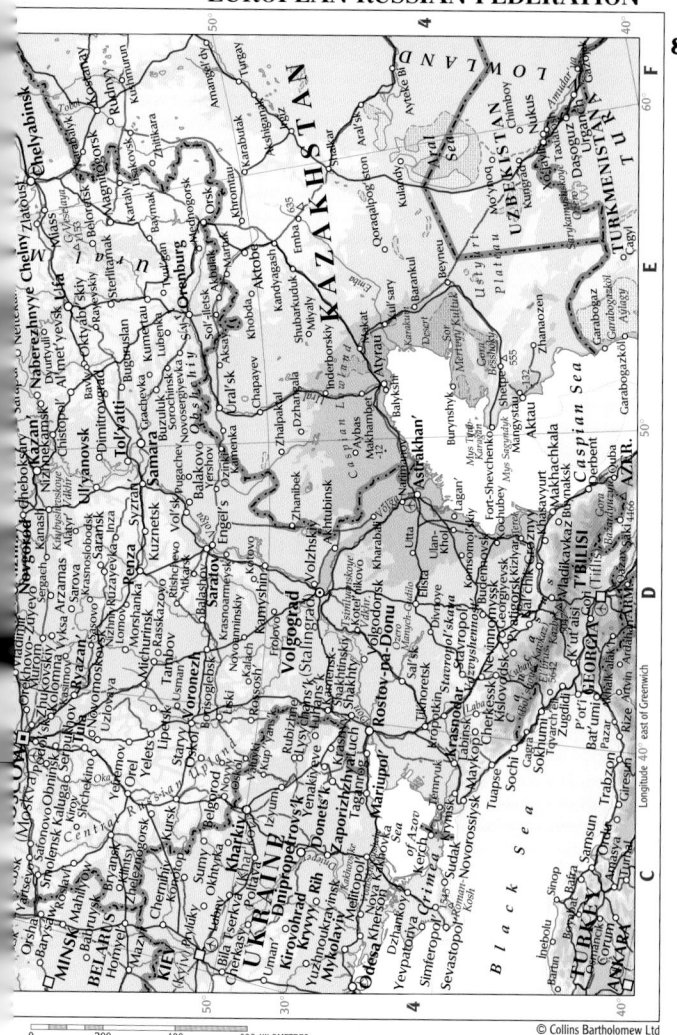

0   200   400   600 KILOMETRES

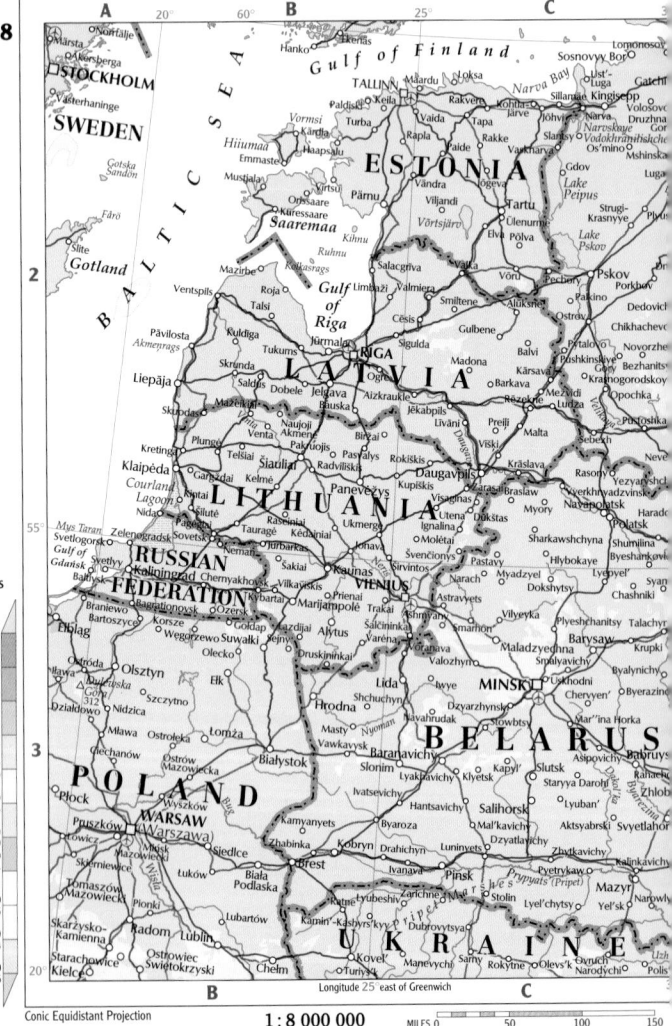

A   20°   60°   B   25°   C

SWEDEN

Märsta ○ Norrtälje
Korsberga
STOCKHOLM
Västerhaninge

Gotska
Sandön

Fårö
Slite
Gotland

Ventspils

Pāvilosta
Akmeņrags

B A L T I C   S E A

Hanko
Gulf of Finland
TALLINN Maardu Loksa
Paldiski Keila
Vormsi Vaida Rakvere Kohtla-Järve Sillamäe
Hiiumaa Kärdla Turba Rapla Paide Rakke Vaeküla
Emmaste Haapsalu
Orissaare **ESTONIA**
Kuressaare Pärnu Vändra Viljandi Tartu
Saaremaa Kihnu Võrtsjärv Elva Põlva
Ruhnu Salacgrīva Valga Võru
Mazirbe Roja Limbaži Valmiera Smiltene Aluksne
Kolkasrags **Gulf of Riga** Cēsis Gulbene Balvi
Talsi Sigulda Madona Kārsava
Kuldīga Jūrmala **RIGA** Barkava Rēzekne
LATVIA Mežvidi

Narva Bay
Sosnovyy Bor
Ust'-Luga Gatchi
Narva Volosov
Slantsy Druzhna Gor
Vodokhranilishche
Os'mino Mshinska
Gdov Luga
Lake Peipus
Strugi-Krasnyye
Lake Pskov Pskov Porkhov
Pechory Pakino Dedovic
Ostrov Chikhachev
Novorzhe
Pöshkinskiye Gory Bezhanits
Krasnogorodskoy Opochka
Pustoška

Kretinga
Klaipėda
Courland
Lagoon
Nida

Mys Taran
Svetlogorsk
Zelenogradsk
RUSSIAN
Gulf of
Gdansk Baltiysk
Svetlyy
Kaliningrad
Chernyakhovsk
FEDERATION
Bagrationovsk
Gvardeysk Ozersk

Skrunda
Liepāja Saldus Dobele Jelgava
Skuodas Mažeikiai Naujoji Bauska
Akmene
Plungė Venta Pakruojis
Telšiai Šiauliai Pasvalys
Radviliškis
Garždai Kelmė **LITHUANIA**
Gargždai Kėdainiai Panevėžys
Plungė Kelmė
Šilutė Tauragė
Sovetsk Jurbarkas Kaunas
Neman Šakiai
Vilkaviškis
Braniewo Elbląg
Bartoszyce Korsze Goldap
Węgorzewo Suwałki
Olecko

Aizkraukle Jēkabpils
Līvāni Preiļi
Krustpils Malta
Birži Viški
Rokiškis Kraslava
Kupiškis Krāslava
Daugavpils
Utena Braslaw
Visaginas Zarasas
Ignalina Dukštas
Molėtai Myory
Švenčionys Pastavy
Širvintos Narach
Ukmergė Astravyets
Jonava **VILNIUS** Myadzyel
Prienai Trakai Dokshytsy
Marijampolė Ashmyany
Kaišiadorys Smarhon'
Kazlų Rūda Varėna Hlybokaye
Jieznas Vilyeyka
Alytus Maladzyechna
Druskininkai

Rāzekne
Ludza
Rasony
Verkhnyadzvinsk Yezyaryshcł
Navapolatsk
Polatsk Harado
Syan
Shumilina
Byeshankovich
Ul'yanovichy
Chashniki
Talachyn
Krupki

Preiļi

Viski

Ashmyany Smarhon'
Hlybokaye
Vilyeyka **MINSK** Byerazino
Usachy Dzyarzhynsk Syelyava
Lahoysk Barysaw
Plyeshchanitsy Talachyn
Krupki
Byalynichy

Plesky

Plyeshchanitsy

Ostróda
Iława
Olsztyn
Działdowo Nidzica
Mława Szczytno
Olecko
Ełk
Grajewo
Łomża
Ostrów Mazowiecka
Ostrołęka

POLAND
Płock
Pruszków
Wyszków
WARSAW
(Warszawa)
Żyrardów
Łowicz
Skierniewice Mazowiecki
Tomaszów Piotrków
Mazowiecki Pionki
Skarżysko-
Kamienna Radom
Starachowice
Kielce Świętokrzyski
Ostrowiec
Świętokrzyski

Hrodna
Mosty
Vawkavysk
Baranavichy
Slonim
Lyakhavichy
Ivatsevichy
Hantsavichy

Shchuchyn
Iwye
Lida
Nyoman
Navahrudak
Slowtsy
Klyetsk Kapyl'
Staryya Darohi
Salihorsk
Mal'savichy

Valozhyn
Dzyarzhynsk

Ivanava Kobryn Drahichyn Luninyets
Byaroza Mal'savichy
Zhabinka
Brest Pinsk
Pryp'yats (Pripet)
Kamyanyets
Biała Podlaska
Łuków Siedlce
Węgrów
Międzyrzec

BELARUS
Asipovichy Babruysk
Slutsk Rahac
Lyuban' Zhlobin
Svyetlahorsk
Zhytkavichy
Petrykaw
Kalinkavichy
Mazyr Narowl
Yel'sk
Narodychi

Włodawa
Chełm
Lublin
Krasnystaw

Kowel
Turiysk
Kamin'-Kashyrs'kyy
Lyubeshiv
Ratne Zarichne
Dubrovytsya
Manevychi
Sarny
Rokytne
Olevs'k

UKRAINE

METRES FEET
5000 16404
3000 9843
2000 6562
1000 3281
500 1640
200 656
0 LAND B.S.L.
200 656
4000 13124
6000 19686

55°
2
3
20°

Longitude 25° east of Greenwich

Conic Equidistant Projection

B   C

1 : 8 000 000

MILES 0   50   100   150

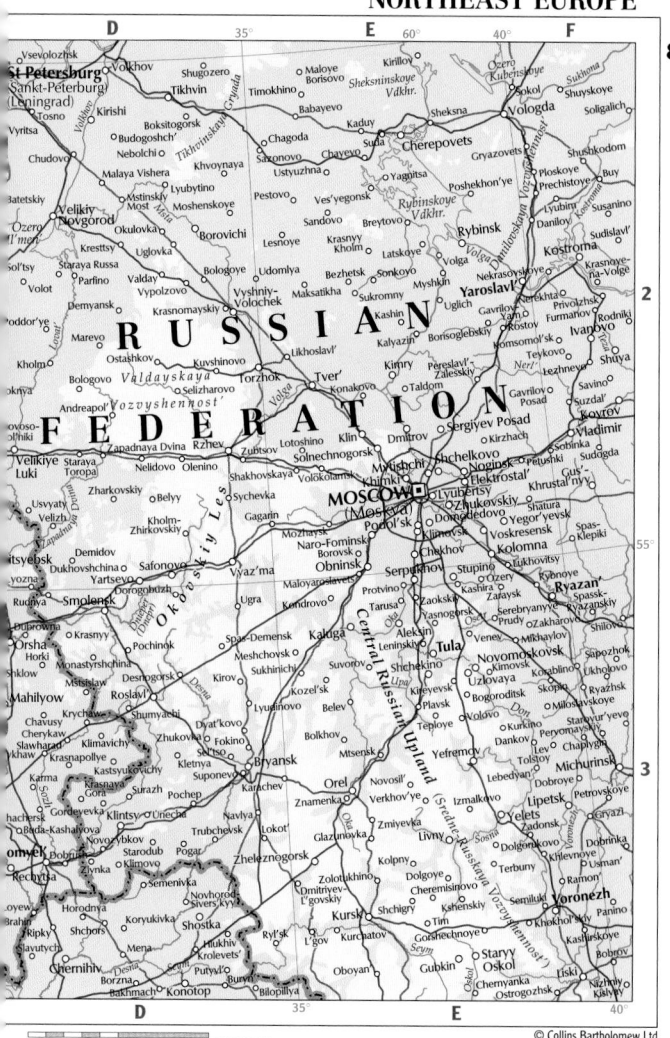

D · · · 35° · · · E · · · 60° · · · · · 40° · · · F

Vsevolozhsk
St Petersburg
(Sankt-Peterburg)
(Leningrad)
Volkhov
Shugozero
Tikhvin
Maloye
Borisovo
Kirillov
Timokhino
Babayevo
Ozero
Kubenskoye
Sokol
Vologda
Shuyskoye
Soligalich
Sukhona
Shushkodom
Tosno
Kirishi
Budogoshch'
Chagoda
Kaduy
Sheksna
Cherepovets
Gryazovets
Ploskove
Prechistoye
Buy
Vyritsa
Chudovo
Nebolichi
Khvoynaya
Sazonovo
Chayevo
Suda
Yagodnya
Poshekhon'ye
Danilov
Susanino
Malaya Vishera
Lyubytino
Ustyuzhna
Ves'yegonsk
Rybinskoye
Vdkhr.
Lyubim
Batetskiy
Velikiy
Novgorod
Mstinskiy
Most
Moshenskoye
Pestovo
Sandovo
Breytovo
Rybinsk
Kostroma
Krasnoye-
na-Volge
Ozero
Il'men'
Kresttsy
Uglovka
Borovichi
Lesnoye
Krasnyy
Kholm
Latskoye
Nekrasovskoye
Gavrilov-
Yam
Nerekhta
Sol'tsy
Staraya Russa
Parfino
Valday
Bologoye
Udomlya
Bezhetsk
Sonkovo
Myshkin
Yaroslavl'
Privolzhsk
Rodniki
Volot
Demyansk
Vypolzovo
Krasnomayskiy
Vyshniy-
Volochek
Maksatikha
Sukromny
Kalyazin
Pereslavl'-
Zalesskiy
Borisoglebskiy
Rostov
Komsomol'sk
Teykovo
Furmanov
Ivanovo
Poddor'ye
Marevo
Ostashkov
Kuvshinovo
Likhoslavl'
Kimry
Nerl'
Savino
Shuya
Kholm
Bologovo
Selizharovo
Torzhok
Tver'
Konakovo
Taldom
Sergiyev Posad
Lezhnevo
Suzdal'
Kovrov
Andreapol'
Zapadnaya Dvina
Rzhev
Zubtsov
Lotoshino
Klin
Dmitrov
Kirzhach
Vladimir
Sudogda
Velikiye
Luki
Staraya
Toropa
Nelidovo
Olenino
Shakhovskaya
Volokolamsk
Istra
Solnechnogorsk
Shchelkovo
Noginsk
Elektrostal'
Petushki
Gus'-
Khrustal'nyy
Usyvaty
Velizh
Belyy
Sychevka
Gagarin
Mytishchi
Khimki
MOSCOW
(Moskva)
Lyubertsy
Zhukovskiy
Yegor'yevsk
Shatura
Spas-
Klepiki
Demidov
Dukhovshchina
Safonovo
Vyaz'ma
Mozhaysk
Naro-Fominsk
Podol'sk
Domodedovo
Ramenskoye
Voskresensk
Kolomna
Smolensk
Yartsevo
Dorogobuzh
Ugra
Maloyaroslavets
Obninsk
Protvino
Chekhov
Stupino
Lukhovitsy
Rudnya
Krasnyy
Pochinok
Spas-Demensk
Kondrovo
Tarusa
Serpukhov
Kashira
Zaraysk
Ryazan'
Orsha
Horki
Monastyrshchina
Desnogorsk
Kirova
Kaluga
Aleksin
Yasnogorsk
Venev
Serebryannyye
Prudy
Mikhaylov
Spozhok
Spassk-
Ryazanskiy
Mstsislaw
Roslavl'
Kozel'sk
Sukhinichi
Suvorov
Leninskiy
Shchekino
Tula
Novomoskovsk
Skopin
Shilovo
Mahilyow
Chavusy
Krychaw
Shumyachi
Dyat'kovo
Belev
Plavsk
Bogoroditsk
Uzlovaya
Kimovsk
Kireyevsk
Skopin
Ukholovo
Ryazhsk
Cherykaw
Klimavichy
Zhukovka
Fokino
Bolkhov
Teploye
Volovo
Kurkino
Milovslavskoye
Slawharad
Kastsyukovichy
Kletnya
Suponevo
Karachev
Mtsensk
Yefremov
Lev
Tolstoy
Dankov
Chaplygin
Michurinsk
Karma
Krasnaya
Gora
Surazh
Pochep
Bryansk
Orel
Novosil'
Verkhov'ye
Izmalkovo
Lebedyan'
Petrovskoye
hachersk
Klintsy
Unecha
Navlya
Lokot'
Znamenka
Zmiyevka
Livny
Yelets
Zadonsk
Lipetsk
Dobrinka
Beda-Kashalyova
Novo-
zybkov
Starodub
Pogar
Trubchevsk
Glazunovka
Dolgoye
Terbuny
Usman'
omyel'
Dobrush
Zlynka
Klimovo
Dmitriyev-
L'govskiy
Zheleznogorsk
Kolpny
Zolotukhino
Cheremisinovo
Semiluki
Voronezh
Rechytsa
Semenivka
Novhorod-
Sivers'kyy
Shostka
Kursk
Shchigry
Tim
Gorshechnoye
Ramon'
Panino
Brahin
Ripky
Horodnya
Koryukivka
Hlukhiv
Ryl'sk
L'gov
Kurchatov
Gubkin
Staryy
Oskol
Kshen'sky
Khokhol'skiy
Slavutych
Shchors
Mena
Krolevets'
Putyvl'
Oboyan'
Stariy
Oskol
Kashir
Liski
Chernihiv
Borzna
Bakhmach
Konotop
Bilopillya
Seym
Ostrogozhsk
Bobrov

D · · · 35° · · · E · · · · · 40°

0 · · 100 · · 200 KILOMETRES

METRES
FEET

5000
16404

3000
9843

2000
6562

1000
3281

500
1640

200
656

0
0
LAND
B.S.L.

200
656

4000
13124

6000
19686

Conic Equidistant Projection

1 : 8 000 000

MILES 0   50   100   150

Longitude 25° east of Greenwich

POLAND

BELARUS

UKRA

KIEV
(Kyïv)

HUNGARY

SLA

ROMANIA

MOLDOVA

CHIŞINĂU
(Kishinev)

BUCHAREST
(Bucureşti)

WARSAW
(Warszawa)

Ostrów
Mazowiecka
Białystok
Wyszków
Siedlce
Radom
Lublin
Zamość
Chełm
Kovel'
Rivne
Zhytomyr

Ternopil'
L'viv
(Lvov)

Chernivtsi

Iaşi

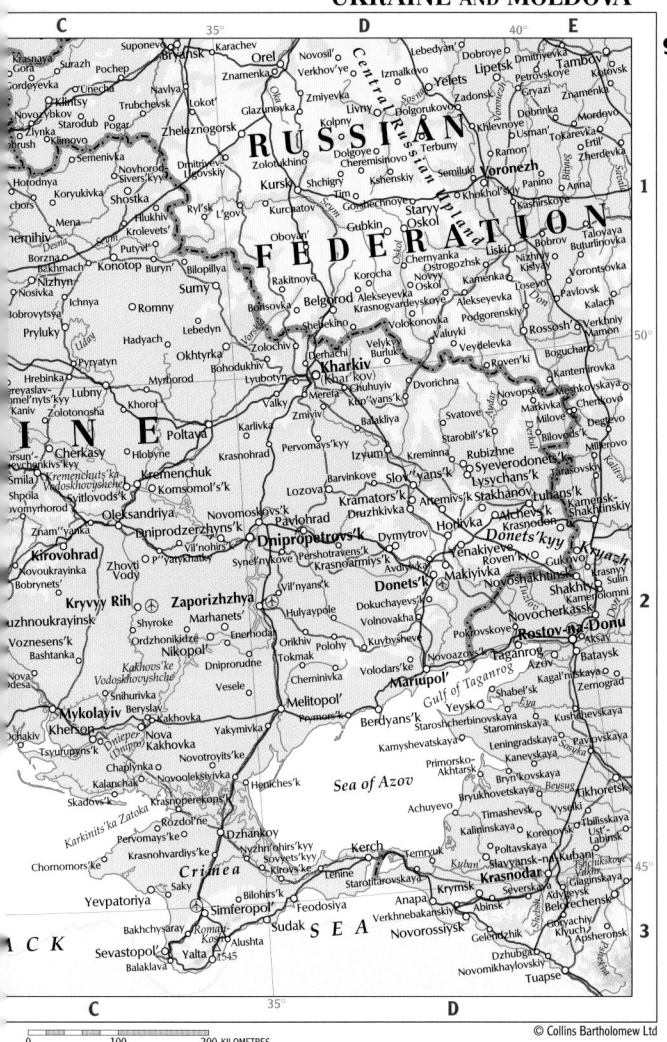

0   100   200 KILOMETRES

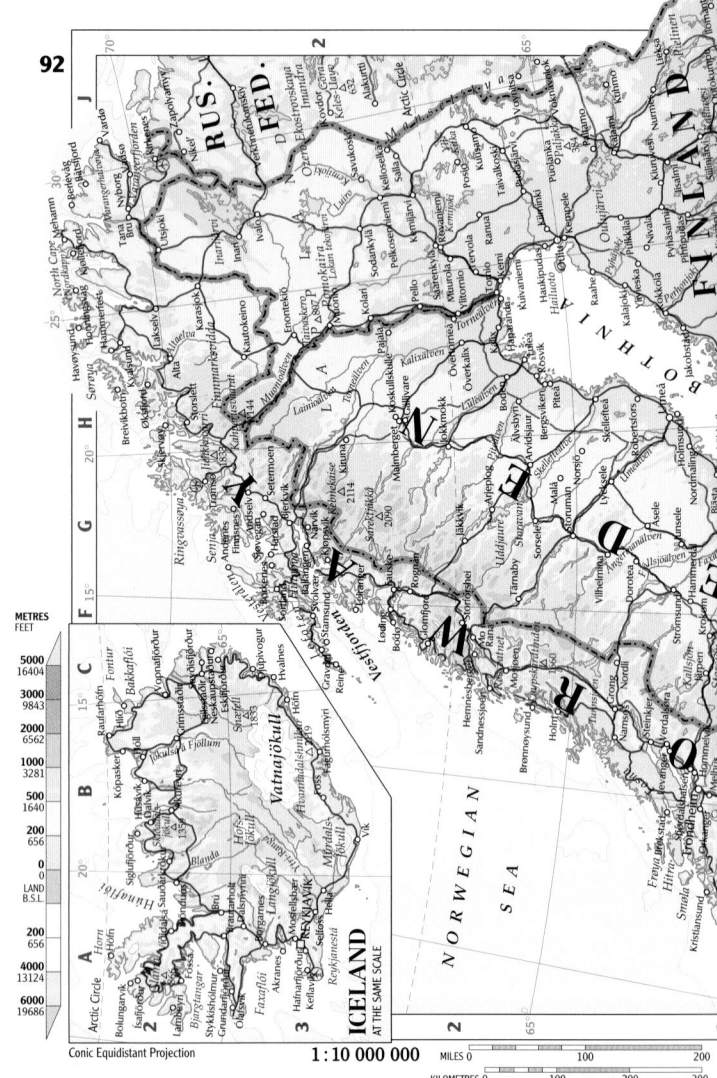

RUS. FED.

FINLAND

BOTHNIA

NORWAY

North Cape

Arctic Circle

Vardø

Kola

ICELAND
AT THE SAME SCALE

Vatnajökull

REYKJAVIK

Arctic Circle

NORWEGIAN SEA

METRES
FEET

5000
16404

3000
9843

2000
6562

1000
3281

500
1640

200
656

0
0

LAND
B.S.L.

200
656

4000
13124

6000
19686

Conic Equidistant Projection

1:10 000 000

MILES 0   100   200

KILOMETRES 0   100   200   300

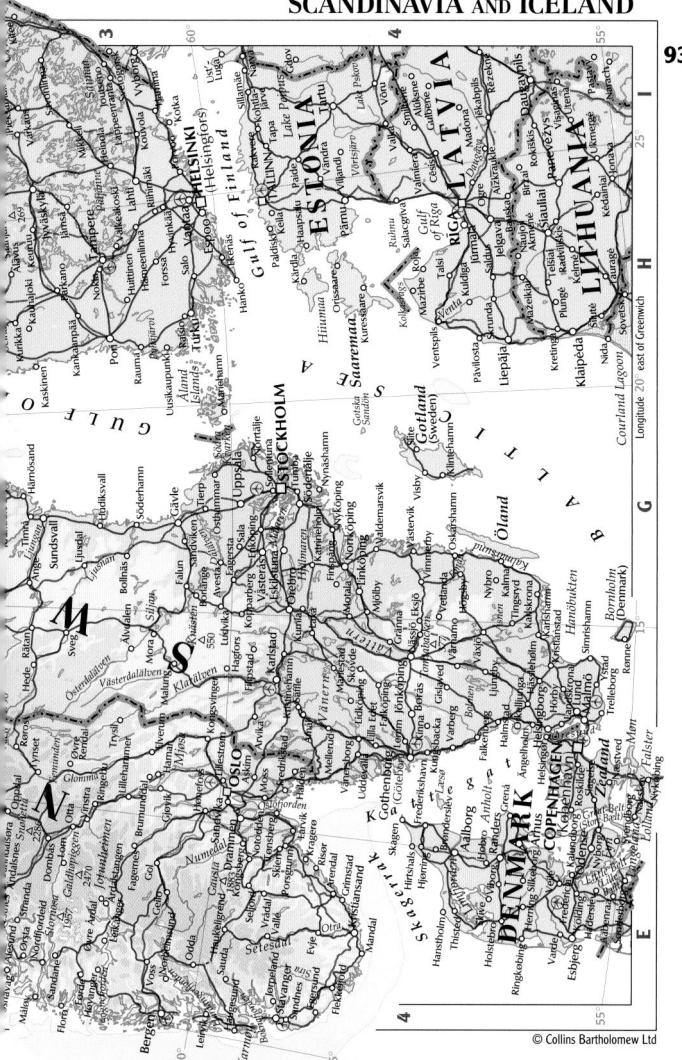

© Collins Bartholomew Ltd

94

1   2

D   C   B   A

60°   0°   5°   10°   60°

N O R T H   S E A

Shetland Islands
Herma Ness · Unist · Fetlar · Isbister · Mainland · Foula · Lerwick · Sumburgh Head · Fair Isle

Orkney Islands
Mainland · Kirkwall · Hoy · John o'Groats · Wick

SCOTLAND
Fraserburgh · Peterhead · Aberdeen · Banff · Elgin · Nairn · Inverness · Kingussie · Ballater · Brechin · Montrose · Arbroath · Dundee · St Andrews · North Berwick · Kirkcaldy · Stirling · Crianlarich · Grampian · Monadhliath · Perth · Dee · Don · Spey · Moray Firth · Dingwall · Ross · Helmsdale · Thurso · Tongue · Durness · Cape Wrath · Scourie · Lochinver · Ullapool · Ben Hope 927 · Ben More 1062 · 1309 · 1214 · 1130

Faroe Islands (Denmark)
Nordoyar · Klaksvik · Bordoy · Eysturoy · Sandoy · TORSHAVN · Sandur · Vestmanna · Midvagur · Vagar · Sudur · Vagur · Suduroy · 882

A T L A N T I C   O C E A N

Outer Hebrides
Butt of Lewis · Isle of Lewis · Stornoway · Harris · North Uist · Benbecula · South Uist · Barra · St Kilda · The Minch · Little Minch · Rum · Coll · Tiree · Loch Linnhe · Fort William

METRES FEET
5000 16404
3000 9843
2000 6562
1000 3281
500 1640
200 656
0 0
LAND B.S.L.
200 656
4000 13124
6000 19686

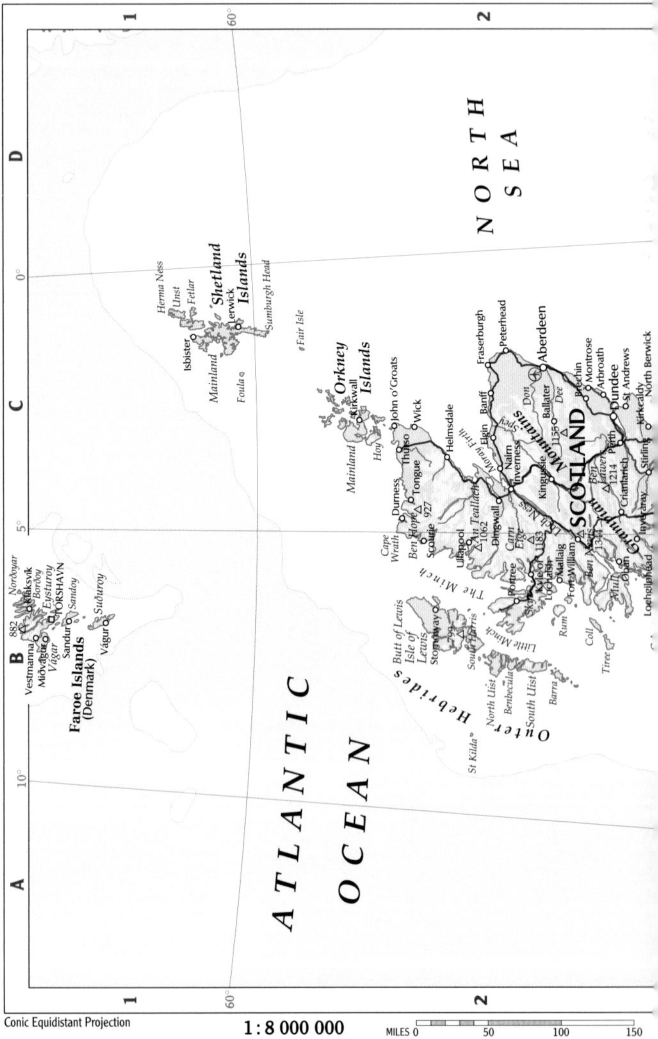

Conic Equidistant Projection   1:8 000 000   MILES 0   50   100   150

UNITED
KINGDOM

PENNINES

ENGLAND

WALES

LONDON

IRELAND

NORTHERN
IRELAND

DUBLIN

FRANCE

Irish
Sea

North Channel

St George's Channel

Bristol Channel

English Channel
(La Manche)

Celtic Sea

Chapnel Islands
(Iles Normandes)

Guernsey
(U.K.)

St Helier

Isle of Man
(U.K.)

DOUGLAS

Longitude 5 west of Greenwich

Isles of Scilly

0   100   200 KILOMETRES

© Collins Bartholomew Ltd

A 10° B 8° C 6° D

ATLANTIC OCEAN

Islay
Mull of Oa
Gigha
Port Ellen
Kintyre
Campbeltown
Mull of Kintyre

West Town   Tory Island
Bloody Foreland
Inishowen
Malin Head
Carndonagh
Rathlin Island
Ballycastle
North Channel

Gweedore   Errigal   752
Aran Island
Burtonport
Gweebarra Bay
Glenties
Letterkenny
Lifford
Buncrana
Londonderry
Portrush
Giant's Causeway
Portstewart
Coleraine
Limavady
Dungiven
Ballymoney
Cullybackey
Ballymena   Larne

ULSTER
NORTHERN
IRELAND

Malin More
Rossan Point
Killybegs
Donegal
Blue Stack Mts
676
Strabane
Castlederg
Omagh
Newtownstewart
Cookstown
Magherafelt
Antrim
Ballyclare
Newtownabbey
Belfast
Lisburn
Whitehead
Bangor
Newtownards
Strangford Lough

Donegal Bay
Ballyshannon
Bundoran
Lower Lough Erne
Lough Erne
Enniskillen
Lisnaskea
Lough Neagh
Dungannon
Portadown
Armagh
Keady
Dromore
Ballynahinch
Donaghadee
Portaferry
Downpatrick

Benwee Head
Erris Head
Belmullet
Killala
Killala Bay
Ballycastle
Ballina
Sligo Bay
Sligo
Colooney
Monaghan
Clones
Castleblayney
Newry
Warrenpoint
Carlingford Lough
Newcastle
Dundrum Bay
Kilkeel
Mourne Mts

Blacksod Bay
Achill Island
Clare Island
Louisburgh
Inishbofin
Slyne Head

Nephin Beg Range
Nephin 806
Lough Conn
Crough Patrick 765
Westport
Castlebar
Boyle
Ballaghaderreen
Cavan
Carrick-on-Shannon
Carrickmacross
Dundalk
Dundalk Bay

54°

Gorumna Islands
Galway
Clifden
Connemara
Lough Corrib
Lough Mask
Claremorris
Ballinrobe
Tuam
Roscommon
Longford
Lough Ree
Lough Sheelin
Navan
Trim
Kells
Drogheda
Balbriggan
Skerries

Inishmore
Aran Islands
Galway Bay
Burren
Ennistymon
Liscannor Bay
Hag's Head
CONNAUGHT
IRELAND
Ballinasloe
Athlone
Mullingar
Edenderry
Bog of Allen
Tullamore
Newbridge
Naas
Leixlip
Lucan
DUBLIN
Dún Laoghaire
Bray
Greystones
LEINSTER

Spanish Point
Ennis
Killaloe
Lough Derg
Roscrea
Birr
Portlaoise
Athy
Lugnaquilla 926
Wicklow
Wicklow Head
Wicklow Mts

2

Kilkee
Loop Head
Mouth of the Shannon
Kilrush
Nenagh
Templemore
Thurles
Carlow
Muine Bheag
Gorey
Cahore Point

Listowel
Tralee
Brandon Mountain 953
Dingle
Slea Head
Dingle Bay
Castleisland
Newcastle West
Tipperary
Cashel
Clonmel
Kilkenny
Thomastown
Carrick-on-Suir
Enniscorthy
Wexford
Rosslare
Carnsore Point
St George's Channel

Caherciveen
Cahermore
Dursey Island
Macgillycuddy's Reeks
Carrauntoohil 1041
Killarney
Lough Leane
Kenmare
Kenmare River
Caha Mts
Macroom
Bandon
Kinsale
Old Head of Kinsale
Midleton
Youghal
Cobh
Cork
Mallow
Fermoy
Dungarvan
Tramore
Waterford
Waterford Harbour
Helvick Head

52°

MUNSTER
Newtown
Kanturk
Mitchelstown
Blackwater
Comeragh Mountains
Galtymore 920
Galty Mts
Knockmealdown Mts
Slieve Bloom Mts

Mizen Head
Cape Clear
Skibbereen
Clonakilty
Bantry
Bantry Bay
Caha Mts

3

Longitude 8° west of Greenwich

0   50   100 KILOMETRES

1 : 4 000 000

METRES
FEET

5000 16404
3000 9843
2000 6562
1000 3281
500 1640
200 656
0
0
LAND B.S.L.
200 656
4000 13124
6000 19686

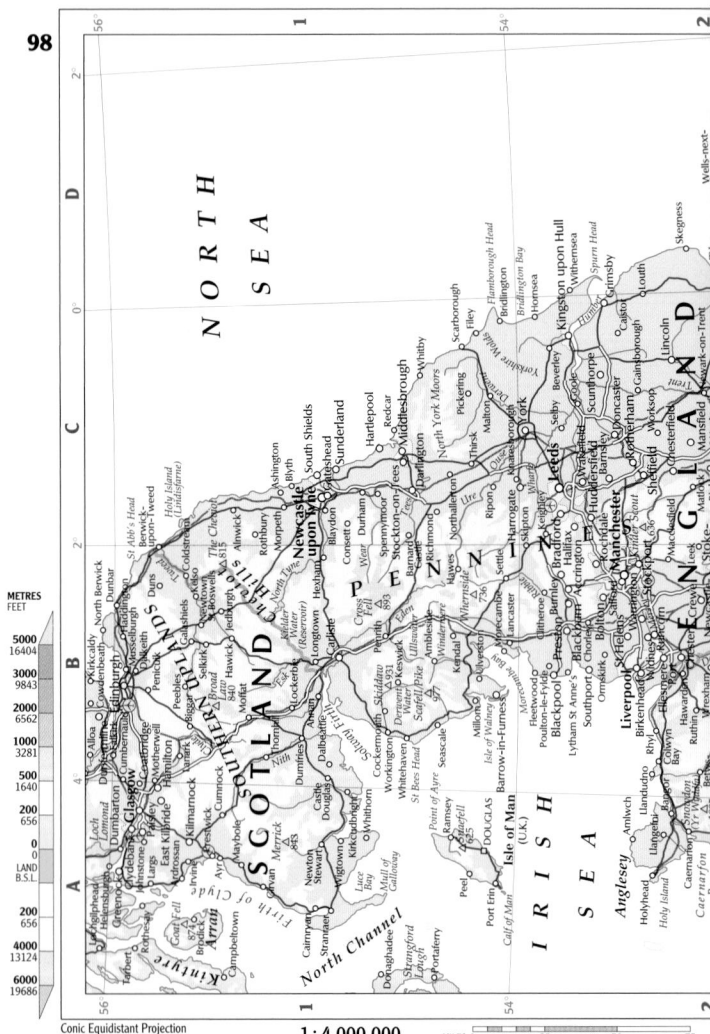

METRES
FEET

5000
16404

3000
9843

2000
6562

1000
3281

500
1640

200
656

0
LAND
B.S.L.

200
656

4000
13124

6000
19686

Conic Equidistant Projection

1 : 4 000 000

MILES 0   25   50   75

N O R T H

S E A

I R I S H

S E A

S C O T L A N D

E N G L A N D

P E N N I N E S

C H E V I O T   H I L L S

S O U T H E R N   U P L A N D S

Newcastle upon Tyne

Kingston upon Hull

Liverpool

Manchester

Leeds

Sheffield

Edinburgh

Glasgow

Isle of Man
(U.K.)

North Channel

Firth of Clyde

Anglesey

Wells-next-

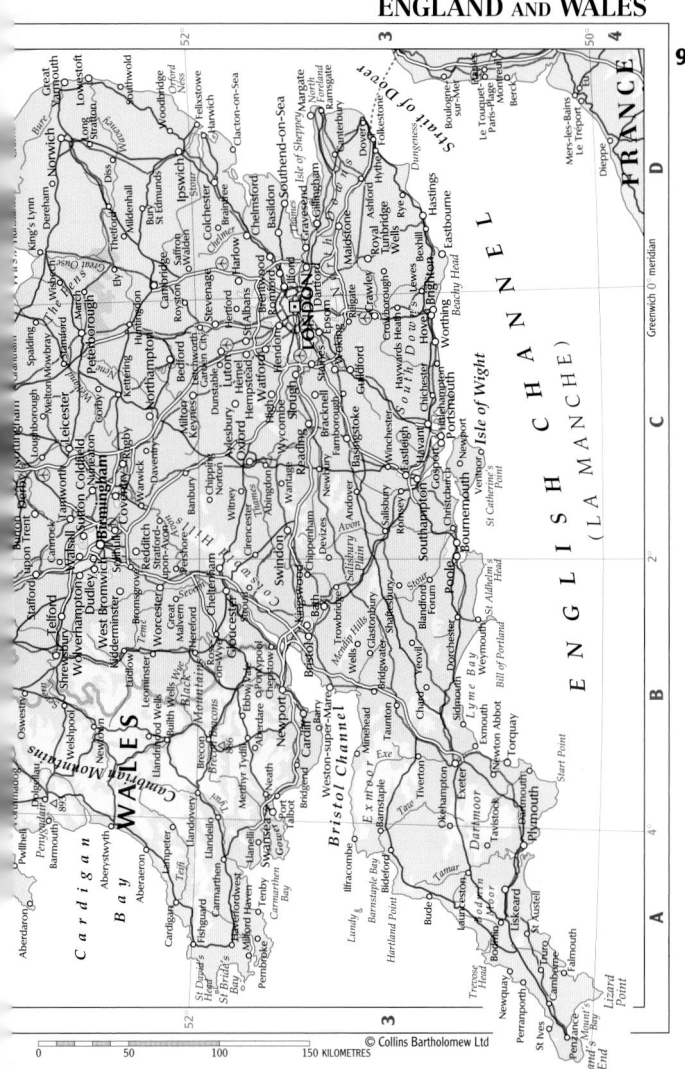

0   50   100   150 KILOMETRES

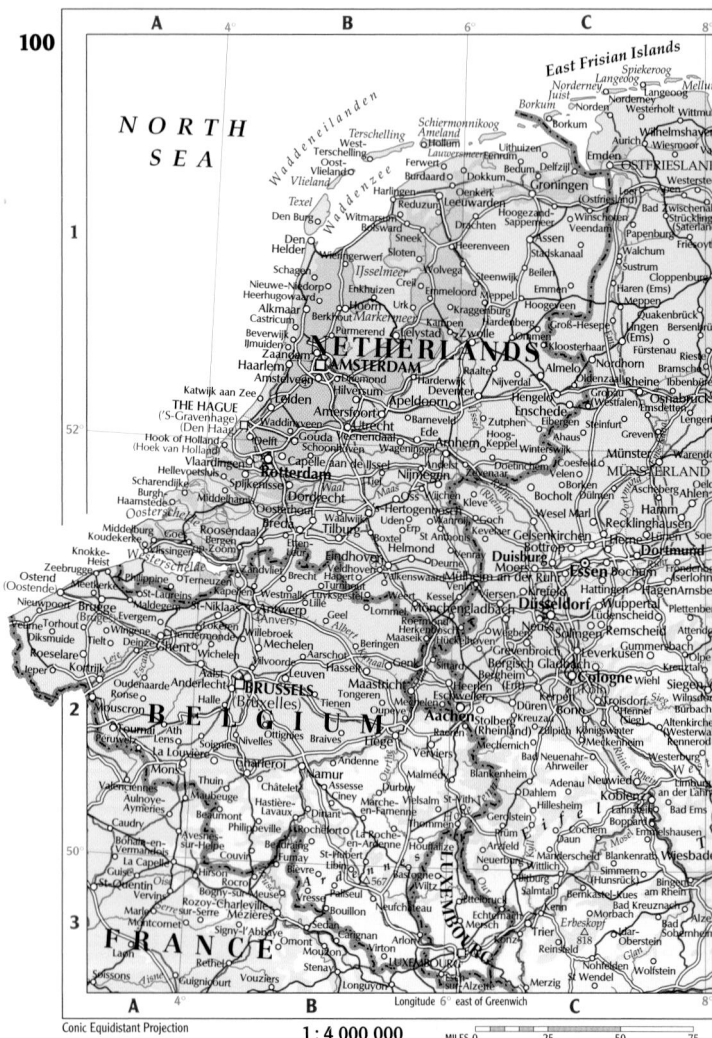

A   4°   B   6°   C   8°

NORTH SEA

East Frisian Islands

Waddeneilanden
Terschelling West-Terschelling
Schiermonnikoog
Ameland
Langeoog Spiekeroog
Norderney Juist
Borkum Borkum
Norden Wilhelmshaven
Wittmund

OSTFRIESLAND

NETHERLANDS
□AMSTERDAM

THE HAGUE
('S-Gravenhage)
(Den Haag)

Rotterdam
Dordrecht

MÜNSTERLAND

BELGIUM
□BRUSSELS
(Bruxelles)

Cologne

Düsseldorf

Aachen

Koblenz

Wiesbaden

LUXEMBOURG
□LUXEMBOURG

FRANCE

A   4°   B   Longitude 6° east of Greenwich   C   8°

Conic Equidistant Projection

1 : 4 000 000

MILES 0   25   50   75

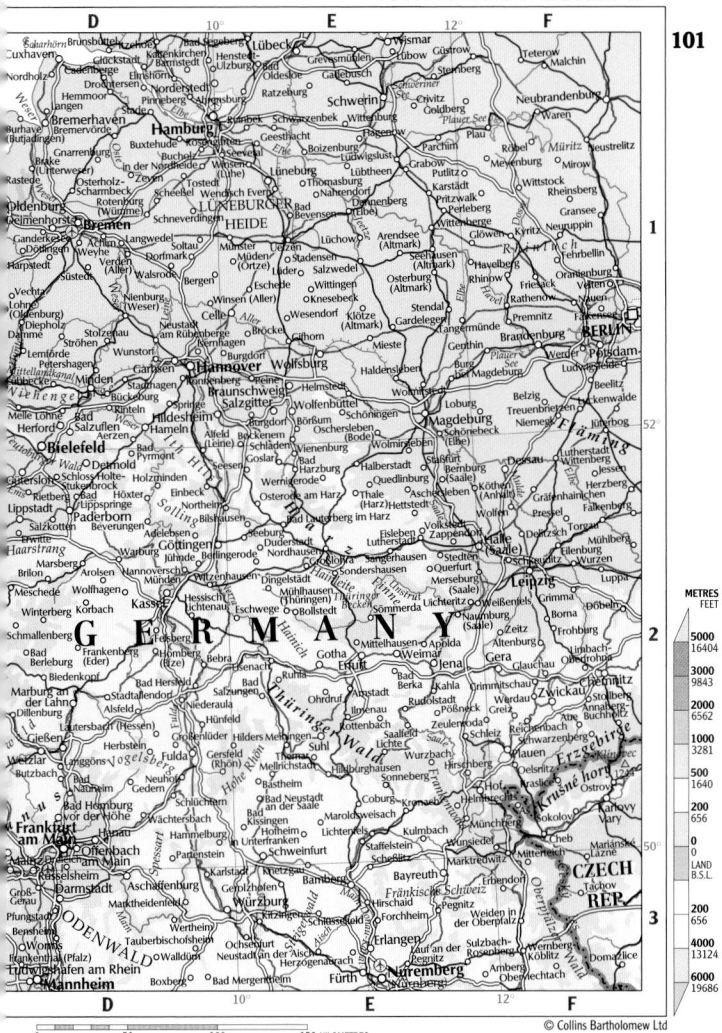

NORTH SEA

Helgoländer Bucht

Helgoland

BALTIC

Pomerania

East Frisian Islands

Waddeneilanden

NETHERLANDS

AMSTERDAM

Hamburg

Bremen

Hannover

BERLIN

BEL

Düsseldorf

Essen

Dortmund

Cologne (Köln)

GERMANY

Leipzig

Dresden

PRAGUE (PRAHA)

Frankfurt am Main

Wiesbaden

Mainz

CZECH

LUX

Mannheim

Heidelberg

Nuremberg (Nürnberg)

FRANCE

Stuttgart

Munich (München)

AUS

Zürich

BERN

LIECHTEN STEIN

Innsbruck

SWITZERLAND

A

LJUBLJANA

ITALY

Lake Garda

Lake Como

SLOV

METRES FEET

5000	16404
3000	9843
2000	6562
1000	3281
500	1640
200	656
0 LAND B.S.L.	0
200	656
4000	13124
6000	19686

Conic Equidistant Projection

Longitude 10° east of Greenwich

1 : 8 000 000

MILES 0   50   100   150

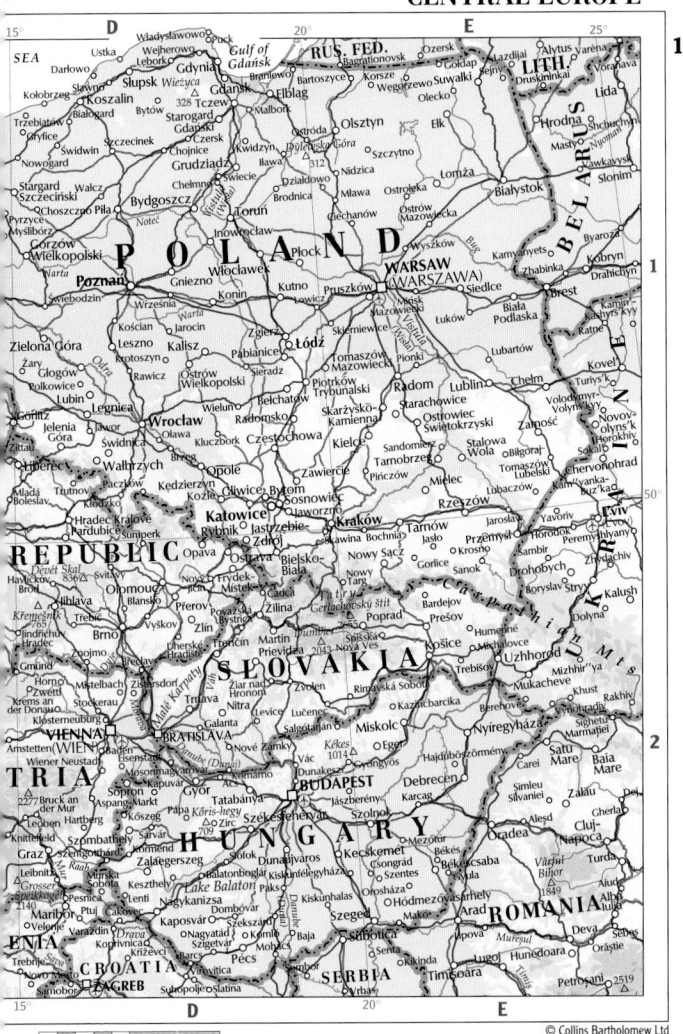

0   100   200 KILOMETRES

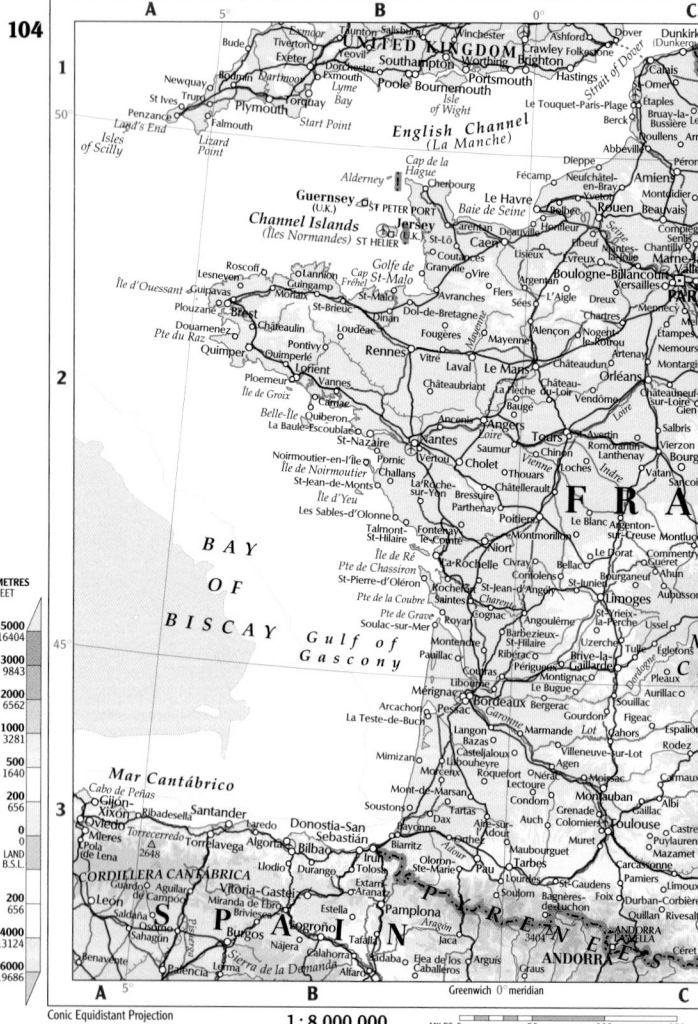

A   5°   **B**   0°   **C**

1

Bude
Exmoor
Taunton
Salisbury
Winchester
Ashford
Dover
Dunkirk
(Dunkerque)
Tiverton
Exeter
Dorchester
Bodmin
Dartmoor
Exmouth
UNITED KINGDOM
Southampton
Worthing
Brighton
Crawley
Folkestone
Hastings
Calais
St-Omer
Newquay
Torquay
Lyme
Bay
Poole
Bournemouth
Portsmouth
Le Touquet-Paris-Plage
Étaples
Bruay-la-
Bussière
Lens
St Ives
Truro
Penzance
Land's End
Lizard
Point
Start Point
Isle
of Wight
Le Havre
Berck
Doullens
Arras
Isles
of Scilly
Falmouth
Plymouth
English Channel
(La Manche)
Dieppe
Neufchâtel-
en-Bray
Abbeville
Péronne
Amiens
Montdidier
Beauvais
50

Cap de la
Hague
Cherbourg
Fécamp
Étretat
Bolbec

Alderney
Guernsey
(U.K.)
ST PETER PORT
Channel Islands
(Îles Normandes)
Jersey
(U.K.)
ST HELIER
Baie de Seine
Le Havre
Honfleur
Pont-l'Évêque
Rouen
Évreux
Compiègne
Senlis
Chantilly
Marne-la-Vallée
PARIS
Golfe de
St-Malo
Coutances
Granville
Caen
Lisieux
Versailles

Roscoff
Lannion
Guingamp
Cap
Fréhel
St-Brieuc
St-Malo
Avranches
Vire
Flers
Argentan
Sées
L'Aigle
Dreux
Chartres
Nogent-le-Rotrou
Mennecy
Étampes
Nemours
Montargis
Île d'Ouessant
Guipavas
Brest
Plouzané
Douarnenez
Pte du Raz
Quimper
Morlaix
Châteaulin
Quimperlé
Lorient
Pontivy
Loudéac
Dinan
Dol-de-Bretagne
Fougères
Mayenne
Laval
Le Mans
Châteaudun
Orléans
Châteauneuf-
sur-Loire
Gien
Salbris

2

Ploemeur
Île de Groix
Belle-Île
Quiberon
La Baule-Escoublac
St-Nazaire
Vannes
Carnac
Redon
Rennes
Vitré
Châteaubriant
Ancenis
Angers
Baugé
La Flèche
Château-du-Loir
Tours
Loches
Amboise
Vendôme
Romorantin-
Lanthenay
Vierzon
Bourges
Vatan
Sancoins

F R A

Noirmoutier-en-l'Île
Île de Noirmoutier
St-Jean-de-Monts
Île d'Yeu
Pornic
Challans
Nantes
Vertou
Cholet
Thouars
Saumur
Chinon
Bressuire
Châtellerault
Poitiers
Le Blanc
Argenton-
sur-Creuse
Montluçon
Commentry

Les Sables-d'Olonne
Talmont-
St-Hilaire
La Roche-
sur-Yon
Parthenay
Fontenay-
le-Comte
Montmorillon
La Châtre
Aigurande
Guéret
Aubusson
Ahun

BAY
OF
BISCAY

Île de Ré
La Rochelle
Niort
St-Jean-d'Angély
Civray
Confolens
St-Junien
Limoges
Eymoutiers
Ussel

Pte de Chassiron
St-Pierre-d'Oléron
Rochefort
Saintes
Cognac
Angoulême
St-Yrieix-
la-Perche
Uzerche
Tulle
Égletons

Pte de la Coubre
Pte de Grave
Soulac-sur-Mer
Royan
Montendre
Barbezieux-
St-Hilaire
Ribérac
Périgueux
Brive-la-
Gaillarde
Pleaux

Gulf of
Gascony
Pauillac
Libourne
Coutras
Montignac
Le Bugue
Sarlat-la-Canéda
Souillac
Gourdon
Aurillac
Espalion

Arcachon
La Teste-de-Buch
Mérignac
Pessac
Bordeaux
Bergerac
Marmande
Lot
Cahors
Figeac
Rodez

45

Mimizan
Langon
Bazas
Casteljaloux
Libourne
Nérac
Villeneuve-sur-Lot
Agen
Moissac
Montauban
Villefranche-de-Rouergue
Carmaux
Albi

Mar Cantábrico
Cabo de Peñas
Santander
Mont-de-Marsan
Soustons
Dax
Tartas
Aire-sur-l'Adour
Auch
Grenade
Colomiers
Toulouse
Gaillac
Castres
Mazamet

Gijón
Xixón
Bilbadesella
Oviedo
Mieres
Pola
de Lena
Torrecerredo
2648
Torrelavega
Laredo
Algorta
Bilbao
Donostia-San
Sebastián
Biarritz
Bayonne
Peyrehorade
St-Jean-Pied-de-Port
Orthez
Mauléon-Licharre
Pau
Lourdes
Tarbes
Maubourguet
St-Gaudens
Muret
Carcassonne
Limoux
Castelnaudary
Pamiers
Foix
Mazères
Puylaurens

3

CORDILLERA CANTÁBRICA
León
Aguilar
de Campoo
Saldaña
Osorno
Sahagún
Benavente
Llodio
Durango
Vitoria-Gasteiz
Miranda de Ebro
Aranjuez
Irún
Tolosa
Estella
Pamplona
Jaca
Aragón
Bagnères-
de-Luchon
ANDORRA
ANDORRA
3404
Durban-Corbières
Céret
Rivesaltes

Burgos
Aguilar
Briviesca
Logroño
Nájera
Calahorra
Tafalla
Tudela
Ejea de los
Caballeros
Arguis
Graus

Sierra de la Demanda
Palencia
Lerma
Aranda
Alfaro

P Y R É N É E S

A   5°   **B**   Greenwich 0° meridian   **C**

S P A I N

METRES
FEET

METRES	FEET
5000	16404
3000	9843
2000	6562
1000	3281
500	1640
200	656
0	0
LAND	B.S.L.
200	656
4000	13124
6000	19686

Conic Equidistant Projection

1 : 8 000 000

MILES 0   50   100   150

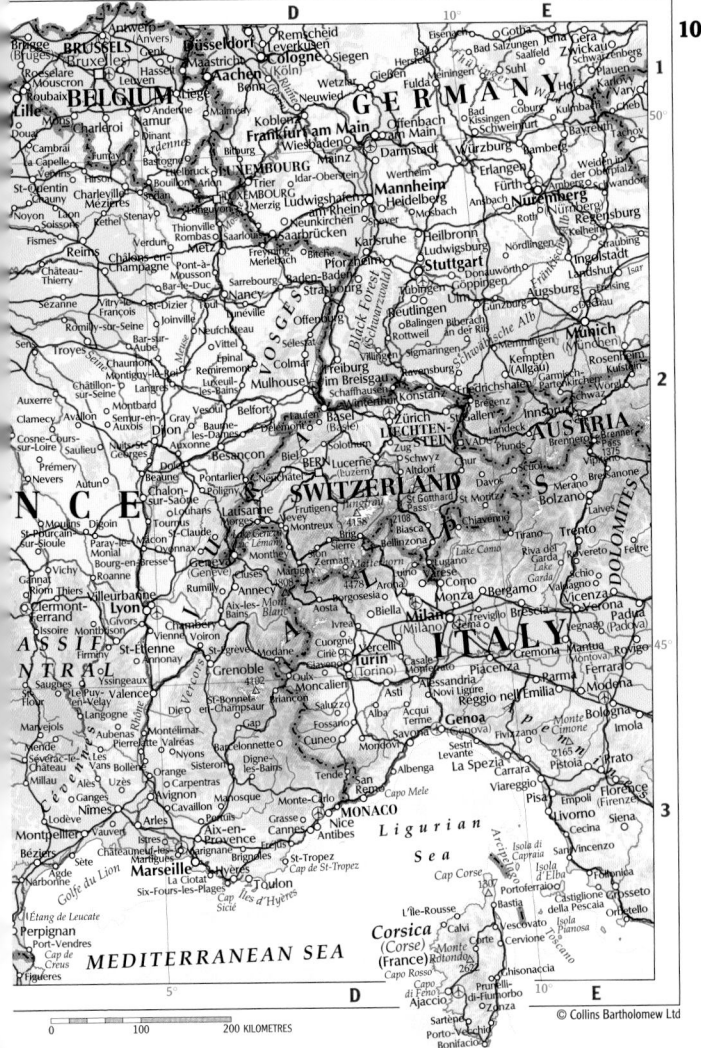

0   100   200 KILOMETRES

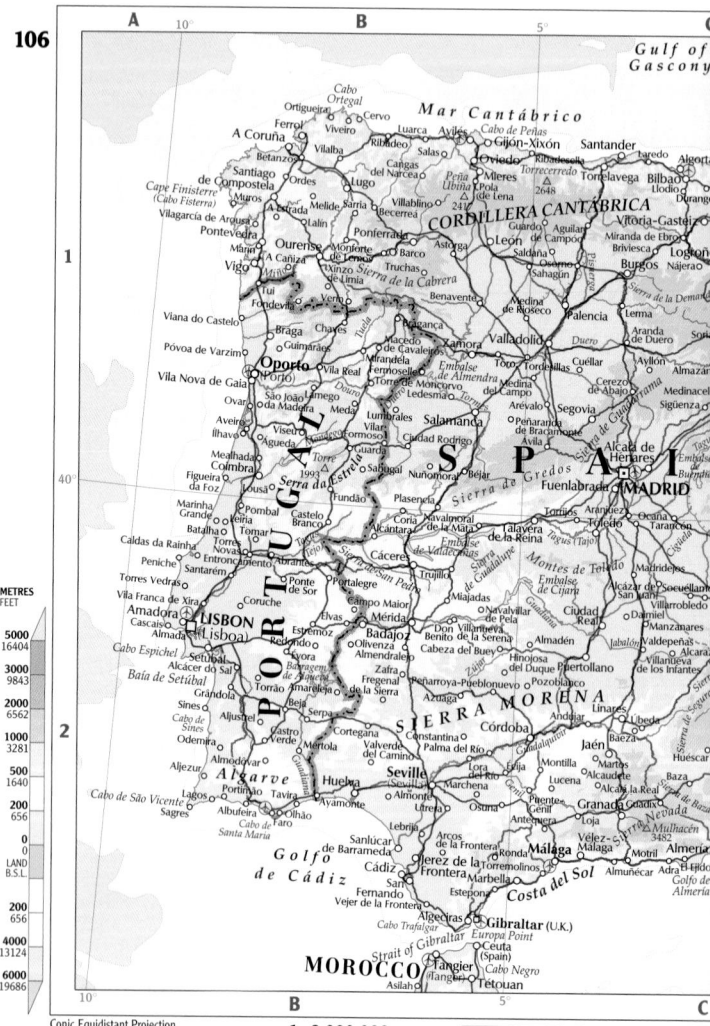

Gulf of Gascony

Mar Cantábrico

Cabo Ortegal
Ortigueira Cervo
Ferrol Viveiro Luarca Avilés Cabo de Peñas
A Coruña Vilalba Ribadeo Cangas Gijón-Xixón Santander Laredo Algorta
Betanzos Salas Oviedo Ribadesella Torrelavega Bilbao Llodio Durango
Santiago Ordes Lugo del Narcea Mieres Peña Torrecerredo Vitoria-Gasteiz
de Compostela Melide Sarria Becerreá Pola Ubiña 2648 Miranda de Ebro Briviesca Logroño
Cape Finisterre Arzúa de Lena 2418 Briviesca Nájerao
(Cabo Fisterra) Vilagarcía de Arousa Monforte Ponferrada Astorga León Guardo de Campoo Burgos Sierra de la Demanda
Pontevedra A Cañiza de Lemos Barco Truchas Saldaña Aguilar Lerma Soria
Vigo Ourense Sierra de la Cabrera Benavente Medina Palencia Aranda Ayllón Almazán
Tui Xinzo Bragança de Ríoseco de Duero Medinaceli
Fonteveda de Limia Chaves Zamora Valladolid Cuéllar Cerezo Sigüenza
Viana do Castelo Braga Macedo Toro Tordesillas de Abajo Segovia
Póvoa de Varzim Guimarães de Cavaleiros Mirandela Medina Arévalo Peñaranda Sierra de Guadarrama Alcalá de
Oporto Vila Real Torre de Moncorvo del Campo de Bracamonte Henares MADRID
(Porto) Ledesma Salamanca Béjar Fuenlabrada Embalse MADRID
Vila Nova de Gaia São João Lamego Medo Lumbrales Vilar Ciudad Rodrigo Sierra de Gredos Aranjuez Buendía
Ovar da Madeira Formoso Nuñomoral Ocaña Tarancón
Aveiro Viseu Vilar Guarda Sabugal Plasencia Talavera Toledo Cigüela
Ílhavo Águeda Formoso Tondela de la Reina Madridejos
Mealhada Serra da Estrela Coria Sierra de San Pedro Montes de Toledo Alcázar de Socuéllamos
Coimbra 1991 Castelo Navalmoral San Juan Villarrobledo
Figueira Bouçã Branco de la Mata Embalse Daimiel
da Foz Batalha Tomar Abrantes Cáceres de Valdecañas Ciudad Manzanares
Marinha Pombal Ponte Trujillo Navalvillar Real Valdepeñas Alcaraz
Grande Nova de Sor Portalegre de Pela Almadén Villanueva
Caldas da Rainha Entroncamento Campo Maior Miajadas Benito El Viso Puertollano de los Infantes
Peniche Santarém Elvas Mérida Don Villanueva del Duque Pozoblanco
Torres Vedras Coruche Badajoz de la Serena Cabeza del Buey Hinojosa Linares
Vila Franca de Xira Estremoz Olivenza Almendralejo del Duque Puertollano Úbeda
Amadora Cascais Campo de Brócia Azuaga Peñarroya-Pueblonuevo Andújar Jaén Baeza
LISBON Alcácer do Sal Torrão Amareleja Fregenal SIERRA MORENA Martos La Real
Lisboa Almada Barragem de la Sierra Córdoba Alcaudete Huéscar
Cabo Espichel Setúbal do Maranhão Beja Cortegana Constantina Montilla Lucena Baza
Baía de Setúbal Grândola Serpa Valverde Palma del Río Fuentes Granada Guadix
Sines Ajustrel del Camino Écija de León Nevada Mulhacén
Cabo de Aljezur Castro Mértola Huelva Sevilla Marchena Osuna 3482
Sines Odemira Verde Seville Antequera Vélez- Guadix Almería
Aljezur Algarve Ayamonte Almonte Utrera Montilla Ronda Málaga Motril Adra
Cabo de São Vicente Lagos Portimão Tavira Lebrija Arcos Marbella Costa del Sol Almuñécar Golfo de
Sagres Albufeira Olhão Sanlúcar de la Frontera Toremolinos Almería
Cabo de de Barrameda Jerez de la Estepona
Santa Maria Cádiz Frontera Algeciras Gibraltar (U.K.)
Golfo San Vejer de la Frontera Europa Point
de Cádiz Fernando Cabo Trafalgar Ceuta
Strait of Gibraltar (Spain) Cabo Negro
MOROCCO Tangier Tetouan
(Tánger) Asilah

PORTUGAL SPAIN

Duero Douro Tajo Tejo Guadiana Guadalquivir Júcar

CORDILLERA CANTÁBRICA

METRES
FEET

5000	16404
3000	9843
2000	6562
1000	3281
500	1640
200	656
0	LAND B.S.L.
200	656
4000	13124
6000	19686

Conic Equidistant Projection

1 : 8 000 000

MILES 0   50   100   150

© Collins Bartholomew Ltd

A

B

METRES
FEET

5000
16404

3000
9843

2000
6562

1000
3281

500
1640

200
656

0
0
LAND
B.S.L.

200
656

4000
13124

6000
19686

45

40

Conic Equidistant Projection

1 : 8 000 000

Longitude 10° east of Greenwich

MILES 0   50   100   150

A

B

Annecy Cluses Martigny Matterhorn
Rumilly 3905
Aix-les-Bains
Chambéry
Grenoble
Gap
Briançon
Barcelonnette
Sisteron
Digne-les-Bains
Verdon
Monte-Carlo
Grasse
Cannes Nice
Antibes MONACO
Fréjus
St-Tropez
Brignoles Cap de St-Tropez
Îles d'Hyères

Mt Blanc Aosta
Ivrea
Biella
Vercelli
Turin (Torino)
Ciriè
Oulx
Susa
Pinerolo
Saluzzo
Savigliano
Cuneo
Fossano
Mondovì
Alba
Acqui Terme
Tende
Col de Tende 1871
Albenga
San Remo Savona
Imperia
Capo Mele

Verbania
Lecco
Lake Como
Lugano
Varese Como
Bergamo
Milan (Milano)
Monza
Pavia
Treviglio
Brescia
Cremona
Casale Monferrato
Alessandria
Novi Ligure
Piacenza
Asti
Genoa (Genova)
Sestri Levante
La Spezia
Massa
Viareggio
Pisa

Bolzano
Merano
Bressanone
Tirano
Sondrio
Riva del Garda
Rovereto
Schio
Valdagno
Vicenza
Verona
Padua (Padova)
Mantua (Mantova)
Rovigo
Modena
Reggio nell'Emilia
Parma
Ferrara
Bologna
Imola
Faenza
Forlì
Cesena
Rimini
Monte Cimone 2165
Pistoia
Arno
Florence (Firenze)
Empoli
Livorno
Cecina
San Vincenzo
Montepulciano
Piombino
Grosseto
Orbetello
Tarquinia
Civitavecchia

Dolomites
3205
Cortina d'Ampezzo
Tolmezzo
Maniago
Udine
Belluno
Vittorio Veneto
Conegliano
Pordenone
Portogruaro
Chioggia
Porto Tolle
Po
Porto Garibaldi
Comacchio
Ravenna
Cervia
San Marino
SAN MARINO
Pesaro
Fano
Senigallia
Siena
Arezzo
Perugia
Foligno
Terni
Rieti
Guidonia
Tivoli
ROME (ROMA)
VATICAN CITY
Pomezia
Aprilia
Anzio
Sabaudia
Fossa
Gaeta
Isole Ponziane

Tarvisio
2864
SLOV
LJUBLJANA
Gorizia
Trieste
Pula
Rovinj
ADRIATIC

Rijeka

Lošinj
Rt Kamenjak
Cres
Lošinj

Ancona
Osimo
Macerata
Civitanova Marche
Fermo
San Benedetto del Tronto
Giulianova
Pescara
Monte Corno 2912
Penne
Chieti
Monte Amaro 2793
Vasto
Alessa
Benevento
Campobasso
Isernia
Venafro
Teano
Caserta
Naples (Napoli)
Pozzuoli
Vesuvius 1281
Isola d'Ischia
Isola di Capri

Ascoli Piceno
Fabriano
Jesi
Cagli
Montecassino
Frosinone
Latina
Fondi

Ligurian
Sea

Cap Corse
Isola di Capraia
1307
Isola di Elba
Portoferraio
St-Florent
Bastia
l'Île-Rousse
Calvi
Corsica (Corse) (France)
Monte Rotondo
Capo Rosso
Corte
Ajaccio
Vescovato
Cervione
Ghisonaccia
Pranelli-di-Fiumorbo
Sartène
Porto-Vecchio
Zonza
Capo Pertusato
Bonifacio
Strait of Bonifacio
Pta Caprara
Maddalena
Asinara
Golfo dell'Asinara
Punta Falcone
Capo Ferro
Porto Torres
Sassari
Capo Caccia
Alghero
Buddusò
Oschiri
Budoni
Bonorva
Nuoro
Macomer
Capo Comino
Siniscola
Orosei
Abbasanta
Punta La Marmora 1834
Golfo di Orosei
Capo di Monte Santu
Oristano
Laconi
Tortolì
Capo della Frasca
Mandas
Guspini
Tertenia
San Gavino Monreale
Iglesias
Villaputzu
Isola di San Pietro
Punta Maxia 1017
Quartu Sant'Elena
Sant'Antioco
Cagliari
Isola di Sant'Antioco
Capo Carbonara
Pula
Golfo di Cagliari

Arcipelago
Isola di Montecristo

Sardinia (Sardegna) (Italy)

Orvieto
Bolsena
Viterbo
Terni

Isola di Ustica

TYRRHENIAN
SEA

Isole Lipari

Sicily (Sicilia)
Capo San Vito
Monte Sparagio
Trapani
Isola Marettimo
Alcamo
Rocca Busambra 1613
Palermo
Monti
Cefalù
Capo d'Orlando
Imerese
Termini
Marsala
Mazara del Vallo
Castelvetrano
Caltanissetta
Caltagirone
Niscemi
Gela
Vittoria
Ragusa
Licata
Agrigento
Sciacca
Capo Granitola
Sicilian Channel

MEDITERRANEAN SEA

La Galite

Cap de Fer

Bizerte

SEA

MAP LABELS (reading the map):

Maribor · Varaždin · HUNGARY · Nagyatád · Komló · Baja · Subotica · Senta · Makó · Lipova · Mureş · Deva · Orăştie · Sebeş

ZAGREB · CROATIA · Karlovac · Sisak · VOJVODINA · Sombor · Kikinda · Zrenjanin · Timişoara · Hunedoara · Transylvanian Alps (Carpaţii Meridionali) · Petroşani

Banja Luka · Prijedor · BELGRADE (BEOGRAD) · Novi Sad · Vršac · ROMANIA · Târgu

BOSNIA-HERZEGOVINA · Tuzla · Bijeljina · Loznica · Smederevo · Požarevac · Drobeta-Turnu Severin

SARAJEVO · Srebrenica · Valjevo · SERBIA · Kragujevac · Paraćin · Zaječar · Calafat

Mostar · Nikšić · MONTENEGRO · Novi Pazar · Niš · Pirot · SOFIA (SOFIYA) · BUL.

PODGORICA · Cetinje · KOSOVO · Priština · Vranje · Kyustendil

Bar · Shkodër · ALBANIA · Prizren · SKOPJE · Tetovo · Štip · Blagoevgrad

Dubrovnik · Lezhë · Debar · MACEDONIA (F.Y.R.O.M.) · Strumica

Termoli · TIRANA (Tiranë) · Elbasan · Ohrid · Bitola · Kilkis

Foggia · Bari · Durrës · Vlorë · Berat · Florina · Thessaloniki · Veroia · Katerini · Mount Olympus 2911

Taranto · Brindisi · Lecce · GREECE · Ioannina · Larisa

Golfo di Taranto · Corfu (Kerkyra) · Karditsa · Lamia

Cosenza · Catanzaro · Crotone · LA SILA · Gulf of Corinth · Patras

IONIAN SEA · Cephalonia (Kefallonia) · Ionian Islands (Ionioi Nisoi) · Zakynthos · Olympia · Tripoli

Reggio di Calabria · Messina · Catania · Syracuse · Mount Etna 3323

0   100   200 KILOMETRES

© Collins Bartholomew Ltd

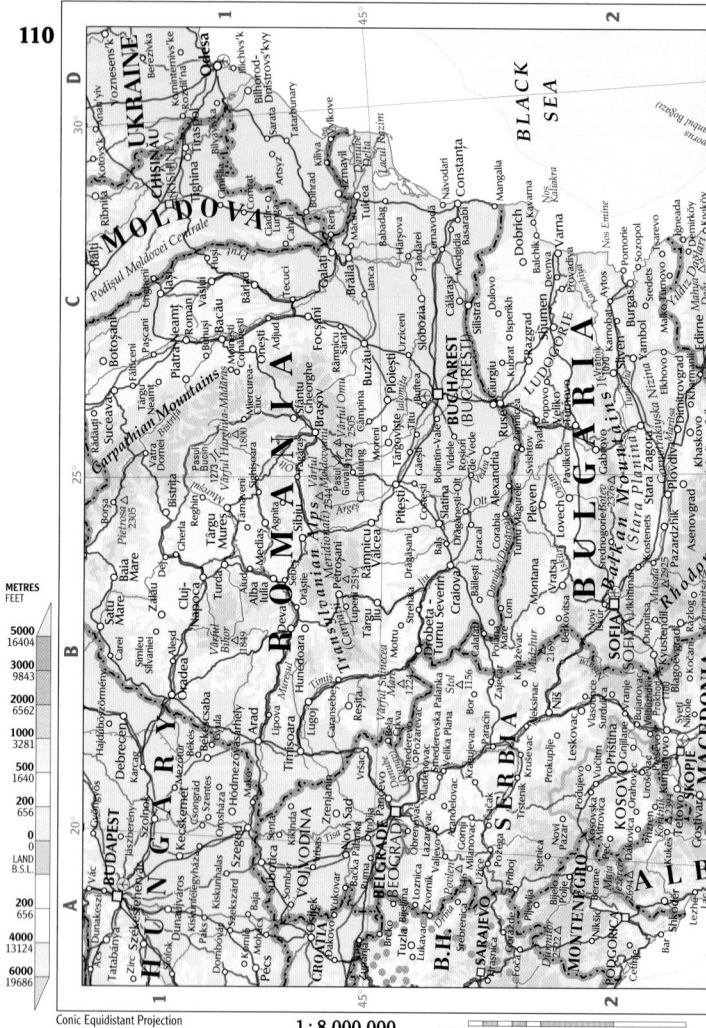

110

1 : 8 000 000

MILES 0   50   100   150

METRES
FEET

5000
16404

3000
9843

2000
6562

1000
3281

500
1640

200
656

0
0

LAND
B.S.L.

200
656

4000
13124

6000
19686

TURKEY

GREECE

(F.Y.R.O.M.)

ALBANIA

BULGARIA

Seas and water bodies:
MEDITERRANEAN SEA

AEGEAN SEA

IONIAN SEA

Sea of Marmara (Marmara Denizi)

Krytiko Pelagos

Mirtoö Pelagos

Thermaïkos Kolpos

Argolikos Kolpos

Messiniakos Kolpos

Lakonikos Kolpos

Patraïkos Kolpos

Korinthiakos Kolpos

Saronikos Kolpos

Kolpos Agiou Oros

Strait of Otranto

Islands and regions:
CRETE (KRITI)

Rhodes (Rodos)

Karpathos (Scarpanto)

Kasos

Dodecanese (Dodekanisos)

Cyclades (Kyklades)

Leshos (Lesvos)

Chios

Samos

Ikaria

Thira (Santorini)

Naxos

Paros

Mykonos

Andros

Tinos

Evvoia (Euboea)

Skyros

Skopelos

Limnos

Samothraki

Thasos

Corfu (Kerkyra)

Cephalonia (Kefallonia)

Zakynthos (Zakinthos)

Ithaki

Lefkada

Ionian Islands (Ionioi Nisoi)

Symi

Tilos

Chalki

Kalymnos

Kos

Astypalaia

Amorgos

Ios

Sifnos

Serifos

Kythnos

Kea

Milos

Kythira

Antikythira

Gavdos

Cities and towns:
ATHENS (ATHINA)

Thessaloniki

Istanbul

Bursa

TIRANA (TIRANË)

Bitola

Patras (Patra)

Tripoli

Sparti

Kalamata

Pyrgos

Olympia (Olimpia)

Corinth (Korinthos)

Piraeus (Peiraias)

Lamia

Volos

Larisa

Trikala

Karditsa

Ioannina

Arta

Preveza

Igoumenitsa

Kozani

Kastoria

Florina

Edessa

Veroia

Katerini

Serres

Drama

Kavala

Komotini

Xanthi

Alexandroupoli

Orestiada

Mudanya

Balikesir

Çanakkale

Bandirma

Tekirdağ

Gelibolu

Edirne

Kirklareli

İzmir

Manisa

Aydin

Denizli

Muğla

Bodrum

Marmaris

Fethiye

Kütahya

Uşak

Afyon

Isparta

Burdur

Mesolongi

Nafpaktos

Amfissa

Livadeia

Thiva

Chalkida

Nafplio

Argos

Pindus Mountains (Pindos)

Olympus

Grid and scale:
Longitude 20 east of Greenwich

0   100   200 KILOMETRES

ASIA

EUROPE

Mediterranean Sea

Gulf of Sirte

Tropic of Cancer

Gulf of Aden

Red Sea

ALGERIA

Atlas Mountains

MOROCCO

Rabat

Madeira (Portugal)

Canary Islands (Spain)

Laâyoune

WESTERN SAHARA

Algiers

Tunis

TUNISIA

Tripoli

LIBYA

Libyan Desert

EGYPT

Alexandria

Cairo

Aswan

Lake Nasser

Nile

SUDAN

Khartoum

Blue Nile

White Nile

Wau

S a h a r a

MAURITANIA

Nouakchott

Senegal

MALI

Bamako

Niger

BURKINA

Ouagadougou

NIGER

Niamey

Lake Chad

Ndjamena

CHAD

ERITREA

Asmara

DJIBOUTI

Djibouti

Addis Ababa

ETHIOPIA

SOMALIA

CENTRAL AFRICAN REPUBLIC

Bangui

Kano

Abuja

NIGERIA

CAMEROON

Douala

Yaoundé

Malabo

Lake Volta

BENIN

Porto-Novo

TOGO

Lomé

GHANA

Accra

CÔTE D'IVOIRE

Yamoussoukro

Abidjan

LIBERIA

Monrovia

SIERRA LEONE

Freetown

GUINEA

Conakry

GUINEA BISSAU

Bissau

THE GAMBIA

Banjul

SENEGAL

Dakar

Praia

CAPE VERDE

1 : 66 000 000

MILES 0   400   800

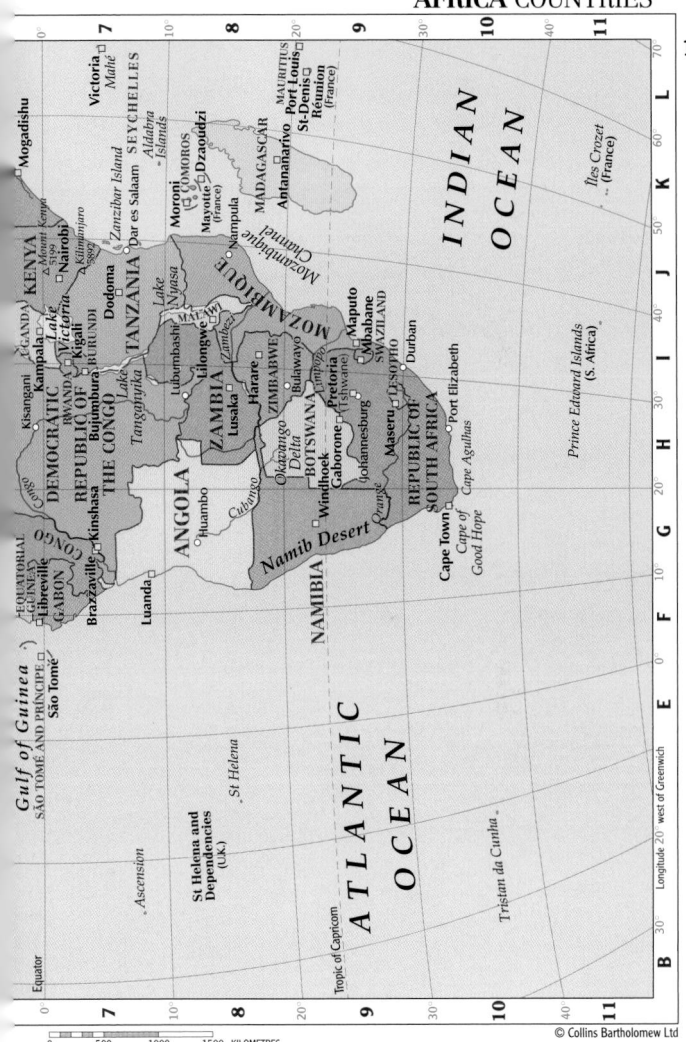

Gulf of Guinea

SÃO TOMÉ AND PRÍNCIPE
São Tomé

EQUATORIAL GUINEA
Libreville
GABON
Brazzaville
Kinshasa
CONGO
REPUBLIC OF THE CONGO
Luanda

DEMOCRATIC REPUBLIC OF THE CONGO

Kisangani
Kampala
UGANDA
KENYA
Nairobi
Mogadishu

RWANDA
Kigali
BURUNDI
Bujumbura

Lake Victoria
Mount Kenya
5199
Kilimanjaro
5895

Dodoma
Dar es Salaam
Zanzibar Island

TANZANIA
Lake Tanganyika
Lake Nyasa
Lubumbashi

ANGOLA
Huambo
Cubango
Okavango Delta
Zambezi

ZAMBIA
Lusaka
MALAWI
Lilongwe

MOZAMBIQUE
Nampula
Mozambique Channel

Moroni
COMOROS
Mayotte (France)
Dzaoudzi

SEYCHELLES
Victoria
Mahé
Aldabra Islands

MADAGASCAR
Antananarivo

MAURITIUS
Port Louis
Réunion (France)
St-Denis

ZIMBABWE
Harare
Bulawayo
Limpopo

BOTSWANA
Gaborone

NAMIBIA
Windhoek
Namib Desert

Maputo
Mbabane
SWAZILAND
Pretoria (Tshwane)
Johannesburg
LESOTHO
Maseru

REPUBLIC OF SOUTH AFRICA
Orange
Durban
Port Elizabeth
Cape Town
Cape of Good Hope
Cape Agulhas

INDIAN OCEAN

Îles Crozet (France)

Prince Edward Islands (S. Africa)

ATLANTIC OCEAN

St Helena
St Helena and Dependencies (U.K.)
Ascension

Tristan da Cunha

Tropic of Capricorn

Equator
Longitude 20 west of Greenwich

© Collins Bartholomew Ltd

0   500   1000   1500   KILOMETRES

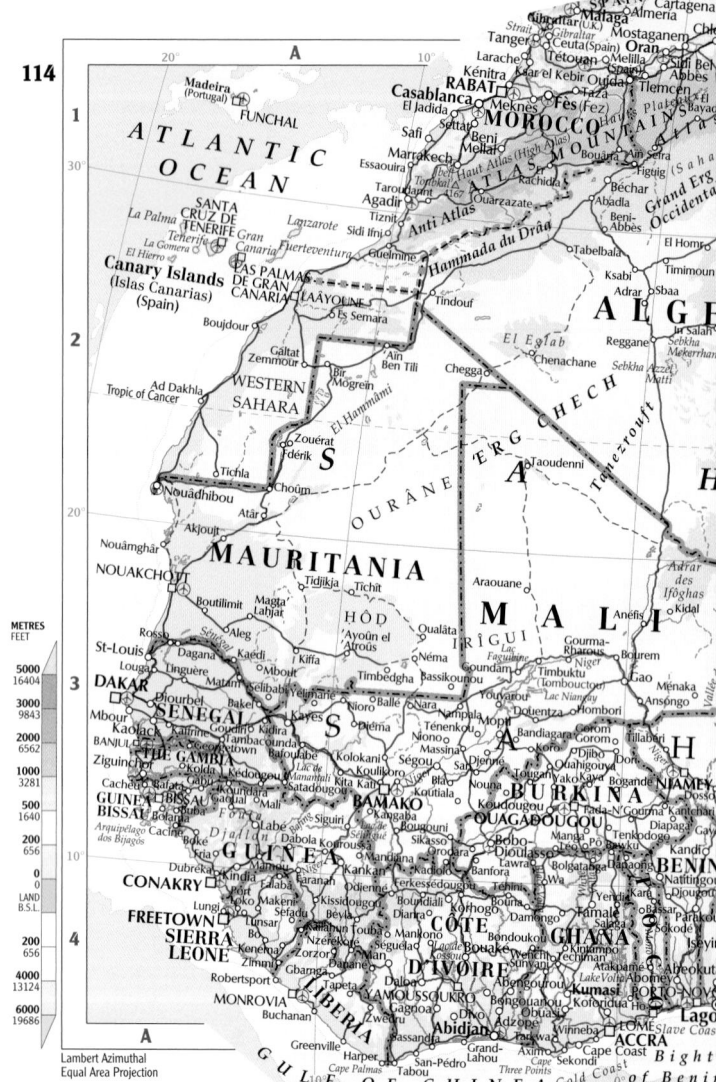

A

1

2

3

4

A

ATLANTIC

OCEAN

Madeira
(Portugal)
FUNCHAL

SANTA
CRUZ DE
TENERIFE
La Palma
Tenerife
El Hierro
La Gomera
Gran
Canaria
Canary Islands
(Islas Canarias)
(Spain)
LAS PALMAS
DE GRAN
CANARIA
Lanzarote
Fuerteventura

Boujdour

Ad Dakhla

Tropic of Cancer

WESTERN
SAHARA

Nouâdhibou

Nouâmghâr
NOUAKCHOTT

St-Louis
Rosso
Louga
DAKAR
Mbour
Kaolack
SENEGAL
BANJUL
THE GAMBIA
Ziguinchor
GUINEA-
BISSAU
Cacheu
BISSAU
Arquipélago
dos Bijagós
Cacine

CONAKRY

FREETOWN
SIERRA
LEONE

Robertsport
MONROVIA
Buchanan

LIBERIA
Greenville
Harper
Cape Palmas
Tabou

GULF

OF

GUINEA

Cartagena
Almería
SPAIN
Gibraltar (U.K.)
Ceuta (Spain)
Tangier
Larache
Kenitra
RABAT
Casablanca
El Jadida
Safi
Essaouira
Meknes
MOROCCO
Fès
(Fez)

ATLAS MOUNTAINS

Marrakech
Haut Atlas (High Atlas)
Taroudannt
Agadir
Tiznit
Anti Atlas
Guelmine
Tan-Tan
Hammada du Drâa

Ksabi

Tindouf

El Eglab

Chegga

Chenachane

Sebkha
Mekkarrhane
Sebkha Azzel
Matti

ERG CHECH

Taoudenni

Araouane

Timbuktu
(Tombouctou)

MAURITANIA

Boutilimit
Magta
Lahjar
Tidjikja
Tichit
HODH
Ayoûn el
Atroûs
Néma
Bassikounou

MALI

IRÎGUI

Gourma-
Rharous
Goundam

Lac
Faguibine
Niger

Gao
Ménaka
Ansongo

Timbédgha
Youvarou
Nampala
Douentza
Hombori
Mopti
Bandiagara
Douenza
Gorom-
Gorom
Djibo

NIGER

NIAMEY

Tillabéri

BURKINA

OUAGADOUGOU

Bobo-
Dioulasso

BENIN

GHANA

CÔTE

D'IVOIRE

Yamoussoukro
Gagnoa
Abidjan

ACCRA

Kumasi

LOMÉ

PORTO-
NOVO

Lagos

Gulf of Guinea

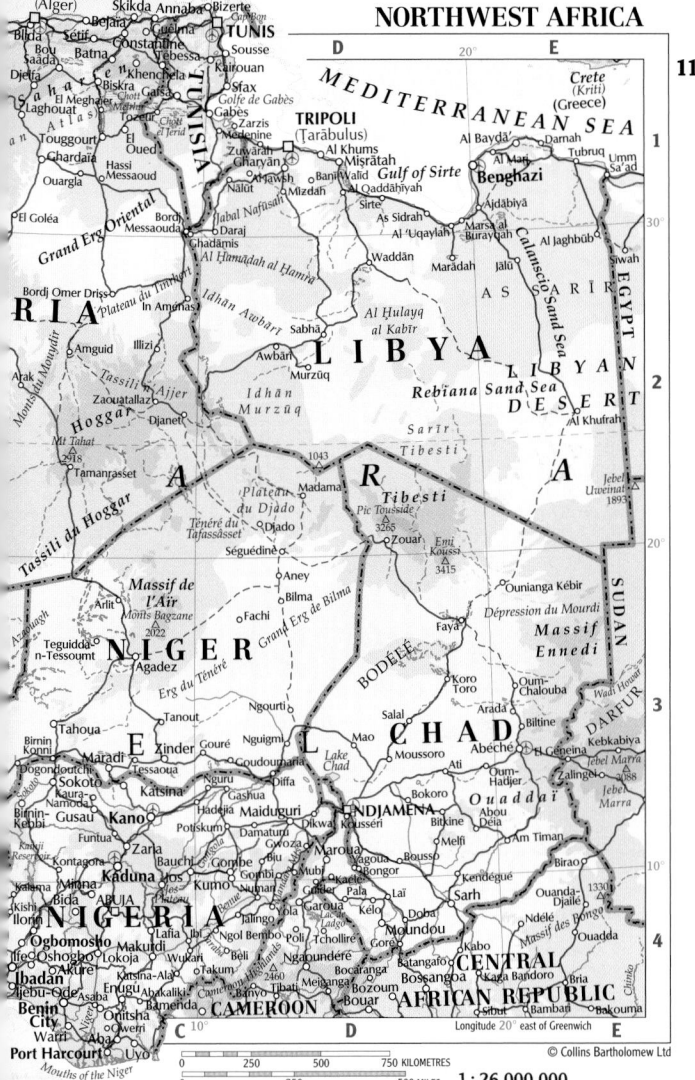

ALGIERS
(Alger)
Skikda Annaba Bizerte
Bêjaïa
Bilda Sétif
Bou Batna
Saâda
Djelfa El Meghaïer Sousse
Laghouat Biskra Gabès
Touggourt El Oued Zarzis
Ghardaïa Hassi Ghadāmis
Messaoud Al Khums Misrātah
Ouargla Darah
El Goléa Gharyān
Nālūt Mizdah
Bordj Omer Driss Al Ḩamādah al Ḩamrā
Bordj
In Amguid Messaouda
Illizi Sabhā
Tamanrasset
Djanet Murzūq
Mt Tahat Idhān
2918 Murzūq
Tassili du Hoggar

MEDITERRANEAN SEA
Crete
(Kriti)
(Greece)
TRIPOLI
(Tarābulus)
Al Baydā'
Banī Darnah
Tubruq
Umm
al Walīd Benghazi
Al Qaddāhiyah Ajdābiyā
Sirte
As Sidrah
Al 'Uqaylah Marsá al
Burayqah Al Jaghbūb
Siwah
Waddān Maradah Jālū

LIBYA
Al Hulayq
al Kabīr
Awbāri
Rebiana Sand Sea
Al Khufrah
Sarir Tibesti

SAHARA
1043
Madama
Tibesti
Pic Toussidé
3265
Zouar Emi
Koussi
3415
Jebel
Uweinat
1893

Plateau
du Djado
Ténéré du
Tafassasset
Séguédine
Aney
Djado
Bilma
Erg de Bilma
Fachi
Ouaniânga Kébir

Arlit
Monts Bagzane
2022
Teguidda-
n-Tessoum
Agadez
Erg du Ténéré

NIGER
Massif de
l'Aïr

Depression du Mourdi
Massif
Ennedi
Faya
Koro
Toro
Oum-
Chalouba

SUDAN

Tahoua
Konni
Maradi
Dogondoutchi
Sokoto
Katsina
Gusau
Funtua
Zaria
Birni-
Kebbi
Kontagora
Minna
KADUNA
Ilorin
Kaiama
Bida
Ogbomosho
Ilesha
Oyo AKURE
Ibadan
Benin
City
Warri
Port Harcourt
Mouths of the Niger

Zinder Gouré
Tessaoua
Tanout
Nguigmi
Ngourti
Magaria
Coudoumaoua
Gashua
Nguru
Diffa
Maiduguri
Potiskum
Damaturu
Biu

CHAD
Mao
Lake
Chad
Salal
Arada
Biltine
Abéché
Kebkabiya
El Geneina
Zalingei

DARFUR
Jebel Marra
3088
Jebel
Marra

N'DJAMENA
Massaguet
Bokoro
Ati
Oum-
Hadjer
Moussoro
Moundou
Bongor
Melfi
Bitkine
G0z Beida
Am Timan
Birao

NIGERIA
Katsina
Kaura-
Namoda
Birnin-

CAMEROON

CENTRAL
AFRICAN REPUBLIC

Longitude 20° east of Greenwich
© Collins Bartholomew Ltd

0   250   500   750 KILOMETRES
0   250   500 MILES

1 : 26 000 000

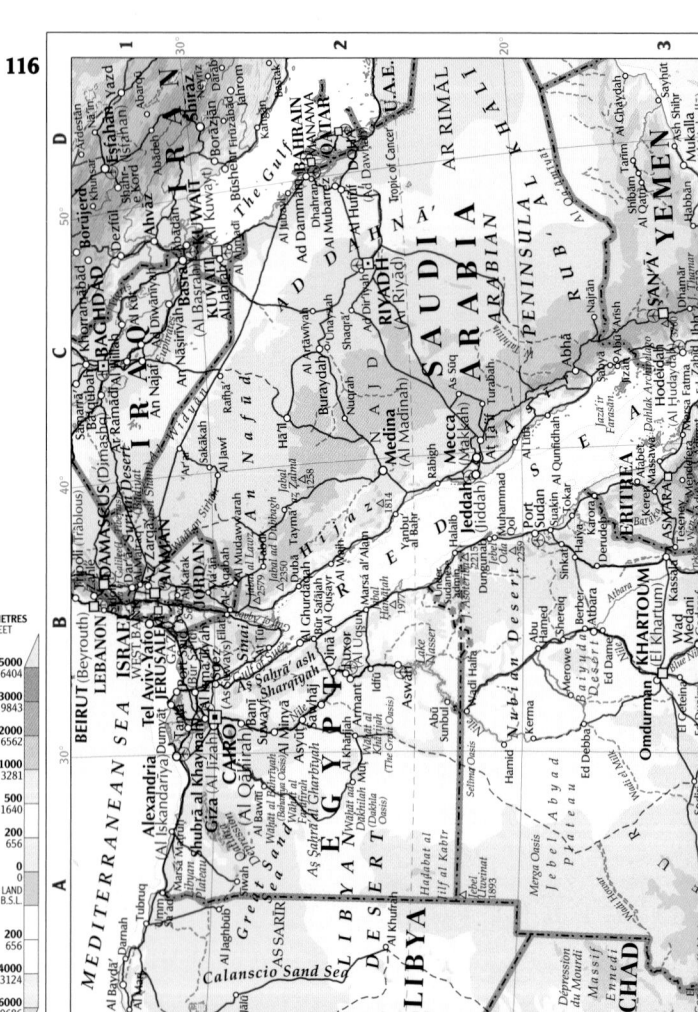

116

MEDITERRANEAN SEA

BEIRUT (Beyrouth)
LEBANON
DAMASCUS (Dimashq)
Tel Aviv-Yafo
ISRAEL
JERUSALEM
WEST BANK
AMMAN
JORDAN

Tripoli (Tarābulus)
Al Bayḍā'
Darnah
Tubruq

Alexandria
(Al Iskandarīyah)
Shubrā al Khaymah
Giza (Al Jīzah)
CAIRO (Al Qāhirah)
Al Fayyūm
EGYPT

Siwah Oasis
(Wāḥat Sīwah)
Qattâra Depression
(Munkhafaḍ al Qaṭṭârah)

Ad Dākhlah Oasis
Bahariya Oasis
(Wāḥat al Baḥrīyah)
Farafra Oasis
Aswân
Asyûṭ
Al Minyâ
Banī Suwayf
El Khârga Oasis
(Al Wāḥat al Khārijah)
The Great Oasis

L I B Y A   D E S E R T

Abū
Sumbul

Great Sand Sea

AS SARīR

Calanscio Sand Sea

Ḥafūbat al
Ilf al Kabīr
Jebel
Ûweinat 1893

Jebel Abyad
Plateau

Merga Oasis

Selîma Oasis

N u b i a n   D e s e r t

Wādī Ḥalfā
Ḥamīd
Ed Debba
Kerma
Merowe
Dongola

LIBYA

Depression
du Mourdi

Massif
Ennedi

CHAD

Kebkabiya
Geneina

Wādī Howar

SYRIA

Al Qāmishlī
BAGHDAD (Baghdād)
I R A Q
Karbalā'
An Najaf
An Nāṣirīyah
Al Baṣrah
KUWAIT (Al Kuwayt)

Kirkūk
Ar Ramādī
Ḥadīthah

At Taʾmīm

Dezful
Khurramābād
Borūjerd
Eṣfahān
Yazd
Ārdestān
Ābādān
Khorramshahr
Abādān

I R A N

Shīrāz
Būshehr
Fīrūzābād
Kāzerūn
Jahrom
Lār

The Gulf
BAHRAIN
MANAMA
QATAR
DOHA (Ad Dawḥah)
U.A.E.

Ad Dammām
Dhahran
Al Jubayl
AI Hufūf
Abū Dhabi

Ḥāʾil
Buraydah
Medina (Al Madīnah)
RIYADH (Ar Riyāḍ)
As Sulayyil
Shaqrāʾ
Ad Dawādimī
Az Zilfī
Unayzah

S A U D I   A R A B I A

N a f ū d

N a j d

Rabigh
Jeddah (Jiddah)
Mecca (Makkah)
Aṭ Ṭāʾif
At Ṭurabah

Yanbuʿ
al Baḥr

Al Qunfidhah
Abhā
Najrān
Abū ʿArīsh

Tropic of Cancer

AR RIMĀL

RUBʿ AL KHĀLĪ

PENINSULA

ARABIAN

Al Qaṭan

Tarīm
Shibām
Shiḥr
Al Ghaydaḥ

Ash Shiḥr
Al Mukallā
(Al Mukalla)

YEMEN
SANAʿ (Ṣanʿāʾ)
Dhamār

Shaqrāʾ

Ḥodeida
(Al Ḥudaydah)

Zabīd
Taʿizz
Jīzān
Farasān

Jazāʾir Farasān

ERITREA
ASMARA

Port Sudan
Sawākin
Tokar

Sinkāt
Halaib
Ḥalfa
Dongola

Abū
Ḥamed
Berber
Atbara
Shereiq

KHARTOUM
(Al Kharṭūm)
Omdurman
Wad Medani
El Obeid
Ed Dueim
Kosti

Blue Nile
White Nile

SUDAN

METRES
FEET

5000 16404
3000 9843
2000 6562
1000 3281
500   1640
200   656
0   LAND B.S.L.
200   656
4000 13124
6000 19686

Lambert Azimuthal Equal Area Projection

1 : 26 000 000

MILES 0   250   500

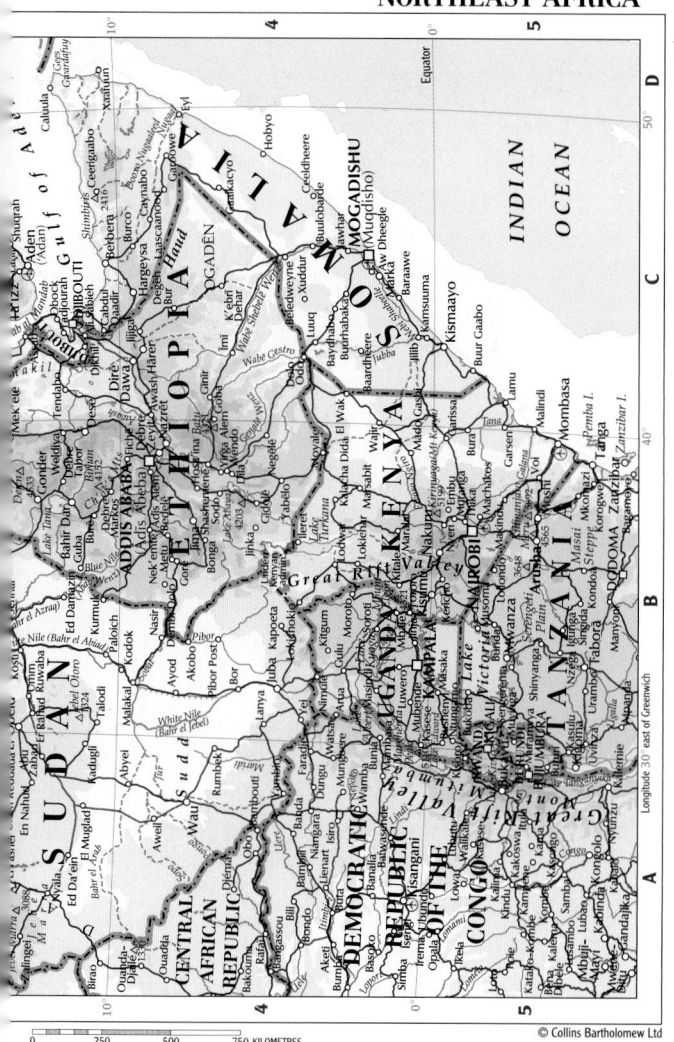

0   250   500   750 KILOMETRES

A 10° B 20°

10°

Bauchi
Jos
Gombe
Biu
Gwoza
Maroua
Yagoua
Bousso
Mélfi
Am Timan
Kumo
Gombi
Mubi
Kaélé
Bongor
Kendougé
Birao
Shendam
NIGERIA
Numan
Guider
Garoua
Pala
Laï
Doba
Sarh
CHAD
Ouanda-
Djallé
1330
Ibi
Ngol Bembol
Yola
Poli
Tcholliré
Moundou
Goré
Ndélé
Massif des Bongo
Ouadda
Wukari
Beli
Jalingo
Takum
Katsina-
Ala
2460
Banyo
Ngaoundéré
Kabo
Batangalo
Kaga
Bandoro
Ippy
Bria
Bamenda
Meiganga
Bocaranga
Bossangoa
CENTRAL
Bambari
Bakouma
CAMEROON
Bafoussam
Yoko
Tibati
Bétaré
Oya
Bouar
AFRICAN REPUBLIC
Sibut
Bangassou
Rafaï
Mbouda
Bamenda
Banyo
Bélabo
Bertoua
Bozoum
Bossembélé
Carnot
Boda
Bosobolo
Mobayi-
Mbongo
Uele
Bondo
Kumba
Mbanga
Bafia
Nanga
Eboko
Batouri
Berbérati
Mbaïki
BANGUI
Bimbo
Libenge
Gemena
Businga
Aketi
Bu
DOUALA
Edéa
Obala
Nanga Mbang
Nola
Dongou
Kungu
Lisala
Bumba
Basoko
MALABO
Bioco
Kribi
YAOUNDÉ
Mbalmayo
Sangmélima
Boumba
Molondou
Impfondo
Bongandanga
Lomela
Simba
Iseng
Bata
Niefang
Ebolowa
Ntem
Souanké
Ouesso
Congo
Losombo
DEMOCR
Cogo
Evinayong
Mitzic
Makokou
Sembé
Mbomo
Bolomba
Lisala
EQ. GUINEA
Oyem
Equator
Bifoun
Alembe
Dongou
Mbandaka
Boende
Tshuapa
Busanga
Irema
Iket
REPUI
LIBREVILLE
Port-
Gentil
GABON
Lastoursville
Koulamoutou
Okondja
Owando
Obouya
Bokatola
Kengo
Lac
Tumba
Boleko
Bokele
Loto
OF TH
Lambaréné
Mouila
Franceville
Okoyo
Gamboma
Inongo
Lac Mai-
Ndombe
Poie
Kataka-Kombe
Iguéla
Ndendé
Tchibanga
Mayoko
Bongango
Tékana
Bolobo
Kutu
Mushie
Bunia
Oshwe
Lukenie
Dekese
Kole
CONG
METRES
FEET
5000
16404
3000
9843
2000
6562
1000
3281
500
1640
200
656
0
0
LAND
B.S.L.
200
656
4000
13124
6000
19686
Mayumba
Mossendjo
Djambala
Ngo
Bandundu
Bunanga
Ilebo
Bena
Dibele
Kalema
Loubomo (Dolisie)
Pointe-
Noire
Madingou
BRAZZAVILLE
KINSHASA
Kasangulu
Manga
Bulungu
Mweka
Luebo
Lusambo
CABINDA
(Angola)
Cabinda
Tshela
Kimpese
Kisantu
Kenge
Kikwit
Idiofa
Dekese
Denba
Kananga
Kabind
Muanda
Bopa
Kitona
Maquela
do Zombo
Mawanga
Feshi
Popokabaka
Gungu
Kilembe
Tshikapa
Mbuji-Mayi
Kamonia
Gandajika
Mwene-
Ditu
Matadi
M'banza
Congo
Kasongo-Lunda
Bibaya
N'zeto
Songo
Quimbele
Tembo
Aluma
Bindu
Kahemba
Chitato
Luiza
Kamonia
Tshitanzu
Ambriz
Uige
Negage
Muxaluando
Massango
Cuilo
Lucapa
Kapanga
Caxito
LUANDA
Ndalatando
ANGOLA
Calandula
Capenda-
Camulemba
Saurimo
Sombo
Mwimba
Sandoa
ATLANTIC
OCEAN
Dondo
Lucala
Malanje
Muriege
Muconda
Kasaji
10°
Gabela
Quibala
Quitapa
Cacolo
Dala
Luau
Dilolo
Malonga
Sumbe
Andúlo
Luacano
Caianta

A 10° B

Longitude 20° east of Greenwich

Lambert Azimuthal Equal Area Projection

1 : 20 000 000

MILES 0   100   200   300   400

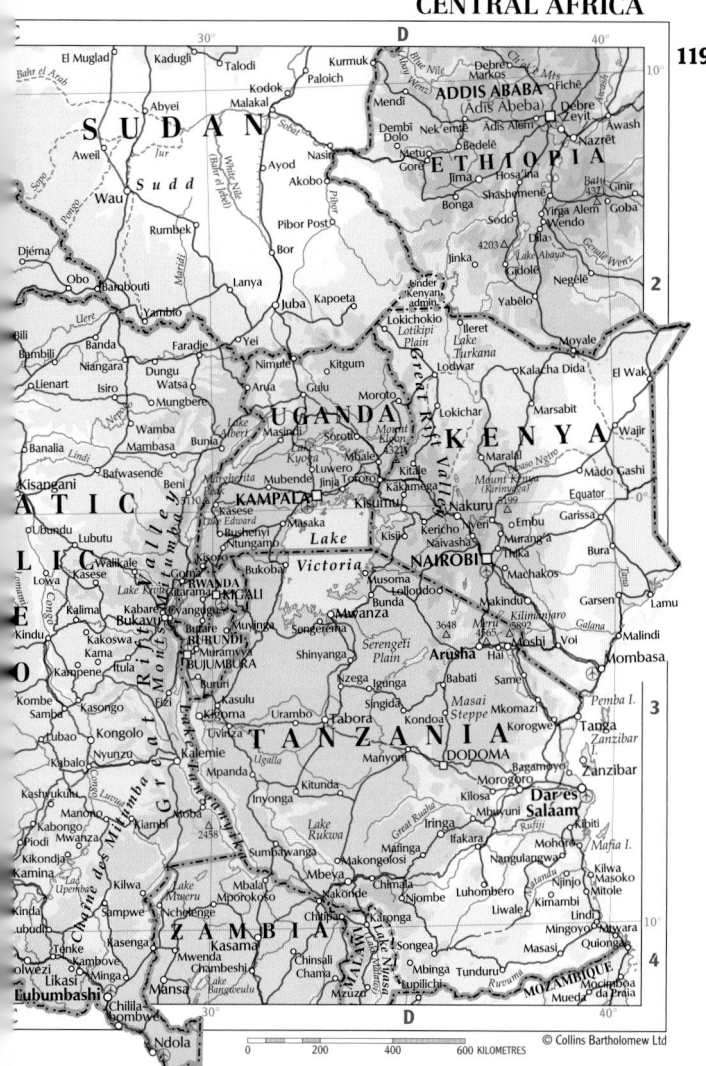

© Collins Bartholomew Ltd

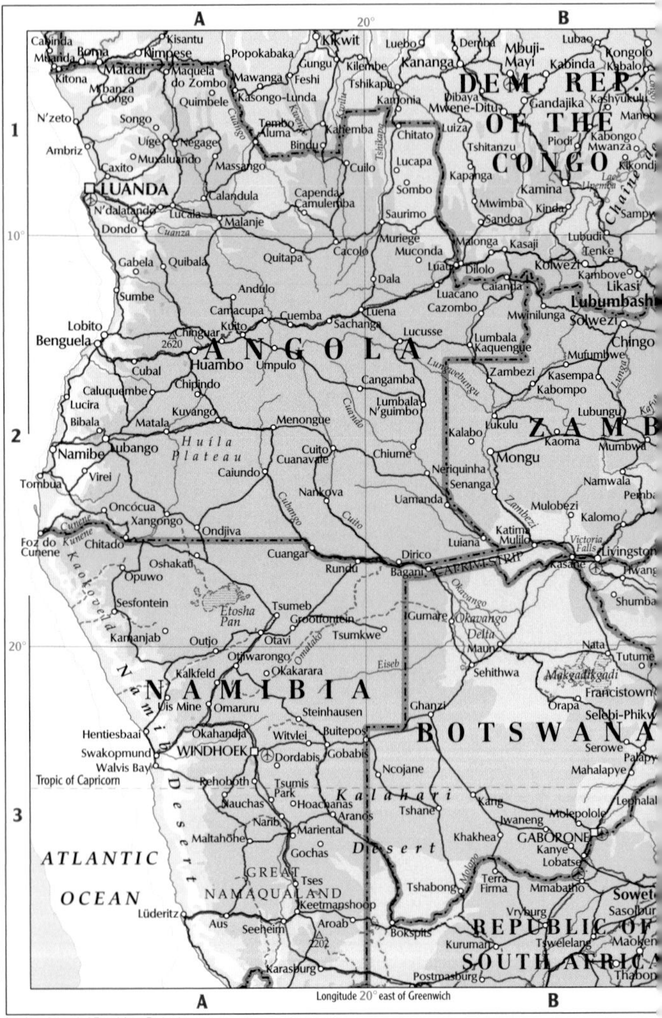

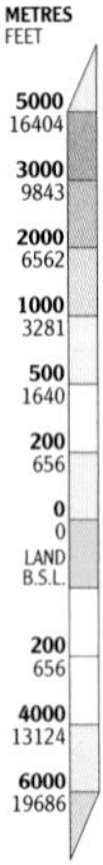

A 20° B

DEM. REP. OF THE CONGO

ANGOLA

ZAMBIA

NAMIBIA

BOTSWANA

REPUBLIC OF SOUTH AFRICA

ATLANTIC OCEAN

Huíla Plateau

Namib Desert

Kalahari Desert

GREAT NAMAQUALAND

Etosha Pan

Okavango Delta

Makgadikgadi

Caprivi Strip

Tropic of Capricorn

METRES / FEET

5000	16404
3000	9843
2000	6562
1000	3281
500	1640
200	656
0 LAND B.S.L.	0
200	656
4000	13124
6000	19686

Lambert Azimuthal Equal Area Projection

Longitude 20° east of Greenwich

1 : 20 000 000

MILES 0   100   200   300   400

0   200   400   600 KILOMETRES

REPUBLIC OF SOUTH AFRICA

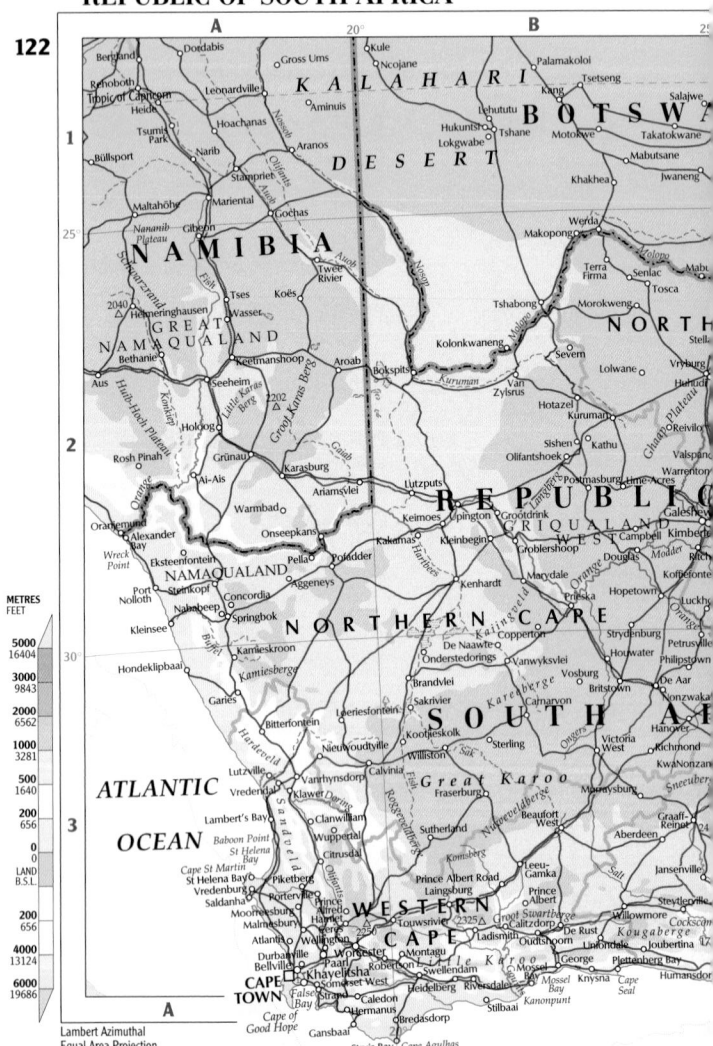

A · 20° · B · 25

KALAHARI

Berkland · Dordabis · Gross Ums · Kule · Ncojane · Palamakoloi · Tsetseng

Rehoboth · Kang · Salajwe · BOTSW

Heide · Tropic of Capricorn · Leonardville · Aminuis · Hukuntsi · Tshane · Motokwe · Takatokwane

Tsumis · Hoachanas · Lokgwabe · Mabutsane · Jwaneng

Park · Narib · Aranos · Khakhea

Büllsport

Maltahöhe · Stampriet · Werda · Kolope

Mariental · Gochas · Makopong · Terra · Senlac · Mabu

Nananib · Gibeon · Firma · Tosca

Plateau

NAMIBIA · Twee · Tshabong · Morokweng · Stella

Tses · River · NORTH

Hameringhausen · Koës · Kolonkwaneng · Severn · Vryburg

Wasser · Hühud

GREAT · Aroab · Van · Lolwane

Bethanie · Keetmanshoop · Zylsrus · Hotazel · Chad Plateau

NAMAQUALAND · Bokspits · Kuruman · Reivilo · Valspan

Aus · Seeheim · Kuruman · Warrenton

Holoog · Grünau · Sishen · Kathu · Hine Acres

Rosh Pinah · Karasburg · Olifantshoek · Postmasburg · Galeshwe

Ai-Ais · Lutzputs · Grootdrink · **REPUBLIC** · Kimberle

Orangemund · Ariamsvlei · Keimoes · Upington · **GRIQUALAND** · Campbell · Modder · Koffiefonte

Alexander · Warmbad · Onseepkans · Kleinbegin · Groblershoop · **WEST** · Douglas · Lucky

Bay · Eksteenfontein · Pella · Kakamas · Marydale · Hopetown · Trang

Wreck · Port · Pofadder · Kenhardt · Priska · Petrusville

Point · Nolloth · Aggeneys · **NORTHERN CAPE** · Copperton · Strydenburg · Philipstown

Concordia · De Naawte · Houwater · De Aar

Kleinsee · Springbok · Onderstedorings · Vanwyksvlei · Vosburg · Britstown · Nonzwakar

Kamieskroon · Brandvlei · Sakrivier · Carnarvon · Victoria · Hanover · Richmond

Hondeklipbaai · Kamiesberg · Loeriesfontein · **SOUTH A** · West · KwaNobuhle

Garies · Nieuwoudtville · Williston · Sterling · Onnys · Sneeuber

Bitterfontein · Williston · **Great Karoo** · Fraserburg · Middelburg · Graaff-

METRES / FEET · Lutzville · Calvinia · Sutherland · Niekerksberge · Beaufort · Reinet · Jansenville

5000 / 16404 · Vredendal · Vanrhynsdorp · West · Aberdeen · Steytlerville

3000 / 9843 · **ATLANTIC** · Klawer · Clanwilliam · Komsberg · Salt · Willowmore · Cockscom

2000 / 6562 · Lambert's Bay · Wuppertal · Kougabe · Joubertina · V

1000 / 3281 · **OCEAN** · St Helena · Citrusdal · Leeu- · Prince Albert Road · Uniondale · Humansdo

500 / 1640 · Baboon Point · Bay · Gamka · Langsburg · Plettenberg

200 / 656 · St Martin · Cape St Martin · Piketberg · Prince · Groot Swartberge · George · Cape

0 · St Helena · Albert · Oudtshoorn · Knysna · Seal

LAND / B.S.L. · Bay · Vredenburg · Porterville · 2325△ · Little Karoo · Mossel

200 / 656 · Saldanha · Moorreesburg · Hopefield · Ladismith · Calitzdorp · De Rust · Mossel · Kanonpunt

4000 / 13124 · Malmesbury · Atlantis · Wellington · 225 · Montagu · Bay

6000 / 19686 · Durbanville · Paarl · **WESTERN** · Robertson · Swellendam · Riversdale

Bellville · Khayelitsha · **CAPE** · Worcester · Heidelberg · Bredasdorp

CAPE · False · Strand · Somerset West · Caledon · Stilbaai · Cape Agulhas

TOWN · Bay · Grabouw · Hermanus · Struis Bay

Cape of · Gansbaai

Good Hope

Lambert Azimuthal

Equal Area Projection

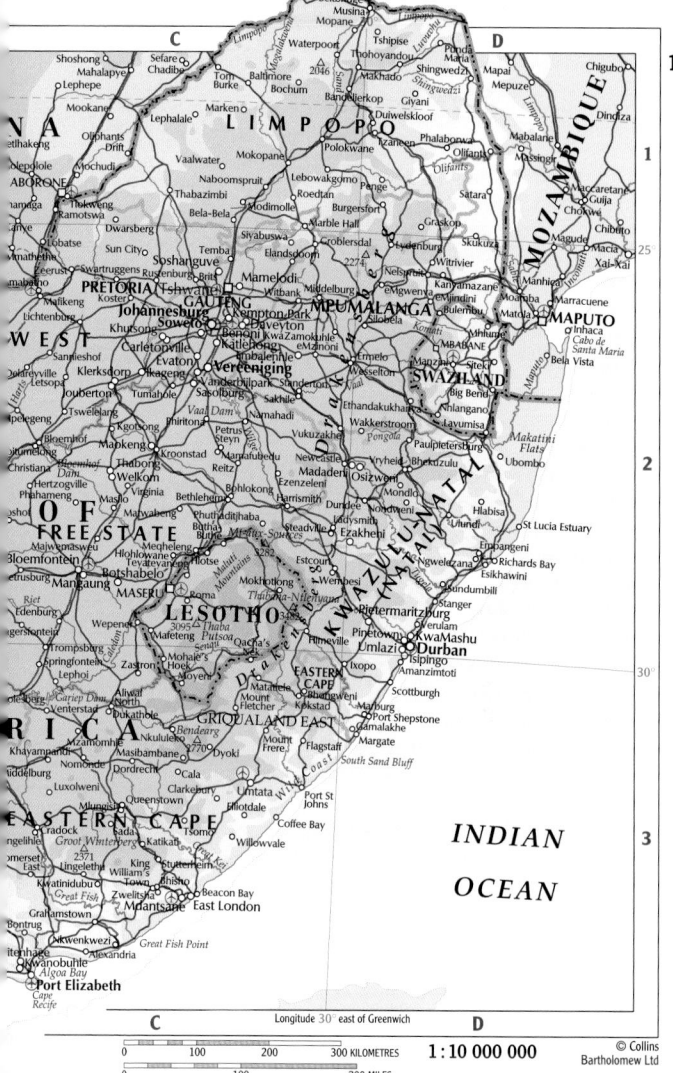

C

D

Beitbridge
Musina
Mopani
Shoshong
Sefare
Chadibo
Mahalapye
Shipise
Tshipise
Tshohoyandou
Makhado
Shingwedzi
Waterpoort
Tom
Burke
Baltimore
Bochum
2046
Thohoyandou
Makhado
Shingwedzi
Mapai
Mepuze
Chigubo
Dindza
Lephepe
Mookane
Ramotswa
Lephalale
Marken
Duiwelskloof
Phalaborwa
Mabalane
Massingir

ABORONE
Olifants
Drift
Vaalwater
Mokopane
Polokwane
Lebowakgomo
Panje
Olifants
Satara
Maccaretane
Guija
Chibuto
Macia
Xai-Xai

NA
Thokweng
Mochudi
Thabazimbi
Naboomspruit
Roedtan
Burgersfort
Graskop
Skukuza
Magude
25

Tlobatse
Dwarsberg
Bela-Bela
Siyabuswa
Modimolle
Marble Hall
Groblersdal
Lydenburg
Witrivier
Kanyamazane
Manhiça

Sun City
Soshanguve
Rustenburg
Temba
Elandsdoorn
Middelburg
Nelspruit
Mgwenya
Bulembu
Matola
MAPUTO

PRETORIA
Tshwane
Mamelodi
Witbank
Emgweni
Mbombela
Inhaca
Cabo de
Santa Maria
Koster
JOHANNESBURG
GAUTENG
Kempton Park
KwaZamokuhle
Mzinoni
Mbabane
Siteki
Bela Vista

WEST
Khutsong
Soweto
Benoni
Daveyton
Ermelo
SWAZILAND
Big Bend

Carletonville
Evaton
Katlehong
Standerton
Ethandakukhanya
Nhlangano

Klerksdorp
Vanderbijlpark
Sasolburg
Sakhile
Wesselton
Pongola
Paulpietersburg
Ubombo

Louberton
Tumahole
Namahadi
Vukuzakhe
Wakkerstroom
Makatini
Flats

Kgotsong
Kroonstad
Petrus
Steyn
Newcastle
Vryheid
Ngwelezana
Hlabisa
St Lucia Estuary

Bothaville
Thabong
Welkom
Reitz
Madadeni
Osizweni
Nongoma
Ulundi
Empangeni
Richards Bay

Virginia
Bethlehem
Blokkong
Ladysmith
Nqutu
Eshowe
Esikhawini

Mapheng
Senekal
Harrismith
Dundee
Nkandla
Mtunzini

OF
Masilo
Malwabeng
Phuthaditjhaba
Steadville
Ezakheni

Bloemhof
Dam
Maboloka
Bethlehem
Mooi River
Wembesi
Stanger
KwaDukuza

FREE
STATE
Hlohlowane
Tweling
Qalabotjha
Estcourt
Mokhotlong
Thaba-Tseka
Greytown
Verulam
Durban

Bloemfontein
Mangaung
Botshabelo
MASERU
Mafeteng
Roma
Pietermaritzburg
Pinetown
KwaMashu

Riet
Thaba
Bosiu
3095
LESOTHO
Himeville
Umlazi
Isipingo
Amanzimtoti

Wepener
Qacha's
Nek
Ixopo
Scottburgh

Trompsburg
Zastron
Mohale's
Hoek
Matatiele
Kokstad
Ugie
Port Shepstone
Hibberdene
Margate

Springfontein
Lephoi
Moyeni
EASTERN
CAPE
Mount
Fletcher
Mngeni
Maburg

RICA
Gariep Dam
Aliwal
North
Dukathole
Bendearg
Nkululeko
GRIQUALAND EAST
Mount
Frere
Flagstaff
South Sand Bluff

Khayamnandi
Masibambane
Mzamomhle
2709
Dyoki
Cala

EASTERN
CAPE
Nomonde
Dordrecht
Clarkebury
Umtata
Port St
Johns

Luxolweni
Queenstown
Mthatha
Coffee Bay

Radock
Sada
Katikati
Willowvale

Somerset
East
Groot Winterberg
2371
Stutterheim
Beacon Bay

Kwatinidubo
King
William's
Town
Bhisho
East London

Great Fish
Zwelitsha
Mdantsane

Bontrug
Nkwenkwezi
Grahamstown
Alexandria
Great Fish Point

Port Elizabeth
Cape
Recife
Algoa Bay

LIMPOPO

MPUMALANGA

MOZAMBIQUE

KWAZULU-NATAL

INDIAN

OCEAN

C
Longitude 30° east of Greenwich
D

0   100   200   300 KILOMETRES
0   100   200 MILES
1 : 10 000 000

© Collins
Bartholomew Ltd

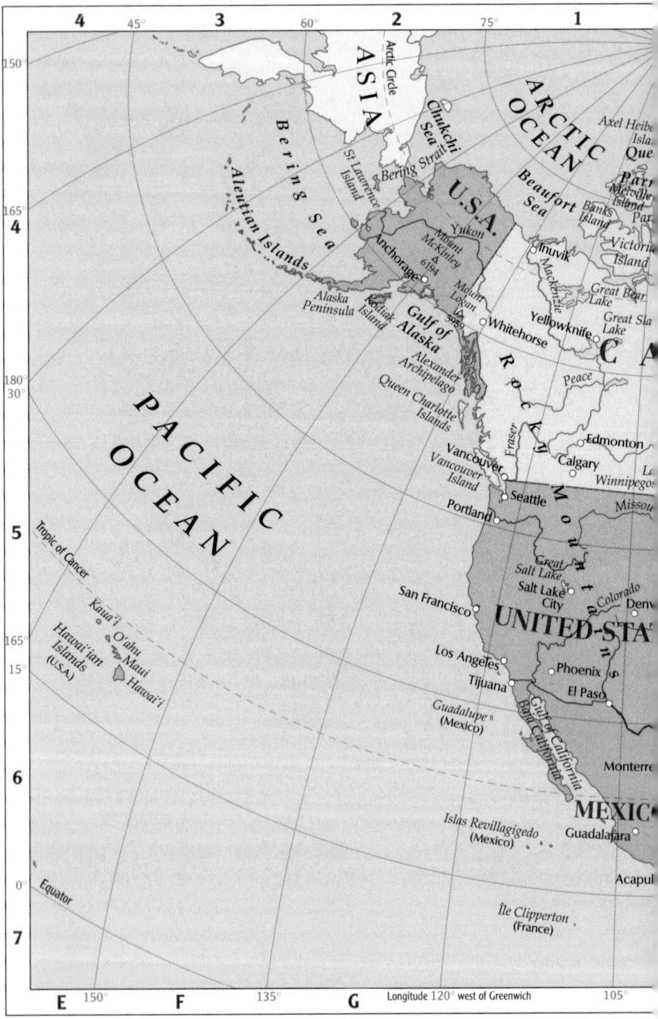

4 45° **3** 60° **2** 75° **1**

150°

Arctic Circle

ASIA

A R C T I C
O C E A N

Axel Heibe
Isla
Que

Chukchi
Sea

Bering Strait

Par
Melville
Island Par

Beaufort
Sea

Banks
Island

U.S.A.

Inuvik

Victoria
Island

165°
4

St Lawrence
Island

Anchorage

Mount
McKinley
6194

Yukon

Mackenzie

Great Bear
Lake

Aleutian Islands

B e r i n g   S e a

Alaska
Peninsula

Kodiak
Island

Mackenzie

Whitehorse

Yellowknife

C A

Great Sla
Lake

Gulf of
Alaska

180°
30°

Alexander
Archipelago

Peace

Queen Charlotte
Islands

Fraser

Edmonton

Calgary

L
Winnipegos

P A C I F I C

O C E A N

Vancouver

Vancouver
Island

Seattle

Portland

Rocky Mountains

Misso

5

Tropic of Cancer

Kaua'i

Great
Salt Lake

Salt Lake
City

Colorado

Denv

San Francisco

UNITED-STA

165°
15°

Hawai'ian
Islands
(U.S.A.)

O'ahu

Maui

Hawai'i

Los Angeles

Tijuana

Phoenix

El Paso

Guadalupe °
(Mexico)

Gulf of California
Baja California

Monterre

6

MEXIC

Islas Revillagigedo
(Mexico)

Guadalajara

Acapul

0°

Equator

Île Clipperton
(France)

7

E 150° F 135° G Longitude 120° west of Greenwich 105°

1 : 72 000 000   MILES 0   500   1000

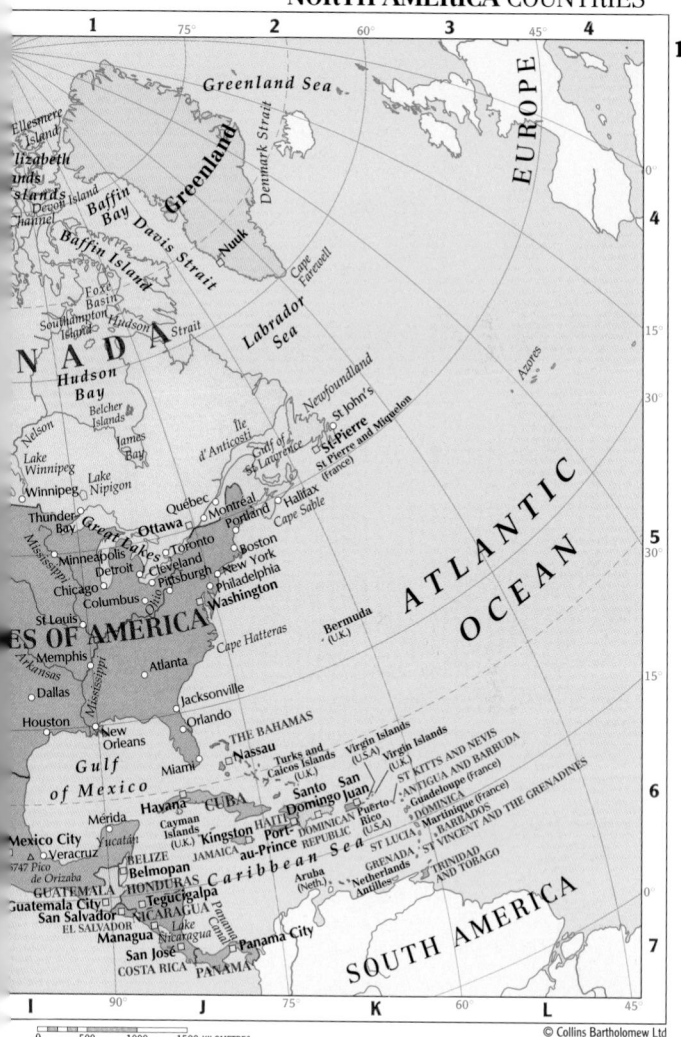

Greenland Sea

EUROPE

Ellesmere
Island

Elizabeth
Islands
Islands
Devon Island
Channel

Baffin
Bay

Greenland

Denmark Strait

Baffin Bay Davis Strait

Baffin Island

Nuuk

Cape
Farewell

Foxe
Basin

Southampton
Island

Hudson Strait

Labrador
Sea

CANADA

Hudson
Bay

Belcher
Islands

Nelson

James
Bay

Newfoundland

St John's

Lake
Winnipeg

Lake
Nipigon

Île
d'Anticosti

Gulf of
St Lawrence

St Pierre
St Pierre and Miquelon
(France)

St-Pierre

Winnipeg

Thunder
Bay

Great Lakes

Québec

Montreal

Ottawa

Portland

Azores

Mississippi

Minneapolis

Toronto

Detroit

Cleveland

Halifax
Cape Sable

Boston

Chicago

Pittsburgh

New York

ATLANTIC

Columbus

Ohio

Philadelphia

St Louis

Washington

ES OF AMERICA

Memphis

Arkansas

Cape Hatteras

Bermuda
(U.K.)

OCEAN

Dallas

Atlanta

Mississippi

Jacksonville

Houston

New
Orleans

Orlando

THE BAHAMAS

Gulf

Miami

Nassau

Turks and
Caicos Islands
(U.K.)

Virgin Islands
(U.K.)

Virgin Islands
(U.S.A)

of Mexico

Merida

Havana

CUBA

Santo
Domingo

San
Juan

ST KITTS AND NEVIS

ANTIGUA AND BARBUDA

Guadeloupe (France)

DOMINICA

Mexico City

Veracruz

Yucatán

Cayman
Islands
(U.K.)

Kingston

HAITI

Port-
au-Prince

DOMINICAN
REPUBLIC

Puerto
Rico
(U.S.A)

ST LUCIA

Martinique (France)

BARBADOS

5747 Pico
de Orizaba

BELIZE

JAMAICA

Caribbean Sea

GRENADA

ST VINCENT AND THE GRENADINES

GUATEMALA

Belmopan

HONDURAS

Aruba
(Neth.)

Netherlands
Antilles

TRINIDAD
AND TOBAGO

Guatemala City

Tegucigalpa

San Salvador

EL SALVADOR

NICARAGUA

Managua

Lake
Nicaragua

Panama
Canal

SOUTH AMERICA

San José

COSTA RICA

PANAMA

Panama City

0   500   1000   1500 KILOMETRES

© Collins Bartholomew Ltd

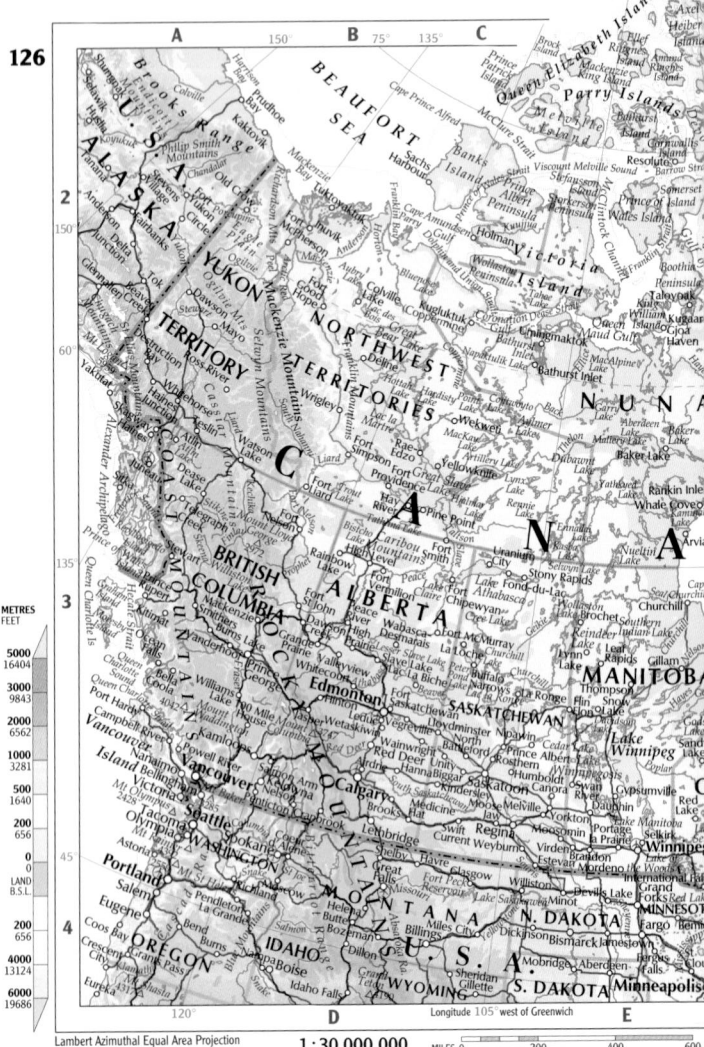

Lambert Azimuthal Equal Area Projection

1:30 000 000

MILES 0   200   400   600

Longitude 105° west of Greenwich

METRES FEET

METRES	FEET
5000	16404
3000	9843
2000	6562
1000	3281
500	1640
200	656
0	0
LAND	B.S.L.
200	656
4000	13124
6000	19686

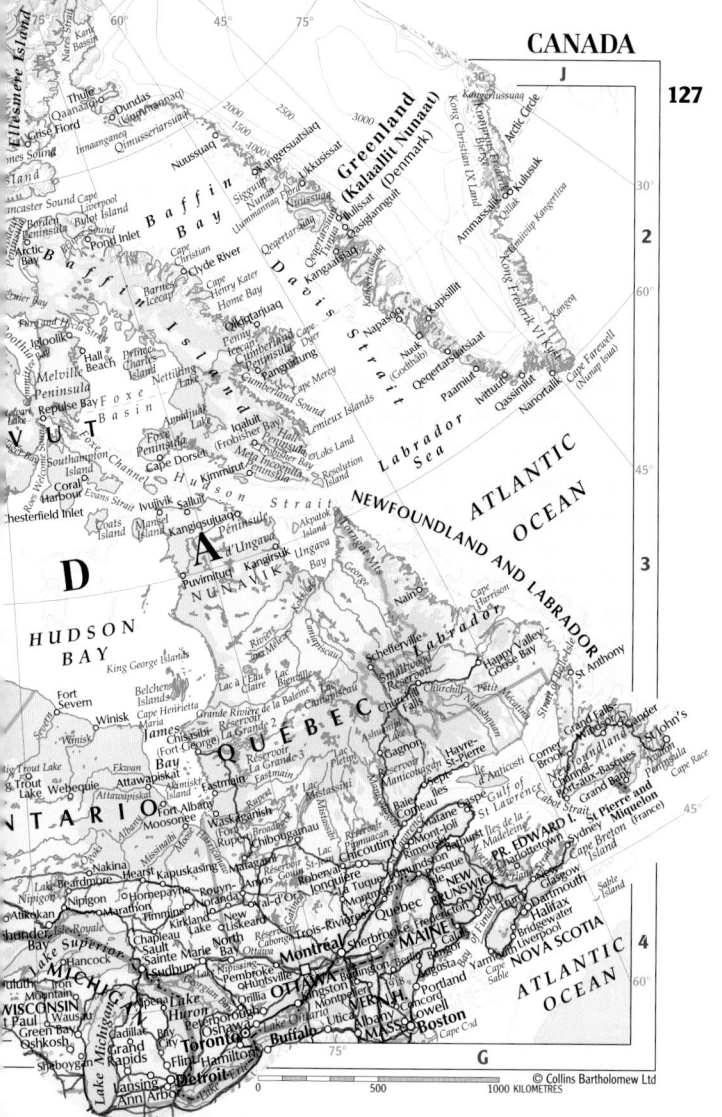

ATLANTIC OCEAN

HUDSON BAY

JAMES BAY

NEWFOUNDLAND AND LABRADOR

Labrador Sea

Greenland (Kalaallit Nunaat) (Denmark)

Baffin Bay

Davis Strait

Baffin Island

Foxe Basin

NUNAVUT

QUÉBEC

ONTARIO

NOVA SCOTIA

MAINE

MICHIGAN

WISCONSIN

Hudson Strait

NUNAVIK

© Collins Bartholomew Ltd

500   1000 KILOMETRES

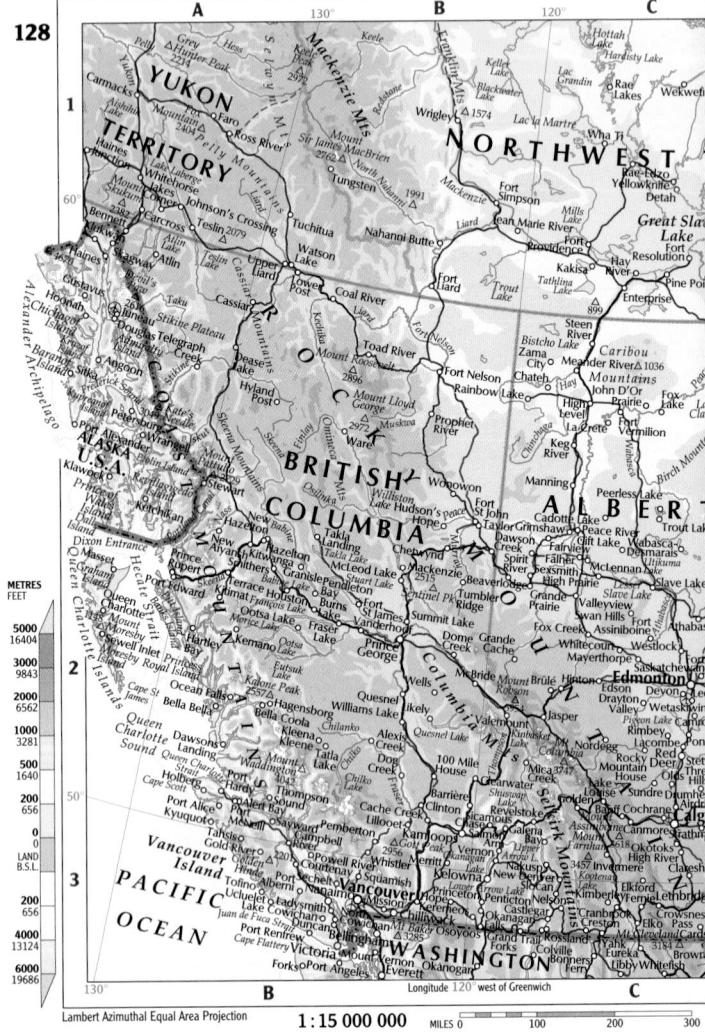

A · 130° · B · 120° · C

YUKON

TERRITORY

Carmacks

Grey Hunter Peak 2224

Keele

Franklin Mts △ 1574

Wrigley

Hottah Lake

Hardisty Lake

Rae Lakes

Wekweti

N O R T H W E S T

Fort Faro

Ross River

Mount Keele 2404

Mount MacBrien 2762

North Nahanni 1991

Lac la Martre

Wha Ti

Rae-Edzo Yellowknife

Detah

Haines Junction

Whitehorse

Johnson's Crossing

Tungsten

Mackenzie

Fort Simpson

Mills Lake

Carcross

Teslin 2079

Jean Marie River

Fort Providence

Hay River

Great Slave Lake

Fort Resolution

Pine Point

Bennett

Atlin

Upper Liard

Watson Lake

Nahanni Butte

Liard

Fort Liard

Trout Lake

Kakisa

Enterprise

Skagway

Haines

Lower Post

Coal River

Steen River

Bistcho Lake

Zama City

Chateh

Meander River △1036

Caribou

Haines

Juneau

Cassiar

Dease Lake

Toad River

Mount Roosevelt 2096

Fort Nelson

Rainbow Lake

High Level

John D'Or Prairie

La Crete

Vermilion

Telegraph Creek

Dease Lake

Hyland Post

Mount Lloyd George 2972

Muskwa

Prophet River

Keg River

Manning

Birch Mts

ALASKA U.S.A.

Petersburg Wrangell

Ketchikan

Stewart

Ware

Wonowon

Hudson's Hope

A L B E R

Fox Creek

Trout Lake

Alexander Archipelago

Masset

British Columbia

Takla Landing

McLeod Lake

Williston Lake

Taylor

Dawson Creek

Peace River

Cadotte

Grimshaw

Spirit River

Fairview

High Prairie

Slave Lake

Swan Hills

Fort Assiniboine

Athab

Prince Rupert

New Hazelton

Smithers

Granisle Pendleton

Mackenzie

Beaverlodge

Grande Prairie

Valleyview

Whitecourt

Westlock

Queen Charlotte Islands

Terrace Kitimat

Houston

Burns Lake

Fort St James

Summit Lake

Tumbler Ridge

Dome Creek

Grande Cache

Fox Creek

Edson

Hinton

Edmonton

Devon

Kemano

Fraser Lake

Vanderhoof

Prince George

McBride

Mount Robson

Jasper

Drayton Valley

Wetaskiwin

Ootsa Lake

Bella Coola

Hagensborg

Wells

Rimbey

Lacombe

Red Deer

Anahim Lake

Williams Lake

Quesnel

Likely

Valemount

Nordegg

Rocky Mountain House

Sundre

Drumheller

Hazelton

Dawsons Landing

Bella Bella

Ocean Falls

Kleena Kleene

Tatla Lake

Chilanko

Alexis Creek

Quesnel Lake

Mica

Clearwater

Golden

Olds

Cochrane

Calg

Okotoks

High River

Port Hardy

Holberg

Waddington

Tahsis

Gold River

Powell River

Squamish

Pemberton

Whistler

Kamloops

Barrière

Revelstoke

Salmon Arm

Vernon

Arrow Lakes

Nakusp

Kelowna

Rossland

Invermere

Kimberley

Fernie

Claresholm

Lethbridge

Vancouver Island

Nanaimo

Duncan

Victoria

Ladysmith

Courtenay

Campbell River

Port Alberni

Ucluelet

Tofino

Merritt

Princeton

Penticton

Osoyoos

Okanagan

Grand Forks

Trail

Castlegar

Nelson

Creston

Cranbrook

Elko

Crowsnest

P A C I F I C

O C E A N

Juan de Fuca Strait

Cape Flattery

Port Angeles

Port Renfrew

WASHINGTON

Bellingham

Mount Baker

Everett

Vernon

Okanogan

Colville

Bonners Ferry

Libby

Whitefish

Eureka

Port Townsend

Forks

Lambert Azimuthal Equal Area Projection

1 : 15 000 000

MILES 0 · 100 · 200 · 300

Longitude 120° west of Greenwich

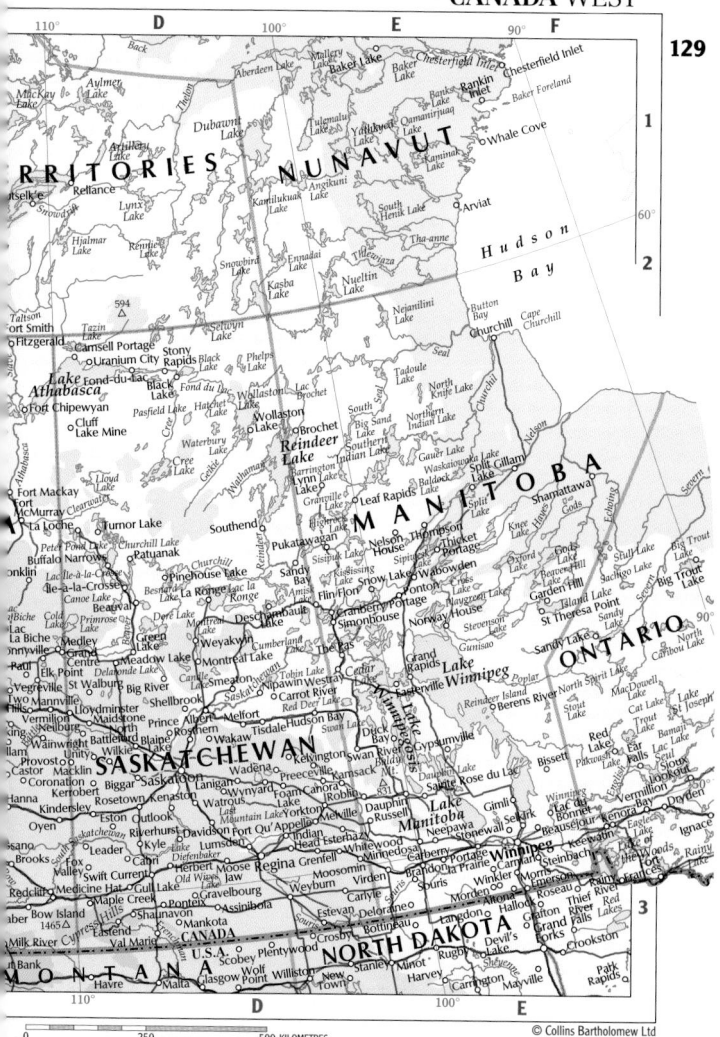

0   250   500 KILOMETRES

© Collins Bartholomew Ltd

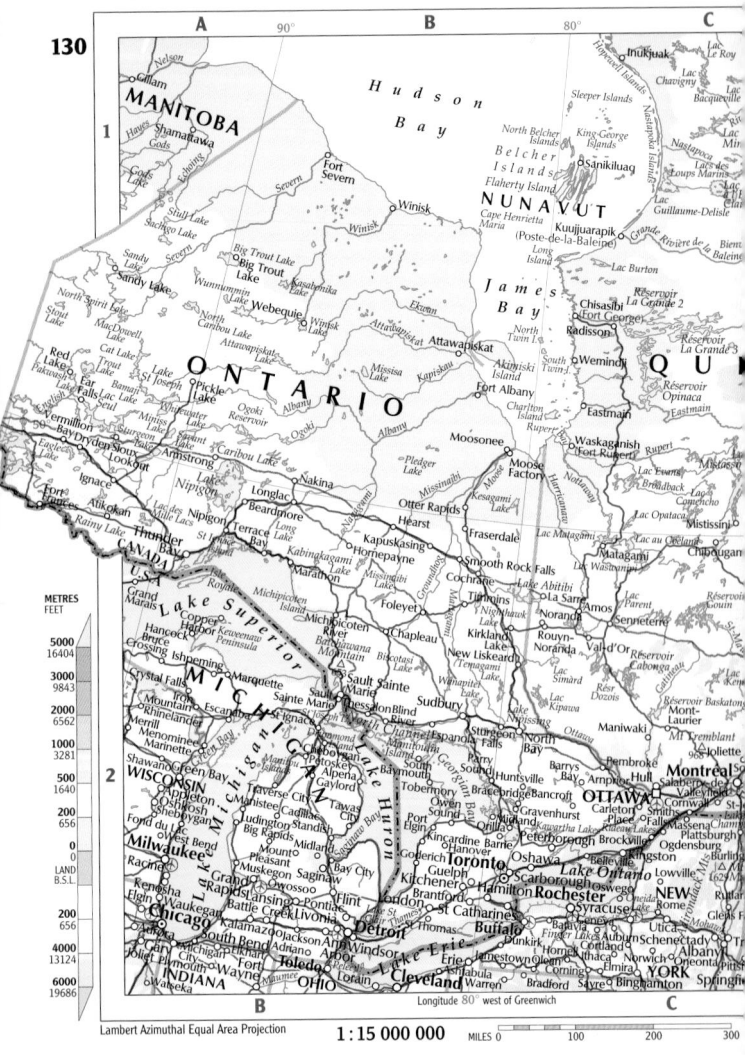

130

A 90° B 80° C

MANITOBA

Hudson Bay

Gillam
Nelson
Shamattawa
Gods
Gods Lake
Island Lake
Fort Severn
Severn
Winisk

NUNAVUT

Inukjuak
Lac Le Roy
Lac Chavigny
Lac Bacquerville

Sleeper Islands
North Belcher Islands
King George Islands
Nastapoca Islands
Belcher Islands
Sanikiluaq
Flaherty Island
Cape Henrietta Maria
Long Island

Lac Guillaume-Delisle
Lac des Loups Marins
Rivière de la
Bient

Stull Lake
Sachigo Lake
North Spirit Lake
Stout Lake
Sandy Lake
Big Trout Lake
Wunnummin Lake
Kasabonika Lake
Webequie
North Caribou Lake
Attawapiskat
Winisk
Ekwan
Kuujjuarapik (Poste-de-la-Baleine)
Lac Burton

Sandy Lake
Red Lake
MacDowell Lake
Cat Lake
St Joseph Lake
Pickle Lake
Osnaburgh
Lake St Joseph
Ogoki Reservoir
Lansdowne House
Ozhiski Lake
Attawapiskat
Missisa Lake
Lansdowne
Fort Albany
Attawapiskat
Akimiski Island
Kapiskau
South Twin Island
Weminji

QU

Réservoir La Grande 3
Réservoir Opinaca
Eastmain

ONTARIO

J a m e s B a y

Chisasibi
Fort George
Radisson
Réservoir La Grande 2

Pakwash Lake
Ear Falls
Vermillion Bay
Eagle Lake
Dryden
Sioux Lookout
Pelican Lake
Savant Lake
Armstrong
Caribou Lake
Nakina
Pledger Lake
Moosonee
Moose Factory
Waskaganish Fort Rupert
Rupert
Lac Evans
Broadback
Lac Opataca
Comenha
Lac au Goéland
Mistissini
Lac Mistassini

Fort Frances
Ignace
Atikokan
Rainy Lake
CANADA
Thunder Bay
Nipigon
Lake Nipigon
Beardmore
Longlac
Otter Rapids
Kesagami Lake
Fraserdale
Lac Matagami
Matagami
Lac Waswanipi
Chibougamau
Réservoir Gouin

Grand Marais
Hancock
Keweenaw Peninsula
Lake Superior
Marathon
Terrace Bay
Kabinakagami Lake
Hornepayne
Kapuskasing
Hearst
Smooth Rock Falls
Cochrane
Nighthawk Lake
La Sarre
Noranda
Amos
Val-d'Or
Senneterre
Lac Parent
Réservoir Cabonga

Bruce Crossing
Ishpeming
Crystal Falls
Iron Mountain
Rhinelander
Marquette
MICHIGAN
Sainte Marie
Michipicoten River
Wawa
Michipicoten Island
Michipicoten Mountain
Chapleau
Biscotasi Lake
Foleyet
Timmins
Kirkland Lake
New Liskeard
Temagami
Rouyn-Noranda
Lac Simard
Lac Kipawa
Lac Dozois
Réservoir Baskatong
Mont-Laurier
Mt Tremblant

WISCONSIN
Escanaba
Menominee
Marinette
Green Bay
Appleton
Shawano
Fond du Lac
Sheboygan
Manistique
St Ignace
Mackinaw City
Petoskey
Charlevoix
Traverse City
Gaylord
Alpena
Sault Sainte Marie
Blind River
Thessalon
Manitoulin Island
Espanola
Sudbury
Sturgeon Falls
North Bay
Lake Nipissing
Huntsville
Bracebridge
Bancroft
Pembroke
Arnprior
Carleton Place
Hull
OTTAWA
Maniwaki
Joliette
Cornwall
Valleyfield
Montréal

Milwaukee
Waukesha
Racine
Kenosha
West Bend
Oshkosh
Cadillac
Ludington
Big Rapids
Manistee
Mount Pleasant
Midland
Bay City
Saginaw
Owosso
Flint
Tawas City
Standish
Owen Sound
Goderich
Tobermory
Parry Sound
Midland
Orillia
Barrie
Peterborough
Kawartha Lakes
Belleville
Kingston
Brockville
Ogdensburg
Plattsburgh
Burlington

Chicago
Elgin
Aurora
Waukegan
Joliet
Wheaton
Gary
South Bend
Elkhart
Kalamazoo
Battle Creek
Jackson
Ann Arbor
Lansing
Livonia
Detroit
Windsor
Pontiac
Flint
Port Huron
Sarnia
Toronto
Guelph
Kitchener
Brantford
Hamilton
St Catharines
Oshawa
Scarborough
Lake Ontario
Rochester
Syracuse
Utica
Rome
Schenectady
Albany
Oneonta

INDIANA
Wabash
Wayne
Fort Wayne
OHIO
Toledo
Cleveland
Lorain
Warren
Ashtabula
Erie
Lake Erie
Buffalo
Dunkirk
Jamestown
Olean
Corning
Elmira
Ithaca
Auburn
Binghamton
Norwich
Sayre
Bradford
Warren
NEW YORK

METRES FEET
5000 16404
3000 9843
2000 6562
1000 3281
500 1640
200 656
0 LAND B.S.L.
200 656
4000 13124
6000 19686

Lambert Azimuthal Equal Area Projection

Longitude 80° west of Greenwich

1:15 000 000

MILES 0   100   200   300

A   B   C

Tasiujaq Kangiqsualujjuaq *Korok* Hebron
Kangiqsualujjuaq   *Cod*
aux Feuilles Kuujjuaq   *Island*
Lac *Thévenet* (Fort Chimo)
Duffreboy   Nain
aux *Lac Moyne* *Lac Bélanger*   *Voisey Bay*
Medlous *aux* *Lac* *Renée*   Nutuashish
Ghakomout *Lac* *Jeannin*   Davis Inlet
Lac *Cambrien* Mistinibi   Hopedale

N E W F O U N D L A N D   A T L A N T I C
                                              O C E A N
Caniapiscau   Makkovik
Caniapiscau   Schefferville   Cape Harrison
Laforge Menihek   *Nipishish*
Réservoir Esker   *Lake*   Rigolet *Grosswater Bay*
La Grande 4 *Lac*   Cartwright
          Bermen *Hope* *Mts* 1128
          Labrador Churchill *Lake Melville*
B E C   Copscotéo City Falls North West River Port Hope
          Fermont   Happy Valley-Goose Bay   Simpson
Lac *Naococane* *Churchill Goose Bay* *Mealy Mountains* Red *Belle Isle*
                                              Bay Cook's Harbour
                    Joseph *Minipi Lake 'Petit* St Anthony *Grey*
Lac Plétipi Gagnon *Lac* *Mecatina*   Blanc-   *Islands*
          Réservoir *Joseph* Minipi Lake Sablon Roddickton
          Manicouagan   St-Augustin Port aux *Horse Islands*
Lac *Lac* *Lac* *Sac Magpie* La Tabatière Choix *Notre Dame* Fogo
Manouane *Berté*   *Lac*   Harrington Springdale *Bay* *Island*
aux *Lac* *Magpie*   Harbour Twillingate
Réservoir *Quatre*   Mingan Havre-St-Pierre Deer Lake *Grand Falls-Windsor* Gander *Bonavista*
Pipmuacan *Péribonka* Natashquan Corner Brook Newfoundland Round *Bay* Polich
Lac St-Jean *Port-Menier* *Île d'Anticosti* Stephenville *Pond* Clarenville *Cove*
Alma Chicoutimi Baie- Gulf of St Lawrence Terrenceville *Avalon*
boreal Jonquière Comeau Ste-Anne- (Golfe du Saint-Laurent) Channel-Port- Burgeo *Peninsula*
  Rivière-du-Loup Hauterive des-Monts Cabot Strait aux-Basques Harbour Breton *Placentia*
Tuque Baie- Forestville Matane Gaspé St Pierre and Grand Bank *Placentia*
  St-Siméon Rimouski Grande-Rivière Miquelon Burin Trepassey
Montmagny St-Paul Pén. de Gaspé (France) ST-PIERRE
Québec Edmundston St Quentin Bathurst Chaleur Havre Aubert *Cape Race*
rois Mines St-Georges Caraquet Îles de la
  Thetford Van Madeleine
kières Buren Nepisiguit PRINCE EDWARD
Drummondville Presque Isle Miramichi ISLAND Chéticamp Cape Breton
  Asbestos Caribou Tignish *Island*
erbrookee Woodstock Minto Bouctouche Summerside Souris *Inverness* Glace Bay
Richelieu Bingham Mt Katahdin NEW Moncton Charlottetown North Sydney
E. Newport 1606 BRUNSWICK Riverview Sydney *Bras d'Or Lake*
chester Grovetown Millinocket Amherst New Hawkesbury
  Bangor Fredericton Sussex Glasgow Antigonish
llton Augusta Lincoln St Wolfville NOVA SCOTIA Sherbrooke
N.H. Conway Foxcroft John Truro
Laconia Dover Calais Saint Digby Dartmouth
torchester Sanford John Bridgewater Halifax
thelon Augusta Brunswick Yarmouth Liverpool Sable Island
eene Nashua Belfast Bar Bay of Fundy Shelburne
mbridge Lowell Harbor *Cape* A T L A N T I C
ASS Quincy Massachusetts Bay *Sable*
  Worcester Cape Cod O C E A N

70° D *60°* E

© Collins Bartholomew Ltd

0 250 500 KILOMETRES

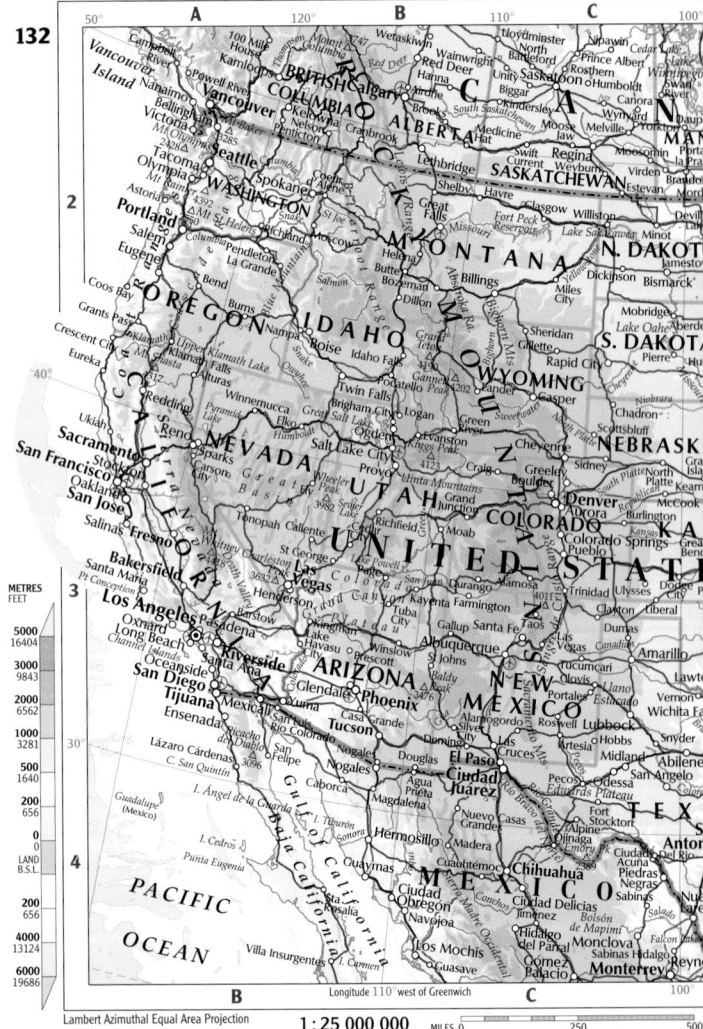

50°   A   120°   B   110°   C   100°

2

METRES
FEET

5000
16404

3000
9843

2000
6562

1000
3281

500
1640

200
656

0
LAND
B.S.L.

200
656

4000
13124

6000
19686

3

4

Lambert Azimuthal Equal Area Projection

1 : 25 000 000

MILES 0   250   500

B   Longitude 110° west of Greenwich   C   100°

UNITED STATES OF AMERICA

133

0   250   500   750 KILOMETRES

© Collins Bartholomew Ltd

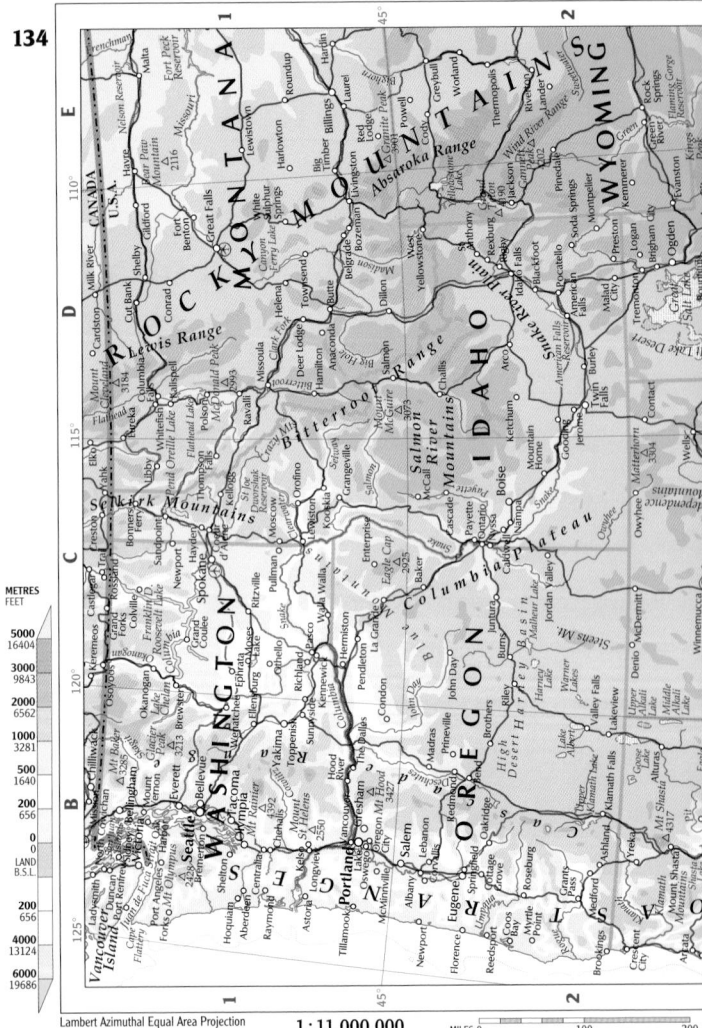

Lambert Azimuthal Equal Area Projection 1:11 000 000 MILES 0   100   200

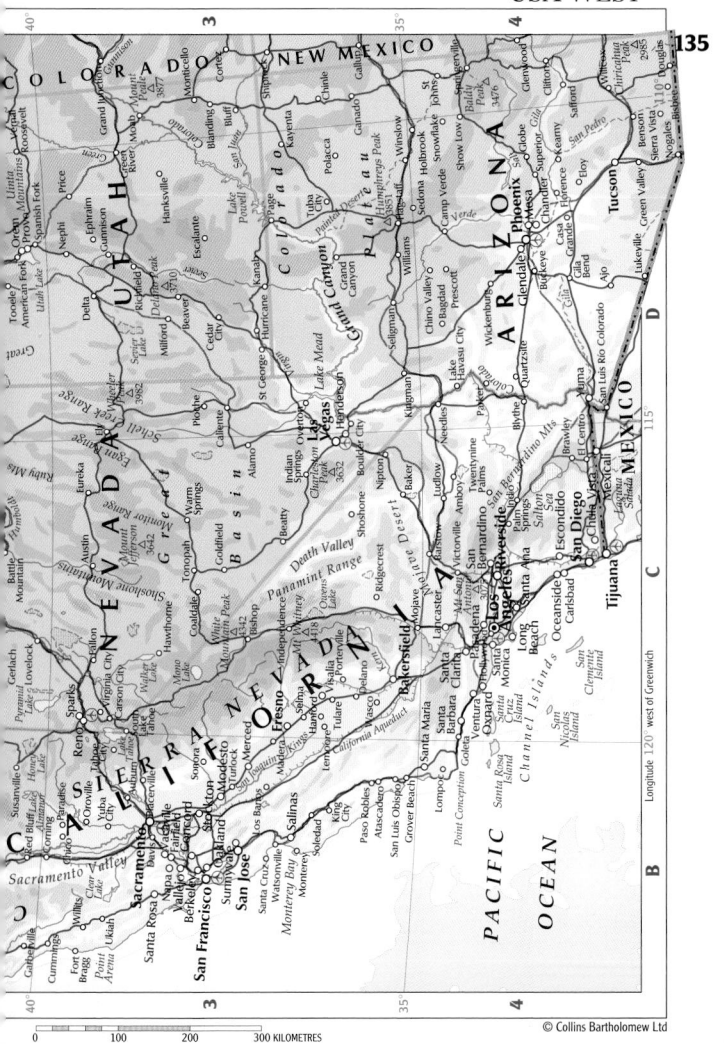

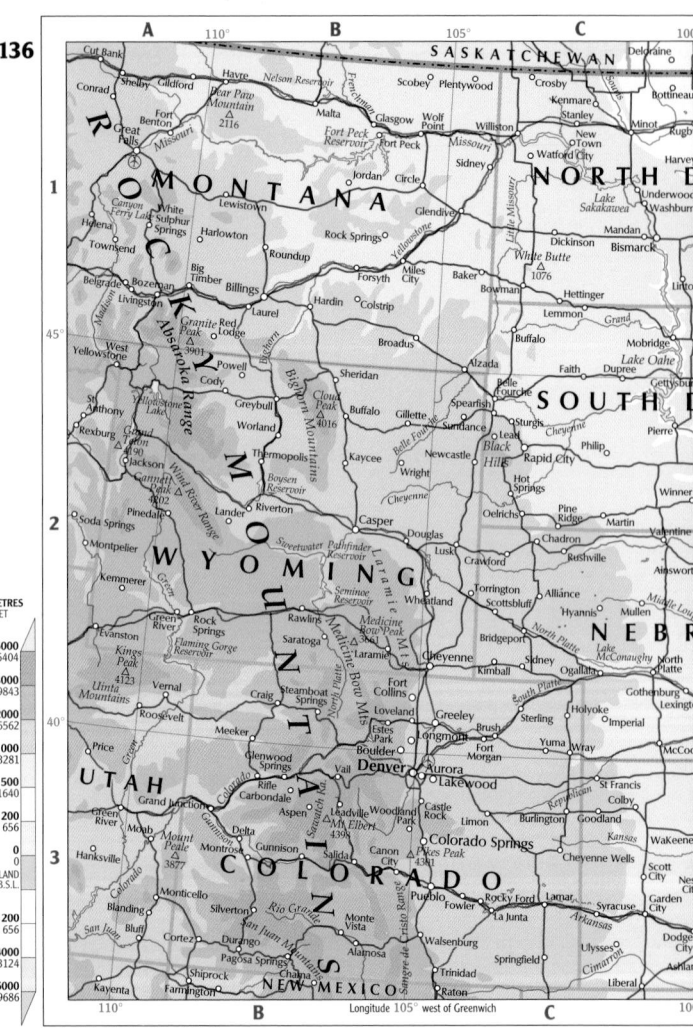

METRES
FEET

METRES	FEET
5000	16404
3000	9843
2000	6562
1000	3281
500	1640
200	656
0	0
LAND	B.S.L.
200	656
4000	13124
6000	19686

Lambert Azimuthal Equal Area Projection

1 : 11 000 000

MILES 0   100   200

© Collins Bartholomew Ltd

0   100   200   300 KILOMETRES

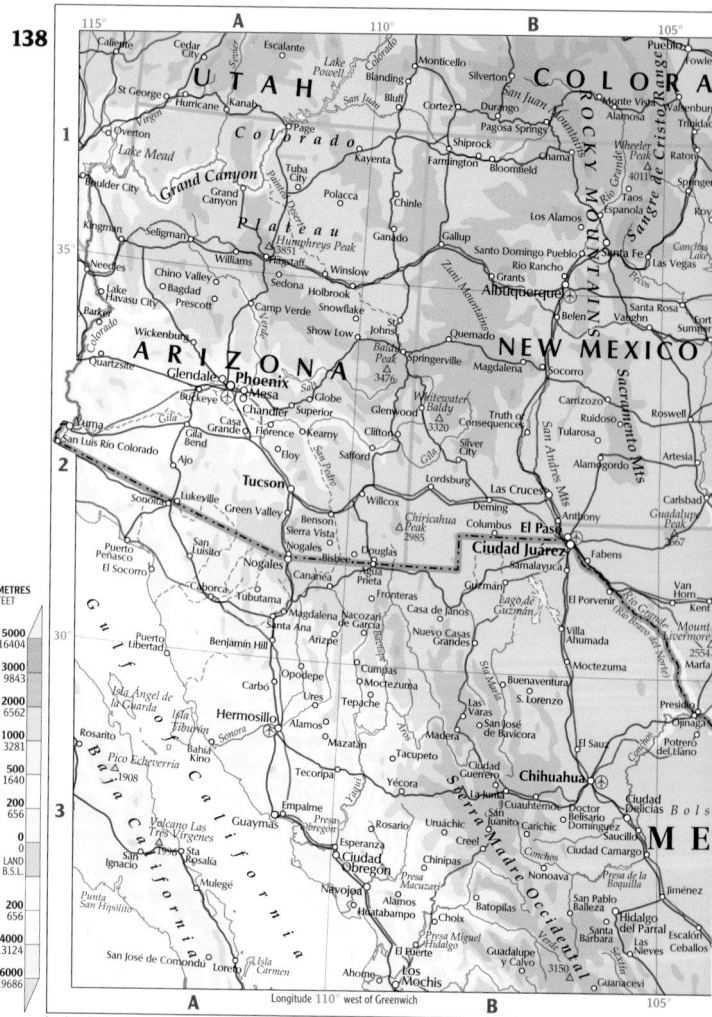

138

UTAH

COLORA

ARIZONA

NEW MEXICO

ME

Longitude 110° west of Greenwich

METRES
FEET

5000
16404

3000
9843

2000
6562

1000
3281

500
1640

200
656

0
0

LAND
B.S.L.

200
656

4000
13124

6000
19686

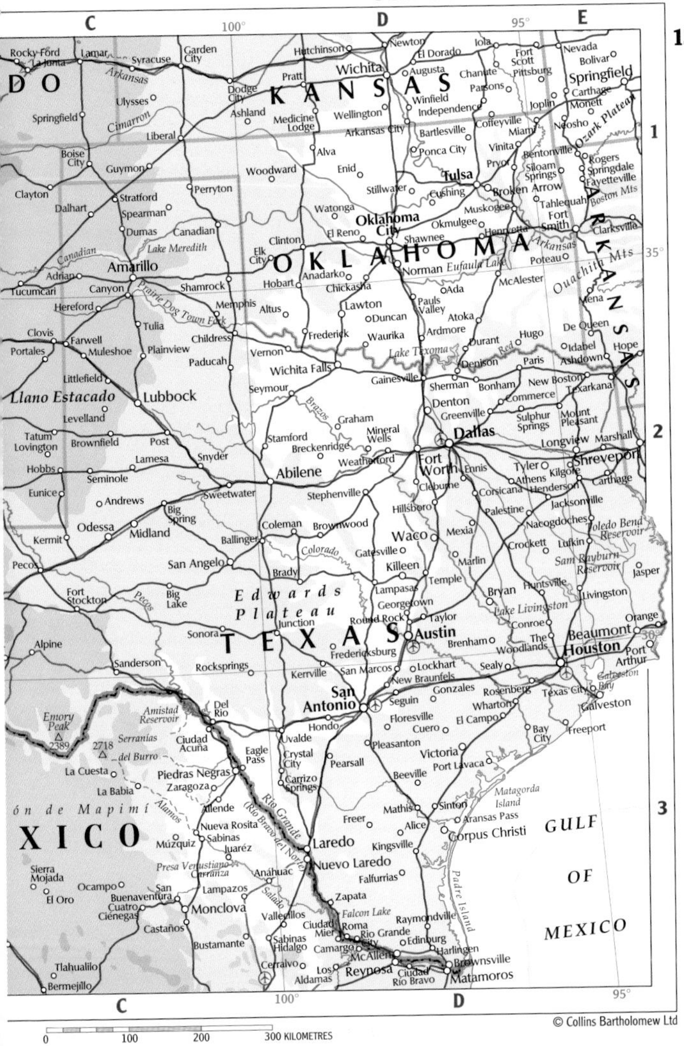

C
D
E
100°
95°
1
2
3
35°
30°
KANSAS
OKLAHOMA
TEXAS
ARKANSAS
DO
XICO
Rocky Ford
La Junta
Lamar
Syracuse
Garden City
Hutchinson
Newton
El Dorado
Iola
Fort Scott
Nevada
Bolivar
Pittsburg
Springfield
Arkansas
Dodge City
Pratt
Wichita
Augusta
Chanute
Parsons
Carthage
Monett
Joplin
Ulysses
Ashland
Medicine Lodge
Wellington
Winfield
Independence
Springfield
Cimarron
Liberal
Arkansas City
Bartlesville
Coffeyville
Miami
Neosho
Ozark Plateau
Boise City
Alva
Ponca City
Vinita
Bentonville
Rogers
Springdale
Fayetteville
Guymon
Woodward
Enid
Tulsa
Pryor
Siloam Springs
Clayton
Stratford
Perryton
Stillwater
Cushing
Broken Arrow
Tahlequah
Boston Mts
Dalhart
Spearman
Watonga
Oklahoma City
Muskogee
Fort Smith
Okmulgee
Dumas
Canadian
El Reno
Henryetta
Clarksville
Lake Meredith
Clinton
Shawnee
Canadian
Elk City
Arkansas
Poteau
Amarillo
Adrian
Norman
Eufaula Lake
Tucumcari
Canyon
Shamrock
Hobart
Anadarko
Chickasha
Ada
McAlester
Ouachita Mts
Hereford
Prairie Dog Town Fork
Memphis
Altus
Lawton
Pauls Valley
Mena
Duncan
Atoka
Tulia
Clovis
Farwell
Childress
Frederick
Waurika
Ardmore
De Queen
Portales
Muleshoe
Plainview
Vernon
Durant
Hugo
Idabel
Hope
Lake Texoma
Red
Paducah
Wichita Falls
Denison
Paris
Ashdown
Littlefield
Gainesville
Sherman
Bonham
New Boston
Texarkana
Seymour
Llano Estacado
Lubbock
Brazos
Denton
Commerce
Levelland
Graham
Greenville
Sulphur Springs
Mount Pleasant
Tatum
Lovington
Brownfield
Post
Stamford
Mineral Wells
Dallas
Longview
Marshall
Breckenridge
Snyder
Lamesa
Weatherford
Fort Worth
Tyler
Kilgore
Shreveport
Hobbs
Seminole
Abilene
Ennis
Athens
Carthage
Eunice
Sweetwater
Stephenville
Cleburne
Corsicana
Henderson
Andrews
Big Spring
Hillsboro
Palestine
Jacksonville
Odessa
Midland
Coleman
Brownwood
Nacogdoches
Toledo Bend Reservoir
Kermit
Ballinger
Waco
Mexia
Colorado
Gatesville
Crockett
Lufkin
Pecos
San Angelo
Marlin
Sam Rayburn Reservoir
Jasper
Killeen
Brady
Temple
Fort Stockton
Pecos
Big Lake
Edwards Plateau
Lampasas
Bryan
Huntsville
Livingston
Georgetown
Junction
Round Rock
Taylor
Lake Livingston
Conroe
Orange
Sonora
Austin
The Woodlands
Beaumont
Alpine
Fredericksburg
Brenham
Houston
Port Arthur
Sanderson
Rocksprings
Kerrville
San Marcos
Lockhart
Sealy
New Braunfels
Galveston Bay
Gonzales
Rosenberg
Texas City
San Antonio
Seguin
Wharton
Galveston
Del Rio
Amistad Reservoir
Emory Peak
2389
2718
Serranías del Burro
Ciudad Acuña
Hondo
Floresville
Cuero
El Campo
Uvalde
Bay City
Freeport
Eagle Pass
Crystal City
Pleasanton
Victoria
La Cuesta
Piedras Negras
Pearsall
Port Lavaca
Zaragoza
Carrizo Springs
Beeville
La Babia
Matagorda Island
Álamos
Allende
Rio Grande (Río Bravo del Norte)
Mathis
Sinton
Aransas Pass
ón de Mapimí
Nueva Rosita
Freer
Alice
Corpus Christi
GULF OF MEXICO
Sabinas
Múzquiz
Laredo
Kingsville
Juaréz
Sierra Mojada
Presa Venustiano Carranza
Anáhuac
Nuevo Laredo
Padre Island
Falfurrias
Ocampo
El Oro
San Buenaventura
Lampazos
Zapata
Cuatro Ciénegas
Monclova
Salado
Falcon Lake
Raymondville
Vallecillos
Ciudad Mier
Roma
Rio Grande City
Castaños
Sabinas Hidalgo
Edinburg
Bustamante
Camargo
McAllen
Harlingen
Brownsville
Cerralvo
Los Aldamas
Reynosa
Ciudad Río Bravo
Matamoros
Tlahualilo
Bermejillo
0
100
200
300 KILOMETRES

140

METRES
FEET

5000
16404

3000
9843

2000
6562

1000
3281

500
1640

200
656

0
0
LAND
B.S.L.

200
656

4000
13124

6000
19686

Lambert Azimuthal Equal Area Projection

1 : 11 000 000

MILES 0   100   200

Longitude 85° west of Greenwich

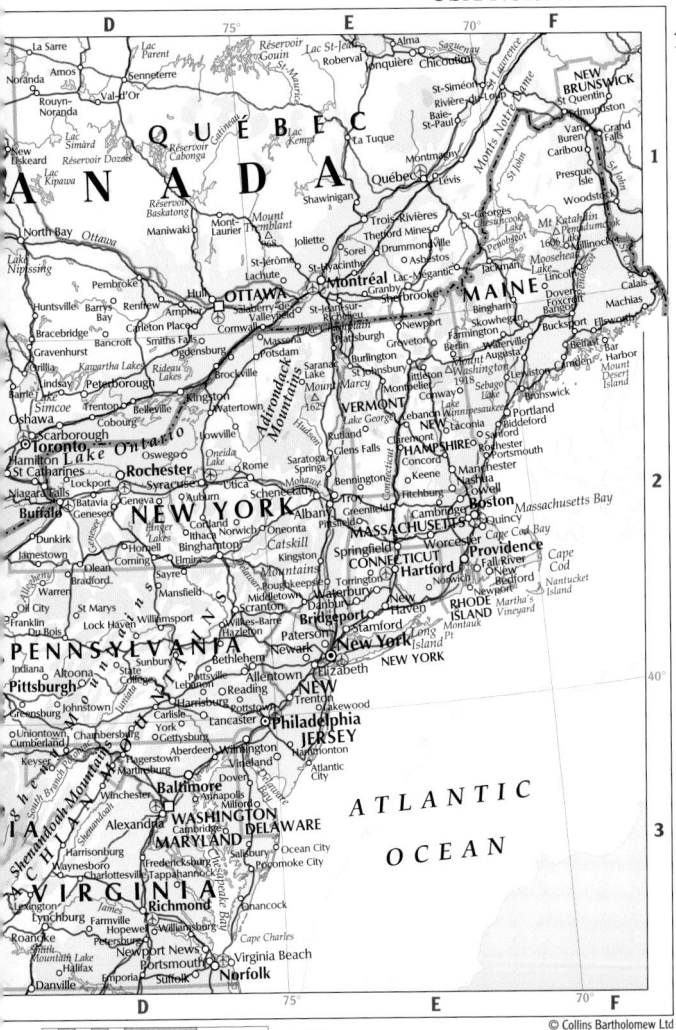

0   100   200   300 KILOMETRES

METRES
FEET

5000
16404

3000
9843

2000
6562

1000
3281

500
1640

200
656

0
0
LAND
B.S.L.

200
656

4000
13124

6000
19686

Lambert Azimuthal Equal Area Projection

1:11 000 000

MILES 0   100   200

Longitude 90° west of Greenwich

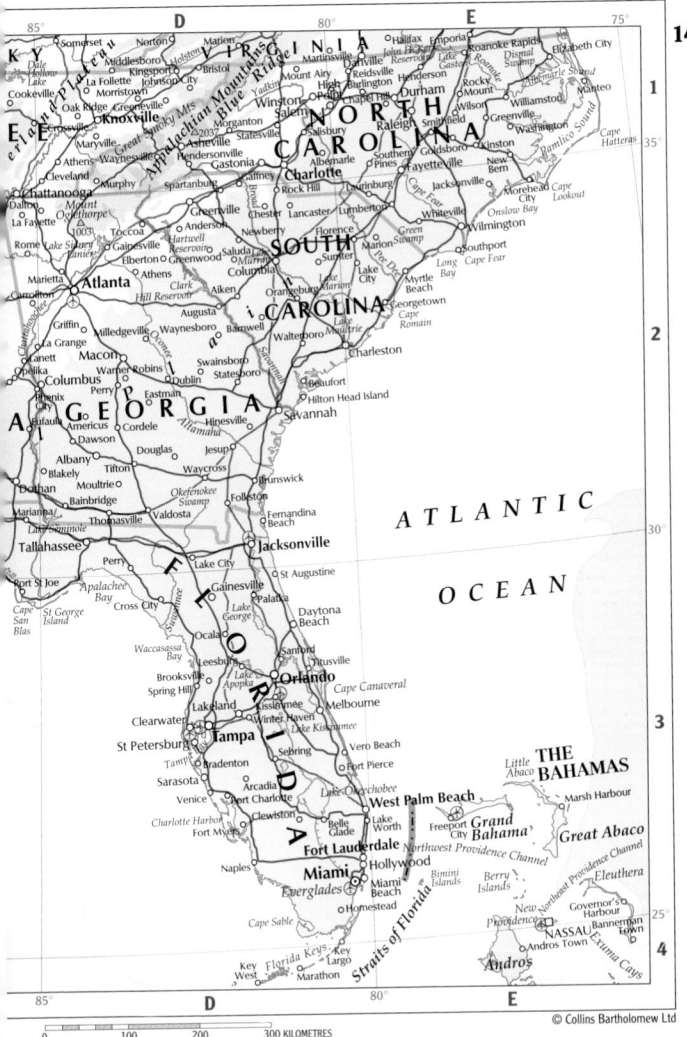

85°   D   80°   E   75°

Somerset   Norton   Marion   Halifax Emporia   Roanoke Rapids   Elizabeth City
K Y   Middlesboro   Mansville   John H Kerr   Gaston   Dismal   1
Cookeville   Kingsport Bristol   Mount Airy   Reidsville   Henderson   Swamp
Oak Ridge   La Follette Johnson City   Winston   Reidsville   Burlington   Durham   Rocky   Wilson   Williamston   Nanteo
Knoxville   Morristown   Salem   High Point   Mount   Cape
Maryville   Waynesville Hendersonville   N O R T H   Raleigh   Goldsboro   Greenville   Washington   Hatteras   35°
Athens   Murphy   Statesville   C A R O L I N A   Southern   New   Pamlico Sound
Cleveland   Spartanburg   Gastonia   Charlotte   Pines   Fayetteville   Bern   Cape
Chattanooga   Greenville   Rock Hill   Lancaster   Lumberton   Whiteville   Wilmington   Lookout
Dalton   Anderson   Newberry   Florence   Marion   Long   Cape Fear
Rome   Toccoa   Greenwood   Saluda   Sumter   Green   Bay   Onslow Bay
Elberton   Clark   Columbia   Lake   Swamp   Myrtle
Atlanta   Athens   Hill Reservoir   S O U T H   City   Georgetown   Beach
Marietta   Aiken   Orangeburg   C A R O L I N A   Cape   2
Griffin   Augusta   Barnwell   Walterboro   Lake   Romain
La Grange   Milledgeville   Waynesboro   Swainsboro   Marion   Charleston
Macon   Warner Robins   Statesboro
Columbus   Perry   Eastman   Beaufort
Phenix   G E O R G I A   Hinesville   Hilton Head Island
Americus   Cordele   Dawson   Savannah
Albany   Tifton   Douglas   Jesup
Dothan   Moultrie   Waycross   Brunswick   A T L A N T I C
Marianna   Thomasville   Valdosta   Folkston   Fernandina
Tallahassee   Okefenokee   Swamp   O C E A N   30°
Cape St Joe   Apalachee   Lake City   St Augustine
Bay   F L O R I D A   Gainesville   Palatka
St George   Cross City   Ocala   Daytona
Island   Lake   George   Beach
Waccasassa   Leesburg   Sanford
Bay   Brooksville   Lake   Titusville
Spring Hill   Apopka   Orlando   Cape Canaveral
Clearwater   Lakeland   Kissimmee   Melbourne   3
St Petersburg   Tampa   Winter Haven   Vero Beach   Little
Bradenton   Arcadia   Sebring   Fort Pierce   Abaco   T H E
Sarasota   B A H A M A S
Venice   Port Charlotte   Lake Okeechobee   West Palm Beach   Marsh Harbour
Charlotte Harbor   Clewiston   Lake   Freeport Grand   Great Abaco
Fort Myers   Belle   Worth   City Bahama   Northeast Providence Channel
Glade   Fort Lauderdale   Northwest Providence Channel   Eleuthera
Naples   Miami   Berry   New Northeast Providence Channel
Everglades   Miami   Bimini   Islands   Providence
Cape Sable   Homestead   Beach   Islands   Governor's   Bannerman
Key   Florida   Key   NASSAU   Harbour   Town
West   Largo   Andros Town   Exuma Cays   4
Marathon   Straits of Florida   Andros   25°

85°   D   80°   E

0   100   200   300 KILOMETRES

© Collins Bartholomew Ltd

100° C 90° D

Snyder Abilene Weatherford Fort Worth Longview Marshall Monroe Winnsboro Jackson ALABAMA
Sweetwater Stephenville Jefferson Tyler Henderson Jonesboro Meridian Laurel Jackson 1
S T A T E S O F A M E R I C A MISSISSIPPI Hattiesburg Atmore
Ballinger Brownwood Gatesville Waco Marlin Palestine Bend Reef McComb Bogalusa Picayune Mobile
San Angelo T E X A S Crockett Lufkin Leesville Oakdale Ville Platte Biloxi Pascagoula
Sonora Junction Georgetown Temple Bryan Huntsville De Ridder L O U I S I A N A Bay 30°
E d w a r d s Round Rock Taylor Brenham Livingston Jasper Lafayette Baton Rouge Chandeleur
Fredericksburg AUSTIN Woodland Orange Jennings Thibodaux New Orleans Sound
Kerrville New Braunfels Lockhart Houston Beaumont Vinton Houma Breton Islands
Rocksprings San Antonio Seguin Gonzales Port Arthur Marsh Grand Mississippi
Del Rio Floresville El Campo Texas City Island Isle Delta
Piedras Uvalde Pleasanton Victoria Wharton Galveston
Negras Crystal Pearsall Beeville Bay City
Allende City Sinton Port Lavaca Matagorda
Nueva Rosita Mathis Aransas Pass Island
Sabinas Freer Alice Corpus Christi
Juárez Laredo Kingsville
Anáhuac Nuevo Laredo Padre
Lampazos Zapata Falfurrias Island
Valle Mier Falcon Lake Raymondville
Hidalgo Ciudad Camargo McAllen Harlingen
Garza Cerralvo Reynosa Brownsville
Monterrey China Matamoros
Saltillo Cadereyta Allende Méndez Valle Hermoso
Montemorelos Laguna Madre
El Salado Linares Burgos San
Galeana Fernando
Matehuala Doctor Nevada El Temascal
Arroyo Ciudad La Pesca
Chertas Victoria Soto la Marina

C O Moctezuma Palmillas G U L F
Cerritos Jaumave
San Luis Tula O F
Potosí Rayón Aldama
Ebano Gonzales Tampico M E X I C O
Ciudad Antiguo Morelos
de Valles El Higo Pánuco Tropic of Cancer
Naranjos
Tamazunchco Cerro Azul
Jalpan Tempoal Tuxpan
Zimapán Tlacan Molango Tihuatlán Bahía de
Querétaro Huejutla Poza Rica la Ascensión
Actopán Tulancingo Chignahuapan Nautla Campeche YUCATÁN Felipe
Celaya Zumpango Jalapa Champotón Tenabo Cárdenas
Morelia Toluca MEXICO Puebla Veracruz Chetumal
Zitácuaro CITY Huatusco BAHÍA Ciudad del Carmen Escárcega
Cuernavaca Cuautla Córdoba Alvarado DE CAMPECHE Frontera Laguna de Términos
Altamirano Iguala Chietla Orizaba Tlacotalpan Paraíso Candelaria
Arcelia Taxco Acatlán Tehuacán Andrés Tuxtla Coatzacoalcos Villahermosa Balancán BELIZE
S I E R R A Chilpancingo Huajuapan Minatitlán Macuspana Tenosique
Acapulco Tlapa Oaxaca Salina Tuxtla San Cristóbal de las Casas La Libertad
Pinotepa Nacional Miahuatlán Gutiérrez Comitán de Domínguez
Puerto Escondido Juchitán GUATEMALA
100° C Puerto Ángel Gulf of Tehuantepec 90° D
Tapachula

0 250 KILOMETRES

© Collins Bartholomew Ltd

C 70° D 60° E 30°

ATLANTIC

OCEAN

BAHAMAS

Cat Island

Long Island

Mayaguana

Acklins Island

Great Inagua

Tropic of Cancer

20°

W E S T   I N D I E S

Turks and Caicos Islands (U.K.)
□ GRAND TURK (Cockburn Town)

Caicos Islands

LEEWARD ISLANDS

Baracoa

Guantánamo

Windward Passage

Cap-Haïtien

Port-de-Paix

Gonaïves

Santiago

Puerto Plata

Hispaniola

Puerto Rico (U.S.A.)

Virgin Is (U.K.)

Anguilla (U.K.)

St Maarten (Neth.)

ANTIGUA AND BARBUDA

Jérémie

HAITI

DOMINICAN REPUBLIC

Barahona

SAN JUAN

Virgin Is (U.S.A.)

St John's

St John's Antigua

Île de la Gonâve

Les Cayes

Jacmel

PORT-AU-PRINCE

SANTO DOMINGO

La Romana

Ponce

St Croix

BASSETERRE

Plymouth □ BRADES

ST KITTS AND NEVIS

Montserrat (U.K.)

Guadeloupe (Fr.)

Isla Beata

Cabo Beata

BASSE-TERRE

Marie-Galante (Fr.)

DOMINICA

ROSEAU

A N T I L L E S

Lesser Antilles

Martinique (Fr.)

FORT-DE-FRANCE

CASTRIES

ST LUCIA

BARBADOS

BRIDGETOWN

PORT OF SPAIN

E A N   S E A

ST VINCENT AND THE GRENADINES

Kingstown

Netherlands Antilles

Aruba (Neth.)

Curaçao

Bonaire

GRENADA

ST GEORGE'S

WINDWARD ISLANDS

Scarborough

Tobago

Ríohacha

Pta Gallinas

Península de la Guajira

WILLEMSTAD

Punta Fijo

Coro

Islas Los Roques

Isla La Tortuga

La Asunción

Isla de Margarita

TRINIDAD AND TOBAGO

Trinidad

Golfo de Venezuela

Santa Marta

Barranquilla

Valledupar

Maracaibo

Cabimas

Maicao

San Felipe

Barquisimeto

Maracay

CARACAS

Cumaná

Barcelona

San Carlos

Los Teques

Valencia

G. of Paria

Fernando

Maturín

Orinoco Delta

10°

Sincelejo

Lake Maracaibo

El Banco

Plato

San Carlos del Zulia

Valle de la Pascua

Zaraza

El Tigre

Tucupita

Magangué

Mérida

Trujillo

Acarigua

Guanare

VENEZUELA

Ciudad Guayana

COLOMBIA

El Baúl

Barinas

Calabozo

Ciudad Bolívar

Orinoco

Valera

Bucaramanga 5007

Libertad

Longitude 70° west of Greenwich

60°

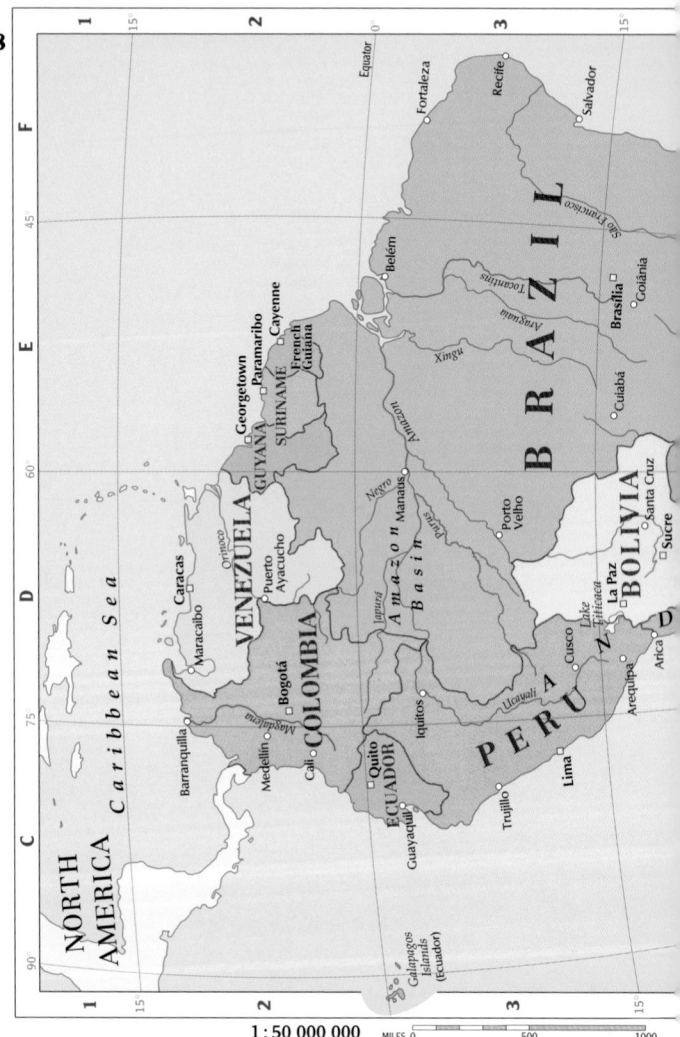

NORTH AMERICA

Caribbean Sea

Barranquilla
Maracaibo

VENEZUELA

Caracas

Orinoco

Puerto
Ayacucho

Georgetown
Paramaribo
Cayenne

GUYANA
SURINAME
French
Guiana

Negro
Manaus

Amazon

*A m a z o n
B a s i n*

Japurá

Xingu

Tocantins

Araguaia

Belém

BRAZIL

Fortaleza
Recife
Salvador

São Francisco

Goiânia
Brasília
Cuiabá

Porto
Velho

Purus

BOLIVIA

Santa Cruz
Sucre
La Paz

Lake
Titicaca

Arica

Cusco
Arequipa

PERU

Ucayali

Marañón

Iquitos

COLOMBIA

Bogotá

Medellín
Cali

Magdalena

Quito

ECUADOR

Guayaquil

Trujillo

Lima

Galapagos
Islands
(Ecuador)

Equator

1 : 50 000 000   MILES 0   500   1000

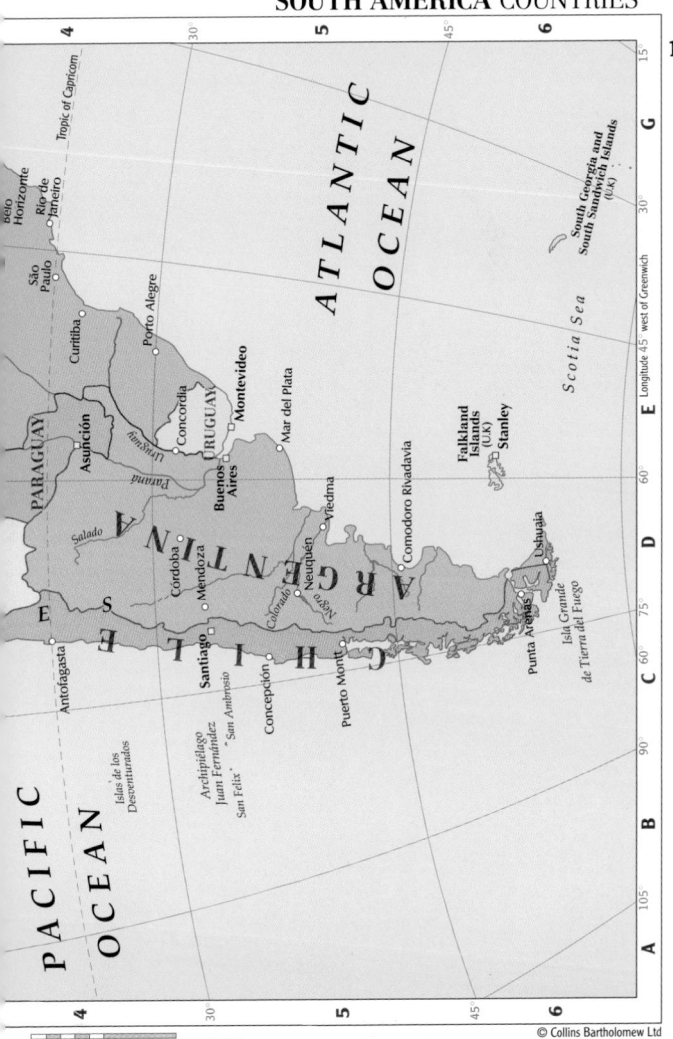

0   500   1000 KILOMETRES

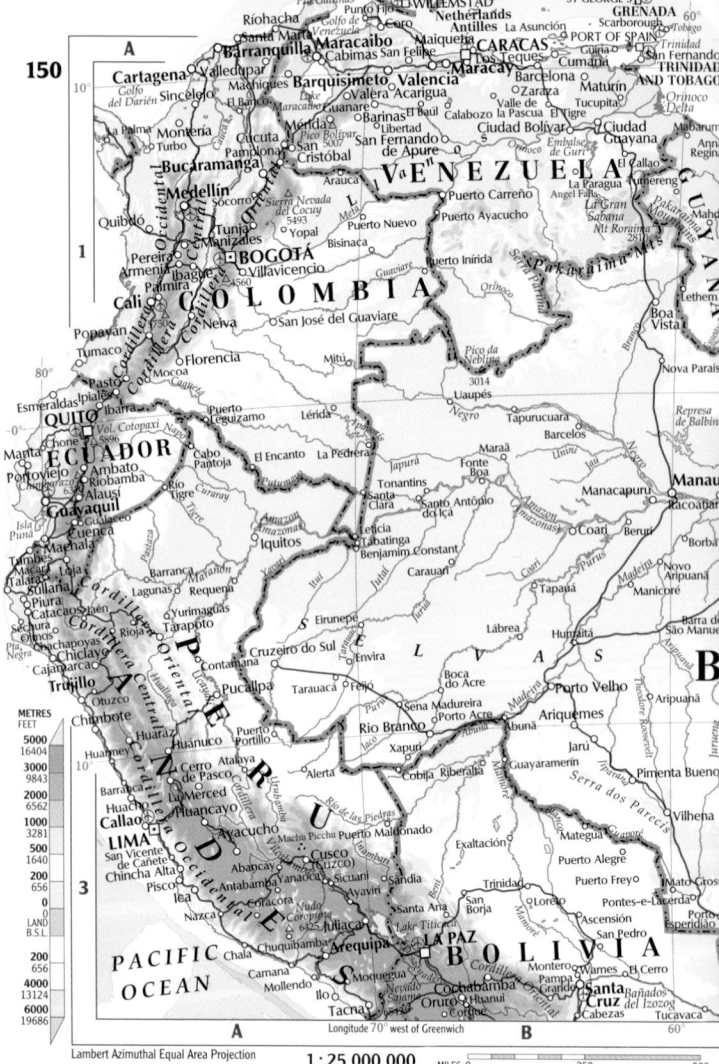

150

A

Cartagena
Golfo del Darién
Santa Marta
Barranquilla
Maracaibo
Golfo de Venezuela
Punta Fijo
WILLEMSTAD
Netherlands
ST GEORGE'S
GRENADA
La Asunción
Tobago
Coro
Maicaibo
Cabimas San Felipe
La Asunción
Scarborough
PORT OF SPAIN
TRINIDAD
AND TOBAGO
Valledupar
Maiquetía
CARACAS
Los Teques
Cumaná
San Fernando
Cúcuta
Magdalena
Barquisimeto
Valencia
Maturín
Barcelona
Sincelejo
El Banco
Acarigua
Zaraza
El Tigre
Tucupita
Orinoco Delta
Montería
Ciudad Bolívar
Mompós
Maiguetia
Mérida
Guanare
Calabozo
La Pasqua
Turbo
Pico Bolívar
San Fernando de Apure
Barinas
Quibdó
Bucaramanga
Pamplona
Socorro
Arauca
Medellín
Sierra Nevada del Cocuy
5493
Puerto Carreño
Puerto Ayacucho
GUIANA
Manizales
Pereira
Yopal
Bisinaca
Puerto Nuevo
Armenia
Ibagué
Tunja
BOGOTÁ
Villavicencio
4560
COLOMBIA
Palmira
Cali
Popayán
Neiva
San José del Guaviare
Mitú
Uaupés
Tumaco
Florencia
Mocoa
Pasto
Puerto Leguízamo
Lérida
Pico da Neblina
3014
Nova Paraís
QUITO
El Encanto
La Pedrera
Tapurucuara
Boa Vista
ECUADOR
Ambato
Cabo Pantoja
Iquitos
Leticia
Tabatinga
Benjamim Constant
Barcelos
Manacapuru
Manau
Coari
Guayaquil
Cuenca
Loja
Yurimaguas
Requena
Eirunepé
Lábrea
Humaitá
Novo Aripuanã
Manicoré
Piura
Cajamarca
Trujillo
PERÚ
Pucallpa
Cruzeiro do Sul
Feijó
Boca do Acre
Porto Velho
Ariquemes
Barra do São Manuel
Chimbote
Huaraz
Puerto Portillo
Rio Branco
Porto Acre
Abunã
Jaru
Pimenta Bueno
Vilhena
Cerro de Pasco
Atalaya
Alerta
Riberalta
Cobija
Guayaramerín
Serra dos Parecis
Callao
LIMA
Huancayo
Ayacucho
Puerto Maldonado
Exaltación
Mategua
Porto Alegre
Pisco
Cusco
Sandia
Trinidad
Loreto
Pontes-e-Lacerda
Nazca
Juliaca
Santa Ana
San Borja
San Pedro
Arequipa
LA PAZ
BOLIVIA
Montero
Santa Cruz
PACIFIC OCEAN
Moquegua
Oruro
Cochabamba
Warnes
Tacna
Longitude 70° west of Greenwich

METRES FEET
5000 16404
3000 9843
2000 6562
1000 3281
500 1640
200 656
0 0
LAND B.S.L.
200 656
4000 13124
6000 19686

Lambert Azimuthal Equal Area Projection

1 : 25 000 000

MILES 0   250   500

0   250   500   750 KILOMETRES

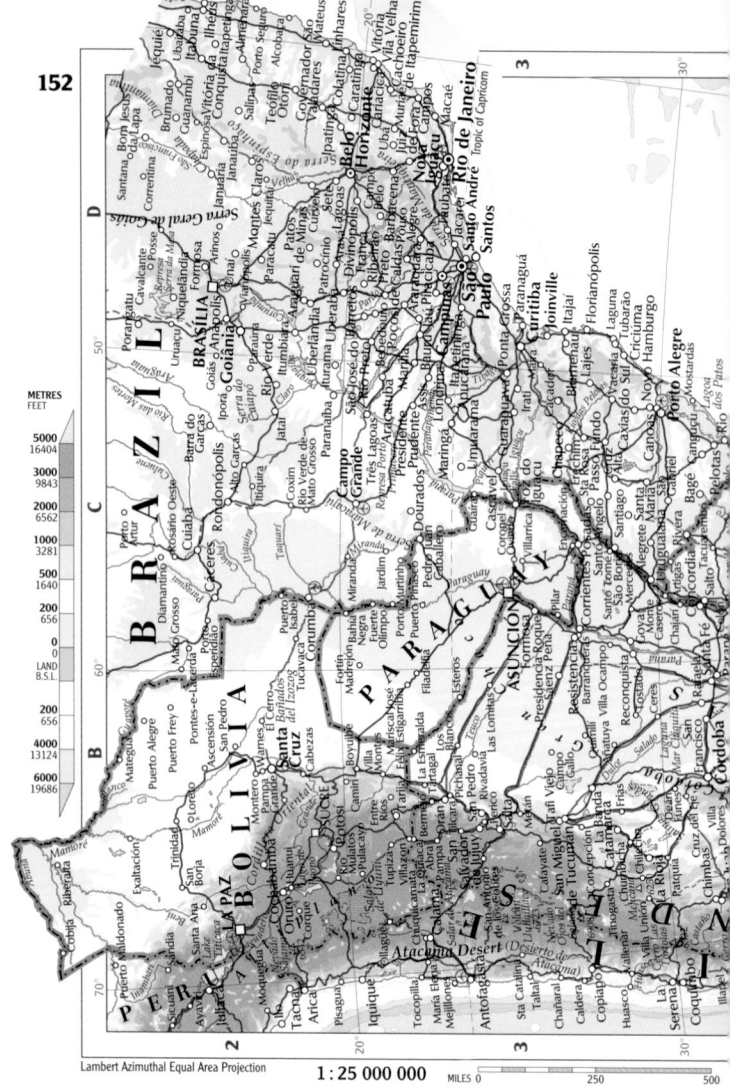

ATLANTIC

OCEAN

Falkland Islands
(U.K.)
STANLEY
East
Falkland
West
Falkland

Longitude 50 west of Greenwich

MONTEVIDEO
Mar
del Plata

A R G E N T I N A

SANTIAGO

URUGUAY

BUENOS AIRES

Mendoza

Valparaíso

Viña del Mar

Concepción

Bahía Blanca

P A T A G O N I A

Comodoro Rivadavia

Río Gallegos

Punta Arenas

Río Grande

© Collins Bartholomew Ltd

B 50° **C**

Rio das Mortes
Planalto do
Mato Grosso
Poxoréu
Tesouro
Batovi
Torixoréu
Barra do Garças
Aragarças
Itapuranga
Ceres
Rianópolis Brasilândia
Jaraguá
Planaltina
Formosa
BRASÍLIA
Gama
Una

Rondonópolis
Guiratinga
Piranhas
Iporá
Anicuns
Goiás
Goiânia
Nerópolis
Trindade
Anápolis
Vianópolis
Luziânia
Cristalina

Anhumas
Alto Garças
Alto Araguaia
Sta Rita do Araguaia
Caiapônia
Aurilândia
Paraúna
Hidrolândia
Edéia
Piracanjuba
Pires do Rio
Paracatu

Correntes
Iúquira
Mineiros
Serranópolis
Alto Taquari
Jataí
Santa Helena de Goiás
Rio Verde
Pontalina
Morrinhos
Caldas Novas
Ipameri
Guarda Mor

Pedro Gomes
Serra do Caiapó
Serra Verdinho
Caçu
Cachoeira Alta
Itumbiara
Tupaciguara
Goiandira Catalão
Coromandel

Coxim
Jauru
Costa Rica
Baús
Serra da Mombuca
Aporé
Itarumã
São Simão
Gurinhatã
Prata
Ituiutaba
Uberlândia
Araguari
Patrocínio
Represa de Emborcação

Rio Verde de Mato Grosso
Paraíso
Cassilândia
Alto Sucuriú
Paranaíba
Iturama
Campina Verde
Campo Florido
Araxá

Camapuã
Rochedo
Jaraguari
Água Clara
Inocência
Aparecida do Tabuado
Jales
Votuporanga
Colômbia
Itapipe
Uberaba
Igarapava

Campo Grande
Ribas do Rio Pardo
Pereira Barreto
Represa Ilha Solteira
Fernandópolis
Nova Granada
Olímpia
Barretos
São Joaquim da Barra
Pedregulho
Orlândia
Franca
Cássia

Sidrolândia
Três Lagoas
Andradina
São José do Rio Preto
Catanduva
Bebedouro
Sertãozinho
São Sebastião do Paraíso
Ribeirão Preto

Rio Brilhante
Bataguassu
Mirandópolis
Panorama
Araçatuba
Valparaíso
Birigui
Penápolis
Taquaritinga
Jaboticabal
Mococa
Casa Branca

Dourados
Presidente Epitácio
Dracena
Lucélia
Tupã
Lins
Novo Horizonte
Araraquara
São Carlos
Piracununga

Presidente Prudente
Represa Porto Primavera
Pirajuí
Garça
Rio Claro
Leme

Caarapó
Teodoro Sampaio
Iepê
Marília
Bauru
Jaú
Limeira
Mogi Mirim

Amambaí
Represa Ilha Grande
Nova Londrina
Paranavaí
Itaguaje
Assis
Ourinhos
São Manuel
Botucatu
Conchas
Piracicaba
Campinas

Iguatemi
Querência do Norte
Rondon
Cornélio Procópio
Santa Antônio da Platina
Avaré
Tatuí
Itu
Salto

Umuarama
Nova Esperança
Maringá
Rolândia
Arapongas
Londrina
Apucarana
Vencesláu Brás
Itapeva
Itapetininga
Sorocaba

Saltó del Guairá
Guaíra
Cianorte
Campo Mourão
Telêmaco Borba
Jaguariaíva
Itararé
Capão Bonito
Juquiá
Itanhaém
Peruíbe
Iguape

Porto Mendes
Toledo
Pitanga
Reserva
Castro
Piraí do Sul
Serra Paranapiacaba
Apiaí
Cerro Azul
Jacupiranga
Cananéia

Cascavel
Catanduvas
Represa de Itaipu
Prudentópolis
Ipiranga
Ponta Grossa
Irati
Rio Branco do Sul
Antonina
Guaraqueçaba

Foz do Iguaçu
Laranjeiras do Sul
Guarapuava
Curitiba
Palmeira
Lapa
Paranaguá

Dionísio Cerqueira
Chapimzinho
Represa de Foz de Areia
Canoinhas
São José dos Pinhais
Rio Negro
Ilha de São Francisco
São Francisco do Sul

Wanda
Manguerinha
Pato Branco
Palmas
União da Vitória
Mafra
Araquari
Joinville

PARAGUAY
ARG.

25°
20°

55° **B** Longitude 50° west of Greenwich **C**

Lambert Azimuthal Equal Area Projection

1 : 10 000 000

MILES 0   100   200

METRES
FEET
5000 / 16404
3000 / 9843
2000 / 6562
1000 / 3281
500 / 1640
200 / 656
0 / 0
LAND / B.S.L.
200 / 656
4000 / 13124
6000 / 19686

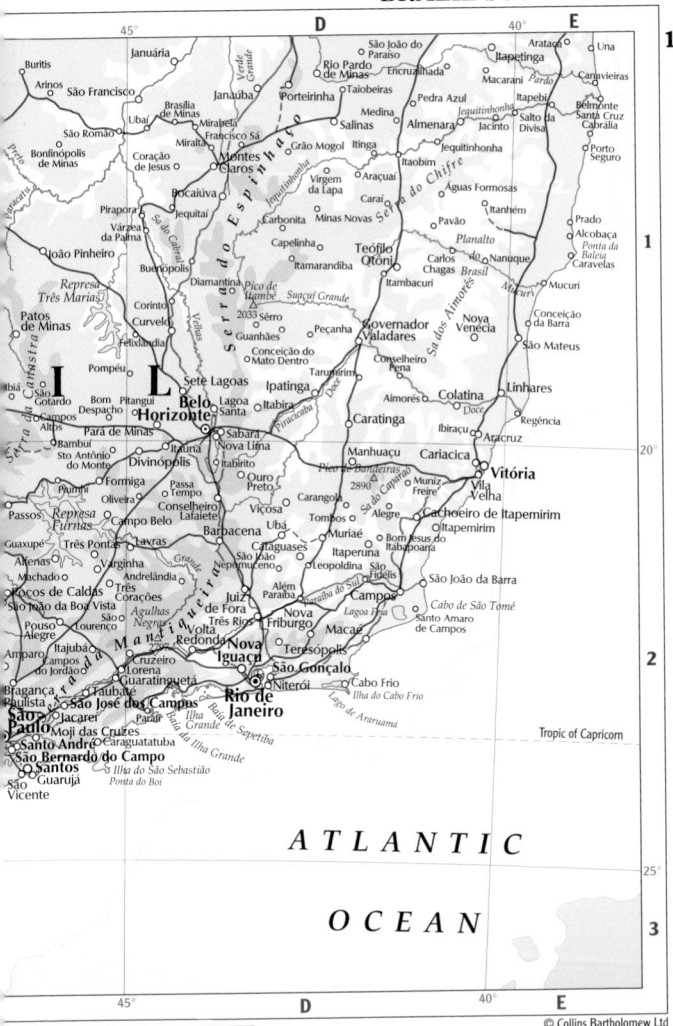

ATLANTIC

OCEAN

Tropic of Capricorn

0   100   200   300 KILOMETRES

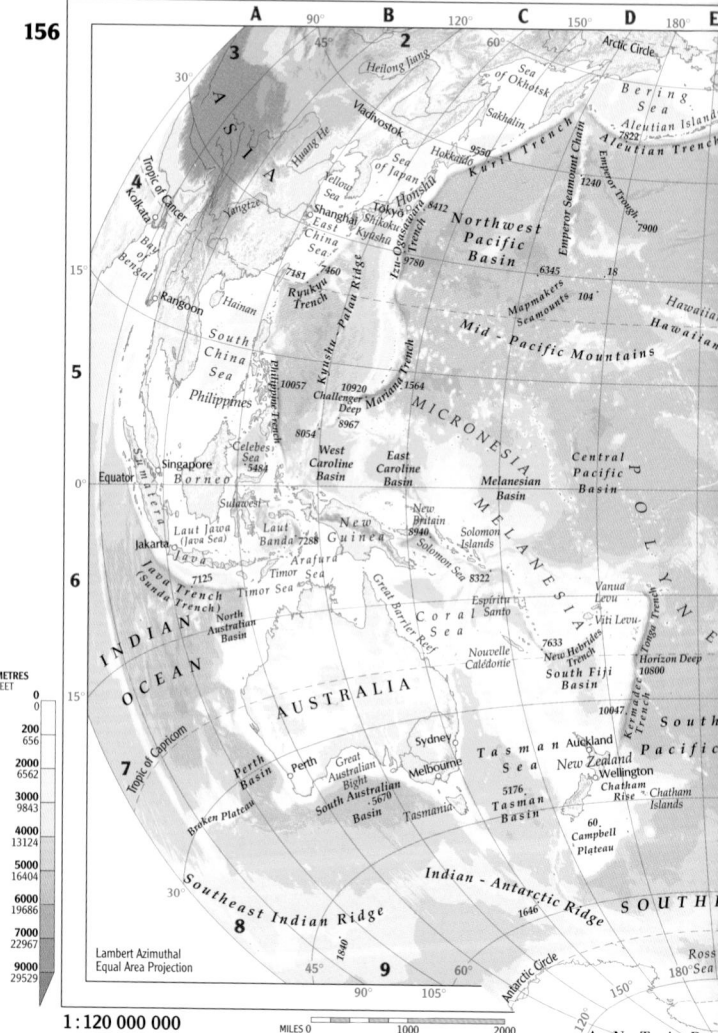

156

A 90° 45° B 120° 60° C 150° D 180° E

30°

3 A S I A

Heilong Jiang

2

Sea of Okhotsk

Arctic Circle

Bering Sea

Aleutian Islands

Vladivostok

Sakhalin

Kuril Trench

Tropic of Cancer

4

Kolkata

Huang He

Yellow Sea

Hokkaido

9550

Aleutian Trench 7822

Emperor Seamount Chain

Emperor Trough 1240

7900

Yangtze

Sea of Japan

Honshu

Tokyo

Shikoku 8412

Japan Trench

Bay of Bengal

Shanghai

East China Sea

Kyushu

Izu Ogasawara

Ryukyu Trench 7181 7460

9780

Northwest Pacific Basin

6345

18

Rangoon

Hainan

Kyushu-Palau Ridge

Mariana Trench 1564

Mapmakers Seamounts 104

Hawaiian

Hawaiian

15°

South China Sea

Philippines

Philippine Trench 10057

Challenger Deep 10920

8967

Mariana Trench

Mid-Pacific Mountains

5

8054

West Caroline Basin

East Caroline Basin

MICRONESIA

Central Pacific Basin

P O L Y N E

Singapore

Celebes Sea 5484

Melanesian Basin

Equator

Borneo

Sulawesi

New Britain 8940

Solomon Islands

Sumatra

Laut Jawa (Java Sea)

Laut Banda 7788

New Guinea

Solomon Sea 8322

MELANESIA

Jakarta

Java

Arafura Sea

Vanua Levu

6

Java Trench (Sunda Trench)

Timor Sea 7125

Timor Sea

North Australian Basin

Great Barrier Reef

Coral Sea

Espíritu Santo

Viti Levu

I N D I A N

Nouvelle Calédonie

New Hebrides Trench 7633

South Fiji Basin

Horizon Deep 10800

Tonga Trench

15°

O C E A N

A U S T R A L I A

10047

Kermadec Trench

S o u t h

Tropic of Capricorn

Sydney

Tasman Sea

Auckland

Pacific

7

Perth Basin

Perth

Great Australian Bight

Melbourne

New Zealand

Wellington

Broken Plateau

South Australian Basin 5670

Tasmania

5176

Tasman Basin

Chatham Rise

Chatham Islands

60

Campbell Plateau

METRES FEET

0 0

200 656

2000 6562

3000 9843

4000 13124

5000 16404

6000 19686

7000 22967

8000

9000 29529

Southeast Indian Ridge

1840

Indian-Antarctic Ridge

1646

SOUTHE

8

Lambert Azimuthal Equal Area Projection

9

45° 90° 60° 105°

Antarctic Circle

120°

150°

Ross Sea 180°

1:120 000 000

MILES 0 1000 2000

A N T A R

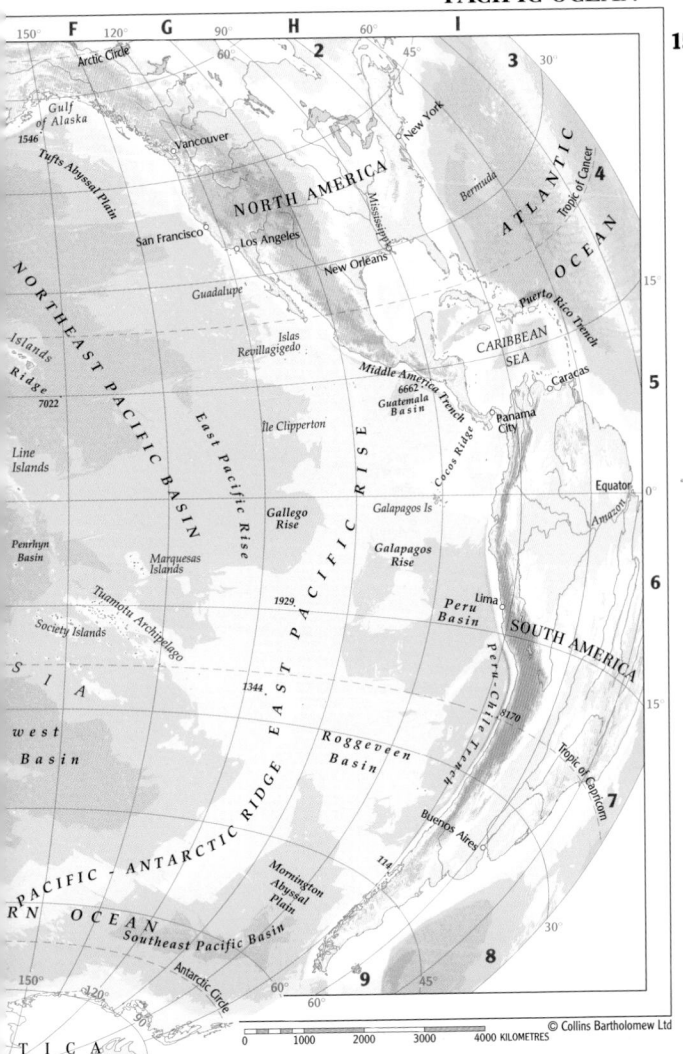

Arctic Circle

Gulf of Alaska
1546

Tufts Abyssal Plain

Vancouver

NORTH AMERICA

San Francisco

Los Angeles

Guadalupe

New York

Bermuda

ATLANTIC

Tropic of Cancer

OCEAN

New Orleans

Mississippi

Islas Revillagigedo

Puerto Rico Trench

CARIBBEAN SEA

Middle America Trench
6662
Guatemala Basin

Caracas

Panama City

N O R T H E A S T   P A C I F I C   B A S I N

Islands Ridge
7022

Line Islands

Penrhyn Basin

Île Clipperton

East Pacific Rise

Cocos Ridge

Equator

Amazon

Gallego Rise

Galapagos Is

Galapagos Rise

Marquesas Islands

Tuamotu Archipelago

Society Islands

1929

Lima

Peru Basin

SOUTH AMERICA

E A S T   P A C I F I C   R I S E

Peru-Chile Trench

S I A

1344

8170

west Basin

Roggeveen Basin

Tropic of Capricorn

Buenos Aires

114

P A C I F I C – A N T A R C T I C   R I D G E

Mornington Abyssal Plain

R N   O C E A N

Southeast Pacific Basin

Antarctic Circle

T I C A

© Collins Bartholomew Ltd

0   1000   2000   3000   4000 KILOMETRES

ATLANTIC OCEAN

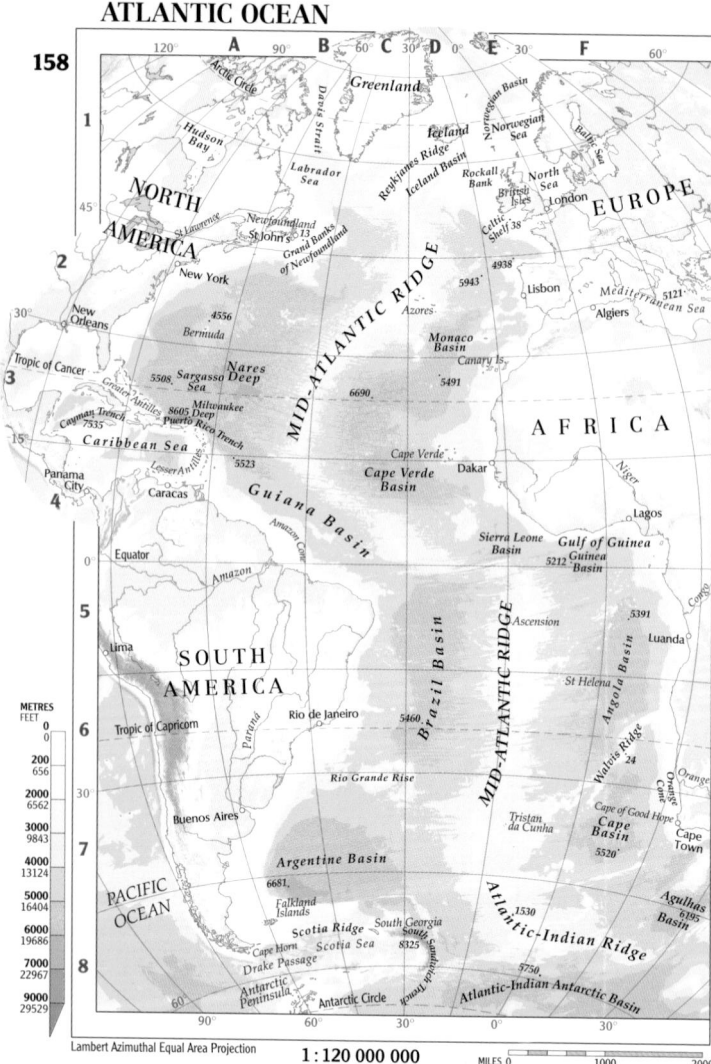

NORTH AMERICA

Arctic Circle
Hudson Bay
Greenland
Davis Strait
Iceland
Norwegian Sea
Baltic Sea
North Sea
Reykjanes Ridge
Iceland Basin
Labrador Sea
Rockall Bank
British Isles
London
EUROPE
Celtic Shelf 38
St Lawrence
Newfoundland
St John's
Grand Banks of Newfoundland
13
New York
4938
5943
Lisbon
Mediterranean Sea
5121
4556
Azores
Monaco Basin
Algiers
Bermuda
Tropic of Cancer
New Orleans
Nares Deep
Sargasso Sea
5508
Canary Is.
5491
Greater Antilles
8605
Milwaukee
Cayman Trench
7535
Puerto Rico Trench
AFRICA
6690
Caribbean Sea
Lesser Antilles
5523
Cape Verde
Cape Verde Basin
Dakar
Niger
Panama City
Caracas
Guiana Basin
Amazon Cone
Lagos
Sierra Leone Basin
Gulf of Guinea
Guinea Basin
Equator
Amazon
5212
MID-ATLANTIC RIDGE
Ascension
5391
Luanda
Lima
SOUTH AMERICA
Brazil Basin
St Helena
Angola Basin
Paraná
Rio de Janeiro
5460
MID-ATLANTIC RIDGE
Tropic of Capricorn
Rio Grande Rise
Walvis Ridge
24
Orange Cone
Orange
Buenos Aires
Cape Basin
Cape of Good Hope
Cape Town
Tristan da Cunha
5520
Agulhas Basin
6195
Argentine Basin
6681
PACIFIC OCEAN
1530
Atlantic-Indian Ridge
Falkland Islands
Scotia Ridge
South Georgia
8325
5750
Cape Horn
Drake Passage
Scotia Sea
Antarctic Peninsula
Antarctic Circle
Atlantic-Indian Antarctic Basin

METRES FEET
0	0
200	656
2000	6562
3000	9843
4000	13124
5000	16404
6000	19686
7000	22967
9000	29529

Lambert Azimuthal Equal Area Projection

1 : 120 000 000

MILES 0   1000   2000

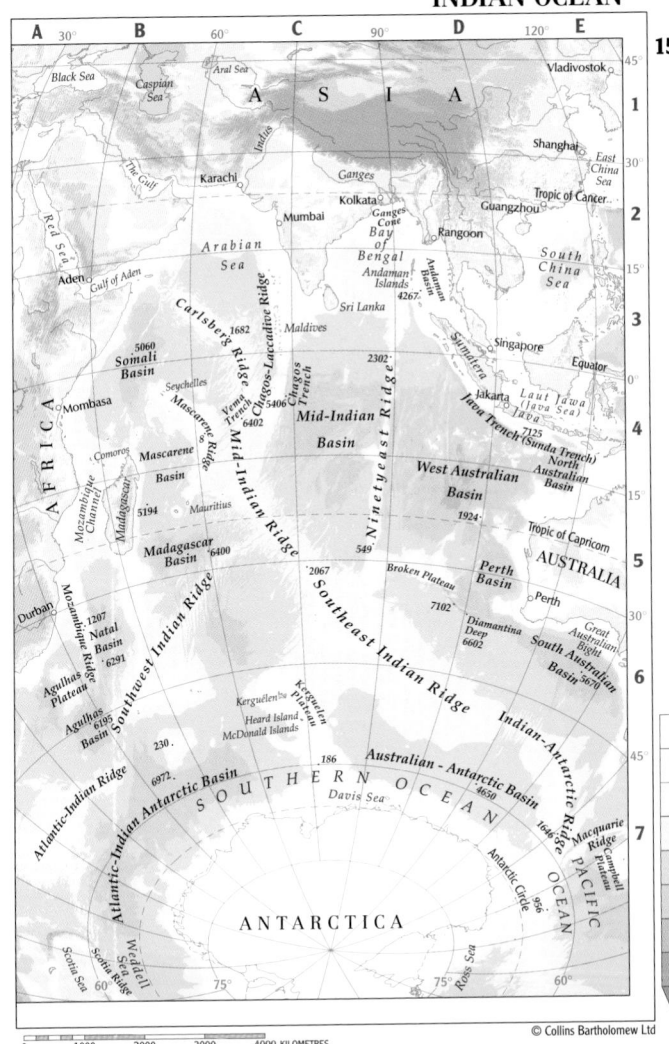

A 30° B 60° C 90° D 120° E

45°

Black Sea
Caspian Sea
Aral Sea
Vladivostok

1

A S I A

Shanghai

The Gulf
Karachi
Ganges
Kolkata
East China Sea

30°

Tropic of Cancer

2

Aden
Red Sea
Gulf of Aden
Mumbai
Ganges Cone
Bay of Bengal
Andaman Islands 4267
Rangoon
Guangzhou

Arabian Sea

South China Sea

15°

3

Carlsberg Ridge 1682
Chagos-Laccadive Ridge
Maldives
Sri Lanka
Andaman Basin
Sumatra
Singapore

AFRICA

Mombasa
5060
Somali Basin
Seychelles
Mascarene Ridge
Vema Trench 6402
Chagos Trench 5406
2302
Mid-Indian Basin
Ninetyeast Ridge
7125
Java Trench (Sunda Trench)
Laut Jawa (Java Sea)
Jakarta
Java
Equator

0°

4

Comoros
Mascarene Basin
North Australian Basin

Mozambique Channel
Madagascar
5194
Mauritius
Mid-Indian Ridge
West Australian Basin
1924

15°

5

Durban
1207
Natal Basin
6291
Madagascar Basin 6400
2067
549
Broken Plateau
7102
Perth Basin
Perth
Tropic of Capricorn

AUSTRALIA

Southeast Indian Ridge

Agulhas Plateau
Agulhas Basin 6195
Southwest Indian Ridge
Diamantina Deep 6602
South Australian Basin 5670
Great Australian Bight

30°

6

Mozambique Ridge

Kerguelen Plateau
Heard Island
McDonald Islands
230
Indian-Antarctic Ridge
Macquarie Ridge
Campbell Plateau

Atlantic-Indian Ridge

45°

6972
186
Australian-Antarctic Basin 4650
5466

7

S O U T H E R N   O C E A N
Davis Sea
956
PACIFIC OCEAN

Scotia Sea
Scotia Ridge
Weddell Sea
60°
Antarctic Circle
75°
75°
60°

A N T A R C T I C A

METRES	FEET
0	0
200	656
2000	6562
3000	9843
4000	13124
5000	16404
6000	19686
7000	22967
9000	29529

© Collins Bartholomew Ltd

0   1000   2000   3000   4000 KILOMETRES

ARCTIC OCEAN

K 160° **J** 180° **I** 160° **H**

PACIFIC OCEAN
Bering Sea

Gulf of Alaska

Kodiak Island

Sea of Okhotsk

St Lawrence Island

Bering Strait

Anchorage

Nome

Arctic Circle

L

Chukchi Sea

A S I A

G

Barrow

3990

Wrangel Island

East Siberian Sea

70°

Mackenzie

Beaufort Sea

Canada Basin

Novosibirskiye Ostrova

60

Lena

Laptev Sea

120°

M

N O R T H   A M E R I C A

Victoria Island

80°

F

3700

North Magnetic Pole (2005)

Alpha Ridge

Mendeleyev Ridge

100°

Lomonosov Ridge

Amerasian Basin

4000

N 3 2 1 North Pole 4346 Arctic Mid-Ocean Ridge 1 2 **E**

Ellesmere Island

North Geomagnetic Pole (2005)

3800

Nansen Basin

Yenisey

Zemlya
Frantsa-Iosifa

80°

304

Baffin Island

Baffin Bay

GREENLAND

Station Nord

Kara Sea

Zemlya

Novaya Zemlya

O **D**

Davis Strait

Greenland Sea

Spitsbergen

Barents Sea

60°

3884
Greenland Basin

Bjørnøya

METRES
FEET

0 / 0

200 / 656

Nuuk

Tromsø Murmansk

Archangel

C

2000 / 6562

3000 / 9843

P

Denmark Strait

Norwegian Basin

4000 / 13124

Reykjavik

Iceland

Arctic Circle

Norwegian Sea

5000 / 16404

6000 / 19686

ATLANTIC OCEAN

3970

40°

E U R O P E

7000 / 22967

Faroe Islands

Bergen

9000 / 29529

North Sea

Baltic Sea

Polar Stereographic Projection

Q 20° **R** 0° **A** 20° **B**

1 : 60 000 000

MILES 0   400   800

KILOMETRES 0   500   1000   1500

INTRODUCTION TO THE INDEX

The index includes all names shown on the maps in the Atlas of the World. Names are referenced by page number and by a grid reference. The grid reference correlates to the alphanumeric values which appear within each map frame. Each entry also includes the country or geographical area in which the feature is located. Entries relating to names appearing on insets are indicated by a small box symbol: □, followed by a grid reference if the inset has its own alphanumeric values.

Name forms are as they appear on the maps, with additional alternative names or name forms included as cross-references which refer the user to the entry for the map form of the name. Names beginning with Mc or Mac are alphabetized exactly as they appear. The terms Saint, Sainte, etc, are abbreviated to St, Ste, etc, but alphabetized as if in the full form.

Names of physical features beginning with generic, geographical terms are permuted – the descriptive term is placed after the main part of the name. For example, Lake Superior is indexed as Superior, Lake; Mount Everest as Everest, Mount. This policy is applied to all languages.

Entries, other than those for towns and cities, include a descriptor indicating the type of geographical feature. Descriptors are not included where the type of feature is implicit in the name itself.

Administrative divisions are included to differentiate entries of the same name and feature type within the one country. In such cases, duplicate names are alphabetized in order of administrative division. Additional qualifiers are also included for names within selected geographical areas.

INDEX ABBREVIATIONS

admin. div.	administrative division	for.	forest	Pol.	Poland
Afgh.	Afghanistan	g.	gulf	Port.	Portugal
Alg.	Algeria	Ger.	Germany	prov.	province
Arg.	Argentina	Guat.	Guatemala	reg.	region
Austr.	Australia	hd	headland	Rep.	Republic
aut. reg.	autonomous region	Hond.	Honduras	Rus. Fed.	Russian Federation
aut. rep.	autonomous republic	imp. l.	impermanent lake	S.	South
Azer.	Azerbaijan	Indon.	Indonesia	Serb. and Mont.	Serbia and Montenegro*
Bangl.	Bangladesh	isth.	isthmus	Switz.	Switzerland
Bol.	Bolivia	Kazakh.	Kazakhstan	Tajik.	Tajikistan
Bos.-Herz.	Bosnia Herzegovina	Kyrg.	Kyrgyzstan	Tanz.	Tanzania
Bulg.	Bulgaria	lag.	lagoon	terr.	territory
Can.	Canada	Lith.	Lithuania	Thai.	Thailand
C.A.R.	Central African Republic	Lux.	Luxembourg	Trin. and Tob.	Trinidad and Tobago
		Madag.	Madagascar	Turkm.	Turkmenistan
Col.	Colombia	Maur.	Mauritania	U.A.E.	United Arab Emirates
Czech Rep.	Czech Republic	Mex.	Mexico	U.K.	United Kingdom
Dem. Rep. Congo	Democratic Republic of the Congo	Moz.	Mozambique	Ukr.	Ukraine
		mun.	municipality	Uru.	Uruguay
depr.	depression	N.	North	U.S.A.	United States of America
des.	desert	Neth.	Netherlands		
Dom. Rep.	Dominican Republic	Nic.	Nicaragua	Uzbek.	Uzbekistan
		N.Z.	New Zealand	val.	valley
esc.	escarpment	Pak.	Pakistan	Venez.	Venezuela
est.	estuary	Para.	Paraguay		
Eth.	Ethiopia	Phil.	Philippines		
Fin.	Finland	plat.	plateau		
		P.N.G.	Papua New Guinea		

*Places in Serbia and Montenegro are indexed to the country as it was before the split in 2006.

1

128 B2 100 Mile House Can.

A

93 E4 Aabenraa Denmark
100 C2 Aachen Ger.
93 E4 Aalborg Denmark
100 B3 Aalst Belgium
100 B2 Aarschot Belgium
68 C2 Aba China
115 C4 Aba Nigeria
81 D2 Ābādān Iran
81 D2 Ābādeh Iran
114 B1 Abadla Alg.
115 C4 Abakaliki Nigeria
83 H3 Abakan Rus. Fed.
150 A3 Abancay Peru
81 D2 Abarqū Iran
66 D2 Abashiri Japan
117 B4 Abaya, Lake Eth.
       Ābay Wenz r. Eth./Sudan
       see Blue Nile
82 G3 Abaza Rus. Fed.
108 A2 Abbasanta Sardinia Italy
104 C1 Abbeville France
142 B3 Abbeville U.S.A.
55 O2 Abbot Ice Shelf Antarctica
74 B1 Abbottabad Pak.
115 E3 Abéché Chad
114 B4 Abengourou Côte d'Ivoire
114 C4 Abeokuta Nigeria
99 A2 Aberaeron U.K.
96 C2 Aberchirder U.K.
99 B3 Aberdare U.K.
99 A2 Aberdare U.K.
122 B3 Aberdeen S. Africa
96 C2 Aberdeen U.K.
141 D3 Aberdeen MD U.S.A.
137 D1 Aberdeen SD U.S.A.
134 B1 Aberdeen WA U.S.A.
129 E1 Aberdeen Lake Can.
99 A2 Aberystwyth U.K.
86 F2 Abez' Rus. Fed.
78 B3 Abhā Saudi Arabia
       Abiad, Bahr el r.
       see Sudan/Uganda see
       White Nile
114 B4 Abidjan Côte d'Ivoire
137 D3 Abilene KS U.S.A.
139 D2 Abilene TX U.S.A.
99 C3 Abingdon U.K.
91 D3 Abinsk Rus. Fed.
130 B2 Abitibi, Lake Can.
       Åbo Fin. see Turku
74 B1 Abohar India
114 C4 Abomey Benin
60 A1 Abongabong, Gunung mt.
       Indon.
118 B2 Abong Mbang Cameroon
64 A2 Aborlan Phil.
115 D3 Abou Déïa Chad
106 B2 Abrantes Port.
152 B3 Abra Pampa Arg.
136 A2 Absaroka Range mts U.S.A.
81 C1 Abşeron Yarımadası pen.
       Azer.
78 B3 Abū 'Arīsh Saudi Arabia
79 C2 Abu Dhabi U.A.E.
116 B3 Abu Hamed Sudan
115 C4 Abuja Nigeria
81 C2 Abū Kamāl Syria
152 B1 Abunã r. Bol.
150 B2 Abunã Brazil

74 B2 Abu Road India
116 B2 Abū Sunbul Egypt
117 A3 Abu Zabad Sudan
       Abū Zabī U.A.E. see
       Abu Dhabi
117 A4 Abyei Sudan
145 B2 Acambaro Mex.
106 B1 A Cañiza Spain
144 B2 Acaponeta Mex.
145 C3 Acapulco Mex.
151 D2 Acará Brazil
150 B1 Acarigua Venez.
145 C3 Acatlan Mex.
145 C3 Acayucán Mex.
114 B4 Accra Ghana
98 B2 Accrington U.K.
74 B2 Achalpur India
97 A2 Achill Island Ireland
101 D1 Achim Ger.
96 B2 Achnasheen U.K.
91 D3 Achuyevo Rus. Fed.
111 C3 Acıpayam Turkey
109 C3 Acireale Sicily Italy
147 C2 Acklins Island Bahamas
153 B4 Aconcagua, Cerro mt. Arg.
106 B1 A Coruña Spain
108 A2 Acqui Terme Italy
103 D2 Ács Hungary
145 C2 Actopan Mex.
139 D2 Ada U.S.A.
79 C2 Adam Oman
49 J4 Adamstown Pitcairn Is.
       'Adam Yemen see Aden
80 B2 Adana Turkey
111 D2 Adapazarı Turkey
108 A1 Adda r. Italy
78 B2 Ad Dafinah Saudi Arabia
78 B2 Ad Dahnā' des.
       Saudi Arabia
114 A2 Ad Dakhla Western Sahara
       Ad Dammām Saudi Arabia
       see Dammam
78 A2 Ad Dār al Ḥamrā'
       Saudi Arabia
78 B3 Ad Darb Saudi Arabia
78 B2 Ad Dawādimī Saudi Arabia
       Ad Dawḥah Qatar see Doha
78 B2 Ad Dilam Saudi Arabia
116 C2 Ad Dir'īyah Saudi Arabia
117 B4 Addis Ababa Eth.
81 C2 Ad Dīwānīyah Iraq
52 A2 Adelaide Austr.
50 C1 Adelaide River Austr.
101 D2 Adelebsen Ger.
55 J2 Adélie Land Antarctica
78 B3 Aden Yemen
117 C3 Aden, Gulf of
       Somalia/Yemen
100 C2 Adenau Ger.
79 C2 Adh Dhayd U.A.E.
59 C3 Adi i. Indon.
78 A3 Ādī Ārk'ay Eth.
116 B3 Adigrat Eth.
75 B3 Adilabad India
141 E2 Adirondack Mountains
       U.S.A.
       Ādīs Ābeba Eth. see
       Addis Ababa
117 B4 Ādīs Alem Eth.
110 C1 Adjud Romania
50 B1 Admiralty Gulf Austr.
128 A2 Admiralty Island U.S.A.
104 B3 Adour r. France
106 C2 Adra Spain
114 B2 Adrar Alg.
140 C2 Adrian MI U.S.A.
139 C1 Adrian TX U.S.A.
108 B2 Adriatic Sea Europe
116 B3 Adwa Eth.
83 K2 Adycha r. Rus. Fed.

91 D3 Adygeysk Rus. Fed.
114 B4 Adzopé Côte d'Ivoire
111 B3 Aegean Sea Greece/Turkey
101 D1 Aerzen Ger.
106 B1 A Estrada Spain
116 B3 Afabet Eritrea
76 C3 Afghanistan country Asia
78 B2 'Afif Saudi Arabia
80 B2 Afyon Turkey
115 C3 Agadez Niger
114 B1 Agadir Morocco
77 D2 Agadyr' Kazakh.
74 B2 Agar India
75 D2 Agartala India
81 C2 Ağdam Azer.
105 C3 Agde France
104 C3 Agen France
122 A2 Aggeneys S. Africa
111 B3 Agia Vervara Greece
111 B3 Agios Dimitrios Greece
111 C3 Agios Efstratios i. Greece
111 C3 Agios Nikolaos Greece
110 B1 Agnita Romania
75 B2 Agra India
81 C2 Ağrı Turkey
       Ağrı Dağı mt. Turkey see
       Ararat, Mount
108 B3 Agrigento Sicily Italy
111 B3 Agrinio Greece
109 B2 Agropoli Italy
154 B2 Água Clara Brazil
146 B4 Aguadulce Panama
144 B2 Aguanaval r. Mex.
144 B1 Agua Prieta Mex.
144 B2 Aguascalientes Mex.
155 D1 Águas Formosas Brazil
106 B1 Águeda Port.
106 C1 Aguilar de Campóo Spain
107 C2 Águilas Spain
144 B3 Aguililla Mex.
122 B3 Agulhas, Cape S. Africa
155 D2 Agulhas Negras mt. Brazil
111 C2 Ağva Turkey
81 C2 Ahar Iran
100 C1 Ahaus Ger.
81 C2 Ahlat Turkey
100 C2 Ahlen Ger.
74 B2 Ahmadabad India
73 B3 Ahmadnagar India
74 B2 Ahmadpur East Pak.
74 B1 Ahmadpur Sial Pak.
144 B2 Ahome Mex.
79 C2 Ahram Iran
101 E1 Ahrensburg Ger.
104 C2 Ahun France
81 C2 Ahvāz Iran
122 A2 Ai-Ais Namibia
80 B2 Aigialousa Cyprus
111 B3 Aigio Greece
143 D2 Aiken U.S.A.
155 D1 Aimorés Brazil
155 D1 Aimorés, Serra dos hills
       Brazil
114 B2 'Aïn Ben Tili Maur.
107 D2 Aïn Defla Alg.
114 B1 Aïn Sefra Alg.
136 D2 Ainsworth U.S.A.
       Aintab Turkey see Gaziantep
107 D2 Aïn Taya Alg.
107 D2 Aïn Tédélès Alg.
115 C3 Aïr, Massif de l' mts Niger
60 A1 Airbangis Indon.
128 C2 Airdrie Can.
104 B3 Aire-sur-l'Adour France
101 E3 Aisch r. Ger.
128 A1 Aishihik Lake Can.
100 A3 Aisne r. France
59 D3 Aitape P.N.G.
110 B1 Aiud Romania
105 D3 Aix-en-Provence France

105 D2 **Aix-les-Bains** France
62 A1 **Aizawl** India
88 C2 **Aizkraukle** Latvia
67 C3 **Aizu-wakamatsu** Japan
105 D3 **Ajaccio** *Corsica* France
115 E1 **Ajdābiyā** Libya
74 B2 **Ajmer** India
138 A2 **Ajo** U.S.A.
87 E3 **Akbulak** Rus. Fed.
80 B2 **Akçakale** Turkey
80 B2 **Akdağmadeni** Turkey
88 A2 **Åkersberga** Sweden
118 C2 **Aketi** Dem. Rep. Congo
87 D4 **Akhalk'alak'i** Georgia
79 C2 **Akhḍar, Jabal** *mts* Oman
111 C3 **Akhisar** Turkey
87 D4 **Akhtubinsk** Rus. Fed.
130 B1 **Akimiski Island** Can.
66 D3 **Akita** Japan
114 A3 **Akjoujt** Maur.
77 D1 **Akkol'** Kazakh.
88 B2 **Akmenrags** *pt* Latvia
    Akmola Kazakh. *see* Astana
117 B4 **Akobo** Sudan
74 B2 **Akola** India
78 A3 **Akordat** Eritrea
127 G2 **Akpatok Island** Can.
92 □A3 **Akranes** Iceland
111 B2 **Akrathos, Akra** *pt* Greece
140 E2 **Akron** U.S.A.
75 B1 **Aksai Chin** *terr.* Asia
80 B2 **Aksaray** Turkey
76 B1 **Aksay** Kazakh.
91 D2 **Aksay** Rus. Fed.
80 B2 **Akşehir** Turkey
76 C2 **Akshiganak** Kazakh.
77 E2 **Aksu** China
74 A3 **Āksum** Eth.
76 B2 **Aktau** Kazakh.
76 B1 **Aktobe** Kazakh.
77 D2 **Aktogay** Kazakh.
88 C3 **Aktsyabrski** Belarus
115 C4 **Akure** Nigeria
92 □B2 **Akureyri** Iceland
142 C2 **Alabama** *r.* U.S.A.
142 C2 **Alabama** *state* U.S.A.
111 C3 **Alaçatı** Turkey
81 C1 **Alagir** Rus. Fed.
151 E3 **Alagoinhas** Brazil
107 C1 **Alagón** Spain
79 B2 **Al Aḥmadī** Kuwait
77 E2 **Alakol', Ozero** *salt l.* Kazakh.
92 J2 **Alakurtti** Rus. Fed.
78 B3 **Al 'Alayyah** Saudi Arabia
81 C2 **Al 'Amādīyah** Iraq
80 A2 **Al 'Āmirīyah** Egypt
135 C3 **Alamo** U.S.A.
138 B2 **Alamogordo** U.S.A.
144 A2 **Alamos** *Sonora* Mex.
144 B2 **Alamos** *Sonora* Mex.
144 B2 **Alamos** *r.* Mex.
136 B3 **Alamosa** U.S.A.
93 G3 **Åland Islands** Fin.
80 B2 **Alanya** Turkey
80 B3 **Al 'Aqabah** Jordan
78 B2 **Al 'Aqīq** Saudi Arabia
107 C2 **Alarcón, Embalse de** *resr* Spain
80 B2 **Al 'Arish** Egypt
78 B2 **Al Arṭāwīyah** Saudi Arabia
61 C2 **Alas** Indon.
111 C3 **Alaşehir** Turkey
128 A2 **Alaska** *state* U.S.A.
124 F3 **Alaska, Gulf of** U.S.A.
81 C1 **Ālāt** Azer.
87 D3 **Alatyr'** Rus. Fed.
150 A2 **Alausí** Ecuador
93 H3 **Alavus** Fin.
52 B2 **Alawoona** Austr.

108 A2 **Alba** Italy
107 C2 **Albacete** Spain
110 B1 **Alba Iulia** Romania
109 C2 **Albania** *country* Europe
50 A3 **Albany** Austr.
130 B1 **Albany** *r.* Can.
143 D2 **Albany** *GA* U.S.A.
141 E2 **Albany** *NY* U.S.A.
134 B2 **Albany** *OR* U.S.A.
    Al Başrah Iraq *see* Basra
51 D1 **Albatross Bay** Austr.
116 A2 **Al Bawīṭī** Egypt
115 E1 **Al Baydā'** Libya
78 B3 **Al Baydā'** Yemen
143 D1 **Albemarle** U.S.A.
143 E1 **Albemarle Sound** *sea chan.* U.S.A.
108 A2 **Albenga** Italy
51 C2 **Alberga** *watercourse* Austr.
119 D2 **Albert, Lake** Dem. Rep. Congo/Uganda
134 B2 **Albert, Lake** U.S.A.
128 C2 **Alberta** *prov.* Can.
100 B2 **Albert Kanaal** *canal* Belgium
137 E2 **Albert Lea** U.S.A.
104 C3 **Albi** France
78 A2 **Al Bi'r** Saudi Arabia
78 B3 **Al Birk** Saudi Arabia
78 B2 **Al Biyāḍh** *reg.* Saudi Arabia
    Alborz, Reshteh-ye *mts* Iran *see* Elburz Mountains
106 B2 **Albufeira** Port.
138 B1 **Albuquerque** U.S.A.
79 C2 **Al Buraymī** Oman
53 C3 **Albury** Austr.
106 B2 **Alcácer do Sal** Port.
106 C1 **Alcalá de Henares** Spain
106 C2 **Alcalá la Real** Spain
108 B3 **Alcamo** *Sicily* Italy
107 C1 **Alcañiz** Spain
106 B2 **Alcántara** Spain
106 C2 **Alcaraz** Spain
106 C2 **Alcaraz, Sierra de** *mts* Spain
106 C2 **Alcaudete** Spain
106 C2 **Alcázar de San Juan** Spain
91 D2 **Alchevs'k** Ukr.
155 E1 **Alcobaça** Brazil
107 C2 **Alcoy-Alcoi** Spain
107 D2 **Alcúdia** Spain
145 C2 **Aldama** Mex.
83 J2 **Aldan** Rus. Fed.
83 J2 **Aldan** *r.* Rus. Fed.
95 C4 **Alderney** *i.* Channel Is
114 A3 **Aleg** Maur.
155 D2 **Alegre** Brazil
152 C3 **Alegrete** Brazil
83 K3 **Aleksandrovsk-Sakhalinskiy** Rus. Fed.
91 D1 **Alekseyevka** *Belgorodskaya Oblast'* Rus. Fed.
91 D1 **Alekseyevka** *Belgorodskaya Oblast'* Rus. Fed.
89 E3 **Aleksin** Rus. Fed.
109 D2 **Aleksinac** Serb. and Mont.
155 D2 **Além Paraíba** Brazil
93 F3 **Ålen** Norway
104 C2 **Alençon** France
80 B2 **Aleppo** Syria
150 A3 **Alerta** Peru
128 B2 **Alert Bay** Can.
105 D2 **Alès** France
110 B1 **Aleşd** Romania
108 A2 **Alessandria** Italy
93 E3 **Ålesund** Norway
124 C3 **Aleutian Islands** U.S.A.
83 L3 **Alevina, Mys** *c.* Rus. Fed.

128 A2 **Alexander Archipelago** *is* U.S.A.
122 A2 **Alexander Bay** S. Africa
142 C2 **Alexander City** U.S.A.
55 O2 **Alexander Island** Antarctica
53 C3 **Alexandra** Austr.
54 A3 **Alexandra** N.Z.
111 B2 **Alexandreia** Greece
    Alexandretta Turkey *see* İskenderun
116 A1 **Alexandria** Egypt
110 C2 **Alexandria** Romania
123 C3 **Alexandria** S. Africa
142 B2 **Alexandria** *LA* U.S.A.
137 D1 **Alexandria** *MN* U.S.A.
141 D3 **Alexandria** *VA* U.S.A.
52 A3 **Alexandrina, Lake** Austr.
111 C2 **Alexandroupoli** Greece
131 E1 **Alexis** *r.* Can.
128 B2 **Alexis Creek** Can.
77 E1 **Aleysk** Rus. Fed.
107 C1 **Alfaro** Spain
81 C3 **Al Fāw** Iraq
101 D2 **Alfeld (Leine)** Ger.
155 C2 **Alfenas** Brazil
    Al Fujayrah U.A.E. *see* Fujairah
    Al Furāt *r.* Iraq/Syria *see* Euphrates
106 B2 **Algeciras** Spain
107 C2 **Algemesí** Spain
78 A3 **Algena** Eritrea
    Alger Alg. *see* Algiers
114 C2 **Algeria** *country* Africa
79 C3 **Al Ghaydah** Yemen
108 A2 **Alghero** *Sardinia* Italy
116 B2 **Al Ghurdaqah** Egypt
79 B2 **Al Ghwaybiyah** Saudi Arabia
115 C1 **Algiers** Alg.
123 C3 **Algoa Bay** S. Africa
137 E2 **Algona** U.S.A.
81 C2 **Al Ḥadīthah** Iraq
79 C2 **Al Hajar al Gharbī** *mts* Oman
115 D2 **Al Ḥamādah al Ḥamrā'** *plat.* Libya
107 C2 **Alhama de Murcia** Spain
80 A2 **Al Ḥammām** Egypt
78 B2 **Al Ḥanākīyah** Saudi Arabia
81 C2 **Al Ḥasakah** Syria
81 C2 **Al Ḥayy** Iraq
78 B3 **Al Ḥazm al Jawf** Yemen
79 B3 **Al Ḥibāk** *des.* Saudi Arabia
78 B2 **Al Ḥillah** Saudi Arabia
79 B2 **Al Ḥinnāh** Saudi Arabia
    Al Ḥudaydah Yemen *see* Hodeidah
79 B2 **Al Ḥufūf** Saudi Arabia
115 D2 **Al Ḥulayq al Kabir** *hills* Libya
79 C2 **'Alīābād** Iran
111 C3 **Aliağa** Turkey
111 B2 **Aliakmonas** *r.* Greece
107 C2 **Alicante** Spain
139 D3 **Alice** U.S.A.
109 C3 **Alice, Punta** *pt* Italy
51 C2 **Alice Springs** Austr.
75 B2 **Aligarh** India
81 C2 **Aligüdarz** Iran
69 E1 **Alihe** China
118 B3 **Alima** *r.* Congo
111 C3 **Aliova** *r.* Turkey
117 C3 **Ali Sabieh** Djibouti
    Al Iskandarīyah Egypt *see* Alexandria
116 B1 **Al Ismā'īlīyah** Egypt
123 C3 **Aliwal North** S. Africa

115 E2 Al Jaghbūb Libya
78 B2 Al Jahrah Kuwait
79 C2 Al Jamaliyah Qatar
78 A2 Al Jawf Saudi Arabia
115 D1 Al Jawsh Libya
106 B2 Aljezur Port.
78 A2 Al Jizah Egypt see Giza
79 B2 Al Jubayl Saudi Arabia
78 B2 Al Junaynah Saudi Arabia
106 B2 Aljustrel Port.
78 B2 Al Kahfah Saudi Arabia
80 B2 Al Karak Jordan
79 C2 Al Khābūrah Oman
78 B2 Al Khamāsin Saudi Arabia
116 B2 Al Kharijah Egypt
79 C2 Al Khaşab Oman
78 B3 Al Khawkhah Yemen
79 C2 Al Khawr Qatar
115 E2 Al Khufrah Libya
115 D1 Al Khums Libya
79 B2 Al Khunn Saudi Arabia
79 C2 Al Kir'ānah Qatar
100 B1 Alkmaar Neth.
81 C3 Al Kūt Iraq
Al Kuwayt Kuwait see Kuwait
Al Lādhiqīyah Syria see Latakia
75 C2 Allahabad India
83 K2 Allakh-Yun' Rus. Fed.
141 D2 Allegheny r. U.S.A.
140 C3 Allegheny Mountains U.S.A.
97 B1 Allen, Lough l. Ireland
145 B2 Allende Coahuila Mex.
145 B2 Allende Nuevo León Mex.
141 D2 Allentown U.S.A.
73 B4 Alleppey India
101 D1 Aller r. Ger.
136 C1 Alliance NE U.S.A.
140 C2 Alliance OH U.S.A.
78 B2 Al Lith Saudi Arabia
96 C2 Alloa U.K.
131 C2 Alma Can.
Alma-Ata Kazakh. see Almaty
106 B2 Almada Port.
106 C2 Almadén Spain
Al Madīnah Saudi Arabia see Medina
116 B1 Al Mafraq Jordan
78 B3 Al Maḥwit Yemen
78 B2 Al Majma'ah Saudi Arabia
135 B2 Almanor, Lake U.S.A.
107 C2 Almansa Spain
80 B2 Al Manşūrah Egypt
79 C2 Al Mariyyah U.A.E.
115 E1 Al Marj Libya
77 D2 Almaty Kazakh.
106 C1 Almazán Spain
151 C2 Almeirim Brazil
100 C1 Almelo Neth.
155 D1 Almenara Brazil
106 B1 Almendra, Embalse de resr Spain
106 B2 Almendralejo Spain
106 C2 Almería Spain
106 C2 Almería, Golfo de b. Spain
87 E3 Al'met'yevsk Rus. Fed.
78 B2 Al Mindak Saudi Arabia
116 B2 Al Minyā Egypt
79 B2 Al Mish'āb Saudi Arabia
106 B2 Almodôvar Port.
106 B2 Almonte Spain
75 B2 Almora India
79 B2 Al Mubarrez Saudi Arabia
79 C2 Al Muḍaibī Oman
80 B3 Al Mudawwarah Jordan

Al Mukallā Yemen see Mukalla
Al Mukhā Yemen see Mocha
106 C2 Almuñécar Spain
78 A2 Al Muwaylih Saudi Arabia
111 B3 Almyros Greece
96 B2 Alness U.K.
98 C1 Alnwick U.K.
49 G4 Alofi Niue
111 B3 Alonnisos i. Greece
59 C3 Alor i. Indon.
59 C3 Alor, Kepulauan is Indon.
60 B1 Alor Setar Malaysia
Alost Belgium see Aalst
86 C2 Alozero Rus. Fed.
140 C1 Alpena U.S.A.
139 C2 Alpine U.S.A.
105 D2 Alps mts Europe
79 B3 Al Qa'āmīyāt reg. Saudi Arabia
115 D1 Al Qaddāḥīyah Libya
Al Qāhirah Egypt see Cairo
78 B2 Al Qā'īyah Saudi Arabia
81 C2 Al Qāmishlī Syria
80 B2 Al Qaryatayn Syria
79 B3 Al Qaţn Yemen
106 B2 Alqueva, Barragem de resr Port.
80 B2 Al Qunayţirah Syria
78 B3 Al Qunfidhah Saudi Arabia
116 B2 Al Quşayr Egypt
78 B2 Al Quwayyiyah Saudi Arabia
101 D2 Alsfeld Ger.
92 H2 Alta Norway
92 H2 Altaelva r. Norway
68 B1 Altai Mountains Asia
143 D2 Altamaha r. U.S.A.
151 C2 Altamira Brazil
109 C2 Altamura Italy
68 B1 Altay China
68 C1 Altay Mongolia
105 D2 Altdorf Switz.
107 C2 Altea Spain
101 F2 Altenburg Ger.
100 C2 Altenkirchen (Westerwald) Ger.
111 C3 Altınoluk Turkey
111 D3 Altıntaş Turkey
152 B2 Altiplano plain Bol.
154 B1 Alto Araguaia Brazil
107 C1 Alto del Moncayo mt. Spain
154 B1 Alto Garças Brazil
121 C2 Alto Molócuè Moz.
129 E3 Altona Can.
141 D2 Altoona U.S.A.
154 B1 Alto Sucuriú Brazil
154 B1 Alto Taquari Brazil
102 C2 Altötting Ger.
68 B2 Altun Shan mts China
134 B2 Alturas U.S.A.
139 D2 Altus U.S.A.
88 C2 Alūksne Latvia
78 A2 Al 'Ulā Saudi Arabia
115 D1 Al 'Uqaylah Libya
Al Uqşur Egypt see Luxor
91 C3 Alushta Ukr.
139 D1 Alva U.S.A.
145 C2 Alvarado Mex.
93 F3 Älvdalen Sweden
92 H2 Älvsbyn Sweden
78 A2 Al Wajh Saudi Arabia
74 B2 Alwar India
81 C2 Al Widyān plat. Iraq/Saudi Arabia
Alxa Youqi China see Ehen Hudag
Alxa Zuoqi China see Bayan Hot

51 C1 Alyangula Austr.
88 B3 Alytus Lith.
136 C1 Alzada U.S.A.
100 D3 Alzey Ger.
50 C2 Amadeus, Lake salt flat Austr.
127 G2 Amadjuak Lake Can.
106 B2 Amadora Port.
78 B2 Amā'ir Saudi Arabia
93 F4 Åmål Sweden
111 B3 Amaliada Greece
59 D3 Amamapare Indon.
154 B2 Amambaí Brazil
154 B2 Amambaí r. Brazil
69 E3 Amami-Ō-shima i. Japan
69 E3 Amami-shotō is Japan
77 C1 Amangel'dy Kazakh.
109 C3 Amantea Italy
123 D3 Amanzimtoti S. Africa
151 C1 Amapá Brazil
106 B2 Amareleja Port.
139 C1 Amarillo U.S.A.
108 B2 Amaro, Monte mt. Italy
80 B1 Amasya Turkey
150 C1 Amazon r. S. America
151 D1 Amazon, Mouths of the Brazil
Amazonas r. S. America see Amazon
74 B1 Ambala India
121 □D3 Ambalavao Madag.
121 □D2 Ambanja Madag.
150 A2 Ambato Ecuador
121 □D2 Ambato Boeny Madag.
121 □D3 Ambato Finandrahana Madag.
121 □D2 Ambatolampy Madag.
121 □D2 Ambatondrazaka Madag.
101 E3 Amberg Ger.
146 B3 Ambergris Cay i. Belize
75 C2 Ambikapur India
121 □D2 Ambilobe Madag.
98 B1 Ambleside U.K.
121 □D3 Amboasary Madag.
121 □D2 Ambohimahasoa Madag.
59 C3 Ambon Indon.
59 C3 Ambon i. Indon.
121 □D3 Ambositra Madag.
121 □D3 Ambovombe Madag.
135 C4 Amboy U.S.A.
120 A1 Ambriz Angola
145 B2 Amealco Mex.
144 B2 Ameca Mex.
100 B1 Ameland i. Neth.
134 D2 American Falls U.S.A.
134 D2 American Falls Reservoir U.S.A.
135 D2 American Fork U.S.A.
49 G3 American Samoa terr. S. Pacific Ocean
143 D2 Americus U.S.A.
100 B1 Amersfoort Neth.
55 F2 Amery Ice Shelf Antarctica
137 E2 Ames U.S.A.
111 B3 Amfissa Greece
83 J2 Amga Rus. Fed.
66 C1 Amgu Rus. Fed.
115 C2 Amguid Alg.
83 K3 Amgun' r. Rus. Fed.
131 D2 Amherst Can.
104 C2 Amiens France
73 B3 Amindivi Islands India
122 A1 Aminuis Namibia
74 A2 Amir Chah Pak.
129 D2 Amisk Lake Can.
139 C3 Amistad Reservoir Mex./U.S.A.
98 A2 Amlwch U.K.
80 B2 'Ammān Jordan
127 I2 Ammassalik Greenland

78 B3 **Am Nābiyah** Yemen
81 D2 **Amol** Iran
111 C3 **Amorgos** *i.* Greece
142 C2 **Amory** U.S.A.
130 C2 **Amos** Can.
Amoy China *see* Xiamen
155 C2 **Amparo** Brazil
107 D1 **Amposta** Spain
75 B2 **Amravati** India
74 B1 **Amritsar** India
100 B1 **Amstelveen** Neth.
100 B1 **Amsterdam** Neth.
103 C2 **Amstetten** Austria
115 E3 **Am Timan** Chad
76 B2 **Amudar'ya** *r.* Asia
126 E1 **Amund Ringnes Island** Can.
126 C2 **Amundsen Gulf** Can.
55 M2 **Amundsen Sea** Antarctica
61 C2 **Amuntai** Indon.
Amur *r.* China/Rus. Fed. *see* Heilong Jiang
78 A3 **'Amur, Wadi** *watercourse* Sudan
83 I2 **Anabar** *r.* Rus. Fed.
83 I2 **Anabarskiy Zaliv** *b.* Rus. Fed.
134 D1 **Anaconda** U.S.A.
139 D1 **Anadarko** U.S.A.
80 B1 **Anadolu Dağları** *mts* Turkey
83 M2 **Anadyr'** *r.* Rus. Fed.
81 C2 **'Ānah** Iraq
145 B2 **Anáhuac** Mex.
60 B1 **Anambas, Kepulauan** *is* Indon.
137 E2 **Anamosa** U.S.A.
80 B2 **Anamur** Turkey
67 B4 **Anan** Japan
73 B3 **Anantapur** India
74 B1 **Anantnag** Jammu and Kashmir
90 B2 **Anan'yiv** Ukr.
91 C3 **Anapa** Rus. Fed.
154 C1 **Anápolis** Brazil
152 B3 **Añatuya** Arg.
65 B2 **Anbyon** N. Korea
104 B2 **Ancenis** France
108 B2 **Ancona** Italy
153 A5 **Ancud** Chile
Anda China *see* Daqing
93 E3 **Åndalsnes** Norway
142 C2 **Andalusia** U.S.A.
73 D3 **Andaman Islands** India
63 A2 **Andaman Sea** Indian Ocean
121 □D2 **Andapa** Madag.
100 B2 **Andelst** Neth.
92 G2 **Andenes** Norway
100 B2 **Andenne** Belgium
100 B2 **Anderlecht** Belgium
126 C2 **Anderson** *r.* Can.
126 B2 **Anderson** *AK* U.S.A.
140 B2 **Anderson** *IN* U.S.A.
143 D2 **Anderson** *SC* U.S.A.
148 D3 **Andes** *mts* S. America
77 D2 **Andijon** Uzbek.
121 □D2 **Andilamena** Madag.
121 □D2 **Andilanatoby** Madag.
121 □D2 **Andoany** Madag.
Andong China *see* Dandong
65 B2 **Andong** S. Korea
107 D1 **Andorra** *country* Europe
107 D1 **Andorra la Vella** Andorra
99 C3 **Andover** U.K.
154 B2 **Andradina** Brazil
89 D2 **Andreapol'** Rus. Fed.
155 D2 **Andrelândia** Brazil
139 C2 **Andrews** U.S.A.
109 C2 **Andria** Italy

121 □D3 **Androka** Madag.
146 C2 **Andros** *i.* Bahamas
111 B3 **Andros** *i.* Greece
143 E4 **Andros Town** Bahamas
73 B3 **Andrott** *i.* India
90 B1 **Andrushivka** Ukr.
92 G2 **Andselv** Norway
106 C2 **Andújar** Spain
120 A2 **Andulo** Angola
114 C3 **Anéfis** Mali
115 D3 **Aney** Niger
83 H3 **Angara** *r.* Rus. Fed.
69 C1 **Angarsk** Rus. Fed.
93 G3 **Ånge** Sweden
144 A2 **Ángel de la Guarda, Isla** *i.* Mex.
64 B1 **Angeles** Phil.
150 B1 **Angel Falls** Venez.
93 F4 **Ängelholm** Sweden
92 G3 **Ångermanälven** *r.* Sweden
104 B2 **Angers** France
129 E1 **Angikuni Lake** Can.
98 A2 **Anglesey** *i.* U.K.
121 C2 **Angoche** Moz.
79 C2 **Angohrān** Iran
120 A2 **Angola** *country* Africa
140 C2 **Angola** U.S.A.
128 A2 **Angoon** U.S.A.
145 C3 **Angostura, Presa de la** *resr* Mex.
104 C2 **Angoulême** France
77 D2 **Angren** Uzbek.
147 D3 **Anguilla** *terr.* West Indies
75 C2 **Angul** India
93 F4 **Anholt** *i.* Denmark
71 B3 **Anhua** China
70 B2 **Anhui** *prov.* China
154 B1 **Anhumas** Brazil
154 C1 **Anicuns** Brazil
66 D1 **Aniva, Mys** *c.* Rus. Fed.
65 B2 **Anjŭ** N. Korea
70 A2 **Ankang** China
80 B2 **Ankara** Turkey
70 B2 **Anlu** China
91 E1 **Anna** Rus. Fed.
115 C1 **Annaba** Alg.
101 F2 **Annaberg-Buchholtz** Ger.
78 B2 **An Nafūd** *des.* Saudi Arabia
81 C2 **An Najaf** Iraq
96 C3 **Annan** U.K.
141 D3 **Annapolis** U.S.A.
75 C2 **Annapurna I** *mt.* Jammu and Kashmir/Nepal
140 C2 **Ann Arbor** U.S.A.
150 C1 **Anna Regina** Guyana
81 C2 **An Nāşiriyah** Iraq
105 D2 **Annecy** France
78 B3 **An Nimāş** Saudi Arabia
62 B1 **Anning** China
142 C2 **Anniston** U.S.A.
105 C2 **Annonay** France
79 B2 **An Nu'ayriyah** Saudi Arabia
121 □D2 **Anorontany, Tanjona** *hd* Madag.
111 C3 **Ano Viannos** Greece
71 B3 **Anpu** China
70 B2 **Anqing** China
102 C2 **Ansbach** Ger.
70 C1 **Anshan** China
71 A3 **Anshun** China
114 C3 **Ansongo** Mali
150 A3 **Antabamba** Peru
80 B2 **Antakya** Turkey
121 □E2 **Antalaha** Madag.
80 B2 **Antalya** Turkey
80 B2 **Antalya Körfezi** *g.* Turkey
121 □D2 **Antananarivo** Madag.
55 Q3 **Antarctic Peninsula** Antarctica
96 B2 **An Teallach** *mt.* U.K.

106 C2 **Antequera** Spain
138 B2 **Anthony** U.S.A.
114 B2 **Anti Atlas** *mts* Morocco
105 D3 **Antibes** France
131 D2 **Anticosti, Île d'** *i.* Can.
131 D2 **Antigonish** Can.
147 D3 **Antigua** *i.* Antigua
147 D3 **Antigua and Barbuda** *country* West Indies
145 C2 **Antiguo-Morelos** Mex.
111 B3 **Antikythira** *i.* Greece
Antioch Turkey *see* Antakya
49 F6 **Antipodes Islands** N.Z.
152 A3 **Antofagasta** Chile
154 C3 **Antonina** Brazil
97 C1 **Antrim** U.K.
97 C1 **Antrim Hills** U.K.
121 □D2 **Antsalova** Madag.
121 □D2 **Antsirabe** Madag.
121 □D2 **Antsirañana** Madag.
121 □D2 **Antsohihy** Madag.
100 B2 **Antwerp** Belgium
An Uaimh Ireland *see* Navan
74 B2 **Anupgarh** India
73 C4 **Anuradhapura** Sri Lanka
Anvers Belgium *see* Antwerp
68 C2 **Anxi** China
51 C3 **Anxious Bay** Austr.
70 B2 **Anyang** China
65 B2 **Anyang** S. Korea
108 B2 **Anzio** Italy
66 D2 **Aomori** Japan
54 B2 **Aoraki** *mt.* N.Z.
108 A1 **Aosta** Italy
143 D3 **Apalachee Bay** U.S.A.
150 B2 **Apaporis** *r.* Col.
154 B2 **Aparecida do Tabuado** Brazil
64 B1 **Aparri** Phil.
86 C2 **Apatity** Rus. Fed.
144 B3 **Apatzingán** Mex.
100 B1 **Apeldoorn** Neth.
100 C1 **Apen** Ger.
108 A2 **Apennines** *mts* Italy
49 G3 **Apia** Samoa
64 B2 **Apiaí** Brazil
101 E2 **Apolda** Ger.
52 B3 **Apollo Bay** Austr.
143 D3 **Apopka, Lake** U.S.A.
154 B1 **Aporé** Brazil
154 B1 **Aporé** *r.* Brazil
80 B2 **Apostolos Andreas, Cape** Cyprus
133 E3 **Appalachian Mountains** U.S.A.
53 D2 **Appin** Austr.
140 B2 **Appleton** U.S.A.
108 B2 **Aprilia** Italy
91 D3 **Apsheronsk** Rus. Fed.
154 B2 **Apucarana** Brazil
154 B2 **Apucarana, Serra da** *hills* Brazil
78 B2 **Aqaba, Gulf of** Asia
154 A1 **Aquidauana** *r.* Brazil
72 B2 **Ara** India
117 A4 **Arab, Bahr el** *watercourse* Sudan
78 B2 **Arabian Peninsula** Asia
56 G5 **Arabian Sea** Indian Ocean
151 E3 **Aracaju** Brazil
151 E2 **Aracati** Brazil
154 B2 **Araçatuba** Brazil
155 D1 **Aracruz** Brazil
155 D1 **Araçuaí** Brazil
110 B1 **Arad** Romania
115 E3 **Arada** Chad
156 C6 **Arafura Sea** Austr./Indon.

154 B1 Aragarças Brazil
107 C1 Aragón r. Spain
151 D2 Araguaia r. Brazil
151 D2 Araguaína Brazil
154 C1 Araguari Brazil
67 C3 Arai Japan
115 C2 Arak Alg.
81 C2 Arāk Iran
62 A1 Arakan Yoma mts Myanmar
81 C1 Arak's r. Armenia/Turkey
76 C2 Aral Sea salt l.
Kazakh./Uzbek.
76 C2 Aral'sk Kazakh.
Aral'skoye More salt l.
Kazakh./Uzbek. see Aral Sea
106 C2 Aranda de Duero Spain
109 D2 Arandelovac
Serb. and Mont.
97 B1 Aran Island Ireland
97 B2 Aran Islands Ireland
106 C1 Aranjuez Spain
122 A1 Aranos Namibia
139 D3 Aransas Pass U.S.A.
67 B4 Arao Japan
114 B3 Araouane Mali
151 E2 Arapiraca Brazil
154 B2 Arapongas Brazil
154 C3 Araquari Brazil
78 B1 'Ar'ar Saudi Arabia
154 C2 Araraquara Brazil
151 C2 Araras Brazil
154 B3 Araras, Serra das mts
Brazil
52 B1 Ararat Austr.
81 C2 Ararat, Mount Turkey
155 D2 Araruama, Lago de lag.
Brazil
155 E1 Arataca Brazil
150 A1 Aratürük China see Yiwu
154 C1 Araúca Brazil
81 C2 Arbil Iraq
96 C2 Arbroath U.K.
74 A2 Arba Lut, Dasht-e des.
Afgh.
104 B3 Arcachon France
143 D3 Arcadia U.S.A.
134 B2 Arcata U.S.A.
145 B3 Arcelia Mex.
86 D2 Archangel Rus. Fed.
51 D1 Archer r. Austr.
134 D2 Arco U.S.A.
106 B2 Arcos de la Frontera Spain
127 F2 Arctic Bay Can.
160 Arctic Ocean
126 C2 Arctic Red r. Can.
81 C2 Ardabil Iran
81 C1 Ardahan Turkey
93 E3 Årdalstangen Norway
100 B3 Ardennes plat. Belgium
81 D2 Ardestān Iran
53 C2 Ardfinnan Austr.
139 D2 Ardmore U.S.A.
96 A2 Ardnamurchan, Point of U.K.
52 A2 Ardrossan Austr.
96 B3 Ardrossan U.K.
135 B3 Arena, Point U.S.A.
93 E4 Arendal Norway
101 E1 Arendsee (Altmark) Ger.
150 A3 Arequipa Peru
129 C2 Arere Brazil
106 C1 Arévalo Spain
108 B2 Arezzo Italy
104 B2 Argentan France
153 B4 Argentina country
S. America
153 A6 Argentino, Lago l. Arg.
104 C2 Argenton-sur-Creuse
France
110 C2 Argeş r. Romania

74 A1 Arghandab r. Afgh.
111 B3 Argolikos Kolpos b. Greece
111 B3 Argos Greece
111 B3 Argostoli Greece
107 C1 Arguís Spain
69 E1 Argun' r. China/Rus. Fed.
50 B1 Argyle, Lake Austr.
93 F4 Århus Denmark
122 A2 Arimsvlei Namibia
152 A2 Arica Chile
96 A2 Arinagour U.K.
155 C1 Arinos Brazil
150 C3 Aripuanã Brazil
150 B2 Aripuanã r. Brazil
150 B2 Ariquemes Brazil
154 B1 Arirahã r. Brazil
138 A2 Arizona state U.S.A.
144 A1 Arizpe Mex.
78 B2 'Arjah Saudi Arabia
92 G2 Arjeplog Sweden
142 D2 Arkadelphia U.S.A.
77 C1 Arkalyk Kazakh.
142 B2 Arkansas r. U.S.A.
142 B1 Arkansas state U.S.A.
137 D3 Arkansas City U.S.A.
Arkhangel'sk Rus. Fed. see
Archangel
97 C2 Arklow Ireland
102 C1 Arkona, Kap c. Ger.
82 G1 Arkticheskogo Instituta,
Ostrova is Rus. Fed.
105 C3 Arles France
115 C3 Arlit Niger
100 B3 Arlon Belgium
97 C1 Armagh U.K.
116 B2 Armant Egypt
81 C1 Armavir Rus. Fed.
150 A1 Armenia Col.
144 B3 Armería Mex.
53 D2 Armidale Austr.
130 B1 Armstrong Can.
81 C1 Armyans'k Ukr.
80 B2 Arnauti, Cape Cyprus
100 B2 Arnhem Neth.
51 C1 Arnhem, Cape Austr.
51 C1 Arnhem Bay Austr.
51 C1 Arnhem Land reg. Austr.
108 B2 Arno r. Italy
52 A2 Arno Bay Austr.
130 C2 Arnprior Can.
100 D2 Arnsberg Ger.
101 E2 Arnstadt Ger.
122 A2 Aroab Namibia
101 D2 Arolsen Ger.
78 A3 Aroma Sudan
108 A1 Arona Italy
144 B3 Aros r. Mex.
81 C2 Ar Ramādī Iraq
96 B3 Arran i. U.K.
80 B2 Ar Raqqah Syria
104 C1 Arras France
78 B2 Ar Rass Saudi Arabia
79 C2 Arriagá Mex.
79 C2 Ar Rimāl reg. Saudi Arabia
Ar Riyāḍ Saudi Arabia see
Riyadh
145 C3 Arroyo Seco Mex.
79 C2 Ar Rustāq Oman
81 C2 Ar Rutbah Iraq
81 D3 Arsenajān Iran
66 E2 Arsen'yev Rus. Fed.
111 B3 Arta Greece
144 B3 Arteaga Mex.
66 B2 Artem Rus. Fed.
91 D2 Artemivs'k Ukr.
104 C2 Artenay France
138 C2 Artesia U.S.A.
51 E2 Arthur Point Austr.
54 B2 Arthur's Pass N.Z.

152 C4 Artigas Uru.
129 D1 Artillery Lake Can.
90 B2 Artsyz Ukr.
77 D3 Artux China
81 C1 Artvin Turkey
59 C3 Aru, Kepulauan is Indon.
119 D2 Arua Uganda
147 D3 Aruba terr. West Indies
119 D3 Arusha Tanz.
69 C1 Arvayheer Mongolia
129 E1 Arviat Can.
92 G2 Arvidsjaur Sweden
93 F4 Arvika Sweden
87 D3 Arzamas Rus. Fed.
107 C2 Arzew Alg.
100 C2 Arzfeld Ger.
101 F2 Aš Czech Rep.
115 C4 Asaba Nigeria
66 D2 Asahi-dake vol. Japan
66 D2 Asahikawa Japan
78 B3 Asäle l. Eth.
75 C2 Asansol India
131 C2 Asbestos Can.
109 C2 Ascea Italy
152 B2 Ascensión Bol.
113 D7 Ascension i.
S. Atlantic Ocean
145 D3 Ascensión, Bahía de la b.
Mex.
101 D3 Aschaffenburg Ger.
100 C2 Ascheberg Ger.
101 E2 Aschersleben Ger.
108 B2 Ascoli Piceno Italy
92 G3 Åsele Sweden
110 B2 Asenovgrad Bulg.
76 B3 Aşgabat Turkm.
50 A2 Ashburton watercourse
Austr.
54 B2 Ashburton N.Z.
142 B2 Ashdown U.S.A.
143 D1 Asheville U.S.A.
53 D1 Ashford Austr.
99 D3 Ashford U.K.
Ashgabat Turkm. see
Aşgabat
98 C1 Ashington U.K.
67 B4 Ashizuri-misaki pt Japan
136 D3 Ashland KS U.S.A.
140 C3 Ashland KY U.S.A.
140 C2 Ashland OH U.S.A.
134 B2 Ashland OR U.S.A.
140 A1 Ashland WI U.S.A.
88 C3 Ashmyany Belarus
78 B3 Ash Sharawrah
Saudi Arabia
Ash Shāriqah U.A.E. see
Sharjah
81 C2 Ash Sharqāţ Iraq
81 C2 Ash Shaţrah Iraq
79 B3 Ash Shiḩr Yemen
79 C2 Ash Shināş Oman
78 B2 Ash Shu'bah Saudi Arabia
78 B2 Ash Shumlūl Saudi Arabia
140 C2 Ashtabula U.S.A.
131 C1 Ashuanipi Lake Can.
106 B2 Asilah Morocco
82 B3 Asino Rus. Fed.
88 C3 Asipovichy Belarus
78 B2 'Asir reg. Saudi Arabia
93 F4 Askim Norway
68 C1 Askiz Rus. Fed.
116 B3 Asmara Eritrea
93 F4 Åsnen l. Sweden
116 B3 Asoteriba, Jebel mt. Sudan
103 D2 Aspang-Markt Austria
136 B3 Aspen U.S.A.
54 A2 Aspiring, Mount N.Z.
117 C3 Assab Eritrea
116 A2 Aş Şaḩrā' al Gharbīyah
des. Egypt

116 B2   Aş Şaḩrā' ash Sharqīyah *des.* Egypt
78 B2   As Salamīyah Saudi Arabia
81 C2   As Samāwah Iraq
79 C2   Aş Şanām *reg.* Saudi Arabia
115 E2   As Sarīr *reg.* Libya
100 C1   Assen Neth.
100 B2   Assesse Belgium
115 D1   As Sidrah Libya
129 D3   Assiniboia Can.
128 C2   Assiniboine, Mount Can.
154 B2   Assis Brazil
78 B2   Aş Şubayḩīyah Kuwait
81 C2   As Sulaymānīyah Iraq
78 B2   As Sulaymī Saudi Arabia
78 B2   As Sulayyil Saudi Arabia
78 B2   As Sūq Saudi Arabia
80 B2   As Suwaydā' Syria
79 C2   As Suwayq Oman
       As Suways Egypt *see* Suez
111 B3   Astakos Greece
77 H1   Astana Kazakh.
81 C2   Āstārā Iran
108 A2   Asti Italy
74 H1   Astor Jammu and Kashmir
106 B1   Astorga Spain
134 B1   Astoria U.S.A.
87 D4   Astrakhan' Rus. Fed.
88 C3   Astravyets Belarus
111 C3   Astypalaia *i.* Greece
152 C3   Asunción Para.
116 B2   Aswān Egypt
116 B2   Asyūţ Egypt
152 B3   Atacama, Desert *des.* Chile
       Atacama, Desierto *des.* Chile *see* Atacama, Desert
152 B3   Atacama, Salar de *salt flat* Chile
114 C4   Atakpamé Togo
111 B3   Atalanti Greece
150 A3   Atalaya Peru
77 C3   Atamyrat Turkm.
78 B3   'Ataq Yemen
114 A2   Atâr Maur.
135 B3   Atascadero U.S.A.
77 D2   Atasu Kazakh.
116 B3   Atbara Sudan
116 B3   Atbara *r.* Sudan
77 C1   Atbasar Kazakh.
137 D3   Atchison U.S.A.
108 B2   Aterno *r.* Italy
108 B2   Atessa Italy
100 A2   Ath Belgium
128 C2   Athabasca Can.
129 C2   Athabasca *r.* Can.
129 D2   Athabasca, Lake Can.
111 B3   Athens Greece
143 D2   Athens *GA* U.S.A.
140 C3   Athens *OH* U.S.A.
143 D1   Athens *TN* U.S.A.
139 D2   Athens *TX* U.S.A.
       Athina Greece *see* Athens
97 C2   Athlone Ireland
111 B2   Athos *mt.* Greece
97 C2   Athy Ireland
115 D3   Ati Chad
130 A2   Atikokan Can.
87 D3   Atkarsk Rus. Fed.
143 D2   Atlanta U.S.A.
137 D2   Atlantic U.S.A.
141 E3   Atlantic City U.S.A.
158   Atlantic Ocean
122 A3   Atlantis S. Africa
114 B1   Atlas Mountains Africa
114 C1   Atlas Saharien *mts* Alg.
128 A2   Atlin Can.
128 A2   Atlin Lake Can.
142 C2   Atmore U.S.A.

139 D2   Atoka U.S.A.
75 C2   Atrai *r.* India
81 C2   Aţ Ţā'if Saudi Arabia
63 B2   Attapu Laos
111 C3   Attavyros *mt.* Greece
130 B1   Attawapiskat Can.
130 B1   Attawapiskat *r.* Can.
130 B1   Attawapiskat Lake Can.
100 C2   Attendorn Ger.
116 B2   Aţ Ţūr Egypt
78 B3   At Turbah Yemen
76 B2   Atyrau Kazakh.
105 C3   Aubenas France
126 C2   Aubry Lake Can.
142 C2   Auburn *AL* U.S.A.
135 B3   Auburn *CA* U.S.A.
137 D2   Auburn *NE* U.S.A.
141 D2   Auburn *NY* U.S.A.
104 C2   Aubusson France
104 C3   Auch France
54 B1   Auckland N.Z.
48 F6   Auckland Islands N.Z.
101 F2   Aue Ger.
102 C2   Augsburg Ger.
109 C3   Augusta *Sicily* Italy
143 D2   Augusta *GA* U.S.A.
137 D3   Augusta *KS* U.S.A.
141 F2   Augusta *ME* U.S.A.
50 A2   Augustus, Mount Austr.
100 A2   Aulnoye-Aymeries France
62 A2   Aunglan Myanmar
122 B2   Auob *watercourse* Namibia/S. Africa
74 B3   Aurangabad India
100 C1   Aurich Ger.
154 B1   Aurilândia Brazil
104 C3   Aurillac France
136 C3   Aurora *CO* U.S.A.
140 B2   Aurora *IL* U.S.A.
137 D2   Aurora *NE* U.S.A.
122 A2   Aus Namibia
137 E2   Austin *MN* U.S.A.
135 C3   Austin *NV* U.S.A.
139 D2   Austin *TX* U.S.A.
50 B2   Australia *country* Oceania
159 D7   Australian-Antarctic Basin *sea feature* Southern Ocean
53 C3   Australian Capital Territory *admin. div.* Austr.
102 C2   Austria *country* Europe
144 B3   Autlán Mex.
105 C2   Autun France
105 C2   Auxerre France
105 D2   Auxonne France
105 C2   Avallon France
131 E2   Avalon Peninsula Can.
154 C2   Avaré Brazil
49 H4   Avarua Cook Is
91 D2   Avdiyivka Ukr.
106 B1   Aveiro Port.
109 B2   Avellino Italy
100 A2   Avesnes-sur-Helpe France
93 G3   Avesta Sweden
108 B2   Avezzano Italy
96 C2   Aviemore U.K.
105 C2   Avignon France
106 C1   Ávila Spain
106 B1   Avilés Spain
109 C3   Avola *Sicily* Italy
99 B2   Avon *r. England* U.K.
99 C3   Avon *r. England* U.K.
104 B2   Avranches France
54 B1   Awanui N.Z.
117 C4   Āwash Eth.
117 C4   Āwash *r.* Eth.
115 D2   Awbārī Libya
117 C4   Aw Dheegle Somalia
96 B2   Awe, Loch *l.* U.K.
117 A4   Aweil Sudan

126 E1   Axel Heiberg Island Can.
114 B4   Axim Ghana
150 A3   Ayacucho Peru
77 E2   Ayagoz Kazakh.
68 B2   Ayakkum Hu *salt l.* China
106 B2   Ayamonte Spain
83 K3   Ayan Rus. Fed.
150 A3   Ayaviri Peru
76 A2   Aybas Kazakh.
91 D2   Aydar *r.* Ukr.
77 C2   Aydarko'l ko'li *l.* Uzbek.
111 C3   Aydın Turkey
77 C2   Ayeat, Gora *hill* Kazakh.
       Ayers Rock *hill* Austr. *see* Uluru
99 C3   Aylesbury U.K.
106 C1   Ayllón Spain
129 D1   Aylmer Lake Can.
117 B4   Ayod Sudan
83 M2   Ayon, Ostrov *i.* Rus. Fed.
114 B3   'Ayoûn el 'Atroûs Maur.
51 D1   Ayr Austr.
96 B3   Ayr U.K.
98 A1   Ayre, Point of Isle of Man
76 C2   Ayteke Bi Kazakh.
110 C2   Aytos Bulg.
145 C3   Ayutla Mex.
63 B2   Ayutthaya Thai.
111 C3   Ayvacık Turkey
111 C3   Ayvalık Turkey
114 C3   Azaouagh, Vallée de *watercourse* Mali/Niger
       Azbine *mts* Niger *see* Aïr, Massif de l'
81 C1   Azerbaijan *country* Asia
86 D2   Azopol'ye Rus. Fed.
84 D5   Azores *aut. reg.* N. Atlantic Ocean
91 D2   Azov Rus. Fed.
91 D2   Azov, Sea of Rus. Fed./Ukr.
       Azraq, Bahr el *r.* Eth./Sudan *see* Blue Nile
106 B2   Azuaga Spain
146 B4   Azuero, Península de *pen.* Panama
153 C4   Azul Arg.
80 B2   Az Zaqāzīq Egypt
80 B2   Az Zarqā' Jordan
78 B3   Az Zaydīyah Yemen
114 C2   Azzel Matti, Sebkha *salt pan* Alg.
78 B2   Az Zilfī Saudi Arabia
78 B3   Az Zuqur *i.* Yemen

B

117 C4   Baardheere Somalia
77 C3   Bābā, Kūh-e *mts* Afgh.
110 C2   Babadag Romania
111 C2   Babaeski Turkey
117 C3   Bāb al Mandab *str.* Africa/Asia
61 C2   Babana Indon.
59 C3   Babar *i.* Indon.
119 D3   Babati Tanz.
89 E2   Babayevo Rus. Fed.
128 B2   Babine *r.* Can.
128 B2   Babine Lake Can.
59 C3   Babo Indon.
81 D2   Bābol Iran
122 A3   Baboon Point S. Africa
88 C3   Babruysk Belarus
64 B1   Babuyan *i.* Phil.
64 B1   Babuyan Islands Phil.
151 D2   Bacabal Brazil
59 C3   Bacan *i.* Indon.
110 C1   Bacău Romania

52	B3	**Bacchus Marsh** Austr.
77	D3	**Bachu** China
129	E1	**Back** r. Can.
109	C1	**Bacŏlod** Phil.
		Bắc Liêu Vietnam see
63	B3	**Bac Liêu** Vietnam
64	B1	**Bacolod** Phil.
130	C1	**Bacqueville, Lac** l. Can.
106	B2	**Badajoz** Spain
62	A1	**Badarpur** India
101	E2	**Bad Berka** Ger.
101	D2	**Bad Berleburg** Ger.
101	E1	**Bad Bevensen** Ger.
100	C2	**Bad Ems** Ger.
103	D2	**Baden** Austria
102	B2	**Baden-Baden** Ger.
101	E2	**Bad Harzburg** Ger.
101	D2	**Bad Hersfeld** Ger.
102	C2	**Bad Hofgastein** Austria
101	D2	**Bad Homburg vor der Höhe** Ger.
74	A2	**Badin** Pak.
		Bādiyat ash Shām des. Asia see Syrian Desert
101	E2	**Bad Kissingen** Ger.
100	C3	**Bad Kreuznach** Ger.
101	E2	**Bad Lauterberg im Harz** Ger.
101	D2	**Bad Lippspringe** Ger.
101	D3	**Bad Mergentheim** Ger.
101	D2	**Bad Nauheim** Ger.
100	C2	**Bad Neuenahr-Ahrweiler** Ger.
101	E2	**Bad Neustadt an der Saale** Ger.
101	E1	**Bad Oldesloe** Ger.
101	D2	**Bad Pyrmont** Ger.
78	A2	**Badr Ḩunayn** Saudi Arabia
101	D1	**Bad Salzuflen** Ger.
101	E2	**Bad Salzungen** Ger.
102	C1	**Bad Schwartau** Ger.
101	E1	**Bad Segeberg** Ger.
100	C3	**Bad Sobernheim** Ger.
73	C4	**Badulla** Sri Lanka
100	D1	**Bad Zwischenahn** Ger.
106	C2	**Baeza** Spain
114	A3	**Bafatá** Guinea-Bissau
160	O2	**Baffin Bay** sea Can./Greenland
127	C2	**Baffin Island** Can.
118	B2	**Bafia** Cameroon
114	A3	**Bafing** r. Guinea/Mali
114	A3	**Bafoulabé** Mali
118	B2	**Bafoussam** Cameroon
76	B3	**Bāfq** Iran
80	B1	**Bafra** Turkey
79	C2	**Bāft** Iran
119	C2	**Bafwasende** Dem. Rep. Congo
119	D3	**Bagamoyo** Tanz.
60	B1	**Bagan Datuk** Malaysia
120	B2	**Bagani** Namibia
60	B1	**Bagansiapiapi** Indon.
138	A2	**Bagdad** U.S.A.
152	C4	**Bagé** Brazil
81	C2	**Baghdād** Iraq
77	C3	**Baghlān** Afgh.
104	C3	**Bagnères-de-Luchon** France
88	B3	**Bagrationovsk** Rus. Fed.
		Bagrax China see Bohu
64	B1	**Baguio** Phil.
115	C3	**Bagzane, Monts** mts Niger
146	C2	**Bahamas, The** country West Indies
75	C2	**Baharampur** India
		Bahariya Oasis Egypt see Baḩrīyah, Wāḩāt al
76	B3	**Baharly** Turkm.

60	B1	**Bahau** Malaysia
72	B2	**Bahawalnagar** Pak.
74	B2	**Bahawalpur** Pak.
153	B4	**Bahía Blanca** Arg.
144	A2	**Bahía Kino** Mex.
152	C3	**Bahía Negra** Para.
144	A2	**Bahía Tortugas** Mex.
117	B3	**Bahir Dar** Eth.
75	C2	**Bahraich** India
79	C2	**Bahrain** country Asia
116	A2	**Baḩrīyah, Wāḩāt al** oasis Egypt
79	D2	**Bāhū Kālāt** Iran
110	B1	**Baia Mare** Romania
69	E1	**Baicheng** China
131	D2	**Baie-Comeau** Can.
		Baie-du-Poste Can. see Mistissini
131	D2	**Baie-St-Paul** Can.
65	B1	**Baihe** China
69	D1	**Baikal, Lake** Rus. Fed.
110	B2	**Băileşti** Romania
68	C2	**Baima** China
143	D2	**Bainbridge** U.S.A.
48	F2	**Bairiki** Kiribati
		Bairin Youqi China see Daban
53	C3	**Bairnsdale** Austr.
65	B1	**Baishan** Jilin China
65	B1	**Baishanzhen** Jilin China
70	A2	**Baiyin** China
116	B3	**Baiyuda Desert** Sudan
103	D2	**Baja** Hungary
144	A1	**Baja** Yemen
114	A3	**Bakel** Senegal
135	C3	**Baker** CA U.S.A.
136	C1	**Baker** MT U.S.A.
134	C2	**Baker** OR U.S.A.
134	B1	**Baker, Mount** vol. U.S.A.
129	E1	**Baker Foreland** hd Can.
49	G2	**Baker Island** terr. N. Pacific Ocean
129	E1	**Baker Lake** Can.
129	E1	**Baker Lake** l. Can.
135	C3	**Bakersfield** U.S.A.
91	C3	**Bakhchysaray** Ukr.
91	C1	**Bakhmach** Ukr.
		Bākhtarān Iran see Kermānshāh
		Bakı Azer. see Baku
111	C2	**Bakırköy** Turkey
92	□C2	**Bakkaflói** b. Iceland
118	C2	**Bakouma** C.A.R.
81	C1	**Baku** Azer.
64	A2	**Balabac** Phil.
64	A2	**Balabac** i. Phil.
64	A2	**Balabac Strait** Malaysia/Phil.
61	C2	**Balaiberkuak** Indon.
52	A3	**Balaklava** Austr.
91	C3	**Balaklava** Ukr.
91	D2	**Balakliya** Ukr.
87	D3	**Balakovo** Rus. Fed.
76	C3	**Bālā Morghāb** Afgh.
145	C3	**Balancán** Mex.
111	C3	**Balan Dağı** hill Turkey
64	B1	**Balanga** Phil.
87	D3	**Balashov** Rus. Fed.
103	D2	**Balaton, Lake** Hungary
103	D2	**Balatonboglár** Hungary
150	D2	**Balbina, Represa de** resr Brazil
97	C2	**Balbriggan** Ireland
52	A2	**Balcanoona** Austr.
110	C2	**Balchik** Bulg.
54	A3	**Balclutha** N.Z.
129	E2	**Baldock Lake** Can.
129	E2	**Baldy Mountain** hill Can.
138	B2	**Baldy Peak** U.S.A.

		Baleares, Islas is Spain see Balearic Islands
107	D2	**Balearic Islands** is Spain
155	E1	**Baleia, Ponta da** pt Brazil
130	C1	**Baleine, Grande Rivière de la** r. Can.
131	D1	**Baleine, Rivière à la** r. Can.
75	C2	**Baleshwar** India
61	C2	**Bali** i. Indon.
61	C2	**Bali, Laut** sea Indon.
60	A1	**Balige** Indon.
75	C2	**Baliguda** India
111	C3	**Balıkesir** Turkey
61	C2	**Balikpapan** Indon.
59	D3	**Balimo** P.N.G.
102	B2	**Balingen** Ger.
		Bali Sea Indon. see Bali, Laut
76	B3	**Balkanabat** Turkm.
110	B2	**Balkan Mountains** Bulg./Serb. and Mont.
77	D2	**Balkhash** Kazakh.
77	D2	**Balkhash, Lake** Kazakh.
		Balkhash, Ozero l. Kazakh. see Balkhash, Lake
50	B3	**Balladonia** Austr.
97	B2	**Ballaghaderreen** Ireland
92	G2	**Ballangen** Norway
52	B3	**Ballarat** Austr.
50	B2	**Ballard, Lake** salt flat Austr.
96	C2	**Ballater** U.K.
114	B3	**Ballé** Mali
53	D1	**Ballina** Austr.
97	B1	**Ballina** Ireland
97	B2	**Ballinasloe** Ireland
139	D2	**Ballinger** U.S.A.
97	B2	**Ballinrobe** Ireland
97	C1	**Ballycastle** Ireland
97	C1	**Ballycastle** U.K.
97	C1	**Ballyclare** U.K.
97	C1	**Ballymena** U.K.
97	C1	**Ballymoney** U.K.
97	D1	**Ballynahinch** U.K.
97	B1	**Ballyshannon** Ireland
95	B2	**Ballyvoy** U.K.
51	D2	**Balonne** r. Austr.
74	B2	**Balotra** India
75	C2	**Balrampur** India
52	B2	**Balranald** Austr.
110	B2	**Balş** Romania
151	D2	**Balsas** Brazil
145	C3	**Balsas** Mex.
90	B2	**Balta** Ukr.
90	B2	**Bălţi** Moldova
93	G4	**Baltic Sea** g. Europe
123	C1	**Baltîm** Egypt
123	C1	**Baltimore** S. Africa
141	D3	**Baltimore** U.S.A.
88	A3	**Baltiysk** Rus. Fed.
62	A1	**Balu** India
88	C2	**Balvi** Latvia
77	D2	**Balykchy** Kyrg.
87	E4	**Balykshi** Kazakh.
79	C2	**Bam** Iran
51	D1	**Bamaga** Austr.
130	A1	**Bamaji Lake** Can.
114	B3	**Bamako** Mali
118	C2	**Bambari** C.A.R.
101	E3	**Bamberg** Ger.
119	C2	**Bambili** Dem. Rep. Congo
119	C2	**Bambouti** C.A.R.
155	C2	**Bambuí** Brazil
118	B2	**Bamenda** Cameroon
74	A1	**Bāmīān** Afgh.
152	B2	**Bañados del Izozog** swamp Bol.
119	C2	**Banalia** Dem. Rep. Congo
151	C3	**Bananal, Ilha do** i. Brazil
74	B2	**Banas** r. India
111	C3	**Banaz** Turkey

62	B2	Ban Ban Laos
97	C1	Banbridge U.K.
99	C2	Banbury U.K.
130	C2	Bancroft Can.
119	C2	Banda Dem. Rep. Congo
75	C2	Banda India
59	C3	Banda, Kepulauan *is* Indon.
59	C3	Banda, Laut *sea* Indon.
60	A1	Banda Aceh Indon.
79	C2	Bandar-e 'Abbās Iran
81	C2	Bandar-e Anzali Iran
79	C2	Bandar-e Chārak Iran
81	C2	Bandar-e Emām Khomeynī Iran
79	C2	Bandar-e Lengeh Iran
79	C2	Bandar-e Maqām Iran
60	B2	Bandar Lampung Indon.
61	C1	Bandar Seri Begawan Brunei
		Banda Sea Indon. *see* Banda, Laut
155	D2	Bandeiras, Pico de *mt.* Brazil
123	C1	Bandelierkop S. Africa
144	B2	Banderas, Bahía de *b.* Mex.
114	B3	Bandiagara Mali
111	C2	Bandırma Turkey
97	B3	Bandon Ireland
118	B3	Bandundu Dem. Rep. Congo
61	B2	Bandung Indon.
128	C2	Banff Can.
96	C2	Banff U.K.
114	B3	Banfora Burkina
64	B2	Banga Phil.
73	B3	Bangalore India
118	C2	Bangassou C.A.R.
59	C3	Banggai Indon.
59	C3	Banggai, Kepulauan *is* Indon.
61	C1	Banggi *i.* Sabah Malaysia
60	B2	Bangka *i.* Indon.
61	C2	Bangkalan Indon.
60	B1	Bangkinang Indon.
60	B2	Bangko Indon.
63	B2	Bangkok Thai.
75	C2	Bangladesh *country* Asia
63	B2	Ba Ngoi Vietnam
97	D1	Bangor *Northern Ireland* U.K.
98	A2	Bangor *Wales* U.K.
141	F2	Bangor U.S.A.
63	A2	Ban Saphan Yai Thai.
64	B1	Bangued Phil.
118	B2	Bangui C.A.R.
121	B2	Bangweulu, Lake Zambia
62	B2	Ban Huai Khon Thai.
116	B2	Banī Suwayf Egypt
115	E1	Banī Walīd Libya
80	B2	Bāniyās Syria
109	C2	Banja Luka Bos.-Herz.
114	A3	Banjul Gambia
126	C2	Banks Island *N.W.T.* Can.
48	F3	Banks Islands Vanuatu
129	E1	Banks Lake Can.
54	B2	Banks Peninsula N.Z.
75	C2	Bankura India
62	A1	Banmauk Myanmar
62	B2	Ban Mouang Laos
97	C1	Bann *r.* U.K.
62	B2	Ban Napè Laos
63	A3	Ban Na San Thai.
143	E4	Bannerman Town Bahamas
74	B1	Bannu Pak.
74	B2	Banswara India
63	A3	Ban Tha Kham Thai.
62	A2	Ban Tha Song Yang Thai.
63	B2	Ban Tôp Laos
97	B3	Bantry Ireland
97	B3	Bantry Bay Ireland
118	B2	Banyo Cameroon
107	D1	Banyoles Spain
61	C2	Banyuwangi Indon.
		Bao'an China *see* Shenzhen
69	D2	Baochang China
70	B2	Baoding China
70	A2	Baoji China
62	B1	Bao Lac Vietnam
63	B2	Bao Lôc Vietnam
66	B1	Baoqing China
62	A1	Baoshan China
70	B1	Baotou China
65	B1	Baotou Shan *mt.* China/N. Korea
81	C2	Ba'qūbah Iraq
109	C2	Bar Serb. and Mont.
117	C4	Baraawe Somalia
147	C2	Baracoa Cuba
147	C3	Baradine Austr.
116	B3	Baraka *watercourse* Eritrea/Sudan
61	C1	Baram *r.* Sarawak Malaysia
88	C3	Baranavichy Belarus
78	A2	Baranis Egypt
90	B1	Baranivka Ukr.
76	B2	Barankul Kazakh.
128	A2	Baranof Island U.S.A.
59	C3	Barat Daya, Kepulauan *is* Indon.
155	D2	Barbacena Brazil
147	E3	Barbados *country* West Indies
107	D1	Barbastro Spain
104	B2	Barbezieux-St-Hilaire France
51	D2	Barcaldine Austr.
107	D1	Barcelona Spain
150	B1	Barcelona Venez.
105	D3	Barcelonnette France
150	B2	Barcelos Brazil
		Barcoo Creek *watercourse* Austr. *see* Cooper Creek
103	D2	Barcs Hungary
75	C2	Barddhaman India
103	E2	Bardejov Slovakia
79	C2	Bardsīr Iran
75	B2	Bareilly India
160	B2	Barents Sea Arctic Ocean
116	B3	Barentu Eritrea
75	C2	Barh India
141	F2	Bar Harbor U.S.A.
109	C2	Bari Italy
74	B1	Barikot Afgh.
150	A1	Barinas Venez.
75	C2	Baripada India
75	D2	Barisal Bangl.
60	B2	Barisan, Pegunungan *mts* Indon.
61	C2	Barito *r.* Indon.
79	C2	Bark Oman
88	C2	Barkava Latvia
51	C1	Barkly Tableland *reg.* Austr.
68	C2	Barkol China
110	C1	Bârlad Romania
105	D2	Bar-le-Duc France
50	A2	Barlee, Lake *salt flat* Austr.
109	C2	Barletta Italy
53	C2	Barmedman Austr.
74	B2	Barmer India
99	A2	Barmouth U.K.
101	D1	Barmstedt Ger.
98	C1	Barnard Castle U.K.
53	B2	Barnato Austr.
82	G3	Barnaul Rus. Fed.
127	G2	Barnes Icecap Can.
100	B1	Barneveld Neth.
98	C2	Barnsley U.K.
99	A3	Barnstaple U.K.
99	A3	Barnstaple Bay U.K.
143	D2	Barnwell U.S.A.
		Baroda India *see* Vadodara
150	B1	Barquisimeto Venez.
96	A2	Barra *i.* U.K.
53	D2	Barraba Austr.
151	D2	Barra do Corda Brazil
154	B1	Barra do Garças Brazil
150	C2	Barra do São Manuel Brazil
150	A3	Barranca *Lima* Peru
150	A2	Barranca *Loreto* Peru
152	C3	Barranqueras Arg.
150	A1	Barranquilla Col.
151	D2	Barreiras Brazil
154	C2	Barretos Brazil
130	C2	Barrie Can.
128	B2	Barrière Can.
52	B2	Barrier Range *hills* Austr.
53	D2	Barrington, Mount Austr.
129	D2	Barrington Lake Can.
53	C1	Barringun Austr.
97	C2	Barrow *r.* Ireland
51	C2	Barrow Creek Austr.
98	B1	Barrow-in-Furness U.K.
50	A2	Barrow Island Austr.
126	E2	Barrow Strait Can.
99	B3	Barry U.K.
130	C2	Barrys Bay Can.
74	B2	Barsalpur India
135	C4	Barstow U.S.A.
105	C2	Bar-sur-Aube France
80	B1	Bartın Turkey
51	D1	Bartle Frere, Mount Austr.
139	D1	Bartlesville U.S.A.
103	E1	Bartoszyce Pol.
61	C2	Barung *i.* Indon.
69	D1	Baruun-Urt Mongolia
91	D2	Barvinkove Ukr.
52	A1	Barwon *r.* Austr.
88	C3	Barysaw Belarus
110	C2	Basarabi Romania
105	D2	Basel Switz.
91	C2	Bashtanka Ukr.
64	B2	Basilan *i.* Phil.
99	D3	Basildon U.K.
99	C3	Basingstoke U.K.
81	C2	Başkale Turkey
130	C2	Baskatong, Réservoir *resr* Can.
		Basle Switz. *see* Basel
118	C2	Basoko Dem. Rep. Congo
81	C2	Basra Iraq
128	C2	Bassano Can.
108	B1	Bassano del Grappa Italy
114	C4	Bassar Togo
63	A2	Bassein Myanmar
147	D3	Basse-Terre Guadeloupe
147	D3	Basseterre St Kitts and Nevis
114	A3	Bassikounou Maur.
51	D3	Bass Strait Austr.
79	C2	Bastak Iran
101	E2	Bastheim Ger.
75	C2	Basti India
105	D3	Bastia *Corsica* France
100	B2	Bastogne Belgium
142	B2	Bastrop U.S.A.
		Basuo China *see* Dongfang
118	A2	Bata Equat. Guinea
83	J2	Batagay Rus. Fed.
154	B2	Bataguassu Brazil
106	B2	Batalha Port.
71	C3	Batan *i.* Phil.
118	B2	Batangafo C.A.R.
64	B1	Batangas Phil.
60	B2	Batanghari *r.* Indon.

71 C3 **Batan Islands** Phil.
141 D2 **Batavia** U.S.A.
91 D2 **Bataysk** Rus. Fed.
130 B2 **Batchawana Mountain**
hill Can.
50 C1 **Batchelor** Austr.
63 B2 **Bătdâmbâng** Cambodia
53 D3 **Batemans Bay** Austr.
142 B1 **Batesville** U.S.A.
89 D2 **Batetskiy** Rus. Fed.
99 B3 **Bath** U.K.
74 B1 **Bathinda** India
53 C2 **Bathurst** Austr.
131 D2 **Bathurst** Can.
126 D2 **Bathurst Inlet** Can.
126 D2 **Bathurst Inlet** Can.
50 C1 **Bathurst Island** Austr.
126 E1 **Bathurst Island** Can.
78 B1 **Bāţin, Wādī al** *watercourse*
Asia
81 C1 **Batman** Turkey
115 C1 **Batna** Alg.
142 B2 **Baton Rouge** U.S.A.
144 B2 **Batopilas** Mex.
118 B2 **Batouri** Cameroon
154 B1 **Batovi** Brazil
92 I1 **Båtsfjord** Norway
73 C4 **Batticaloa** Sri Lanka
109 B2 **Battipaglia** Italy
129 D2 **Battle** *r.* Can.
140 B2 **Battle Creek** U.S.A.
135 C2 **Battle Mountain** U.S.A.
74 B1 **Battura Glacier**
Jammu and Kashmir
117 B4 **Batu** *mt.* Eth.
60 A2 **Batu, Pulau-pulau** *is* Indon.
81 C1 **Bat'umi** Georgia
60 B1 **Batu Pahat** Malaysia
59 C3 **Baubau** Indon.
115 C3 **Bauchi** Nigeria
104 B2 **Baugé** France
105 D2 **Baume-les-Dames** France
154 B2 **Bauru** Brazil
154 B1 **Baús** Brazil
88 B2 **Bauska** Latvia
102 C1 **Bautzen** Ger.
144 B2 **Bavispe** *r.* Mex.
87 E3 **Bavly** Rus. Fed.
62 A1 **Bawdwin** Myanmar
61 C2 **Bawean** *i.* Indon.
114 B3 **Bawku** Ghana
146 C2 **Bayamo** Cuba
Bayan Gol China *see*
Dengkou
68 C2 **Bayanhongor** Mongolia
70 A2 **Bayan Hot** China
64 B2 **Bayawan** Phil.
80 C1 **Bayburt** Turkey
140 C2 **Bay City** *MI* U.S.A.
139 D3 **Bay City** *TX* U.S.A.
86 F2 **Baydaratskaya Guba**
Rus. Fed.
117 C4 **Baydhabo** Somalia
81 C2 **Bayji** Iraq
Baykal, Ozero *l.* Rus. Fed.
see **Baikal, Lake**
83 I3 **Baykal'skiy Khrebet** *mts*
Rus. Fed.
76 C2 **Baykonyr** Kazakh.
87 E3 **Baymak** Rus. Fed.
64 B1 **Bayombong** Phil.
104 B3 **Bayonne** France
111 C3 **Bayramiç** Turkey
101 E3 **Bayreuth** Ger.
78 B3 **Bayt al Faqīh** Yemen
106 C2 **Baza** Spain
106 C2 **Baza, Sierra de** *mts* Spain
76 A2 **Bazardyuzyu, Gora** *mt.*
Azer./Rus. Fed.
104 B3 **Bazas** France

74 A2 **Bazdar** Pak.
70 A2 **Bazhong** China
79 D2 **Bazmān** Iran
79 D2 **Bazmān, Kūh-e** *mt.* Iran
121 □D2 **Bé, Nosy** *i.* Madag.
99 D3 **Beachy Head** U.K.
123 C3 **Beacon Bay** S. Africa
50 B1 **Beagle Gulf** Austr.
121 □D2 **Bealanana** Madag.
130 B2 **Beardmore** Can.
Bear Island Arctic Ocean
see **Bjørnøya**
134 E1 **Bear Paw Mountain** U.S.A.
147 C3 **Beata, Cabo** *c.* Dom. Rep.
147 C3 **Beata, Isla** *i.* Dom. Rep.
137 D2 **Beatrice** U.S.A.
135 C3 **Beatty** U.S.A.
53 D1 **Beaudesert** Austr.
52 B3 **Beaufort** Austr.
61 C1 **Beaufort** *Sabah* Malaysia
143 D2 **Beaufort** U.S.A.
160 L2 **Beaufort Sea** Can./U.S.A.
122 B3 **Beaufort West** S. Africa
96 B2 **Beauly** *r.* U.K.
100 A2 **Beaumont** Belgium
54 A3 **Beaumont** N.Z.
139 E2 **Beaumont** U.S.A.
105 C2 **Beaune** France
100 B2 **Beauraing** Belgium
129 E2 **Beauséjour** Can.
104 C2 **Beauvais** France
129 D2 **Beauval** Can.
135 D3 **Beaver** *r.* Can.
135 D3 **Beaver** U.S.A.
126 B2 **Beaver Creek** Can.
140 B2 **Beaver Dam** U.S.A.
129 E2 **Beaver Hill Lake** Can.
140 B1 **Beaver Island** U.S.A.
128 C2 **Beaverlodge** Can.
74 B2 **Beawar** India
154 C2 **Bebedouro** Brazil
101 D2 **Bebra** Ger.
106 B1 **Becerreá** Spain
114 B1 **Béchar** Alg.
140 C3 **Beckley** U.S.A.
117 B4 **Bedelē** Eth.
99 C2 **Bedford** U.K.
140 B3 **Bedford** U.S.A.
100 C1 **Bedum** Neth.
53 D2 **Beecroft Peninsula** Austr.
101 F1 **Beelitz** Ger.
53 D1 **Beenleigh** Austr.
80 B2 **Beersheba** Israel
139 D3 **Beeville** U.S.A.
53 C3 **Bega** Austr.
107 D1 **Begur, Cap de** *c.* Spain
81 D2 **Behshahr** Iran
69 E1 **Bei'an** China
71 A3 **Beihai** China
70 B2 **Beijing** China
100 C1 **Beilen** Neth.
96 A2 **Beinn Mhòr** *hill* U.K.
121 C2 **Beira** Moz.
80 B2 **Beirut** Lebanon
123 C1 **Beitbridge** Zimbabwe
106 B2 **Beja** Port.
115 C1 **Bejaïa** Alg.
106 B1 **Béjar** Spain
74 A2 **Beji** *r.* Pak.
103 E2 **Békés** Hungary
103 E2 **Békéscsaba** Hungary
121 □D3 **Bekily** Madag.
74 A2 **Bela** Pak.
123 C1 **Bela-Bela** S. Africa
118 B2 **Bélabo** Cameroon
109 D2 **Bela Crkva** Serb. and Mont.
61 C1 **Belaga** Malaysia
88 C3 **Belarus** *country* Europe
Belau *country*
N. Pacific Ocean *see* **Palau**

123 D2 **Bela Vista** Moz.
60 A1 **Belawan** Indon.
83 M2 **Belaya** *r.* Rus. Fed.
103 D1 **Bełchatów** Pol.
130 C1 **Belcher Islands** Can.
117 C4 **Bebedweyne** Somalia
151 D2 **Belém** Brazil
138 B2 **Belen** U.S.A.
89 E3 **Belev** Rus. Fed.
97 D1 **Belfast** U.K.
141 F2 **Belfast** U.S.A.
105 D2 **Belfort** France
73 B3 **Belgaum** India
100 B2 **Belgium** *country* Europe
91 D1 **Belgorod** Rus. Fed.
134 D1 **Belgrade** U.S.A.
109 D2 **Belgrade** Serbia
115 D4 **Beli** Nigeria
60 B2 **Belinyu** Indon.
61 B2 **Belitung** *i.* Indon.
146 B3 **Belize** Belize
146 B3 **Belize** *country*
Central America
83 K1 **Bel'kovskiy, Ostrov** *i.*
Rus. Fed.
128 B2 **Bella Bella** Can.
104 C2 **Bellac** France
128 B2 **Bella Coola** Can.
53 C1 **Bellata** Austr.
136 C2 **Belle Fourche** U.S.A.
136 C2 **Belle Fourche** *r.* U.S.A.
143 D3 **Belle Glade** U.S.A.
104 B2 **Belle-Île** *i.* Can.
131 E1 **Belle Isle** *i.* Can.
131 E1 **Belle Isle, Strait of** Can.
130 C2 **Belleville** Can.
140 B3 **Belleville** *IL* U.S.A.
137 D3 **Belleville** *KS* U.S.A.
134 B1 **Bellevue** U.S.A.
134 B1 **Bellingham** U.S.A.
55 O2 **Bellingshausen Sea**
Antarctica
105 D2 **Bellinzona** Switz.
108 B1 **Belluno** Italy
122 A3 **Bellville** S. Africa
155 E1 **Belmonte** Brazil
146 B3 **Belmopan** Belize
97 B1 **Belmullet** Ireland
69 E1 **Belogorsk** Rus. Fed.
121 □D3 **Beloha** Madag.
155 D1 **Belo Horizonte** Brazil
140 B2 **Beloit** U.S.A.
86 C2 **Belomorsk** Rus. Fed.
91 D3 **Belorechensk** Rus. Fed.
87 E3 **Beloretsk** Rus. Fed.
Belorussia *country* Europe
see **Belarus**
86 F2 **Beloyarskiy** Rus. Fed.
86 C2 **Beloye, Ozero** *l.* Rus. Fed.
Beloye More *sea* Rus. Fed.
see **White Sea**
86 C2 **Belozersk** Rus. Fed.
77 E2 **Belukha, Gora** *mt.*
Kazakh./Rus. Fed.
86 D2 **Belush'ye** Rus. Fed.
89 D2 **Belyy** Rus. Fed.
86 G2 **Belyy, Ostrov** *i.* Rus. Fed.
101 F1 **Belzig** Ger.
137 E1 **Bemidji** U.S.A.
118 C3 **Bena Dibele**
Dem. Rep. Congo
53 C3 **Benalla** Austr.
106 B1 **Benavente** Spain
96 A2 **Benbecula** *i.* U.K.
134 B2 **Bend** U.S.A.
123 C3 **Bendearg** *mt.* S. Africa
53 B3 **Bendigo** Austr.
121 C2 **Bene** Moz.
102 C2 **Benešov** Czech Rep.
109 B2 **Benevento** Italy

159 C2 Bengal, Bay of *sea* Indian Ocean
70 B2 Bengbu China
115 E1 Benghazi Libya
61 B1 Bengkayang Indon.
60 B2 Bengkulu Indon.
120 A2 Benguela Angola
96 B1 Ben Hope *hill* U.K.
152 B2 Beni *r.* Bol.
119 C2 Beni Dem. Rep. Congo
114 B1 Beni-Abbès Alg.
107 C2 Benidorm Spain
114 B1 Beni Mellal Morocco
114 C3 Benin *country* Africa
114 C4 Benin, Bight of *g.* Africa
115 C4 Benin City Nigeria
153 C3 Benito Juárez Arg.
150 B2 Benjamim Constant Brazil
144 A1 Benjamin Hill Mex.
59 C3 Benjina Indon.
96 B1 Ben Lawers *mt.* U.K.
96 B2 Ben Lomond *hill* U.K.
96 C2 Ben Macdui *mt.* U.K.
96 A2 Ben More *hill* U.K.
54 B2 Benmore, Lake N.Z.
96 B1 Ben More Assynt *hill* U.K.
128 A2 Bennett Can.
83 N1 Bennetta, Ostrov *i.* Rus. Fed.
96 B2 Ben Nevis *mt.* U.K.
141 E2 Bennington U.S.A.
123 C2 Benoni S. Africa
101 D3 Bensheim Ger.
138 A2 Benson U.S.A.
58 C3 Benteng Indon.
140 B2 Benton Harbor U.S.A.
142 B1 Bentonville U.S.A.
115 C4 Benue *r.* Nigeria
97 B1 Benwee Head Ireland
96 B2 Ben Wyvis *mt.* U.K.
70 C1 Benxi China
Beograd Serbia *see* Belgrade
75 C2 Beohari India
67 B4 Beppu Japan
109 C2 Berane Serb. and Mont.
109 C2 Berat Albania
59 C3 Berau, Teluk *b.* Indon.
116 B3 Berber Sudan
117 C3 Berbera Somalia
118 B2 Berbérati C.A.R.
104 C1 Berck France
91 D2 Berdyans'k Ukr.
91 D2 Berdychiv Ukr.
90 A2 Berehove Ukr.
59 D3 Bereina P.N.G.
76 B3 Bereket Turkm.
129 E2 Berens River Can.
90 A2 Berezhany Ukr.
90 C2 Berezivka Ukr.
90 B1 Berezne Ukr.
86 D2 Bereznik Rus. Fed.
86 E3 Berezniki Rus. Fed.
86 F2 Berezovo Rus. Fed.
107 D1 Berga Spain
111 C3 Bergama Turkey
108 A1 Bergamo Italy
102 C2 Bergen *Mecklenburg-Vorpommern* Ger.
101 D1 Bergen *Niedersachsen* Ger.
93 E3 Bergen Norway
100 B2 Bergen op Zoom Neth.
104 C3 Bergerac France
100 C2 Bergheim (Erft) Ger.
100 C2 Bergisch Gladbach Ger.
122 A1 Bergland Namibia
92 H2 Bergsviken Sweden
88 M3 Berguia, Ostrov *i.* Rus. Fed.
100 B2 Beringen Belgium

124 C3 Bering Sea N. Pacific Ocean
83 N2 Bering Strait Rus. Fed./U.S.A.
135 B3 Berkeley U.S.A.
100 B1 Berkhout Neth.
55 Q2 Berkner Island Antarctica
110 B2 Berkovitsa Bulg.
92 I1 Berlevåg Norway
101 F1 Berlin Ger.
141 E2 Berlin U.S.A.
101 E2 Berlingerode Ger.
53 D3 Bermagui Austr.
144 B2 Bermejillo Mex.
152 B3 Bermejo Bol.
131 D1 Bermen, Lac *l.* Can.
125 K4 Bermuda *terr.* N. Atlantic Ocean
105 D2 Bern Switz.
101 E2 Bernburg (Saale) Ger.
127 F2 Bernier Bay Can.
101 E2 Bernkastel-Kues Ger.
121 □D3 Beroroha Madag.
52 B2 Berri Austr.
107 D2 Berrouaghia Alg.
146 C2 Berry Islands Bahamas
100 C1 Bersenbrück Ger.
90 B2 Bershad' Ukr.
131 D1 Berté, Lac *l.* Can.
118 B2 Bertoua Cameroon
150 B2 Beruri Brazil
98 B1 Berwick-upon-Tweed U.K.
91 C2 Beryslav Ukr.
121 □D2 Besalampy Madag.
105 D2 Besançon France
129 D2 Besnard Lake Can.
142 C2 Bessemer U.S.A.
76 B2 Besshoky, Gora *hill* Kazakh.
106 B1 Betanzos Spain
118 B2 Bétaré Oya Cameroon
122 A2 Bethanie Namibia
123 C2 Bethlehem S. Africa
141 D2 Bethlehem U.S.A.
121 □D2 Betioky Madag.
77 D2 Betpak-Dala *plain* Kazakh.
121 □D3 Betroka Madag.
131 D2 Betsiamites Can.
121 □D2 Betsiboka *r.* Madag.
137 E2 Bettendorf U.S.A.
75 C2 Bettiah India
75 B2 Betul India
74 B2 Betwa *r.* India
98 B2 Betws-y-coed U.K.
98 C2 Beverley U.K.
101 D2 Beverungen Ger.
100 B1 Beverwijk Neth.
99 D3 Bexhill U.K.
111 C2 Beykoz Turkey
114 B4 Beyla Guinea
76 B2 Beyneu Kazakh.
80 B1 Beypazarı Turkey
Beyrouth Lebanon *see* Beirut
80 B2 Beyşehir Turkey
80 B2 Beyşehir Gölü *l.* Turkey
91 D2 Beysug *r.* Rus. Fed.
88 C2 Bezhanitsy Rus. Fed.
89 E2 Bezhetsk Rus. Fed.
105 C3 Béziers France
75 C2 Bhadrak India
73 B3 Bhadravati India
75 C2 Bhagalpur India
74 B1 Bhairi Hol *mt.* Pak.
74 B1 Bhakkar Pak.
62 A1 Bhamo Myanmar
75 C3 Bhanjanagar India
74 B2 Bharatpur India
74 B2 Bharuch India
74 B2 Bhavnagar India
75 C3 Bhawanipatna India

123 D2 Bhekuzulu S. Africa
123 C3 Bhisho S. Africa
74 B2 Bhilwara India
73 B3 Bhima *r.* India
74 B2 Bhiwani India
123 C3 Bhongweni S. Africa
75 C2 Bhubaneshwar India
74 A2 Bhuj India
62 A2 Bhumiphol Dam Thai.
74 B2 Bhusawal India
75 D2 Bhutan *country* Asia
62 B2 Bia, Phou *mt.* Laos
59 D3 Biak Indon.
59 D3 Biak *i.* Indon.
103 E1 Biała Podlaska Pol.
103 D1 Białogard Pol.
103 E1 Białystok Pol.
109 C3 Bianco Italy
104 B3 Biarritz France
105 D2 Biasca Switz.
66 D2 Bibai Japan
120 A2 Bibala Angola
102 B2 Biberach an der Riß Ger.
129 C2 Bic, Île du *i.* Can.
115 C4 Bida Nigeria
141 E2 Biddeford U.S.A.
99 A3 Bideford U.K.
101 D2 Biedenkopf Ger.
105 D2 Biel Switz.
101 D1 Bielefeld Ger.
108 A1 Biella Italy
103 D1 Bielsko-Biała Pol.
63 B2 Biên Hoa Vietnam
130 C1 Bienville, Lac *l.* Can.
100 B3 Bièvre Belgium
118 B3 Bifoun Gabon
111 C2 Biga Turkey
123 D2 Big Bend Swaziland
129 D2 Biggar Can.
96 C3 Biggar U.K.
134 D1 Big Hole *r.* U.S.A.
136 B1 Bighorn *r.* U.S.A.
136 B2 Bighorn Mountains U.S.A.
139 C2 Big Lake U.S.A.
140 B2 Big Rapids U.S.A.
129 D2 Big River Can.
129 E2 Big Sand Lake Can.
137 D2 Big Sioux *r.* U.S.A.
139 C2 Big Spring U.S.A.
134 E1 Big Timber U.S.A.
130 B1 Big Trout Lake Can.
130 A1 Big Trout Lake Can.
109 C2 Bihać Bos.-Herz.
75 C2 Bihar Sharif India
110 B1 Bihor, Vârful *mt.* Romania
114 A3 Bijagós, Arquipélago dos *is* Guinea-Bissau
81 C2 Bijär Iran
109 C2 Bijeljina Bos.-Herz.
109 C2 Bijelo Polje Serb. and Mont.
71 A3 Bijie China
74 B2 Bikaner India
69 E1 Bikin Rus. Fed.
118 B3 Bikoro Dem. Rep. Congo
79 C2 Bilād Banī Bū 'Alī Oman
75 C2 Bilaspur India
90 C2 Bila Tserkva Ukr.
63 A2 Bilauktaung Range *mts* Myanmar/Thai.
106 C1 Bilbao Spain
111 C2 Bilecik Turkey
103 E1 Biłgoraj Pol.
90 C2 Bilhorod-Dnistrovs'kyy Ukr.
119 C2 Bili Dem. Rep. Congo
83 M2 Bilibino Rus. Fed.
134 E1 Billings U.S.A.
99 B3 Bill of Portland *hd* U.K.

115 D3	Bilma Niger	
51 E2	Biloela Austr.	
91 C2	Bilohirs'k Ukr.	
90 B1	Bilohir"ya Ukr.	
91 C1	Bilopillya Ukr.	
91 D2	Bilovods'k Ukr.	
142 C2	Biloxi U.S.A.	
51 C2	Bilpa Morea Claypan salt flat Austr.	
101 C2	Bilshausen Ger.	
115 E3	Biltine Chad	
91 C2	Bilyayivka Ukr.	
143 E3	Bimini Islands Bahamas	
75 B2	Bina-Etawa India	
59 C3	Binaija, Gunung mt. Indon.	
118 B3	Bindu Dem. Rep. Congo	
121 C2	Bindura Zimbabwe	
107 D1	Binefar Spain	
53 D1	Bingara Austr.	
100 C3	Bingen am Rhein Ger.	
141 F1	Bingham U.S.A.	
141 D2	Binghamton U.S.A.	
81 C2	Bingöl Turkey	
60 A1	Binjai Indon.	
60 B2	Bintuhan Indon.	
61 C1	Bintulu Sarawak Malaysia	
70 B2	Binzhou China	
118 A2	Bioco i. Equat. Guinea	
109 C2	Biograd na Moru Croatia	
118 C1	Birao C.A.R.	
75 C2	Biratnagar Nepal	
128 C2	Birch Mountains Can.	
51 C2	Birdsville Austr.	
80 B2	Birecik Turkey	
60 A1	Bireun Indon.	
75 C2	Birganj Nepal	
117 B3	Birhan mt. Eth.	
154 B2	Birigüi Brazil	
76 B3	Birjand Iran	
98 B2	Birkenhead U.K.	
99 C2	Birmingham U.K.	
142 C2	Birmingham U.S.A.	
114 A4	Bir Mogreïn Maur.	
115 C3	Birnin-Kebbi Nigeria	
115 C3	Birnin Konni Niger	
69 E1	Birobidzhan Rus. Fed.	
97 C2	Birr Ireland	
96 C1	Birsay U.K.	
78 A2	Bi'r Shalatayn Egypt	
88 B2	Biržai Lith.	
75 B2	Bisalpur India	
138 B2	Bisbee U.S.A.	
104 A2	Biscay, Bay of sea France/Spain	
102 C2	Bischofshofen Austria	
130 B2	Biscotasi Lake Can.	
77 D2	Bishkek Kyrg.	
135 C3	Bishop U.S.A.	
69 E1	Bishui China	
150 B1	Bisinaca Col.	
115 C1	Biskra Alg.	
136 C1	Bismarck U.S.A.	
48 D3	Bismarck Sea P.N.G.	
107 C1	Bissa, Djebel mt. Alg.	
114 A3	Bissau Guinea-Bissau	
129 E2	Bissett Can.	
128 C2	Bistcho Lake Can.	
110 B1	Bistrița Romania	
110 C1	Bistrița r. Romania	
100 C3	Bitburg Ger.	
105 D2	Bitche France	
115 D3	Bitkine Chad	
109 C2	Bitola Macedonia	
109 C2	Bitonto Italy	
122 A3	Bitterfontein S. Africa	
134 D1	Bitterroot r. U.S.A.	
134 D1	Bitterroot Range mts U.S.A.	
91 D2	Bityug r. Rus. Fed.	
115 D3	Biu Nigeria	
67 C3	Biwa-ko l. Japan	
68 B1	Biysk Rus. Fed.	
115 C1	Bizerte Tunisia	
92 □A2	Bjargtangar hd Iceland	
92 G3	Bjästa Sweden	
92 G2	Bjerkvik Norway	
82 C2	Bjørnøya i. Arctic Ocean	
114 B3	Bla Mali	
137 E3	Black r. U.S.A.	
51 D2	Blackall Austr.	
98 B2	Blackburn U.K.	
134 D2	Blackfoot U.S.A.	
102 B2	Black Forest mts Ger.	
136 C2	Black Hills U.S.A.	
96 B2	Black Isle pen. U.K.	
129 D2	Black Lake l. Can.	
129 D2	Black Lake Can.	
99 B3	Black Mountains hills U.K.	
98 B2	Blackpool U.K.	
62 B1	Black River r. Vietnam	
140 A2	Black River Falls U.S.A.	
140 C3	Blacksburg U.S.A.	
80 B1	Black Sea Asia/Europe	
97 A1	Blacksod Bay Ireland	
97 C2	Blackstairs Mountains hills Ireland	
114 B4	Black Volta r. Africa	
97 C2	Blackwater r. Ireland	
128 B1	Blackwater Lake Can.	
50 A3	Blackwood r. Austr.	
76 A2	Blagodarnyy Rus. Fed.	
110 B2	Blagoevgrad Bulg.	
69 E1	Blagoveshchensk Rus. Fed.	
129 D2	Blaine Lake Can.	
137 D2	Blair U.S.A.	
96 C2	Blair Atholl U.K.	
96 C2	Blairgowrie U.K.	
143 D2	Blakely U.S.A.	
153 B4	Blanca, Bahía b. Arg.	
52 A1	Blanche, Lake salt flat Austr.	
152 B2	Blanco r. Bol.	
131 E1	Blanc-Sablon Can.	
92 □A2	Blanda r. Iceland	
99 B3	Blandford Forum U.K.	
135 E3	Blanding U.S.A.	
107 D1	Blanes Spain	
60 A1	Blangkejeren Indon.	
100 C2	Blankenheim Ger.	
100 C2	Blankenrath Ger.	
103 D2	Blansko Czech Rep.	
121 C2	Blantyre Malawi	
98 C1	Blaydon U.K.	
53 C2	Blayney Austr.	
54 B2	Blenheim N.Z.	
115 C1	Blida Alg.	
130 B2	Blind River Can.	
123 C2	Bloemfontein S. Africa	
123 C2	Bloemhof S. Africa	
123 C2	Bloemhof Dam S. Africa	
92 □A2	Blönduós Iceland	
97 B1	Bloody Foreland pt Ireland	
138 B1	Bloomfield U.S.A.	
140 B3	Bloomington IL U.S.A.	
140 B3	Bloomington IN U.S.A.	
140 C3	Bluefield U.S.A.	
146 B3	Bluefields Nic.	
53 C2	Blue Mountains Austr.	
134 C1	Blue Mountains U.S.A.	
116 B3	Blue Nile r. Eth./Sudan	
126 D2	Bluenose Lake Can.	
140 C3	Blue Ridge mts U.S.A.	
97 B1	Blue Stack Mountains hills Ireland	
54 A3	Bluff N.Z.	
135 E3	Bluff U.S.A.	
152 D3	Blumenau Brazil	
52 A2	Blyth Austr.	
98 C1	Blyth U.K.	
135 D4	Blythe U.S.A.	
142 C1	Blytheville U.S.A.	
114 A4	Bo Sierra Leone	
64 B1	Boac Phil.	
151 D2	Boa Esperança, Açude resr Brazil	
150 B1	Boa Vista Brazil	
53 C2	Bobadah Austr.	
71 B3	Bobai China	
121 □D2	Bobaomby, Tanjona c. Madag.	
114 B3	Bobo-Dioulasso Burkina	
91 C1	Bobrov Rus. Fed.	
91 C1	Bobrovytsya Ukr.	
91 C2	Bobrynets' Ukr.	
121 □D3	Boby mt. Madag.	
150 B2	Boca do Acre Brazil	
155 D1	Bocaiúva Brazil	
118 B2	Bocaranga C.A.R.	
103 E2	Bochnia Pol.	
100 C2	Bocholt Ger.	
100 C2	Bochum Ger.	
123 C1	Bochum S. Africa	
101 E1	Bockenem Ger.	
118 B2	Boda C.A.R.	
83 I3	Bodaybo Rus. Fed.	
115 D3	Bodélé reg. Chad	
92 H2	Boden Sweden	
99 A3	Bodmin U.K.	
99 A3	Bodmin Moor moorland U.K.	
92 F2	Bodø Norway	
111 C3	Bodrum Turkey	
118 C3	Boende Dem. Rep. Congo	
142 C2	Bogalusa U.S.A.	
114 B3	Bogandé Burkina	
68 B2	Bogda Shan mts China	
53 D1	Boggabilla Austr.	
97 B2	Boggeragh Mountains hills Ireland	
100 B3	Bogny-sur-Meuse France	
97 C2	Bog of Allen reg. Ireland	
53 C3	Bogong, Mount Austr.	
60 B2	Bogor Indon.	
89 E3	Bogoroditsk Rus. Fed.	
89 F2	Bogorodsk Rus. Fed.	
150 A1	Bogotá Col.	
82 G3	Bogotol Rus. Fed.	
83 H3	Boguchany Rus. Fed.	
91 E2	Boguchar Rus. Fed.	
70 B2	Bo Hai g. China	
100 A3	Bohain-en-Vermandois France	
70 B2	Bohai Wan b. China	
123 C2	Bohlokong S. Africa	
102 C2	Böhmer Wald mts Ger.	
91 D1	Bohodukhiv Ukr.	
64 B2	Bohol i. Phil.	
64 B2	Bohol Sea Phil.	
68 B2	Bohu China	
155 C2	Boi, Ponta do pt Brazil	
154 B1	Bois r. Brazil	
126 C2	Bois, Lac des l. Can.	
134 C2	Boise U.S.A.	
139 C1	Boise City U.S.A.	
123 C2	Boitumelong S. Africa	
101 E1	Boizenburg Ger.	
76 B2	Bojnürd Iran	
118 B3	Bokatola Dem. Rep. Congo	
114 A3	Boké Guinea	
118 C3	Bokele Dem. Rep. Congo	
93 E4	Boknafjorden sea chan. Norway	
115 D3	Bokoro Chad	
63 A2	Bokpyin Myanmar	
89 D2	Boksitogorsk Rus. Fed.	
122 B2	Bokspits S. Africa	
114 A3	Bolama Guinea-Bissau	
75 C2	Bolangir India	
104 C2	Bolbec France	
77 E2	Bole China	
118 B3	Boleko Dem. Rep. Congo	
114 B3	Bolgatanga Ghana	

90 B2	**Bolhrad** Ukr.	
66 B1	**Boli** China	
110 C2	**Bolintin-Vale** Romania	
137 E3	**Bolivar** U.S.A.	
150 A1	**Bolívar, Pico** mt. Venez.	
152 B2	**Bolivia** country S. America	
89 E3	**Bolkhov** Rus. Fed.	
105 C3	**Bolkhne** France	
93 G3	**Bolnäs** Sweden	
53 C1	**Bolo, Mount** Austr.	
101 E2	**Bollstedt** Ger.	
93 F4	**Bolmen** l. Sweden	
118 C3	**Bolobo** Dem. Rep. Congo	
108 B2	**Bologna** Italy	
89 D2	**Bologovo** Rus. Fed.	
89 D2	**Bologoye** Rus. Fed.	
118 B3	**Bolomba** Dem. Rep. Congo	
63 B2	**Bolovens, Phouphieng** plat. Laos	
83 H1	**Bol'shevik, Ostrov** i. Rus. Fed.	
86 E2	**Bol'shezemel'skaya Tundra** lowland Rus. Fed.	
83 L2	**Bol'shoy Aluy** r. Rus. Fed.	
66 B2	**Bol'shoy Kamen'** Rus. Fed.	
	Bol'shoy Kavkaz mts Asia/Europe see **Caucasus**	
83 K2	**Bol'shoy Lyakhovskiy, Ostrov** i. Rus. Fed.	
100 B1	**Bolsward** Neth.	
98 B2	**Bolton** U.K.	
80 B1	**Bolu** Turkey	
92 □A2	**Bolungarvik** Iceland	
108 B1	**Bolzano** Italy	
118 B3	**Boma** Dem. Rep. Congo	
53 D2	**Bomaderry** Austr.	
53 C3	**Bombala** Austr.	
	Bombay India see **Mumbai**	
155 C1	**Bom Despacho** Brazil	
75 D2	**Bomdila** India	
151 D3	**Bom Jesus da Lapa** Brazil	
155 D2	**Bom Jesus do Itabapoana** Brazil	
115 C2	**Bon, Cap** c. Tunisia	
147 D3	**Bonaire** i. Neth. Antilles	
50 E1	**Bonaparte Archipelago** is Austr.	
131 E2	**Bonavista** Can.	
131 E2	**Bonavista Bay** Can.	
118 C2	**Bondo** Dem. Rep. Congo	
114 B4	**Bondoukou** Côte d'Ivoire	
58 C3	**Bonerate, Kepulauan** is Indon.	
155 C1	**Bonfinópolis de Minas** Brazil	
117 B4	**Bonga** Eth.	
75 D2	**Bongaigaon** India	
118 C2	**Bongandanga** Dem. Rep. Congo	
118 C2	**Bongo, Massif des** mts C.A.R.	
115 C2	**Bongor** Chad	
114 B4	**Bongouanou** Côte d'Ivoire	
63 B2	**Bông Son** Vietnam	
139 D2	**Bonham** U.S.A.	
105 D3	**Bonifacio** Corsica France	
108 A2	**Bonifacio, Strait of** France/Italy	
100 C2	**Bonn** Ger.	
134 C1	**Bonners Ferry** U.S.A.	
50 A3	**Bonnie Rock** Austr.	
129 C2	**Bonnyville** Can.	
108 A2	**Bonorva** Sardinia Italy	
61 C1	**Bontang** Indon.	
64 B1	**Bontoc** Phil.	
58 B3	**Bontosunggu** Indon.	
123 C3	**Bontrug** S. Africa	
52 B2	**Booligal** Austr.	
53 C1	**Boomi** Austr.	
53 D1	**Boonah** Austr.	
137 E2	**Boone** U.S.A.	
142 C2	**Booneville** U.S.A.	
137 E3	**Boonville** U.S.A.	
53 C2	**Boorowa** Austr.	
126 F2	**Boothia, Gulf of** Can.	
126 E2	**Boothia Peninsula** Can.	
100 C2	**Boppard** Ger.	
144 B2	**Boquilla, Presa de la** resr Mex.	
117 B4	**Bor** Sudan	
80 B2	**Bor** Turkey	
109 D2	**Bor** Serb. and Mont.	
121 □E2	**Boraha, Nosy** i. Madag.	
93 F4	**Borås** Sweden	
79 C2	**Borāzjān** Iran	
150 C2	**Borba** Brazil	
104 B3	**Bordeaux** France	
127 F2	**Borden Peninsula** Can.	
52 B3	**Bordertown** Austr.	
107 D2	**Bordj Bou Arréridj** Alg.	
107 D2	**Bordj Bounaama** Alg.	
115 C2	**Bordj Messaouda** Alg.	
115 C2	**Bordj Omer Driss** Alg.	
94 B1	**Borðoy** i. Faroe Is	
92 □A3	**Borgarnes** Iceland	
108 A1	**Borgosesia** Italy	
87 D3	**Borisoglebsk** Rus. Fed.	
89 E2	**Borisoglebskiy** Rus. Fed.	
91 D1	**Borisovka** Rus. Fed.	
100 C2	**Borken** Ger.	
92 G2	**Borkenes** Norway	
100 C1	**Borkum** Ger.	
100 C1	**Borkum** i. Ger.	
93 G3	**Borlänge** Sweden	
101 F2	**Borna** Ger.	
61 C1	**Borneo** i. Asia	
93 F4	**Bornholm** i. Denmark	
111 C3	**Bornova** Turkey	
90 B1	**Borodyanka** Ukr.	
89 D2	**Borovichi** Rus. Fed.	
89 E2	**Borovsk** Rus. Fed.	
51 C1	**Borroloola** Austr.	
110 B1	**Borşa** Romania	
90 B2	**Borshchiv** Ukr.	
69 D1	**Borshchovochnyy Khrebet** mts Rus. Fed.	
101 E1	**Börßum** Ger.	
	Bortala China see **Bole**	
81 C2	**Borüjerd** Iran	
90 A2	**Boryslav** Ukr.	
90 C1	**Boryspil'** Ukr.	
91 C1	**Borzna** Ukr.	
69 D1	**Borzya** Rus. Fed.	
109 C1	**Bosanska Dubica** Bos.-Herz.	
109 C1	**Bosanska Gradiška** Bos.-Herz.	
109 C1	**Bosanska Krupa** Bos.-Herz.	
109 C1	**Bosanski Novi** Bos.-Herz.	
109 C2	**Bosansko Grahovo** Bos.-Herz.	
71 A3	**Bose** China	
123 C3	**Boshof** S. Africa	
109 C2	**Bosnia-Herzegovina** country Europe	
118 B3	**Bosobolo** Dem. Rep. Congo	
110 C2	**Bosporus** str. Turkey	
118 B2	**Bossangoa** C.A.R.	
118 B2	**Bossembélé** C.A.R.	
68 B2	**Bosten Hu** l. China	
98 C2	**Boston** U.K.	
141 E2	**Boston** U.S.A.	
142 B1	**Boston Mountains** U.S.A.	
53 D2	**Botany Bay** Austr.	
110 B2	**Botev** mt. Bulg.	
93 G3	**Bothnia, Gulf of** Fin./Sweden	
110 C1	**Botoşani** Romania	
123 C2	**Botshabelo** S. Africa	
120 B3	**Botswana** country Africa	
109 C3	**Botte Donato, Monte** mt. Italy	
136 C1	**Bottineau** U.S.A.	
100 C2	**Bottrop** Ger.	
154 C2	**Botucatu** Brazil	
114 B4	**Bouaké** Côte d'Ivoire	
118 B2	**Bouar** C.A.R.	
114 B1	**Bouârfa** Morocco	
131 D2	**Bouctouche** Can.	
107 E2	**Bougaa** Alg.	
114 B3	**Bougouni** Mali	
100 B3	**Bouillon** Belgium	
107 D2	**Bouira** Alg.	
114 A2	**Boujdour** Western Sahara	
136 B2	**Boulder** U.S.A.	
135 D3	**Boulder City** U.S.A.	
51 C2	**Boulia** Austr.	
104 C2	**Boulogne-Billancourt** France	
99 D3	**Boulogne-sur-Mer** France	
118 B3	**Boumango** Gabon	
118 B2	**Boumba** r. Cameroon	
107 D2	**Boumerdes** Alg.	
114 B4	**Bouna** Côte d'Ivoire	
114 B4	**Boundiali** Côte d'Ivoire	
134 D2	**Bountiful** U.S.A.	
114 B3	**Bourem** Mali	
104 C2	**Bourganeuf** France	
105 D2	**Bourg-en-Bresse** France	
104 C2	**Bourges** France	
53 C2	**Bourke** Austr.	
99 C3	**Bournemouth** U.K.	
115 C1	**Bou Saâda** Alg.	
115 D3	**Bousso** Chad	
114 A3	**Boutilimit** Maur.	
129 C3	**Bow** r. Can.	
51 D2	**Bowen** Austr.	
129 C3	**Bow Island** Can.	
140 B3	**Bowling Green** KY U.S.A.	
140 C2	**Bowling Green** OH U.S.A.	
136 C1	**Bowman** U.S.A.	
101 D3	**Boxberg** Ger.	
100 B2	**Boxtel** Neth.	
80 B1	**Boyabat** Turkey	
71 B3	**Boyang** China	
97 B2	**Boyle** Ireland	
97 C2	**Boyne** r. Ireland	
136 B2	**Boysen Reservoir** U.S.A.	
152 B3	**Boyuibe** Bol.	
111 C3	**Bozburun** Turkey	
111 C3	**Bozcaada** i. Turkey	
111 C3	**Bozdağ** mt. Turkey	
111 C3	**Boz Dağları** mts Turkey	
111 C3	**Bozdoğan** Turkey	
134 D1	**Bozeman** U.S.A.	
118 B2	**Bozoum** C.A.R.	
111 D3	**Bozüyük** Turkey	
109 C2	**Brač** i. Croatia	
130 C2	**Bracebridge** Can.	
131 D2	**Brachet, Lac au** l. Can.	
99 C3	**Bracknell** U.K.	
109 C2	**Bradano** r. Italy	
143 D3	**Bradenton** U.S.A.	
147 D3	**Brades** Montserrat	
98 C2	**Bradford** U.K.	
141 D2	**Bradford** U.S.A.	
139 D2	**Brady** U.S.A.	
96 C2	**Braemar** U.K.	
106 B1	**Braga** Port.	
151 D2	**Bragança** Brazil	
106 B1	**Bragança** Port.	
155 C2	**Bragança Paulista** Brazil	
89 D3	**Brahin** Belarus	
73 C3	**Brahmapur** India	
62 A1	**Brahmaputra** r. China/India	
110 C1	**Brăila** Romania	
137 E1	**Brainerd** U.S.A.	
99 D3	**Braintree** U.K.	
100 B2	**Braives** Belgium	

101 D1 Brake (Unterweser) Ger.
100 D1 Bramsche Ger.
150 B2 Branco r. Brazil
101 F1 Brandenburg Ger.
129 E3 Brandon Can.
97 A2 Brandon Mountain hill Ireland
122 B3 Brandvlei S. Africa
103 D1 Braniewo Pol.
130 B2 Brantford Can.
131 D2 Bras d'Or Lake Can.
155 D1 Brasil, Planalto do plat. Brazil
154 C1 Brasilândia Brazil
154 C1 Brasília Brazil
155 D1 Brasília de Minas Brazil
88 C2 Braslaw Belarus
110 C1 Braşov Romania
103 D2 Bratislava Slovakia
83 H3 Bratsk Rus. Fed.
102 C2 Braunau am Inn Austria
101 E1 Braunschweig Ger.
92 ☐A2 Brautarholt Iceland
Bravo del Norte, Río r. Mex./U.S.A. see Rio Grande
135 C4 Brawley U.S.A.
97 C2 Bray Ireland
150 C2 Brazil country S. America
139 D3 Brazos r. U.S.A.
118 B3 Brazzaville Congo
109 C2 Brčko Bos.-Herz.
96 C2 Brechin U.K.
100 B2 Brecht Belgium
139 D2 Breckenridge U.S.A.
103 D2 Břeclav Czech Rep.
99 B3 Brecon U.K.
99 B3 Brecon Beacons reg. U.K.
100 B2 Breda Neth.
122 B3 Bredasdorp S. Africa
102 B2 Bregenz Austria
92 H1 Breivikbotn Norway
92 E3 Brekstad Norway
101 D1 Bremen Ger.
134 B1 Bremerton U.S.A.
101 D1 Bremervörde Ger.
139 D2 Brenham U.S.A.
108 B1 Brennero Italy
102 C2 Brenner Pass Austria/Italy
99 D3 Brentwood U.K.
108 B1 Brescia Italy
108 B1 Bressanone Italy
96 ☐1 Bressay i. U.K.
104 B2 Bressuire France
88 B3 Brest Belarus
104 B2 Brest France
142 C3 Breton Sound b. U.S.A.
151 C2 Breves Brazil
53 C1 Brewarrina Austr.
134 C1 Brewster U.S.A.
81 E2 Breytovo Rus. Fed.
109 C1 Brezovo Polje hill Croatia
118 C2 Bria C.A.R.
105 D3 Briançon France
90 B2 Briceni Moldova
99 B3 Bridgend U.K.
141 E2 Bridgeport CT U.S.A.
136 C2 Bridgeport NE U.S.A.
147 E3 Bridgetown Barbados
131 D2 Bridgewater Can.
99 B3 Bridgwater U.K.
98 C1 Bridlington U.K.
98 C1 Bridlington Bay U.K.
105 D2 Brig Switz.
134 D2 Brigham City U.S.A.
54 B3 Brighton N.Z.
99 C3 Brighton U.K.
105 D3 Brignoles France
101 D2 Brilon Ger.
109 C2 Brindisi Italy

53 D1 Brisbane Austr.
99 B3 Bristol U.K.
143 D1 Bristol U.S.A.
99 A3 Bristol Channel est. U.K.
128 B2 British Columbia prov. Can.
56 G7 British Indian Ocean Territory terr. Indian Ocean
123 C2 Brits S. Africa
122 B3 Britstown S. Africa
104 C2 Brive-la-Gaillarde France
106 C1 Briviesca Spain
103 D2 Brno Czech Rep.
143 D2 Broad r. U.S.A.
130 C1 Broadback r. Can.
96 C3 Broad Law hill U.K.
136 B1 Broadus U.S.A.
129 D2 Brochet Can.
129 D2 Brochet, Lac l. Can.
101 E1 Bröckel Ger.
126 D1 Brock Island Can.
130 C2 Brockville Can.
127 F2 Brodeur Peninsula Can.
96 B3 Brodick U.K.
103 D1 Brodnica Pol.
90 B1 Brody Ukr.
139 D1 Broken Arrow U.S.A.
137 D2 Broken Bow U.S.A.
52 B2 Broken Hill Austr.
93 E4 Brønderslev Denmark
92 F2 Brønnøysund Norway
64 A2 Brooke's Point Phil.
142 B2 Brookhaven U.S.A.
134 B2 Brookings OR U.S.A.
137 D2 Brookings SD U.S.A.
129 C2 Brooks Can.
126 B2 Brooks Range mts U.S.A.
143 D3 Brooksville U.S.A.
96 B2 Broom, Loch inlet U.K.
50 B1 Broome Austr.
134 B2 Brothers U.S.A.
Broughton Island Can. see Qikiqtarjuaq
90 C1 Brovary Ukr.
139 C2 Brownfield U.S.A.
128 C3 Browning U.S.A.
142 C1 Brownsville TN U.S.A.
139 D3 Brownsville TX U.S.A.
139 D2 Brownwood U.S.A.
92 ☐A2 Brú Iceland
104 C1 Bruay-la-Buissière France
140 B1 Bruce Crossing U.S.A.
103 D2 Bruck an der Mur Austria
Bruges Belgium see Brugge
100 A2 Brugge Belgium
128 C2 Brûlé Can.
151 D3 Brumado Brazil
93 F3 Brumunddal Norway
61 C1 Brunei country Asia
108 B1 Brunico Italy
101 D1 Brunsbüttel Ger.
143 D2 Brunswick GA U.S.A.
141 F2 Brunswick ME U.S.A.
53 D1 Brunswick Heads Austr.
136 C2 Brush U.S.A.
100 B2 Brussels Belgium
Bruxelles Belgium see Brussels
139 D2 Bryan U.S.A.
89 D3 Bryansk Rus. Fed.
91 D2 Bryn'kovskaya Rus. Fed.
91 D2 Bryukhovetskaya Rus. Fed.
103 D1 Brzeg Pol.
114 A3 Buba Guinea-Bissau
80 B2 Bucak Turkey
150 A1 Bucaramanga Col.
53 C3 Buchan Austr.
114 A4 Buchanan Liberia
110 C2 Bucharest Romania

101 D1 Bucholz in der Nordheide Ger.
110 C1 Bucin, Pasul pass Romania
101 D1 Bückeburg Ger.
138 A2 Buckeye U.S.A.
96 C2 Buckhaven U.K.
96 C2 Buckie U.K.
51 C1 Buckingham Bay Austr.
51 D2 Buckland Tableland reg. Austr.
52 A2 Buckleboo Austr.
141 F2 Bucksport U.S.A.
Bucureşti Romania see Bucharest
89 D3 Buda-Kashalyova Belarus
103 D2 Budapest Hungary
75 B2 Budaun India
108 A2 Buddusò Sardinia Italy
99 A3 Bude U.K.
87 D4 Budennovsk Rus. Fed.
89 D2 Bodogoshch' Rus. Fed.
108 A2 Budoni Sardinia Italy
118 A2 Buea Cameroon
144 B2 Buenaventura Mex.
106 C1 Buendia, Embalse de resr Spain
155 D1 Buenópolis Brazil
153 C4 Buenos Aires Arg.
153 A5 Buenos Aires, Lago l. Arg./Chile
141 D2 Buffalo NY U.S.A.
136 C1 Buffalo SD U.S.A.
136 B2 Buffalo WY U.S.A.
129 D2 Buffalo Narrows Can.
122 A2 Buffels watercourse S. Africa
110 C2 Buftea Romania
103 E1 Bug r. Pol.
61 C2 Bugel, Tanjung pt Indon.
109 C2 Bugojno Bos.-Herz.
64 A2 Bugsuk i. Phil.
87 E3 Buguruslan Rus. Fed.
110 C1 Buhuşi Romania
99 B2 Builth Wells U.K.
69 D1 Buir Nur l. Mongolia
120 A3 Buitepos Namibia
109 D2 Bujanovac Serb. and Mont.
119 C3 Bujumbura Burundi
69 D1 Bukachacha Rus. Fed.
119 C3 Bukavu Dem. Rep. Congo
60 B2 Bukittinggi Indon.
119 D3 Bukoba Tanz.
53 D2 Bulahdelah Austr.
121 B3 Bulawayo Zimbabwe
111 C3 Buldan Turkey
123 D2 Bulembu Swaziland
69 C1 Bulgan Mongolia
110 C2 Bulgaria country Europe
54 B2 Buller r. N.Z.
51 C1 Bulloo Downs Austr.
122 A1 Bülsport Namibia
58 C3 Bukumba Indon.
118 B3 Bulungu Dem. Rep. Congo
118 C3 Bumba Dem. Rep. Congo
62 A1 Bumhkang Myanmar
118 B3 Buna Dem. Rep. Congo
50 A3 Bunbury Austr.
97 C1 Buncrana Ireland
119 D3 Bunda Tanz.
51 E2 Bundaberg Austr.
123 D2 Bundarra Austr.
74 B2 Bundi India
97 B1 Bundoran Ireland
53 C3 Bungendore Austr.
67 B4 Bungo-suidō sea chan. Japan
119 D2 Bunia Dem. Rep. Congo
118 C3 Buniunga Dem. Rep. Congo
63 B2 Buôn Ma Thuột Vietnam
119 D3 Bura Kenya

78	B2	**Buraydah** Saudi Arabia
100	D2	**Burbach** Ger.
117	C4	**Burco** Somalia
100	B1	**Burdaard** Neth.
80	B2	**Burdur** Turkey
117	B3	**Burē** Eth.
99	D2	**Bure** r. U.K.
110	C2	**Burgas** Bulg.
101	E1	**Burg bei Magdeburg** Ger.
101	E1	**Burgdorf** *Niedersachsen* Ger.
101	E1	**Burgdorf** *Niedersachsen* Ger.
131	E2	**Burgeo** Can.
123	D1	**Burgersfort** S. Africa
100	A2	**Burgh-Haamstede** Neth.
145	E2	**Burgos** Mex.
106	C1	**Burgos** Spain
111	C3	**Burhaniye** Turkey
74	B2	**Burhanpur** India
101	D1	**Burhave (Butjadingen)** Ger.
131	E2	**Burin** Can.
151	D2	**Buriti Bravo** Brazil
155	C1	**Buritis** Brazil
51	C1	**Burketown** Austr.
114	B3	**Burkina** *country* Africa
134	D2	**Burley** U.S.A.
136	C3	**Burlington** *CO* U.S.A.
137	E2	**Burlington** *IA* U.S.A.
143	E1	**Burlington** *NC* U.S.A.
141	E2	**Burlington** *VT* U.S.A.
		Burma *country* Asia *see* Myanmar
134	B2	**Burney** U.S.A.
51	D4	**Burnie** Austr.
98	B2	**Burnley** U.K.
134	C2	**Burns** U.S.A.
128	B2	**Burns Lake** Can.
77	E2	**Burqin** China
52	A2	**Burra** Austr.
109	D2	**Burrel** Albania
97	B2	**Burren** *reg.* Ireland
53	C2	**Burrendong, Lake** *resr* Austr.
53	C2	**Burren Junction** Austr.
107	C2	**Burriana** Spain
53	C2	**Burrinjuck Reservoir** Austr.
144	B2	**Burro, Serranías del** *mts* Mex.
111	C2	**Bursa** Turkey
116	B2	**Būr Safājah** Egypt
		Būr Sa'īd Egypt *see* Port Said
130	C1	**Burton, Lac** *l.* Can.
97	B1	**Burtonport** Ireland
99	C2	**Burton upon Trent** U.K.
59	C3	**Buru** *i.* Indon.
119	C3	**Burundi** *country* Africa
119	C3	**Bururi** Burundi
91	C1	**Buryn'** Ukr.
76	B2	**Burynshyk** Kazakh.
99	D2	**Bury St Edmunds** U.K.
118	C3	**Busanga** Dem. Rep. Congo
79	C2	**Būshehr** Iran
119	D3	**Bushenyi** Uganda
118	C2	**Busigina** Dem. Rep. Congo
50	A3	**Busselton** Austr.
139	C2	**Bustamante** Mex.
64	A1	**Busuanga** Phil.
118	C2	**Buta** Dem. Rep. Congo
119	C3	**Butare** Rwanda
123	C2	**Butha-Buthe** Lesotho
140	D2	**Butler** U.S.A.
59	C3	**Buton** *i.* Indon.
134	D1	**Butte** U.S.A.
60	B1	**Butterworth** Malaysia
96	A1	**Butt of Lewis** *hd* U.K.
129	E2	**Button Bay** Can.
64	B2	**Butuan** Phil.
91	E1	**Buturlinovka** Rus. Fed.
75	C2	**Butwal** Nepal
101	D2	**Butzbach** Ger.
117	C4	**Buulobarde** Somalia
117	C5	**Buur Gaabo** Somalia
117	C4	**Buurhabaka** Somalia
76	C3	**Buxoro** Uzbek.
101	D1	**Buxtehude** Ger.
89	F2	**Buy** Rus. Fed.
87	D4	**Buynaksk** Rus. Fed.
111	C3	**Büyükmenderes** *r.* Turkey
110	C1	**Buzău** Romania
121	C2	**Búzi** Moz.
87	E3	**Buzuluk** Rus. Fed.
110	C2	**Byala** Bulg.
88	C3	**Byalynichy** Belarus
88	D3	**Byarezina** *r.* Belarus
88	B3	**Byaroza** Belarus
103	D1	**Bydgoszcz** Pol.
88	C3	**Byerazino** Belarus
88	C2	**Byeshankovichy** Belarus
89	D3	**Bykhaw** Belarus
127	F2	**Bylot Island** Can.
53	D1	**Byrock** Austr.
53	D2	**Byron Bay** Austr.
83	J2	**Bytantay** *r.* Rus. Fed.
103	D1	**Bytom** Pol.
103	D1	**Bytów** Pol.

C

154	B2	**Caarapó** Brazil
64	B1	**Cabanatuan** Phil.
117	C3	**Cabdul Qaadir** Somalia
106	B2	**Cabeza del Buey** Spain
152	B2	**Cabezas** Bol.
150	A1	**Cabimas** Venez.
120	A1	**Cabinda** Angola
118	B3	**Cabinda** *prov.* Angola
155	D2	**Cabo Frio** Brazil
155	D2	**Cabo Frio, Ilha do** *i.* Brazil
130	C2	**Cabonga, Réservoir** *resr* Can.
51	E2	**Caboolture** Austr.
150	A2	**Cabo Pantoja** Peru
144	A1	**Caborca** Mex.
131	D2	**Cabot Strait** Can.
155	D1	**Cabral, Serra de** *mts* Brazil
107	D2	**Cabrera** *i.* Spain
129	D2	**Cabri** Can.
107	C2	**Cabriel** *r.* Spain
152	C3	**Caçador** Brazil
109	D2	**Čačak** Serb. and Mont.
108	A2	**Caccia, Capo** *c.* Sardinia Italy
151	D3	**Cáceres** Brazil
106	B2	**Cáceres** Spain
128	B2	**Cache Creek** Can.
114	A3	**Cacheu** Guinea-Bissau
151	C2	**Cachimbo, Serra do** *hills* Brazil
154	B1	**Cachoeira Alta** Brazil
155	D2	**Cachoeiro de Itapemirim** Brazil
114	A3	**Cacine** Guinea-Bissau
120	A2	**Cacolo** Angola
154	B1	**Caçu** Brazil
103	D2	**Čadca** Slovakia
101	D1	**Cadenberge** Ger.
145	B2	**Cadereyta** Mex.
106	B2	**Cadillac** U.S.A.
106	B2	**Cádiz** Spain
106	B2	**Cádiz, Golfo de** *g.* Spain
128	C2	**Cadotte Lake** Can.
104	B2	**Caen** France
98	A2	**Caernarfon** U.K.
98	A2	**Caernarfon Bay** U.K.
152	B3	**Cafayate** Arg.
64	B2	**Cagayan de Oro** Phil.
64	A2	**Cagayan de Tawi-Tawi** *i.* Phil.
108	A3	**Cagli** Italy
108	A3	**Cagliari** *Sardinia* Italy
108	A3	**Cagliari, Golfo di** *b.* Sardinia Italy
76	B2	**Çagyl** Turkm.
97	B3	**Caha Mountains** *hills* Ireland
97	A3	**Cahermore** Ireland
97	C2	**Cahir** Ireland
97	A3	**Cahirciveen** Ireland
97	C2	**Cahore Point** Ireland
104	C3	**Cahors** France
90	B2	**Cahul** Moldova
121	C2	**Caia** Moz.
151	C3	**Caiabis, Serra dos** *hills* Brazil
120	B2	**Caianda** Angola
154	B1	**Caiapó, Serra de** *mts* Brazil
154	B1	**Caiapônia** Brazil
147	C2	**Caicos Islands** Turks and Caicos Is
96	C2	**Cairngorm Mountains** U.K.
98	A1	**Cairnryan** U.K.
51	D1	**Cairns** Austr.
116	B1	**Cairo** Egypt
98	C2	**Caistor** U.K.
120	A2	**Caiundo** Angola
150	A2	**Cajamarca** Peru
109	C1	**Cakovec** Croatia
123	C3	**Cala** S. Africa
150	B1	**Calabozo** Venez.
110	B2	**Calafat** Romania
153	A6	**Calafate** Arg.
107	C1	**Calahorra** Spain
104	C1	**Calais** France
141	F1	**Calais** U.S.A.
152	B3	**Calama** Chile
64	A1	**Calamian Group** *is* Phil.
107	C1	**Calamocha** Spain
120	A1	**Calandula** Angola
60	A1	**Calang** Indon.
115	E1	**Calanscio Sand Sea** *des.* Libya
64	B1	**Calapan** Phil.
110	C2	**Călăraşi** Romania
107	C1	**Calatayud** Spain
64	B1	**Calayan** *i.* Phil.
64	B1	**Calbayog** Phil.
151	E2	**Calcanhar, Ponta do** *pt* Brazil
151	C1	**Calçoene** Brazil
		Calcutta India *see* Kolkata
106	B2	**Caldas da Rainha** Port.
154	C1	**Caldas Novas** Brazil
152	A3	**Caldera** Chile
134	C2	**Caldwell** U.S.A.
123	C3	**Caledon** *r.* Lesotho/S. Africa
122	A3	**Caledon** S. Africa
153	B5	**Caleta Olivia** Arg.
98	A1	**Calf of Man** *i.* Isle of Man
128	C2	**Calgary** Can.
150	A1	**Cali** Col.
73	B3	**Calicut** India
135	D3	**Caliente** U.S.A.
135	B3	**California** *state* U.S.A.
144	A1	**California, Gulf of** Mex.
135	B3	**California Aqueduct** *canal* U.S.A.
122	B3	**Calitzdorp** S. Africa
145	C2	**Calkiní** Mex.
52	B1	**Callabonna, Lake** *salt flat* Austr.
96	B2	**Callander** U.K.
150	A3	**Callao** Peru
108	B3	**Caltagirone** *Sicily* Italy
108	B3	**Caltanissetta** *Sicily* Italy

Caluquembe

120 A2	Caluquembe Angola	
117 D3	Caluula Somalia	
105 D3	Calvi Corsica France	
107 D2	Calvià Spain	
144 B2	Calvillo Mex.	
122 A3	Calvinia S. Africa	
109 C2	Calvo, Monte mt. Italy	
144 B2	Camacho Mex.	
120 A2	Camacupa Angola	
146 C2	Camagüey Cuba	
150 A3	Camana Peru	
154 B1	Camapuã Brazil	
145 C2	Camargo Mex.	
63 B3	Ca Mau Vietnam	
63 B3	Cambodia country Asia	
99 A3	Camborne U.K.	
105 C1	Cambrai France	
99 B2	Cambrian Mountains hills U.K.	
54 C1	Cambridge N.Z.	
99 D2	Cambridge U.K.	
141 E2	Cambridge MA U.S.A.	
141 D3	Cambridge MD U.S.A.	
137 E1	Cambridge MN U.S.A.	
140 C2	Cambridge OH U.S.A.	
131 D1	Cambrien, Lac l. Can.	
53 D2	Camden Austr.	
142 B2	Camden AR U.S.A.	
141 F2	Camden ME U.S.A.	
118 B2	Cameroon country Africa	
118 B2	Cameroon Highlands slope Cameroon/Nigeria	
151 D2	Cametá Brazil	
64 B1	Camiguin i. Phil.	
152 B3	Camiri Bol.	
151 D2	Camocim Brazil	
51 C1	Camooweal Austr.	
63 A3	Camorta i. India	
153 A5	Campana, Isla i. Chile	
122 B2	Campbell S. Africa	
54 B2	Campbell, Cape N.Z.	
48 F6	Campbell Island N.Z.	
128 B2	Campbell River Can.	
140 B3	Campbellsville U.S.A.	
128 B2	Campbellton Can.	
96 B3	Campbeltown U.K.	
145 C3	Campeche Mex.	
145 C3	Campeche, Bahía de g. Mex.	
52 B3	Camperdown Austr.	
110 C1	Câmpina Romania	
151 E2	Campina Grande Brazil	
154 C2	Campinas Brazil	
154 C1	Campina Verde Brazil	
108 B2	Campobasso Italy	
155 C2	Campo Belo Brazil	
154 C1	Campo Florido Brazil	
152 B3	Campo Gallo Arg.	
154 B2	Campo Grande Brazil	
151 D2	Campo Maior Brazil	
106 B2	Campo Maior Port.	
154 B2	Campo Mourão Brazil	
155 D2	Campos Brazil	
155 C1	Campos Altos Brazil	
155 C2	Campos do Jordão Brazil	
110 C1	Câmpulung Romania	
138 A2	Camp Verde U.S.A.	
128 C2	Camrose Can.	
129 D2	Camsell Portage Can.	
111 C2	Çan Turkey	
126 F2	Canada country N. America	
139 C1	Canadian U.S.A.	
139 D1	Canadian r. U.S.A.	
111 C2	Çanakkale Turkey	
144 A1	Cananea Mex.	
154 C2	Cananéia Brazil	
	Canarias, Islas terr. N. Atlantic Ocean see Canary Islands	
114 A2	Canary Islands terr. N. Atlantic Ocean	
155 C1	Canastra, Serra da mts Brazil	
144 B2	Canatlán Mex.	
143 D3	Canaveral, Cape U.S.A.	
155 E1	Canavieiras Brazil	
53 C3	Canberra Austr.	
145 D2	Cancún Mex.	
111 C3	Çandarlı Turkey	
145 C3	Candelaria Mex.	
129 D2	Candle Lake Can.	
120 A2	Cangamba Angola	
106 B1	Cangas del Narcea Spain	
152 C4	Canguçu Brazil	
70 B2	Cangzhou China	
131 D1	Caniapiscau Can.	
131 D1	Caniapiscau r. Can.	
131 C1	Caniapiscau, Lac l. Can.	
108 B3	Canicattì Sicily Italy	
151 E2	Canindé Brazil	
144 B2	Cañitas de Felipe Pescador Mex.	
80 B1	Çankırı Turkey	
128 C2	Canmore Can.	
96 A2	Canna i. U.K.	
73 B3	Cannanore India	
105 D3	Cannes France	
99 B2	Cannock U.K.	
53 C3	Cann River Austr.	
152 C3	Canoas Brazil	
129 D2	Canoe Lake Can.	
154 B3	Canoinhas Brazil	
136 B3	Canon City U.S.A.	
129 D2	Canora Can.	
53 C2	Canowindra Austr.	
106 C1	Cantábrica, Cordillera mts Spain	
106 B1	Cantábrico, Mar sea Spain	
99 D3	Canterbury U.K.	
54 B2	Canterbury Bight b. N.Z.	
54 B2	Canterbury Plains N.Z.	
63 B2	Cân Thơ Vietnam	
151 D2	Canto do Buriti Brazil	
	Canton China see Guangzhou	
142 C2	Canton MS U.S.A.	
140 C2	Canton OH U.S.A.	
139 C1	Canyon U.S.A.	
134 D1	Canyon Ferry Lake U.S.A.	
62 B1	Cao Băng Vietnam	
154 C2	Capão Bonito Brazil	
155 D2	Caparaó, Serra do mts Brazil	
51 C4	Cape Barren Island Austr.	
52 A3	Cape Borda Austr.	
131 D2	Cape Breton Island Can.	
114 B4	Cape Coast Ghana	
141 E2	Cape Cod Bay U.S.A.	
127 F2	Cape Dorset Can.	
143 E2	Cape Fear r. U.S.A.	
137 F3	Cape Girardeau U.S.A.	
155 D1	Capelinha Brazil	
100 B2	Capelle aan de IJssel Neth.	
120 A1	Caponda-Camulemba Angola	
122 A3	Cape Town S. Africa	
112 C5	Cape Verde country N. Atlantic Ocean	
51 D1	Cape York Peninsula Austr.	
147 C3	Cap-Haïtien Haiti	
151 D2	Capim r. Brazil	
58 D1	Capitol Hill N. Mariana Is	
109 C2	Capljina Bos.-Herz.	
109 B3	Capo d'Orlando Sicily Italy	
108 A2	Capraia, Isola di i. Italy	
108 A2	Caprara, Punta pt Sardinia Italy	
108 B2	Capri, Isola di i. Italy	
120 B2	Caprivi Strip reg. Namibia	
150 B2	Caquetá r. Col.	
110 B2	Caracal Romania	
150 B1	Caracas Venez.	
151 D2	Caracol Brazil	
155 C2	Caraguatatuba Brazil	
153 A4	Carahue Chile	
155 D1	Caraí Brazil	
155 D2	Carangola Brazil	
110 B1	Caransebeş Romania	
131 D2	Caraquet Can.	
146 B3	Caratasca, Laguna de lag. Hond.	
155 D1	Caratinga Brazil	
150 B2	Carauari Brazil	
107 C2	Caravaca de la Cruz Spain	
155 E1	Caravelas Brazil	
129 E3	Carberry Can.	
144 A2	Carbó Mex.	
108 A3	Carbonara, Capo c. Sardinia Italy	
136 B3	Carbondale CO U.S.A.	
140 B3	Carbondale IL U.S.A.	
131 E2	Carbonear Can.	
155 D1	Carbonita Brazil	
107 C2	Carcaixent Spain	
104 C3	Carcassonne France	
128 A1	Carcross Can.	
145 C3	Cárdenas Mex.	
99 B3	Cardiff U.K.	
99 A2	Cardigan U.K.	
99 A2	Cardigan Bay U.K.	
128 C3	Cardston Can.	
110 B1	Carei Romania	
104 B2	Carentan France	
50 B2	Carey, Lake salt flat Austr.	
155 D2	Cariacica Brazil	
146 B3	Caribbean Sea N. Atlantic Ocean	
141 F1	Caribou U.S.A.	
130 B1	Caribou Lake Can.	
128 C2	Caribou Mountains Can.	
127 G3	Carichíc Mex.	
100 B3	Carignan France	
53 C2	Carinda Austr.	
107 C1	Cariñena Spain	
130 C2	Carleton Place Can.	
123 C2	Carletonville S. Africa	
97 C1	Carlingford Lough inlet Ireland/U.K.	
98 B1	Carlisle U.K.	
141 D2	Carlisle U.S.A.	
155 D1	Carlos Chagas Brazil	
97 C2	Carlow Ireland	
135 C4	Carlsbad CA U.S.A.	
138 C2	Carlsbad NM U.S.A.	
129 D3	Carlyle Can.	
128 A1	Carmacks Can.	
129 E3	Carman Can.	
99 A3	Carmarthen U.K.	
99 A3	Carmarthen Bay U.K.	
104 C3	Carmaux France	
145 C3	Carmelita Guat.	
144 A2	Carmen, Isla i. Mex.	
104 B2	Carnac France	
122 B3	Carnarvon S. Africa	
97 C1	Carndonagh Ireland	
50 B2	Carnegie, Lake salt flat Austr.	
96 B2	Carn Eige mt. U.K.	
63 A3	Car Nicobar i. India	
118 B2	Carnot C.A.R.	
52 A2	Carnot, Cape Austr.	
97 C2	Carnsore Point Ireland	
151 D2	Carolina Brazil	
48 D2	Caroline Islands N. Pacific Ocean	
59 D2	Caroline Islands N. Pacific Ocean	

103 D2 Carpathian Mountains Europe
Carpaţii Meridionali *mts* Romania *see* Transylvanian Alps
51 C1 Carpentaria, Gulf of Austr.
105 D3 Carpentras France
97 B3 Carrantuohill *mt.* Ireland
105 E3 Carrara Italy
97 C2 Carrickmacross Ireland
97 B2 Carrick-on-Shannon Ireland
97 C2 Carrick-on-Suir Ireland
137 D1 Carrington U.S.A.
139 D3 Carrizo Springs U.S.A.
138 B2 Carrizozo U.S.A.
137 E2 Carroll U.S.A.
143 C2 Carrollton U.S.A.
129 C2 Carrot River Can.
135 C3 Carson City U.S.A.
150 A1 Cartagena Col.
107 C2 Cartagena Spain
146 B4 Cartago Costa Rica
137 E3 Carthage *MO* U.S.A.
139 E2 Carthage *TX* U.S.A.
131 E1 Cartwright Can.
151 E2 Caruaru Brazil
114 B1 Casablanca Morocco
154 C2 Casa Branca Brazil
144 B1 Casa de Janos Mex.
138 A2 Casa Grande U.S.A.
108 A1 Casale Monferrato Italy
109 C2 Casarano Italy
134 C2 Cascade U.S.A.
134 B2 Cascade Range *mts* Can./U.S.A.
106 B2 Cascais Port.
154 B2 Cascavel Brazil
108 B2 Caserta Italy
97 C2 Cashel Ireland
53 D1 Casino Austr.
107 C1 Caspe Spain
136 B2 Casper U.S.A.
76 A2 Caspian Lowland Kazakh./Rus. Fed.
81 C1 Caspian Sea Asia/Europe
154 C2 Cássia Brazil
128 B2 Cassiar Can.
128 A2 Cassiar Mountains Can.
154 B1 Cassilândia Brazil
96 B2 Cassley *r.* U.K.
151 D2 Castanhal Brazil
152 B4 Castaño *r.* Arg.
144 B2 Castaños Mex.
104 C3 Casteljaloux France
107 C2 Castellón de la Plana Spain
106 B2 Castelo Branco Port.
108 B3 Castelvetrano *Sicily* Italy
52 B3 Casterton Austr.
108 B2 Castiglione della Pescaia Italy
97 C1 Castlebar Ireland
96 A2 Castlebay U.K.
97 C1 Castleblayney Ireland
97 C1 Castlederg U.K.
96 C3 Castle Douglas U.K.
128 C3 Castlegar Can.
97 B2 Castleisland Ireland
52 B3 Castlemaine Austr.
97 B2 Castlerea Ireland
53 C2 Castlereagh *r.* Austr.
136 C3 Castle Rock U.S.A.
129 C2 Castor Can.
104 C3 Castres France
100 B1 Castricum Neth.
147 D3 Castries St Lucia
154 C2 Castro Brazil
153 A5 Castro Chile

106 B2 Castro Verde Port.
109 C3 Castrovillari Italy
150 A2 Catacaos Peru
155 D2 Cataguases Brazil
154 C1 Catalão Brazil
152 B3 Catamarca Arg.
64 B1 Catanduanes *i.* Phil.
154 B1 Catanduva Brazil
154 B3 Catanduvas Brazil
109 C3 Catania *Sicily* Italy
109 C3 Catanzaro Italy
64 B1 Catarman Phil.
64 B1 Catbalogan Phil.
145 C3 Catemaco Mex.
147 C2 Cat Island Bahamas
130 A1 Cat Lake Can.
145 D2 Catoche, Cabo *c.* Mex.
141 E2 Catskill Mountains U.S.A.
64 B2 Cauayan Phil.
150 A1 Cauca *r.* Col.
151 E2 Caucaia Brazil
81 C1 Caucasus *mts* Asia/Europe
100 A2 Caudry France
109 C3 Caulonia Italy
131 D2 Causapscal Can.
105 D3 Cavaillon France
151 D3 Cavalcante Brazil
97 C2 Cavan Ireland
154 B3 Cavernoso, Serra de *mts* Brazil
151 D2 Caxias Brazil
152 C3 Caxias do Sul Brazil
120 A1 Caxito Angola
151 C1 Cayenne Fr. Guiana
146 B3 Cayman Islands *terr.* West Indies
117 C4 Caynabo Somalia
120 B2 Cazombo Angola
144 B2 Ceballos Mex.
64 B1 Cebu Phil.
64 B1 Cebu *i.* Phil.
108 B2 Cecina Italy
137 F2 Cedar *r.* U.S.A.
135 D3 Cedar City U.S.A.
137 E2 Cedar Falls U.S.A.
129 C2 Cedar Lake Can.
137 E2 Cedar Rapids U.S.A.
144 A2 Cedros, Isla *i.* Mex.
51 C3 Ceduna Austr.
117 C4 Ceeldheere Somalia
117 C3 Ceerigaabo Somalia
108 B3 Cefalù *Sicily* Italy
145 B2 Celaya Mex.
58 C3 Celebes *i.* Indon.
156 B5 Celebes Sea Indon./Phil.
145 C2 Celestún Mex.
101 E1 Celle Ger.
95 B3 Celtic Sea Ireland/U.K.
59 D3 Cenderawasih, Teluk *b.* Indon.
150 A1 Central, Cordillera *mts* Col.
150 A3 Central, Cordillera *mts* Peru
64 B1 Central, Cordillera *mts* Phil.
118 C2 Central African Republic *country* Africa
74 A2 Central Brahui Range *mts* Pak.
137 D2 Central City U.S.A.
140 B3 Centralia *IL* U.S.A.
134 B1 Centralia *WA* U.S.A.
74 A2 Central Makran Range *mts* Pak.
59 D3 Central Range *mts* P.N.G.
89 E3 Central Russian Upland *hills* Rus. Fed.
83 I2 Central Siberian Plateau Rus. Fed.

111 B3 Cephalonia *i.* Greece
Ceram Sea Indon. *see* Seram, Laut
152 B3 Ceres Arg.
154 C1 Ceres Brazil
122 A3 Ceres S. Africa
104 C3 Céret France
106 C1 Cerezo de Abajo Spain
109 C2 Cerignola Italy
110 C2 Cernavodă Romania
145 C2 Cerralvo Mex.
144 B2 Cerralvo, Isla *i.* Mex.
145 B2 Cerritos Mex.
145 C2 Cerro Azul Brazil
145 C2 Cerro Azul Mex.
150 A3 Cerro de Pasco Peru
105 D3 Cervione *Corsica* France
106 B1 Cervo Spain
108 B2 Cesena Italy
88 C2 Cēsis Latvia
102 C2 České Budějovice Czech Rep.
101 F3 Český les *mts* Czech Rep./Ger.
111 C3 Çeşme Turkey
53 D2 Cessnock Austr.
109 C2 Cetinje Serb. and Mont.
109 C3 Cetraro Italy
106 B2 Ceuta N. Africa
105 C3 Cévennes *mts* France
Ceylon *country* Asia *see* Sri Lanka
79 D2 Châbahār Iran
75 C1 Chabyêr Caka *salt l.* China
150 A2 Chachapoyas Peru
89 D3 Chachersk Belarus
63 B2 Chachoengsao Thai.
115 D3 Chad *country* Africa
115 D3 Chad, Lake Africa
69 C1 Chadaasan Mongolia
68 C1 Chadan Rus. Fed.
123 C1 Chadibe Botswana
136 C2 Chadron U.S.A.
65 B2 Chaeryŏng N. Korea
74 A2 Chagai Pak.
77 C3 Chaghcharān Afgh.
89 E2 Chagoda Rus. Fed.
75 C2 Chaibasa India
63 B2 Chainat Thai.
63 B2 Chaiyaphum Thai.
152 C4 Chajarí Arg.
131 D1 Chakonipau, Lac *l.* Can.
150 A3 Chala Peru
74 A1 Chalap Dalam *mts* Afgh.
131 D2 Chaleur Bay *inlet* Can.
74 B2 Chalisgaon India
111 C3 Chalki *i.* Greece
111 B3 Chalkida Greece
104 B2 Challans France
134 D2 Challis U.S.A.
105 C2 Châlons-en-Champagne France
105 C2 Chalon-sur-Saône France
138 B1 Chama U.S.A.
121 C2 Chama Zambia
74 A1 Chaman Pak.
74 B1 Chamba India
74 B2 Chambal *r.* India
137 D2 Chamberlain U.S.A.
141 D3 Chambersburg U.S.A.
105 D2 Chambéry France
121 C2 Chambeshi Zambia
140 B2 Champaign U.S.A.
141 E2 Champlain, Lake Can./U.S.A.
145 C3 Champotón Mex.
152 A3 Chañaral Chile
126 B2 Chandalar *r.* U.S.A.
142 C3 Chandeleur Islands U.S.A.
74 B1 Chandigarh India

138 A2 **Chandler** U.S.A.
75 B3 **Chandrapur** India
63 B2 **Chang, Ko** i. Thai.
Chang'an China see
Rong'an
121 C3 **Changane** r. Moz.
121 C2 **Changara** Moz.
65 B1 **Changbai** China
65 B1 **Changbai Shan** mts
China/N. Korea
69 E2 **Changchun** China
71 B3 **Changde** China
65 B2 **Ch'angdo** N. Korea
71 C3 **Changhua** Taiwan
65 B3 **Changhŭng** S. Korea
Chang Jiang r. China see
Yangtze
65 B1 **Changjin** N. Korea
65 B1 **Changjin-gang** r. N. Korea
71 B3 **Changsha** China
65 B2 **Changsŏng** S. Korea
71 B3 **Changting** China
65 B2 **Ch'angwŏn** S. Korea
70 B2 **Changyuan** China
70 B2 **Changzhi** China
70 B2 **Changzhou** China
111 B3 **Chania** Greece
95 C4 **Channel Islands** Europe
135 C4 **Channel Islands** U.S.A.
131 E2 **Channel-Port-aux-
Basques** Can.
63 B2 **Chanthaburi** Thai.
104 C2 **Chantilly** France
137 D3 **Chanute** U.S.A.
82 G3 **Chany, Ozero** salt l.
Rus. Fed.
71 B3 **Chaoyang** China
Chaoyang China see
Huinan
71 B3 **Chaozhou** China
144 B2 **Chapala, Laguna de** l.
Mex.
76 B3 **Chapayev** Kazakh.
152 C3 **Chapecó** Brazil
143 E1 **Chapel Hill** U.S.A.
130 B2 **Chapleau** Can.
89 E3 **Chaplygin** Rus. Fed.
91 C2 **Chaplynka** Ukr.
145 B2 **Charcas** Mex.
99 B3 **Chard** U.K.
104 B2 **Charente** r. France
77 C3 **Chärikär** Afgh.
86 E2 **Charkayuvom** Rus. Fed.
104 B2 **Charleroi** Belgium
141 D3 **Charles, Cape** U.S.A.
137 E2 **Charles City** U.S.A.
140 B3 **Charleston** IL U.S.A.
143 E2 **Charleston** SC U.S.A.
140 C3 **Charleston** WV U.S.A.
135 C3 **Charleston Peak** U.S.A.
51 D2 **Charleville** Austr.
105 C2 **Charleville-Mézières**
France
143 D1 **Charlotte** U.S.A.
143 D3 **Charlotte Harbor** b. U.S.A.
141 D3 **Charlottesville** U.S.A.
131 D2 **Charlottetown** Can.
52 B3 **Charlton** Austr.
130 C1 **Charlton Island** Can.
51 D2 **Charters Towers** Austr.
104 C2 **Chartres** France
128 C2 **Chase** Can.
88 C3 **Chashniki** Belarus
54 A3 **Chaslands Mistake** c. N.Z.
65 B1 **Chasŏng** N. Korea
104 B2 **Chassiron, Pointe de** pt
France
104 B2 **Châteaubriant** France
104 C2 **Château-du-Loir** France
104 C2 **Châteaudun** France

104 B2 **Châteaulin** France
105 D3 **Châteauneuf-les-
Martigues** France
104 C2 **Châteauneuf-sur-Loire**
France
105 C2 **Château-Thierry** France
128 C2 **Châtelet** Belgium
100 B2 **Châtelet** Belgium
104 C2 **Châtellerault** France
140 C2 **Chatham** Ont. Can.
49 G5 **Chatham Islands** N.Z.
105 C2 **Châtillon-sur-Seine** France
143 D2 **Chattahoochee** r. U.S.A.
143 C1 **Chattanooga** U.S.A.
63 B2 **Châu Đôc** Vietnam
62 A1 **Chauk** Myanmar
105 C2 **Chaumont** France
105 C2 **Chauny** France
106 B1 **Chaves** Brazil
106 B1 **Chaves** Port.
130 C1 **Chavigny, Lac** l. Can.
89 D3 **Chavusy** Belarus
82 E3 **Chayevo** Rus. Fed.
86 E3 **Chaykovskiy** Rus. Fed.
102 C1 **Cheb** Czech Rep.
87 D3 **Cheboksary** Rus. Fed.
140 C1 **Cheboygan** U.S.A.
65 B2 **Chech'ŏn** S. Korea
114 B2 **Chegga** Maur.
134 B1 **Chehalis** U.S.A.
65 B3 **Cheju** S. Korea
65 B3 **Cheju-do** i. S. Korea
65 B3 **Cheju-haehyŏp** sea chan.
S. Korea
89 E2 **Chekhov** Rus. Fed.
134 B1 **Chelan, Lake** U.S.A.
107 D2 **Chélif, Oued** r. Alg.
103 E1 **Chełm** Pol.
99 D3 **Chelmer** r. U.K.
103 D1 **Chełmno** Pol.
99 D3 **Chelmsford** U.K.
99 B3 **Cheltenham** U.K.
87 F3 **Chelyabinsk** Rus. Fed.
101 F2 **Chemnitz** Ger.
114 B2 **Chenachane** Alg.
70 B2 **Chengde** China
70 A2 **Chengdu** China
71 B4 **Chengmai** China
Chengshou China see
Yingshan
70 A2 **Chengxian** China
Chengyang China see
Juxian
73 C3 **Chennai** India
71 B3 **Chenzhou** China
99 B3 **Chepstow** U.K.
104 B2 **Cherbourg** France
89 E3 **Cheremisinovo** Rus. Fed.
69 C1 **Cheremkhovo** Rus. Fed.
89 E2 **Cherepovets** Rus. Fed.
91 C2 **Cherkasy** Ukr.
87 D4 **Cherkessk** Rus. Fed.
91 C1 **Chernihiv** Ukr.
91 D2 **Cherninivka** Ukr.
90 B2 **Chernivtsi** Ukr.
90 B1 **Chernyakhiv** Ukr.
88 B3 **Chernyakhovsk** Rus. Fed.
89 E3 **Chernyanka** Rus. Fed.
83 I2 **Chernyshevskiy** Rus. Fed.
137 D2 **Cherokee** U.S.A.
83 K2 **Cherskogo, Khrebet** mts
Rus. Fed.
91 E2 **Chertkovo** Rus. Fed.
90 A1 **Chervonohrad** Ukr.
88 C3 **Chervyen'** Belarus
89 E3 **Cherykaw** Belarus
141 D3 **Chesapeake** U.S.A.
86 D2 **Cheshskaya Guba** b.
Rus. Fed.
98 B2 **Chester** U.K.

140 B3 **Chester** IL U.S.A.
143 D2 **Chester** SC U.S.A.
99 B2 **Chester** U.K.
129 E1 **Chesterfield Inlet** Can.
129 E1 **Chesterfield Inlet** inlet Can.
141 F1 **Chesuncook Lake** U.S.A.
131 D2 **Chéticamp** Can.
145 D3 **Chetumal** Mex.
128 B2 **Chetwynd** Can.
98 B1 **Cheviot Hills** U.K.
136 C2 **Cheyenne** U.S.A.
136 C2 **Cheyenne** r. U.S.A.
136 C3 **Cheyenne Wells** U.S.A.
75 B2 **Chhapra** India
75 B2 **Chhatarpur** India
71 C3 **Chiai** Taiwan
62 A2 **Chiang Dao** Thai.
62 A2 **Chiang Mai** Thai.
62 A2 **Chiang Rai** Thai.
108 A1 **Chiavenno** Italy
70 B3 **Chibi** China
121 C3 **Chiboma** Moz.
130 C2 **Chibougamau** Can.
123 D1 **Chibuto** Moz.
140 B2 **Chicago** U.S.A.
128 A2 **Chichagof Island** U.S.A.
99 C3 **Chichester** U.K.
50 A2 **Chichester Range** mts
Austr.
139 D1 **Chickasha** U.S.A.
150 A2 **Chiclayo** Peru
153 B5 **Chico** r. Arg.
135 B3 **Chico** U.S.A.
122 E1 **Chicoutimi** Can.
108 B2 **Chieti** Italy
145 C3 **Chietla** Mex.
69 D2 **Chifeng** China
155 D1 **Chifre, Serra do** mts Brazil
77 D2 **Chiganak** Kazakh.
145 C3 **Chignahuapán** Mex.
121 C3 **Chigubo** Moz.
144 B2 **Chihuahua** Mex.
88 C2 **Chikhachevo** Rus. Fed.
67 C3 **Chikuma-gawa** r. Japan
128 B2 **Chilanko** r. Can.
74 B1 **Chilas** Jammu and Kashmir
139 C2 **Childress** U.S.A.
153 A4 **Chile** country S. America
152 B3 **Chilecito** Arg.
75 C2 **Chilika Lake** India
121 B2 **Chililabombwe** Zambia
128 B2 **Chilko** r. Can.
128 B2 **Chilko Lake** Can.
153 A4 **Chillán** Chile
137 E3 **Chillicothe** MO U.S.A.
140 C3 **Chillicothe** OH U.S.A.
128 B3 **Chilliwack** Can.
153 A5 **Chiloé, Isla de** i. Chile
145 C3 **Chilpancingo** Mex.
53 C3 **Chiltern** Austr.
71 C3 **Chilung** Taiwan
119 D3 **Chimala** Tanz.
152 B4 **Chimbas** Arg.
150 A2 **Chimborazo** mt. Ecuador
150 A2 **Chimbote** Peru
87 E4 **Chimkent** Uzbek.
Chimkent Kazakh. see
Shymkent
121 C2 **Chimoio** Moz.
77 C3 **Chimtargha, Qullai** mt.
Tajik.
68 C2 **China** country Asia
145 C2 **China** Mex.
150 A3 **Chincha Alta** Peru
128 C2 **Chinchaga** r. Can.
145 D3 **Chinchorro, Banco**
sea feature Mex.
121 C2 **Chinde** Moz.
65 B3 **Chindo** S. Korea
65 B3 **Chin-do** i. S. Korea

68 C2	Chindu China	
62 A1	Chindwin *r.* Myanmar	
65 B2	Chinhae N. Korea	
120 B2	Chingola Zambia	
120 A2	Chinguar Angola	
65 B2	Chinhae S. Korea	
121 C2	Chinhoyi Zimbabwe	
74 B1	Chiniot Pak.	
144 B2	Chinipas Mex.	
65 B2	Chinju S. Korea	
118 C2	Chinko *r.* C.A.R.	
138 B1	Chinle U.S.A.	
71 B3	Chinmen Taiwan	
67 C3	Chino Japan	
104 C2	Chinon France	
138 A2	Chino Valley U.S.A.	
108 B1	Chioggia Italy	
111 C3	Chios Greece	
111 C3	Chios *i.* Greece	
121 C2	Chipata Zambia	
120 A2	Chipindo Angola	
121 C3	Chipinge Zimbabwe	
73 B3	Chiplun India	
99 B3	Chippenham U.K.	
99 C3	Chipping Norton U.K.	
77 C2	Chirchiq Uzbek.	
121 C3	Chiredzi Zimbabwe	
138 B2	Chiricahua Peak *mt.* U.S.A.	
146 B4	Chiriquí, Golfo de *b.* Panama	
65 B2	Chiri-san *mt.* S. Korea	
146 B4	Chirripó *mt.* Costa Rica	
121 B2	Chirundu Zimbabwe	
130 C1	Chisasibi Can.	
137 E1	Chisholm U.S.A.	
90 B2	Chişinău Moldova	
87 E3	Chistopol' Rus. Fed.	
69 D1	Chita Rus. Fed.	
120 A2	Chitado Angola	
121 C2	Chitambo Zambia	
120 B1	Chitato Angola	
121 C1	Chitipa Malawi	
73 B3	Chitradurga India	
74 B1	Chitral Pak.	
146 B4	Chitré Panama	
75 D2	Chittagong Bangl.	
74 B2	Chittaurgarh India	
121 C2	Chitungwiza Zimbabwe	
120 B2	Chiume Angola	
121 C2	Chivhu Zimbabwe	
70 B2	Chizhou China	
114 C2	Chlef Alg.	
153 B4	Choele Choel Arg.	
144 B2	Choix Mex.	
103 D1	Chojnice Pol.	
117 B3	Ch'ok'ē Mountains Eth.	
83 K2	Chokurdakh Rus. Fed.	
121 C3	Chokwé Moz.	
104 B2	Cholet France	
102 C1	Chomutov Czech Rep.	
83 I2	Chona *r.* Rus. Fed.	
65 B2	Ch'ŏnan S. Korea	
150 A3	Chone Ecuador	
65 B1	Ch'ŏngjin N. Korea	
65 B2	Chŏngju N. Korea	
65 B2	Chŏngp'yŏng N. Korea	
70 A3	Chongqing China	
70 A2	Chongqing *mun.* China	
71 A3	Chongzuo China	
65 B2	Chŏnju S. Korea	
153 A5	Chonos, Archipiélago de los *is* Chile	
154 B3	Chopimzinho Brazil	
98 B3	Chorley U.K.	
91 C2	Chornomors'ke Ukr.	
90 B2	Chortkiv Ukr.	
65 B2	Ch'ŏrwŏn S. Korea	
65 B1	Ch'osan N. Korea	
67 D3	Chōshi Japan	

103 D1	Choszczno Pol.	
114 A2	Choûm Maur.	
69 D1	Choybalsan Mongolia	
69 D1	Choyr Mongolia	
54 B2	Christchurch N.Z.	
99 C3	Christchurch U.K.	
127 G2	Christian, Cape Can.	
123 C2	Christiana S. Africa	
54 A2	Christina, Mount N.Z.	
111 C3	Chrysi *i.* Greece	
153 B5	Chubut *r.* Arg.	
90 B1	Chudniv Ukr.	
89 D2	Chudovo Rus. Fed.	
	Chudskoye Ozero *l.* Estonia/Rus. Fed. *see* Peipus, Lake	
126 B2	Chugach Mountains U.S.A.	
67 B4	Chūgoku-sanchi *mts* Japan	
66 B2	Chuguyevka Rus. Fed.	
91 D2	Chuhuyiv Ukr.	
160 J3	Chukchi Sea Rus. Fed./U.S.A.	
83 N2	Chukotskiy Poluostrov *pen.* Rus. Fed.	
135 C4	Chula Vista U.S.A.	
82 G3	Chulym Rus. Fed.	
152 B3	Chumbicha Arg.	
83 K3	Chumikan Rus. Fed.	
63 A2	Chumphon Thai.	
65 B2	Ch'unch'ŏn S. Korea	
	Chungking China *see* Chongqing	
83 H2	Chunya *r.* Rus. Fed.	
150 A3	Chuquibamba Peru	
152 B3	Chuquicamata Chile	
105 D2	Chur Switz.	
62 A1	Churachandpur India	
129 E2	Churchill Can.	
129 E2	Churchill *r. Man.* Can.	
131 D1	Churchill *r. Nfld.* Can.	
129 E2	Churchill, Cape Can.	
131 D1	Churchill Falls Can.	
129 D2	Churchill Lake Can.	
74 B2	Churu India	
131 C2	Chute-des-Passes Can.	
62 B1	Chuxiong China	
90 B2	Ciadîr-Lunga Moldova	
61 B2	Ciamis Indon.	
60 B2	Cianjur Indon.	
154 B2	Cianorte Brazil	
103 E1	Ciechanów Pol.	
146 C2	Ciego de Ávila Cuba	
146 B2	Cienfuegos Cuba	
107 C2	Cieza Spain	
106 C2	Cigüela *r.* Spain	
80 B2	Cihanbeyli Turkey	
144 B3	Cihuatlán Mex.	
106 C2	Cijara, Embalse de *resr* Spain	
61 B2	Cilacap Indon.	
139 C1	Cimarron *r.* U.S.A.	
90 B2	Cimişlia Moldova	
108 B2	Cimone, Monte *mt.* Italy	
140 C3	Cincinnati U.S.A.	
111 C3	Çine Turkey	
100 B2	Ciney Belgium	
145 C3	Cintalapa Mex.	
126 B2	Circle AK U.S.A.	
136 B1	Circle MT U.S.A.	
58 B3	Cirebon Indon.	
99 C3	Cirencester U.K.	
108 A1	Cirié Italy	
109 C3	Cirò Marina Italy	
109 C2	Čitluk Bos.-Herz.	
122 A3	Citrusdal S. Africa	
145 B2	Ciudad Acuña Mex.	
145 B3	Ciudad Altamirano Mex.	
150 B1	Ciudad Bolívar Venez.	
144 B2	Ciudad Camargo Mex.	

144 A2	Ciudad Constitución Mex.	
145 C3	Ciudad del Carmen Mex.	
144 B2	Ciudad Delicias Mex.	
145 C2	Ciudad de Valles Mex.	
150 B1	Ciudad Guayana Venez.	
138 B3	Ciudad Guerrero Mex.	
144 B3	Ciudad Guzmán Mex.	
145 C3	Ciudad Hidalgo Mex.	
145 C3	Ciudad Ixtepec Mex.	
144 B1	Ciudad Juárez Mex.	
145 C2	Ciudad Mante Mex.	
145 C2	Ciudad Mier Mex.	
144 B2	Ciudad Obregón Mex.	
106 C2	Ciudad Real Spain	
145 C2	Ciudad Río Bravo Mex.	
106 B1	Ciudad Rodrigo Spain	
145 C2	Ciudad Victoria Mex.	
107 D1	Ciutadella de Menorca Spain	
111 C3	Civan Dağ *mt.* Turkey	
108 B1	Cividale del Friuli Italy	
108 B2	Civitanova Marche Italy	
108 B2	Civitavecchia Italy	
104 C2	Civray France	
111 C3	Çivril Turkey	
70 C2	Cixi China	
99 D3	Clacton-on-Sea U.K.	
128 C2	Claire, Lake Can.	
105 C2	Clamecy France	
122 A3	Clanwilliam S. Africa	
52 A2	Clare Austr.	
97 A2	Clare Island Ireland	
141 E2	Claremont U.S.A.	
97 B2	Claremorris Ireland	
54 B2	Clarence N.Z.	
131 E2	Clarenville Can.	
128 C2	Claresholm Can.	
137 D2	Clarinda U.S.A.	
123 C3	Clarkebury S. Africa	
134 C1	Clark Fork *r.* U.S.A.	
143 D2	Clark Hill Reservoir U.S.A.	
140 C3	Clarksburg U.S.A.	
142 B2	Clarksdale U.S.A.	
142 B1	Clarksville AR U.S.A.	
142 C1	Clarksville TN U.S.A.	
154 B1	Claro *r.* Brazil	
139 C1	Clayton U.S.A.	
97 B3	Clear, Cape Ireland	
137 E2	Clear Lake U.S.A.	
135 B3	Clear Lake U.S.A.	
128 C2	Clearwater Can.	
129 C2	Clearwater *r.* Can.	
143 D3	Clearwater U.S.A.	
134 C1	Clearwater *r.* U.S.A.	
139 D2	Cleburne U.S.A.	
51 D2	Clermont Austr.	
105 C2	Clermont-Ferrand France	
51 D2	Cleve Austr.	
142 B2	Cleveland MS U.S.A.	
140 C2	Cleveland OH U.S.A.	
143 D1	Cleveland TN U.S.A.	
134 D1	Cleveland, Mount U.S.A.	
143 D3	Clewiston U.S.A.	
97 A2	Clifden Ireland	
53 D1	Clifton Austr.	
138 B2	Clifton U.S.A.	
128 B2	Clinton Can.	
137 E2	Clinton IA U.S.A.	
137 E3	Clinton MO U.S.A.	
139 D1	Clinton OK U.S.A.	
124 H6	Clipperton, Île *i.* N. Pacific Ocean	
96 A2	Clisham *hill* U.K.	
98 B2	Clitheroe U.K.	
97 B3	Clonakilty Ireland	
51 D2	Cloncurry Austr.	
97 C1	Clones Ireland	
97 C2	Clonmel Ireland	
100 D1	Cloppenburg Ger.	
136 B2	Cloud Peak U.S.A.	

139	C2	**Clovis** U.S.A.
129	D2	**Cluff Lake Mine** Can.
110	B1	**Cluj-Napoca** Romania
51	C2	**Cluny** Austr.
105	D2	**Cluses** France
54	A3	**Clutha** r. N.Z.
96	B3	**Clyde** r. U.K.
96	B3	**Clyde, Firth of** est. U.K.
96	B3	**Clydebank** U.K.
127	G2	**Clyde River** Can.
144	B3	**Coalcomán** Mex.
135	C3	**Coaldale** U.S.A.
128	B2	**Coal River** Can.
150	B2	**Coari** Brazil
150	B2	**Coari** r. Brazil
142	B2	**Coastal Plain** U.S.A.
128	B2	**Coast Mountains** Can.
135	B2	**Coast Ranges** mts U.S.A.
96	B3	**Coatbridge** U.K.
127	F2	**Coats Island** Can.
55	R2	**Coats Land** reg. Antarctica
145	C3	**Coatzacoalcos** Mex.
146	A3	**Cobán** Guat.
53	C2	**Cobar** Austr.
97	B3	**Cobh** Ireland
152	B2	**Cobija** Bol.
141	D2	**Cobourg** Can.
53	C1	**Cobourg Peninsula** Austr.
53	C1	**Cobram** Austr.
101	E2	**Coburg** Ger.
152	B2	**Cochabamba** Bol.
100	C2	**Cochem** Ger.
73	B4	**Cochin** India
128	C2	**Cochrane** Alta Can.
130	B2	**Cochrane** Ont. Can.
153	A5	**Cochrane** Chile
52	B2	**Cockburn** Austr.
		Cockburn Town Turks and Caicos Is see **Grand Turk**
98	B1	**Cockermouth** U.K.
122	B3	**Cockscomb** mt. S. Africa
146	B3	**Coco** r. Hond./Nic.
144	B2	**Cocula** Mex.
150	A1	**Cocuy, Sierra Nevada del** mt. Col.
141	D2	**Cod, Cape** U.S.A.
108	B2	**Codigoro** Italy
131	D1	**Cod Island** Can.
151	D2	**Codó** Brazil
129	C3	**Cody** U.S.A.
51	D1	**Coen** Austr.
100	C2	**Coesfeld** Ger.
134	C1	**Coeur d'Alene** U.S.A.
123	C3	**Coffee Bay** S. Africa
137	D3	**Coffeyville** U.S.A.
53	D2	**Coffs Harbour** Austr.
104	B2	**Cognac** France
118	A2	**Cogo** Equat. Guinea
52	B3	**Cohuna** Austr.
146	B4	**Coiba, Isla de** i. Panama
153	A5	**Coihaique** Chile
73	B3	**Coimbatore** India
106	B1	**Coimbra** Port.
52	B3	**Colac** Austr.
155	D1	**Colatina** Brazil
136	C3	**Colby** U.S.A.
99	D3	**Colchester** U.K.
129	C2	**Cold Lake** Can.
96	C3	**Coldstream** U.K.
139	D2	**Coleman** U.S.A.
52	B3	**Coleraine** Austr.
97	C1	**Coleraine** U.K.
123	C3	**Colesberg** S. Africa
144	B3	**Colima** Mex.
144	B3	**Colima, Nevado de** vol. Mex.
96	A2	**Coll** i. U.K.
53	C2	**Collarenebri** Austr.
50	B1	**Collier Bay** Austr.
54	B2	**Collingwood** N.Z.
97	B1	**Collooney** Ireland
105	D2	**Colmar** France
100	C2	**Cologne** Ger.
154	C2	**Colômbia** Brazil
150	A1	**Colombia** country S. America
73	B4	**Colombo** Sri Lanka
104	C3	**Colomiers** France
152	C4	**Colón** Arg.
146	C4	**Colón** Panama
109	C3	**Colonna, Capo** c. Italy
96	A2	**Colonsay** i. U.K.
153	B4	**Colorado** r. Arg.
135	D4	**Colorado** r. Mex./U.S.A.
139	D2	**Colorado** r. U.S.A.
136	B3	**Colorado** state U.S.A.
135	E3	**Colorado Plateau** U.S.A.
136	C3	**Colorado Springs** U.S.A.
144	B2	**Colotlán** Mex.
136	B1	**Colstrip** U.S.A.
137	E3	**Columbia** MO U.S.A.
143	D2	**Columbia** SC U.S.A.
142	C1	**Columbia** TN U.S.A.
134	B1	**Columbia** r. U.S.A.
128	C2	**Columbia, Mount** Can.
134	D1	**Columbia Falls** U.S.A.
128	B2	**Columbia Mountains** Can.
134	C1	**Columbia Plateau** U.S.A.
143	D2	**Columbus** GA U.S.A.
140	B3	**Columbus** IN U.S.A.
142	C2	**Columbus** MS U.S.A.
137	D2	**Columbus** NE U.S.A.
138	B2	**Columbus** NM U.S.A.
140	C3	**Columbus** OH U.S.A.
134	C1	**Colville** U.S.A.
126	A2	**Colville** r. U.S.A.
126	C2	**Colville Lake** Can.
98	B2	**Colwyn Bay** U.K.
108	B2	**Comacchio** Italy
110	C1	**Comăneşti** Romania
130	C1	**Comencho, Lac** l. Can.
97	C2	**Comeragh Mountains** hills Ireland
75	D2	**Comilla** Bangl.
108	A2	**Comino, Capo** c. Sardinia Italy
145	C3	**Comitán de Domínguez** Mex.
104	C2	**Commentry** France
139	D2	**Commerce** U.S.A.
127	F2	**Committee Bay** Can.
108	A1	**Como** Italy
153	B5	**Comodoro Rivadavia** Arg.
121	D2	**Comoros** country Africa
104	C2	**Compiègne** France
144	B2	**Compostela** Mex.
90	B3	**Comrat** Moldova
114	A4	**Conakry** Guinea
155	E1	**Conceição da Barra** Brazil
151	D2	**Conceição do Araguaia** Brazil
155	D1	**Conceição do Mato Dentro** Brazil
152	B3	**Concepción** Arg.
153	A4	**Concepción** Chile
144	B2	**Concepción** Mex.
135	B4	**Conception, Point** U.S.A.
154	C2	**Conchas** Brazil
138	C1	**Conchas Lake** U.S.A.
144	B2	**Conchos** r. Chihuahua Mex.
145	C2	**Conchos** r. Nuevo León/Tamaulipas Mex.
135	B3	**Concord** CA U.S.A.
141	E2	**Concord** NH U.S.A.
152	C4	**Concordia** Arg.
122	A2	**Concordia** S. Africa
137	D3	**Concordia** U.S.A.
53	C2	**Condobolin** Austr.
104	C3	**Condom** France
134	B1	**Condon** U.S.A.
108	B1	**Conegliano** Italy
104	C2	**Confolens** France
75	C2	**Congdü** China
118	B3	**Congo** country Africa
118	B3	**Congo** r. Congo/Dem. Rep. Congo
118	C3	**Congo, Democratic Republic of the** country Africa
129	C2	**Conklin** Can.
97	B1	**Conn, Lough** l. Ireland
97	B2	**Connaught** reg. Ireland
141	E2	**Connecticut** r. U.S.A.
141	E2	**Connecticut** state U.S.A.
97	B2	**Connemara** reg. Ireland
134	D1	**Conrad** U.S.A.
139	D2	**Conroe** U.S.A.
155	D2	**Conselheiro Lafaiete** Brazil
155	D1	**Conselheiro Pena** Brazil
98	C1	**Consett** U.K.
63	B3	**Côn Son, Đao** i. Vietnam
110	C2	**Constanţa** Romania
106	B2	**Constantina** Spain
115	C1	**Constantine** Alg.
134	D2	**Contact** U.S.A.
150	A2	**Contamana** Peru
153	A6	**Contreras, Isla** i. Chile
126	D2	**Contwoyto Lake** Can.
142	B1	**Conway** AR U.S.A.
141	E2	**Conway** NH U.S.A.
51	C2	**Coober Pedy** Austr.
		Cook, Mount N.Z. see **Aoraki**
143	C1	**Cookeville** U.S.A.
49	H4	**Cook Islands** S. Pacific Ocean
131	E1	**Cook's Harbour** Can.
97	C1	**Cookstown** U.K.
54	B2	**Cook Strait** N.Z.
51	D1	**Cooktown** Austr.
53	C2	**Coolabah** Austr.
53	C2	**Coolamon** Austr.
53	D1	**Coolangatta** Austr.
50	B3	**Coolgardie** Austr.
53	C3	**Cooma** Austr.
52	B2	**Coombah** Austr.
53	C2	**Coonabarabran** Austr.
52	A3	**Coonalpyn** Austr.
53	C2	**Coonamble** Austr.
52	A1	**Cooper Creek** watercourse Austr.
134	B2	**Coos Bay** U.S.A.
53	C2	**Cootamundra** Austr.
145	C3	**Copainalá** Mex.
145	C3	**Copala** Mex.
93	F4	**Copenhagen** Denmark
109	C2	**Copertino** Italy
152	A3	**Copiapó** Chile
140	B1	**Copper Harbor** U.S.A.
		Coppermine Can. see **Kugluktuk**
126	D2	**Coppermine** r. Can.
122	B2	**Copperton** S. Africa
152	A3	**Coquimbo** Chile
110	B2	**Corabia** Romania
155	D1	**Coração de Jesus** Brazil
150	A3	**Coracora** Peru
144	C1	**Coral** U.S.A.
80	A2	**Coral Bay** Austr.
127	F2	**Coral Harbour** Can.
156	D7	**Coral Sea** S. Pacific Ocean
48	D4	**Coral Sea Islands Territory** Austr.
52	B3	**Corangamite, Lake** Austr.
99	C2	**Corby** U.K.
153	A5	**Corcovado, Golfo de** sea chan. Chile
143	D2	**Cordele** U.S.A.

64 B1 Cordilleras Range mts Phil.
152 B4 Córdoba Arg.
145 C3 Córdoba Mex.
106 C2 Córdoba Spain
153 B4 Córdoba, Sierras de mts Arg.
111 A3 Corfu i. Greece
106 B2 Coria Spain
111 B3 Corinth Greece
142 C2 Corinth U.S.A.
155 D1 Corinto Brazil
97 B3 Cork Ireland
111 C2 Corlu Turkey
154 B2 Cornélio Procópio Brazil
131 E2 Corner Brook Can.
53 C3 Corner Inlet b. Austr.
135 B3 Corning CA U.S.A.
141 D2 Corning NY U.S.A.
Corn Islands is Nic. see Maíz, Islas del
108 B2 Corno, Monte mt. Italy
130 C2 Cornwall Can.
126 E1 Cornwallis Island Can.
150 B1 Coro Venez.
154 C1 Coromandel Brazil
54 C1 Coromandel Peninsula N.Z.
129 C2 Coronation Can.
126 E2 Coronation Gulf Can.
152 C3 Coronel Oviedo Para.
153 B4 Coronel Suárez Arg.
109 D2 Çorovodë Albania
139 D3 Corpus Christi U.S.A.
152 B2 Corque Bol.
151 D3 Corrente Brazil
154 B1 Correntes Brazil
151 D3 Correntina Brazil
97 B3 Corrib, Lough l. Ireland
152 C3 Corrientes Arg.
144 B2 Corrientes, Cabo c. Mex.
53 C3 Corryong Austr.
Corse i. France see Corsica
105 D3 Corse, Cap c. Corsica France
105 D3 Corsica i. France
139 D2 Corsicana U.S.A.
105 D3 Corte Corsica France
106 B2 Cortegana Spain
136 B3 Cortez U.S.A.
108 B1 Cortina d'Ampezzo Italy
141 D2 Cortland U.S.A.
108 B2 Cortona Italy
106 B2 Coruche Port.
80 B1 Çoruh Turkey
152 C2 Çorum Turkey
152 C2 Corumbá Brazil
154 C1 Corumbá r. Brazil
134 B2 Corvallis U.S.A.
98 B2 Corwen U.K.
144 B2 Cosalá Mex.
145 C3 Cosamaloapan Mex.
109 C3 Cosenza Italy
105 C2 Cosne-Cours-sur-Loire France
107 C2 Costa Blanca coastal area Spain
107 D1 Costa Brava coastal area Spain
106 B2 Costa del Sol coastal area Spain
146 B3 Costa de Mosquitos coastal area Nic.
154 B1 Costa Rica Brazil
146 B3 Costa Rica country Central America
144 B2 Costa Rica Mex.
110 B2 Costeşti Romania
64 B3 Cotabato Phil.
114 B4 Côte d'Ivoire country Africa
150 A2 Cotopaxi, Volcán vol. Ecuador

99 B3 Cotswold Hills U.K.
134 B2 Cottage Grove U.S.A.
102 C1 Cottbus Ger.
104 B2 Coubre, Pointe de la pt France
52 A3 Couedic, Cape du Austr.
137 D2 Council Bluffs U.S.A.
88 B2 Courland Lagoon b. Lith./Rus. Fed.
128 B3 Courtenay Can.
104 C2 Coutances France
104 B2 Coutras France
100 B3 Couvin Belgium
99 C2 Coventry U.K.
140 C3 Covington U.S.A.
50 B3 Cowan, Lake salt flat Austr.
96 C2 Cowdenbeath U.K.
53 C3 Cowes Austr.
134 B1 Cowlitz r. U.S.A.
53 C2 Cowra Austr.
154 B1 Coxim Brazil
75 D2 Cox's Bazar Bangl.
145 B3 Coyuca de Benitez Mex.
145 D2 Cozumel Mex.
145 D2 Cozumel, Isla de i. Mex.
123 C3 Cradock S. Africa
136 B2 Craig U.S.A.
102 C2 Crailsheim Ger.
110 B2 Craiova Romania
129 C2 Cranberry Portage Can.
53 C3 Cranbourne Austr.
128 C3 Cranbrook Can.
134 C1 Cranbrook Can.
157 D2 Crateús Brazil
151 E2 Crato Brazil
136 C2 Crawford U.S.A.
140 B3 Crawfordsville U.S.A.
99 C3 Crawley U.K.
134 D1 Crazy Mountains U.S.A.
129 D2 Cree r. Can.
144 B2 Creel Mex.
129 D2 Cree Lake Can.
100 B1 Creil Neth.
105 D2 Crema Italy
108 B1 Cremona Italy
108 B2 Cres i. Croatia
134 B2 Crescent City U.S.A.
128 C3 Creston Can.
137 E2 Creston U.S.A.
142 C2 Crestview U.S.A.
111 B3 Crete i. Greece
107 D1 Creus, Cap de c. Spain
98 B2 Crewe U.K.
96 B2 Crianlarich U.K.
152 D3 Criciúma Brazil
96 C2 Crieff U.K.
108 B1 Crikvenica Croatia
91 C2 Crimea pen. Ukr.
101 F2 Crimmitschau Ger.
154 C1 Cristalina Brazil
101 E1 Crivitz Ger.
109 C1 Črnomelj Slovenia
97 B2 Croagh Patrick hill Ireland
109 C1 Croatia country Europe
61 C1 Crocker, Banjaran mts Malaysia
139 D2 Crockett U.S.A.
59 C3 Croker Island Austr.
99 D2 Cromer U.K.
54 A3 Cromwell N.Z.
137 D1 Crookston U.S.A.
53 C2 Crookwell Austr.
143 D3 Crosby U.S.A.
142 B2 Cross City U.S.A.
143 C2 Crossett U.S.A.
98 B1 Cross Fell hill U.K.
129 E2 Cross Lake Can.
143 C1 Crossville U.S.A.
109 C3 Crotone Italy
99 D3 Crowborough U.K.

142 B2 Crowley U.S.A.
128 C3 Crowsnest Pass Can.
113 K11 Crozet, Îles is Indian Ocean
146 C3 Cruz, Cabo c. Cuba
152 C3 Cruz Alta Brazil
152 B4 Cruz del Eje Arg.
155 D2 Cruzeiro Brazil
150 A2 Cruzeiro do Sul Brazil
52 A2 Crystal Brook Austr.
139 D3 Crystal City U.S.A.
140 B1 Crystal Falls U.S.A.
103 E2 Csongrád Hungary
120 B2 Cuando r. Angola/Zambia
120 A2 Cuangar Angola
118 B3 Cuango r. Angola/Dem. Rep. Congo
120 A1 Cuanza r. Angola
139 C3 Cuatro Ciénegas Mex.
144 B2 Cuauhtémoc Mex.
145 C3 Cuautla Mex.
146 B2 Cuba country West Indies
120 A2 Cubal Angola
120 B2 Cubango r. Angola/Namibia
150 A1 Cúcuta Col.
73 B3 Cuddalore India
73 B3 Cuddapah India
106 C1 Cuéllar Spain
120 A2 Cuemba Angola
150 A2 Cuenca Ecuador
107 C1 Cuenca Spain
145 C3 Cuenca, Serranía de mts Spain
145 C3 Cuernavaca Mex.
139 D3 Cuero U.S.A.
151 C3 Cuiabá Brazil
151 C3 Cuiabá r. Brazil
96 A2 Cuillin Sound sea chan. U.K.
120 A1 Cuilo Angola
120 A2 Cuito r. Angola
120 A2 Cuito Cuanavale Angola
60 B1 Cukai Malaysia
53 C3 Culcairn Austr.
53 C1 Culgoa r. Austr.
144 B2 Culiacán Mex.
64 A1 Culion i. Phil.
107 C2 Cullera Spain
142 C2 Cullman U.S.A.
97 C1 Cullybackey U.K.
151 C3 Culuene r. Brazil
150 B1 Cumaná Venez.
141 D3 Cumberland U.S.A.
140 B3 Cumberland r. U.S.A.
129 D2 Cumberland Lake Can.
127 G2 Cumberland Peninsula Can.
142 C1 Cumberland Plateau U.S.A.
127 G2 Cumberland Sound sea chan. Can.
96 C3 Cumbernauld U.K.
135 B3 Cummings U.S.A.
96 B3 Cumnock U.K.
144 B1 Cumpas Mex.
145 C3 Cunduacán Mex.
120 A2 Cunene r. Angola
108 A2 Cuneo Italy
53 C1 Cunnamulla Austr.
108 A1 Cuorgnè Italy
96 C2 Cupar U.K.
147 D3 Curaçao i. Neth. Antilles
150 A2 Curaray r. Ecuador
153 A4 Curicó Chile
154 C3 Curitiba Brazil
52 A2 Curnamona Austr.
51 D3 Currie Austr.
51 E2 Curtis Island Austr.
151 C2 Curuá r. Brazil
60 B2 Curup Indon.
151 D2 Cururupu Brazil
155 D1 Curvelo Brazil

150 A3 **Cusco** Peru
139 D1 **Cushing** U.S.A.
134 C1 **Cut Bank** U.S.A.
75 C2 **Cuttack** India
101 D1 **Cuxhaven** Ger.
64 B1 **Cuyo Islands** Phil.
Cuzco Peru *see* **Cusco**
119 C3 **Cyangugu** Rwanda
111 B3 **Cyclades** *is* Greece
129 C3 **Cypress Hills** Can.
80 B2 **Cyprus** *country* Asia
102 C2 **Czech Republic** *country*
Europe
103 D1 **Czersk** Pol.
103 D1 **Częstochowa** Pol.

D

Đa, Sông *r.* Vietnam *see*
Black River
69 D2 **Daban** China
114 A3 **Dabola** Guinea
Dacca Bangl. *see* **Dhaka**
102 C2 **Dachau** Ger.
74 A2 **Dadu** Pak.
64 B1 **Daet** Phil.
114 A3 **Dagana** Senegal
64 B1 **Dagupan** Phil.
74 B3 **Dahanu** India
69 D2 **Da Hinggan Ling** *mts* China
116 C3 **Dahlak Archipelago** *is*
Eritrea
100 C2 **Dahlem** Ger.
60 B2 **Daik** Indon.
106 C2 **Daimiel** Spain
51 C3 **Dajarra** Austr.
114 A3 **Dakar** Senegal
116 A2 **Dākhilah, Wāḥāt al** *oasis*
Egypt
Dakhla Oasis Egypt *see*
Dākhilah, Wāḥāt al
63 A3 **Dakoank** India
88 C3 **Dakol'ka** *r.* Belarus
109 D2 **Đakovica** Serb. and Mont.
109 C1 **Đakovo** Croatia
120 B2 **Dala** Angola
68 C2 **Dalain Hob** China
93 G3 **Dalälven** *r.* Sweden
111 C3 **Dalaman** Turkey
111 C3 **Dalaman** *r.* Turkey
69 C2 **Dalandzadgad** Mongolia
63 B2 **Đa Lat** Vietnam
74 A2 **Dalbandin** Pak.
96 C3 **Dalbeattie** U.K.
51 E2 **Dalby** Austr.
143 C1 **Dale Hollow Lake** U.S.A.
53 C3 **Dalgety** Austr.
139 C1 **Dalhart** U.S.A.
131 D2 **Dalhousie** Can.
62 B1 **Dali** China
70 C2 **Dalian** China
96 C3 **Dalkeith** U.K.
138 C2 **Dallas** U.S.A.
128 A2 **Dall Island** U.S.A.
109 C2 **Dalmatia** *reg.* Croatia
66 C2 **Dal'negorsk** Rus. Fed.
66 B1 **Dal'nerechensk** Rus. Fed.
114 B4 **Daloa** Côte d'Ivoire
51 D2 **Dalrymple, Mount** Austr.
92 □A3 **Dalsmynni** Iceland
75 C2 **Daltenganj** India
143 D2 **Dalton** U.S.A.
60 B1 **Daludalu** Indon.
92 □B2 **Dalvík** Iceland
50 C1 **Daly** *r.* Austr.
51 C1 **Daly Waters** Austr.
74 B2 **Daman** India

80 B2 **Damanhūr** Egypt
59 C3 **Damar** *i.* Indon.
80 B2 **Damascus** Syria
115 D3 **Damaturu** Nigeria
76 B3 **Dāmāvand, Qolleh-ye**
mt. Iran
81 D2 **Damazin** Sudan
79 D2 **Dammam** Saudi Arabia
101 D1 **Damme** Ger.
75 B2 **Damoh** India
114 B4 **Damongo** Ghana
59 C3 **Dampir, Selat** *sea chan.*
Indon.
75 D1 **Damxung** China
114 B4 **Danané** Côte d'Ivoire
63 B2 **Đa Nẵng** Vietnam
141 E2 **Danbury** U.S.A.
65 A1 **Dandong** China
146 B3 **Dangriga** Belize
70 B2 **Dangshan** China
89 F2 **Danilov** Rus. Fed.
89 E2 **Danilovskaya**
Vozvyshennost' *hills*
Rus. Fed.
70 B2 **Danjiangkou** China
89 E3 **Dankov** Rus. Fed.
146 B3 **Danlí** Hond.
101 E1 **Dannenberg (Elbe)** Ger.
54 C2 **Dannevirke** N.Z.
62 B2 **Dan Sai** Thai.
70 C2 **Dantu** China
110 A1 **Danube** *r.* Europe
110 C1 **Danube Delta** Romania
76 B2 **Danville** *IL.* U.S.A.
140 C3 **Danville** *KY* U.S.A.
141 D3 **Danville** *VA* U.S.A.
71 A4 **Danzhou** China
71 B3 **Daoxian** China
114 C3 **Dapaong** Togo
64 B2 **Dapitan** Phil.
68 C2 **Da Qaidam Zhen** China
69 E1 **Daqing** China
80 B2 **Dar'ā** Syria
77 D2 **Dārāb** Iran
115 D1 **Daraj** Libya
81 D2 **Dārān** Iran
75 C2 **Darbhanga** India
119 D3 **Dar es Salaam** Tanz.
117 A3 **Darfur** *reg.* Sudan
74 B1 **Dargai** Pak.
54 B1 **Dargaville** N.Z.
53 C3 **Dargo** Austr.
69 D1 **Darhan** Mongolia
150 A1 **Darién, Golfo del** *g.* Col.
75 C2 **Darjiling** India
75 C2 **Darling** China
52 B2 **Darling** *r.* Austr.
53 C1 **Darling Downs** *hills* Austr.
50 A3 **Darling Range** *hills* Austr.
98 C1 **Darlington** U.K.
53 C2 **Darlington Point** Austr.
103 D1 **Darłowo** Pol.
101 D3 **Darmstadt** Ger.
115 E1 **Darnah** Libya
52 B2 **Darnick** Austr.
107 C1 **Daroca** Spain
99 D3 **Dartford** U.K.
99 A3 **Dartmoor** *hills* U.K.
99 B3 **Dartmouth** Can.
99 B3 **Dartmouth** U.K.
59 D3 **Daru** P.N.G.
50 C1 **Darwin** Austr.
74 A2 **Dasht** *r.* Pak.
76 B2 **Daşoguz** Turkm.
61 C1 **Datadian** Indon.
111 C3 **Datça** Turkey
70 B1 **Datong** China
64 B2 **Datu Piang** Phil.
74 B1 **Daud Khel** Pak.
88 B2 **Daugava** *r.* Latvia

88 C2 **Daugavpils** Latvia
100 C2 **Daun** Ger.
129 D2 **Dauphin** Can.
129 E2 **Dauphin Lake** Can.
73 B3 **Davangere** India
64 B2 **Davao** Phil.
64 B2 **Davao Gulf** Phil.
137 E2 **Davenport** U.S.A.
99 C2 **Daventry** U.K.
123 C2 **Daveyton** S. Africa
146 B4 **David** Panama
126 C2 **Davidson** Can.
126 E3 **Davidson Lake** Can.
135 B3 **Davis** U.S.A.
131 D1 **Davis Inlet** Can.
159 F3 **Davis Sea** Antarctica
160 P3 **Davis Strait**
Can./Greenland
105 D2 **Davos** Switz.
79 C3 **Dawqah** Oman
126 B2 **Dawson** Can.
143 D2 **Dawson** U.S.A.
128 B2 **Dawson Creek** Can.
128 B2 **Dawsons Landing** Can.
68 C2 **Dawu** China
Dawukou China *see*
Shizuishan
104 B3 **Dax** France
68 C2 **Da Xueshan** *mts* China
80 C2 **Dayr az Zawr** Syria
140 C3 **Dayton** U.S.A.
143 D3 **Daytona Beach** U.S.A.
70 B2 **Dazhou** China
71 B3 **Dazhu** China
122 B3 **De Aar** S. Africa
80 B2 **Dead Sea** *salt l.* Asia
68 C2 **De'an** China
152 B4 **Deán Funes** Arg.
128 B2 **Dease Lake** Can.
126 D2 **Dease Strait** Can.
135 C3 **Death Valley** *depr.* U.S.A.
104 C2 **Deauville** France
61 C1 **Debak** Sarawak Malaysia
109 D2 **Debar** Macedonia
126 D2 **Debrecen** Hungary
117 B3 **Debre Markos** Eth.
117 B3 **Debre Tabor** Eth.
117 B4 **Debre Zeyit** Eth.
142 C2 **Decatur** *AL.* U.S.A.
140 B3 **Decatur** *IL.* U.S.A.
73 B3 **Deccan** *plat.* India
102 C1 **Děčín** Czech Rep.
137 E2 **Decorah** U.S.A.
88 C2 **Dedovichi** Rus. Fed.
121 C2 **Dedza** Malawi
98 B2 **Dee** *r.* England/Wales U.K.
96 C2 **Dee** *r.* Scotland U.K.
53 D1 **Deepwater** Austr.
131 E2 **Deer Lake** Can.
134 D1 **Deer Lodge** U.S.A.
140 C2 **Defiance** U.S.A.
68 C2 **Dêgê** China
117 C4 **Degeh Bur** Eth.
102 C2 **Deggendorf** Ger.
91 E2 **Degtevo** Rus. Fed.
75 B1 **Dehra Dun** India
75 C2 **Dehri** India
69 E2 **Dehui** China
100 A2 **Deinze** Belgium
110 B1 **Dej** Romania
140 B2 **De Kalb** U.S.A.
78 A3 **Dekemhare** Eritrea
118 C3 **Dekese** Dem. Rep. Congo
135 C3 **Delano** U.S.A.
135 D3 **Delano Peak** U.S.A.
74 B1 **Delārām** Afgh.
123 C2 **Delareyville** S. Africa
129 D2 **Delaronde Lake** Can.
140 C2 **Delaware** U.S.A.
141 D3 **Delaware** *r.* U.S.A.
141 D3 **Delaware** *state* U.S.A.

141 D3 Delaware Bay U.S.A.
53 C3 Delegate Austr.
105 D2 Delémont Switz.
100 B1 Delft Neth.
100 C1 Delfzijl Neth.
121 D2 Delgado, Cabo c. Moz.
75 B2 Delhi India
60 B2 Deli i. Indon.
126 C2 Déline Can.
101 F2 Delitzsch Ger.
107 D2 Dellys Alg.
101 D1 Delmenhorst Ger.
109 B1 Delnice Croatia
83 L1 De-Longa, Ostrova is
Rus. Fed.
129 D3 Deloraine Can.
111 B3 Delphi tourist site Greece
139 C3 Del Rio U.S.A.
136 B3 Delta CO U.S.A.
135 D3 Delta UT U.S.A.
126 B2 Delta Junction U.S.A.
109 D3 Delvinë Albania
118 C3 Demba Dem. Rep. Congo
117 B4 Dembi Dolo Eth.
89 D2 Demidov Rus. Fed.
138 B2 Deming U.S.A.
111 C3 Demirci Turkey
110 C2 Demirköy Turkey
102 C1 Demmin Ger.
142 C2 Demopolis U.S.A.
60 B2 Dempo, Gunung vol. Indon.
89 D2 Demyansk Rus. Fed.
122 B3 De Naawte S. Africa
117 C3 Denakil reg. Eritrea/Eth.
100 B1 Den Burg Neth.
100 B2 Dendermonde Belgium
70 A1 Dengkou China
70 B2 Dengzhou China
— Den Haag Neth. see
The Hague
50 A2 Denham Austr.
100 B1 Den Helder Neth.
52 B3 Deniliquin Austr.
134 C2 Denio U.S.A.
137 D2 Denison IA U.S.A.
139 D2 Denison TX U.S.A.
111 C3 Denizli Turkey
53 D2 Denman Austr.
50 A3 Denmark Austr.
93 E4 Denmark country Europe
160 Q3 Denmark Strait
Greenland/Iceland
61 C2 Denpasar Indon.
139 D2 Denton U.S.A.
50 A3 D'Entrecasteaux, Point
Austr.
136 B3 Denver U.S.A.
75 C2 Deogarh Orissa India
74 B2 Deogarh Rajasthan India
75 C2 Deoghar India
83 K2 Deputatskiy Rus. Fed.
68 C3 Dêqên China
142 B2 De Queen U.S.A.
74 A2 Dera Bugti Pak.
74 B1 Dera Ghazi Khan Pak.
74 B1 Dera Ismail Khan Pak.
87 D4 Derbent Rus. Fed.
50 B1 Derby Austr.
99 C2 Derby U.K.
99 D2 Dereham U.K.
97 B2 Derg, Lough l. Ireland
91 D1 Derhachi Ukr.
142 B2 De Ridder U.S.A.
91 D2 Derkul r. Rus. Fed./Ukr.
75 B1 Dêrub China
116 B3 Derudeb Sudan
122 B3 De Rust S. Africa
109 C2 Derventa Bos.-Herz.
98 C2 Derwent r. U.K.
98 B1 Derwent Water l. U.K.

77 C1 Derzhavinsk Kazakh.
152 B2 Desaguadero r. Bol.
49 I3 Désappointement, Îles du
is Fr. Polynesia
129 D2 Deschambault Lake Can.
134 B1 Deschutes r. U.S.A.
117 B3 Desë Eth.
153 B5 Deseado Arg.
153 B5 Deseado r. Arg.
137 E2 Des Moines U.S.A.
137 E2 Des Moines r. U.S.A.
91 C1 Desna r. Rus. Fed./Ukr.
89 D3 Desnogorsk Rus. Fed.
101 F2 Dessau Ger.
126 B2 Destruction Bay Can.
128 C1 Detah Can.
101 D2 Detmold Ger.
140 C2 Detroit U.S.A.
137 D1 Detroit Lakes U.S.A.
100 B2 Deurne Neth.
110 B1 Deva Romania
100 C1 Deventer Neth.
96 C2 Deveron r. U.K.
103 D2 Devét Skal hill Czech Rep.
137 D1 Devil's Lake U.S.A.
128 A2 Devil's Paw mt. U.S.A.
99 C3 Devizes U.K.
74 B2 Devli India
110 C2 Devnya Bulg.
128 C2 Devon i. Can.
126 E1 Devon Island Can.
51 D4 Devonport Austr.
74 B2 Dewas India
59 D3 Dewa, Tanjung pt Indon.
81 C2 Dezful Iran
70 B2 Dezhou China
75 C2 Dhahran Saudi Arabia
75 B3 Dhaka Bangl.
78 B3 Dhamār Yemen
75 C2 Dhamtari India
75 C2 Dhanbad India
75 C2 Dhankuta Nepal
62 A1 Dharmanagar India
75 C2 Dharmjaygarh India
73 B3 Dharwad India
74 B2 Dhasa India
78 B3 Dhubāb Yemen
74 B2 Dhule India
144 A1 Diablo, Picacho del
mt. Mex.
51 C2 Diamantina watercourse
Austr.
151 D1 Diamantina Brazil
151 D3 Diamantina, Chapada
plat. Brazil
151 C3 Diamantino Brazil
71 B3 Dianbai China
151 D3 Dianópolis Brazil
114 B4 Dianra Côte d'Ivoire
79 C2 Diapaga Burkina
79 C2 Dibā al Ḥişn U.A.E.
118 C3 Dibaya Dem. Rep. Congo
62 A1 Dibrugarh India
136 C1 Dickinson U.S.A.
142 C1 Dickson U.S.A.
— Dicle r. Turkey see Tigris
105 D3 Die France
129 D2 Diefenbaker, Lake Can.
114 B3 Diéma Mali
62 B2 Diên Châu Vietnam
101 D1 Diepholz Ger.
104 C2 Dieppe France
115 D3 Diffa Niger
131 D2 Digby Can.
105 D3 Digne-les-Bains France
105 C2 Digoin France
64 B2 Digos Phil.
59 D3 Digul r. Indon.

— Dihang r. China/India see
Brahmaputra
— Dihang r. China/India see
Yarlung Zangbo
105 D2 Dijon France
117 C3 Dikhil Djibouti
111 C3 Dikili Turkey
100 A2 Diksmuide Belgium
115 D3 Dikwa Nigeria
117 B4 Dila Eth.
59 C3 Dili East Timor
101 D2 Dillenburg Ger.
134 D1 Dillon U.S.A.
118 C4 Dilolo Dem. Rep. Congo
62 A1 Dimapur India
— Dimashq Syria see
Damascus
52 B3 Dimboola Austr.
110 C2 Dimitrovgrad Bulg.
87 D3 Dimitrovgrad Rus. Fed.
100 B2 Dinan France
100 B2 Dinant Belgium
111 D3 Dinar Turkey
81 D2 Dīnār, Kūh-e mt. Iran
73 B3 Dindigul India
123 D1 Dindiza Moz.
101 E2 Dingelstädt Ger.
97 A2 Dingle Ireland
97 A2 Dingle Bay Ireland
96 B2 Dingwall U.K.
70 A2 Dingxi China
154 B3 Dionísio Cerqueira Brazil
114 A3 Diourbel Senegal
74 B1 Dir Pak.
51 D1 Direction, Cape Austr.
117 C4 Dirē Dawa Eth.
120 A2 Dirico Angola
50 A2 Dirk Hartog Island Austr.
53 C1 Dirranbandi Austr.
78 B3 Dirs Saudi Arabia
50 B2 Disappointment, Lake
salt flat Austr.
52 B3 Discovery Bay Austr.
143 E1 Dismal Swamp U.S.A.
99 D2 Diss U.K.
108 B3 Dittaino r. Sicily Italy
74 B2 Diu India
155 D2 Divinópolis Brazil
87 D4 Divnoye Rus. Fed.
114 B4 Divo Côte d'Ivoire
80 B2 Divriği Turkey
140 B2 Dixon U.S.A.
128 A2 Dixon Entrance sea chan.
Can./U.S.A.
80 C2 Diyarbakır Turkey
74 A2 Diz Pak.
115 D3 Djado Niger
115 D3 Djado, Plateau du Niger
118 B3 Djambala Congo
115 C1 Djanet Alg.
115 C1 Djelfa Alg.
119 C2 Djéma C.A.R.
114 B3 Djenné Mali
114 B3 Djenné Mali
117 C3 Djibouti country Africa
117 C3 Djibouti Djibouti
114 C4 Djougou Benin
92 □C3 Djúpivogur Iceland
91 E1 Dmitriyevka Rus. Fed.
89 E3 Dmitriyev-L'govskiy
Rus. Fed.
89 E2 Dmitrov Rus. Fed.
— Dnepr r. Rus. Fed. see
Dnieper
91 C2 Dnieper r. Europe
90 B2 Dniester r. Ukr.
— Dnipro r. Ukr. see Dnieper
91 C2 Dniprodzerzhyns'k Ukr.

91	D2	**Dnipropetrovs'k** Ukr.
91	D2	**Dniprorudne** Ukr.
		Dnister *r.* Ukr. *see* **Dniester**
88	C2	**Dno** Rus. Fed.
115	D4	**Doba** Chad
88	B2	**Dobele** Latvia
101	F2	**Döbeln** Ger.
59	C3	**Doberai, Jazirah** *pen.* Indon.
59	C3	**Dobo** Indon.
109	C2	**Doboj** Bos.-Herz.
110	C2	**Dobrich** Bulg.
89	F3	**Dobrinka** Rus. Fed.
89	D3	**Dobroye** Rus. Fed.
89	D3	**Dobrush** Belarus
155	E1	**Doce** *r.* Brazil
145	B2	**Doctor Arroyo** Mex.
144	B2	**Doctor Belisario Domínguez** Mex.
111	C3	**Dodecanese** *is* Greece
		Dodekanisos *is* Greece *see* **Dodecanese**
136	C3	**Dodge City** U.S.A.
119	D3	**Dodoma** Tanz.
100	C2	**Doetinchem** Neth.
59	C3	**Dofa** Indon.
75	C1	**Dogai Coring** *salt l.* China
128	B2	**Dog Creek** Can.
67	B3	**Dōgo** *i.* Japan
115	C3	**Dogondoutchi** Niger
81	C2	**Doğubeyazıt** Turkey
79	C2	**Doha** Qatar
62	A2	**Doi Saket** Thai.
100	B1	**Dokkum** Neth.
88	C3	**Dokshytsy** Belarus
91	D2	**Dokuchayevs'k** Ukr.
59	D3	**Dolak, Pulau** *i.* Indon.
131	C2	**Dolbeau** Can.
104	B2	**Dol-de-Bretagne** France
105	D2	**Dole** France
99	B2	**Dolgellau** U.K.
89	E3	**Dolgorukovo** Rus. Fed.
89	E3	**Dolgoye** Rus. Fed.
		Dolisie Congo *see* **Loubomo**
108	B1	**Dolomites** *mts* Italy
117	C4	**Dolo Odo** Eth.
126	D2	**Dolphin and Union Strait** Can.
90	A2	**Dolyna** Ukr.
102	C2	**Domažlice** Czech Rep.
93	E3	**Dombås** Norway
103	D2	**Dombóvár** Hungary
128	B2	**Dome Creek** Can.
147	D3	**Dominica** *country* West Indies
147	C3	**Dominican Republic** *country* West Indies
89	E2	**Domodedovo** Rus. Fed.
111	B3	**Domokos** Greece
61	C2	**Dompu** Indon.
89	E3	**Don** *r.* Rus. Fed.
96	C2	**Don** *r.* U.K.
97	D1	**Donaghadee** U.K.
52	B3	**Donald** Austr.
		Donau *r.* Austria/Ger. *see* **Danube**
102	C2	**Donauwörth** Ger.
106	B2	**Don Benito** Spain
98	C2	**Doncaster** U.K.
120	A1	**Dondo** Angola
121	C2	**Dondo** Moz.
73	C4	**Dondra Head** Sri Lanka
97	B1	**Donegal** Ireland
97	B1	**Donegal Bay** Ireland
91	D2	**Donets'k** Ukr.
91	D2	**Donets'kyy Kryazh** *hills* Rus. Fed./Ukr.
50	A2	**Dongara** Austr.
62	B1	**Dongchuan** China
71	A4	**Dongfang** China
66	B1	**Dongfanghong** China
58	B3	**Donggala** Indon.
65	A2	**Donggang** China
71	B3	**Dongguan** China
62	B2	**Đông Ha** Vietnam
		Dong Hai *sea* N. Pacific Ocean *see* **East China Sea**
62	B2	**Đông Hơi** Vietnam
118	B2	**Dongou** Congo
71	B3	**Dongshan** China
70	C2	**Dongtai** China
71	B3	**Dongting Hu** *l.* China
70	B2	**Dongying** China
54	B1	**Donnellys Crossing** N.Z.
107	C1	**Donostia-San Sebastián** Spain
117	C4	**Dooxo Nugaaleed** *val.* Somalia
99	B3	**Dorchester** U.K.
122	A1	**Dordabis** Namibia
104	B2	**Dordogne** *r.* France
100	B2	**Dordrecht** Neth.
123	C3	**Dordrecht** S. Africa
129	C2	**Doré Lake** Can.
101	D1	**Dorfmark** Ger.
114	B3	**Dori** Burkina
122	A3	**Doring** *r.* S. Africa
96	B2	**Dornoch** U.K.
96	B2	**Dornoch Firth** *est.* U.K.
89	D3	**Dorogobuzh** Rus. Fed.
90	B2	**Dorohoi** Romania
68	C1	**Döröö Nuur** *salt l.* Mongolia
92	G3	**Dorotea** Sweden
50	A2	**Dorre Island** Austr.
53	D2	**Dorrigo** Austr.
100	C2	**Dortmund** Ger.
100	C2	**Dortmund-Ems-Kanal** *canal* Ger.
153	B5	**Dos Bahías, Cabo** *c.* Arg.
101	F1	**Dosse** *r.* Ger.
114	C3	**Dosso** Niger
143	C2	**Dothan** U.S.A.
101	D1	**Dötlingen** Ger.
105	C1	**Douai** France
118	A2	**Douala** Cameroon
104	B2	**Douarnenez** France
114	B3	**Douentza** Mali
98	A1	**Douglas** Isle of Man
122	B2	**Douglas** S. Africa
128	A2	**Douglas** *AK* U.S.A.
138	B2	**Douglas** *AZ* U.S.A.
143	D2	**Douglas** *GA* U.S.A.
136	B2	**Douglas** *WY* U.S.A.
104	C1	**Doullens** France
154	B1	**Dourada, Serra** *hills* Brazil
154	B2	**Dourados** Brazil
154	B2	**Dourados, Serra dos** *hills* Brazil
106	B1	**Douro** *r.* Port.
99	D3	**Dover** U.K.
141	D3	**Dover** U.S.A.
95	D3	**Dover, Strait of** France/U.K.
141	F1	**Dover-Foxcroft** U.S.A.
79	C2	**Dowlatābād** *Būshehr* Iran
79	C2	**Dowlatābād** *Kermān* Iran
97	D1	**Downpatrick** U.K.
77	C3	**Dowshī** Afgh.
67	B3	**Dōzen** *is* Japan
130	C2	**Dozois, Réservoir** *resr* Can.
154	B2	**Dracena** Brazil
100	C1	**Drachten** Neth.
110	B2	**Drăgănești-Olt** Romania
110	B2	**Drăgășani** Romania
88	C3	**Drahichyn** Belarus
123	C2	**Drakensberg** *mts* Lesotho/S. Africa
123	C2	**Drakensberg** *mts* S. Africa
158	B8	**Drake Passage** S. Atlantic Ocean
111	B2	**Drama** Greece
93	F4	**Drammen** Norway
109	C1	**Drava** *r.* Europe
128	C2	**Drayton Valley** Can.
101	D2	**Dreieich** Ger.
111	B3	**Drepano, Akra** *pt* Greece
102	C1	**Dresden** Ger.
104	C2	**Dreux** France
100	B1	**Driemond** Neth.
109	C2	**Drina** *r.* Bos.-Herz./Serb. and Mont.
109	C2	**Drniš** Croatia
110	B1	**Drobeta-Turnu Severin** Romania
101	D1	**Drochtersen** Ger.
97	C2	**Drogheda** Ireland
90	A2	**Drohobych** Ukr.
97	C1	**Dromore** U.K.
74	B1	**Drosh** Pak.
53	C3	**Drouin** Austr.
128	C2	**Drumheller** Can.
140	C1	**Drummond Island** U.S.A.
131	C2	**Drummondville** Can.
88	B3	**Druskininkai** Lith.
91	D2	**Druzhkivka** Ukr.
88	D2	**Druzhnaya Gorka** Rus. Fed.
130	A2	**Dryden** Can.
78	A2	**Dubā** Saudi Arabia
79	C2	**Dubai** U.A.E.
129	D1	**Dubawnt Lake** Can.
		Dubayy U.A.E. *see* **Dubai**
78	A2	**Dubbagh, Jabal ad** *mt.* Saudi Arabia
53	C2	**Dubbo** Austr.
97	C2	**Dublin** Ireland
143	D2	**Dublin** U.S.A.
90	B1	**Dubno** Ukr.
140	C2	**Du Bois** U.S.A.
114	A4	**Dubréka** Guinea
109	C2	**Dubrovnik** Croatia
90	B1	**Dubrovytsya** Ukr.
89	D3	**Dubrowna** Belarus
137	E2	**Dubuque** U.S.A.
129	D2	**Duck Bay** Can.
101	E2	**Duderstadt** Ger.
82	G2	**Dudinka** Rus. Fed.
99	B2	**Dudley** U.K.
106	B1	**Duero** *r.* Spain
131	C1	**Duffreboy, Lac** *l.* Can.
96	C2	**Dufftown** U.K.
109	C2	**Dugi Rat** Croatia
100	C2	**Duisburg** Ger.
123	D1	**Duiwelskloof** S. Africa
123	C3	**Dukathole** S. Africa
79	C2	**Dukhān** Qatar
89	D2	**Dukhovshchina** Rus. Fed.
		Dukou China *see* **Panzhihua**
88	C2	**Dūkštas** Lith.
68	C2	**Dulan** China
152	B4	**Dulce** *r.* Arg.
100	C2	**Dülmen** Ger.
110	C2	**Dulovo** Bulg.
137	E1	**Duluth** U.S.A.
64	B2	**Dumaguete** Phil.
60	B1	**Dumai** Indon.
64	B1	**Dumaran** *i.* Phil.
142	B2	**Dumas** *AR* U.S.A.
139	C1	**Dumas** *TX* U.S.A.
96	C3	**Dumbarton** U.K.
103	D2	**Dumbier** *mt.* Slovakia
96	C3	**Dumfries** U.K.
55	J3	**Dumont d'Urville Sea** Antarctica

116 B1 **Dumyâṭ** Egypt
Duna r. Hungary see Danube
103 D2 **Dunaj** r. Slovakia see Danube
91 D2 **Dymytrov** Ukr.
103 D2 **Dunakeszi** Hungary
Dunârea r. Romania see Danube
103 D2 **Dunaújváros** Hungary see Danube
90 B2 **Dunayivtsi** Ukr.
96 C2 **Dunbar** U.K.
96 C1 **Dunbeath** U.K.
128 B3 **Duncan** Can.
139 D2 **Duncan** U.S.A.
96 C1 **Duncansby Head** U.K.
97 C1 **Dundalk** Ireland
97 C2 **Dundalk Bay** Ireland
127 G1 **Dundas** Greenland
123 D2 **Dundee** S. Africa
96 C2 **Dundee** U.K.
97 D1 **Dundrum Bay** U.K.
54 A1 **Dunedin** N.Z.
96 C2 **Dunfermline** U.K.
97 C1 **Dungannon** U.K.
74 B2 **Dungarpur** India
97 C2 **Dungarvan** Ireland
99 D3 **Dungeness** hd U.K.
97 C1 **Dungiven** U.K.
53 D2 **Dungog** Austr.
119 C2 **Dungu** Dem. Rep. Congo
60 B1 **Dungun** Malaysia
116 B2 **Dungunab** Sudan
69 E2 **Dunhua** China
68 C2 **Dunhuang** China
Dunkerque France see Dunkirk
104 C1 **Dunkirk** France
141 D2 **Dunkirk** U.S.A.
97 C2 **Dún Laoghaire** Ireland
97 D1 **Dunmurry** U.K.
96 C1 **Dunnet Head** U.K.
96 C3 **Duns** U.K.
99 C3 **Dunstable** U.K.
110 B2 **Dupnitsa** Bulg.
136 C1 **Dupree** U.S.A.
50 B1 **Durack** r. Austr.
144 B2 **Durango** Mex.
106 C1 **Durango** Spain
136 B3 **Durango** U.S.A.
139 D2 **Durant** U.S.A.
153 C4 **Durazno** Uru.
123 D2 **Durban** S. Africa
104 C3 **Durban-Corbières** France
122 A3 **Durbanville** S. Africa
100 B2 **Durbuy** Belgium
100 C2 **Düren** Ger.
73 C2 **Durg** India
98 C1 **Durham** U.K.
143 E1 **Durham** U.S.A.
60 B1 **Duri** Indon.
109 C2 **Durmitor** mt. Serb. and Mont.
96 B1 **Durness** U.K.
109 C2 **Durrës** Albania
97 A3 **Dursey Island** Ireland
111 C3 **Dursunbey** Turkey
54 B2 **D'Urville Island** N.Z.
71 A3 **Dushan** China
77 C3 **Dushanbe** Tajik.
100 C2 **Düsseldorf** Ger.
71 A3 **Duyun** China
91 D2 **Dvorichna** Ukr.
74 A2 **Dwarka** India
123 C1 **Dwarsberg** S. Africa
134 C1 **Dworshak Reservoir** U.S.A.
89 D3 **Dyat'kovo** Rus. Fed.
96 C2 **Dyce** U.K.
127 G2 **Dyer, Cape** Can.

142 C1 **Dyersburg** U.S.A.
103 D2 **Dyje** r. Austria/Czech Rep.
103 D1 **Dylewska Góra** hill Pol.
91 D2 **Dymytrov** Ukr.
123 C3 **Dyoki** S. Africa
87 E3 **Dyurtyuli** Rus. Fed.
69 D2 **Dzamïn Üüd** Mongolia
120 D2 **Dzaoudzi** Mayotte
Dzhambul Kazakh. see Taraz
76 B2 **Dzhangala** Kazakh.
91 C2 **Dzhankoy** Ukr.
91 D3 **Dzhubga** Rus. Fed.
83 K3 **Dzhugdzhur, Khrebet** mts Rus. Fed.
77 D2 **Dzhungarskiy Alatau, Khrebet** mts China/Kazakh.
76 C2 **Dzhusaly** Kazakh.
103 E1 **Działdowo** Pol.
69 D1 **Dzuunmod** Mongolia
88 C3 **Dzyarzhynsk** Belarus
88 C3 **Dzyatlavichy** Belarus

E

131 E1 **Eagle** r. Can.
134 C1 **Eagle Cap** mt. U.S.A.
130 A2 **Eagle Lake** Can.
134 B2 **Eagle Lake** U.S.A.
139 C3 **Eagle Pass** U.S.A.
126 B2 **Eagle Plain** Can.
130 A1 **Ear Falls** Can.
99 D3 **Eastbourne** U.K.
156 C3 **East China Sea** N. Pacific Ocean
54 B1 **East Coast Bays** N.Z.
129 D3 **Eastend** Can.
123 C3 **Eastern Cape** prov. S. Africa
Eastern Desert Egypt see Aş Şaḥrāʾ ash Sharqiyah
73 B3 **Eastern Ghats** mts India
52 C3 **East Falkland** i. Falkland Is
100 C1 **East Frisian Islands** Ger.
96 B3 **East Kilbride** U.K.
99 C3 **Eastleigh** U.K.
140 C2 **East Liverpool** U.S.A.
123 C3 **East London** S. Africa
130 C1 **Eastmain** Can.
130 C1 **Eastmain** r. Can.
143 D2 **Eastman** U.S.A.
140 A3 **East St Louis** U.S.A.
East Sea N. Pacific Ocean see Japan, Sea of
83 K2 **East Siberian Sea** Rus. Fed.
59 C3 **East Timor** country Asia
140 A2 **Eau Claire** U.S.A.
130 C1 **Eau Claire, Lac à l'** l. Can.
59 D2 **Eauripik** atoll Micronesia
145 C2 **Ebano** Mex.
99 B3 **Ebbw Vale** U.K.
102 C1 **Eberswalde-Finow** Ger.
109 C2 **Eboli** Italy
118 B2 **Ebolowa** Cameroon
107 D1 **Ebro** r. Spain
144 A2 **Echeverria, Pico** mt. Mex.
129 E2 **Echoing** r. Can.
100 C3 **Echternach** Lux.
52 B3 **Echuca** Austr.
106 B2 **Écija** Spain
102 B1 **Eckernförde** Ger.
127 F2 **Eclipse Sound** sea chan. Can.
150 A2 **Ecuador** country S. America
116 C3 **Ed** Eritrea

117 A3 **Ed Da'ein** Sudan
117 B3 **Ed Damazin** Sudan
116 B3 **Ed Damer** Sudan
116 B3 **Ed Debba** Sudan
116 B3 **Ed Dueim** Sudan
51 D4 **Eddystone Point** Austr.
100 B1 **Ede** Neth.
118 B2 **Edéa** Cameroon
154 C1 **Edéia** Brazil
53 C3 **Eden** Austr.
98 B1 **Eden** r. U.K.
123 C2 **Edenburg** S. Africa
97 C2 **Edenderry** Ireland
52 B3 **Edenhope** Austr.
111 B2 **Edessa** Greece
82 C1 **Edgeøya** i. Svalbard
139 D3 **Edinburg** U.S.A.
96 C3 **Edinburgh** U.K.
110 C2 **Edirne** Turkey
128 C2 **Edmonton** Can.
131 D2 **Edmundston** Can.
111 C3 **Edremit** Turkey
111 C3 **Edremit Körfezi** b. Turkey
128 C2 **Edson** Can.
119 C3 **Edward, Lake** Dem. Rep. Congo/Uganda
139 C2 **Edwards Plateau** TX U.S.A.
100 C1 **Eenrum** Neth.
48 F4 **Éfaté** i. Vanuatu
140 B3 **Effingham** U.S.A.
135 C3 **Egan Range** mts U.S.A.
103 E2 **Eger** Hungary
93 E4 **Egersund** Norway
92 □C2 **Egilsstaðir** Iceland
80 B2 **Eğirdir** Turkey
80 B2 **Eğirdir Gölü** l. Turkey
104 C2 **Égletons** France
Egmont, Mount vol. N.Z. see Taranaki, Mount
83 M2 **Egvekinot** Rus. Fed.
68 C2 **Ehen Hudag** China
100 C1 **Eibergen** Neth.
100 C2 **Eifel** hills Ger.
96 A2 **Eigg** i. U.K.
73 B4 **Eight Degree Channel** India/Maldives
50 B1 **Eighty Mile Beach** Austr.
80 B2 **Eilat** Israel
101 F2 **Eilenburg** Ger.
100 D1 **Einbeck** Ger.
100 B2 **Eindhoven** Neth.
150 B2 **Eirunepé** Brazil
120 B2 **Eiseb** watercourse Namibia
101 E2 **Eisenach** Ger.
102 C1 **Eisenhüttenstadt** Ger.
103 D2 **Eisenstadt** Austria
101 E2 **Eisleben Lutherstadt** Ger.
Eivissa Spain see Ibiza
Eivissa i. Spain see Ibiza
107 C1 **Ejea de los Caballeros** Spain
121 □D3 **Ejeda** Madag.
Ejin Qi China see Dalain Hob
93 H4 **Ekenäs** Fin.
77 D1 **Ekibastuz** Kazakh.
92 J2 **Ekostrovskaya Imandra, Ozero** l. Rus. Fed.
93 F4 **Eksjö** Sweden
122 A3 **Eksteenfontein** S. Africa
130 B1 **Ekwan** r. Can.
62 A2 **Ela** Myanmar
123 C2 **Elandsdoorn** S. Africa
111 B3 **Elassona** Greece
80 B2 **Elazığ** Turkey
150 A1 **El Banco** Col.
109 C2 **Elbasan** Albania
150 B1 **El Baúl** Venez.
114 C1 **El Bayadh** Alg.
101 D1 **Elbe** r. Ger.

136 B3 Elbert, Mount U.S.A.
143 D2 Elberton U.S.A.
104 C2 Elbeuf France
80 B2 Elblag Pol.
103 D1 Elbląg Pol.
87 D4 El'brus mt. Rus. Fed.
81 C2 Elburz Mountains Iran
150 B1 El Callao Venez.
139 D3 El Campo U.S.A.
135 C4 El Centro U.S.A.
152 B2 El Cerro Bol.
107 C2 Elche-Elx Spain
107 C2 Elda Spain
137 E3 Eldon U.S.A.
144 B2 El Dorado Mex.
142 B2 El Dorado AR U.S.A.
137 D3 El Dorado KS U.S.A.
114 B2 El Eglab plat. Alg.
106 C2 El Ejido Spain
89 E2 Elektrostal' Rus. Fed.
150 A2 El Encanto Col.
146 C2 Eleuthera i. Bahamas
117 A3 El Fasher Sudan
144 B2 El Fuerte Mex.
117 A3 El Geneina Sudan
116 B3 El Geteina Sudan
96 C2 Elgin U.K.
140 B2 Elgin U.S.A.
115 C1 El Goléa Alg.
144 A1 El Golfo de Santa Clara Mex.
119 D3 Elgon, Mount Uganda
114 A2 El Hammâmi reg. Maur.
114 A2 El Hierro i. Canary Is
145 C2 El Higo Mex.
114 C2 El Homr Alg.
87 D4 Elista Rus. Fed.
141 E2 Elizabeth U.S.A.
143 E1 Elizabeth City U.S.A.
140 B3 Elizabethtown U.S.A.
114 B1 El Jadida Morocco
103 E1 Elk Pol.
139 D1 Elk City U.S.A.
128 C2 Elkford Can.
140 B2 Elkhart U.S.A.
El Khartum Sudan see Khartoum
110 C2 Elkhovo Bulg.
140 D3 Elkins U.S.A.
128 C3 Elko Can.
134 C2 Elko U.S.A.
129 C2 Elk Point Can.
126 E1 Ellef Ringnes Island Can.
137 D2 Ellendale U.S.A.
134 B1 Ellensburg U.S.A.
54 B2 Ellesmere, Lake N.Z.
127 F1 Ellesmere Island Can.
98 B2 Ellesmere Port U.K.
116 E2 Ellice r. Can.
Ellice Islands country S. Pacific Ocean see Tuvalu
123 C3 Elliotdale S. Africa
96 C3 Ellon U.K.
141 F2 Ellsworth U.S.A.
55 O2 Ellsworth Mountains Antarctica
111 C3 Elmalı Turkey
115 C3 El Meghaïer Alg.
141 D2 Elmira U.S.A.
107 C2 El Moral Spain
101 D1 Elmshorn Ger.
117 A3 El Muglad Sudan
64 A1 El Nido Phil.
117 B3 El Obeid Sudan
144 B2 El Oro Mex.
115 C1 El Oued Alg.
138 A2 Eloy U.S.A.
138 B2 El Paso U.S.A.
144 B1 El Porvenir Mex.
107 D1 El Prat de Llobregat Spain

139 D1 El Reno U.S.A.
145 B2 El Salado Mex.
144 B2 El Salto Mex.
146 B3 El Salvador country Central America
145 B2 El Salvador Mex.
138 B3 El Sauz Mex.
144 A1 El Socorro Mex.
145 C2 El Temascal Mex.
150 B1 El Tigre Venez.
147 D4 El Tocuyo Venez.
88 C2 Elva Estonia
106 B2 Elvas Port.
93 F3 Elverum Norway
119 E2 El Wak Kenya
99 D2 Ely U.K.
137 E1 Ely MN U.S.A.
135 D3 Ely NV U.S.A.
81 D2 Emāmrūd Iran
93 G4 Emån r. Sweden
76 B2 Emba Kazakh.
76 B2 Emba r. Kazakh.
123 C2 Embalenhle S. Africa
154 C1 Emborcação, Represa de resr Brazil
119 D3 Emba Kenya
100 C1 Emden Ger.
51 C1 Emerald Austr.
123 E3 Emerson Can.
111 C3 Emet Turkey
123 D2 eMgwenya S. Africa
115 D3 Emi Koussi mt. Chad
110 C2 Emine, Nos pt Bulg.
80 B2 Emirdağ Turkey
123 D2 eMjindini S. Africa
88 B2 Emmaste Estonia
100 B1 Emmeloord Neth.
100 C2 Emmelshausen Ger.
100 C1 Emmen Neth.
139 C3 Emory Peak U.S.A.
144 A2 Empalme Mex.
123 D2 Empangeni S. Africa
108 B2 Empoli Italy
137 D3 Emporia KS U.S.A.
141 D3 Emporia VA U.S.A.
100 C1 Ems r. Ger.
100 C1 Emsdetten Ger.
123 C2 eMzinoni S. Africa
59 D3 Enarotali Indon.
144 B2 Encarnación Mex.
152 C3 Encarnación Para.
155 D1 Encruzilhada Brazil
58 C3 Ende Indon.
126 A2 Endicott Mountains U.S.A.
91 C2 Enerhodar Ukr.
87 D3 Engel's Rus. Fed.
60 B2 Enggano i. Indon.
98 C2 England admin. div. U.K.
130 A1 English r. Can.
95 C4 English Channel France/U.K.
139 D1 Enid U.S.A.
100 B1 Enkhuizen Neth.
93 G4 Enköping Sweden
108 B3 Enna Sicily Italy
129 D1 Ennadai Lake Can.
117 A3 En Nahud Sudan
115 E3 Ennedi, Massif mts Chad
53 C1 Enngonia Austr.
97 B2 Ennis Ireland
139 D2 Ennis U.S.A.
97 C2 Enniscorthy Ireland
97 C1 Enniskillen U.K.
97 B2 Ennistymon Ireland
102 C2 Enns r. Austria
92 H2 Enontekiö Fin.
53 C3 Ensay Austr.
100 C1 Enschede Neth.
144 B2 Ensenada Mex.
70 A2 Enshi China

128 C1 Enterprise Can.
142 C2 Enterprise AL U.S.A.
134 C1 Enterprise OR U.S.A.
152 B3 Entre Ríos Bol.
106 B2 Entroncamento Port.
115 C4 Enugu Nigeria
150 A2 Envira Brazil
135 D3 Ephraim U.S.A.
134 C1 Ephrata U.S.A.
105 D2 Épinal France
99 C3 Epsom U.K.
118 A2 Equatorial Guinea country Africa
101 F3 Erbendorf Ger.
100 C3 Erbeskopf hill Ger.
81 C2 Erciş Turkey
65 B1 Erdao Jiang r. China
111 C2 Erdek Turkey
80 B2 Erdemli Turkey
152 C3 Erechim Brazil
69 D1 Ereentsav Mongolia
80 B2 Ereğli Konya Turkey
80 B1 Ereğli Zonguldak Turkey
69 D2 Erenhot China
Erevan Armenia see Yerevan
101 E2 Erfurt Ger.
80 B2 Ergani Turkey
114 B2 'Erg Chech des. Alg./Mali
115 D3 Erg du Ténéré des. Niger
111 C2 Ergene r. Turkey
140 C2 Erie U.S.A.
140 C2 Erie, Lake Can./U.S.A.
66 D2 Erimo-misaki c. Japan
116 B3 Eritrea country Africa
101 E3 Erlangen Ger.
50 C2 Erldunda Austr.
123 C2 Ermelo S. Africa
80 B2 Ermenek Turkey
111 B3 Ermoupoli Greece
73 B4 Ernakulam India
73 B3 Erode India
100 B2 Erp Neth.
114 B1 Er Rachidia Morocco
117 B3 Er Rahad Sudan
97 B1 Errigal hill Ireland
97 A1 Erris Head Ireland
109 D2 Erseke Albania
91 E1 Ertil' Rus. Fed.
101 D2 Erwitte Ger.
102 C1 Erzgebirge mts Czech Rep./Ger.
80 B2 Erzincan Turkey
81 C2 Erzurum Turkey
93 E4 Esbjerg Denmark
135 D3 Escalante U.S.A.
144 B2 Escalón Mex.
140 B1 Escanaba U.S.A.
145 C3 Escárcega Mex.
107 C1 Escatrón Spain
100 A2 Escaut r. Belgium
101 E1 Eschede Ger.
100 B3 Esch-sur-Alzette Lux.
101 E2 Eschwege Ger.
100 C2 Eschweiler Ger.
135 C4 Escondido U.S.A.
144 B2 Escuinapa Mex.
111 C3 Eşen Turkey
81 D2 Eşfahān Iran
123 D2 Esikhawini S. Africa
98 B1 Esk r. U.K.
131 D1 Esker Can.
92 □C2 Eskifjörður Iceland
93 G4 Eskilstuna Sweden
Eskimo Point Can. see Arviat
80 B2 Eskişehir Turkey
81 C2 Eslāmābād-e Gharb Iran
111 C3 Esler Dağı mt. Turkey
111 C3 Eşme Turkey

150 A1 **Esmeraldas** Ecuador
79 D2 **Espakeh** Iran
104 C3 **Espalion** France
130 B2 **Espanola** Can.
138 B1 **Espanola** U.S.A.
50 B3 **Esperance** Austr.
144 B2 **Esperanza** Mex.
106 B2 **Espichel, Cabo** c. Port.
155 D1 **Espinhaço, Serra do** mts Brazil
151 D3 **Espinosa** Brazil
48 F4 **Espíritu Santo** i. Vanuatu
144 A2 **Espíritu Santo, Isla** i. Mex.
93 H3 **Espoo** Fin.
153 A5 **Esquel** Arg.
114 A2 **Essaouira** Morocco
114 A2 **Es Semara** Western Sahara
100 C2 **Essen** Ger.
150 C1 **Essequibo** r. Guyana
83 L3 **Esso** Rus. Fed.
79 C2 **Eştahbān** Iran
151 E3 **Estância** Brazil
123 C2 **Estcourt** S. Africa
107 C1 **Estella** Spain
106 B2 **Estepona** Spain
106 C1 **Esteras de Medinaceli** Spain
129 D2 **Esterhazy** Can.
152 B3 **Esteros** Para.
136 B2 **Estes Park** U.S.A.
129 D3 **Estevan** Can.
137 E2 **Estherville** U.S.A.
129 D2 **Eston** Can.
88 C2 **Estonia** country Europe
106 B1 **Estrela, Serra da** mts Port.
106 B2 **Estremoz** Port.
52 A1 **Etadunna** Austr.
104 C2 **Étampes** France
104 C1 **Étaples** France
75 B2 **Etawah** India
123 D2 **Ethandakukhanya** S. Africa
117 B4 **Ethiopia** country Africa
109 C3 **Etna, Mount** vol. Sicily Italy
128 A2 **Etolin Island** U.S.A.
120 A2 **Etosha Pan** salt pan Namibia
100 C3 **Ettelbrück** Lux.
100 B2 **Etten-Leur** Neth.
107 C1 **Etxarri-Aranatz** Spain
99 C3 **Eu** France
53 C2 **Euabalong** Austr.
Euboea i. Greece see Evvoia
50 B3 **Eucla** Austr.
143 C2 **Eufaula** U.S.A.
139 D1 **Eufaula Lake** resr U.S.A.
132 B2 **Eugene** U.S.A.
144 A2 **Eugenia, Punta** pt Mex.
53 C1 **Eulo** Austr.
53 C2 **Eumungerie** Austr.
139 C2 **Eunice** U.S.A.
80 C2 **Euphrates** r. Asia
134 B2 **Eureka** CA U.S.A.
134 C1 **Eureka** MT U.S.A.
135 C3 **Eureka** NV U.S.A.
52 B2 **Euriowie** Austr.
53 C2 **Euroa** Austr.
106 B2 **Europa Point** Gibraltar
128 B2 **Eutsuk Lake** Can.
130 C1 **Evans, Lac** l. Can.
53 D1 **Evans Head** Austr.
127 F2 **Evans Strait** Can.
136 A2 **Evanston** U.S.A.
140 B3 **Evansville** U.S.A.
123 C2 **Evaton** S. Africa
79 C2 **Evaz** Iran
82 E3 **Evensk** Rus. Fed.
54 C2 **Everard Range** hills Austr.
75 C2 **Everest, Mount** China/Nepal

134 B1 **Everett** U.S.A.
100 A2 **Evergem** Belgium
143 D3 **Everglades** swamp U.S.A.
118 B2 **Evinayong** Equat. Guinea
93 E4 **Evje** Norway
106 B2 **Évora** Port.
104 C2 **Évreux** France
111 C2 **Evros** r. Greece/Turkey
111 B3 **Evrotas** r. Greece
80 B2 **Evrychou** Cyprus
111 B3 **Evvoia** i. Greece
119 E2 **Ewaso Ngiro** r. Kenya
152 B2 **Exaltación** Bol.
99 B3 **Exe** r. U.K.
99 B3 **Exeter** U.K.
99 B3 **Exmoor** hills U.K.
99 B3 **Exmouth** U.K.
50 A2 **Exmouth Gulf** Austr.
146 C2 **Exuma Cays** is Bahamas
91 D2 **Eya** r. Rus. Fed.
117 C4 **Eyl** Somalia
52 A1 **Eyre, Lake (North)** salt flat Austr.
51 C3 **Eyre Peninsula** Austr.
94 B1 **Eysturoy** i. Faroe Is
123 C2 **Ezakheni** S. Africa
123 C2 **Ezenzeleni** S. Africa
70 B2 **Ezhou** China
86 E2 **Ezhva** Rus. Fed.
111 C3 **Ezine** Turkey

F

138 B2 **Fabens** U.S.A.
108 B2 **Fabriano** Italy
115 D3 **Fachi** Niger
114 C3 **Fada-N'Gourma** Burkina
108 B2 **Faenza** Italy
59 C3 **Fafanlap** Indon.
110 B1 **Făgăraş** Romania
49 G3 **Fagatogo** American Samoa
93 E3 **Fagernes** Norway
93 G4 **Fagersta** Sweden
153 B6 **Fagnano, Lago** l. Arg./Chile
114 B3 **Faguibine, Lac** l. Mali
92 □B3 **Fagurhólsmýri** Iceland
126 B2 **Fairbanks** U.S.A.
137 D2 **Fairbury** U.S.A.
135 B3 **Fairfield** U.S.A.
96 □ **Fair Isle** i. U.K.
137 E2 **Fairmont** MN U.S.A.
140 C3 **Fairmont** WV U.S.A.
128 C2 **Fairview** Can.
59 D2 **Fais** i. Micronesia
74 B1 **Faisalabad** Pak.
136 C1 **Faith** U.S.A.
75 C2 **Faizabad** India
59 C3 **Fakfak** Indon.
65 A1 **Faku** China
114 A4 **Falaba** Sierra Leone
139 D3 **Falcon Lake** Mex./U.S.A.
93 G3 **Falfurrias** U.S.A.
138 D3 **Falher** Can.
101 F2 **Falkenberg** Ger.
93 F4 **Falkenberg** Sweden
101 F1 **Falkensee** Ger.
96 C3 **Falkirk** U.K.
153 C6 **Falkland Islands** terr. S. Atlantic Ocean
93 F4 **Falköping** Sweden
135 C3 **Fallon** U.S.A.
141 E2 **Fall River** U.S.A.
137 D2 **Falls City** U.S.A.
99 A3 **Falmouth** U.K.
122 A3 **False Bay** S. Africa
93 F4 **Falster** i. Denmark

110 C1 **Fălticeni** Romania
93 G3 **Falun** Sweden
71 A3 **Fangchenggang** China
71 C3 **Fangshan** Taiwan
69 E1 **Fangzheng** China
108 B2 **Fano** Italy
119 C2 **Faradje** Dem. Rep. Congo
121 □D3 **Farafangana** Madag.
116 A2 **Farāfirah, Wāḥāt al** oasis Egypt
76 C3 **Farāh** Afgh.
114 A3 **Faranah** Guinea
78 B3 **Farasān, Jazā'ir** is Saudi Arabia
127 J3 **Farewell, Cape** Greenland
54 B2 **Farewell, Cape** N.Z.
137 D1 **Fargo** U.S.A.
77 D2 **Farg'ona** Uzbek.
137 E2 **Faribault** U.S.A.
141 E2 **Farmington** ME U.S.A.
138 B1 **Farmington** NM U.S.A.
141 D3 **Farmville** U.S.A.
99 C3 **Farnborough** U.K.
128 C2 **Farnham, Mount** Can.
128 A1 **Faro** Can.
106 B2 **Faro** Port.
88 A2 **Fårö** i. Sweden
94 B1 **Faroe Islands** terr. N. Atlantic Ocean
79 C2 **Farrāshband** Iran
139 C2 **Farwell** U.S.A.
79 C2 **Fāryāb** Iran
79 C2 **Fasā** Iran
109 C2 **Fasano** Italy
90 B1 **Fastiv** Ukr.
75 B2 **Fatehgarh** India
75 C2 **Fatehpur** India
92 G2 **Fauske** Norway
92 □A3 **Faxaflói** b. Iceland
92 G3 **Faxälven** r. Sweden
115 D3 **Faya** Chad
142 B1 **Fayetteville** AR U.S.A.
143 E1 **Fayetteville** NC U.S.A.
142 C1 **Fayetteville** TN U.S.A.
74 B1 **Fazilka** India
114 A2 **Fdérik** Maur.
143 E2 **Fear, Cape** U.S.A.
54 C2 **Featherston** N.Z.
104 C2 **Fécamp** France
102 C1 **Fehmarn** i. Ger.
101 F1 **Fehrbellin** Ger.
155 D1 **Feia, Lagoa** lag. Brazil
150 A2 **Feijó** Brazil
54 C2 **Feilding** N.Z.
151 E3 **Feira de Santana** Brazil
107 D2 **Felanitx** Spain
131 D3 **Felipe C. Puerto** Mex.
155 D1 **Felixlândia** Brazil
99 D3 **Felixstowe** U.K.
108 B1 **Feltre** Italy
93 F3 **Femunden** l. Norway
71 B3 **Fengcheng** Jiangxi China
65 A1 **Fengcheng** Liaoning China
62 A1 **Fengqing** China
70 B2 **Fengqiu** China
Fengxiang China see Lincang
71 C3 **Fengyüan** Taiwan
70 B1 **Fengzhen** China
105 D3 **Feno, Capo di** c. Corsica France
121 □D2 **Fenoarivo Atsinanana** Madag.
91 D2 **Feodosiya** Ukr.
108 A3 **Fer, Cap de** c. Alg.
137 D1 **Fergus Falls** U.S.A.
114 B4 **Ferkessédougou** Côte d'Ivoire
108 B2 **Fermo** Italy

131 D1	**Fermont** Can.	
106 B1	**Fermoselle** Spain	
97 B2	**Fermoy** Ireland	
143 D2	**Fernandina Beach** U.S.A.	
154 A3	**Fernandópolis** Brazil	
128 C3	**Fernie** Can.	
106 B2	**Ferrara** Italy	
154 B2	**Ferreiros** Brazil	
108 A2	**Ferro, Capo** c. Sardinia Italy	
106 B1	**Ferrol** Spain	
100 B1	**Ferwert** Neth.	
114 B1	**Fès** Morocco	
118 B3	**Feshi** Dem. Rep. Congo	
137 E3	**Festus** U.S.A.	
111 C3	**Fethiye** Turkey	
96 □	**Fetlar** i. U.K.	
130 C1	**Feuilles, Rivière aux** r. Can.	
77 D3	**Feyzābād** Afgh.	
	Fez Morocco see **Fès**	
121 □D3	**Fianarantsoa** Madag.	
117 B4	**Fichē** Eth.	
109 C2	**Fier** Albania	
96 C2	**Fife Ness** pt U.K.	
104 C3	**Figeac** France	
106 B1	**Figueira da Foz** Port.	
107 D1	**Figueres** Spain	
114 B1	**Figuig** Morocco	
48 F3	**Fiji** country S. Pacific Ocean	
152 B3	**Filadelfia** Para.	
55 Q2	**Filchner Ice Shelf** Antarctica	
98 C1	**Filey** U.K.	
111 B3	**Filippiada** Greece	
93 F4	**Filipstad** Sweden	
96 C2	**Findhorn** r. U.K.	
140 C2	**Findlay** U.S.A.	
51 D4	**Fingal** Austr.	
141 D2	**Finger Lakes** U.S.A.	
106 B1	**Finisterre, Cape** Spain	
92 I3	**Finland** country Europe	
93 H4	**Finland, Gulf of** Europe	
128 B2	**Finlay** r. Can.	
53 C2	**Finley** Austr.	
101 E2	**Finne** ridge Ger.	
92 H2	**Finnmarksvidda** reg. Norway	
92 G2	**Finnsnes** Norway	
93 G4	**Finspång** Sweden	
96 A2	**Fionnphort** U.K.	
	Firat r. Turkey see **Euphrates**	
	Firenze Italy see **Florence**	
105 C2	**Firminy** France	
75 C2	**Firozabad** India	
74 B1	**Firozpur** India	
79 C2	**Fīrūzābād** Iran	
122 A2	**Fish** watercourse Namibia	
122 B3	**Fish** r. S. Africa	
99 A3	**Fishguard** U.K.	
105 C2	**Fismes** France	
	Fisterra, Cabo c. Spain see **Finisterre, Cape**	
141 D2	**Fitchburg** U.S.A.	
129 C2	**Fitzgerald** Can.	
50 B1	**Fitzroy Crossing** Austr.	
108 B2	**Fivizzano** Italy	
119 C3	**Fizi** Dem. Rep. Congo	
92 G3	**Fjällsjöälven** r. Sweden	
123 C3	**Flagstaff** S. Africa	
138 A1	**Flagstaff** U.S.A.	
130 C1	**Flaherty Island** Can.	
98 C1	**Flamborough Head** U.K.	
101 F1	**Fläming** hills Ger.	
136 B3	**Flaming Gorge Reservoir** U.S.A.	
134 B1	**Flathead** r. U.S.A.	
134 D1	**Flathead Lake** U.S.A.	
51 D1	**Flattery, Cape** Austr.	
134 B1	**Flattery, Cape** U.S.A.	
98 B2	**Fleetwood** U.K.	
93 E4	**Flekkefjord** Norway	
102 B1	**Flensburg** Ger.	
104 B2	**Flers** France	
51 D1	**Flinders** r. Austr.	
50 A3	**Flinders Bay** Austr.	
51 D3	**Flinders Island** Austr.	
52 A2	**Flinders Ranges** mts Austr.	
129 D2	**Flin Flon** Can.	
140 C2	**Flint** U.S.A.	
107 D1	**Florac** France	
108 B2	**Florence** Italy	
142 C2	**Florence** AL U.S.A.	
138 A2	**Florence** AZ U.S.A.	
134 B2	**Florence** OR U.S.A.	
143 E2	**Florence** SC U.S.A.	
150 A1	**Florencia** Col.	
146 B3	**Flores** Guat.	
58 C3	**Flores** i. Indon.	
58 B3	**Flores, Laut** sea Indon.	
	Flores Sea Indon. see **Flores, Laut**	
151 E2	**Floresta** Brazil	
139 D3	**Floresville** U.S.A.	
151 D2	**Floriano** Brazil	
152 D3	**Florianópolis** Brazil	
153 C4	**Florida** Uru.	
143 D2	**Florida** state U.S.A.	
143 D4	**Florida, Straits of** Bahamas/U.S.A.	
143 D4	**Florida Keys** is U.S.A.	
111 B2	**Florina** Greece	
93 E3	**Floro** Norway	
129 C2	**Foam Lake** Can.	
109 C2	**Foča** Bos.-Herz.	
110 C1	**Focşani** Romania	
71 B3	**Fogang** China	
72 □	**Foggia** Italy	
131 E2	**Fogo Island** Can.	
104 C3	**Foix** France	
89 D3	**Fokino** Rus. Fed.	
130 C2	**Foleyet** Can.	
108 B2	**Foligno** Italy	
99 D3	**Folkestone** U.K.	
143 D2	**Folkston** U.S.A.	
108 B2	**Follonica** Italy	
129 C2	**Fond-du-Lac** Can.	
129 D2	**Fond du Lac** r. Can.	
140 B2	**Fond du Lac** U.S.A.	
106 B1	**Fonsagrada** Spain	
108 B2	**Fondi** Italy	
146 B3	**Fonseca, Golfo de** b. Central America	
150 B2	**Fonte Boa** Brazil	
104 B2	**Fontenay-le-Comte** France	
92 □C2	**Fontur** pt Iceland	
53 C2	**Forbes** Austr.	
101 E3	**Forchheim** Ger.	
93 E3	**Førde** Norway	
53 C1	**Fords Bridge** Austr.	
142 B2	**Fordyce** U.S.A.	
142 C2	**Forest** U.S.A.	
53 C3	**Forest Hill** Austr.	
131 D2	**Forestville** Can.	
96 C2	**Forfar** U.K.	
134 B1	**Forks** U.S.A.	
108 B2	**Forlì** Italy	
107 D2	**Formentera** i. Spain	
107 D2	**Formentor, Cap de** c. Spain	
155 C2	**Formiga** Brazil	
152 C3	**Formosa** Arg.	
	Formosa country Asia see **Taiwan**	
154 C1	**Formosa** Brazil	
96 C2	**Forres** U.K.	
50 B3	**Forrest** Austr.	
142 B1	**Forrest City** U.S.A.	
51 D1	**Forsayth** Austr.	
93 H3	**Forssa** Fin.	
53 D2	**Forster** Austr.	
136 B1	**Forsyth** U.S.A.	
74 B2	**Fort Abbas** Pak.	
130 B1	**Fort Albany** Can.	
151 E2	**Fortaleza** Brazil	
129 C2	**Fort Assiniboine** Can.	
96 B2	**Fort Augustus** U.K.	
134 D1	**Fort Benton** U.S.A.	
135 B3	**Fort Bragg** U.S.A.	
	Fort Chimo Can. see **Kuujjuaq**	
129 C2	**Fort Chipewyan** Can.	
136 B2	**Fort Collins** U.S.A.	
147 D3	**Fort-de-France** Martinique	
137 E2	**Fort Dodge** U.S.A.	
130 A2	**Fort Frances** Can.	
	Fort Franklin Can. see **Déline**	
	Fort George Can. see **Chisasibi**	
126 C2	**Fort Good Hope** Can.	
96 C2	**Forth** r. U.K.	
96 C2	**Forth, Firth of** est. U.K.	
152 C3	**Fortín Madrejón** Para.	
143 D3	**Fort Lauderdale** U.S.A.	
128 B1	**Fort Liard** Can.	
129 C2	**Fort Mackay** Can.	
129 C2	**Fort McMurray** Can.	
126 C2	**Fort McPherson** Can.	
136 C2	**Fort Morgan** U.S.A.	
143 D3	**Fort Myers** U.S.A.	
128 B2	**Fort Nelson** Can.	
128 B2	**Fort Nelson** r. Can.	
142 C2	**Fort Payne** U.S.A.	
136 B1	**Fort Peck** U.S.A.	
136 B1	**Fort Peck Reservoir** U.S.A.	
143 D3	**Fort Pierce** U.S.A.	
128 C1	**Fort Providence** Can.	
129 D2	**Fort Qu'Appelle** Can.	
128 C1	**Fort Resolution** Can.	
	Fort Rupert Can. see **Waskaganish**	
128 B2	**Fort St James** Can.	
128 B2	**Fort St John** Can.	
128 C2	**Fort Saskatchewan** Can.	
137 E3	**Fort Scott** U.S.A.	
130 B1	**Fort Severn** Can.	
76 B2	**Fort-Shevchenko** Kazakh.	
128 B1	**Fort Simpson** Can.	
129 C1	**Fort Smith** Can.	
142 B1	**Fort Smith** U.S.A.	
139 C2	**Fort Stockton** U.S.A.	
138 C2	**Fort Sumner** U.S.A.	
128 C2	**Fort Vermilion** Can.	
142 C2	**Fort Walton Beach** U.S.A.	
140 B2	**Fort Wayne** U.S.A.	
96 B2	**Fort William** U.K.	
139 D2	**Fort Worth** U.S.A.	
126 B2	**Fort Yukon** U.S.A.	
71 B3	**Foshan** China	
92 F3	**Fosna** pen. Norway	
93 E3	**Fosnavåg** Norway	
92 □B3	**Foss** Iceland	
92 □A2	**Fossá** Iceland	
108 A2	**Fossano** Italy	
53 C3	**Foster** Austr.	
104 B2	**Fougères** France	
96 □	**Foula** i. U.K.	
111 C1	**Fournoi** i. Greece	
114 A3	**Fouta Djallon** reg. Guinea	
54 A3	**Foveaux Strait** N.Z.	
136 C3	**Fowler** U.S.A.	
50 C3	**Fowlers Bay** Austr.	
128 C2	**Fox Creek** Can.	
127 F2	**Foxe Basin** g. Can.	
127 F2	**Foxe Channel** Can.	
127 F2	**Foxe Peninsula** Can.	
54 B2	**Fox Glacier** N.Z.	
128 C2	**Fox Lake** Can.	
128 A1	**Fox Mountain** Can.	
54 C2	**Foxton** N.Z.	

129 D2 **Fox Valley** Can.
97 C1 **Foyle, Lough** b. Ireland/U.K.
154 B3 **Foz de Areia, Represa de** resr Brazil
120 A2 **Foz do Cunene** Angola
154 B3 **Foz do Iguaçu** Brazil
107 D1 **Fraga** Spain
154 C2 **Franca** Brazil
109 C2 **Francavilla Fontana** Italy
104 C2 **France** country Europe
118 B3 **Franceville** Gabon
137 D2 **Francis Case, Lake** U.S.A.
155 D1 **Francisco Sá** Brazil
155 D5 **Francistown** Botswana
128 B2 **François Lake** Can.
101 D2 **Frankenberg (Eder)** Ger.
101 D3 **Frankenthal (Pfalz)** Ger.
101 E2 **Frankenwald** mts Ger.
140 C3 **Frankfort** U.S.A.
101 D2 **Frankfurt am Main** Ger.
102 C1 **Frankfurt an der Oder** Ger.
102 C2 **Fränkische Alb** mts Ger.
101 E3 **Fränkische Schweiz** reg. Ger.
141 D2 **Franklin** U.S.A.
126 C2 **Franklin Bay** Can.
134 C1 **Franklin D. Roosevelt Lake** U.S.A.
128 B1 **Franklin Mountains** Can.
126 E2 **Franklin Strait** Can.
82 E1 **Frantsa-Iosifa, Zemlya** is Rus. Fed.
54 B2 **Franz Josef Glacier** N.Z.
   Franz Josef Land is Rus. Fed. see Frantsa-Iosifa, Zemlya
108 A3 **Frasca, Capo della** c. Sardinia Italy
128 B3 **Fraser** r. B.C. Can.
131 D1 **Fraser** r. Nfld. Can.
122 B3 **Fraserburg** S. Africa
96 C2 **Fraserburgh** U.K.
130 B2 **Fraserdale** Can.
51 E2 **Fraser Island** Austr.
128 C2 **Fraser Lake** Can.
153 C4 **Fray Bentos** Uru.
93 E4 **Fredericia** Denmark
139 D2 **Frederick** U.S.A.
139 D2 **Fredericksburg** TX U.S.A.
141 D3 **Fredericksburg** VA U.S.A.
128 A2 **Frederick Sound** sea chan. U.S.A.
131 D2 **Fredericton** Can.
93 F4 **Frederikshavn** Denmark
   Frederikshamn Fin. see Hamina
93 F4 **Fredrikstad** Norway
140 B2 **Freeport** IL U.S.A.
139 D3 **Freeport** TX U.S.A.
146 C2 **Freeport City** Bahamas
139 D3 **Freer** U.S.A.
123 C2 **Free State** prov. S. Africa
114 A4 **Freetown** Sierra Leone
106 B2 **Fregenal de la Sierra** Spain
104 B2 **Fréhel, Cap** c. France
102 B2 **Freiburg im Breisgau** Ger.
102 C2 **Freising** Ger.
102 C2 **Freistadt** Austria
105 D3 **Fréjus** France
50 A3 **Fremantle** Austr.
137 D2 **Fremont** NE U.S.A.
140 C2 **Fremont** OH U.S.A.
151 C1 **French Guiana** terr. S. America
134 E1 **Frenchman** r. U.S.A.
49 I4 **French Polynesia** terr. S. Pacific Ocean
144 B2 **Fresnillo** Mex.

135 C3 **Fresno** U.S.A.
107 D2 **Freu, Cap des** c. Spain
105 D2 **Freyming-Merlebach** France
114 A3 **Fria** Guinea
152 B3 **Frías** Arg.
102 B2 **Friedrichshafen** Ger.
101 F1 **Friesack** Ger.
100 C1 **Friesoythe** Ger.
   Frobisher Bay Can. see Iqaluit
127 G2 **Frobisher Bay** Can.
101 F2 **Frohburg** Ger.
87 D4 **Frolovo** Rus. Fed.
52 A2 **Frome, Lake** salt flat Austr.
52 A2 **Frome Downs** Austr.
100 C2 **Fröndenberg** Ger.
145 C3 **Frontera** Mex.
144 B1 **Fronteras** Mex.
108 B2 **Frosinone** Italy
92 E3 **Frøya** i. Norway
   Frunze Kyrg. see Bishkek
105 D2 **Frutigen** Switz.
103 D2 **Frýdek-Místek** Czech Rep.
71 B3 **Fu'an** China
106 C1 **Fuenlabrada** Spain
152 C3 **Fuerte Olimpo** Para.
114 A2 **Fuerteventura** i. Canary Is
64 B1 **Fuga** i. Phil.
79 C2 **Fujairah** U.A.E.
67 C3 **Fuji** Japan
71 B3 **Fujian** prov. China
67 C3 **Fujinomiya** Japan
67 C3 **Fuji-san** vol. Japan
67 B4 **Fukui** Japan
67 B4 **Fukuoka** Japan
67 D3 **Fukushima** Japan
101 D2 **Fulda** Ger.
101 D2 **Fulda** r. Ger.
70 A3 **Fuling** China
137 E3 **Fulton** U.S.A.
105 C2 **Fumay** France
114 A1 **Funchal** Madeira
106 B1 **Fundão** Port.
131 D2 **Fundy, Bay of** g. Can.
70 B2 **Funing** Jiangsu China
71 A3 **Funing** Yunnan China
115 C3 **Funtua** Nigeria
79 C2 **Fürgun, Küh-e** mt. Iran
89 F2 **Furmanov** Rus. Fed.
155 C2 **Furnas, Represa** resr Brazil
51 D4 **Furneaux Group** is Austr.
100 C1 **Fürstenau** Ger.
101 E3 **Fürth** Ger.
66 D3 **Furukawa** Japan
127 F2 **Fury and Hecla Strait** Can.
65 A1 **Fushun** China
65 B1 **Fusong** China
79 C2 **Fuwayriṭ** Qatar
70 B2 **Fuyang** China
69 E1 **Fuyu** China
68 B1 **Fuyun** China
71 B3 **Fuzhou** Jiangxi China
71 B3 **Fuzhou** Fujian China
93 F4 **Fyn** i. Denmark
   F.Y.R.O.M. country Europe see Macedonia

G

117 C4 **Gaalkacyo** Somalia
120 A2 **Gabela** Angola
115 D1 **Gabès** Tunisia
115 D1 **Gabès, Golfe de** g. Tunisia
118 B3 **Gabon** country Africa

123 C1 **Gaborone** Botswana
110 C2 **Gabrovo** Bulg.
114 A3 **Gabú** Guinea-Bissau
73 B3 **Gadag** India
75 C2 **Gadchiroli** India
120 A2 **Gadebusch** Ger.
142 C2 **Gadsden** U.S.A.
110 C2 **Găești** Romania
108 B2 **Gaeta** Italy
143 D1 **Gaffney** U.S.A.
115 C1 **Gafsa** Tunisia
89 E2 **Gagarin** Rus. Fed.
114 B4 **Gagnoa** Côte d'Ivoire
131 D1 **Gagnon** Can.
81 C1 **Gagra** Georgia
122 A2 **Gaiab** watercourse Namibia
104 C3 **Gaillac** France
143 D3 **Gainesville** FL U.S.A.
143 D2 **Gainesville** GA U.S.A.
139 D2 **Gainesville** TX U.S.A.
98 C2 **Gainsborough** U.K.
52 A2 **Gairdner, Lake** salt flat Austr.
96 B2 **Gairloch** U.K.
119 E3 **Galana** r. Kenya
103 D2 **Galanta** Slovakia
148 B3 **Galapagos Islands** Pacific Ocean
96 C3 **Galashiels** U.K.
110 C1 **Galați** Romania
93 E3 **Galdhøpiggen** mt. Norway
145 B2 **Galeana** Mex.
128 C2 **Galena Bay** Can.
140 A2 **Galesburg** U.S.A.
122 B2 **Galeshewe** S. Africa
86 D3 **Galich** Rus. Fed.
116 B1 **Galilee, Sea of** l. Israel
142 C1 **Gallatin** U.S.A.
73 C4 **Galle** Sri Lanka
150 A1 **Gallinas, Punta** pt Col.
109 C2 **Gallipoli** Italy
111 C2 **Gallipoli** Turkey
92 H2 **Gällivare** Sweden
138 B1 **Gallup** U.S.A.
114 A2 **Galtat Zemmour** Western Sahara
97 B2 **Galtymore** hill Ireland
139 E3 **Galveston** U.S.A.
139 E3 **Galveston Bay** U.S.A.
97 B2 **Galway** Ireland
97 B2 **Galway Bay** Ireland
154 C1 **Gamá** Brazil
123 D3 **Gamalakhe** S. Africa
114 A3 **Gambia, The** country Africa
49 I4 **Gambier, Îles** is Fr. Polynesia
52 A3 **Gambier Islands** Austr.
130 C2 **Gambo** Can.
118 B3 **Gamboma** Congo
138 B1 **Ganado** U.S.A.
81 D3 **Gänäveh** Iran
81 C1 **Gäncä** Azer.
   Gand Belgium see Ghent
61 C2 **Gandadiwata, Bukit** mt. Indon.
118 C3 **Gandajika** Dem. Rep. Congo
131 E2 **Gander** Can.
131 E2 **Gander** r. Can.
101 D1 **Ganderkesee** Ger.
107 D1 **Gandesa** Spain
74 B2 **Gandhidham** India
74 B2 **Gandhinagar** India
74 B2 **Gandhi Sagar** resr India
107 C2 **Gandia** Spain
   Ganga r. Bangl./India see Ganges
74 A2 **Gangán** Arg.
74 B2 **Ganganagar** India

68 C2 **Gangca** China
75 C1 **Gangdisê Shan** *mts* China
75 C2 **Ganges** *r.* Bangl./India
105 C3 **Ganges** France
75 C2 **Ganges, Mouths of the** Bangl./India
75 C2 **Gangtok** India
105 C2 **Gannat** France
136 B2 **Gannett Peak** U.S.A.
122 A3 **Gansbaai** S. Africa
70 A1 **Gansu** *prov.* China
71 B3 **Ganzhou** China
114 B3 **Gao** Mali
114 A3 **Gaoual** Guinea
70 B2 **Gaoyou** China
70 B2 **Gaoyou Hu** *l.* China
105 D3 **Gap** France
107 C2 **Gap Carbon** *hd* Alg.
75 C1 **Gar** China
76 B2 **Garabogaz** Turkm.
76 B2 **Garabogazköl** Turkm.
76 B2 **Garabogazköl Aýlagy** *b.* Turkm.
Garagum Turkm. see **Karakum Desert**
53 C1 **Garah** Austr.
151 E2 **Garanhuns** Brazil
135 B2 **Garberville** U.S.A.
101 D1 **Garbsen** Ger.
154 C2 **Garça** Brazil
101 E1 **Gardelegen** Ger.
136 C3 **Garden City** U.S.A.
129 E2 **Garden Hill** Can.
77 C3 **Gardêz** Afgh.
88 B2 **Gargždai** Lith.
123 C3 **Gariep Dam** *resr* S. Africa
122 A3 **Garies** S. Africa
119 D3 **Garissa** Kenya
102 C2 **Garmisch-Partenkirchen** Ger.
52 B2 **Garnpung Lake** *imp. l.* Austr.
104 B3 **Garonne** *r.* France
117 C4 **Garoowe** Somalia
74 B2 **Garoth** India
118 B2 **Garoua** Cameroon
96 B2 **Garry** *r.* U.K.
126 E2 **Garry Lake** Can.
119 E3 **Garsen** Kenya
61 B2 **Garut** Indon.
140 B2 **Gary** U.S.A.
145 B2 **Garza García** Mex.
68 C2 **Garzê** China
104 B2 **Gascony, Gulf of** France/Spain
50 A2 **Gascoyne** *r.* Austr.
115 D3 **Gashua** Nigeria
131 D2 **Gaspé** Can.
131 D2 **Gaspé, Péninsule de** *pen.* Can.
143 E1 **Gaston, Lake** U.S.A.
143 D1 **Gastonia** U.S.A.
107 C2 **Gata, Cabo de** *c.* Spain
88 D2 **Gatchina** Rus. Fed.
98 C1 **Gateshead** U.K.
139 D2 **Gatesville** U.S.A.
130 C2 **Gatineau** *r.* Can.
53 D1 **Gatton** Austr.
129 E2 **Gauer Lake** Can.
93 E4 **Gausta** *mt.* Norway
123 C2 **Gauteng** *prov.* S. Africa
79 C2 **Gāvbandī** Iran
111 B3 **Gavdos** *i.* Greece
93 G3 **Gävle** Sweden
89 F2 **Gavrilov Posad** Rus. Fed.
89 E2 **Gavrilov-Yam** Rus. Fed.
62 A1 **Gawai** Myanmar
52 A2 **Gawler** Austr.

52 A2 **Gawler Ranges** *hills* Austr.
75 C2 **Gaya** India
114 C3 **Gaya** Niger
140 C1 **Gaylord** U.S.A.
86 E2 **Gayny** Rus. Fed.
80 B2 **Gaza** *terr.* Asia
80 B2 **Gaziantep** Turkey
76 C2 **Gazojak** Turkm.
114 B4 **Gbarnga** Liberia
103 D1 **Gdańsk** Pol.
88 A3 **Gdańsk, Gulf of** Pol./Rus. Fed.
88 C2 **Gdov** Rus. Fed.
103 D1 **Gdynia** Pol.
116 B3 **Gedaref** Sudan
101 D2 **Gedern** Ger.
111 C3 **Gediz** *r.* Turkey
102 C1 **Gedser** Denmark
100 B2 **Geel** Belgium
52 B3 **Geelong** Austr.
101 E1 **Geesthacht** Ger.
75 C1 **Gê'gyai** China
129 D2 **Geikie** *r.* Can.
93 E3 **Geilo** Norway
62 B1 **Gejiu** China
108 B3 **Gela** *Sicily* Italy
91 D3 **Gelendzhik** Rus. Fed.
Gelibolu Turkey see **Gallipoli**
100 C2 **Gelsenkirchen** Ger.
118 C2 **Gemena** Dem. Rep. Congo
111 C2 **Gemlik** Turkey
117 C4 **Genalē Wenz** *r.* Eth.
153 B4 **General Acha** Arg.
153 B4 **General Alvear** Arg.
153 C4 **General Belgrano** Arg.
144 B2 **General Cepeda** Mex.
153 B4 **General Pico** Arg.
153 B4 **General Roca** Arg.
64 B2 **General Santos** Phil.
141 D2 **Genesee** *r.* U.S.A.
141 D2 **Geneseo** U.S.A.
105 D2 **Geneva** Switz.
141 D2 **Geneva** U.S.A.
105 D2 **Geneva, Lake** France/Switz.
Genève Switz. see **Geneva**
106 B2 **Genil** *r.* Spain
100 B2 **Genk** Belgium
108 A2 **Genoa** Italy
Genova Italy see **Genoa**
101 F1 **Genthin** Ger.
50 A2 **Geographe Bay** Austr.
131 D1 **George** *r.* Can.
122 B3 **George** S. Africa
143 D3 **George, Lake** *FL* U.S.A.
141 E2 **George, Lake** *NY* U.S.A.
114 A3 **Georgetown** Gambia
151 C1 **Georgetown** Guyana
60 B1 **George Town** Malaysia
143 E2 **Georgetown** *SC* U.S.A.
139 D2 **Georgetown** *TX* U.S.A.
55 I2 **George V Land** *reg.* Antarctica
81 C1 **Georgia** *country* Asia
143 D2 **Georgia** *state* U.S.A.
130 B2 **Georgian Bay** Can.
51 C2 **Georgina** *watercourse* Austr.
77 E2 **Georgiyevka** Kazakh.
87 D4 **Georgiyevsk** Rus. Fed.
101 F2 **Gera** Ger.
151 D3 **Geral de Goiás, Serra** *hills* Brazil
54 B2 **Geraldine** N.Z.
50 A2 **Geraldton** Austr.
80 B1 **Gerede** Turkey
74 A1 **Gereshk** Afgh.
135 C2 **Gerlach** U.S.A.

103 E2 **Gerlachovský štít** *mt.* Slovakia
102 C1 **Germany** *country* Europe
100 C2 **Gerolstein** Ger.
101 E3 **Gerolzhofen** Ger.
101 D2 **Gersfeld (Rhön)** Ger.
75 C1 **Gêrzê** China
141 D3 **Gettysburg** *PA* U.S.A.
136 D1 **Gettysburg** *SD* U.S.A.
109 D2 **Gevgelija** Macedonia
111 C3 **Geyikli** Turkey
122 B2 **Ghaap Plateau** S. Africa
115 C1 **Ghadāmis** Libya
75 C2 **Ghaghara** *r.* India
114 B4 **Ghana** *country* Africa
120 B3 **Ghanzi** Botswana
115 C1 **Ghardaïa** Alg.
115 D1 **Gharyān** Libya
75 C2 **Ghatal** India
75 B2 **Ghaziabad** India
75 C2 **Ghazipur** India
77 C3 **Ghaznī** Afgh.
100 A2 **Ghent** Belgium
110 B1 **Gherla** Romania
105 D3 **Ghisonaccia** *Corsica* France
74 B2 **Ghotaru** India
74 A2 **Ghotki** Pak.
91 E3 **Giaginskaya** Rus. Fed.
97 C1 **Giant's Causeway** *lava field* U.K.
61 C2 **Gianyar** Indon.
109 C3 **Giarre** *Sicily* Italy
108 A1 **Giaveno** Italy
122 A2 **Gibeon** Namibia
106 B2 **Gibraltar** *terr.* Europe
106 B2 **Gibraltar, Strait of** Morocco/Spain
50 B2 **Gibson Desert** Austr.
68 C1 **Gichgeniyn Nuruu** *mts* Mongolia
117 B4 **Gīdolē** Eth.
104 C2 **Gien** France
101 D2 **Gießen** Ger.
101 E1 **Gifhorn** Ger.
128 C2 **Gift Lake** Can.
67 C3 **Gifu** Japan
96 B3 **Gigha** *i.* U.K.
106 B1 **Gijón-Xixón** Spain
138 A2 **Gila** *r.* U.S.A.
138 A2 **Gila Bend** U.S.A.
51 D1 **Gilbert** *r.* Austr.
49 F2 **Gilbert Islands** *country* Pacific Ocean
134 D1 **Gildford** U.S.A.
53 C2 **Gilgandra** Austr.
74 B1 **Gilgit** Jammu and Kashmir
74 B1 **Gilgit** *r.* Jammu and Kashmir
53 C2 **Gilgunnia** Austr.
129 E2 **Gillam** Can.
136 B2 **Gillette** U.S.A.
99 D3 **Gillingham** U.K.
129 E2 **Gimli** Can.
117 C4 **Gīnīr** Eth.
109 C2 **Ginosa** Italy
53 C3 **Gippsland** *reg.* Austr.
74 A2 **Girdar Dhor** *r.* Pak.
80 B1 **Giresun** Turkey
107 D1 **Girona** Spain
96 B3 **Girvan** U.K.
54 C1 **Gisborne** N.Z.
93 F4 **Gislaved** Sweden
119 C3 **Gitarama** Rwanda
110 C2 **Giurgiu** Romania
110 C1 **Giuvala, Pasul** *pass* Romania
105 C2 **Givors** France
123 D1 **Giyani** S. Africa
116 B2 **Giza** Egypt

109 D2 **Gjirokastër** Albania
126 E2 **Gjoa Haven** Can.
93 F3 **Gjøvik** Norway
131 E2 **Glace Bay** Can.
134 B1 **Glacier Peak** vol. U.S.A.
51 E2 **Gladstone** Austr.
92 □A2 **Gláma** mts Iceland
109 C2 **Glamoč** Bos.-Herz.
100 C3 **Glan** r. Ger.
97 B2 **Glanaruddery Mountains** hills Ireland
96 B3 **Glasgow** U.K.
140 B3 **Glasgow** KY U.S.A.
136 B1 **Glasgow** MT U.S.A.
99 B3 **Glastonbury** U.K.
101 F2 **Glauchau** Ger.
86 E3 **Glazov** Rus. Fed.
89 E3 **Glazunovka** Rus. Fed.
96 B2 **Glen Coe** val. U.K.
138 A2 **Glendale** U.S.A.
53 D2 **Glen Davis** Austr.
136 C1 **Glendive** U.S.A.
52 B3 **Glenelg** r. Austr.
53 D1 **Glen Innes** Austr.
126 B2 **Glennallen** U.S.A.
96 C2 **Glenrothes** U.K.
141 E2 **Glens Falls** U.S.A.
96 C2 **Glen Shee** val. U.K.
97 B1 **Glenties** Ireland
138 B2 **Glenwood** U.S.A.
136 B3 **Glenwood Springs** U.S.A.
103 D1 **Gliwice** Pol.
138 A2 **Globe** U.S.A.
103 D1 **Głogów** Pol.
92 F2 **Glomfjord** Norway
93 F4 **Glomma** r. Norway
53 D2 **Gloucester** Austr.
99 B3 **Gloucester** U.K.
101 F1 **Glöwen** Ger.
77 E1 **Glubokoye** Kazakh.
101 D1 **Glückstadt** Ger.
103 C2 **Gmünd** Austria
102 C2 **Gmunden** Austria
101 D1 **Gnarrenburg** Ger.
103 D1 **Gniezno** Pol.
109 D2 **Gnjilane** Serb. and Mont.
75 D2 **Goalpara** India
96 B3 **Goat Fell** hill U.K.
78 B3 **Goba** Eth.
120 A3 **Gobabis** Namibia
153 A5 **Gobernador Gregores** Arg.
69 D2 **Gobi** des. China/Mongolia
100 C2 **Goch** Ger.
122 A1 **Gochas** Namibia
74 B3 **Godavari** r. India
73 C3 **Godavari, Mouths of the** India
130 B2 **Goderich** Can.
74 B2 **Godhra** India
129 E2 **Gods** r. Can.
129 E2 **Gods Lake** Can.
Godthåb Greenland see Nuuk
Godwin-Austen, Mount China/Jammu and Kashmir see K2
130 C2 **Goéland, Lac au** l. Can.
131 D1 **Goélands, Lac aux** l. Can.
100 A2 **Goes** Neth.
154 C1 **Goianira** Brazil
154 B1 **Goiânia** Brazil
154 B1 **Goiás** Brazil
154 B2 **Goio-Erê** Brazil
111 C2 **Gökçeada** i. Turkey
111 C3 **Gökçedağ** Turkey
121 B2 **Gokwe** Zimbabwe
93 E3 **Gol** Norway
62 A1 **Golaghat** India
111 C2 **Gölcük** Turkey
103 E1 **Gołdap** Pol.

101 F1 **Goldberg** Ger.
53 D1 **Gold Coast** Austr.
114 B4 **Gold Coast** Ghana
128 C2 **Golden** Can.
54 B2 **Golden Bay** N.Z.
128 B3 **Golden Hinde** mt. Can.
97 B2 **Golden Vale** lowland Ireland
135 C3 **Goldfield** U.S.A.
135 D3 **Gold River** Can.
143 E1 **Goldsboro** U.S.A.
135 C4 **Goleta** U.S.A.
108 A2 **Golfo dell'Asinara** b. Sardinia Italy
68 C2 **Golmud** China
81 D2 **Golpāyegān** Iran
96 C2 **Golspie** U.K.
119 C3 **Goma** Dem. Rep. Congo
75 C2 **Gomati** r. India
115 D3 **Gombe** Nigeria
115 D3 **Gombi** Nigeria
Gomel' Belarus see Homyel'
144 B3 **Gómez Palacio** Mex.
147 C3 **Gonaïves** Haiti
147 C3 **Gonâve, Île de la** i. Haiti
81 D2 **Gonbad-e Kavus** Iran
117 B3 **Gonder** Eth.
75 C2 **Gondia** India
111 C2 **Gönen** Turkey
115 D4 **Gongola** r. Nigeria
53 C2 **Gongolgon** Austr.
145 C2 **Gonzáles** Mex.
139 D3 **Gonzales** U.S.A.
122 A3 **Good Hope, Cape of** S. Africa
134 D2 **Gooding** U.S.A.
136 C3 **Goodland** U.S.A.
53 C1 **Goodooga** Austr.
98 C2 **Goole** U.K.
52 A3 **Goolgowi** Austr.
53 D1 **Goondiwindi** Austr.
134 B2 **Goose Lake** U.S.A.
102 B2 **Göppingen** Ger.
75 C2 **Gorakhpur** India
109 C2 **Goražde** Bos.-Herz.
111 C3 **Gördes** Turkey
91 D3 **Gordeyevka** Rus. Fed.
51 D4 **Gordon, Lake** Austr.
115 D4 **Goré** Chad
117 B4 **Goré** Eth.
54 A3 **Gore** N.Z.
97 C2 **Gorey** Ireland
81 D2 **Gorgān** Iran
81 C1 **Gori** Georgia
108 B1 **Gorizia** Italy
Gor'kiy Rus. Fed. see Nizhniy Novgorod
103 E2 **Gorlice** Pol.
103 C1 **Görlitz** Ger.
109 D2 **Gornji Milanovac** Serb. and Mont.
109 C2 **Gornji Vakuf** Bos.-Herz.
77 E1 **Gorno-Altaysk** Rus. Fed.
110 C2 **Gornotrakiyska Nizina** lowland Bulg.
77 E1 **Gornyak** Rus. Fed.
59 D3 **Goroka** P.N.G.
114 B3 **Gorom Gorom** Burkina
59 C2 **Gorontalo** Indon.
89 E3 **Gorshechnoye** Rus. Fed.
97 B2 **Gorumna Island** Ireland
91 D3 **Goryachiy Klyuch** Rus. Fed.
103 D1 **Gorzów Wielkopolski** Pol.
53 D2 **Gosford** U.K.
66 D2 **Goshogawara** Japan
101 E2 **Goslar** Ger.
109 C2 **Gospić** Croatia

99 C3 **Gosport** U.K.
109 D2 **Gostivar** Macedonia
Göteborg Sweden see Gothenburg
101 E2 **Gotha** Ger.
93 F4 **Gothenburg** Sweden
136 C2 **Gothenburg** U.S.A.
93 G4 **Gotland** i. Sweden
111 B2 **Gotse Delchev** Bulg.
93 G4 **Gotska Sandön** i. Sweden
67 B4 **Gōtsu** Japan
101 D2 **Göttingen** Ger.
128 B2 **Gott Peak** Can.
100 B1 **Gouda** Neth.
114 A3 **Goudiri** Senegal
115 D3 **Goudoumaria** Niger
130 C2 **Gouin, Réservoir** resr Can.
53 C2 **Goulburn** Austr.
53 B3 **Goulburn** r. N.S.W. Austr.
53 B3 **Goulburn** r. Vic. Austr.
114 B3 **Goundam** Mali
107 D2 **Gouraya** Alg.
104 C3 **Gourdon** France
115 D3 **Gouré** Niger
122 B3 **Gourits** r. S. Africa
114 B3 **Gourma-Rharous** Mali
53 C3 **Gourock Range** mts Austr.
155 D1 **Governador Valadares** Brazil
143 E3 **Governor's Harbour** Bahamas
68 C2 **Govi Altayn Nuruu** mts Mongolia
99 C3 **Gower** pen. U.K.
152 E3 **Goya** Arg.
81 C1 **Göyçay** Azer.
75 C1 **Gozha Co** salt l. China
122 B3 **Graaff-Reinet** S. Africa
109 E1 **Grabow** Ger.
109 C2 **Gračac** Croatia
87 E3 **Grachevka** Rus. Fed.
101 F2 **Gräfenhainichen** Ger.
53 D1 **Grafton** Austr.
137 D1 **Grafton** U.S.A.
139 D2 **Graham** U.S.A.
128 A2 **Graham Island** Can.
55 P3 **Graham Land** reg. Antarctica
123 C3 **Grahamstown** S. Africa
151 D2 **Grajaú** Brazil
111 B2 **Grammos** mt. Greece
96 B2 **Grampian Mountains** U.K.
146 B3 **Granada** Nic.
106 C2 **Granada** Spain
141 E1 **Granby** Can.
114 A2 **Gran Canaria** i. Canary Is
152 B3 **Gran Chaco** reg. Arg./Para.
136 C1 **Grand** r. U.S.A.
146 C2 **Grand Bahama** i. Bahamas
131 E2 **Grand Bank** Can.
158 C2 **Grand Banks of Newfoundland** sea feature N. Atlantic Ocean
138 A1 **Grand Canyon** U.S.A.
138 A1 **Grand Canyon** gorge U.S.A.
146 B3 **Grand Cayman** i. Cayman Is
129 C2 **Grand Centre** Can.
134 C1 **Grand Coulee** U.S.A.
52 B2 **Grande** r. Bol.
154 B2 **Grande** r. Brazil
153 B6 **Grande, Bahía** b. Arg.
128 C2 **Grande, Ilha** i. Brazil
128 C2 **Grand Cache** Can.
128 C2 **Grand Prairie** Can.
115 D3 **Grand Erg de Bilma** des. Niger

114 B1 **Grand Erg Occidental** *des.* Alg.
115 C2 **Grand Erg Oriental** *des.* Alg.
131 D2 **Grande-Rivière** Can.
152 B4 **Grandes, Salinas** *salt marsh* Arg.
131 D2 **Grand Falls** *N.B.* Can.
131 E2 **Grand Falls-Windsor** Nfld. Can.
128 C3 **Grand Forks** Can.
137 D1 **Grand Forks** U.S.A.
128 C1 **Grandin, Lac** *l.* Can.
137 D2 **Grand Isle** U.S.A.
142 B3 **Grand Isle** U.S.A.
136 B3 **Grand Junction** U.S.A.
114 B4 **Grand-Lahou** Côte d'Ivoire
131 D2 **Grand Lake** *N.B.* Can.
131 E2 **Grand Lake** Nfld. Can.
137 E1 **Grand Marais** U.S.A.
106 B2 **Grândola** Port.
129 E2 **Grand Rapids** Can.
140 B2 **Grand Rapids** *MI* U.S.A.
137 E1 **Grand Rapids** *MN* U.S.A.
136 A2 **Grand Teton** *mt.* U.S.A.
147 C3 **Grand Turk** Turks and Caicos Is
134 C1 **Grangeville** U.S.A.
128 B2 **Granisle** Can.
134 E1 **Granite Peak** U.S.A.
108 B3 **Granitola, Capo** *c.* Sicily Italy
93 F4 **Gränna** Sweden
101 F1 **Gransee** Ger.
99 C2 **Grantham** U.K.
96 C2 **Grantown-on-Spey** U.K.
138 B1 **Grants** U.S.A.
134 B2 **Grants Pass** U.S.A.
104 B2 **Granville** France
129 D2 **Granville Lake** Can.
155 D1 **Grão Mogol** Brazil
123 D1 **Graskop** S. Africa
105 D3 **Grasse** France
107 D1 **Grassington** U.K.
92 F2 **Gravdal** Norway
104 B2 **Grave, Pointe de** *pt* France
129 D3 **Gravelbourg** Can.
130 C2 **Gravenhurst** Can.
53 D1 **Gravesend** Austr.
99 D3 **Gravesend** U.K.
105 D2 **Gray** France
103 D2 **Graz** Austria
146 C2 **Great Abaco** *i.* Bahamas
50 B3 **Great Australian Bight** *g.* Austr.
54 C1 **Great Barrier Island** N.Z.
51 D1 **Great Barrier Reef** Austr.
135 C3 **Great Basin** U.S.A.
126 D2 **Great Bear Lake** Can.
93 F4 **Great Belt** *sea chan.* Denmark
137 D3 **Great Bend** U.S.A.
63 A2 **Great Coco Island** Cocos Is
53 D3 **Great Dividing Range** *mts* Austr.
146 B2 **Greater Antilles** *is* Caribbean Sea
134 D1 **Great Falls** U.S.A.
123 C3 **Great Fish** *r.* S. Africa
123 C3 **Great Fish Point** S. Africa
147 C2 **Great Inagua** *i.* Bahamas
122 B3 **Great Karoo** *plat.* S. Africa
123 C3 **Great Kei** *r.* S. Africa
99 B2 **Great Malvern** U.K.
122 A2 **Great Namaqualand** *reg.* Namibia
63 A3 **Great Nicobar** *i.* India
99 D2 **Great Ouse** *r.* U.K.

119 D3 **Great Rift Valley** Africa
119 D3 **Great Ruaha** *r.* Tanz.
134 D2 **Great Salt Lake** U.S.A.
135 D2 **Great Salt Lake Desert** U.S.A.
116 A2 **Great Sand Sea** *des.* Egypt/Libya
50 B1 **Great Sandy Desert** Austr.
128 C1 **Great Slave Lake** Can.
143 D1 **Great Smoky Mountains** U.S.A.
50 B2 **Great Victoria Desert** Austr.
70 B1 **Great Wall** *tourist site* China
99 D2 **Great Yarmouth** U.K.
106 B1 **Gredos, Sierra de** *mts* Spain
111 B3 **Greece** *country* Europe
136 C2 **Greeley** U.S.A.
82 F1 **Greem-Bell, Ostrov** *i.* Rus. Fed.
140 B3 **Green** *r.* *KY* U.S.A.
136 B3 **Green** *r.* *WY* U.S.A.
140 B1 **Green Bay** U.S.A.
140 B1 **Green Bay** *b.* U.S.A.
140 C3 **Greenbrier** *r.* U.S.A.
140 B3 **Greencastle** U.S.A.
143 D1 **Greeneville** U.S.A.
141 E2 **Greenfield** U.S.A.
129 D2 **Green Lake** Can.
127 I2 **Greenland** *terr.* N. America
160 R2 **Greenland Sea** Greenland/Svalbard
96 B3 **Greenock** U.K.
135 D3 **Green River** *UT* U.S.A.
136 B2 **Green River** *WY* U.S.A.
140 B3 **Greensburg** *IN* U.S.A.
141 D2 **Greensburg** *PA* U.S.A.
143 E2 **Green Swamp** U.S.A.
138 A2 **Green Valley** U.S.A.
114 B4 **Greenville** Liberia
142 C2 **Greenville** *AL* U.S.A.
142 B2 **Greenville** *MS* U.S.A.
143 E1 **Greenville** *NC* U.S.A.
143 D2 **Greenville** *SC* U.S.A.
139 D2 **Greenville** *TX* U.S.A.
53 D2 **Greenwell Point** Austr.
143 D2 **Greenwood** U.S.A.
50 B2 **Gregory, Lake** *salt flat* Austr.
51 D1 **Gregory Range** *hills* Austr.
102 C1 **Greifswald** Ger.
93 F4 **Greià** Denmark
142 C2 **Grenada** U.S.A.
147 D3 **Grenada** *country* West Indies
104 C3 **Grenade** France
53 C2 **Grenfell** Austr.
129 D2 **Grenfell** Can.
105 D2 **Grenoble** France
51 D1 **Grenville, Cape** Austr.
134 B1 **Gresham** U.S.A.
100 C1 **Greven** Ger.
111 B2 **Grevena** Greece
100 C2 **Grevenbroich** Ger.
101 E1 **Grevesmühlen** Ger.
136 B2 **Greybull** U.S.A.
128 A1 **Grey Hunter Peak** Can.
131 E1 **Grey Islands** Can.
54 B2 **Greymouth** N.Z.
52 B2 **Grey Range** *hills* Austr.
97 C2 **Greystones** Ireland
143 D2 **Griffin** U.S.A.
53 C2 **Griffith** Austr.
101 F2 **Grimma** Ger.
102 C1 **Grimmen** Ger.
98 C2 **Grimsby** U.K.
128 C2 **Grimshaw** Can.

92 □B2 **Grímsstaðir** Iceland
93 E4 **Grimstad** Norway
137 E2 **Grinnell** U.S.A.
123 C3 **Griqualand East** *reg.* S. Africa
122 B2 **Griqualand West** *reg.* S. Africa
127 F1 **Grise Fiord** Can.
96 C1 **Gritley** U.K.
123 C2 **Groblersdal** S. Africa
122 B2 **Groblershoop** S. Africa
Grodno Belarus *see* Hrodna
104 B2 **Groix, Île de** *i.* France
100 C1 **Gronau (Westfalen)** Ger.
92 F3 **Grong** Norway
100 C1 **Groningen** Neth.
122 B2 **Grootdrink** S. Africa
51 C1 **Groote Eylandt** *i.* Austr.
120 A2 **Grootfontein** Namibia
122 A2 **Groot Karas Berg** *plat.* Namibia
122 B3 **Groot Swartberge** *mts* S. Africa
123 C3 **Groot Winterberg** *mt.* S. Africa
101 D2 **Großenlüder** Ger.
102 C2 **Großer Rachel** *mt.* Ger.
103 C2 **Grosser Speikkogel** *mt.* Austria
108 B2 **Grosseto** Italy
101 D3 **Groß-Gerau** Ger.
102 C2 **Großglockner** *mt.* Austria
100 C1 **Groß-Hesepe** Ger.
101 E2 **Großlohra** Ger.
122 A1 **Gross Ums** Namibia
131 E1 **Groswater Bay** Can.
130 B2 **Groundhog** *r.* Can.
49 I4 **Groupe Actéon** *i.* Fr. Polynesia
135 B3 **Grover Beach** U.S.A.
141 E2 **Groveton** U.S.A.
87 D4 **Groznyy** Rus. Fed.
109 C1 **Grubišno Polje** Croatia
103 D1 **Grudziądz** Pol.
122 A2 **Grünau** Namibia
92 □A3 **Grundarfjörður** Iceland
89 E3 **Gryazi** Rus. Fed.
89 F2 **Gryazovets** Rus. Fed.
103 D1 **Gryfice** Pol.
102 C1 **Gryfino** Pol.
146 C2 **Guacanayabo, Golfo de** *b.* Cuba
144 B2 **Guadalajara** Mex.
49 E3 **Guadalcanal** *i.* Solomon Is
107 C1 **Guadalope** *r.* Spain
106 B2 **Guadalquivir** *r.* Spain
132 B4 **Guadalupe** *i.* Mex.
106 B2 **Guadalupe, Sierra de** *mts* Spain
138 C2 **Guadalupe Peak** U.S.A.
144 B2 **Guadalupe Victoria** Mex.
144 B2 **Guadalupe y Calvo** Mex.
106 C1 **Guadarrama, Sierra de** *mts* Spain
147 D3 **Guadeloupe** *terr.* West Indies
106 B2 **Guadiana** *r.* Port./Spain
106 C2 **Guadix** Spain
154 B2 **Guaíra** Brazil
147 C3 **Guajira, Península de la** *pen.* Col.
150 A2 **Gualaceo** Ecuador
59 D2 **Guam** *terr.* N. Pacific Ocean
144 B2 **Guamúchil** Mex.
144 B2 **Guanacevi** Mex.
151 D3 **Guanambi** Brazil
150 B1 **Guanare** Venez.
146 B2 **Guane** Cuba
70 A2 **Guang'an** China
71 B3 **Guangchang** China

71 B3 Guangdong *prov.* China
71 A3 Guangxi Zhuangzu Zizhiqu
        aut. reg. China
70 A2 Guangyuan China
71 B3 Guangzhou China
155 D1 Guanhães Brazil
147 D4 Guanipa *r.* Venez.
71 A3 Guanling China
65 A1 Guanshui China
        Guansuo China *see*
        Guanling
147 C2 Guantánamo Cuba
150 B3 Guaporé *r.* Bol./Brazil
154 B3 Guarapuava Brazil
154 C3 Guaraqueçaba Brazil
155 C2 Guaratinguetá Brazil
106 B1 Guarda Port.
154 C1 Guarda Mor Brazil
106 C1 Guardo Spain
155 C2 Guarujá Brazil
144 B2 Guasave Mex.
146 A3 Guatemala *country*
        Central America
146 A3 Guatemala City Guat.
150 B1 Guaviare *r.* Col.
155 C2 Guaxupé Brazil
150 A2 Guayaquil Ecuador
150 B3 Guayaramerín Bol.
144 A2 Guaymas Mex.
117 B3 Guba Eth.
86 E1 Guba Dolgaya Rus. Fed.
89 E3 Gubkin Rus. Fed.
115 C1 Guelma Alg.
114 A2 Guelmine Morocco
130 B2 Guelph Can.
145 C2 Guémez Mex.
104 C2 Guéret France
95 C4 Guernsey *terr.* Channel Is
144 A2 Guerrero Negro Mex.
131 D1 Guers, Lac *l.* Can.
118 B2 Guider Cameroon
108 B2 Guidonia-Montecelio Italy
71 A3 Guigang China
100 A3 Guignicourt France
123 D1 Guija Moz.
99 C3 Guildford U.K.
71 B3 Guilin China
130 C1 Guillaume-Delisle, Lac *l.*
        Can.
106 B1 Guimarães Port.
114 A3 Guinea *country* Africa
113 F6 Guinea, Gulf of Africa
114 A3 Guinea-Bissau *country*
        Africa
104 B2 Guingamp France
104 B2 Guipavas France
104 B2 Guiratinga Brazil
150 B1 Güiria Venez.
100 A3 Guise France
64 B1 Guiuan Phil.
71 A3 Guiyang China
71 A3 Guizhou *prov.* China
74 B1 Gujranwala Pak.
74 B1 Gujrat Pak.
91 D2 Gukovo Rus. Fed.
53 C2 Gulargambone Austr.
73 B3 Gulbarga India
88 C2 Gulbene Latvia
79 C2 Gulf, the Asia
111 B3 Gulf of Corinth *sea chan.*
        Greece
142 C2 Gulfport U.S.A.
69 E1 Gulian China
77 C2 Guliston Uzbek.
        Gulja China *see* Yining
129 D2 Gull Lake Can.
111 C3 Gülük Turkey
119 D2 Gulu Uganda
120 B2 Gumare Botswana
76 B3 Gumdag Turkm.

75 C2 Gumla India
100 C2 Gummersbach Ger.
74 B2 Guna India
53 C3 Gundagai Austr.
111 C3 Güney Turkey
118 B3 Gungu Dem. Rep. Congo
129 E2 Gunisao *r.* Can.
53 D2 Gunnedah Austr.
136 B3 Gunnison *CO* U.S.A.
135 D3 Gunnison *UT* U.S.A.
136 B3 Gunnison *r.* U.S.A.
73 B3 Guntakal India
60 A1 Gunungsitoli Indon.
60 A1 Gunungtua Indon.
102 C2 Günzburg Ger.
102 C2 Gunzenhausen Ger.
70 B2 Guojiaba China
74 B2 Gurgaon India
151 D2 Gurgueia *r.* Brazil
150 B1 Guri, Embalse de *resr*
        Venez.
154 C1 Gurinhatã Brazil
151 D2 Gurupi *r.* Brazil
74 B2 Guru Sikhar *mt.* India
115 C3 Gusau Nigeria
65 A2 Gushan China
70 B2 Gushi China
83 I3 Gusinoozersk Rus. Fed.
89 F2 Gus'-Khrustal'nyy
        Rus. Fed.
108 A3 Guspini *Sardinia* Italy
128 A2 Gustavus U.S.A.
101 F1 Güstrow Ger.
101 D2 Gütersloh Ger.
121 C2 Gutu Zimbabwe
75 D2 Guwahati India
150 C1 Guyana *country* S. America
        Guyi China *see* Sanjiang
139 C1 Guymon U.S.A.
53 D2 Guyra Austr.
70 A2 Guyuan China
144 B3 Guzmán Mex.
144 B1 Guzmán, Lago de *l.* Mex.
74 A2 Gwadar Pak.
75 B2 Gwalior India
121 B3 Gwanda Zimbabwe
117 D3 Gwardafuy, Gees *c.*
        Somalia
97 B1 Gweebarra Bay Ireland
97 B1 Gweedore Ireland
121 B2 Gweru Zimbabwe
115 D3 Gwoza Nigeria
53 D2 Gwydir *r.* Austr.
75 C2 Gyangzê China
75 C1 Gyaring Co *l.* China
68 C2 Gyaring Hu *l.* China
86 G1 Gydan Peninsula Rus. Fed.
        Gydanskiy Poluostrov
        pen. Rus. Fed. *see*
        Gydan Peninsula
        Gyêgu China *see* Yushu
68 C3 Gyigang China
51 E2 Gympie Austr.
103 D2 Gyöngyös Hungary
103 D2 Győr Hungary
129 E2 Gypsumville Can.
103 E2 Gyula Hungary
81 C1 Gyumri Armenia

H

88 B2 Haapsalu Estonia
100 B1 Haarlem Neth.
101 C2 Haarstrang *ridge* Ger.
54 A2 Haast N.Z.
78 B3 Habbān Yemen

81 C2 Ḩabbānīyah, Hawr al
        l. Iraq
67 C4 Hachijō-jima *i.* Japan
66 D2 Hachinohe Japan
121 C3 Hacufera Moz.
79 C2 Ḩadd, Ra's al *pt* Oman
96 C3 Haddington U.K.
115 C3 Hadejia Nigeria
93 E4 Haderslev Denmark
91 C1 Hadyach Ukr.
65 B2 Haeju N. Korea
65 B2 Haeju-man *b.* N. Korea
65 B3 Haenam S. Korea
78 B2 Ḩafar al Bāṭin Saudi Arabia
62 A1 Haflong India
92 □A3 Hafnarfjörður Iceland
78 A3 Hagar Nish Plateau Eritrea
48 D2 Hagåtña Guam
100 C2 Hagen Ger.
101 E1 Hagenow Ger.
128 B2 Hagensborg Can.
141 D3 Hagerstown U.S.A.
93 F3 Hagfors Sweden
67 B4 Hagi Japan
62 B1 Ha Giang Vietnam
97 B2 Hag's Head Ireland
104 B2 Hague, Cap de la *c.*
        France
119 D3 Hai Tanz.
62 B1 Hai Duong Vietnam
80 B2 Haifa Israel
71 B3 Haifeng China
71 B3 Haikou China
78 B2 Ḩā'il Saudi Arabia
92 H2 Hailuoto *i.* Fin.
71 C3 Hainan *i.* China
71 A4 Hainan *prov.* China
128 A2 Haines U.S.A.
128 A1 Haines Junction Can.
101 E2 Hainich *ridge* Ger.
101 E2 Hainleite *ridge* Ger.
62 B1 Hai Phong Vietnam
147 C3 Haiti *country* West Indies
116 B3 Haiya Sudan
103 E2 Hajdúböszörmény
        Hungary
78 B3 Ḩajjah Yemen
79 C2 Ḩājjīābād Iran
62 A1 Haka Myanmar
81 C2 Hakkâri Turkey
66 D2 Hakodate Japan
        Ḩalab Syria *see* Aleppo
78 B2 Ḩalabān Saudi Arabia
81 C2 Ḩalabja Iraq
116 B2 Halaib Sudan
78 A2 Halaib Triangle *terr.*
        Egypt/Sudan
79 C3 Ḩalāniyāt, Juzur al *is*
        Oman
78 A2 Ḩālat 'Ammār
        Saudi Arabia
68 C1 Halban Mongolia
101 E2 Halberstadt Ger.
64 B1 Halcon, Mount Phil.
93 F4 Halden Norway
101 E1 Haldensleben Ger.
75 C2 Haldwani India
79 C2 Ḩāleh Iran
54 A3 Halfmoon Bay N.Z.
131 D2 Halifax Can.
98 C2 Halifax U.K.
141 D3 Halifax U.S.A.
65 B3 Halla-san *mt.* S. Korea
127 F2 Hall Beach Can.
100 B2 Halle Belgium
101 E2 Halle (Saale) Ger.
102 C2 Hallein Austria
137 D1 Hallock U.S.A.
127 G2 Hall Peninsula Can.
50 B1 Halls Creek Austr.

59	C2	Halmahera *i.* Indon.
93	F4	Halmstad Sweden
62	B1	Ha Long Vietnam
67	B4	Hamada Japan
81	C2	Hamadān Iran
80	B2	Hamāh Syria
67	C4	Hamamatsu Japan
93	F3	Hamar Norway
116	B2	Hamāţah, Jabal *mt.* Egypt
73	C4	Hambantota Sri Lanka
101	D1	Hamburg Ger.
78	A2	Ḩamḑ, Wādī al *watercourse* Saudi Arabia
78	B3	Ḩamḑah Saudi Arabia
93	H3	Hämeenlinna Fin.
101	D1	Hameln Ger.
50	A2	Hamersley Range *mts* Austr.
65	B2	Hamhŭng N. Korea
68	C2	Hami China
116	B2	Hamid Sudan
52	B3	Hamilton Austr.
130	C2	Hamilton Can.
54	C1	Hamilton N.Z.
96	B3	Hamilton U.K.
142	C2	Hamilton *AL* U.S.A.
134	D1	Hamilton *MT* U.S.A.
140	C3	Hamilton *OH* U.S.A.
93	I3	Hamina Fin.
100	C2	Hamm Ger.
114	B2	Hammada du Drâa *plat.* Alg.
81	C2	Hammār, Hawr al *imp. l.* Iraq
101	D2	Hammelburg Ger.
92	G3	Hammerdal Sweden
92	H1	Hammerfest Norway
142	B2	Hammond U.S.A.
141	E3	Hammonton U.S.A.
79	C2	Hāmūn-e Jaz Mūriān *salt marsh* Iran
74	A2	Hamun-i-Lora *dry lake* Pak.
74	A2	Hamun-i-Mashkel *salt flat* Pak.
78	A2	Ḩanak Saudi Arabia
66	D3	Hanamaki Japan
101	D2	Hanau Ger.
70	B2	Hancheng China
140	B1	Hancock U.S.A.
70	B2	Handan China
135	C3	Hanford U.S.A.
68	C1	Hangayn Nuruu *mts* Mongolia
		Hanggin Houqi China *see* Xamba
		Hangö Fin. *see* Hanko
70	C2	Hangzhou China
70	C2	Hangzhou Wan *b.* China
		Hanjia China *see* Pengshui
		Hanjiang China *see* Yangzhou
93	H4	Hanko Fin.
135	D3	Hanksville U.S.A.
54	B2	Hanmer Springs N.Z.
129	C2	Hanna Can.
137	E3	Hannibal U.S.A.
101	D1	Hannover Ger.
101	D2	Hannoversch Münden Ger.
93	F4	Hanöbukten *b.* Sweden
62	B1	Ha Nôi Vietnam
		Hanoi Vietnam *see* Ha Nôi
130	B2	Hanover Can.
122	B3	Hanover S. Africa
93	E4	Hanstholm Denmark
88	C3	Hantsavichy Belarus
75	C2	Hanumana India
74	B2	Hanumangarh India
70	A2	Hanzhong China
92	H2	Haparanda Sweden
100	B2	Hapert Neth.

131	D1	Happy Valley-Goose Bay Can.
78	A2	Ḩaql Saudi Arabia
79	B2	Ḩaraḑh Saudi Arabia
88	C2	Haradok Belarus
78	B3	Ḩarajā Saudi Arabia
121	C2	Harare Zimbabwe
79	C3	Ḩarāsīs, Jiddat al *des.* Oman
69	D1	Har-Ayrag Mongolia
69	E1	Harbin China
131	E2	Harbour Breton Can.
74	B2	Harda India
93	E4	Hardangerfjorden Norway
100	C1	Hardenberg Neth.
100	B1	Harderwijk Neth.
122	A3	Hardeveld *mts* S. Africa
134	E1	Hardin U.S.A.
128	C1	Hardisty Lake Can.
100	C1	Haren (Ems) Ger.
117	C4	Hārer Eth.
117	C4	Hargeysa Somalia
110	C1	Harghita-Mădăraş, Vârful *mt.* Romania
68	C2	Har Hu *l.* China
74	B1	Haripur Pak.
74	A1	Hari Rūd *r.* Afgh./Iran
100	B1	Harlingen Neth.
139	D3	Harlingen U.S.A.
99	D3	Harlow U.K.
134	E1	Harlowton U.S.A.
134	C2	Harney Basin U.S.A.
134	C2	Harney Lake U.S.A.
93	G3	Härnösand Sweden
69	E1	Har Nur China
68	C1	Har Nuur *l.* Mongolia
114	B4	Harper Liberia
101	D1	Harpstedt Ger.
130	C1	Harricanaw *r.* Can.
52	D2	Harrington Austr.
131	E1	Harrington Harbour Can.
96	A2	Harris, Sound of *sea chan.* U.K.
140	B3	Harrisburg *IL* U.S.A.
141	D2	Harrisburg *PA* U.S.A.
123	C2	Harrismith S. Africa
142	B1	Harrison U.S.A.
131	E1	Harrison, Cape Can.
126	A2	Harrison Bay U.S.A.
141	D3	Harrisonburg U.S.A.
137	E3	Harrisonville U.S.A.
98	C2	Harrogate U.K.
110	C2	Hârşova Romania
92	G2	Harstad Norway
122	B2	Hartbees *watercourse* S. Africa
103	D2	Hartberg Austria
141	E2	Hartford U.S.A.
99	A3	Hartland Point U.K.
98	C1	Hartlepool U.K.
128	B2	Hartley Bay Can.
123	B2	Harts *r.* S. Africa
143	D1	Hartwell Reservoir U.S.A.
68	C1	Har Us Nuur *l.* Mongolia
136	C1	Harvey U.S.A.
99	D3	Harwich U.K.
101	E2	Harz *hills* Ger.
73	B3	Hassan India
100	B2	Hasselt Belgium
115	C1	Hassi Messaoud Alg.
93	F4	Hässleholm Sweden
100	B2	Hastière-Lavaux Belgium
53	C3	Hastings Austr.
54	C1	Hastings N.Z.
99	D3	Hastings U.K.
137	E2	Hastings *MN* U.S.A.
137	D2	Hastings *NE* U.S.A.
129	D2	Hatchet Lake Can.
52	B2	Hatfield Austr.

68	C1	Hatgal Mongolia
62	B2	Ha Tinh Vietnam
143	E1	Hatteras, Cape U.S.A.
142	C2	Hattiesburg U.S.A.
100	C2	Hattingen Ger.
63	B3	Hat Yai Thai.
117	C4	Haud *reg.* Eth.
93	E4	Haugesund Norway
93	E4	Haukeligrend Norway
92	I2	Haukipudas Fin.
54	C1	Hauraki Gulf N.Z.
114	B1	Haut Atlas *mts* Morocco
131	D2	Hauterive Can.
114	B1	Hauts Plateaux Alg.
146	B2	Havana Cuba
99	C3	Havant U.K.
101	E1	Havel *r.* Ger.
101	F1	Havelberg Ger.
54	B2	Havelock N.Z.
54	C1	Havelock North N.Z.
99	A3	Haverfordwest U.K.
103	D2	Havlíčkův Brod Czech Rep.
92	H1	Havøysund Norway
111	C3	Havran Turkey
134	E1	Havre U.S.A.
131	D1	Havre Aubert Can.
131	D1	Havre-St-Pierre Can.
124	E5	Hawai'i *i.* N. Pacific Ocean
124	E5	Hawai'ian Islands N. Pacific Ocean
98	B2	Hawarden U.K.
54	A2	Hawea, Lake N.Z.
54	B1	Hawera N.Z.
98	B1	Hawes U.K.
96	C3	Hawick U.K.
54	C1	Hawke Bay N.Z.
52	A2	Hawker Austr.
52	B1	Hawkers Gate Austr.
135	C3	Hawthorne U.S.A.
52	B2	Hay Austr.
128	C1	Hay *r.* Can.
134	C1	Hayden U.S.A.
129	E2	Hayes *r. Man.* Can.
126	E2	Hayes *r. Nunavut* Can.
79	C3	Haymā' Oman
77	C2	Hayotboshi tog'i *mt.* Uzbek.
111	C2	Hayrabolu Turkey
128	C1	Hay River Can.
137	D3	Hays U.S.A.
78	B3	Hays Yemen
90	B2	Haysyn Ukr.
99	C3	Haywards Heath U.K.
81	D2	Hazar Turkm.
74	A1	Hazarajat *reg.* Afgh.
140	C3	Hazard U.S.A.
75	C2	Hazaribagh India
75	C2	Hazaribagh Range *mts* India
128	B2	Hazelton Can.
141	D2	Hazleton U.S.A.
53	C3	Healesville Austr.
130	B2	Hearst Can.
70	B2	Hebei *prov.* China
53	C1	Hebel Austr.
142	B1	Heber Springs U.S.A.
70	B2	Hebi China
131	D1	Hebron Can.
128	A2	Hecate Strait Can.
71	A3	Hechi China
93	F3	Hede Sweden
100	B1	Heerenveen Neth.
100	B1	Heerhugowaard Neth.
100	B2	Heerlen Neth.
		Hefa Israel *see* Haifa
70	B2	Hefei China
70	B3	Hefeng China
69	E1	Hegang China
102	B1	Heide Ger.
122	A1	Heide Namibia

102 B2 **Heidelberg** Ger.
122 B3 **Heidelberg** S. Africa
102 B2 **Heilbronn** Ger.
69 E1 **Heilong Jiang** *r.*
China/Rus. Fed.
93 I3 **Heinola** Fin.
92 F3 **Helagsfjället** *mt.* Sweden
142 B2 **Helena** *AR* U.S.A.
134 D1 **Helena** *MT* U.S.A.
96 B2 **Helensburgh** U.K.
102 B1 **Helgoland** *i.* Ger.
102 B1 **Helgoländer Bucht** *b.* Ger.
Helixi China *see* Ningguo
92 □A3 **Hella** Iceland
100 B2 **Hellevoetsluis** Neth.
107 C2 **Hellín** Spain
76 C3 **Helmand** *r.* Afgh.
101 E2 **Helmbrechts** Ger.
122 A2 **Helmeringhausen** Namibia
100 B2 **Helmond** Neth.
96 C1 **Helmsdale** U.K.
96 C1 **Helmsdale** *r.* U.K.
101 E1 **Helmstedt** Ger.
65 B1 **Helong** China
93 F4 **Helsingborg** Sweden
Helsingfors Fin. *see*
Helsinki
93 F4 **Helsingør** Denmark
93 H3 **Helsinki** Fin.
97 C2 **Helvick Head** Ireland
99 C3 **Hemel Hempstead** U.K.
101 D1 **Hemmoor** Ger.
92 F2 **Hemnesberget** Norway
70 B2 **Henan** *prov.* China
140 D3 **Henderson** *KY* U.S.A.
143 E1 **Henderson** *NC* U.S.A.
135 D3 **Henderson** *NV* U.S.A.
139 E2 **Henderson** *TX* U.S.A.
143 D1 **Hendersonville** U.S.A.
99 C3 **Hendon** U.K.
62 A1 **Hengduan Shan** *mts* China
100 C1 **Hengelo** Neth.
Hengnan China *see*
Hengyang
70 B2 **Hengshui** China
71 A3 **Hengxian** China
71 B3 **Hengyang** China
Hengzhou China *see*
Hengxian
91 C2 **Heniches'k** Ukr.
100 C2 **Hennef (Sieg)** Ger.
130 B1 **Henrietta Maria, Cape** Can.
139 D1 **Henryetta** U.S.A.
127 G2 **Henry Kater, Cape** Can.
101 D1 **Henstedt-Ulzburg** Ger.
120 A3 **Hentiesbaai** Namibia
71 A3 **Hepu** China
76 C3 **Herāt** Afgh.
129 D2 **Herbert** Can.
101 D2 **Herbstein** Ger.
99 B2 **Hereford** U.K.
139 C2 **Hereford** U.S.A.
101 D1 **Herford** Ger.
100 C2 **Herkenbosch** Neth.
96 □ **Herma Ness** *hd* U.K.
123 C2 **Hermanus** S. Africa
53 C2 **Hermidale** Austr.
134 C1 **Hermiston** U.S.A.
59 D3 **Hermit Islands** P.N.G.
144 B3 **Hermosillo** Mex.
154 B3 **Hernandarias** Para.
100 C2 **Herne** Ger.
93 E4 **Herning** Denmark
99 C3 **Hertford** U.K.
123 C2 **Hertzogville** S. Africa
51 E2 **Hervey Bay** Austr.
101 F2 **Herzberg** Ger.
101 E3 **Herzogenaurach** Ger.
71 A3 **Heshan** China
128 A1 **Hess** *r.* Can.

101 D2 **Hessisch Lichtenau** Ger.
136 C1 **Hettinger** U.S.A.
101 E2 **Hettstedt** Ger.
98 B1 **Hexham** U.K.
71 B3 **Heyuan** China
52 B3 **Heywood** Austr.
70 B2 **Heze** China
71 B3 **Hezhou** China
137 D3 **Hiawatha** U.S.A.
137 E1 **Hibbing** U.S.A.
54 C1 **Hicks Bay** N.Z.
66 D2 **Hidaka-sanmyaku** *mts*
Japan
145 C2 **Hidalgo** Mex.
144 B2 **Hidalgo del Parral** Mex.
154 C1 **Hidrolândia** Brazil
High Atlas *mts* Morocco
see Haut Atlas
134 B2 **High Desert** U.S.A.
128 C2 **High Level** Can.
143 E1 **High Point** U.S.A.
128 C2 **High Prairie** Can.
128 C2 **High River** Can.
129 D2 **Highrock Lake** Can.
99 C3 **High Wycombe** U.K.
88 B2 **Hiiumaa** *i.* Estonia
78 A2 **Ḥijaz** *reg.* Saudi Arabia
54 C1 **Hikurangi** *mt.* N.Z.
101 E2 **Hildburghausen** Ger.
101 D2 **Hilders** Ger.
101 D1 **Hildesheim** Ger.
81 C2 **Ḥillah** Iraq
100 C2 **Hillesheim** Ger.
140 C3 **Hillsboro** *OH* U.S.A.
139 D2 **Hillsboro** *TX* U.S.A.
53 C2 **Hillston** Austr.
143 D2 **Hilton Head Island** U.S.A.
100 B1 **Hilversum** Neth.
68 B2 **Himalaya** *mts* Asia
67 B4 **Himeji** Japan
123 C2 **Himeville** S. Africa
51 D1 **Hinchinbrook Island** Austr.
74 A1 **Hindu Kush** *mts* Afgh./Pak.
143 D2 **Hinesville** U.S.A.
75 B2 **Hinganghat** India
81 C2 **Ḥinis** Turkey
92 G2 **Hinnøya** *i.* Norway
106 B2 **Hinojosa del Duque** Spain
62 A2 **Hinthada** Myanmar
128 C2 **Hinton** Can.
75 C2 **Hirakud Reservoir** India
66 D2 **Hirosaki** Japan
67 B4 **Hiroshima** Japan
101 E3 **Hirschaid** Ger.
101 E2 **Hirschberg** Ger.
105 C2 **Hirson** France
93 E4 **Hirtshals** Denmark
74 B2 **Hisar** India
147 C3 **Hispaniola** *i.* Caribbean Sea
81 C2 **Ḥit** Iraq
67 D3 **Hitachi** Japan
67 D3 **Hitachinaka** Japan
92 E3 **Hitra** *i.* Norway
49 I3 **Hiva Oa** *i.* Fr. Polynesia
93 G4 **Hjälmaren** *l.* Sweden
129 D1 **Hjalmar Lake** Can.
93 F4 **Hjørring** Denmark
123 D2 **Hlabisa** S. Africa
92 □B2 **Hlíð** Iceland
91 C2 **Hlobyne** Ukr.
123 C2 **Hlohlowane** S. Africa
123 C2 **Hlotse** Lesotho
91 C1 **Hlukhiv** Ukr.
88 C2 **Hlybokaye** Belarus
114 C4 **Ho** Ghana
62 B2 **Hoa Binh** Vietnam
122 A1 **Hoachanas** Namibia
51 D4 **Hobart** Austr.
139 C1 **Hobart** U.S.A.
139 C2 **Hobbs** U.S.A.

93 E4 **Hobro** Denmark
117 C4 **Hobyo** Somalia
63 B2 **Ho Chi Minh City** Vietnam
114 B3 **Ḥōḍ** *reg.* Maur.
78 B3 **Hodeidah** Yemen
103 E2 **Hódmezővásárhely**
Hungary
Hoek van Holland Neth.
see Hook of Holland
65 B2 **Hoeyang** N. Korea
101 E2 **Hof** Ger.
101 E2 **Hofheim in Unterfranken**
Ger.
92 □B3 **Höfn** *Austurland* Iceland
92 □A2 **Höfn** *Vestfirðir* Iceland
92 □B3 **Hofsjökull** *ice cap* Iceland
67 B3 **Hōfu** Japan
115 C2 **Hoggar** *plat.* Alg.
93 G4 **Högsby** Sweden
101 D2 **Hohe Rhön** *mts* Ger.
100 C2 **Hohe Venn** *moorland*
Belgium
70 B1 **Hohhot** China
75 C1 **Hoh Xil Shan** *mts* China
62 A1 **Hojai** India
54 B2 **Hokitika** N.Z.
66 D2 **Hokkaidō** *i.* Japan
128 B2 **Holberg** Can.
138 A2 **Holbrook** U.S.A.
137 D2 **Holdrege** U.S.A.
146 C2 **Holguín** Cuba
92 □B2 **Hóll** Iceland
Holland *country* Europe *see*
Netherlands
140 B2 **Holland** U.S.A.
100 B1 **Hollum** Neth.
142 C2 **Holly Springs** U.S.A.
135 C4 **Hollywood** U.S.A.
143 D3 **Hollywood** U.S.A.
92 F2 **Holm** Norway
126 D2 **Holman** Can.
92 H3 **Holmsund** Sweden
122 A2 **Holoog** Namibia
93 E4 **Holstebro** Denmark
143 D1 **Holston** *r.* U.S.A.
98 A2 **Holyhead** U.K.
98 C1 **Holy Island** *England* U.K.
98 A2 **Holy Island** *Wales* U.K.
136 C2 **Holyoke** U.S.A.
101 D2 **Holzminden** Ger.
62 A1 **Homalin** Myanmar
101 D2 **Homberg (Efze)** Ger.
114 B3 **Hombori** Mali
127 G2 **Home Bay** Can.
143 D3 **Homestead** U.S.A.
92 F3 **Hommelvik** Norway
80 B2 **Ḥoms** Syria
89 D3 **Homyel'** Belarus
122 A3 **Hondeklipbaai** S. Africa
145 D3 **Hondo** *r.* Belize/Mex.
139 D3 **Hondo** U.S.A.
146 B3 **Honduras** *country*
Central America
93 F3 **Hønefoss** Norway
135 B2 **Honey Lake** U.S.A.
104 C2 **Honfleur** France
70 B3 **Honghu** China
71 A3 **Hongjiang** China
71 B3 **Hong Kong** China
71 B3 **Hong Kong**
special admin. reg. China
65 B1 **Hongwŏn** N. Korea
70 B2 **Hongze Hu** *l.* China
49 E3 **Honiara** Solomon Is.
66 D3 **Honjō** Japan
92 I1 **Honningsvåg** Norway
67 B3 **Honshū** *i.* Japan
134 B1 **Hood, Mount** *vol.* U.S.A.
50 A3 **Hood Point** Austr.

134	B1	**Hood River** U.S.A.
100	C1	**Hoogeveen** Neth.
100	C1	**Hoogezand-Sappemeer** Neth.
100	C2	**Hoog-Keppel** Neth.
100	B2	**Hook of Holland** Neth.
128	A2	**Hoonah** U.S.A.
100	B1	**Hoorn** Neth.
128	B3	**Hope** Can.
142	B2	**Hope** U.S.A.
83	N2	**Hope, Point** U.S.A.
131	D1	**Hopedale** Can.
131	D1	**Hope Mountains** Can.
52	B3	**Hopetoun** Austr.
122	B2	**Hopetown** S. Africa
141	D3	**Hopewell** U.S.A.
130	C1	**Hopewell Islands** Can.
50	B2	**Hopkins, Lake** salt flat Austr.
140	B3	**Hopkinsville** U.S.A.
134	B1	**Hoquiam** U.S.A.
81	C1	**Horasan** Turkey
93	F4	**Hörby** Sweden
89	D3	**Horki** Belarus
91	D2	**Horlivka** Ukr.
79	D2	**Hormak** Iran
79	C2	**Hormuz, Strait of** Iran/Oman
103	D2	**Horn** Austria
92	□A2	**Horn** c. Iceland
153	B6	**Horn, Cape** Chile
141	D2	**Hornell** U.S.A.
130	B2	**Hornepayne** Can.
98	C2	**Hornsea** U.K.
90	B2	**Horodenka** Ukr.
91	C1	**Horodnya** Ukr.
90	B2	**Horodok** Khmel'nyts'ka Oblast' Ukr.
90	A2	**Horodok** L'vivs'ka Oblast' Ukr.
90	A1	**Horokhiv** Ukr.
		Horqin Youyi Qianqi China see Ulanhot
131	E1	**Horse Islands** Can.
52	B3	**Horsham** Austr.
126	C2	**Horton** r. Can.
117	B4	**Hosa'ina** Eth.
74	C2	**Hoshab** Pak.
74	B1	**Hoshiarpur** India
77	E3	**Hotan** China
122	B2	**Hotazel** S. Africa
142	B2	**Hot Springs** AR U.S.A.
136	C2	**Hot Springs** SD U.S.A.
128	C1	**Hottah Lake** Can.
100	B2	**Houffalize** Belgium
70	B2	**Houma** China
142	B3	**Houma** U.S.A.
128	B2	**Houston** Can.
139	D3	**Houston** U.S.A.
122	B3	**Houwater** S. Africa
68	C1	**Hovd** Mongolia
99	C3	**Hove** U.K.
68	C1	**Hövsgöl Nuur** l. Mongolia
68	C2	**Hövüün** Mongolia
116	A3	**Howar, Wadi** watercourse Sudan
53	C3	**Howe, Cape** Austr.
49	G2	**Howland Island** N. Pacific Ocean
53	C2	**Howlong** Austr.
101	D2	**Höxter** Ger.
96	C1	**Hoy** i. U.K.
93	E3	**Høyanger** Norway
102	C1	**Hoyerswerda** Ger.
62	A2	**Hpapun** Myanmar
103	D1	**Hradec Králové** Czech Rep.
109	C2	**Hrasnica** Bos.-Herz.
91	C1	**Hrebinka** Ukr.
88	B3	**Hrodna** Belarus
62	A1	**Hsi-hseng** Myanmar
71	C3	**Hsinchu** Taiwan
71	C3	**Hsinying** Taiwan
62	A1	**Hsipaw** Myanmar
70	A2	**Huachi** China
150	A3	**Huacho** Peru
69	D2	**Huade** China
65	B1	**Huadian** China
70	B2	**Huai'an** China
70	B2	**Huaibei** China
71	A3	**Huaihua** China
70	B2	**Huainan** China
70	B2	**Huaiyang** China
145	C3	**Huajuápan de León** Mex.
59	C3	**Huaki** Indon.
71	C3	**Hualien** Taiwan
150	A2	**Huallaga** r. Peru
120	A2	**Huambo** Angola
150	A3	**Huancayo** Peru
		Huangcaoba China see Xingyi
70	B2	**Huangchuan** China
		Huang Hai sea N. Pacific see Yellow Sea
		Huang He r. China see Yellow River
71	A4	**Huangliu** China
71	B3	**Huangshan** China
70	B2	**Huangshi** China
70	A2	**Huangtu Gaoyuan** plat. China
71	B3	**Huangyan** China
65	B1	**Huanren** China
150	A2	**Huánuco** Peru
152	B2	**Huanuni** Bol.
150	A2	**Huaraz** Peru
150	A3	**Huarmey** Peru
152	A3	**Huasco** Chile
152	A3	**Huasco** r. Chile
144	B2	**Huatabampo** Mex.
145	C3	**Huatusco** Mex.
71	A3	**Huayuan** China
62	B1	**Huayxay** Laos
70	B2	**Hubei** prov. China
73	B3	**Hubli** India
100	C2	**Hückelhoven** Ger.
98	C2	**Hucknall** U.K.
98	C2	**Huddersfield** U.K.
93	G3	**Hudiksvall** Sweden
141	E2	**Hudson** r. U.S.A.
129	D2	**Hudson Bay** Can.
127	F3	**Hudson Bay** sea Can.
128	B2	**Hudson's Hope** Can.
127	G2	**Hudson Strait** Can.
63	B2	**Huê** Viet.
146	A3	**Huehuetenango** Guat.
144	B2	**Huehueto, Cerro** mt. Mex.
145	C2	**Huejutla** Mex.
106	B2	**Huelva** Spain
107	C2	**Huércal-Overa** Spain
107	C1	**Huesca** Spain
106	C2	**Huéscar** Spain
51	D2	**Hughes** Austr.
139	D2	**Hugo** U.S.A.
122	B2	**Huhudi** S. Africa
122	A2	**Huib-Hoch Plateau** Namibia
71	B3	**Huichang** China
65	B1	**Huich'ŏn** N. Korea
71	B3	**Huilai** China
120	A2	**Huila Plateau** Angola
62	A1	**Huili** China
65	B1	**Huinan** China
93	H3	**Huittinen** Fin.
145	C3	**Huixtla** Mex.
		Huiyang China see **Huizhou**
62	B1	**Huize** China
71	B3	**Huizhou** China
69	C1	**Hujirt** Mongolia
78	B2	**Hujr** Saudi Arabia
122	B1	**Hukuntsi** Botswana
78	B2	**Ḩulayfah** Saudi Arabia
66	B1	**Hulin** China
130	C2	**Hull** Can.
		Hulun China see **Hulun Buir**
69	D1	**Hulun Buir** China
69	D1	**Hulun Nur** l. China
91	D2	**Hulyaypole** Ukr.
69	E1	**Huma** China
150	B2	**Humaitá** Brazil
122	B3	**Humansdorp** S. Africa
98	C2	**Humber** est. U.K.
126	D3	**Humboldt** Can.
142	C1	**Humboldt** U.S.A.
135	C2	**Humboldt** r. U.S.A.
103	E2	**Humenné** Slovakia
53	C3	**Hume Reservoir** Austr.
138	A1	**Humphreys Peak** U.S.A.
92	□A2	**Húnaflói** b. Iceland
71	B3	**Hunan** prov. China
65	C1	**Hunchun** China
110	B1	**Hunedoara** Romania
101	D2	**Hünfeld** Ger.
102	D2	**Hungary** country Europe
52	B1	**Hungerford** Austr.
65	B2	**Hŭngnam** N. Korea
65	A1	**Hun He** r. China
99	D2	**Hunstanton** U.K.
101	D1	**Hunte** r. Ger.
51	D4	**Hunter Islands** Austr.
99	C2	**Huntingdon** U.K.
140	B2	**Huntington** IN U.S.A.
140	C3	**Huntington** WV U.S.A.
54	C1	**Huntly** N.Z.
96	C2	**Huntly** U.K.
130	C2	**Huntsville** Can.
142	C2	**Huntsville** AL U.S.A.
139	D2	**Huntsville** TX U.S.A.
59	D3	**Huon Peninsula** P.N.G.
70	B2	**Huozhou** China
137	D2	**Huron** U.S.A.
140	C2	**Huron, Lake** Can./U.S.A.
135	D3	**Hurricane** U.S.A.
92	□B2	**Húsavík** Iceland
110	C1	**Huşi** Romania
93	G4	**Huskvarna** Sweden
78	B3	**Ḩuşn Āl 'Abr** Yemen
102	B1	**Husum** Ger.
69	C1	**Hutag** Mongolia
60	A1	**Hutanopan** Indon.
137	D3	**Hutchinson** U.S.A.
70	C2	**Huzhou** China
92	□C3	**Hvalnes** Iceland
92	□B3	**Hvannadalshnúkur** vol. Iceland
109	C2	**Hvar** i. Croatia
120	B2	**Hwange** Zimbabwe
136	C2	**Hyannis** U.S.A.
68	C1	**Hyargas Nuur** salt l. Mongolia
50	A3	**Hyden** Austr.
73	B3	**Hyderabad** India
74	A2	**Hyderabad** Pak.
105	D3	**Hyères** France
65	B1	**Hyesan** N. Korea
128	B2	**Hyland Post** Can.
67	B3	**Hyŏno-sen** mt. Japan
99	D3	**Hythe** U.K.
93	H3	**Hyvinkää** Fin.

I

150	B2	**Iaco** r. Brazil
110	C1	**Ialomiţa** r. Romania
110	C1	**Ianca** Romania
110	C1	**Iaşi** Romania
64	A1	**Iba** Phil.

115	C4	Ibadan Nigeria
150	A1	Ibagué Col.
150	A1	Ibarra Ecuador
78	B3	Ibb Yemen
100	C1	Ibbenbüren Ger.
115	C4	Ibi Nigeria
155	C1	Ibiá Brazil
155	D1	Ibiraçu Brazil
107	D2	Ibiza Spain
107	D2	Ibiza i. Spain
151	D3	Ibotirama Brazil
79	C2	Ibrā' Oman
79	C2	Ibrī Oman
150	A3	Ica Peru
92	□B2	Iceland country Europe
152	A4	Içel Turkey
66	D3	Ichinoseki Japan
91	C1	Ichnya Ukr.
65	B2	Ich'ŏn N. Korea
139	E2	Idabel U.S.A.
134	D2	Idaho state U.S.A.
134	D2	Idaho Falls U.S.A.
100	C3	Idar-Oberstein Ger.
116	B2	Idfū Egypt
115	D2	Idhān Awbārī des. Libya
115	D2	Idhān Murzūq des. Libya
118	B3	Idiofa Dem. Rep. Congo
80	B2	Idlib Syria
154	B2	Iepê Brazil
100	A2	Ieper Belgium
119	D3	Ifakara Tanz.
121	□D3	Ifanadiana Madag.
115	C4	Ife Nigeria
114	C3	Ifôghas, Adrar des hills Mali
61	C1	Igan Sarawak Malaysia
154	C2	Igarapava Brazil
82	G2	Igarka Rus. Fed.
74	B3	Igatpuri India
81	C2	Iğdır Turkey
108	A3	Iglesias Sardinia Italy
127	F2	Igloolik Can.
		Iglulligaarjuk Can. see Chesterfield Inlet
130	A2	Ignace Can.
88	C2	Ignalina Lith.
110	C2	Iğneada Turkey
111	B3	Igoumenitsa Greece
86	E3	Igra Rus. Fed.
86	F2	Igrim Rus. Fed.
154	B3	Iguaçu r. Brazil
154	B3	Iguaçu Falls Arg./Brazil
145	C3	Iguala Mex.
107	D1	Igualada Spain
154	C2	Iguape Brazil
154	B2	Iguatemi Brazil
154	B2	Iguatemi r. Brazil
151	E3	Iguatu Brazil
118	A3	Iguéla Gabon
119	D3	Igunga Tanz.
69	D2	Ihbulag Mongolia
121	□D3	Ihosy Madag.
92	I3	Iisalmi Fin.
115	C4	Ijebu-Ode Nigeria
100	B1	IJmuiden Neth.
100	B1	IJssel r. Neth.
100	B1	IJsselmeer l. Neth.
123	C2	Ikageng S. Africa
111	C3	Ikaria i. Greece
118	C3	Ikela Dem. Rep. Congo
110	B2	Ikhtiman Bulg.
67	A4	Iki-shima i. Japan
121	□D3	Ikongo Madag.
65	B2	Iksan S. Korea
64	B1	Ilagan Phil.
81	C2	Īlām Iran
75	C2	Ilam Nepal
103	D1	Iława Pol.
79	C2	Ilazārān, Kūh-e mt. Iran
129	D2	Île-à-la-Crosse Can.
129	D2	Île-à-la-Crosse, Lac l. Can.
118	C3	Ilebo Dem. Rep. Congo
119	D2	Ileret Kenya
105	D3	Îles d'Hyères is France
99	D3	Ilford U.K.
99	A3	Ilfracombe U.K.
155	D2	Ilha Grande, Baía da b. Brazil
154	B2	Ilha Grande, Represa resr Brazil
154	B2	Ilha Solteira, Represa resr Brazil
106	B1	Ílhavo Port.
151	E3	Ilhéus Brazil
64	B2	Iligan Phil.
152	A4	Illapel Chile
90	C2	Illichivs'k Ukr.
140	A3	Illinois r. U.S.A.
140	B3	Illinois state U.S.A.
90	B1	Illintsi Ukr.
115	D2	Illizi Alg.
89	D2	Il'men', Ozero l. Rus. Fed.
101	E2	Ilmenau Ger.
150	A3	Ilo Peru
64	B1	Iloilo Phil.
92	J3	Ilomantsi Fin.
115	C4	Ilorin Nigeria
53	D1	Iluka Austr.
127	H2	Ilulissat Greenland
67	A4	Imari Japan
117	C5	Īmī Eth.
108	B2	Imola Italy
151	D2	Imperatriz Brazil
136	C2	Imperial U.S.A.
118	B2	Impfondo Congo
62	A1	Imphal India
111	C2	İmroz Turkey
150	B3	Inambari r. Peru
115	C2	In Aménas Alg.
59	C3	Inanwatan Indon.
92	I2	Inari Fin.
92	I2	Inarijärvi l. Fin.
67	D3	Inawashiro-ko l. Japan
80	B1	İnce Burun pt Turkey
65	B2	Inch'ŏn S. Korea
123	D2	Incomati r. Moz.
78	A3	Inda Silasē Eth.
144	B2	Indé Mex.
135	C3	Independence CA U.S.A.
137	E2	Independence IA U.S.A.
137	D3	Independence KS U.S.A.
137	E3	Independence MO U.S.A.
134	D2	Independence Mountains U.S.A.
76	B2	Inderborskiy Kazakh.
72	B2	India country Asia
141	D2	Indiana U.S.A.
140	B2	Indiana state U.S.A.
140	B3	Indianapolis U.S.A.
129	D2	Indian Head Can.
159		Indian Ocean
137	E2	Indianola IA U.S.A.
142	B2	Indianola MS U.S.A.
135	C3	Indian Springs U.S.A.
86	D2	Indiga Rus. Fed.
83	K2	Indigirka r. Rus. Fed.
109	D1	Indija Serbia and Mont.
135	C4	Indio U.S.A.
58	B3	Indonesia country Asia
74	B2	Indore India
61	B2	Indramayu, Tanjung pt Indon.
104	C2	Indre r. France
74	A2	Indus r. China/Pak.
74	A2	Indus, Mouths of the Pak.
80	B1	İnebolu Turkey
111	C2	İnegöl Turkey
144	B3	Infiernillo, Presa resr Mex.
53	D1	Inglewood Austr.
75	C2	İngraj Bazar India
123	D2	Inhaca Moz.
121	C3	Inhambane Moz.
97	A2	Inishbofin i. Ireland
97	A2	Inishmore i. Ireland
97	C1	Inishowen pen. Ireland
54	B2	Inland Kaikoura Range mts N.Z.
102	C2	Inn r. Europe
127	G1	Innaanganeq c. Greenland
96	B2	Inner Sound sea chan. U.K.
51	D1	Innisfail Austr.
102	C2	Innsbruck Austria
154	B1	Inocência Brazil
118	B3	Inongo Dem. Rep. Congo
103	D1	Inowrocław Pol.
114	C2	In Salah Alg.
62	A2	Insein Myanmar
86	F2	Inta Rus. Fed.
137	E1	International Falls U.S.A.
130	C1	Inukjuak Can.
126	C2	Inuvik Can.
96	B2	Inveraray U.K.
54	A3	Invercargill N.Z.
53	D1	Inverell Austr.
96	B2	Invergordon U.K.
128	C2	Invermere Can.
131	D2	Inverness Can.
96	B2	Inverness U.K.
96	C2	Inverurie U.K.
52	A3	Investigator Strait Austr.
77	E1	Inya Rus. Fed.
119	D3	Inyonga Tanz.
87	D3	Inza Rus. Fed.
111	B3	Ioannina Greece
137	D3	Iola U.S.A.
96	A2	Iona i. U.K.
111	B3	Ionian Islands Greece
109	C3	Ionian Sea Greece/Italy
		Ionioi Nisoi is Greece see Ionian Islands
111	C3	Ios i. Greece
137	E2	Iowa state U.S.A.
137	E2	Iowa City U.S.A.
154	C1	Ipameri Brazil
81	C1	Ipatovo Rus. Fed.
123	C2	Ipelegeng S. Africa
150	A1	Ipiales Col.
154	B3	Ipiranga Brazil
60	B1	Ipoh Malaysia
154	B1	Iporá Brazil
118	C2	Ippy C.A.R.
111	C2	İpsala Turkey
53	D1	Ipswich Austr.
99	D2	Ipswich U.K.
127	G2	Iqaluit Can.
152	A3	Iquique Chile
150	A2	Iquitos Peru
111	C3	Iraklio Greece see Iraklion
111	C3	Iraklion Greece
76	B3	Iran country Asia
61	C1	Iran, Pegunungan mts Indon.
79	D2	Īrānshahr Iran
144	B2	Irapuato Mex.
81	C2	Iraq country Asia
154	B3	Irati Brazil
80	B2	Irbid Jordan
86	F3	Irbit Rus. Fed.
151	D3	Irecê Brazil
97	C2	Ireland country Europe
118	C3	Irema Dem. Rep. Congo
76	C2	Irgiz Kazakh.
114	B3	Irigui reg. Mali/Maur.
119	D3	Iringa Tanz.
151	D2	Iriri r. Brazil
95	B3	Irish Sea Ireland/U.K.
69	C1	Irkutsk Rus. Fed.
106		Iron Knob Austr.
140	B1	Iron Mountain U.S.A.

140 A1 **Ironwood** U.S.A.
64 B1 **Irosin** Phil.
67 C4 **Irō-zaki** *pt* Japan
90 C1 **Irpin'** Ukr.
92 A2 **Irrawaddy** *r.* Myanmar
63 A2 **Irrawaddy, Mouths of the** Myanmar
86 F2 **Irtysh** *r.* Kazakh./Rus. Fed.
107 C1 **Irun** Spain
96 B3 **Irvine** U.K.
64 B2 **Isabela** Phil.
146 B3 **Isabelia, Cordillera** *mts* Nic.
92 □A2 **Ísafjörður** Iceland
67 B4 **Isahaya** Japan
105 E2 **Isar** *r.* Ger.
96 □ **Isbister** U.K.
67 C4 **Ise** Japan
118 C2 **Isengi** Dem. Rep. Congo
100 C2 **Iserlohn** Ger.
101 D1 **Isernhagen** Ger.
67 C4 **Ise-wan** *b.* Japan
114 C4 **Iseyin** Nigeria
   Isfahan Iran *see* **Eşfahān**
66 D2 **Ishikari-wan** *b.* Japan
77 D1 **Ishim** *r.* Kazakh./Rus. Fed.
66 D3 **Ishinomaki** Japan
67 D3 **Ishioka** Japan
140 B1 **Ishpeming** U.S.A.
111 C2 **Işıklar Dağı** *mts* Turkey
111 C3 **Işıklı** Turkey
123 C2 **Isipingo** S. Africa
119 C2 **Isiro** Dem. Rep. Congo
80 B2 **İskenderun** Turkey
82 G3 **Iskitim** Rus. Fed.
110 B2 **Iskŭr** *r.* Bulg.
128 A2 **Iskut** *r.* Can.
74 B1 **Islamabad** Pak.
52 A2 **Island Lagoon** *salt flat* Austr.
129 E2 **Island Lake** Can.
54 B1 **Islands, Bay of** N.Z.
96 A3 **Islay** *i.* U.K.
98 A1 **Isle of Man** *i.* Irish Sea
77 D3 **Ismoili Somoni, Qullai** *mt.* Tajik.
108 B2 **Isola d'Elba** *i.* Italy
109 C3 **Isola di Capo Rizzuto** Italy
108 B2 **Isola d'Ischia** *i.* Italy
110 C2 **Isperikh** Bulg.
80 B2 **Israel** *country* Asia
105 C2 **Issoire** France
111 C2 **İstanbul** Turkey
   İstanbul Boğazı *str.* Turkey *see* **Bosporus**
111 B3 **Istiaia** Greece
105 C3 **Istres** France
108 B1 **Istria** *pen.* Croatia
151 D3 **Itaberaba** Brazil
155 D1 **Itabira** Brazil
155 D2 **Itabirito** Brazil
151 E3 **Itabuna** Brazil
150 C2 **Itacoatiara** Brazil
154 B2 **Itaguajé** Brazil
154 B2 **Itaí** Brazil
154 B3 **Itaipu, Represa de** *resr* Brazil
151 C2 **Itaituba** Brazil
152 D3 **Itajaí** Brazil
155 C2 **Itajubá** Brazil
108 B2 **Italy** *country* Europe
155 D1 **Itamarandiba** Brazil
155 D1 **Itambacuri** Brazil
155 D1 **Itambé, Pico de** *mt.* Brazil
62 A1 **Itanagar** India
154 C2 **Itanhaém** Brazil
155 D1 **Itanhém** Brazil
155 D1 **Itaobim** Brazil
155 C2 **Itapajipe** Brazil
155 E1 **Itapebi** Brazil

155 D2 **Itapemirim** Brazil
155 D2 **Itaperuna** Brazil
155 D1 **Itapetinga** Brazil
154 C2 **Itapetininga** Brazil
151 E3 **Itapeva** Brazil
151 C2 **Itapicuru** *r.* Brazil
151 D2 **Itapicuru Mirim** Brazil
154 C1 **Itapuranga** Brazil
154 C2 **Itararé** Brazil
75 B2 **Itarsi** India
154 B1 **Itarumã** Brazil
155 D2 **Itaúna** Brazil
71 C3 **Itbayat** *i.* Phil.
141 D2 **Ithaca** U.S.A.
119 D2 **Ith Hils** *ridge* Ger.
118 C2 **Itimbiri** *r.* Dem. Rep. Congo
155 D1 **Itinga** Brazil
154 B1 **Itiquira** Brazil
154 A1 **Itiquira** *r.* Brazil
67 C4 **Itō** Japan
154 C2 **Itu** Brazil
150 A2 **Itui** *r.* Brazil
154 C1 **Ituiutaba** Brazil
119 C3 **Itula** Dem. Rep. Congo
154 C1 **Itumbiara** Brazil
154 B1 **Iturama** Brazil
101 D1 **Itzehoe** Ger.
83 N2 **Iul'tin** Rus. Fed.
154 B2 **Ivaí** *r.* Brazil
92 I2 **Ivalo** Fin.
88 C3 **Ivanava** Belarus
52 B2 **Ivanhoe** Austr.
90 B1 **Ivankiv** Ukr.
90 A2 **Ivano-Frankivs'k** Ukr.
89 F2 **Ivanovo** Rus. Fed.
88 C3 **Ivatsevichy** Belarus
111 C2 **Ivaylovgrad** Bulg.
86 F2 **Ivdel'** Rus. Fed.
154 B2 **Ivinheima** Brazil
154 B2 **Ivinheima** *r.* Brazil
127 H2 **Ivittuut** Greenland
   Ivory Coast *country* Africa *see* **Côte d'Ivoire**
108 A1 **Ivrea** Italy
111 C3 **İvrindi** Turkey
127 F2 **Ivujivik** Can.
67 D3 **Iwaki** Japan
67 B4 **Iwakuni** Japan
66 D2 **Iwamizawa** Japan
66 D2 **Iwanai** Japan
88 C3 **Iwye** Belarus
123 D3 **Ixopo** S. Africa
145 B2 **Ixtlán** Mex.
145 D2 **Izamal** Mex.
81 C1 **Izberbash** Rus. Fed.
86 E3 **Izhevsk** Rus. Fed.
86 E2 **Izhma** Rus. Fed.
89 E3 **Izmalkovo** Rus. Fed.
90 B2 **Izmayil** Ukr.
111 C3 **İzmir** Turkey
111 C2 **İznik Gölü** *l.* Turkey
67 B3 **Izumo** Japan
90 B1 **Izyaslav** Ukr.
91 D2 **Izyum** Ukr.

J

   Jabal, Bahr el *r.* Sudan/Uganda *see* **White Nile**
106 C2 **Jabalón** *r.* Spain
75 B2 **Jabalpur** India
50 C1 **Jabiru** Austr.
109 C2 **Jablanica** Bos.-Herz.
151 E2 **Jaboatão** Brazil
154 C2 **Jaboticabal** Brazil
107 C1 **Jaca** Spain
145 C2 **Jacala** Mex.

151 C2 **Jacareacanga** Brazil
155 C2 **Jacareí** Brazil
155 D1 **Jacinto** Brazil
141 E1 **Jackman** U.S.A.
142 C2 **Jackson** *AL* U.S.A.
140 C2 **Jackson** *MI* U.S.A.
142 B2 **Jackson** *MS* U.S.A.
142 C1 **Jackson** *TN* U.S.A.
136 A2 **Jackson** *WY* U.S.A.
54 A2 **Jackson Head** N.Z.
142 B2 **Jacksonville** *AR* U.S.A.
143 D2 **Jacksonville** *FL* U.S.A.
140 A3 **Jacksonville** *IL* U.S.A.
143 E2 **Jacksonville** *NC* U.S.A.
139 D2 **Jacksonville** *TX* U.S.A.
147 C3 **Jacmel** Haiti
74 A2 **Jacobabad** Pak.
151 D3 **Jacobina** Brazil
131 D2 **Jacques Cartier, Mont** *mt.* Can.
151 C2 **Jacunda** Brazil
154 C2 **Jacupiranga** Brazil
109 C2 **Jadovnik** *mt.* Bos.-Herz.
150 A2 **Jaén** Peru
106 C2 **Jaén** Spain
52 B3 **Jaffa, Cape** Austr.
73 B4 **Jaffna** Sri Lanka
73 C3 **Jagdalpur** India
123 C2 **Jagersfontein** S. Africa
79 C2 **Jaghin** Iran
154 C2 **Jaguariaíva** Brazil
79 C2 **Jahrom** Iran
74 B2 **Jaipur** India
74 B2 **Jaisalmer** India
75 C2 **Jajarkot** Nepal
109 C2 **Jajce** Bos.-Herz.
60 B2 **Jakarta** Indon.
128 A1 **Jakes Corner** Can.
92 G2 **Jäkkvik** Sweden
92 H3 **Jakobstad** Fin.
77 D3 **Jalālābād** Afgh.
77 D2 **Jalal-Abad** Kyrg.
74 B1 **Jalandhar** India
145 C3 **Jalapa** Mex.
154 B2 **Jales** Brazil
74 B2 **Jalgaon** India
115 D4 **Jalingo** Nigeria
144 B3 **Jalpa** Mex.
75 C2 **Jalpaiguri** India
145 C2 **Jalpan** Mex.
115 E2 **Jālū** Libya
146 C3 **Jamaica** *country* West Indies
146 C3 **Jamaica Channel** Haiti/Jamaica
75 C2 **Jamalpur** Bangl.
60 B2 **Jambi** Indon.
137 D2 **James** *r. ND/SD* U.S.A.
141 D3 **James** *r. VA* U.S.A.
130 B1 **James Bay** Can.
52 A2 **Jamestown** Austr.
137 D1 **Jamestown** *ND* U.S.A.
141 D2 **Jamestown** *NY* U.S.A.
74 B1 **Jammu** Jammu and Kashmir
74 B1 **Jammu and Kashmir** *terr.* Asia
74 B2 **Jamnagar** India
93 I3 **Jämsä** Fin.
75 C2 **Jamshedpur** India
75 C2 **Jamuna** *r.* Bangl.
75 C2 **Janakpur** Nepal
155 D1 **Janaúba** Brazil
81 D2 **Jandaq** Iran
140 B2 **Janesville** U.S.A.
84 F1 **Jan Mayen** *i.* Arctic Ocean
81 D1 **Jañña** Turkm.
122 B3 **Jansenville** S. Africa
155 D1 **Januária** Brazil
74 B2 **Jaora** India

67 C3 Japan country Asia
156 C3 Japan, Sea of N. Pacific Ocean
150 B2 Japurá r. Brazil
154 C1 Jaraguá Brazil
154 B2 Jaraguari Brazil
152 C3 Jardim Brazil
69 D1 Jargalant Mongolia
103 D1 Jarocin Pol.
103 E1 Jarosław Pol.
92 F3 Järpen Sweden
70 A2 Jartai China
150 B3 Jarú r. Brazil
Jarud China see Lubei
49 H3 Jarvis Island N. Pacific Ocean
79 C2 Jāsk Iran
103 E2 Jasło Pol.
128 C2 Jasper Can.
140 B3 Jasper IN U.S.A.
139 E2 Jasper TX U.S.A.
103 D2 Jastrzębie-Zdrój Pol.
103 D2 Jászberény Hungary
154 B1 Jataí Brazil
74 A2 Jati Pak.
154 C2 Jaú Brazil
150 B2 Jaú r. Brazil
62 A1 Jaumave Mex.
75 C2 Jaunpur India
154 B1 Jauru Brazil
61 B2 Java i. Indon.
69 D1 Javarthushuu Mongolia
Java Sea Indon. see Jawa, Laut
Jawa i. Indon. see Java
159 D4 Jawa, Laut sea Indon.
117 C4 Jawhar Somalia
103 D1 Jawor Pol.
103 D2 Jaworzno Pol.
59 D3 Jaya, Puncak mt. Indon.
59 D3 Jayapura Indon.
128 B1 Jean Marie River Can.
131 D1 Jeannin, Lac l. Can.
116 A3 Jebel Abyad Plateau Sudan
117 A3 Jebel Marra plat. Sudan
96 C3 Jedburgh U.K.
78 A2 Jeddah Saudi Arabia
101 E1 Jeetze r. Ger.
135 C3 Jefferson, Mount U.S.A.
137 E3 Jefferson City U.S.A.
88 C2 Jēkabpils Latvia
103 D1 Jelenia Góra Pol.
88 B2 Jelgava Latvia
61 C2 Jember Indon.
101 E2 Jena Ger.
Jengish Chokusu mt. China/Kyrg. see Pobeda Peak
80 B2 Jenin West Bank
142 B2 Jennings U.S.A.
151 D3 Jequié Brazil
155 D1 Jequitaí Brazil
155 D1 Jequitinhonha Brazil
155 E1 Jequitinhonha r. Brazil
147 C3 Jérémie Haiti
144 B2 Jerez Mex.
106 B2 Jerez de la Frontera Spain
109 D3 Jergucat Albania
115 C1 Jerid, Chott el salt l. Tunisia
134 D2 Jerome U.S.A.
95 C4 Jersey terr. Channel Is
151 D2 Jerumenha Brazil
80 B2 Jerusalem Israel/West Bank
53 D3 Jervis Bay Territory admin. div. Austr.
108 B1 Jesenice Slovenia
108 B2 Jesi Italy

101 F2 Jessen Ger.
75 C2 Jessore Bangl.
143 D2 Jesup U.S.A.
145 C3 Jesús Carranza Mex.
74 B1 Jhalawar India
74 B1 Jhang Pak.
75 B2 Jhansi India
75 C2 Jharsuguda India
74 B1 Jhelum Pak.
70 C2 Jiading China
69 E1 Jiamusi China
71 B3 Ji'an Jiangxi China
65 B1 Ji'an Jilin China
62 A1 Jianchuan China
Jiandaoyu China see Guojiaba
70 B2 Jiangsu prov. China
71 B3 Jiangxi prov. China
70 A2 Jiangyou China
70 B3 Jianli China
70 B2 Jianqiao China
71 B3 Jianyang Fujian China
70 A2 Jianyang Sichuan China
70 C2 Jiaozhou China
70 B2 Jiaozuo China
70 C2 Jiaxing China
68 C2 Jiayuguan China
Jiddah Saudi Arabia see Jeddah
92 G2 Jiehkkevárri mt. Norway
70 B2 Jiexiu China
68 C2 Jigzhi China
107 C4 Jihlava Czech Rep.
116 A2 Jilf al Kabir, Hadabat al plat. Egypt
117 C4 Jilib Somalia
69 E2 Jilin China
65 B1 Jilin prov. China
65 A1 Jilin Hada Ling mts China
117 B4 Jima Eth.
144 B2 Jiménez Chihuahua Mex.
145 C3 Jiménez Tamaulipas Mex.
70 B2 Jinan China
70 B2 Jincheng China
53 D2 Jindabyne Austr.
103 D2 Jindřichův Hradec Czech Rep.
71 B3 Jingdezhen China
71 B3 Jinggangshan China
62 B1 Jinghong China
70 B2 Jingmen China
70 A2 Jingning China
70 A2 Jingtai China
71 A3 Jingxi China
65 B1 Jingyu China
70 A2 Jingyuan China
70 B2 Jingzhou Hubei China
70 B2 Jingzhou Hubei China
71 B3 Jinhua China
70 B1 Jining Nei Mongol China
70 B2 Jining Shandong China
119 D2 Jinja Uganda
117 B4 Jinka Eth.
146 B3 Jinotepe Nic.
71 A3 Jinping China
Jinsha Jiang r. China see Yangtze
70 B3 Jinshi China
70 B2 Jinzhong China
70 C1 Jinzhou China
150 B2 Jiparaná r. Brazil
75 C1 Jirang India
79 C2 Jiroft Iran
71 A3 Jishou China
110 B2 Jiu r. Romania
70 A2 Jiuding Shan mt. China
70 B3 Jiujiang China
66 B1 Jixi China
78 B3 Jīzān Saudi Arabia

77 C2 Jizzax Uzbek.
151 E2 João Pessoa Brazil
155 C1 João Pinheiro Brazil
74 B2 Jodhpur India
92 I3 Joensuu Fin.
67 C3 Jōetsu Japan
121 C3 Jofane Moz.
88 C2 Jõgeva Estonia
123 C2 Johannesburg S. Africa
134 C2 John Day U.S.A.
134 B1 John Day r. U.S.A.
128 C2 John D'Or Prairie Can.
143 E1 John H. Kerr Reservoir U.S.A.
96 C1 John o'Groats U.K.
143 D1 Johnson City U.S.A.
128 A1 Johnson's Crossing Can.
49 H1 Johnston Atoll N. Pacific Ocean
96 B3 Johnstone U.K.
141 D2 Johnstown U.S.A.
60 B1 Johor Bahru Malaysia
88 C2 Jõhvi Estonia
154 C3 Joinville Brazil
105 D2 Joinville France
92 G2 Jokkmokk Sweden
92 □B2 Jökulsá á Fjöllum r. Iceland
140 B2 Joliet U.S.A.
130 C2 Joliette Can.
64 B2 Jolo Phil.
64 B2 Jolo i. Phil.
61 C2 Jombang Indon.
75 C2 Jomsom Nepal
88 B2 Jonava Lith.
142 B1 Jonesboro AR U.S.A.
142 B2 Jonesboro LA U.S.A.
127 F1 Jones Sound sea chan. Can.
93 F4 Jönköping Sweden
131 C2 Jonquière Can.
103 D2 Jonuta Mex.
137 E3 Joplin U.S.A.
80 B2 Jordan country Asia
80 B2 Jordan r. Asia
136 B1 Jordan U.S.A.
134 C2 Jordan Valley U.S.A.
62 A1 Jorhat India
93 E4 Jørpeland Norway
115 C4 Jos Nigeria
145 C3 José Cardel Mex.
131 C2 Joseph, Lac l. Can.
50 B1 Joseph Bonaparte Gulf Austr.
115 C4 Jos Plateau Nigeria
93 E3 Jotunheimen mts Norway
122 B3 Joubertina S. Africa
123 C2 Jouberton S. Africa
93 I3 Joutseno Fin.
134 B1 Juan de Fuca Strait Can./U.S.A.
Juanshui China see Tongcheng
145 B2 Juárez Mex.
151 E2 Juàzeiro Brazil
151 E2 Juàzeiro do Norte Brazil
117 A4 Juba Sudan
117 C5 Jubba r. Somalia
78 B2 Jubbah Saudi Arabia
107 C2 Júcar r. Spain
145 C3 Juchitán Mex.
102 C2 Judenburg Austria
101 D2 Jühnde Ger.
146 B3 Juigalpa Nic.
100 C1 Juist i. Ger.
155 D2 Juiz de Fora Brazil
150 A3 Juliaca Peru
75 C2 Jumla Nepal
74 B2 Junagadh India
139 D2 Junction U.S.A.

137	D3	**Junction City** U.S.A.
154	C2	**Jundiaí** Brazil
128	A2	**Juneau** U.S.A.
53	C2	**Junee** Austr.
105	D2	**Jungfrau** *mt.* Switz.
141	D2	**Juniata** *r.* U.S.A.
92	G3	**Junsele** Sweden
134	C2	**Juntura** U.S.A.
154	C2	**Juquiá** Brazil
117	A4	**Jur** *r.* Sudan
105	D2	**Jura** *mts* France/Switz.
96	B2	**Jura** *i.* U.K.
96	B3	**Jura, Sound of** *sea chan.* U.K.
88	B2	**Jurbarkas** Lith.
88	B2	**Jūrmala** Latvia
150	B2	**Juruá** *r.* Brazil
150	C2	**Juruena** *r.* Brazil
150	B2	**Jutaí** *r.* Brazil
101	F2	**Jüterbog** Ger.
146	B2	**Juventud, Isla de la** *i.* Cuba
70	B2	**Juxian** China
79	C2	**Jūyom** Iran
122	B1	**Jwaneng** Botswana
93	I3	**Jyväskylä** Fin.

K

74	B1	**K2** *mt.* China/Jammu and Kashmir
119	C3	**Kabalo** Dem. Rep. Congo
119	C3	**Kabare** Dem. Rep. Congo
130	B2	**Kabinakagami Lake** Can.
118	C3	**Kabinda** Dem. Rep. Congo
118	B2	**Kabo** C.A.R.
120	B2	**Kabompo** Zambia
119	C3	**Kabongo** Dem. Rep. Congo
77	C3	**Kābul** Afgh.
64	B2	**Kaburuang** *i.* Indon.
121	B2	**Kabwe** Zambia
74	A2	**Kachchh, Gulf of** India
74	B2	**Kachchh, Rann of** *marsh* India
83	I3	**Kachug** Rus. Fed.
81	C1	**Kaçkar Dağı** *mt.* Turkey
111	C2	**Kadoma** Zimbabwe
114	B3	**Kadiolo** Mali
73	B3	**Kadmat** *i.* India
121	B2	**Kadoma** Zimbabwe
63	A2	**Kadonkani** Myanmar
117	A3	**Kadugli** Sudan
115	C3	**Kaduna** Nigeria
89	E2	**Kaduy** Rus. Fed.
86	E2	**Kadzherom** Rus. Fed.
114	A3	**Kaédi** Maur.
118	B1	**Kaélé** Cameroon
65	B2	**Kaesŏng** N. Korea
114	A3	**Kaffrine** Senegal
111	B3	**Kafireas, Akra** *pt* Greece
121	B2	**Kafue** Zambia
120	B2	**Kafue** *r.* Zambia
118	B2	**Kaga Bandoro** C.A.R.
67	B4	**Kagoshima** Japan
90	C2	**Kaharlyk** Ukr.
61	C2	**Kahayan** *r.* Indon.
118	B3	**Kahemba** Dem. Rep. Congo
101	E2	**Kahla** Ger.
79	C2	**Kahnūj** Iran
92	H2	**Kahperusvaarat** *mts* Fin.
80	B2	**Kahramanmaraş** Turkey
79	C2	**Kahūrak** Iran
59	C3	**Kai, Kepulauan** *is* Indon.
115	C4	**Kaiama** Nigeria
54	B2	**Kaiapoi** N.Z.
59	C3	**Kai Besar** *i.* Indon.
70	B2	**Kaifeng** China
		Kaihua China *see* Wenshan
122	B2	**Kaiingveld** *reg.* S. Africa
59	C3	**Kai Kecil** *i.* Indon.
54	B2	**Kaiapoi** N.Z.
114	A4	**Kailahun** Sierra Leone
71	A3	**Kaili** China
59	C3	**Kaimana** Indon.
54	C1	**Kaimanawa Mountains** N.Z.
67	C4	**Kainan** Japan
115	C3	**Kainji Reservoir** Nigeria
54	B1	**Kaipara Harbour** N.Z.
74	B2	**Kairana** India
115	D1	**Kairouan** Tunisia
54	B1	**Kaitaia** N.Z.
54	C1	**Kaitawa** N.Z.
		Kaitong China *see* Tongyu
59	C3	**Kaiwatu** Indon.
65	A1	**Kaiyuan** *Liaoning* China
62	B1	**Kaiyuan** *Yunnan* China
92	I3	**Kajaani** Fin.
51	D2	**Kajabbi** Austr.
122	B2	**Kakamas** S. Africa
119	D2	**Kakamega** Kenya
91	C2	**Kakhovka** Ukr.
91	C2	**Kakhovs'ke Vodoskhovyshche** *resr* Ukr.
73	C3	**Kakinada** India
128	C1	**Kakisa** Can.
119	C3	**Kakoswa** Dem. Rep. Congo
126	B2	**Kaktovik** U.S.A.
		Kalaallit Nunaat *terr.* N. America *see* Greenland
59	C3	**Kalabahi** Indon.
120	B2	**Kalabo** Zambia
91	E1	**Kalach** Rus. Fed.
62	A1	**Kaladan** *r.* India/Myanmar
120	B3	**Kalahari Desert** Africa
92	H3	**Kalajoki** Fin.
111	B2	**Kalamaria** Greece
111	B3	**Kalamata** Greece
140	B2	**Kalamazoo** U.S.A.
111	B3	**Kalampaka** Greece
91	C2	**Kalanchak** Ukr.
63	B2	**Kalasin** Thai.
74	A1	**Kalāt** Afgh.
79	C2	**Kalāt** Iran
74	A2	**Kalat** Pak.
50	A2	**Kalbarri** Austr.
111	C3	**Kale** Turkey
80	B1	**Kalecik** Turkey
118	C3	**Kalema** Dem. Rep. Congo
119	C3	**Kalemie** Dem. Rep. Congo
62	A1	**Kalemyo** Myanmar
		Kalgan China *see* Zhangjiakou
50	B3	**Kalgoorlie** Austr.
109	C2	**Kali** Croatia
110	C2	**Kiakra, Nos** *pt* Bulg.
119	C3	**Kalima** Dem. Rep. Congo
61	C2	**Kalimantan** *reg.* Indon.
88	B3	**Kaliningrad** Rus. Fed.
91	D2	**Kalininskaya** Rus. Fed.
88	C3	**Kalinkavichy** Belarus
134	D1	**Kalispell** U.S.A.
103	D1	**Kalisz** Pol.
91	E2	**Kalitva** *r.* Rus. Fed.
92	H2	**Kalix** Sweden
92	H2	**Kalixälven** *r.* Sweden
111	C3	**Kalkan** Turkey
120	A3	**Kalkfeld** Namibia
92	I3	**Kallavesi** *l.* Fin.
93	F3	**Kallsjön** *l.* Sweden
93	G4	**Kalmar** Sweden
93	G4	**Kalmarsund** *sea chan.* Sweden
120	B2	**Kalomo** Zambia
128	B2	**Kalone Peak** Can.
75	B1	**Kalpa** India
73	B3	**Kalpeni** *i.* India
75	B2	**Kalpi** India
101	D1	**Kaltenkirchen** Ger.
89	E3	**Kaluga** Rus. Fed.
93	F4	**Kalundborg** Denmark
90	A2	**Kalush** Ukr.
89	E2	**Kalyazin** Rus. Fed.
111	C3	**Kalymnos** *i.* Greece
119	C3	**Kama** Dem. Rep. Congo
62	A2	**Kama** Myanmar
86	E3	**Kama** *r.* Rus. Fed.
66	D3	**Kamaishi** Japan
80	B2	**Kaman** Turkey
120	A2	**Kamanjab** Namibia
78	B3	**Kamarān** *i.* Yemen
74	A2	**Kamarod** Pak.
50	B3	**Kambalda** Austr.
119	C4	**Kambove** Dem. Rep. Congo
183	L3	**Kamchatka Peninsula** Rus. Fed.
110	C2	**Kamchiya** *r.* Bulg.
110	B2	**Kamenitsa** *mt.* Bulg.
108	B2	**Kamenjak, Rt** *pt* Croatia
76	B1	**Kamenka** Kazakh.
91	D1	**Kamenka** Rus. Fed.
91	E2	**Kamenolomni** Rus. Fed.
83	M2	**Kamenskoye** Rus. Fed.
91	E2	**Kamensk-Shakhtinskiy** Rus. Fed.
86	F3	**Kamensk-Ural'skiy** Rus. Fed.
122	A3	**Kamiesberge** *mts* S. Africa
122	A3	**Kamieskroon** S. Africa
129	D1	**Kamilukuak Lake** Can.
119	C3	**Kamina** Dem. Rep. Congo
129	E1	**Kaminak Lake** Can.
90	A1	**Kamin'-Kashyrs'kyy** Ukr.
128	B2	**Kamloops** Can.
119	C3	**Kamonia** Dem. Rep. Congo
119	D2	**Kampala** Uganda
60	B1	**Kampar** *r.* Indon.
60	B1	**Kampar** Malaysia
100	B1	**Kampen** Neth.
119	C3	**Kampene** Dem. Rep. Congo
63	A2	**Kamphaeng Phet** Thai.
63	B2	**Kâmpóng Cham** Cambodia
63	B2	**Kâmpóng Chhnăng** Cambodia
		Kâmpóng Saôm Cambodia *see* Sihanoukville
63	B2	**Kâmpóng Spœ** Cambodia
63	B2	**Kâmpôt** Cambodia
129	D2	**Kamsack** Can.
86	E3	**Kamskoye Vodokhranilishche** *resr* Rus. Fed.
117	C4	**Kamsuuma** Somalia
90	B2	**Kam''yanets'-Podils'kyy** Ukr.
90	A1	**Kam''yanka-Buz'ka** Ukr.
88	B3	**Kamyanyets** Belarus
91	D2	**Kamyshevatskaya** Rus. Fed.
87	D3	**Kamyshin** Rus. Fed.
135	D3	**Kanab** U.S.A.
118	C3	**Kananga** Dem. Rep. Congo
87	D3	**Kanash** Rus. Fed.
140	C3	**Kanawha** *r.* U.S.A.
66	C3	**Kanazawa** Japan
62	A1	**Kanbalu** Myanmar
63	A2	**Kanchanaburi** Thai.
73	B3	**Kanchipuram** India
77	C3	**Kandahār** Afgh.
86	C2	**Kandalaksha** Rus. Fed.
61	C2	**Kandangan** Indon.
74	A2	**Kandhkot** Pak.
114	C3	**Kandi** Benin
74	B2	**Kandla** India
53	C2	**Kandos** Austr.

121 □D2 **Kandreho** Madag.
73 C4 **Kandy** Sri Lanka
76 B2 **Kandyagash** Kazakh.
127 G1 **Kane Basin** b. Greenland
91 D2 **Kanevskaya** Rus. Fed.
122 B1 **Kang** Botswana
127 H2 **Kangaatsiaq** Greenland
114 B3 **Kangaba** Mali
80 B2 **Kangal** Turkey
79 C2 **Kangān** Iran
60 B1 **Kangar** Malaysia
52 A3 **Kangaroo Island** Austr.
75 C2 **Kangchenjunga** mt.
 India/Nepal
65 B2 **Kangdong** N. Korea
61 C2 **Kangean, Kepulauan** is
 Indon.
127 I2 **Kangeq** c. Greenland
127 H2 **Kangeruss uaq** inlet
 Greenland
127 I2 **Kangerlussuaq** inlet
 Greenland
127 H2 **Kangersuatsiaq** Greenland
65 B1 **Kanggye** N. Korea
131 D1 **Kangiqsualujjuaq** Can.
127 G2 **Kangiqsujuaq** Can.
127 G2 **Kangirsuk** Can.
75 C2 **Kangmar** China
65 B2 **Kangnŭng** S. Korea
65 A1 **Kangping** China
72 D2 **Kangto** mt. China/India
62 A1 **Kani** Myanmar
86 D2 **Kanin, Poluostrov** pen.
 Rus. Fed.
86 D2 **Kanin Nos** Rus. Fed.
91 C2 **Kaniv** Ukr.
93 H3 **Kankaanpää** Fin.
140 B2 **Kankakee** U.S.A.
114 B3 **Kankan** Guinea
75 C2 **Kanker** India
 Kannur India see
 Cannanore
115 C3 **Kano** Nigeria
122 B3 **Kanonpunt** pt S. Africa
67 C4 **Kanoya** Japan
75 C2 **Kanpur** India
136 C3 **Kansas** r. U.S.A.
137 D3 **Kansas** state U.S.A.
137 E3 **Kansas City** U.S.A.
83 H1 **Kansk** Rus. Fed.
114 C3 **Kantchari** Burkina
91 D2 **Kantemirovka** Rus. Fed.
97 B2 **Kanturk** Ireland
123 D2 **Kanyamazane** S. Africa
123 C1 **Kanye** Botswana
71 C3 **Kaohsiung** Taiwan
120 A2 **Kaokoveld** plat. Namibia
114 A3 **Kaolack** Senegal
120 B2 **Kaoma** Zambia
118 C3 **Kapanga** Dem. Rep. Congo
77 D2 **Kapchagay** Kazakh.
77 D2 **Kapchagayskoye**
 Vodokhranilishche resr
 Kazakh.
100 B2 **Kapellen** Belgium
121 B2 **Kapiri Mposhi** Zambia
127 H2 **Kapisillit** Greenland
130 B1 **Kapiskau** r. Can.
61 C1 **Kapit** Sarawak Malaysia
63 A3 **Kapoe** Thai.
117 B4 **Kapoeta** Sudan
103 D2 **Kaposvár** Hungary
61 B2 **Kapuas** r. Indon.
52 A2 **Kapunda** Austr.
130 B2 **Kapuskasing** Can.
103 D2 **Kapuvár** Hungary
88 C3 **Kapyl'** Belarus
114 C4 **Kara** Togo
111 C3 **Kara Ada** i. Turkey
76 C1 **Karabalyk** Kazakh.

80 B1 **Karabük** Turkey
76 C2 **Karabutak** Kazakh.
110 C2 **Karacaköy** Turkey
89 D3 **Karachev** Rus. Fed.
74 A2 **Karachi** Pak.
 Kara Deniz sea Asia/Europe
 see Black Sea
77 D2 **Karaganda** Kazakh.
77 D2 **Karagayly** Kazakh.
83 L3 **Karaginskiy Zaliv** b.
 Rus. Fed.
81 D2 **Karaj** Iran
64 B2 **Karakelong** i. Indon.
77 D2 **Kara-Köl** Kyrg.
77 D2 **Karakol** Kyrg.
74 B1 **Karakoram Range**
 mts Asia
 Karakum, Peski des. Kazakh.
 see Karakum Desert
76 B2 **Karakum Desert** Kazakh.
76 C3 **Karakum Desert** Turkm.
80 B2 **Karaman** Turkey
68 B2 **Karamay** China
54 B2 **Karamea** N.Z.
54 B2 **Karamea Bight** b. N.Z.
80 B2 **Karapınar** Turkey
122 A2 **Karasburg** Namibia
86 F1 **Kara Sea** Rus. Fed.
92 I2 **Karasjok** Norway
82 G3 **Karasuk** Rus. Fed.
77 D2 **Karatau** Kazakh.
77 C2 **Karatau, Khrebet** mts
 Kazakh.
86 F2 **Karatayka** Rus. Fed.
67 A4 **Karatsu** Japan
60 B2 **Karawang** Indon.
81 C2 **Karbalā'** Iraq
103 E2 **Karcag** Hungary
111 B3 **Karditsa** Greece
88 B2 **Kärdla** Estonia
122 B3 **Kareeberge** mts S. Africa
75 B2 **Kareli** India
74 B1 **Kargil** Jammu and Kashmir
121 B2 **Kariba** Zimbabwe
121 B2 **Kariba, Lake** resr
 Zambia/Zimbabwe
61 B2 **Karimata, Pulau-pulau** is
 Indon.
61 B2 **Karimata, Selat** str. Indon.
73 B3 **Karimnagar** India
61 C2 **Karimunjawa, Pulau-pulau**
 is Indon.
91 C1 **Karkinits'ka Zatoka** g. Ukr.
91 D2 **Karlivka** Ukr.
109 C1 **Karlovac** Croatia
102 C1 **Karlovy Vary** Czech Rep.
93 F4 **Karlshamn** Sweden
93 G4 **Karlskrona** Sweden
102 B2 **Karlsruhe** Ger.
93 F4 **Karlstad** Sweden
101 D3 **Karlstadt** Ger.
89 D3 **Karma** Belarus
93 E4 **Karmøy** i. Norway
75 D2 **Karnafuli Reservoir** Bangl.
74 B2 **Karnal** India
110 C2 **Karnobat** Bulg.
74 A2 **Karodi** Pak.
121 B2 **Karoi** Zimbabwe
121 C1 **Karonga** Malawi
116 B3 **Karora** Eritrea
111 C3 **Karpathos** i. Greece
111 B3 **Karpenisi** Greece
86 D2 **Karpogory** Rus. Fed.
50 A2 **Karratha** Austr.
81 C1 **Kars** Turkey
88 C2 **Kārsava** Latvia
86 E2 **Karskiye Vorota, Proliv** str.
 Rus. Fed.
 Karskoye More sea
 Rus. Fed. see Kara Sea

101 E1 **Karstädt** Ger.
111 C2 **Kartal** Turkey
87 F3 **Kartaly** Rus. Fed.
73 B3 **Karwar** India
83 I3 **Karymskoye** Rus. Fed.
111 B3 **Karystos** Greece
80 A2 **Kaş** Turkey
130 B1 **Kasabonika Lake** Can.
118 C4 **Kasaji** Dem. Rep. Congo
121 C2 **Kasama** Zambia
120 B2 **Kasane** Botswana
118 B3 **Kasangulu**
 Dem. Rep. Congo
73 B3 **Kasaragod** India
129 D1 **Kasba Lake** Can.
120 B2 **Kasempa** Zambia
119 C4 **Kasenga** Dem. Rep. Congo
119 C3 **Kasese** Dem. Rep. Congo
119 D2 **Kasese** Uganda
81 D2 **Kāshān** Iran
 Kashgar China see **Kashi**
77 D3 **Kashi** China
67 D3 **Kashima-nada** b. Japan
89 E2 **Kashin** Rus. Fed.
89 E3 **Kashira** Rus. Fed.
89 E3 **Kashirskoye** Rus. Fed.
67 C3 **Kashiwazaki** Japan
76 B3 **Kāshmar** Iran
74 A2 **Kashmor** Pak.
119 C3 **Kashyukulu**
 Dem. Rep. Congo
87 D3 **Kasimov** Rus. Fed.
93 H3 **Kasinen** Fin.
119 C3 **Kasongo** Dem. Rep. Congo
118 B3 **Kasongo-Lunda**
 Dem. Rep. Congo
111 C3 **Kasos** i. Greece
 Kaspiyskoye More sea
 Asia/Europe see Caspian Sea
116 B3 **Kassala** Sudan
101 D2 **Kassel** Ger.
80 B1 **Kastamonu** Turkey
111 B2 **Kastelli** Greece
111 B2 **Kastoria** Greece
89 D3 **Kastsyukovichy** Belarus
119 D3 **Kasulu** Tanz.
121 C2 **Kasungu** Malawi
141 F1 **Katahdin, Mount** U.S.A.
118 C3 **Katako-Kombe**
 Dem. Rep. Congo
121 C2 **Katete** Zambia
62 A1 **Katha** Myanmar
50 C1 **Katherine** r. Austr.
74 B2 **Kathiawar** pen. India
75 C2 **Kathmandu** Nepal
122 B2 **Kathu** S. Africa
74 B1 **Kathua** Jammu and
 Kashmir
114 B3 **Kati** Mali
75 C2 **Katihar** India
54 C1 **Katikati** N.Z.
123 C3 **Katikati** S. Africa
120 B2 **Katima Mulilo** Namibia
123 C2 **Katlehong** S. Africa
111 B3 **Kato Achaïa** Greece
103 D1 **Katoomba** Austr.
103 D1 **Katowice** Pol.
78 A2 **Kātrīnā, Jabal** mt. Egypt
93 G4 **Katrineholm** Sweden
115 C3 **Katsina** Nigeria
115 C4 **Katsina-Ala** Nigeria
77 C3 **Kattaqo'rg'on** Uzbek.
93 F4 **Kattegat** str. Denmark/
 Sweden
100 B1 **Katwijk aan Zee** Neth.

Kaua'i

124 E5 **Kaua'i** i. N. Pacific Ocean
93 H3 **Kauhajoki** Fin.
88 B3 **Kaunas** Lith.
115 C3 **Kaura-Namoda** Nigeria
91 H2 **Kautokeino** Norway
111 B2 **Kavala** Greece
66 C2 **Kavalerovo** Rus. Fed.
73 C3 **Kavali** India
73 B3 **Kavaratti** i. India
110 C2 **Kavarna** Bulg.
81 D2 **Kavir, Dasht-e** des. Iran
67 C3 **Kawagoe** Japan
54 B1 **Kawakawa** N.Z.
67 C3 **Kawanishi** Japan
130 C2 **Kawartha Lakes** Can.
67 C3 **Kawasaki** Japan
54 C1 **Kawerau** N.Z.
63 A2 **Kawkareik** Myanmar
62 A1 **Kawlin** Myanmar
63 A2 **Kawmapyin** Myanmar
63 A2 **Kawthaung** Myanmar
77 D3 **Kaxgar He** r. China
114 B3 **Kaya** Burkina
61 C1 **Kayan** r. Indon.
136 B2 **Kaycee** U.S.A.
138 A1 **Kayenta** U.S.A.
114 A3 **Kayes** Mali
77 D1 **Kaynar** Kazakh.
80 B2 **Kayseri** Turkey
77 D1 **Kazakhskiy Melkosopochnik** plain Kazakh.
81 D1 **Kazakhskiy Zaliv** b. Kazakh.
76 C2 **Kazakhstan** country Asia
87 D3 **Kazan'** Rus. Fed.
80 A1 **Kazanlŭk** Bulg.
76 A2 **Kazbek** mt. Georgia/Rus. Fed.
81 D3 **Käzerün** Iran
103 E2 **Kazincbarcika** Hungary
86 F2 **Kazymskiy Mys** Rus. Fed.
111 B3 **Kea** i. Greece
97 C1 **Keady** U.K.
137 D2 **Kearney** U.S.A.
138 A2 **Kearny** U.S.A.
116 A3 **Kebkabiya** Sudan
92 G2 **Kebnekaise** mt. Sweden
117 C4 **K'ebri Dehar** Eth.
61 C2 **Kebumen** Indon.
128 B2 **Kechika** r. Can.
103 D2 **Kecskemét** Hungary
88 B2 **Kėdainiai** Lith.
114 A3 **Kédougou** Senegal
103 D1 **Kędzierzyn-Koźle** Pol.
128 B1 **Keele** r. Can.
128 A1 **Keele Peak** Can.
Keelung Taiwan see Chilung
141 E2 **Keene** U.S.A.
122 A2 **Keetmanshoop** Namibia
129 E3 **Keewatin** Can.
Kefallonia i. Greece see Cephalonia
59 C3 **Kefamenanu** Indon.
92 □A3 **Keflavík** Iceland
69 G2 **Kegen** Kazakh.
77 D2 **Keg River** Can.
62 A1 **Kehsi Mansam** Myanmar
98 C2 **Keighley** U.K.
88 B2 **Keila** Estonia
122 B2 **Keimoes** S. Africa
92 I3 **Keitele** l. Fin.
52 B3 **Keith** Austr.
103 E2 **Kékes** mt. Hungary
92 J2 **Keles-Uayv, Gora** hill Rus. Fed.
102 C2 **Kelheim** Ger.
80 B1 **Kelkit** r. Turkey
128 B1 **Keller Lake** Can.
134 C1 **Kellogg** U.S.A.
92 I2 **Kelloselkä** Fin.
97 C2 **Kells** Ireland
88 B2 **Kelmė** Lith.
115 D4 **Kélo** Chad
128 C3 **Kelowna** Can.
96 C3 **Kelso** U.K.
134 B1 **Kelso** U.S.A.
60 B1 **Keluang** Malaysia
129 D2 **Kelvington** Can.
86 C2 **Kem'** Rus. Fed.
128 B2 **Kemano** Can.
111 C3 **Kemer** Turkey
82 G3 **Kemerovo** Rus. Fed.
92 H2 **Kemi** Fin.
92 I2 **Kemijärvi** Fin.
92 I2 **Kemijoki** r. Fin.
136 A2 **Kemmerer** U.S.A.
92 I3 **Kempele** Fin.
53 D2 **Kempsey** Austr.
130 C2 **Kempt, Lac** l. Can.
102 C2 **Kempten (Allgäu)** Ger.
123 C2 **Kempton Park** S. Africa
61 C2 **Kemujan** i. Indon.
129 D2 **Kenaston** Can.
59 B1 **Kendal** U.K.
98 B1 **Kendal** Indon.
61 C2 **Kendawangan** Indon.
115 D3 **Kendégué** Chad
114 A4 **Kenema** Sierra Leone
118 B3 **Kenge** Dem. Rep. Congo
62 A1 **Kengtung** Myanmar
122 B2 **Kenhardt** S. Africa
114 B1 **Kénitra** Morocco
97 B3 **Kenmare** Ireland
136 C1 **Kenmare** U.S.A.
97 A3 **Kenmare River** inlet Ireland
100 C3 **Kenn** Ger.
137 E3 **Kennett** U.S.A.
134 C1 **Kennewick** U.S.A.
129 E3 **Kenora** Can.
140 B2 **Kenosha** U.S.A.
138 C2 **Kent** U.S.A.
77 C2 **Kentau** Kazakh.
140 B3 **Kentucky** r. U.S.A.
140 C3 **Kentucky** state U.S.A.
140 B3 **Kentucky Lake** U.S.A.
119 D2 **Kenya** country Africa
119 D3 **Kenya, Mount** Kenya
137 E2 **Keokuk** U.S.A.
75 C2 **Keonjhar** India
111 C3 **Kepsut** Turkey
52 B3 **Kerang** Austr.
91 D2 **Kerch** Ukr.
59 D3 **Kerema** P.N.G.
128 C3 **Keremeos** Can.
116 B3 **Keren** Eritrea
81 C2 **Kerend** Iran
159 C7 **Kerguelen Plateau** sea feature Indian Ocean
119 D3 **Kericho** Kenya
54 B1 **Kerikeri** N.Z.
60 B2 **Kerinci, Gunung** vol. Indon.
111 A3 **Kerkyra** Greece
Kerkyra i. Greece see Corfu
116 B3 **Kerma** Sudan
49 G4 **Kermadec Islands** S. Pacific Ocean
79 C2 **Kermān** Iran
81 C2 **Kermānshāh** Iran
139 C2 **Kermit** U.S.A.
135 C3 **Kern** r. U.S.A.
100 C2 **Kerpen** Ger.
129 D2 **Kerrobert** Can.
139 D2 **Kerrville** U.S.A.
Kerynaia Cyprus see Kyrenia
130 B1 **Kesagami Lake** Can.
111 C2 **Keşan** Turkey
66 D3 **Kesennuma** Japan
74 B2 **Keshod** India
100 C2 **Kessel** Neth.
98 B1 **Keswick** U.K.
103 D2 **Keszthely** Hungary
82 G3 **Ket'** r. Rus. Fed.
61 C2 **Ketapang** Indon.
128 A2 **Ketchikan** U.S.A.
134 D2 **Ketchum** U.S.A.
99 C2 **Kettering** U.K.
93 H3 **Keuruu** Fin.
100 C2 **Kevelaer** Ger.
140 B2 **Kewanee** U.S.A.
140 B1 **Keweenaw Bay** U.S.A.
140 B1 **Keweenaw Peninsula** U.S.A.
143 D3 **Key Largo** U.S.A.
141 D3 **Keyser** U.S.A.
143 D4 **Key West** U.S.A.
123 C2 **Kgotsong** S. Africa
69 E1 **Khabarovsk** Rus. Fed.
80 B1 **Khadyzhensk** Rus. Fed.
62 A1 **Khagrachari** Bangl.
74 A2 **Khairpur** Pak.
122 B1 **Khakhea** Botswana
68 C1 **Khamar-Daban, Khrebet** mts Rus. Fed.
74 B2 **Khambhat** India
73 B3 **Khambhat, Gulf of** India
74 B2 **Khamgaon** India
78 B3 **Khamir** Yemen
78 B3 **Khamis Mushayt** Saudi Arabia
77 C3 **Khānābād** Afgh.
74 B2 **Khandwa** India
83 K2 **Khandyga** Rus. Fed.
74 B1 **Khanewal** Pak.
66 B2 **Khanka, Lake** China/Rus. Fed.
74 B2 **Khanpur** Pak.
77 D2 **Khantau** Kazakh.
83 H2 **Khantayskoye, Ozero** l. Rus. Fed.
86 F2 **Khanty-Mansiysk** Rus. Fed.
63 A3 **Khao Chum Thong** Thai.
63 A2 **Khao Laem Reservoir** Thai.
87 D4 **Kharabali** Rus. Fed.
75 C2 **Kharagpur** India
79 C2 **Khārān** r. Iran
116 B2 **Khārijah, Wāḥāt al** oasis Egypt
91 D2 **Kharkiv** Ukr.
Khar'kov Ukr. see Kharkiv
110 C2 **Kharmanli** Bulg.
86 D3 **Kharovsk** Rus. Fed.
116 B3 **Khartoum** Sudan
87 D4 **Khasavyurt** Rus. Fed.
79 D2 **Khāsh** Iran
78 A3 **Khashm el Girba** Sudan
78 A3 **Khashm el Girba Dam** Sudan
74 D2 **Khasi Hills** India
110 C2 **Khaskovo** Bulg.
123 C3 **Khayamnandi** S. Africa
78 A2 **Khaybar** Saudi Arabia
122 A3 **Khayelitsha** S. Africa
107 D2 **Khemis Miliana** Alg.
63 B2 **Khemmarat** Thai.
115 C1 **Khenchela** Alg.
81 D3 **Kherämeh** Iran
91 C2 **Kherson** Ukr.
83 H2 **Kheta** r. Rus. Fed.
69 D1 **Khilok** Rus. Fed.
89 E2 **Khimki** Rus. Fed.
89 E3 **Khlevnoye** Rus. Fed.
90 B2 **Khmel'nyts'kyy** Ukr.
76 B1 **Khobda** Kazakh.
89 E3 **Khokhol'skiy** Rus. Fed.

74 B2 Khokhropar Pak.
89 D2 Kholm Rus. Fed.
89 D2 Kholm-Zhirkovskiy Rus. Fed.
79 C2 Khonj Iran
63 B2 Khon Kaen Thai.
62 A1 Khonsa India
83 K2 Khonuu Rus. Fed.
86 E2 Khoreyver Rus. Fed.
69 D1 Khorinsk Rus. Fed.
91 C2 Khorol Ukr.
81 C2 Khorramābād Iran
81 C2 Khorramshahr Iran
77 D3 Khorugh Tajik.
74 A1 Khowst Afgh.
62 A1 Khreum Myanmar
76 B1 Khromtau Kazakh.
90 B2 Khrystynivka Ukr.
77 C2 Khŭjand Tajik.
63 B2 Khu Khan Thai.
78 A2 Khulays Saudi Arabia
75 C2 Khulna Bangl.
81 D2 Khunsar Iran
79 B2 Khurays Saudi Arabia
74 B1 Khushab Pak.
90 A2 Khust Ukr.
123 C2 Khutsong S. Africa
74 A2 Khuzdar Pak.
79 C2 Khvormūj Iran
81 C2 Khvoy Iran
89 D2 Khvoynaya Rus. Fed.
77 D3 Khyber Pass Afgh./Pak.
92 B2 Kiama Austr.
119 C3 Kiambi Dem. Rep. Congo
119 D3 Kibiti Tanz.
109 D2 Kičevo Macedonia
114 C3 Kidal Mali
99 B2 Kidderminster U.K.
114 A3 Kidira Senegal
54 C1 Kidnappers, Cape N.Z.
102 C1 Kiel Ger.
103 E1 Kielce Pol.
98 B1 Kielder Water (Reservoir) U.K.
90 C1 Kiev Ukr.
114 A3 Kiffa Maur.
119 D3 Kigali Rwanda
119 C3 Kigoma Tanz.
88 D2 Kihnu i. Estonia
92 I2 Kiiminki Fin.
67 B4 Kii-suidō sea chan. Japan
109 D1 Kikinda Serb. and Mont.
119 C3 Kikondja Dem. Rep. Congo
59 D3 Kikori P.N.G.
59 D3 Kikori r. P.N.G.
118 B3 Kikwit Dem. Rep. Congo
65 B4 Kilchu N. Korea
118 B3 Kilembe Dem. Rep. Congo
139 E2 Kilgore U.S.A.
119 D3 Kilimanjaro vol. Tanz.
80 B2 Kilis Turkey
90 B2 Kiliya Ukr.
97 B2 Kilkee Ireland
97 D1 Kilkeel U.K.
97 C2 Kilkenny Ireland
111 B2 Kilkis Greece
97 B1 Killala Bay Ireland
97 B2 Killaloe Ireland
129 C2 Killam Can.
97 B2 Killarney Ireland
139 D2 Killeen U.S.A.
96 B2 Killin U.K.
97 B1 Killybegs Ireland
96 B3 Kilmarnock U.K.
53 B3 Kilmore Austr.
119 D3 Kilosa Tanz.
97 B2 Kilrush Ireland
119 C3 Kilwa Dem. Rep. Congo
119 D3 Kilwa Masoko Tanz.
119 D3 Kimambi Tanz.

52 A2 Kimba Austr.
136 C2 Kimball U.S.A.
128 C3 Kimberley Can.
122 B2 Kimberley S. Africa
50 B1 Kimberley Plateau Austr.
65 B1 Kimch'aek N. Korea
65 B2 Kimch'ŏn S. Korea
127 G2 Kimmirut Can.
89 E3 Kimovsk Rus. Fed.
118 B3 Kimpese Dem. Rep. Congo
61 C1 Kimry Rus. Fed.
61 C1 Kinabalu, Gunung mt. Sabah Malaysia
128 C2 Kinbasket Lake Can.
130 B2 Kincardine Can.
62 A1 Kinchang Myanmar
119 C3 Kinda Dem. Rep. Congo
98 C2 Kinder Scout hill U.K.
129 D2 Kindersley Can.
114 A3 Kindia Guinea
119 C3 Kindu Dem. Rep. Congo
86 D3 Kineshma Rus. Fed.
51 E2 Kingaroy Austr.
135 B3 King City U.S.A.
130 C1 King George Islands Can.
88 C2 Kingisepp Rus. Fed.
51 D3 King Island Austr.
50 B1 King Leopold Ranges hills Austr.
138 A1 Kingman U.S.A.
135 B3 Kings r. U.S.A.
52 A3 Kingscote Austr.
99 D2 King's Lynn U.K.
48 F3 Kingsmill Group is Kiribati
50 B1 King Sound b. Austr.
134 D2 Kings Peak U.S.A.
143 D1 Kingsport U.S.A.
130 C2 Kingston Can.
146 C3 Kingston Jamaica
141 E2 Kingston U.S.A.
52 A3 Kingston South East Austr.
98 C2 Kingston upon Hull U.K.
147 D3 Kingstown St Vincent
139 D3 Kingsville U.S.A.
99 B3 Kingswood U.K.
96 B2 Kingussie U.K.
126 E2 King William Island Can.
123 C3 King William's Town S. Africa
67 D3 Kinka-san i. Japan
93 F4 Kinna Sweden
97 B3 Kinsale Ireland
118 B3 Kinshasa Dem. Rep. Congo
143 E1 Kinston U.S.A.
88 B2 Kintai Lith.
114 B4 Kintampo Ghana
96 B3 Kintyre pen. U.K.
130 C2 Kipawa, Lac l. Can.
83 I3 Kirensk Rus. Fed.
89 E3 Kireyevsk Rus. Fed.
    Kirghizia country Asia see Kyrgyzstan
49 G3 Kiribati country Pacific Ocean
80 B2 Kırıkkale Turkey
89 E2 Kirillov Rus. Fed.
    Kirin China see Jilin
    Kirinyaga mt. Kenya see Kenya, Mount
89 D2 Kirishi Rus. Fed.
49 H2 Kiritimati i. Kiribati
111 C3 Kırkağaç Turkey
96 C2 Kirkcaldy U.K.
96 B3 Kirkcudbright U.K.
92 I2 Kirkenes Norway
130 B2 Kirkland Lake Can.
137 E2 Kirksville U.S.A.
81 C2 Kirkūk Iraq
96 C1 Kirkwall U.K.

89 D3 Kirov Kaluzhskaya Oblast' Rus. Fed.
86 D3 Kirov Rus. Fed.
    Kirovabad Azer. see Gäncä
86 E3 Kirovo-Chepetsk Rus. Fed.
91 C2 Kirovohrad Ukr.
86 C2 Kirovsk Rus. Fed.
91 D2 Kirovs'ke Ukr.
96 C2 Kirriemuir U.K.
86 E3 Kirs Rus. Fed.
74 A2 Kirthar Range mts Pak.
92 H2 Kiruna Sweden
67 C3 Kiryū Japan
89 E2 Kirzhach Rus. Fed.
119 C2 Kisangani Dem. Rep. Congo
118 B3 Kisantu Dem. Rep. Congo
60 A1 Kisaran Indon.
82 G3 Kiselevsk Rus. Fed.
75 C2 Kishanganj India
115 C4 Kishi Nigeria
    Kishinev Moldova see Chişinău
77 D1 Kishkenekol' Kazakh.
74 B1 Kishtwar Jammu and Kashmir
119 D3 Kisii Kenya
103 D2 Kiskunfélegyháza Hungary
103 D2 Kiskunhalas Hungary
87 D4 Kislovodsk Rus. Fed.
117 C5 Kismaayo Somalia
119 C3 Kisoro Uganda
114 A4 Kissidougou Guinea
143 D3 Kissimmee U.S.A.
143 D3 Kissimmee, Lake U.S.A.
129 D2 Kississing Lake Can.
119 D3 Kisumu Kenya
114 B3 Kita Mali
66 D3 Kitakami Japan
66 D3 Kitakami-gawa r. Japan
67 B4 Kita-Kyūshū Japan
119 D3 Kitale Kenya
66 D2 Kitami Japan
130 B2 Kitchener Can.
93 J3 Kitee Fin.
119 D2 Kitgum Uganda
128 B2 Kitimat Can.
118 B3 Kitona Dem. Rep. Congo
119 D3 Kitunda Tanz.
128 B2 Kitwanga Can.
121 B2 Kitwe Zambia
101 E3 Kitzingen Ger.
92 I3 Kiuruvesi Fin.
119 C3 Kivu, Lake Dem. Rep. Congo/Rwanda
110 C2 Kıyıköy Turkey
86 E3 Kizel Rus. Fed.
111 C3 Kızılca Dağ mt. Turkey
87 D4 Kizlyar Rus. Fed.
92 I1 Kjøllefjord Norway
92 G2 Kjøpsvik Norway
102 C1 Kladno Czech Rep.
102 C2 Klagenfurt Austria
88 B2 Klaipėda Lith.
94 B1 Klaksvík Faroe Is
134 B2 Klamath r. U.S.A.
134 B2 Klamath Falls U.S.A.
134 B2 Klamath Mountains U.S.A.
60 B1 Klang Malaysia
93 F3 Klarälven val. Sweden
102 C2 Klatovy Czech Rep.
122 A3 Klawer S. Africa
128 A2 Klawock U.S.A.
122 B2 Kleena Kleene Can.
122 B2 Kleinbegin S. Africa
122 A2 Kleinsee S. Africa
123 C2 Klerksdorp S. Africa
89 D3 Kletnya Rus. Fed.
100 C2 Kleve Ger.
89 D3 Klimavichy Belarus

89 D3 **Klimovo** Rus. Fed.
89 E2 **Klimovsk** Rus. Fed.
89 E2 **Klin** Rus. Fed.
101 F2 **Klinovec** *mt.* Czech Rep.
93 G4 **Klintehamn** Sweden
89 D3 **Klintsy** Rus. Fed.
109 C2 **Ključ** Bos.-Herz.
103 D1 **Kłodzko** Pol.
100 C1 **Kloosterhaar** Neth.
103 D2 **Klosterneuburg** Austria
101 E1 **Klötze (Altmark)** Ger.
103 D1 **Kluczbork** Pol.
128 A2 **Klukwan** U.S.A.
74 A2 **Klupro** Pak.
88 C3 **Klyetsk** Belarus
98 C1 **Knaresborough** U.K.
93 F3 **Knästen** *hill* Sweden
129 E2 **Knee Lake** Can.
101 E1 **Knesebeck** Ger.
101 E3 **Knetzgau** Ger.
109 C2 **Knin** Croatia
103 C2 **Knittelfeld** Austria
109 D2 **Knjaževac**
          Serb. and Mont.
100 A2 **Knokke-Heist** Belgium
143 D1 **Knoxville** U.S.A.
122 B3 **Knysna** S. Africa
67 C4 **Kōbe** Japan
          København Denmark *see*
          Copenhagen
100 C2 **Koblenz** Ger.
59 C3 **Kobroör** *i.* Indon.
88 B3 **Kobryn** Belarus
109 D2 **Kočani** Macedonia
111 C2 **Kocasu** *r.* Turkey
75 C2 **Koch Bihar** India
          Kochi India *see* **Cochin**
67 B4 **Kōchi** Japan
87 D4 **Kochubey** Rus. Fed.
75 C2 **Kodarma** India
117 B4 **Kodok** Sudan
90 B2 **Kodyma** Ukr.
111 C2 **Kodzhaele** *mt.*
          Bulg./Greece
122 A2 **Koës** Namibia
122 C2 **Koffiefontein** S. Africa
114 B4 **Koforidua** Ghana
67 C3 **Kōfu** Japan
131 D1 **Kogaluk** *r.* Can.
74 B1 **Kohat** Pak.
62 A1 **Kohima** India
88 C4 **Kohtla-Järve** Estonia
92 H3 **Kokkola** Fin.
140 B2 **Kokomo** U.S.A.
77 E2 **Kokpekti** Kazakh.
77 C1 **Koksoak** *r.* Can.
131 D1 **Kokshetau** Kazakh.
123 C3 **Kokstad** S. Africa
          Koktokay China *see*
          Fuyun
58 C3 **Kolaka** Indon.
86 C2 **Kola Peninsula** Rus. Fed.
92 H2 **Kolari** Fin.
114 A3 **Kolda** Senegal
93 E4 **Kolding** Denmark
107 D2 **Koléa** Alg.
86 D2 **Kolguyev, Ostrov** *i.*
          Rus. Fed.
73 B3 **Kolhapur** India
88 B2 **Kolkasrags** *pt* Latvia
75 C2 **Kolkata** India
          Kollam India *see* **Quilon**
          Köln Ger. *see* **Cologne**
103 D1 **Kołobrzeg** Pol.
114 B3 **Kolokani** Mali
89 E2 **Kolomna** Rus. Fed.
90 B2 **Kolomyya** Ukr.
122 B2 **Kolonkwaneng** Botswana
82 G3 **Kolpashevo** Rus. Fed.
89 E3 **Kolpny** Rus. Fed.

          Kol'skiy Poluostrov *pen.*
          Rus. Fed. *see* **Kola Peninsula**
78 B3 **Koluli** Eritrea
119 C4 **Kolwezi** Dem. Rep. Congo
83 L2 **Kolyma** *r.* Rus. Fed.
83 L2 **Kolymskaya Nizmennost'**
          lowland Rus. Fed.
83 M2 **Kolymskiy, Khrebet** *mts*
          Rus. Fed.
67 C3 **Komaki** Japan
83 M3 **Komandorskiye Ostrova** *is*
          Rus. Fed.
103 D2 **Komárno** Slovakia
123 D2 **Komati** *r.* Swaziland
67 C3 **Komatsu** Japan
119 C3 **Kombe** Dem. Rep. Congo
90 C2 **Cominternivs'ke** Ukr.
109 C2 **Komiža** Croatia
103 D2 **Komló** Hungary
118 B3 **Komono** Congo
111 C2 **Komotini** Greece
122 B3 **Komsberg** *mts* S. Africa
83 H1 **Komsomolets, Ostrov** *i.*
          Rus. Fed.
89 F2 **Komsomol'sk** Rus. Fed.
91 C2 **Komsomol's'k** Ukr.
87 D4 **Komsomol'skiy** Rus. Fed.
69 E1 **Komsomol'sk-na-Amure**
          Rus. Fed.
89 E2 **Konakovo** Rus. Fed.
75 C3 **Kondagaon** India
86 F7 **Kondinskoye** Rus. Fed.
119 D3 **Kondoa** Tanz.
86 C2 **Kondopoga** Rus. Fed.
89 E3 **Kondrovo** Rus. Fed.
127 I2 **Kong Christian IX Land**
          reg. Greenland
127 I2 **Kong Frederik VI Kyst**
          coastal area Greenland
65 B2 **Kongju** S. Korea
119 C3 **Kongolo** Dem. Rep. Congo
93 E4 **Kongsberg** Norway
93 F3 **Kongsvinger** Norway
77 D3 **Kongur Shan** *mt.* China
100 C2 **Königswinter** Ger.
103 D1 **Konin** Pol.
109 C2 **Konjic** Bos.-Herz.
122 A2 **Konkiep** *watercourse*
          Namibia
91 C1 **Konotop** Ukr.
102 B2 **Konstanz** Ger.
115 C3 **Kontagora** Nigeria
63 B2 **Kon Tum** Vietnam
63 B2 **Kon Tum, Cao Nguyên**
          plat. Vietnam
80 B2 **Konya** Turkey
100 C3 **Konz** Ger.
86 E3 **Konzhakovskiy Kamen',**
          gora mt. Rus. Fed.
134 C1 **Kooskia** U.S.A.
128 C3 **Kootenay Lake** Can.
122 B3 **Kootjieskolk** S. Africa
92 □B2 **Kópasker** Iceland
108 B1 **Koper** Slovenia
93 G4 **Kopparberg** Sweden
109 C1 **Koprivnica** Croatia
89 F3 **Korablino** Rus. Fed.
73 C3 **Koraput** India
101 D2 **Korbach** Ger.
109 D2 **Korçë** Albania
109 C2 **Korčula** Croatia
109 C2 **Korčula** *i.* Croatia
65 B1 **Korea, North** *country* Asia
65 B2 **Korea, South** *country* Asia
70 C2 **Korea Bay** *g.*
          China/N. Korea
65 B3 **Korea Strait**
          Japan/S. Korea
91 D2 **Korenovsk** Rus. Fed.
90 B1 **Korets'** Rus. Fed.

111 C2 **Körfez** Turkey
114 B4 **Korhogo** Côte d'Ivoire
          Korinthos Greece *see*
          Corinth
103 D2 **Kőris-hegy** *hill* Hungary
109 D2 **Koritnik** *mt.* Albania
67 C3 **Kōriyama** Japan
80 B2 **Korkuteli** Turkey
68 B2 **Korla** China
103 D2 **Körmend** Hungary
114 B3 **Koro** Mali
131 D1 **Koroc** *r.* Can.
91 D1 **Korocha** Rus. Fed.
119 D3 **Korogwe** Tanz.
90 B1 **Korosten'** Ukr.
90 B1 **Korostyshiv** Ukr.
115 D3 **Koro Toro** Chad
91 C2 **Korsun'-Shevchenkivs'kyy**
          Ukr.
103 E1 **Korsze** Pol.
100 A2 **Kortrijk** Belgium
83 L3 **Koryakskaya, Sopka** *vol.*
          Rus. Fed.
83 M2 **Koryakskiy Khrebet** *mts*
          Rus. Fed.
86 D2 **Koryazhma** Rus. Fed.
65 B2 **Koryŏng** S. Korea
91 C1 **Koryukivka** Ukr.
111 C3 **Kos** Greece
111 C3 **Kos** *i.* Greece
65 B2 **Kosan** N. Korea
103 D1 **Kościan** Pol.
53 C3 **Kosciuszko, Mount** Austr.
68 B1 **Kosh-Agach** Rus. Fed.
103 E2 **Košice** Slovakia
92 H2 **Koskullskulle** Sweden
65 B2 **Kosŏng** N. Korea
109 D2 **Kosovo** *prov.*
          Serb. and Mont.
109 D2 **Kosovska Mitrovica**
          Serb. and Mont.
48 E2 **Kosrae** *i.* Micronesia
114 B4 **Kossou, Lac de** *l.*
          Côte d'Ivoire
76 C1 **Kostanay** Kazakh.
110 B2 **Kostenets** Bulg.
123 C2 **Koster** S. Africa
117 B3 **Kosti** Sudan
86 C2 **Kostomuksha** Rus. Fed.
90 B1 **Kostopil'** Ukr.
89 F2 **Kostroma** Rus. Fed.
89 F2 **Kostroma** *r.* Rus. Fed.
102 C1 **Kostrzyn** Pol.
103 D1 **Koszalin** Pol.
103 D2 **Kőszeg** Hungary
74 B2 **Kota** India
60 B2 **Kotaagung** Indon.
61 C2 **Kotabaru** Indon.
60 B1 **Kota Belud** *Sabah* Malaysia
60 B1 **Kota Bharu** Malaysia
60 B2 **Kotabumi** Indon.
61 C1 **Kota Kinabalu** *Sabah*
          Malaysia
61 C1 **Kota Samarahan** *Sarawak*
          Malaysia
86 D3 **Kotel'nich** Rus. Fed.
87 D4 **Kotel'nikovo** Rus. Fed.
83 K1 **Kotel'nyy, Ostrov** *i.*
          Rus. Fed.
101 E2 **Köthen (Anhalt)** Ger.
93 I3 **Kotka** Fin.
86 D2 **Kotlas** Rus. Fed.
109 C2 **Kotor Varoš** Bos.-Herz.
87 D3 **Kotovo** Rus. Fed.
91 E1 **Kotovsk** Rus. Fed.
90 B2 **Kotovs'k** Ukr.
83 H2 **Kotuy** *r.* Rus. Fed.
100 A2 **Koudekerke** Neth.
114 B3 **Koudougou** Burkina
122 B3 **Kougaberge** *mts* S. Africa

118 B3	**Koulamoutou** Gabon	
114 B3	**Koulikoro** Mali	
114 A3	**Koundâra** Guinea	
151 C1	**Kourou** Fr. Guiana	
114 B3	**Kouroussa** Guinea	
115 D3	**Kousséri** Cameroon	
114 B3	**Koutiala** Mali	
93 I3	**Kouvola** Fin.	
92 I2	**Kovdor** Rus. Fed.	
90 A1	**Kovel'** Ukr.	
89 F2	**Kovrov** Rus. Fed.	
54 B3	**Kowhitirangi** N.Z.	
111 C3	**Köyceğiz** Turkey	
86 D2	**Koyda** Rus. Fed.	
126 A2	**Koyukuk** r. U.S.A.	
111 B2	**Kozani** Greece	
90 C1	**Kozelets'** Ukr.	
89 E3	**Kozel'sk** Rus. Fed.	
	Kozhikode India see **Calicut**	
90 B2	**Kozyatyn** Ukr.	
63 A3	**Krabi** Thai.	
63 A2	**Kra Buri** Thai.	
63 B2	**Krâchéh** Cambodia	
93 E4	**Kragerø** Norway	
100 B1	**Kraggenburg** Neth.	
109 D2	**Kragujevac** Serb. and Mont.	
60 B2	**Krakatau** i. Indon.	
103 D1	**Kraków** Pol.	
91 D1	**Kramators'k** Ukr.	
93 G3	**Kramfors** Sweden	
111 B3	**Kranidi** Greece	
86 E1	**Krasino** Rus. Fed.	
88 C2	**Kräslava** Latvia	
101 F2	**Kraslice** Czech Rep.	
89 D3	**Krasnapolye** Belarus	
89 E3	**Krasnaya Gora** Rus. Fed.	
87 D3	**Krasnoarmeysk** Rus. Fed.	
91 D1	**Krasnoarmiys'k** Ukr.	
86 D2	**Krasnoborsk** Rus. Fed.	
91 D2	**Krasnodar** Rus. Fed.	
91 D2	**Krasnodon** Ukr.	
88 C2	**Krasnogorodskoye** Rus. Fed.	
91 D1	**Krasnogvardeyskoye** Rus. Fed.	
91 D2	**Krasnohrad** Ukr.	
91 D1	**Krasnohvardiys'ke** Ukr.	
86 E3	**Krasnokamsk** Rus. Fed.	
89 D2	**Krasnomayskiy** Rus. Fed.	
91 C2	**Krasnoperekops'k** Ukr.	
87 D3	**Krasnoslobodsk** Rus. Fed.	
86 E3	**Krasnoufimsk** Rus. Fed.	
83 H3	**Krasnoyarsk** Rus. Fed.	
89 F2	**Krasnoye-na-Volge** Rus. Fed.	
89 D3	**Krasnyy** Rus. Fed.	
89 E2	**Krasnyy Kholm** Rus. Fed.	
87 C4	**Krasnyy Luch** Ukr.	
91 E2	**Krasnyy Sulin** Rus. Fed.	
90 B2	**Krasyliv** Ukr.	
100 C2	**Krefeld** Ger.	
91 D1	**Kremenchuk** Ukr.	
91 C2	**Kremenchuts'ka Vodoskhovyshche** resr Ukr.	
103 D2	**Křemešník** hill Czech Rep.	
90 B1	**Kreminna** Ukr.	
103 D2	**Krems an der Donau** Austria	
89 D3	**Kresttsy** Rus. Fed.	
88 B2	**Kretinga** Lith.	
100 C3	**Kreuzau** Ger.	
100 C2	**Kreuztal** Ger.	
118 A2	**Kribi** Cameroon	
111 B3	**Krikellos** Greece	
66 D1	**Kril'on, Mys** c. Rus. Fed.	
73 C3	**Krishna** r. India	
73 C3	**Krishna, Mouths of the** India	
75 C2	**Krishnanagar** India	
93 E4	**Kristiansand** Norway	
93 F4	**Kristianstad** Sweden	
92 E3	**Kristiansund** Norway	
93 F4	**Kristinehamn** Sweden	
	Kriti i. Greece see **Crete**	
	Krivoy Rog Ukr. see **Kryvyy Rih**	
109 C1	**Križevci** Croatia	
108 B1	**Krk** i. Croatia	
92 F3	**Krokom** Sweden	
91 C1	**Krolevets'** Ukr.	
101 E2	**Kronach** Ger.	
63 B2	**Krŏng Kaôh Kŏng** Cambodia	
127 I2	**Kronprins Frederik Bjerge** nunataks Greenland	
123 C2	**Kroonstad** S. Africa	
87 D4	**Kropotkin** Rus. Fed.	
103 E2	**Krosno** Pol.	
103 D1	**Krotoszyn** Pol.	
60 B2	**Krui** Indon.	
109 C2	**Krujë** Albania	
111 C2	**Krumovgrad** Bulg.	
	Krung Thep Thai. see **Bangkok**	
88 C3	**Krupki** Belarus	
109 D2	**Kruševac** Serb. and Mont.	
101 F2	**Krušné hory** mts Czech Rep.	
128 A2	**Kruzof Island** U.S.A.	
89 D3	**Krychaw** Belarus	
91 D3	**Krymsk** Rus. Fed.	
111 C3	**Krytiko Pelagos** sea Greece	
91 C2	**Kryvyy Rih** Ukr.	
114 B2	**Ksabi** Alg.	
107 D2	**Ksar el Boukhari** Alg.	
114 B1	**Ksar el Kebir** Morocco	
89 E3	**Kshenskiy** Rus. Fed.	
78 B2	**Kū', Jabal al** hill Saudi Arabia	
61 C1	**Kuala Belait** Brunei	
60 B1	**Kuala Kerai** Malaysia	
60 B1	**Kuala Lipis** Malaysia	
61 C2	**Kuala Lumpur** Malaysia	
60 B1	**Kualapembuang** Indon.	
61 C2	**Kuala Terengganu** Malaysia	
60 B2	**Kualatungal** Indon.	
61 C1	**Kuamut** Sabah Malaysia	
65 A1	**Kuandian** China	
60 B1	**Kuantan** Malaysia	
91 D2	**Kuban'** r. Rus. Fed.	
89 E2	**Kubenskoye, Ozero** l. Rus. Fed.	
110 C2	**Kubrat** Bulg.	
61 C1	**Kubuang** Indon.	
61 C1	**Kuching** Sarawak Malaysia	
109 C2	**Kuçovë** Albania	
61 C1	**Kudat** Sabah Malaysia	
61 C2	**Kudus** Indon.	
102 C2	**Kufstein** Austria	
127 F2	**Kugaaruk** Can.	
126 D2	**Kugluktuk** Can.	
92 I3	**Kuhmo** Fin.	
79 C2	**Kührān, Kūh-e** mt. Iran	
	Kuitin China see **Kuytun**	
120 A2	**Kuito** Angola	
92 I2	**Kuivaniemi** Fin.	
65 B2	**Kujang** N. Korea	
109 D2	**Kukës** Albania	
111 C3	**Kula** Turkey	
75 D2	**Kula Kangri** mt. Bhutan	
76 B2	**Kulandy** Kazakh.	
88 B2	**Kuldīga** Latvia	
122 B1	**Kule** Botswana	
101 E2	**Kulmbach** Ger.	
77 C3	**Kŭlob** Tajik.	
76 B2	**Kul'sary** Kazakh.	
77 D1	**Kulunda** Rus. Fed.	
127 I2	**Kulusuk** Greenland	
67 C3	**Kumagaya** Japan	
67 B4	**Kumamoto** Japan	
109 D2	**Kumanovo** Macedonia	
114 B4	**Kumasi** Ghana	
118 A2	**Kumba** Cameroon	
78 B2	**Kumdah** Saudi Arabia	
87 E3	**Kumertau** Rus. Fed.	
65 B2	**Kumi** S. Korea	
93 G3	**Kumla** Sweden	
115 D3	**Kumo** Nigeria	
62 A1	**Kumon Range** mts Myanmar	
62 B2	**Kumphawapi** Thai.	
	Kumul China see **Hami**	
66 D2	**Kunashir, Ostrov** i. Rus. Fed.	
120 A2	**Kunene** r. Angola/Namibia	
77 D2	**Kungei Alatau** mts Kazakh./Kyrg.	
93 F4	**Kungsbacka** Sweden	
118 B2	**Kungu** Dem. Rep. Congo	
86 E3	**Kungur** Rus. Fed.	
62 A1	**Kunhing** Myanmar	
77 D3	**Kunlun Shan** mts China	
62 B1	**Kunming** China	
65 B2	**Kunsan** S. Korea	
50 B1	**Kununurra** Austr.	
92 I3	**Kuopio** Fin.	
109 C1	**Kupa** r. Croatia/Slovenia	
59 C3	**Kupang** Indon.	
88 B2	**Kupiškis** Lith.	
111 C2	**Küplü** Turkey	
128 A2	**Kupreanof Island** U.S.A.	
91 D2	**Kup"yans'k** Ukr.	
77 E2	**Kuqa** China	
67 B4	**Kurashiki** Japan	
67 B3	**Kurayoshi** Japan	
89 E3	**Kurchatov** Rus. Fed.	
110 C2	**Kürdzhali** Bulg.	
67 B4	**Kure** Japan	
88 B2	**Kuressaare** Estonia	
86 F3	**Kurgan** Rus. Fed.	
93 H3	**Kurikka** Fin.	
156 C3	**Kuril Trench** sea feature N. Pacific Ocean	
89 E3	**Kurkino** Rus. Fed.	
117 B3	**Kurmuk** Sudan	
73 B3	**Kurnool** India	
67 D3	**Kuroiso** Japan	
53 D2	**Kurri Kurri** Austr.	
89 E3	**Kursk** Rus. Fed.	
122 B2	**Kuruman** S. Africa	
122 B2	**Kuruman** watercourse S. Africa	
67 B4	**Kurume** Japan	
83 I3	**Kurumkan** Rus. Fed.	
73 C4	**Kurunegala** Sri Lanka	
111 C3	**Kuşadası** Turkey	
111 C3	**Kuşadası Körfezi** b. Turkey	
111 C3	**Kuş Gölü** l. Turkey	
91 D2	**Kushchevskaya** Rus. Fed.	
66 D2	**Kushiro** Japan	
76 C1	**Kushmurun** Kazakh.	
75 C2	**Kushtia** Bangl.	
66 D2	**Kussharo-ko** l. Japan	
111 C3	**Kütahya** Turkey	
81 C1	**K'ut'aisi** Georgia	
109 C1	**Kutjevo** Croatia	
103 D1	**Kutno** Pol.	
118 B3	**Kutu** Dem. Rep. Congo	
126 D2	**Kuujjua** r. Can.	
131 D1	**Kuujjuaq** Can.	
130 C1	**Kuujjuarapik** Can.	
92 I2	**Kuusamo** Fin.	
120 A2	**Kuvango** Angola	
89 D2	**Kuvshinovo** Rus. Fed.	
78 B2	**Kuwait** country Asia	
79 B2	**Kuwait** Kuwait	

		Kuybyshev Rus. Fed. *see* Samara
91	D2	**Kuybyshev** Ukr.
87	D3	**Kuybyshevskoye Vodokhranilishche** *resr* Rus. Fed.
77	E2	**Kuytun** China
111	C3	**Kuyucak** Turkey
87	D3	**Kuznetsk** Rus. Fed.
90	B1	**Kuznetsovs'k** Ukr.
92	H1	**Kvalsund** Norway
123	D2	**KwaMashu** S. Africa
65	B2	**Kwangju** S. Korea
65	B1	**Kwanmo-bong** *mt.* N. Korea
123	C3	**Kwanobuhle** S. Africa
122	B3	**KwaNonzame** S. Africa
123	C3	**Kwatinidubu** S. Africa
123	C3	**KwaZamokuhle** S. Africa
123	D2	**KwaZulu-Natal** *prov.* S. Africa
121	B2	**Kwekwe** Zimbabwe
118	B3	**Kwenge** *r.* Dem. Rep. Congo
103	D1	**Kwidzyn** Pol.
118	B3	**Kwilu** *r.* Angola/Dem. Rep. Congo
59	C3	**Kwoka** *mt.* Indon.
53	C3	**Kyabram** Austr.
62	A2	**Kyaikto** Myanmar
69	D1	**Kyakhta** Rus. Fed.
52	A2	**Kyancutta** Austr.
62	A1	**Kyaukpadaung** Myanmar
62	A2	**Kyaukpyu** Myanmar
88	B3	**Kybartai** Lith.
62	A2	**Kyebogyi** Myanmar
62	A2	**Kyeintali** Myanmar
74	B1	**Kyelang** India
		Kyiv Ukr. *see* Kiev
		Kyklades *is* Greece *see* Cyclades
129	D2	**Kyle** Can.
96	B2	**Kyle of Lochalsh** U.K.
100	C3	**Kyll** *r.* Ger.
111	B3	**Kyllini** *mt.* Greece
111	B3	**Kymi** Greece
52	B3	**Kyneton** Austr.
119	D2	**Kyoga, Lake** Uganda
53	D1	**Kyogle** Austr.
65	B2	**Kyŏnggi-man** *b.* N. Korea
65	B2	**Kyŏngju** S. Korea
67	C4	**Kyōto** Japan
111	B3	**Kyparissia** Greece
77	C1	**Kypshak,Ozero** *salt l.* Kazakh.
111	B3	**Kyra Panagia** *i.* Greece
80	B2	**Kyrenia** Cyprus
77	D2	**Kyrgyzstan** *country* Asia
101	F1	**Kyritz** Ger.
92	H3	**Kyrönjoki** *r.* Fin.
86	C2	**Kyrta** Rus. Fed.
86	D2	**Kyssa** Rus. Fed.
111	B3	**Kythira** *i.* Greece
111	B3	**Kythnos** *i.* Greece
128	B2	**Kyuquot** Can.
67	B4	**Kyūshū** *i.* Japan
110	B2	**Kyustendil** Bulg.
90	C1	**Kyiv's'ke Vodoskhovyshche** *resr* Ukr.
92	H3	**Kyyjärvi** Fin.
68	C1	**Kyzyl** Rus. Fed.
76	C2	**Kyzylkum Desert** Kazakh./Uzbek.
77	C2	**Kyzylorda** Kazakh.

L

117	C4	**Laascaanood** Somalia
150	B1	**La Asunción** Venez.
114	A2	**Laâyoune** Western Sahara
87	D4	**Laba** *r.* Rus. Fed.
144	B2	**La Babia** Mex.
146	B3	**La Bahia, Islas de** *is* Hond.
152	B3	**La Banda** Arg.
104	D3	**La Baule-Escoublac** France
114	A3	**Labé** Guinea
128	A1	**Laberge, Lake** Can.
87	D4	**Labinsk** Rus. Fed.
64	B1	**Labo** Phil.
104	B3	**Labouheyre** France
131	C1	**Labrador** *reg.* Can.
131	D1	**Labrador City** Can.
158	C1	**Labrador Sea** Can./Greenland
150	B2	**Lábrea** Brazil
61	C1	**Labuan** Malaysia
60	B1	**Labuhanbilik** Indon.
59	C3	**Labuna** Indon.
63	A2	**Labutta** Myanmar
86	F2	**Labytnangi** Rus. Fed.
109	C2	**Laç** Albania
105	C2	**La Capelle** France
73	E3	**Laccadive Islands** India
129	E2	**Lac du Bonnet** Can.
146	B3	**La Ceiba** Hond.
53	B2	**Lachlan** *r.* Austr.
141	E1	**Lachute** Can.
105	D3	**La Ciotat** France
129	C2	**Lac la Biche** Can.
		Lac la Martre Can. *see* Wha Ti
141	E1	**Lac-Mégantic** Can.
128	C2	**Lacombe** Can.
146	B4	**La Concepción** Panama
145	C3	**La Concordia** Mex.
108	A3	**Laconi** *Sardinia* Italy
141	E2	**Laconia** U.S.A.
128	C2	**La Crete** Can.
140	A2	**La Crosse** U.S.A.
144	B2	**La Cruz** Mex.
144	B2	**La Cuesta** Mex.
75	B1	**Ladakh Range** *mts* India
123	B3	**Ladismith** S. Africa
79	D2	**Lādīz** Iran
86	C2	**Ladoga, Lake** Rus. Fed.
		Ladozhskoye Ozero *l.* Rus. Fed. *see* Ladoga, Lake
128	B3	**Ladysmith** Can.
123	C2	**Ladysmith** S. Africa
59	D3	**Lae** P.N.G.
152	B3	**La Esmeralda** Bol.
93	F4	**Læsø** *i.* Denmark
143	C2	**La Fayette** U.S.A.
142	B1	**Lafayette** *IN* U.S.A.
142	B2	**Lafayette** *LA* U.S.A.
115	C4	**Lafia** Nigeria
104	B2	**La Flèche** France
143	D1	**La Follette** U.S.A.
131	C1	**Laforge** Can.
79	C2	**Lāft** Iran
108	A3	**La Galite** *i.* Tunisia
81	C1	**Lagan'** Rus. Fed.
118	B2	**Lagdo, Lac de** *l.* Cameroon
115	C1	**Laghouat** Alg.
155	D1	**Lagoa Santa** Brazil
114	A2	**La Gomera** *i.* Canary Is
114	C4	**Lagos** Nigeria
106	B2	**Lagos** Port.
134	C1	**La Grande** U.S.A.
130	C1	**La Grande 2, Réservoir** *resr* Can.
130	C1	**La Grande 3, Réservoir** *resr* Can.
131	C1	**La Grande 4, Réservoir** *resr* Can.
50	B1	**La Grange** Austr.
143	C2	**La Grange** U.S.A.
150	B1	**La Gran Sabana** *plat.* Venez.
152	D3	**Laguna** Brazil
144	A2	**Laguna, Picacho de la** *mt.* Mex.
150	A2	**Lagunas** Peru
		La Habana Cuba *see* Havana
61	C1	**Lahad Datu** *Sabah* Malaysia
60	B2	**Lahat** Indon.
78	B3	**Laḥij** Yemen
81	C2	**Lāhījān** Iran
100	C2	**Lahnstein** Ger.
74	B1	**Lahore** Pak.
74	A2	**Lahri** Pak.
93	I3	**Lahti** Fin.
115	C4	**Laï** Chad
53	D1	**Laidley** Austr.
104	C2	**L'Aigle** France
122	B3	**Laingsburg** S. Africa
92	H2	**Lainioälven** *r.* Sweden
96	B1	**Lairg** U.K.
108	B1	**Laives** Italy
70	B2	**Laiwu** China
70	C2	**Laiyang** China
70	B2	**Laizhou** China
70	B2	**Laizhou Wan** *b.* China
50	C1	**Lajamanu** Austr.
152	C3	**Lajes** Brazil
144	B2	**La Junta** Mex.
136	C3	**La Junta** U.S.A.
121	C2	**Lake Cabora Bassa** *resr* Moz.
53	C2	**Lake Cargelligo** Austr.
53	D2	**Lake Cathie** Austr.
142	B2	**Lake Charles** U.S.A.
143	D2	**Lake City** *FL* U.S.A.
143	E2	**Lake City** *SC* U.S.A.
108	A1	**Lake Como** Italy
128	B3	**Lake Cowichan** Can.
108	B1	**Lake Garda** Italy
138	A2	**Lake Havasu City** U.S.A.
143	D3	**Lakeland** U.S.A.
128	C2	**Lake Louise** Can.
134	B1	**Lake Oswego** U.S.A.
54	A2	**Lake Paringa** N.Z.
142	B2	**Lake Providence** U.S.A.
54	B2	**Lake Pukaki** N.Z.
53	C3	**Lakes Entrance** Austr.
134	B2	**Lakeview** U.S.A.
136	B3	**Lakewood** *CO* U.S.A.
141	E2	**Lakewood** *NJ* U.S.A.
143	D3	**Lake Worth** U.S.A.
74	A2	**Lakhpat** India
74	B1	**Lakki** Pak.
111	B3	**Lakonikos Kolpos** *b.* Greece
92	H1	**Lakselv** Norway
107	C1	**L'Alcora** Spain
145	C3	**La Libertad** Guat.
106	B1	**Lalín** Spain
75	B2	**Lalitpur** India
129	D2	**La Loche** Can.
100	B2	**La Louvière** Belgium
108	A2	**La Maddalena** *Sardinia* Italy
61	C1	**Lamag** *Sabah* Malaysia
		La Manche *str.* France/U.K. *see* English Channel
136	C3	**Lamar** U.S.A.
79	C2	**Lamard** Iran
108	A3	**La Marmora, Punta** *mt.* *Sardinia* Italy
118	B3	**Lambaréné** Gabon
122	A3	**Lambert's Bay** S. Africa
92	□A2	**Lambeyri** Iceland
106	B2	**Lamego** Port.
150	A3	**La Merced** Peru
52	B3	**Lameroo** Austr.
139	C2	**Lamesa** U.S.A.
111	B3	**Lamia** Greece

137 E2 **Lamoni** U.S.A.
62 A2 **Lampang** Thai.
139 D2 **Lampasas** U.S.A.
145 E2 **Lampazos** Mex.
99 A2 **Lampeter** U.K.
62 A2 **Lamphun** Thai.
119 E3 **Lamu** Kenya
96 C3 **Lanark** U.K.
63 A2 **Lanbi Kyun** i. Myanmar
Lancang Jiang r. China see
Mekong
98 B1 **Lancaster** U.K.
135 C4 **Lancaster** CA U.S.A.
140 C3 **Lancaster** OH U.S.A.
141 D2 **Lancaster** PA U.S.A.
143 D2 **Lancaster** SC U.S.A.
127 F2 **Lancaster Sound** str. Can.
Lanchow China see
Lanzhou
102 C2 **Landeck** Austria
136 B2 **Lander** U.S.A.
99 A3 **Land's End** pt U.K.
102 C2 **Landshut** Ger.
93 F4 **Landskrona** Sweden
143 C2 **Lanett** U.S.A.
122 B2 **Langberg** mts S. Africa
137 D1 **Langdon** U.S.A.
93 F4 **Langeland** i. Denmark
101 D1 **Langen** Ger.
100 C1 **Langeoog** Ger.
100 C1 **Langeoog** i. Ger.
101 D2 **Langgöns** Ger.
92 □A3 **Langjökull** ice cap Iceland
105 C3 **Langogne** France
104 B3 **Langon** France
105 D2 **Langres** France
60 A1 **Langsa** Indon.
62 B1 **Lang Son** Vietnam
101 D1 **Langwedel** Ger.
129 D2 **Lanigan** Can.
153 A4 **Lanín, Volcán** vol.
Arg./Chile
81 C2 **Länkäran** Azer.
104 B2 **Lannion** France
140 C2 **Lansing** U.S.A.
71 B3 **Lanxi** China
117 B4 **Lanya** Sudan
114 A2 **Lanzarote** i. Canary Is
70 A2 **Lanzhou** China
64 B1 **Laoag** Phil.
62 B1 **Lao Cai** Vietnam
70 B2 **Laohekou** China
Laojunmiao China see
Yumen
65 B1 **Laoling** China
65 B1 **Lao Ling** mts China
105 C2 **Laon** France
62 B2 **Laos** country Asia
65 B1 **Laotougou** China
154 C3 **Lapa** Brazil
114 A2 **La Palma** i. Canary Is
146 C4 **La Palma** Panama
150 B1 **La Paragua** Venez.
152 B2 **La Paz** Bol.
144 A2 **La Paz** Mex.
150 B2 **La Pedrera** Col.
66 D1 **La Pérouse Strait**
Japan/Rus. Fed.
145 C2 **La Pesca** Mex.
144 B2 **La Piedad** Mex.
153 C4 **La Plata** Arg.
93 I3 **Lappeenranta** Fin.
92 G2 **Lappland** reg. Europe
111 C2 **Lâpseki** Turkey
83 J1 **Laptev Sea** Rus. Fed.
Laptevykh, More sea
Rus. Fed. see Laptev Sea
92 H3 **Lapua** Fin.
152 B3 **La Quiaca** Arg.
79 C2 **Lār** Iran

114 B1 **Larache** Morocco
136 B2 **Laramie** U.S.A.
136 B2 **Laramie Mountains** U.S.A.
154 B3 **Laranjeiras do Sul** Brazil
59 C3 **Larantuka** Indon.
59 C3 **Larat** i. Indon.
107 D2 **Larba** Alg.
106 C1 **Laredo** Spain
139 D3 **Laredo** U.S.A.
152 B3 **Largs** i. Arg.
La Rioja Arg.
111 B3 **Larisa** Greece
74 A2 **Larkana** Pak.
80 B2 **Larnaca** Cyprus
97 C1 **Larne** U.K.
100 B2 **La Roche-en-Ardenne**
Belgium
104 B2 **La Rochelle** France
104 B2 **La Roche-sur-Yon** France
107 C2 **La Roda** Spain
147 D3 **La Romana** Dom. Rep.
129 D2 **La Ronge** Can.
50 C1 **Larrimah** Austr.
55 P3 **Larsen Ice Shelf** Antarctica
93 F4 **Larvik** Norway
130 C2 **La Sarre** Can.
138 B2 **Las Cruces** U.S.A.
153 C4 **Las Flores** Arg.
153 B4 **Las Heras** Arg.
62 A1 **Lashio** Myanmar
109 C3 **La Sila** reg. Italy
152 B3 **Las Lomitas** Arg.
144 B2 **Las Nieves** Mex.
114 A2 **Las Palmas de Gran
Canaria** Canary Is
108 A2 **La Spezia** Italy
153 B5 **Las Plumas** Arg.
129 D2 **Last Mountain Lake** Can.
152 B3 **Las Tórtolas, Cerro** mt.
Chile
118 B3 **Lastoursville** Gabon
109 C2 **Lastovo** i. Croatia
144 A2 **Las Tres Vírgenes, Volcán**
vol. Mex.
146 C2 **Las Tunas** Cuba
144 B2 **Las Varas** Chihuahua Mex.
144 B2 **Las Varas** Nayarit Mex.
138 B1 **Las Vegas** NM U.S.A.
135 C3 **Las Vegas** NV U.S.A.
131 E1 **La Tabatière** Can.
80 B2 **Latakia** Syria
104 B3 **La Teste-de-Buch** France
108 B2 **Latina** Italy
147 D3 **La Tortuga, Isla** i. Venez.
64 B1 **La Trinidad** Phil.
89 E2 **Latskoye** Rus. Fed.
131 C2 **La Tuque** Can.
88 B2 **Latvia** country Europe
102 C1 **Lauchhammer** Ger.
101 E3 **Lauf an der Pegnitz** Ger.
105 D2 **Laufen** Switz.
51 D4 **Launceston** Austr.
99 A3 **Launceston** U.K.
62 A1 **Laungyyaung** Myanmar
51 D1 **Laura** Austr.
142 C2 **Laurel** MS U.S.A.
134 E1 **Laurel** MT U.S.A.
109 C2 **Lauria** Italy
143 E2 **Laurinburg** U.S.A.
105 D2 **Lausanne** Switz.
61 C2 **Laut** i. Indon.
101 D2 **Lautersbach (Hessen)** Ger.
61 C2 **Laut Kecil, Kepulauan** is
Indon.
100 C1 **Lauwersmeer** l. Neth.
104 B2 **Laval** France
107 C2 **La Vall d'Uixó** Spain
50 B2 **Laverton** Austr.
155 D1 **Lavras** Brazil
123 D2 **Lavumisa** Swaziland

61 C1 **Lawas** Sarawak Malaysia
62 A1 **Lawksawk** Myanmar
114 B3 **Lawra** Ghana
137 D3 **Lawrence** U.S.A.
142 C1 **Lawrenceburg** U.S.A.
139 D2 **Lawton** U.S.A.
78 A2 **Lawz, Jabal al** mt.
Saudi Arabia
93 F4 **Laxå** Sweden
109 D2 **Lazarevac** Serb. and Mont.
144 A1 **Lázaro Cárdenas**
Baja California Norte Mex.
144 B3 **Lázaro Cárdenas**
Michoacán Mex.
88 B3 **Lazdijai** Lith.
136 C2 **Lead** U.S.A.
129 D2 **Leader** Can.
136 B3 **Leadville** U.S.A.
Leaf Bay Can. see Tasiujaq
129 D2 **Leaf Rapids** Can.
97 B2 **Leane, Lough** l. Ireland
137 E3 **Leavenworth** U.S.A.
80 B2 **Lebanon** country Asia
137 E3 **Lebanon** MO U.S.A.
141 E2 **Lebanon** NH U.S.A.
134 B2 **Lebanon** OR U.S.A.
141 D2 **Lebanon** PA U.S.A.
89 E3 **Lebedyan'** Rus. Fed.
91 C1 **Lebedyn** Ukr.
104 C2 **Le Blanc** France
103 D1 **Lębork** Pol.
123 C1 **Lebowakgomo** S. Africa
106 B2 **Lebrija** Spain
153 A4 **Lebu** Chile
104 C3 **Le Bugue** France
109 C2 **Lecce** Italy
108 A1 **Lecco** Italy
102 C2 **Lech** r. Austria/Ger.
111 B3 **Lechaina** Greece
71 B3 **Lechang** China
102 B1 **Leck** Ger.
104 C3 **Lectoure** France
106 B1 **Ledesma** Spain
104 C2 **Le Dorat** France
128 C2 **Leduc** Can.
137 E1 **Leech Lake** U.S.A.
98 C2 **Leeds** U.K.
98 B2 **Leek** U.K.
100 C1 **Leer (Ostfriesland)** Ger.
143 D3 **Leesburg** U.S.A.
142 B2 **Leesville** U.S.A.
53 C2 **Leeton** Austr.
122 B3 **Leeu-Gamka** S. Africa
100 B1 **Leeuwarden** Neth.
50 A3 **Leeuwin, Cape** Austr.
147 D3 **Leeward Islands**
Caribbean Sea
111 B3 **Lefkada** Greece
111 B3 **Lefkada** i. Greece
Lefkosia Cyprus see
Nicosia
64 B1 **Legaspi** Phil.
108 B1 **Legnago** Italy
103 D1 **Legnica** Pol.
75 B1 **Leh** Jammu and Kashmir
104 C2 **Le Havre** France
122 B1 **Lehututu** Botswana
74 B1 **Leiah** Pak.
103 D2 **Leibnitz** Austria
99 C2 **Leicester** U.K.
100 A2 **Leiden** Neth.
100 A2 **Leie** r. Belgium
52 A2 **Leigh Creek** Austr.
93 E3 **Leikanger** Norway
101 D1 **Leine** r. Ger.
97 C2 **Leinster** reg. Ireland
101 F2 **Leipzig** Ger.
92 F2 **Leiranger** Norway
106 B2 **Leiria** Port.

93 E4 **Leirvik** Norway
97 C2 **Leixlip** Ireland
71 B3 **Leiyang** China
71 B3 **Leizhou** China
71 B3 **Leizhou** China
71 A3 **Leizhou Bandao** *pen.* China
118 B3 **Lékana** Congo
100 B1 **Lelystad** Neth.
153 B6 **Le Maire, Estrecho de** *sea chan.* Arg.
Léman, Lac *l.* France/Switz. *see* Geneva, Lake
104 C2 **Le Mans** France
137 D2 **Le Mars** U.S.A.
154 C2 **Leme** Brazil
Lemesos Cyprus *see* Limassol
101 D1 **Lemförde** Ger.
127 G2 **Lemieux Islands** Can.
136 C1 **Lemmon** U.S.A.
135 C3 **Lemoore** U.S.A.
131 D1 **Le Moyne, Lac** *l.* Can.
62 A1 **Lemro** *r.* Myanmar
109 C2 **La Murge** *hills* Italy
83 J2 **Lena** *r.* Rus. Fed.
100 C1 **Lengerich** Ger.
71 B3 **Lengshuijiang** China
71 B3 **Lengshuitan** China
91 D2 **Lenine** Ukr.
Leningrad Rus. Fed. *see* St Petersburg
91 D2 **Leningradskaya** Rus. Fed.
77 D3 **Lenin Peak** Kyrg./Tajik.
Leninsk Kazakh. *see* Baykonyr
89 E3 **Leninskiy** Rus. Fed.
100 A2 **Lens** Belgium
104 C1 **Lens** France
83 I2 **Lensk** Rus. Fed.
103 D2 **Lenti** Hungary
109 C3 **Lentini** *Sicily* Italy
114 B3 **Léo** Burkina
102 G2 **Leoben** Austria
99 B2 **Leominster** U.K.
144 B2 **León** Mex.
146 B3 **León** Nic.
106 B1 **León** Spain
122 A1 **Leonardville** Namibia
50 B2 **Leonora** Austr.
155 D2 **Leopoldina** Brazil
123 C1 **Lephalale** S. Africa
123 C1 **Lephepe** Botswana
123 D3 **Lephoi** S. Africa
71 B3 **Leping** China
105 C2 **Le Puy-en-Velay** France
150 A2 **Lérida** Col.
106 C1 **Lerma** Spain
111 C3 **Leros** *i.* Greece
130 C1 **Le Roy, Lac** *l.* Can.
93 F4 **Lerum** Sweden
96 □ **Lerwick** U.K.
111 C3 **Lesbos** *i.* Greece
147 C3 **Les Cayes** Haiti
69 C3 **Leshan** China
86 D2 **Leshukonskoye** Rus. Fed.
109 D2 **Leskovac** Serb. and Mont.
104 B2 **Lesneven** France
89 E2 **Lesnoye** Rus. Fed.
83 H3 **Lesosibirsk** Rus. Fed.
123 C2 **Lesotho** *country* Africa
66 B1 **Lesozavodsk** Rus. Fed.
104 B2 **Les Sables-d'Olonne** France
147 D3 **Lesser Antilles** *is* Caribbean Sea
81 C1 **Lesser Caucasus** *mts* Asia
128 C2 **Lesser Slave Lake** Can.
105 C3 **Les Vans** France
Lesvos *i.* Greece *see* Lesbos

103 D1 **Leszno** Pol.
99 C3 **Letchworth Garden City** U.K.
128 D2 **Lethbridge** Can.
150 C1 **Lethem** Guyana
59 C3 **Leti, Kepulauan** *is* Indon.
150 B2 **Leticia** Col.
123 C1 **Letlhakane** Botswana
104 C1 **Le Touquet-Paris-Plage** France
99 D3 **Le Tréport** France
63 A2 **Letsok-aw Kyun** *i.* Myanmar
123 C2 **Letsopa** S. Africa
97 C1 **Letterkenny** Ireland
105 C3 **Leucate, Étang de** *l.* France
60 A1 **Leuser, Gunung** *mt.* Indon.
100 B2 **Leuven** Belgium
111 B3 **Levadeia** Greece
92 F3 **Levanger** Norway
139 C2 **Levelland** U.S.A.
50 B1 **Lévêque, Cape** Austr.
100 C2 **Leverkusen** Ger.
103 D2 **Levice** Slovakia
54 C2 **Levin** N.Z.
131 C2 **Lévis** Can.
89 E3 **Lev Tolstoy** Rus. Fed.
99 D3 **Lewes** U.K.
96 A1 **Lewis, Isle of** *i.* U.K.
140 C3 **Lewisburg** U.S.A.
134 D1 **Lewis Range** *mts* U.S.A.
134 C1 **Lewiston** *ID* U.S.A.
141 E2 **Lewiston** *ME* U.S.A.
134 E1 **Lewistown** U.S.A.
140 C3 **Lexington** *KY* U.S.A.
136 D2 **Lexington** *NE* U.S.A.
141 D3 **Lexington** *VA* U.S.A.
64 B1 **Leyte** *i.* Phil.
109 C2 **Lezhë** Albania
89 F2 **Lezhnevo** Rus. Fed.
89 E3 **L'gov** Rus. Fed.
75 C2 **Lhagoi Kangri** *mt.* China
68 C2 **Lharigarbo** China
75 D2 **Lhasa** China
75 C2 **Lhazê** China
60 A1 **Lhokseumawe** Indon.
67 B3 **Liancourt Rocks** *i.* N. Pacific Ocean
71 B3 **Lianhua** China
71 B3 **Lianjiang** China
70 C1 **Lianshan** China
70 B2 **Lianyungang** China
71 B3 **Lianzhou** China
70 B2 **Liaocheng** China
70 C1 **Liaodong Bandao** *pen.* China
70 C1 **Liaodong Wan** *b.* China
65 A1 **Liao He** *r.* China
70 C1 **Liaoning** *prov.* China
65 A1 **Liaoyang** China
65 B1 **Liaoyuan** China
128 B1 **Liard** *r.* Can.
134 C1 **Libby** U.S.A.
118 B2 **Libenge** Dem. Rep. Congo
136 C3 **Liberal** U.S.A.
103 D1 **Liberec** Czech Rep.
114 B4 **Liberia** *country* Africa
146 B3 **Liberia** Costa Rica
150 B1 **Libertad** Venez.
100 B3 **Libin** Belgium
104 B3 **Libourne** France
118 A2 **Libreville** Gabon
115 D2 **Libya** *country* Africa
115 E2 **Libyan Desert** Egypt/Libya
116 A1 **Libyan Plateau** Egypt
108 B3 **Licata** *Sicily* Italy
Licheng China *see* Lipu
121 C2 **Lichinga** Moz.
101 E2 **Lichte** Ger.

123 C2 **Lichtenburg** S. Africa
101 E2 **Lichtenfels** Ger.
88 C3 **Lida** Belarus
93 F4 **Lidköping** Sweden
50 C2 **Liebig, Mount** Austr.
105 D2 **Liechtenstein** *country* Europe
100 B2 **Liège** Belgium
92 J3 **Lieksa** Fin.
119 C2 **Lienart** Dem. Rep. Congo
63 B2 **Liên Nghia** Vietnam
102 C2 **Lienz** Austria
88 B2 **Liepāja** Latvia
102 C2 **Liezen** Austria
97 C2 **Liffey** *r.* Ireland
97 C1 **Lifford** Ireland
53 C1 **Lightning Ridge** Austr.
121 C2 **Ligonha** *r.* Moz.
105 D3 **Ligurian Sea** France/Italy
119 C4 **Likasi** Dem. Rep. Congo
128 B2 **Likely** Can.
89 E2 **Likhoslavl'** Rus. Fed.
61 B1 **Liku** Indon.
L'Île-Rousse *Corsica* France
71 B3 **Liling** China
93 F4 **Lilla Edet** Sweden
100 B2 **Lille** Belgium
105 C1 **Lille** France
Lille Bælt *sea chan.* Denmark *see* Little Belt
93 F3 **Lillehammer** Norway
93 F4 **Lillestrøm** Norway
128 B2 **Lillooet** Can.
121 C2 **Lilongwe** Malawi
64 B2 **Liloy** Phil.
150 A3 **Lima** Peru
140 C2 **Lima** U.S.A.
80 B2 **Limassol** Cyprus
97 C1 **Limavady** U.K.
153 B4 **Limay** *r.* Arg.
101 F2 **Limbach-Oberfrohna** Ger.
88 B2 **Limbaži** Latvia
118 A2 **Limbe** Cameroon
100 C2 **Limburg an der Lahn** Ger.
122 B2 **Lime Acres** S. Africa
154 C2 **Limeira** Brazil
97 B2 **Limerick** Ireland
93 E4 **Limfjorden** *sea chan.* Denmark
111 C3 **Limnos** *i.* Greece
104 C2 **Limoges** France
136 C3 **Limon** U.S.A.
104 C3 **Limoux** France
123 C1 **Limpopo** *prov.* S. Africa
121 C3 **Limpopo** *r.* S. Africa/Zimbabwe
64 A1 **Linapacan** *i.* Phil.
153 A4 **Linares** Chile
145 C2 **Linares** Mex.
106 C2 **Linares** Spain
62 B1 **Lincang** China
98 C2 **Lincoln** U.K.
140 B2 **Lincoln** *IL* U.S.A.
141 F1 **Lincoln** *ME* U.S.A.
137 D2 **Lincoln** *NE* U.S.A.
150 C1 **Linden** Guyana
142 C1 **Linden** U.S.A.
119 C2 **Lindi** *r.* Dem. Rep. Congo
119 D3 **Lindi** Tanz.
Lindisfarne *i.* U.K. *see* Holy Island
80 A2 **Lindos** Greece
141 D2 **Lindsay** Can.
49 H2 **Line Islands** Kiribati
70 B2 **Linfen** China
71 B3 **Lingayen** Phil.
70 B2 **Lingbao** China
123 C3 **Lingelethu** S. Africa
123 C3 **Lingelihle** S. Africa
100 C1 **Lingen (Ems)** Ger.

60	B2	Lingga, Kepulauan is Indon.
71	A3	Lingshan China
71	A4	Lingshui China
114	A3	Linguère Senegal
155	D1	Linhares Brazil
70	A1	Linhe China
93	G4	Linköping Sweden
66	B1	Linkou China
70	B2	Linqing China
154	C2	Lins Brazil
136	C1	Linton U.S.A.
69	D2	Linxi China
69	C2	Linxia China
70	B2	Linyi Shandong China
70	B2	Linyi Shandong China
70	B2	Linying China
102	C2	Linz Austria
105	C3	Lion, Golfe du g. France
109	B3	Lipari Italy
108	B3	Lipari, Isole is Italy
89	E3	Lipetsk Rus. Fed.
110	B1	Lipova Romania
101	D2	Lippstadt Ger.
71	B3	Lipu China
76	C1	Lisakovsk Kazakh.
118	C2	Lisala Dem. Rep. Congo
		Lisboa Port. see Lisbon
106	B2	Lisbon Port.
97	C1	Lisburn U.K.
97	B2	Liscannor Bay Ireland
104	C2	Lisieux France
99	A3	Liskeard U.K.
89	E3	Liski Rus. Fed.
53	D1	Lismore Austr.
97	C1	Lisnaskea U.K.
97	B2	Listowel Ireland
71	A3	Litang Guangxi China
68	C2	Litang Sichuan China
137	E1	Litchfield IL U.S.A.
137	E1	Litchfield MN U.S.A.
53	D2	Lithgow Austr.
111	B3	Lithino, Akra pt Greece
88	B2	Lithuania country Europe
102	C1	Litoměřice Czech Rep.
146	C2	Little Abaco i. Bahamas
73	D3	Little Andaman i. India
93	E4	Little Belt sea chan. Denmark
137	E1	Little Falls U.S.A.
139	C2	Littlefield U.S.A.
99	C3	Littlehampton U.K.
122	A2	Little Karas Berg plat. Namibia
122	B3	Little Karoo plat. S. Africa
96	A2	Little Minch sea chan. U.K.
136	C1	Little Missouri r. U.S.A.
63	A3	Little Nicobar i. India
142	B2	Little Rock U.S.A.
141	E2	Littleton U.S.A.
71	A3	Liujiachang China
68	C2	Liuzhou China
88	C2	Līvāni Latvia
50	B1	Liveringa Austr.
138	C2	Livermore, Mount U.S.A.
131	D2	Liverpool Can.
98	B2	Liverpool U.K.
127	F2	Liverpool, Cape Can.
53	C2	Liverpool Range mts Austr.
134	D1	Livingston MT U.S.A.
139	E2	Livingston TX U.S.A.
139	E2	Livingston, Lake U.S.A.
120	B2	Livingstone Zambia
109	C2	Livno Bos.-Herz.
89	E3	Livny Rus. Fed.
140	C2	Livonia U.S.A.
108	B2	Livorno Italy
119	D3	Liwale Tanz.
70	B2	Liyang China
99	A4	Lizard Point U.K.
108	B1	Ljubljana Slovenia
93	G3	Ljungan r. Sweden
93	F4	Ljungby Sweden
93	G3	Ljusdal Sweden
93	G3	Ljusnan r. Sweden
99	B3	Llandeilo U.K.
99	B3	Llandovery U.K.
99	B2	Llandrindod Wells U.K.
98	B2	Llandudno U.K.
99	A3	Llanelli U.K.
98	A2	Llangefni U.K.
139	C2	Llano Estacado plain U.S.A.
150	B1	Llanos reg. Col./Venez.
107	D1	Lleida Spain
99	A2	Lleyn Peninsula U.K.
107	C2	Lliria Spain
106	C1	Llodio Spain
128	B2	Lloyd George, Mount Can.
129	D2	Lloyd Lake Can.
129	C2	Lloydminster Can.
152	B3	Llullaillaco, Volcán vol. Chile
123	C2	Lobatse Botswana
120	A2	Lobito Angola
101	F1	Loburg Ger.
96	B2	Lochaber mts U.K.
104	C2	Loches France
96	B2	Lochgilphead U.K.
96	B1	Lochinver U.K.
96	A2	Lochmaddy U.K.
96	C2	Lochnagar mt. U.K.
52	A2	Lock Austr.
96	C3	Lockerbie U.K.
139	D3	Lockhart U.S.A.
141	D2	Lock Haven U.S.A.
141	D2	Lockport U.S.A.
63	B2	Lôc Ninh Vietnam
105	C3	Lodève France
86	C2	Lodeynoye Pole Rus. Fed.
92	F2	Løding Norway
119	D2	Lodwar Kenya
103	D1	Łódź Pol.
62	B2	Loei Thai.
122	A3	Loeriesfontein S. Africa
92	F2	Lofoten is Norway
134	D2	Logan U.S.A.
126	B2	Logan, Mount U.S.A.
140	B2	Logansport U.S.A.
108	B1	Logatec Slovenia
106	C1	Logroño Spain
101	D1	Lohne Ger.
101	D1	Lohne (Oldenburg) Ger.
62	A2	Loikaw Myanmar
62	A2	Loi Lan mt. Myanmar/Thai.
104	B2	Loire r. France
150	A2	Loja Ecuador
106	C2	Loja Spain
92	I2	Lokan tekojärvi l. Fin.
100	B2	Lokeren Belgium
122	B1	Lokgwabe Botswana
119	D2	Lokichar Kenya
119	D2	Lokichokio Kenya
89	D2	Loknya Rus. Fed.
115	C4	Lokoja Nigeria
89	D3	Lokot' Rus. Fed.
88	C2	Loksa Estonia
127	G2	Loks Land i. Can.
93	F4	Lolland i. Denmark
119	D3	Lollondo Tanz.
122	B2	Lolwane S. Africa
110	B2	Lom Bulg.
93	E3	Lom Norway
119	C2	Lomami r. Dem. Rep. Congo
153	C4	Lomas de Zamora Arg.
61	C2	Lombok i. Indon.
61	C2	Lombok, Selat sea chan. Indon.
114	C4	Lomé Togo
118	C3	Lomela r. Dem. Rep. Congo
100	B2	Lommel Belgium
96	B2	Lomond, Loch l. U.K.
88	C2	Lomonosov Rus. Fed.
135	B4	Lompoc U.S.A.
63	B2	Lom Sak Thai.
103	E1	Łomża Pol.
130	B2	London Can.
99	C3	London U.K.
140	C3	London U.S.A.
97	C1	Londonderry U.K.
50	B1	Londonderry, Cape Austr.
154	B2	Londrina Brazil
83	M2	Longa, Proliv sea chan. Rus. Fed.
61	C1	Long Akah Sarawak Malaysia
143	E2	Long Bay U.S.A.
135	C4	Long Beach U.S.A.
97	C2	Longford Ireland
61	C2	Longiram Indon.
147	C2	Long Island Bahamas
130	C1	Long Island Can.
59	D3	Long Island P.N.G.
141	E2	Long Island U.S.A.
130		Longlac Can.
130	B2	Long Lake Can.
136	B2	Longmont U.S.A.
140	C2	Long Point Can.
71	B3	Longquan China
131	E2	Long Range Mountains Can.
51	D2	Longreach Austr.
99	D2	Long Stratton U.K.
98	B1	Longtown U.K.
105	D2	Longuyon France
139	E2	Longview TX U.S.A.
134	B1	Longview WA U.S.A.
70	A2	Longxi China
71	B3	Longxi Shan mt. China
63	B2	Long Xuyên Vietnam
71	B3	Longyan China
82	C1	Longyearbyen Svalbard
102	B2	Lons-le-Saunier France
143	E2	Lookout, Cape U.S.A.
52	B1	Loop Head Ireland
63	B2	Lop Buri Thai.
64	B1	Lopez Phil.
68	C2	Lop Nur salt l. China
118	B2	Lopori r. Dem. Rep. Congo
106	B2	Lora del Rio Spain
140	C2	Lorain U.S.A.
74	A2	Loralai Pak.
107	C2	Lorca Spain
48	E5	Lord Howe Island Austr.
138	B2	Lordsburg U.S.A.
155	C2	Lorena Brazil
152	B2	Loreto Bol.
144	A2	Loreto Mex.
104	B2	Lorient France
96	B2	Lorn, Firth of est. U.K.
52	B3	Lorne Austr.
138	B1	Los Alamos U.S.A.
139	C3	Los Aldamas Mex.
153	A4	Los Ángeles Chile
135	C4	Los Angeles U.S.A.
135	B3	Los Banos U.S.A.
152	B3	Los Blancos Arg.
91	E1	Losevo Rus. Fed.
108	B2	Lošinj i. Croatia
144	B2	Los Mochis Mex.
118	B3	Losombo Dem. Rep. Congo
147	D3	Los Roques, Islas is Venez.
96	C2	Lossiemouth U.K.
150	B1	Los Teques Venez.
152	A4	Los Vilos Chile
104	C3	Lot r. France
96	C1	Loth U.K.
119	D2	Lotikipi Plain Kenya
118	C3	Loto Dem. Rep. Congo

89 E2 **Lotoshino** Rus. Fed.
62 B1 **Louangnamtha** Laos
62 B2 **Louangphabang** Laos
118 B3 **Loubomo** Congo
104 B2 **Loudéac** France
71 B3 **Loudi** China
118 B3 **Loudima** Congo
114 A3 **Louga** Senegal
99 C3 **Loughborough** U.K.
97 B2 **Loughrea** Ireland
105 D2 **Louhans** France
97 B2 **Louisburgh** Ireland
142 B2 **Louisiana** state U.S.A.
140 B3 **Louisville** KY U.S.A.
142 C2 **Louisville** MS U.S.A.
86 C2 **Loukhi** Rus. Fed.
130 C1 **Loups Marins, Lacs des** lakes Can.
104 B3 **Lourdes** France
151 E1 **Lourenço** Brazil
106 B1 **Lousã** Port.
53 C2 **Louth** Austr.
98 C2 **Louth** U.K.
Louvain Belgium see Leuven
89 E3 **Lovat'** r. Rus. Fed.
110 B2 **Lovech** Bulg.
136 B3 **Loveland** U.S.A.
135 C2 **Lovelock** U.S.A.
139 C2 **Lovington** U.S.A.
119 C3 **Lowa** Dem. Rep. Congo
141 E2 **Lowell** U.S.A.
128 C3 **Lower Arrow Lake** Can.
54 B2 **Lower Hutt** N.Z.
97 C1 **Lower Lough Erne** l. U.K.
128 B2 **Lower Post** Can.
99 D2 **Lowestoft** U.K.
103 D1 **Łowicz** Pol.
141 D2 **Lowville** U.S.A.
52 B2 **Loxton** Austr.
Loyang China see Luoyang
48 F4 **Loyauté, Îles** is New Caledonia
89 D3 **Loyew** Belarus
92 F2 **Løypskardtinden** mt. Norway
109 C2 **Loznica** Serb. and Mont.
91 D2 **Lozova** Ukr.
120 B2 **Luacano** Angola
70 B2 **Lu'an** China
120 A1 **Luanda** Angola
121 C2 **Luangwa** r. Zambia
121 B2 **Luanshya** Zambia
106 B1 **Luarca** Spain
120 B2 **Luau** Angola
103 E1 **Lubaczów** Pol.
120 A2 **Lubango** Angola
119 C3 **Lubao** Dem. Rep. Congo
103 E1 **Lubartów** Pol.
101 D1 **Lübbecke** Ger.
139 C2 **Lubbock** U.S.A.
101 E1 **Lübeck** Ger.
69 E2 **Lubei** China
87 E3 **Lubenka** Kazakh.
103 D1 **Lubin** Pol.
103 E1 **Lublin** Pol.
91 C1 **Lubny** Ukr.
61 C1 **Lubok Antu** Sarawak Malaysia
101 E1 **Lübow** Ger.
101 E1 **Lübtheen** Ger.
119 C3 **Lubudi** Dem. Rep. Congo
60 B2 **Lubuklinggau** Indon.
119 C4 **Lubumbashi** Dem. Rep. Congo
120 B2 **Lubungu** Zambia
119 C3 **Lubutu** Dem. Rep. Congo
120 A1 **Lucala** Angola

97 C2 **Lucan** Ireland
120 B1 **Lucapa** Angola
96 B3 **Luce Bay** U.K.
154 B2 **Lucélia** Brazil
64 B1 **Lucena** Phil.
106 C2 **Lucena** Spain
103 D2 **Lučenec** Slovakia
109 C2 **Lucera** Italy
105 D2 **Lucerne** Switz.
69 E1 **Lüchow** Ger.
120 A2 **Lucira** Angola
101 F1 **Luckenwalde** Ger.
122 B2 **Luckhoff** S. Africa
75 C2 **Lucknow** India
120 B2 **Lucusse** Angola
Lüda China see Dalian
100 C2 **Lüdenscheid** Ger.
101 E1 **Lüder** Ger.
120 A3 **Lüderitz** Namibia
74 B1 **Ludhiana** India
140 C2 **Ludington** U.S.A.
99 B2 **Ludlow** U.K.
135 C4 **Ludlow** U.S.A.
110 C2 **Ludogorie** reg. Bulg.
93 G3 **Ludvika** Sweden
102 B2 **Ludwigsburg** Ger.
101 F1 **Ludwigsfelde** Ger.
101 D3 **Ludwigshafen am Rhein** Ger.
101 E1 **Ludwigslust** Ger.
88 C2 **Ludza** Latvia
118 C3 **Luebo** Dem. Rep. Congo
120 A2 **Luena** Angola
70 A2 **Lüeyang** China
71 B3 **Lufeng** China
139 E2 **Lufkin** U.S.A.
88 C2 **Luga** Rus. Fed.
88 C2 **Luga** r. Rus. Fed.
105 D2 **Lugano** Switz.
121 C2 **Lugenda** r. Moz.
97 C2 **Lugnaquilla** hill Ireland
106 B1 **Lugo** Spain
110 B1 **Lugoj** Romania
91 D2 **Luhans'k** Ukr.
119 D3 **Luhombero** Tanz.
90 B1 **Luhyny** Ukr.
120 B2 **Luiana** Angola
118 C3 **Luilaka** r. Dem. Rep. Congo
105 D2 **Luino** Italy
92 I2 **Luiro** r. Fin.
118 C3 **Luiza** Dem. Rep. Congo
70 B2 **Lujiang** China
109 C2 **Lukavac** Bos.-Herz.
118 B3 **Lukenie** r. Dem. Rep. Congo
138 A2 **Lukeville** U.S.A.
89 E3 **Lukhovitsy** Rus. Fed.
103 E1 **Łuków** Pol.
120 B2 **Lukulu** Zambia
92 H2 **Luleå** Sweden
92 H2 **Luleälven** r. Sweden
110 C2 **Lüleburgaz** Turkey
70 B2 **Lüliang Shan** mts China
61 C2 **Lumajang** Indon.
75 C1 **Lumajangdong Co** salt l. China
120 B2 **Lumbala Kaquengue** Angola
120 B2 **Lumbala N'guimbo** Angola
143 E2 **Lumberton** U.S.A.
61 C1 **Lumbis** Indon.
106 B1 **Lumbrales** Spain
63 B2 **Lumphăt** Cambodia
129 D2 **Lumsden** Can.
54 A3 **Lumsden** N.Z.
93 F4 **Lund** Sweden
121 C2 **Lundazi** Zambia
99 A3 **Lundy** i. U.K.

101 E1 **Lüneburg** Ger.
101 E1 **Lüneburger Heide** reg. Ger.
100 C2 **Lünen** Ger.
105 D2 **Lunéville** France
120 B2 **Lunga** r. Zambia
114 A4 **Lungi** Sierra Leone
62 A1 **Lunglei** India
120 B2 **Lungwebungu** r. Zambia
74 B2 **Luni** r. India
88 C3 **Luninyets** Belarus
114 A4 **Lunsar** Sierra Leone
77 F2 **Luntai** China
71 A3 **Luodian** China
71 B3 **Luoding** China
70 B2 **Luohe** China
70 B2 **Luoyang** China
121 B2 **Lupane** Zimbabwe
71 A3 **Lupanshui** China
110 B1 **Lupeni** Romania
121 C2 **Lupilichi** Moz.
101 F2 **Luppa** Ger.
121 D2 **Lúrio** Moz.
121 D2 **Lurio** r. Moz.
121 B2 **Lusaka** Zambia
118 C3 **Lusambo** Dem. Rep. Congo
109 C2 **Lushnjë** Albania
136 C2 **Lusk** U.S.A.
76 B3 **Lut, Dasht-e** des. Iran
101 F2 **Lutherstadt Wittenberg** Ger.
99 C3 **Luton** U.K.
61 C1 **Lutong** Sarawak Malaysia
129 C1 **Lutselk'e** Can.
90 B1 **Luts'k** Ukr.
122 B2 **Lutzputs** S. Africa
122 A3 **Lutzville** S. Africa
117 C4 **Luuq** Somalia
137 D2 **Luverne** U.S.A.
119 C3 **Luvua** r. Dem. Rep. Congo
123 D1 **Luvuvhu** r. S. Africa
119 D2 **Luwero** Uganda
59 C3 **Luwuk** Indon.
100 C3 **Luxembourg** country Europe
100 C3 **Luxembourg** Lux.
105 D2 **Luxeuil-les-Bains** France
123 C3 **Luxolweni** S. Africa
116 B2 **Luxor** Egypt
100 B2 **Luyksgestel** Neth.
86 D2 **Luza** Rus. Fed.
Luzern Switz. see Lucerne
71 A3 **Luzhou** China
154 C1 **Luziânia** Brazil
151 D2 **Luzilândia** Brazil
64 B1 **Luzon** i. Phil.
71 C3 **Luzon Strait** Phil.
90 A2 **L'viv** Ukr.
L'vov Ukr. see L'viv
88 C3 **Lyakhavichy** Belarus
92 G3 **Lycksele** Sweden
123 C2 **Lydenburg** S. Africa
88 C2 **Lyel'chytsy** Belarus
88 C3 **Lyepyel'** Belarus
99 B3 **Lyme Bay** U.K.
141 D3 **Lynchburg** U.S.A.
129 D2 **Lynn Lake** Can.
129 D1 **Lynx Lake** Can.
105 C2 **Lyon** France
89 D2 **Lyozna** Belarus
86 E3 **Lys'va** Rus. Fed.
91 D2 **Lysychans'k** Ukr.
98 B2 **Lytham St Anne's** U.K.
88 C3 **Lyuban'** Belarus
89 E2 **Lyubertsy** Rus. Fed.
90 B1 **Lyubeshiv** Ukr.
89 F2 **Lyubim** Rus. Fed.

91 D2 **Lyubotyn** Ukr.
89 D2 **Lyubytino** Rus. Fed.
89 D3 **Lyudinovo** Rus. Fed.

M

80 B2 **Ma'ān** Jordan
88 C2 **Maardu** Estonia
100 B3 **Maas** r. Neth.
100 B2 **Maaseik** Belgium
64 B1 **Maasin** Phil.
100 B2 **Maastricht** Neth.
121 C3 **Mabalane** Moz.
150 C1 **Mabaruma** Guyana
121 C3 **Mabote** Moz.
122 B2 **Mabule** Botswana
122 B1 **Mabutsane** Botswana
155 D2 **Macaé** Brazil
121 C2 **Macaloge** Moz.
126 E2 **MacAlpine Lake** Can.
71 B3 **Macao** special admin. reg.
China
151 C1 **Macapá** Brazil
150 A2 **Macará** Ecuador
155 D2 **Macarani** Brazil
Macassar Strait Indon. see
Makassar, Selat
151 E2 **Macau** Brazil
123 D1 **Maccaretane** Moz.
98 B3 **Macclesfield** U.K.
50 B2 **Macdonald, Lake** salt flat
Austr.
50 C2 **Macdonnell Ranges** mts
Austr.
130 A1 **MacDowell Lake** Can.
106 B1 **Macedo de Cavaleiros**
Port.
52 B2 **Macedon** mt. Austr.
109 D2 **Macedonia** country Europe
151 E2 **Maceió** Brazil
108 B2 **Macerata** Italy
52 A2 **Macfarlane, Lake** salt flat
Austr.
97 B3 **Macgillycuddy's Reeks**
mts Ireland
74 A2 **Mach** Pak.
155 C2 **Machado** Brazil
121 C3 **Machaila** Moz.
119 D3 **Machakos** Kenya
150 A2 **Machala** Ecuador
121 C3 **Machanga** Moz.
70 B2 **Macheng** China
141 F2 **Machias** U.S.A.
150 A1 **Machiques** Venez.
150 A3 **Machu Picchu** Peru
123 D2 **Macia** Moz.
110 C1 **Măcin** Romania
53 D1 **Macintyre** r. Austr.
51 D2 **Mackay** Austr.
50 B2 **Mackay, Lake** salt flat
Austr.
129 C1 **MacKay Lake** Can.
128 B2 **Mackenzie** Can.
128 A1 **Mackenzie** r. Can.
126 D2 **Mackenzie Bay** Can.
126 D1 **Mackenzie King Island**
Can.
128 A1 **Mackenzie Mountains**
Can.
129 D2 **Macklin** Can.
53 D2 **Macksville** Austr.
50 A2 **MacLeod, Lake** imp. l.
Austr.
140 A2 **Macomb** U.S.A.
108 A2 **Macomer** Sardinia Italy
105 C2 **Mâcon** France

143 D2 **Macon** GA U.S.A.
137 E3 **Macon** MO U.S.A.
53 C2 **Macquarie** r. Austr.
48 E6 **Macquarie Island** Austr.
53 C2 **Macquarie Marshes** Austr.
97 B3 **Macroom** Ireland
52 A1 **Macumba** watercourse
Austr.
145 C3 **Macuspana** Mex.
144 B2 **Macuzari, Presa** resr Mex.
123 D2 **Madadeni** S. Africa
121 □D3 **Madagascar** country Africa
115 D2 **Madama** Niger
111 B2 **Madan** Bulg.
59 D3 **Madang** P.N.G.
150 C2 **Madeira** r. Brazil
114 A1 **Madeira** terr.
N. Atlantic Ocean
131 D2 **Madeleine, Îles de la** is
Can.
144 B2 **Madera** Mex.
135 B3 **Madera** U.S.A.
73 B3 **Madgaon** India
118 B3 **Madingou** Congo
140 B3 **Madison** IN U.S.A.
137 D2 **Madison** SD U.S.A.
140 B2 **Madison** WI U.S.A.
140 C3 **Madison** WV U.S.A.
134 D1 **Madison** r. U.S.A.
140 B3 **Madisonville** U.S.A.
61 C2 **Madiun** Indon.
119 D2 **Mado Gashi** Kenya
68 C2 **Madoi** China
88 C2 **Madona** Latvia
78 A2 **Madrakah** Saudi Arabia
Madras India see **Chennai**
134 B2 **Madras** U.S.A.
145 C2 **Madre, Laguna** lag. Mex.
145 B3 **Madre del Sur, Sierra**
mts Mex.
144 B2 **Madre Occidental, Sierra**
mts Mex.
145 B2 **Madre Oriental, Sierra**
mts Mex.
106 C1 **Madrid** Spain
106 C2 **Madridejos** Spain
61 C2 **Madura** i. Indon.
61 C2 **Madura, Selat** sea chan.
Indon.
73 B3 **Madurai** India
67 C3 **Maebashi** Japan
62 A2 **Mae Hong Son** Thai.
62 A1 **Mae Sai** Thai.
62 A2 **Mae Sariang** Thai.
62 A2 **Mae Suai** Thai.
123 C2 **Mafeteng** Lesotho
119 D3 **Mafia Island** Tanz.
123 C2 **Mafikeng** S. Africa
119 D3 **Mafinga** Tanz.
154 C3 **Mafra** Brazil
83 L3 **Magadan** Rus. Fed.
147 C4 **Magangue** Col.
144 A1 **Magdalena** Mex.
138 B2 **Magdalena** U.S.A.
144 A2 **Magdalena, Bahía** b. Mex.
101 E1 **Magdeburg** Ger.
153 A6 **Magellan, Strait of** Chile
97 C1 **Magherafelt** U.K.
87 E3 **Magnitogorsk** Rus. Fed.
142 B2 **Magnolia** U.S.A.
131 D1 **Magpie, Lac** l. Can.
114 A3 **Magta' Lahjar** Maur.
151 D2 **Maguarinho, Cabo** c.
Brazil
123 D2 **Magude** Moz.
62 A1 **Magwe** Myanmar
81 C2 **Mahābād** Iran
74 B2 **Mahajan** India
121 □D2 **Mahajanga** Madag.
61 C2 **Mahakam** r. Indon.

123 C1 **Mahalapye** Botswana
121 □D2 **Mahalevona** Madag.
75 C2 **Mahanadi** r. India
121 □D2 **Mahanoro** Madag.
63 B2 **Maha Sarakham** Thai.
121 □D2 **Mahavavy** r. Madag.
78 B2 **Mahd adh Dhahab**
Saudi Arabia
150 C1 **Mahdia** Guyana
113 K7 **Mahé** i. Seychelles
74 B2 **Mahesana** India
74 B2 **Mahi** r. India
54 C1 **Mahia Peninsula** N.Z.
89 D3 **Mahilyow** Belarus
107 D2 **Mahón** Spain
74 B2 **Mahuva** India
110 C2 **Mahya Daği** mt. Turkey
129 D2 **Maidstone** Can.
99 D4 **Maidstone** U.K.
115 D3 **Maiduguri** Nigeria
75 C2 **Mailani** India
101 D2 **Main** r. Ger.
118 B3 **Mai-Ndombe, Lac** l.
Dem. Rep. Congo
101 E3 **Main-Donau-Kanal**
canal Ger.
141 F1 **Maine** state U.S.A.
62 A1 **Maingkwan** Myanmar
96 C1 **Mainland** i. Scotland U.K.
96 □ **Mainland** i. Scotland U.K.
121 □D2 **Maintirano** Madag.
101 D2 **Mainz** Ger.
150 B1 **Maiquetía** Venez.
53 D2 **Maitland** N.S.W. Austr.
52 A2 **Maitland** S.A. Austr.
146 B3 **Maíz, Islas del** is Nic.
67 C3 **Maizuru** Japan
109 C2 **Maja Jezercë** mt. Albania
61 C2 **Majene** Indon.
107 C2 **Majorca** i. Spain
48 F2 **Majuro** i. Marshall Is
123 C2 **Majwemasweu** S. Africa
118 B3 **Makabana** Congo
58 B3 **Makale** Indon.
77 E2 **Makanchi** Kazakh.
109 C2 **Makarska** Croatia
58 B3 **Makassar** Indon.
61 C2 **Makassar, Selat** str. Indon.
76 B2 **Makat** Kazakh.
123 D2 **Makatini Flats** lowland
S. Africa
114 A4 **Makeni** Sierra Leone
120 B3 **Makgadikgadi** salt pan
Botswana
87 D4 **Makhachkala** Rus. Fed.
123 C1 **Makhado** S. Africa
76 B2 **Makhambet** Kazakh.
119 D3 **Makindu** Kenya
77 D1 **Makinsk** Kazakh.
91 D2 **Makiyivka** Ukr.
Makkah Saudi Arabia see
Mecca
131 E1 **Makkovik** Can.
103 E2 **Makó** Hungary
118 B2 **Makokou** Gabon
119 D3 **Makongolosi** Tanz.
122 B2 **Makopong** Botswana
79 D2 **Makran** reg. Iran/Pak.
74 A2 **Makran Coast Range**
mts Pak.
89 E2 **Maksatikha** Rus. Fed.
81 C2 **Mākū** Iran
62 A1 **Makum** India
67 B4 **Makurazaki** Japan
115 C4 **Makurdi** Nigeria
92 G2 **Malå** Sweden
146 B4 **Mala, Punta** pt Panama
118 A2 **Malabo** Equat. Guinea
60 A1 **Malacca, Strait of**
Indon./Malaysia

134 D2   **Malad** U.S.A.
88 C3   **Maladzyechna** Belarus
106 C2   **Málaga** Spain
48 E3   **Malaita** *i.* Solomon Is
117 B4   **Malakal** Sudan
48 F4   **Malakula** *i.* Vanuatu
61 C2   **Malang** Indon.
120 A1   **Malanje** Angola
93 G4   **Mälaren** *l.* Sweden
153 B4   **Malargüe** Arg.
80 B2   **Malatya** Turkey
121 C2   **Malawi** *country* Africa
        Malawi, Lake Africa *see*
        Nyasa, Lake
89 D3   **Malaya Vishera** Rus. Fed.
64 B2   **Malaybalay** Phil.
81 C2   **Malāyer** Iran
60 B1   **Malaysia** *country* Asia
81 C2   **Malazgirt** Turkey
103 D1   **Malbork** Pol.
101 F1   **Malchin** Ger.
100 A2   **Maldegem** Belgium
49 H3   **Malden Island** Kiribati
56 G6   **Maldives** *country*
        Indian Ocean
153 C4   **Maldonado** Uru.
56 G6   **Male** Maldives
111 B3   **Maleas, Akra** *pt* Greece
103 D2   **Malé Karpaty** *hills* Slovakia
134 C2   **Malheur Lake** U.S.A.
114 B3   **Mali** *country* Africa
114 A3   **Mali** Guinea
58 C3   **Malili** Indon.
119 E3   **Malindi** Kenya
97 C1   **Malin Head** Ireland
97 B1   **Malin More** Ireland
111 C2   **Malkara** Turkey
88 C3   **Mal'kavichy** Belarus
110 C2   **Malko Tŭrnovo** Bulg.
53 C3   **Mallacoota** Austr.
53 C3   **Mallacoota Inlet** *b.* Austr.
96 B2   **Mallaig** U.K.
129 C2   **Mallery Lake** Can.
        Mallorca *i.* Spain *see*
        Majorca
97 C2   **Mallow** Ireland
92 H2   **Malmberget** Sweden
100 C2   **Malmédy** Belgium
122 A3   **Malmesbury** S. Africa
93 F4   **Malmö** Sweden
62 B1   **Malong** China
118 C4   **Malonga** Dem. Rep. Congo
93 E3   **Måløy** Norway
89 E2   **Maloyaroslavets** Rus. Fed.
89 E2   **Maloye Borisovo** Rus. Fed.
85 H5   **Malta** *country* Europe
88 C2   **Malta** Latvia
134 E1   **Malta** U.S.A.
122 A1   **Maltahöhe** Namibia
98 C1   **Malton** U.K.
        Maluku *is* Indon. *see*
        Moluccas
59 C3   **Maluku, Laut** *sea* Indon.
93 F3   **Malung** Sweden
123 C2   **Maluti Mountains** Lesotho
73 B3   **Malvan** India
142 B2   **Malvern** U.S.A.
90 B1   **Malyn** Ukr.
83 L2   **Malyy Anyuy** *r.* Rus. Fed.
83 K2   **Malyy Lyakhovskiy, Ostrov**
        i. Rus. Fed.
123 C2   **Mamafubedu** S. Africa
119 C2   **Mambasa**
        Dem. Rep. Congo
118 B2   **Mambéré** *r.* C.A.R.
123 C2   **Mamelodi** S. Africa
150 B3   **Mamoré** *r.* Bol./Brazil
114 A3   **Mamou** Guinea
61 C2   **Mamuju** Indon.
114 B4   **Man** Côte d'Ivoire

150 B2   **Manacapuru** Brazil
107 D2   **Manacor** Spain
59 C2   **Manado** Indon.
146 B3   **Managua** Nic.
121 □D3   **Manakara** Madag.
78 B3   **Manākhah** Yemen
79 C2   **Manama** Bahrain
59 D3   **Manam Island** P.N.G.
121 □D3   **Mananara** *r.* Madag.
121 □D2   **Mananara Avaratra**
        Madag.
121 □D3   **Mananjary** Madag.
114 A3   **Manantali, Lac de** *l.* Mali
77 E2   **Manas Hu** *l.* China
59 C3   **Manatuto** East Timor
62 A2   **Man-aung Kyun** *i.*
        Myanmar
150 B2   **Manaus** Brazil
80 B2   **Manavgat** Turkey
98 B2   **Manchester** U.K.
141 E2   **Manchester** U.S.A.
121 □D3   **Mandabe** Madag.
93 E4   **Mandal** Norway
59 D3   **Mandala, Puncak** *mt.*
        Indon.
62 A1   **Mandalay** Myanmar
69 D1   **Mandalgovĭ** Mongolia
136 C1   **Mandan** U.S.A.
118 B1   **Mandara Mountains**
        Cameroon/Nigeria
108 A3   **Mandas** *Sardinia* Italy
100 C2   **Manderscheid** Ger.
74 B1   **Mandi** India
114 B3   **Mandiana** Guinea
74 B1   **Mandi Burewala** Pak.
75 C2   **Mandla** India
121 □D2   **Mandritsara** Madag.
74 B2   **Mandsaur** India
50 A3   **Mandurah** Austr.
73 B3   **Mandya** India
108 B1   **Manerbio** Italy
90 B1   **Manevychi** Ukr.
109 C2   **Manfredonia** Italy
114 B3   **Manga** Burkina
118 B3   **Mangai** Dem. Rep. Congo
54 C1   **Mangakino** N.Z.
110 C2   **Mangalia** Romania
73 B3   **Mangalore** India
123 C2   **Mangaung** S. Africa
61 B2   **Manggar** Indon.
68 C2   **Mangnai** China
121 C2   **Mangochi** Malawi
59 C3   **Mangole** *i.* Indon.
154 B3   **Mangueirinha** Brazil
69 E1   **Mangui** China
76 B2   **Mangystau** Kazakh.
137 D3   **Manhattan** U.S.A.
121 C3   **Manhica** Moz.
155 D2   **Manhuaçu** Brazil
121 □D2   **Mania** *r.* Madag.
108 B1   **Maniago** Italy
150 B2   **Manicoré** Brazil
131 D2   **Manicouagan** *r.* Can.
131 D1   **Manicouagan, Réservoir**
        resr Can.
79 B2   **Manifah** Saudi Arabia
64 B1   **Manila** Phil.
53 D2   **Manilla** Austr.
111 C3   **Manisa** Turkey
140 B2   **Manistee** U.S.A.
129 E2   **Manitoba** *prov.* Can.
129 E2   **Manitoba, Lake** Can.
140 B1   **Manitou Islands** U.S.A.
130 B3   **Manitoulin Island** Can.
140 B2   **Manitowoc** U.S.A.
130 C2   **Maniwaki** Can.
150 A1   **Manizales** Col.
137 E2   **Mankato** U.S.A.
114 B4   **Mankono** Côte d'Ivoire
129 D3   **Mankota** Can.

73 C4   **Mankulam** Sri Lanka
74 B2   **Manmad** India
73 B4   **Mannar, Gulf of**
        India/Sri Lanka
101 D3   **Mannheim** Ger.
126 C2   **Manning** Can.
52 A2   **Mannum** Austr.
129 C2   **Mannville** Can.
59 C3   **Manokwari** Indon.
119 C3   **Manono** Dem. Rep. Congo
63 A2   **Manoron** Myanmar
105 D3   **Manosque** France
131 C1   **Manouane, Lac** *l.* Can.
107 D1   **Manresa** Spain
121 B2   **Mansa** Zambia
127 F2   **Mansel Island** Can.
92 I2   **Mansel'ky'a** *ridge*
        Fin./Rus. Fed.
53 C3   **Mansfield** Austr.
98 C2   **Mansfield** U.K.
142 B2   **Mansfield** *LA* U.S.A.
140 C2   **Mansfield** *OH* U.S.A.
141 D2   **Mansfield** *PA* U.S.A.
150 A2   **Manta** Ecuador
143 E1   **Manteo** U.S.A.
104 C2   **Mantes-la-Jolie** France
155 C2   **Mantiqueira, Serra da**
        mts Brazil
        Mantova Italy *see* Mantua
108 B1   **Mantua** Italy
151 C2   **Manuelzinho** Brazil
59 C3   **Manui** *i.* Indon.
54 B1   **Manukau** N.Z.
142 B2   **Many** U.S.A.
87 D4   **Manych-Gudilo, Ozero** *l.*
        Rus. Fed.
119 D3   **Manyoni** Tanz.
106 C2   **Manzanares** Spain
144 B3   **Manzanillo** Mex.
69 D1   **Manzhouli** China
123 D2   **Manzini** Swaziland
115 D3   **Mao** Chad
59 D3   **Maoke, Pegunungan**
        mts Indon.
123 C2   **Maokeng** S. Africa
65 A1   **Maokui Shan** *mt.* China
71 B3   **Maoming** China
121 C3   **Mapai** Moz.
75 C1   **Mapam Yumco** *l.* China
145 C3   **Mapastepec** Mex.
144 B2   **Mapimí** Mex.
144 B2   **Mapimí, Bolsón de** *des.*
        Mex.
121 C3   **Mapinhane** Moz.
129 D3   **Maple Creek** Can.
121 C3   **Maputo** Moz.
123 D2   **Maputo** *r.* Moz./S. Africa
75 C2   **Maquan He** *r.* China
120 A1   **Maquela do Zombo** Angola
153 B5   **Maquinchao** Arg.
137 E2   **Maquoketa** U.S.A.
150 B2   **Maraã** Brazil
151 D2   **Maraba** Brazil
151 C1   **Maracá, Ilha de** *i.* Brazil
150 A1   **Maracaibo** Venez.
150 A1   **Maracaibo, Lake** Venez.
152 C3   **Maracaju, Serra de** *hills*
        Brazil
150 B1   **Maracay** Venez.
115 C2   **Marādah** Libya
115 C3   **Maradi** Niger
81 C2   **Marāgheh** Iran
151 D2   **Marajó, Baía de** *est.* Brazil
151 C2   **Marajó, Ilha de** *i.* Brazil
79 C2   **Marākī** Iran
119 D2   **Maralal** Kenya
50 C3   **Maralinga** Austr.
81 C2   **Marand** Iran
150 A2   **Marañón** *r.* Peru
130 B2   **Marathon** Can.

143 D4 **Marathon** U.S.A.
106 C2 **Marbella** Spain
50 A2 **Marble Bar** Austr.
123 C1 **Marble Hall** S. Africa
123 D3 **Marburg** S. Africa
101 D2 **Marburg an der Lahn** Ger.
99 D2 **March** U.K.
100 B2 **Marche-en-Famenne** Belgium
106 D3 **Marchena** Spain
152 B4 **Mar Chiquita, Laguna** *l.* Arg.
141 E2 **Marcy, Mount** U.S.A.
74 B1 **Mardan** Pak.
153 C4 **Mar del Plata** Arg.
81 C2 **Mardin** Turkey
96 B2 **Maree, Loch** *l.* U.K.
108 B3 **Marettimo, Isola** *i.* Sicily Italy
89 D2 **Marevo** Rus. Fed.
138 C2 **Marfa** U.S.A.
50 A3 **Margaret River** Austr.
147 D3 **Margarita, Isla de** *i.* Venez.
123 D3 **Margate** S. Africa
99 D3 **Margate** U.K.
119 C2 **Margherita Peak** Dem. Rep. Congo/Uganda
76 C3 **Mārgow, Dasht-e** *des.* Afgh.
91 C2 **Marhanets'** Ukr.
62 A1 **Mari** Myanmar
152 B3 **Maria Elena** Chile
156 C5 **Mariana Trench** *sea feature* N. Pacific Ocean
142 B2 **Marianna** *AR* U.S.A.
143 C2 **Marianna** *FL* U.S.A.
102 C2 **Mariánské Lázně** Czech Rep.
144 B2 **Marías, Islas** *is* Mex.
78 B3 **Ma'rib** Yemen
109 C1 **Maribor** Slovenia
117 A4 **Maridi** *watercourse* Sudan
55 M2 **Marie Byrd Land** *reg.* Antarctica
147 D3 **Marie-Galante** *i.* Guadeloupe
93 G3 **Mariehamn** Fin.
122 A1 **Mariental** Namibia
93 F4 **Mariestad** Sweden
143 D2 **Marietta** *GA* U.S.A.
140 C3 **Marietta** *OH* U.S.A.
105 C3 **Marignane** France
83 K3 **Marii, Mys** *pt* Rus. Fed.
88 B3 **Marijampolė** Lith.
154 C2 **Marília** Brazil
106 B1 **Marín** Spain
109 C3 **Marina di Gioiosa Ionica** Italy
88 B3 **Mar"ina Horka** Belarus
140 B1 **Marinette** U.S.A.
154 B2 **Maringá** Brazil
106 B2 **Marinha Grande** Port.
140 B2 **Marion** *IN* U.S.A.
140 C2 **Marion** *OH* U.S.A.
143 E2 **Marion** *SC* U.S.A.
140 C3 **Marion** *VA* U.S.A.
143 D2 **Marion, Lake** U.S.A.
52 A3 **Marion Bay** Austr.
152 B3 **Mariscal José Félix Estigarribia** Para.
110 C2 **Maritsa** *r.* Bulg.
91 D2 **Mariupol'** Ukr.
117 C4 **Marka** Somalia
123 C1 **Marken** S. Africa
100 B1 **Markermeer** *l.* Neth.
83 I2 **Markha** *r.* Rus. Fed.
91 D1 **Markivka** Ukr.
142 B2 **Marksville** U.S.A.
101 D3 **Marktheidenfeld** Ger.
101 F2 **Marktredwitz** Ger.

100 C2 **Marl** Ger.
100 A3 **Marle** France
139 D2 **Marlin** U.S.A.
104 C3 **Marmande** France
111 C2 **Marmara** *Sea of g.* Turkey **Marmara Denizi** *g.* Turkey *see* **Marmara, Sea of**
111 C3 **Marmaris** Turkey
104 C2 **Marne-la-Vallée** France
121 ☐D2 **Maroantsetra** Madag.
101 E2 **Maroldsweisach** Ger.
121 ☐D2 **Maromokotro** *mt.* Madag.
121 C2 **Marondera** Zimbabwe
151 C1 **Maroni** *r.* Fr. Guiana
118 B1 **Maroua** Cameroon
121 ☐D2 **Marovoay** Madag.
49 I3 **Marquesas Islands** Fr. Polynesia
140 B1 **Marquette** U.S.A.
117 A3 **Marra, Jebel** *mt.* Sudan
123 D2 **Marracuene** Moz.
114 B1 **Marrakech** Morocco
52 A1 **Marree** Austr.
86 F2 **Marresale** Rus. Fed.
121 C2 **Marromeu** Moz.
121 C2 **Marrupa** Moz.
116 B2 **Marsá al 'Alam** Egypt
115 D1 **Marsa al Burayqah** Libya
119 D2 **Marsabit** Kenya
108 B3 **Marsala** *Sicily* Italy
116 A1 **Marsá Maṭrūḥ** Egypt
101 D2 **Marsberg** Ger.
108 B2 **Marsciano** Italy
53 C2 **Marsden** Austr.
105 D3 **Marseille** France
137 D2 **Marshall** *MN* U.S.A.
137 E3 **Marshall** *MO* U.S.A.
139 E2 **Marshall** *TX* U.S.A.
48 H2 **Marshall Islands** *country* N. Pacific Ocean
137 E2 **Marshalltown** U.S.A.
140 A2 **Marshfield** U.S.A.
143 E3 **Marsh Harbour** Bahamas
142 B3 **Marsh Island** U.S.A.
88 A2 **Märsta** Sweden
61 C2 **Martapura** *Kalimantan Selatan* Indon.
60 B2 **Martapura** *Sumatera* Indon.
141 E2 **Martha's Vineyard** *i.* U.S.A.
105 D2 **Martigny** Switz.
103 D2 **Martin** Slovakia
136 C2 **Martin** U.S.A.
145 C2 **Martínez** Mex.
147 D3 **Martinique** *terr.* West Indies
141 D3 **Martinsburg** U.S.A.
140 C3 **Martinsville** U.S.A.
54 C2 **Marton** N.Z.
107 D1 **Martorell** Spain
106 C2 **Martos** Spain
128 C1 **Martre, Lac la** *l.* Can.
76 B1 **Martuk** Kazakh.
105 C3 **Marvejols** France
76 C3 **Mary** Turkm.
51 E2 **Maryborough** Austr.
122 B2 **Marydale** S. Africa
141 D3 **Maryland** *state* U.S.A.
137 D3 **Marysville** U.S.A.
137 E2 **Maryville** *MO* U.S.A.
143 D1 **Maryville** *TN* U.S.A.
119 D3 **Masai Steppe** *plain* Tanz.
119 D3 **Masaka** Uganda
65 B2 **Masan** S. Korea
119 D4 **Masasi** Tanz.
64 B1 **Masbate** Phil.
64 B1 **Masbate** *i.* Phil.
123 C2 **Maseru** Lesotho
76 B3 **Mashhad** Iran
122 B3 **Masibambane** S. Africa
79 C3 **Masilah, Wādī al** *watercourse* Yemen

123 C2 **Masilo** S. Africa
119 D2 **Masindi** Uganda
79 C2 **Maṣīrah** *i.* Oman
79 C3 **Maṣīrah, Khalīj** *b.* Oman
81 C2 **Masjed Soleymān** Iran
97 B2 **Mask, Lough** *l.* Ireland
121 ☐E2 **Masoala, Tanjona** *c.* Madag.
137 E2 **Mason City** U.S.A.
Masqaṭ Oman *see* **Muscat**
108 B2 **Massa** Italy
141 E2 **Massachusetts** *state* U.S.A.
141 E2 **Massachusetts Bay** U.S.A.
121 C3 **Massangena** Moz.
120 A1 **Massango** Angola
116 B3 **Massawa** Eritrea
141 E2 **Massena** U.S.A.
128 A2 **Masset** Can.
105 C2 **Massif Central** *mts* France
140 C2 **Massillon** U.S.A.
114 B3 **Massina** Mali
121 C3 **Massinga** Moz.
123 D1 **Massingir** Moz.
78 A2 **Masṭābah** Saudi Arabia
54 C2 **Masterton** N.Z.
74 A2 **Mastung** Pak.
78 A2 **Mastūrah** Saudi Arabia
88 B3 **Masty** Belarus
67 B4 **Masuda** Japan
Masuku Gabon *see* **Franceville**
121 C3 **Masvingo** Zimbabwe
118 B3 **Matadi** Dem. Rep. Congo
146 B3 **Matagalpa** Nic.
130 C2 **Matagami** Can.
130 C2 **Matagami, Lac** *l.* Can.
139 D3 **Matagorda Island** U.S.A.
120 A2 **Matala** Angola
114 A3 **Matam** Senegal
144 B2 **Matamoros** *Coahuila* Mex.
145 C2 **Matamoros** *Tamaulipas* Mex.
119 D3 **Matandu** *r.* Tanz.
131 D2 **Matane** Can.
146 B2 **Matanzas** Cuba
73 C4 **Matara** Sri Lanka
61 C2 **Mataram** Indon.
50 C1 **Mataranka** Austr.
107 D1 **Mataró** Spain
123 C3 **Matatiele** S. Africa
54 A3 **Mataura** N.Z.
49 G3 **Matā'utu** Wallis and Futuna Is
54 C1 **Matawai** N.Z.
152 B2 **Mategua** Bol.
145 B2 **Matehuala** Mex.
109 C3 **Matera** Italy
139 D3 **Mathis** U.S.A.
75 B2 **Mathura** India
64 B2 **Mati** Phil.
98 C3 **Matlock** U.K.
150 C3 **Mato Grosso** Brazil
154 B1 **Mato Grosso, Planalto do** *plat.* Brazil
123 D2 **Matola** Moz.
Matou China *see* **Pingguo**
67 B3 **Matsue** Japan
66 D2 **Matsumae** Japan
67 C4 **Matsusaka** Japan
71 C3 **Matsu Tao** *i.* Taiwan
67 B4 **Matsuyama** Japan
130 B1 **Mattagami** *r.* Can.
105 D2 **Matterhorn** *mt.* Italy/Switz.
134 C2 **Matterhorn** *mt.* U.S.A.
140 B3 **Mattoon** U.S.A.
150 B1 **Maturín** Venez.
123 C2 **Matwabeng** S. Africa
100 A2 **Maubeuge** France
104 C3 **Maubourguet** France

124 E5 **Maui** i. N. Pacific Ocean
140 C2 **Maumee** r. U.S.A.
120 B2 **Maun** Botswana
62 A1 **Maungdaw** Myanmar
50 C2 **Maurice, Lake** salt flat
Austr.
114 A3 **Mauritania** country Africa
113 K9 **Mauritius** country
Indian Ocean
78 B3 **Mäwän, Khashm** hill
Saudi Arabia
118 B3 **Mawanga**
Dem. Rep. Congo
71 B3 **Mawei** China
62 A1 **Mawkmai** Myanmar
62 A1 **Mawlaik** Myanmar
63 A2 **Mawlamyaing** Myanmar
78 B2 **Mawqaq** Saudi Arabia
78 B3 **Mawza** Yemen
108 A3 **Maxia, Punta** mt. Sardinia
Italy
83 J2 **Maya** r. Rus. Fed.
147 C2 **Mayaguana** i. Bahamas
96 B3 **Maybole** U.K.
104 B2 **Mayenne** France
104 B2 **Mayenne** r. France
128 C2 **Mayerthorpe** Can.
140 B3 **Mayfield** U.S.A.
87 D4 **Maykop** Rus. Fed.
126 B2 **Mayo** Can.
118 B3 **Mayoko** Congo
121 D2 **Mayotte** terr. Africa
83 J3 **Mayskiy** Rus. Fed.
140 C3 **Maysville** U.S.A.
118 B3 **Mazabuka** Zambia
137 D1 **Mayville** U.S.A.
151 C2 **Mazagão** Brazil
104 C3 **Mazamet** France
77 D3 **Mazar** China
108 B3 **Mazara del Vallo**
Sicily Italy
77 C3 **Mazār-e Sharīf** Afgh.
144 A2 **Mazatán** Mex.
146 A3 **Mazatenango** Guat.
144 B2 **Mazatlán** Mex.
88 B2 **Mažeikiai** Lith.
88 B2 **Mazirbe** Latvia
121 B3 **Mazunga** Zimbabwe
88 C3 **Mazyr** Belarus
123 D2 **Mbabane** Swaziland
118 B2 **Mbaïki** C.A.R.
121 C1 **Mbala** Zambia
119 D2 **Mbale** Uganda
118 B2 **Mbalmayo** Cameroon
118 B3 **Mbandaka**
Dem. Rep. Congo
118 A2 **Mbanga** Cameroon
120 A1 **M'banza Congo** Angola
119 D3 **Mbeya** Tanz.
119 D4 **Mbinga** Tanz.
118 B3 **Mbomo** Congo
118 B2 **Mbouda** Cameroon
114 A3 **Mbour** Senegal
114 A3 **Mbout** Maur.
118 C3 **Mbuji-Mayi**
Dem. Rep. Congo
119 D3 **Mbuyuni** Tanz.
139 D2 **McAlester** U.S.A.
139 D3 **McAllen** U.S.A.
128 C2 **McBride** Can.
134 C2 **McCall** U.S.A.
126 E2 **McClintock Channel** Can.
126 D2 **McClure Strait** Can.
142 B2 **McComb** U.S.A.
136 C2 **McConaughy, Lake** U.S.A.
136 C2 **McCook** U.S.A.
134 C2 **McDermitt** U.S.A.
134 D1 **McDonald Peak** U.S.A.
134 D1 **McGuire, Mount** U.S.A.
128 C2 **McLennan** Can.

128 B2 **McLeod Lake** Can.
134 B1 **McMinnville** OR U.S.A.
142 C1 **McMinnville** TN U.S.A.
137 D3 **McPherson** U.S.A.
123 C3 **Mdantsane** S. Africa
135 D3 **Mead, Lake** resr U.S.A.
129 D2 **Meadow Lake** Can.
140 C2 **Meadville** U.S.A.
66 D2 **Meaken-dake** vol. Japan
106 B1 **Mealhada** Port.
131 E1 **Mealy Mountains** Can.
128 C2 **Meander River** Can.
78 A2 **Mecca** Saudi Arabia
100 B2 **Mechelen** Belgium
100 B2 **Mechelen** Neth.
100 C2 **Mechernich** Ger.
100 C2 **Meckenheim** Ger.
106 B1 **Meda** Port.
60 A1 **Medan** Indon.
153 B5 **Medanosa, Punta** pt Arg.
73 C4 **Medawachchiya** Sri Lanka
107 D2 **Médéa** Alg.
150 A1 **Medellín** Col.
115 D1 **Medenine** Tunisia
134 B2 **Medford** U.S.A.
110 C2 **Medgidia** Romania
110 B1 **Mediaş** Romania
136 B2 **Medicine Bow Mountains**
U.S.A.
136 B2 **Medicine Bow Peak** U.S.A.
129 C2 **Medicine Hat** Can.
137 D3 **Medicine Lodge** U.S.A.
155 D1 **Medina** Brazil
78 A2 **Medina** Saudi Arabia
106 C1 **Medinaceli** Spain
106 C1 **Medina del Campo** Spain
84 G5 **Medina de Rioseco** Spain
129 C2 **Medley** Can.
87 E3 **Mednogorsk** Rus. Fed.
83 L2 **Medvezh'i, Ostrova** is
Rus. Fed.
86 C2 **Medvezh'yegorsk**
Rus. Fed.
50 A2 **Meekatharra** Austr.
136 B2 **Meeker** U.S.A.
75 B2 **Meerut** India
100 A2 **Meetkerke** Belgium
111 B3 **Megalopoli** Greece
75 C2 **Meghasani** mt. India
80 A2 **Megisti** i. Greece
92 I1 **Mehamn** Norway
50 A2 **Meharry, Mount** Austr.
79 C2 **Mehrān** watercourse Iran
154 C1 **Meia Ponte** r. Brazil
118 B2 **Meiganga** Cameroon
65 B1 **Meihekou** China
Meijiang China see **Ningdu**
62 A1 **Meiktila** Myanmar
101 E2 **Meiningen** Ger.
102 C1 **Meißen** Ger.
71 B3 **Meizhou** China
152 B3 **Mejicana** mt. Arg.
152 A3 **Mejillones** Chile
117 B3 **Mek'elē** Eth.
114 C2 **Mekerrhane, Sebkha**
salt pan Alg.
114 B1 **Meknès** Morocco
63 B2 **Mekong** r. Asia
63 B3 **Mekong, Mouths of the**
Vietnam
60 B1 **Melaka** Malaysia
53 B3 **Melbourne** Austr.
143 D3 **Melbourne** U.S.A.
108 A2 **Mele, Capo** c. Italy
59 C2 **Melekeok** Palau
131 C1 **Mélèzes, Rivière aux**
Can.
115 D3 **Melfi** Chad
109 C2 **Melfi** Italy

129 D2 **Melfort** Can.
92 F3 **Melhus** Norway
106 B1 **Melide** Spain
114 B1 **Melilla** N. Africa
91 D2 **Melitopol'** Ukr.
101 D1 **Melle** Ger.
93 F4 **Mellerud** Sweden
101 E2 **Mellrichstadt** Ger.
100 D1 **Mellum** i. Ger.
152 C4 **Melo** Uru.
115 C1 **Melrhir, Chott** salt l. Alg.
99 C2 **Melton Mowbray** U.K.
104 C2 **Melun** France
129 D2 **Melville** Can.
51 D1 **Melville, Cape** Austr.
131 E1 **Melville, Lake** Can.
50 C1 **Melville Island** Austr.
126 D1 **Melville Island** Can.
127 F2 **Melville Peninsula** Can.
102 C2 **Memmingen** Ger.
61 B1 **Mempawah** Indon.
80 B3 **Memphis** tourist site Egypt
142 B1 **Memphis** TN U.S.A.
139 C2 **Memphis** TX U.S.A.
91 C1 **Mena** Ukr.
142 B2 **Mena** U.S.A.
114 C3 **Ménaka** Mali
Mènam Khong r. Laos/Thai.
see **Mekong**
105 C3 **Mende** France
116 B3 **Mendefera** Eritrea
145 C2 **Méndez** Mex.
119 D2 **Mendī** Eth.
59 D3 **Mendi** P.N.G.
99 B3 **Mendip Hills** U.K.
152 B4 **Mendoza** Arg.
111 C3 **Menemen** Turkey
60 B2 **Menggala** Indon.
62 B1 **Mengzi** China
131 D1 **Menihek** Can.
52 B2 **Menindee** Austr.
52 B2 **Menindee Lake** Austr.
52 A3 **Meningie** Austr.
104 C2 **Mennecy** France
140 B1 **Menominee** U.S.A.
120 A2 **Menongue** Angola
Menorca i. Spain see
Minorca
60 A2 **Mentawai, Kepulauan**
is Indon.
60 B2 **Mentok** Indon.
50 B2 **Menzies** Austr.
100 C1 **Meppel** Neth.
100 C1 **Meppen** Ger.
123 D1 **Mepuze** Moz.
123 C2 **Meqheleng** S. Africa
108 B1 **Merano** Italy
59 D3 **Merauke** Indon.
52 B2 **Merbein** Austr.
135 B3 **Merced** U.S.A.
152 C3 **Mercedes** Arg.
127 G2 **Mercy, Cape** Can.
139 C1 **Meredith, Lake** U.S.A.
91 D2 **Merefa** Ukr.
116 A3 **Merga Oasis** Sudan
63 A2 **Mergui Archipelago** is
Myanmar
110 C2 **Meriç** r. Greece/Turkey
145 D2 **Mérida** Mex.
106 B2 **Mérida** Spain
150 A1 **Mérida** Venez.
142 C2 **Meridian** U.S.A.
53 C3 **Merimbula** Austr.
116 B3 **Merowe** Sudan
50 A3 **Merredin** Austr.
96 B3 **Merrick** hill U.K.
140 B1 **Merrill** U.S.A.
140 B2 **Merrillville** U.S.A.
128 B2 **Merritt** Can.
53 C2 **Merrygoen** Austr.

116 C3 **Mersa Fatma** Eritrea
100 C3 **Mersch** Lux.
101 E2 **Merseburg (Saale)** Ger.
98 B2 **Mersey** r. U.K.
80 B2 **Mersin** Turkey
60 B1 **Mersing** Malaysia
99 D3 **Mers-les-Bains** France
74 B2 **Merta** India
99 B3 **Merthyr Tydfil** U.K.
106 B2 **Mértola** Port.
119 D3 **Meru** vol. Tanz.
100 C3 **Merzig** Ger.
138 A2 **Mesa** U.S.A.
109 C2 **Mesagne** Italy
101 D2 **Meschede** Ger.
87 E2 **Meshchovsk** Rus. Fed.
91 E2 **Meshkovskaya** Rus. Fed.
111 B2 **Mesimeri** Greece
111 B3 **Mesolongi** Greece
121 D2 **Messalo** r. Moz.
109 C3 **Messina** Sicily Italy
109 C3 **Messina, Strait of** Italy
111 B3 **Messiniakos Kolpos** b. Greece
110 B2 **Mesta** r. Bulg.
150 B1 **Meta** r. Col./Venez.
127 G2 **Meta Incognita Peninsula** Can.
152 B3 **Metán** Arg.
111 B3 **Methoni** Greece
109 C2 **Metković** Croatia
60 D2 **Metro** Indon.
117 B4 **Metu** Eth.
105 D2 **Metz** France
100 B2 **Meuse** r. Belgium/France
139 D2 **Mexia** U.S.A.
144 A1 **Mexicali** Mex.
144 B2 **Mexico** country Central America
137 E3 **Mexico** U.S.A.
125 I5 **Mexico, Gulf of** Mex./U.S.A.
145 C3 **Mexico City** Mex.
101 F1 **Meyenburg** Ger.
76 C3 **Meymaneh** Afgh.
86 D2 **Mezen'** Rus. Fed.
86 D2 **Mezen'** r. Rus. Fed.
86 E1 **Mezhdusharskiy, Ostrov** i. Rus. Fed.
103 E2 **Mezőtúr** Hungary
144 B2 **Mezquitic** Mex.
88 C2 **Mežvidi** Latvia
121 C2 **Mfuwe** Zambia
123 D2 **Mhlume** Swaziland
74 B2 **Mhow** India
145 C3 **Miahuatlán** Mex.
106 B2 **Miajadas** Spain
143 D3 **Miami** FL U.S.A.
139 E1 **Miami** OK U.S.A.
143 D3 **Miami Beach** U.S.A.
81 C2 **Miandowāb** Iran
121 □D2 **Miandrivazo** Madag.
81 C2 **Mīāneh** Iran
74 B1 **Mianwali** Pak.
70 A2 **Mianyang** China
121 □D2 **Miarinarivo** Madag.
87 F3 **Miass** Rus. Fed.
128 C2 **Mica Creek** Can.
103 E2 **Michalovce** Slovakia
140 B1 **Michigan** state U.S.A.
140 B2 **Michigan, Lake** U.S.A.
140 B2 **Michigan City** U.S.A.
130 B2 **Michipicoten Island** Can.
130 B2 **Michipicoten River** Can.
89 F3 **Michurinsk** Rus. Fed.
48 D2 **Micronesia, Federated States of** country N. Pacific Ocean
100 A2 **Middelburg** Neth.
123 C3 **Middelburg** E. Cape S. Africa

123 C2 **Middelburg** Mpumalanga S. Africa
100 B2 **Middelharnis** Neth.
134 B2 **Middle Alkali Lake** U.S.A.
73 D3 **Middle Andaman** i. India
136 D2 **Middle Loup** r. U.S.A.
140 C3 **Middlesboro** U.S.A.
98 C1 **Middlesbrough** U.K.
141 E2 **Middletown** NY U.S.A.
140 C3 **Middletown** OH U.S.A.
78 B3 **Midi** Yemen
130 C2 **Midland** Can.
140 C2 **Midland** MI U.S.A.
139 C2 **Midland** TX U.S.A.
97 B3 **Midleton** Ireland
94 B1 **Miðvágur** Faroe Is
109 D2 **Midzhur** mt. Bulg./Serb. and Mont.
103 E1 **Mielec** Pol.
110 C1 **Miercurea-Ciuc** Romania
106 B1 **Mieres** Spain
101 E1 **Mieste** Ger.
75 D1 **Migriggyangzham Co** l. China
145 C3 **Miguel Alemán, Presa** resr Mex.
144 B2 **Miguel Auza** Mex.
144 B2 **Miguel Hidalgo, Presa** resr Mex.
63 A2 **Migyaunglaung** Myanmar
89 E3 **Mikhaylov** Rus. Fed.
Mikhaylovgrad Bulg. see Montana
66 B2 **Mikhaylovka** Rus. Fed.
77 D1 **Mikhaylovskiy** Rus. Fed.
93 I3 **Mikkeli** Fin.
86 E2 **Mikun'** Rus. Fed.
67 C3 **Mikuni-sanmyaku** mts Japan
108 A1 **Milan** Italy
121 C2 **Milange** Moz.
Milano Italy see **Milan**
111 C3 **Milas** Turkey
137 D1 **Milbank** U.S.A.
99 D2 **Mildenhall** U.K.
52 B2 **Mildura** Austr.
62 B1 **Mile** China
136 B1 **Miles City** U.S.A.
141 D3 **Milford** DE U.S.A.
135 D3 **Milford** UT U.S.A.
99 A3 **Milford Haven** U.K.
54 A2 **Milford Sound** N.Z.
107 D2 **Miliana** Alg.
116 B3 **Milk, Wadi** el watercourse Sudan
83 L3 **Mil'kovo** Rus. Fed.
129 C3 **Milk River** Can.
105 C3 **Millau** France
143 D2 **Milledgeville** U.S.A.
137 E1 **Mille Lacs** lakes U.S.A.
130 A2 **Mille Lacs, Lac des** l. Can.
137 D2 **Miller** U.S.A.
91 E2 **Millerovo** Rus. Fed.
52 A2 **Millers Creek** Austr.
53 B3 **Millicent** Austr.
141 F1 **Millinocket** U.S.A.
53 D1 **Millmerran** Austr.
98 B1 **Millom** U.K.
128 C1 **Mills Lake** Can.
111 B3 **Milos** i. Greece
89 E3 **Miloslavskoye** Rus. Fed.
91 E2 **Milove** Rus. Fed.
52 B1 **Milparinka** Austr.
54 A3 **Milton** N.Z.
99 C2 **Milton Keynes** U.K.
140 B2 **Milwaukee** U.S.A.
104 B3 **Mimizan** France
118 B3 **Mimongo** Gabon
79 C2 **Mīnāb** Iran

58 C2 **Minahasa, Semenanjung** pen. Indon.
79 C2 **Mina Jebel Ali** U.A.E.
60 B1 **Minas** Indon.
153 C4 **Minas** Uru.
155 D1 **Minas Novas** Brazil
145 C3 **Minatitlán** Mex.
62 A1 **Minbu** Myanmar
64 B2 **Mindanao** i. Phil.
101 D1 **Minden** Ger.
142 B2 **Minden** LA U.S.A.
137 D2 **Minden** NE U.S.A.
64 B1 **Mindoro** i. Phil.
64 A1 **Mindoro Strait** Phil.
118 B3 **Mindouli** Congo
99 B3 **Minehead** U.K.
154 B1 **Mineiros** Brazil
139 D2 **Mineral Wells** U.S.A.
77 E3 **Minfeng** China
119 C4 **Minga** Dem. Rep. Congo
81 C1 **Mingäçevir** Azer.
131 D1 **Mingan** Can.
52 B2 **Mingary** Austr.
70 B2 **Mingguang** China
62 A1 **Mingin** Myanmar
107 C2 **Minglanilla** Spain
119 D4 **Mingoyo** Tanz.
69 E1 **Mingshui** China
71 B3 **Mingxi** China
73 B4 **Minicoy** i. India
50 A2 **Minilya** Austr.
131 D1 **Minipi Lake** Can.
130 A1 **Miniss Lake** Can.
115 C4 **Minna** Nigeria
137 E2 **Minneapolis** U.S.A.
129 E2 **Minnedosa** Can.
137 E2 **Minnesota** r. U.S.A.
137 E1 **Minnesota** state U.S.A.
106 B1 **Miño** r. Port./Spain
107 D1 **Minorca** i. Spain
136 C1 **Minot** U.S.A.
88 C3 **Minsk** Belarus
103 E1 **Mińsk Mazowiecki** Pol.
131 D2 **Minto** Can.
130 C1 **Minto, Lac** l. Can.
70 A2 **Minxian** China
155 D1 **Mirabela** Brazil
155 D1 **Miralta** Brazil
131 D2 **Miramichi** N.B. Can.
111 C3 **Mirampelou, Kolpos** b. Greece
152 C3 **Miranda** Brazil
152 C2 **Miranda** r. Brazil
106 C1 **Miranda de Ebro** Spain
106 B1 **Mirandela** Port.
154 B2 **Mirandópolis** Brazil
79 C3 **Mirbāţ** Oman
61 C1 **Miri** Sarawak Malaysia
153 C4 **Mirim, Lagoa** l. Brazil
79 D2 **Mirjāveh** Iran
83 I2 **Mirnyy** Rus. Fed.
101 F1 **Mirow** Ger.
74 A2 **Mirpur Khas** Pak.
111 B3 **Mirtoö Pelagos** sea Greece
65 B2 **Miryang** S. Korea
75 C2 **Mirzapur** India
66 B1 **Mishan** China
146 B3 **Miskitos, Cayos** is Nic.
103 E2 **Miskolc** Hungary
59 C3 **Misoöl** i. Indon.
115 D1 **Mişrātah** Libya
130 B1 **Missinaibi** r. Can.
130 B2 **Missinaibi Lake** Can.
128 B3 **Mission** Can.
130 B1 **Missisa Lake** Can.
142 C3 **Mississippi** r. U.S.A.
142 C2 **Mississippi** state U.S.A.
142 C3 **Mississippi Delta** U.S.A.
134 D1 **Missoula** U.S.A.

137 E3 **Missouri** r. U.S.A.
137 E3 **Missouri** state U.S.A.
123 C2 **Mistassibi** r. Can.
130 C1 **Mistassini, Lac** l. Can.
131 D1 **Mistastin Lake** Can.
103 D2 **Mistelbach** Austria
131 D1 **Mistinibi, Lac** l. Can.
130 C1 **Mistissini** Can.
51 D2 **Mitchell** Austr.
51 D1 **Mitchell** r. Austr.
137 D2 **Mitchell** U.S.A.
97 B2 **Mitchelstown** Ireland
74 A2 **Mithi** Pak.
67 D3 **Mito** Japan
119 D3 **Mitole** Tanz.
53 D2 **Mittagong** Austr.
101 E2 **Mittelhausen** Ger.
101 D1 **Mittellandkanal** canal Ger.
101 F3 **Mitterteich** Ger.
150 A1 **Mitú** Col.
119 C4 **Mitumba, Chaîne des** mts
        Dem. Rep. Congo
119 C3 **Mitumba, Monts** mts
        Dem. Rep. Congo
118 B2 **Mitzic** Gabon
78 B2 **Miyah, Wādī al**
        watercourse Saudi Arabia
67 C3 **Miyake-jima** i. Japan
66 D3 **Miyako** Japan
67 B4 **Miyakonojō** Japan
76 B2 **Miyaly** Kazakh.
        Miyang China see Mile
67 B4 **Miyazaki** Japan
115 D1 **Mizdah** Libya
97 B3 **Mizen Head** Ireland
90 A2 **Mizhhir''ya** Ukr.
93 G4 **Mjölby** Sweden
93 F3 **Mjøsa** l. Norway
119 D3 **Mkomazi** Tanz.
103 C1 **Mladá Boleslav**
        Czech Rep.
109 D2 **Mladenovac**
        Serb. and Mont.
103 E1 **Mława** Pol.
123 C3 **Mlungisi** S. Africa
90 B1 **Mlyniv** Ukr.
123 C2 **Mmabatho** S. Africa
123 C2 **Mmathethe** Botswana
135 E3 **Moab** U.S.A.
123 D2 **Moamba** Moz.
119 C3 **Moba** Dem. Rep. Congo
118 C2 **Mobayi-Mbongo**
        Dem. Rep. Congo
137 E3 **Moberly** U.S.A.
142 C2 **Mobile** U.S.A.
142 C2 **Mobile Bay** U.S.A.
136 C1 **Mobridge** U.S.A.
121 D2 **Moçambique** Moz.
62 B1 **Mộc Châu** Vietnam
78 B3 **Mocha** Yemen
123 C1 **Mochudi** Botswana
121 D2 **Mocímboa da Praia** Moz.
150 A1 **Mocoa** Col.
154 C2 **Mococa** Brazil
144 B2 **Mocorito** Mex.
144 B1 **Moctezuma** Chihuahua
        Mex.
145 D2 **Moctezuma** San Luis Potosí
        Mex.
144 B2 **Moctezuma** Sonora Mex.
121 C2 **Mocuba** Moz.
105 D2 **Modane** France
122 B2 **Modder** r. S. Africa
108 B2 **Modena** Italy
135 B3 **Modesto** U.S.A.
123 C1 **Modimolle** S. Africa
53 C3 **Moe** Austr.
100 C2 **Moers** Ger.
96 C3 **Moffat** U.K.
117 C4 **Mogadishu** Somalia

123 C1 **Mogalakwena** r. S. Africa
62 A1 **Mogaung** Myanmar
        Mogilev Belarus see
        Mahilyow
154 C2 **Mogi-Mirim** Brazil
83 I3 **Mogocha** Rus. Fed.
62 A1 **Mogok** Myanmar
103 D2 **Mohács** Hungary
123 C3 **Mohale's Hoek** Lesotho
107 D2 **Mohammadia** Alg.
141 E2 **Mohawk** r. U.S.A.
119 D3 **Mohoro** Tanz.
90 B2 **Mohyliv Podil's'kyy** Ukr.
110 C1 **Moinești** Romania
92 F2 **Mo i Rana** Norway
104 C3 **Moissac** France
135 C3 **Mojave** U.S.A.
135 C3 **Mojave Desert** U.S.A.
62 B1 **Mojiang** China
155 C2 **Moji das Cruzes** Brazil
154 C2 **Moji-Guaçu** r. Brazil
54 B1 **Mokau** N.Z.
123 C2 **Mokhotlong** Lesotho
123 C1 **Mokopane** S. Africa
65 B3 **Mokp'o** S. Korea
145 C2 **Molango** Mex.
        Moldavia country Europe
        see Moldova
92 E3 **Molde** Norway
90 B2 **Moldova** country Europe
110 B1 **Moldoveanu, Vârful** mt.
        Romania
90 B2 **Moldovei Centrale,**
        Podişul plat. Moldova
123 C1 **Molepolole** Botswana
88 C2 **Molėtai** Lith.
109 C2 **Molfetta** Italy
107 C1 **Molina de Aragón** Spain
150 A3 **Mollendo** Peru
53 C2 **Molong** Austr.
122 B2 **Molopo** watercourse
        Botswana/S. Africa
118 B2 **Moloundou** Cameroon
59 C3 **Moluccas** is Indon.
        Molucca Sea Indon. see
        Maluku, Laut
52 B2 **Momba** Austr.
119 D3 **Mombasa** Kenya
154 B1 **Mombuca, Serra de** hills
        Brazil
93 F4 **Møn** i. Denmark
105 D3 **Monaco** country Europe
96 B2 **Monadhliath Mountains**
        U.K.
97 C1 **Monaghan** Ireland
89 D3 **Monastyrshchina** Rus. Fed.
90 B2 **Monastyryshche** Ukr.
66 D2 **Monbetsu** Japan
108 A1 **Moncalieri** Italy
86 C2 **Monchegorsk** Rus. Fed.
100 C2 **Mönchengladbach** Ger.
144 B2 **Monclova** Mex.
131 D2 **Moncton** Can.
106 B1 **Mondego** r. Port.
123 D2 **Mondlo** S. Africa
108 A2 **Mondoví** Italy
111 B3 **Monemvasia** Greece
66 D1 **Moneron, Ostrov** i.
        Rus. Fed.
137 E3 **Monett** U.S.A.
108 B1 **Monfalcone** Italy
106 B1 **Monforte de Lemos** Spain
62 B1 **Mông Cai** Vietnam
62 A1 **Mong Lin** Myanmar
62 A1 **Mong Pawk** Myanmar
62 A1 **Mong Ping** Myanmar
120 B2 **Mongu** Zambia
135 C3 **Monitor Range** mts U.S.A.
114 C4 **Mono** r. Togo

135 C3 **Mono Lake** U.S.A.
109 C2 **Monopoli** Italy
107 C1 **Monreal del Campo** Spain
142 B2 **Monroe** LA U.S.A.
140 B2 **Monroe** WI U.S.A.
142 C2 **Monroeville** U.S.A.
114 A4 **Monrovia** Liberia
100 A2 **Mons** Belgium
122 B3 **Montagu** S. Africa
109 C3 **Montalto** mt. Italy
110 B2 **Montana** Bulg.
134 E1 **Montana** state U.S.A.
104 C2 **Montargis** France
104 C3 **Montauban** France
141 E2 **Montauk Point** U.S.A.
123 C2 **Mont-aux-Sources** mt.
        Lesotho
105 C2 **Montbard** France
105 D2 **Mont Blanc** mt. France/Italy
105 C2 **Montbrison** France
100 B3 **Montcornet** France
104 B3 **Mont-de-Marsan** France
104 C2 **Montdidier** France
151 C2 **Monte Alegre** Brazil
105 D3 **Monte-Carlo** Monaco
152 C4 **Monte Caseros** Arg.
146 C3 **Montego Bay** Jamaica
105 C3 **Montélimar** France
109 C2 **Montella** Italy
145 C2 **Montemorelos** Mex.
104 B2 **Montendre** France
109 C2 **Montenegro** country
        Europe
121 C2 **Montepuez** Moz.
108 B2 **Montepulciano** Italy
135 B3 **Monterey** U.S.A.
135 B3 **Monterey Bay** U.S.A.
150 A1 **Montería** Col.
152 B2 **Montero** Bol.
145 B2 **Monterrey** Mex.
109 C2 **Montesano sulla**
        Marcellana Italy
109 C2 **Monte Sant'Angelo** Italy
151 E3 **Monte Santo** Brazil
108 A2 **Monte Santu, Capo di**
        c. Sardinia Italy
155 D1 **Montes Claros** Brazil
153 C4 **Montevideo** Uru.
137 D2 **Montevideo** U.S.A.
136 B3 **Monte Vista** U.S.A.
142 C2 **Montgomery** U.S.A.
105 D2 **Monthey** Switz.
142 B2 **Monticello** AR U.S.A.
135 E3 **Monticello** UT U.S.A.
104 C2 **Montignac** France
105 D2 **Montigny-le-Roi** France
106 C2 **Montilla** Spain
131 D2 **Mont-Joli** Can.
130 C2 **Mont-Laurier** Can.
104 C2 **Montluçon** France
131 C2 **Montmagny** Can.
104 C2 **Montmorillon** France
51 E2 **Monto** Austr.
134 D2 **Montpelier** ID U.S.A.
141 E2 **Montpelier** VT U.S.A.
105 C3 **Montpellier** France
104 C2 **Montréal** Can.
129 C2 **Montréal** France
129 C2 **Montreal Lake** Can.
129 C2 **Montreal Lake** Can.
99 D3 **Montreuil** France
105 D2 **Montreux** Switz.
96 C2 **Montrose** U.K.
136 B3 **Montrose** U.S.A.
147 D3 **Montserrat** terr.
        West Indies
62 A1 **Monywa** Myanmar
108 A1 **Monza** Italy
107 D1 **Monzón** Spain
123 C1 **Mookane** Botswana
53 D1 **Moonie** Austr.

53 C1 Moonie r. Austr.
52 A2 Moonta Austr.
50 A2 Moore, Lake salt flat Austr.
137 D1 Moorhead U.S.A.
53 C3 Mooroopna Austr.
122 A3 Moorreesburg S. Africa
130 B1 Moose r. Can.
130 B1 Moose Factory Can.
141 F1 Moosehead Lake U.S.A.
129 D2 Moose Jaw Can.
137 E1 Moose Lake U.S.A.
129 D2 Moosomin Can.
130 B1 Moosonee Can.
52 B2 Mootwingee Austr.
123 C1 Mopane S. Africa
114 B3 Mopti Mali
150 A3 Moquegua Peru
93 F3 Mora Sweden
137 E1 Mora U.S.A.
75 B2 Moradabad India
121 □D2 Moramanga Madag.
103 D2 Morava r. Europe
96 B2 Moray Firth b. U.K.
100 C3 Morbach Ger.
74 B2 Morbi India
104 B3 Morcenx France
69 E1 Mordaga China
129 E3 Morden Can.
91 E1 Mordovo Rus. Fed.
98 B1 Morecambe U.K.
98 B1 Morecambe Bay U.K.
53 C1 Moree Austr.
59 D3 Morehead P.N.G.
140 C3 Morehead U.S.A.
143 E2 Morehead City U.S.A.
145 B3 Morelia Mex.
107 C1 Morella Spain
106 B2 Morena, Sierra mts Spain
110 C2 Moreni Romania
128 A2 Moresby, Mount Can.
128 A2 Moresby Island Can.
142 B3 Morgan City U.S.A.
143 D1 Morganton U.S.A.
140 D3 Morgantown U.S.A.
105 D2 Morges Switz.
66 D2 Mori Japan
128 B2 Morice Lake Can.
66 D3 Morioka Japan
53 D2 Morisset Austr.
104 B2 Morlaix France
51 C1 Mornington Island Austr.
59 D3 Morobe P.N.G.
114 B1 Morocco country Africa
119 D3 Morogoro Tanz.
64 B2 Moro Gulf Phil.
122 B3 Morokweng S. Africa
121 □D3 Morombe Madag.
68 C1 Mörön Mongolia
121 □D3 Morondava Madag.
121 C2 Moroni Comoros
59 C2 Morotai i. Indon.
119 D2 Moroto Uganda
98 C1 Morpeth U.K.
154 C1 Morrinhos Brazil
129 E3 Morris Can.
137 D1 Morris U.S.A.
143 D1 Morristown U.S.A.
87 D3 Morshanka Rus. Fed.
154 B1 Mortes, Rio das r. Brazil
52 B3 Mortlake Austr.
53 D3 Moruya Austr.
96 B2 Morvern reg. U.K.
53 C3 Morwell Austr.
102 B2 Mosbach Ger.
89 E2 Moscow Rus. Fed.
134 C1 Moscow U.S.A.
100 C2 Mosel r. Ger.
105 D2 Moselle r. France
134 C1 Moses Lake U.S.A.
92 □A3 Mosfellsbær Iceland

54 B3 Mosgiel N.Z.
89 D2 Moshenskoye Rus. Fed.
119 D3 Moshi Tanz.
92 F2 Mosjøen Norway
       Moskva Rus. Fed. see
       Moscow
103 D2 Mosonmagyaróvár
       Hungary
146 B4 Mosquitos, Golfo de los
       b. Panama
93 F4 Moss Norway
122 A3 Mossel Bay S. Africa
122 B3 Mossel Bay S. Africa
118 B3 Mossendjo Congo
52 B2 Mossgiel Austr.
51 D1 Mossman Austr.
151 E2 Mossoró Brazil
53 D2 Moss Vale Austr.
102 C1 Most Czech Rep.
114 C1 Mostaganem Alg.
109 C2 Mostar Bos.-Herz.
152 C4 Mostardas Brazil
81 C2 Mosul Iraq
93 G4 Motala Sweden
96 C3 Motherwell U.K.
107 C2 Motilla del Palancar
       Spain
122 B1 Motokwe Botswana
106 C2 Motril Spain
110 B2 Motru Romania
63 A2 Mottama, Gulf of Myanmar
145 D2 Motul Mex.
111 C3 Moudros Greece
118 B3 Mouila Gabon
52 B3 Moulamein Austr.
105 C2 Moulins France
143 D2 Moultrie U.S.A.
143 E2 Moultrie, Lake U.S.A.
140 B3 Mound City U.S.A.
115 D4 Moundou Chad
137 E3 Mountain Grove U.S.A.
142 B1 Mountain Home AR U.S.A.
134 C2 Mountain Home ID U.S.A.
143 D1 Mount Airy U.S.A.
52 A3 Mount Barker Austr.
53 C3 Mount Beauty Austr.
123 C3 Mount Darwin Zimbabwe
141 F2 Mount Desert Island
       U.S.A.
123 C3 Mount Fletcher S. Africa
123 C3 Mount Frere S. Africa
52 B3 Mount Gambier Austr.
59 D3 Mount Hagen P.N.G.
53 C2 Mount Hope Austr.
51 C2 Mount Isa Austr.
50 A2 Mount Magnet Austr.
52 B2 Mount Manara Austr.
54 C1 Mount Maunganui N.Z.
111 B2 Mount Olympus Greece
137 E2 Mount Pleasant IA U.S.A.
140 C2 Mount Pleasant MI U.S.A.
139 E2 Mount Pleasant TX U.S.A.
99 A3 Mount's Bay U.K.
134 B2 Mount Shasta U.S.A.
140 B3 Mount Vernon IL U.S.A.
140 C2 Mount Vernon OH U.S.A.
134 B1 Mount Vernon WA U.S.A.
51 D2 Moura Austr.
115 E3 Mourdi, Dépression du
       depr. Chad
97 C1 Mourne Mountains
       hills U.K.
100 A2 Mouscron Belgium
115 D3 Moussoro Chad
58 C2 Moutong Indon.
115 C2 Mouydir, Monts du
       plat. Alg.
100 B3 Mouzon France
97 B1 Moy r. Ireland
117 B4 Moyale Eth.

123 C3 Moyeni Lesotho
76 B2 Mo'ynoq Uzbek.
77 D2 Moyynty Kazakh.
121 C3 Mozambique country
       Africa
113 I9 Mozambique Channel
       Africa
89 E2 Mozhaysk Rus. Fed.
119 D3 Mpanda Tanz.
121 C2 Mpika Zambia
121 C1 Mporokoso Zambia
123 C2 Mpumalanga prov. S. Africa
62 A1 Mrauk-U Myanmar
88 C2 Mshinskaya Rus. Fed.
107 D2 M'Sila Alg.
89 D2 Msta r. Rus. Fed.
89 D2 Mstinskiy Most Rus. Fed.
89 D3 Mstsislaw Belarus
89 E3 Mtsensk Rus. Fed.
119 E4 Mtwara Tanz.
118 B3 Muanda Dem. Rep. Congo
63 B2 Muang Khôngxédôn Laos
62 B1 Muang Ngoy Laos
62 B2 Muang Pakbeng Laos
62 B1 Muang Sing Laos
62 B2 Muang Vangviang Laos
60 B1 Muar Malaysia
60 B2 Muarabungo Indon.
60 B2 Muaradua Indon.
61 C2 Muaralaung Indon.
60 A2 Muarasiberut Indon.
60 B2 Muaratembesi Indon.
61 C2 Muarateweh Indon.
119 D2 Mubende Uganda
115 D3 Mubi Nigeria
120 B2 Muconda Angola
155 E1 Mucuri Brazil
155 E1 Mucuri r. Brazil
66 A2 Mudanjiang China
66 A1 Mudan Jiang r. China
111 C2 Mudanya Turkey
101 E1 Müden (Örtze) Ger.
53 C2 Mudgee Austr.
63 A2 Mudon Myanmar
80 B1 Mudurnu Turkey
121 C2 Mueda Moz.
121 B2 Mufulira Zambia
120 B2 Mufumbwe Zambia
111 C3 Muğla Turkey
116 B2 Muhammad Qol Sudan
101 F2 Mühlberg Ger.
101 E2 Mühlhausen (Thüringen)
       Ger.
63 B3 Mui Ca Mau c. Vietnam
97 C2 Muine Bheag Ireland
121 C2 Muite Moz.
65 B2 Muju S. Korea
90 A2 Mukacheve Ukr.
61 C1 Mukah Sarawak Malaysia
79 B3 Mukalla Yemen
63 B2 Mukdahan Thai.
50 A3 Mukinbudin Austr.
60 B2 Mukomuko Indon.
121 C2 Mulanje, Mount Malawi
101 F2 Mulde r. Ger.
144 A2 Mulegé Mex.
139 C2 Muleshoe U.S.A.
106 C2 Mulhacén mt. Spain
100 C2 Mülheim an der Ruhr Ger.
105 D2 Mulhouse France
66 B2 Muling China
66 B1 Muling He r. China
96 B2 Mull i. U.K.
53 C2 Mullaley Austr.
136 C2 Mullen U.S.A.
61 C1 Muller, Pegunungan
       mts Indon.
50 A2 Mullewa Austr.
97 C2 Mullingar Ireland
96 B3 Mull of Galloway c. U.K.

96 B3 Mull of Kintyre *hd* U.K.
96 A3 Mull of Oa *hd* U.K.
120 B2 Mulobezi Zambia
74 B1 Multan Pak.
73 B3 Mumbai India
120 B2 Mumbwa Zambia
145 D2 Muna Mex.
101 E2 Münchberg Ger.
München Ger. *see* Munich
140 B2 Muncie U.S.A.
50 B3 Mundrabilla Austr.
119 C2 Mungbere
Dem. Rep. Congo
75 C2 Munger India
53 A1 Mungeranie Austr.
53 C1 Mungindi Austr.
102 C2 Munich Ger.
155 D2 Muniz Freire Brazil
101 E1 Münster Niedersachsen Ger.
100 C2 Münster Nordrhein-Westfalen
Ger.
97 B2 Munster reg. Ireland
100 C2 Münsterland reg. Ger.
62 B1 Muong Nhe Vietnam
92 H2 Muonio Fin.
92 H2 Muonioälven r. Fin./Sweden
Mugdisho Somalia see
Mogadishu
103 D1 Mur r. Austria
119 C3 Muramvya Burundi
119 D3 Murang'a Kenya
81 C2 Murat r. Turkey
111 C2 Muratlı Turkey
50 A2 Murchison watercourse
Austr.
107 C2 Murcia Spain
111 C2 Mürefte Turkey
110 B1 Mureşul r. Romania
104 C3 Muret France
142 C1 Murfreesboro U.S.A.
77 C3 Murghab r. Afgh.
77 D3 Murghob Tajik.
155 D2 Muriaé Brazil
120 B1 Muriege Angola
101 F1 Müritz l. Ger.
86 C2 Murmansk Rus. Fed.
87 D3 Murom Rus. Fed.
66 D2 Muroran Japan
106 B1 Muros Spain
67 B4 Muroto Japan
67 B4 Muroto-zaki pt Japan
143 D1 Murphy U.S.A.
53 C1 Murra Murra Austr.
52 A3 Murray r. Austr.
128 B2 Murray r. Can.
140 B3 Murray U.S.A.
143 D2 Murray, Lake U.S.A.
52 A3 Murray Bridge Austr.
122 B3 Murraysburg S. Africa
52 B3 Murrayville Austr.
52 B2 Murrumbidgee r. Austr.
121 C2 Murrupula Moz.
53 D2 Murrurundi Austr.
109 C1 Murska Sobota Slovenia
54 C1 Murupara N.Z.
49 I4 Mururoa i. Fr. Polynesia
75 C2 Murwara India
53 D1 Murwillumbah Austr.
115 D2 Murzūq Libya
81 C2 Muş Turkey
110 B2 Musala mt. Bulg.
65 B1 Musan N. Korea
78 B3 Musaymir Yemen
79 C2 Muscat Oman
137 E2 Muscatine U.S.A.
50 C2 Musgrave Ranges mts
Austr.
118 B3 Mushie Dem. Rep. Congo
60 B2 Musi r. Indon.
123 D1 Musina S. Africa

140 B2 Muskegon U.S.A.
139 D1 Muskogee U.S.A.
128 B2 Muskwa r. Can.
74 A1 Muslimbagh Pak.
78 A3 Musmar Sudan
119 D3 Musoma Tanz.
96 C3 Musselburgh U.K.
88 C2 Mustjala Estonia
53 D2 Muswellbrook Austr.
116 A2 Mūt Egypt
121 C2 Mutare Zimbabwe
66 D2 Mutsu Japan
121 C2 Mutuali Moz.
92 I2 Muurola Fin.
70 A2 Mu Us Shamo des. China
120 A1 Muxaluando Angola
87 D2 Muyezerskiy Rus. Fed.
119 D3 Muyinga Burundi
74 B1 Muzaffargarh Pak.
74 B2 Muzaffarnagar India
75 C2 Muzaffarpur India
144 B2 Múzquiz Mex.
75 C1 Muz Tag mt. China
119 C3 Mwanza Dem. Rep. Congo
119 D3 Mwanza Tanz.
118 C3 Mweka Dem. Rep. Congo
121 B2 Mwenda Zambia
118 C3 Mwene-Ditu
Dem. Rep. Congo
121 C3 Mwenezi Zimbabwe
119 C3 Mweru, Lake
Dem. Rep. Congo/Zambia
118 C3 Mwimba Zambia
120 B2 Mwinilunga Zambia
88 C3 Myadzyel Belarus
62 A2 Myanaung Myanmar
62 A1 Myanmar country Asia
63 A2 Myaungmya Myanmar
63 A2 Myeik Myanmar
Myeik Kyunzu is Myanmar
see Mergui Archipelago
62 A1 Myingyan Myanmar
62 A1 Myitkyina Myanmar
91 C2 Mykolayiv Ukr.
111 C3 Mykonos Greece
111 C3 Mykonos i. Greece
86 F2 Myla Rus. Fed.
75 D2 Mymensingh Bangl.
65 B1 Myŏnggan N. Korea
88 C2 Myory Belarus
92 □B3 Myrdalsjökull ice cap
Iceland
91 C2 Myrhorod Ukr.
90 C2 Myronivka Ukr.
143 E2 Myrtle Beach U.S.A.
53 C3 Myrtleford Austr.
134 B2 Myrtle Point U.S.A.
89 E2 Myshkin Rus. Fed.
103 D1 Myślibórz Pol.
73 B3 Mysore India
83 N2 Mys Shmidta Rus. Fed.
63 B2 My Tho Vietnam
111 C3 Mytilini Greece
89 E3 Mytishchi Rus. Fed.
123 C3 Mzamomhle S. Africa
121 C2 Mzimba Malawi
121 C2 Mzuzu Malawi

N

97 C2 Naas Ireland
122 A2 Nababeep S. Africa
87 E3 Naberezhnyye Chelny
Rus. Fed.
91 D2 Nabire Indon.
80 B2 Nāblus West Bank
123 C1 Naboomspruit S. Africa
121 D2 Nacala Moz.

63 A2 Nachuge India
139 E2 Nacogdoches U.S.A.
144 B1 Nacozari de García Mex.
74 B2 Nadiad India
90 A2 Nadvirna Ukr.
86 C2 Nadvoitsy Rus. Fed.
86 G2 Nadym Rus. Fed.
93 F4 Næstved Denmark
111 B3 Nafpaktos Greece
111 B3 Nafplio Greece
115 D1 Nafūsah, Jabal hills Libya
78 B2 Nafy Saudi Arabia
64 B1 Naga Phil.
130 B1 Nagagami r. Can.
67 C3 Nagano Japan
67 C3 Nagaoka Japan
75 D2 Nagaon India
74 B1 Nagar India
74 B2 Nagar Parkar Pak.
67 A4 Nagasaki Japan
67 B4 Nagato Japan
74 B2 Nagaur India
73 B4 Nagercoil India
74 A2 Nagha Kalat Pak.
75 B2 Nagina India
67 C3 Nagoya Japan
75 B2 Nagpur India
68 C2 Nagqu China
103 D2 Nagyatád Hungary
103 D2 Nagykanizsa Hungary
128 B1 Nahanni Butte Can.
76 A3 Nahāvand Iran
101 E1 Nahrendorf Ger.
153 A5 Nahuel Huapi, Lago l. Arg.
131 D1 Nain Can.
81 D2 Nā'īn Iran
96 C2 Nairn U.K.
119 D3 Nairobi Kenya
119 D3 Naivasha Kenya
81 D2 Najafābād Iran
78 B2 Najd reg. Saudi Arabia
106 C1 Nájera Spain
65 C1 Najin N. Korea
78 B3 Najrān Saudi Arabia
Nakambé watercourse
Burkina/Ghana see
White Volta
67 C3 Nakatsugawa Japan
78 A3 Nakfa Eritrea
66 B2 Nakhodka Rus. Fed.
63 B2 Nakhon Pathom Thai.
63 B2 Nakhon Ratchasima Thai.
63 B2 Nakhon Sawan Thai.
63 A3 Nakhon Si Thammarat
Thai.
130 B1 Nakina Can.
121 C1 Nakonde Zambia
93 F4 Nakskov Denmark
119 D3 Nakuru Kenya
128 C2 Nakusp Can.
75 D2 Nalbari India
87 D4 Nal'chik Rus. Fed.
115 D1 Nālūt Libya
123 C2 Namahadi S. Africa
77 D2 Namangan Uzbek.
122 A2 Namaqualand reg. S. Africa
51 E2 Nambour Austr.
53 D2 Nambucca Heads Austr.
75 D1 Nam Co salt l. China
63 B2 Nam Định Vietnam
120 A3 Namib Desert Namibia
120 A2 Namibe Angola
120 A3 Namibia country Africa
72 D2 Namjagbarwa Feng mt.
China
59 C3 Namlea Indon.
53 C2 Namoi r. Austr.
134 C2 Nampa U.S.A.
114 B3 Nampala Mali
65 B2 Namp'o N. Korea

121 C2	**Nampula** Moz.	
62 A1	**Namrup** India	
62 A1	**Namsang** Myanmar	
92 F3	**Namsos** Norway	
63 A2	**Nam Tok** Thai.	
83 J2	**Namtsy** Rus. Fed.	
62 A1	**Namtu** Myanmar	
100 B2	**Namur** Belgium	
120 B2	**Namwala** Zambia	
65 B2	**Namwŏn** S. Korea	
62 A1	**Namya Ra** Myanmar	
62 B2	**Nan** Thai.	
128 B3	**Nanaimo** Can.	
71 B3	**Nan'an** China	
122 A1	**Nananib Plateau** Namibia	
67 C3	**Nanao** Japan	
71 B3	**Nanchang** *Jiangxi* China	
71 B3	**Nanchang** *Jiangxi* China	
70 A2	**Nanchong** China	
63 A3	**Nancowry** *i.* India	
105 D2	**Nancy** France	
75 C1	**Nanda Devi** *mt.* India	
71 A3	**Nandan** China	
73 B3	**Nanded** India	
74 B2	**Nandurbar** India	
73 B3	**Nandyal** India	
71 B3	**Nanfeng** China	
118 B2	**Nanga Eboko** Cameroon	
61 C2	**Nangahpinoh** Indon.	
74 B1	**Nanga Parbat** *mt.* Jammu and Kashmir	
61 C2	**Nangatayap** Indon.	
70 B2	**Nangong** China	
119 D3	**Nangulangwa** Tanz.	
70 C2	**Nanhui** China	
70 B2	**Nanjing** China	
	Nanking China *see* **Nanjing**	
120 A2	**Nankova** Angola	
71 B3	**Nan Ling** *mts* China	
71 A3	**Nanning** China	
127 H2	**Nanortalik** Greenland	
71 A3	**Nanpan Jiang** *r.* China	
75 C2	**Nanpara** India	
71 B3	**Nanping** China	
	Nansei-shotō *is* Japan *see* **Ryukyu Islands**	
104 B2	**Nantes** France	
70 C2	**Nantong** China	
141 F2	**Nantucket Island** U.S.A.	
155 D1	**Nanuque** Brazil	
64 B2	**Nanusa, Kepulauan** *is* Indon.	
71 B3	**Nanxiong** China	
70 B2	**Nanyang** China	
70 B2	**Nanzhang** China	
107 D2	**Nao, Cabo de la** *c.* Spain	
131 C1	**Naococane, Lac** *l.* Can.	
74 A2	**Naokot** Pak.	
135 B3	**Napa** U.S.A.	
126 D2	**Napaktulik Lake** Can.	
127 H2	**Napasoq** Greenland	
54 C1	**Napier** N.Z.	
108 B2	**Naples** Italy	
143 D3	**Naples** U.S.A.	
150 A2	**Napo** *r.* Ecuador	
	Napoli Italy *see* **Naples**	
114 B3	**Nara** Mali	
93 I4	**Narach** Belarus	
52 B3	**Naracoorte** Austr.	
145 C2	**Naranjos** Mex.	
63 B3	**Narathiwat** Thai.	
105 C3	**Narbonne** France	
63 A2	**Narcondam Island** India	
127 G1	**Nares Strait** Can./Greenland	
122 A1	**Narib** Namibia	
87 D4	**Narimanov** Rus. Fed.	
67 D3	**Narita** Japan	
74 B2	**Narmada** *r.* India	
74 B2	**Narnaul** India	
108 B2	**Narni** Italy	
90 B1	**Narodychi** Ukr.	
89 E2	**Naro-Fominsk** Rus. Fed.	
53 D1	**Narooma** Austr.	
88 C3	**Narowlya** Belarus	
53 C2	**Narrabri** Austr.	
53 C2	**Narrandera** Austr.	
53 C2	**Narromine** Austr.	
88 C2	**Narva** Estonia	
88 C2	**Narva Bay** Estonia/Rus. Fed.	
92 G2	**Narvik** Norway	
88 C2	**Narvskoye Vodokhranilishche** *resr* Estonia/Rus. Fed.	
86 E2	**Nar'yan-Mar** Rus. Fed.	
77 D2	**Naryn** Kyrg.	
74 B2	**Nashik** India	
141 E2	**Nashua** U.S.A.	
142 C1	**Nashville** U.S.A.	
117 B4	**Nasir** India	
128 B2	**Nass** *r.* Can.	
146 C2	**Nassau** Bahamas	
116 B2	**Nasser, Lake** *resr* Egypt	
93 F4	**Nässjö** Sweden	
130 C1	**Nastapoca** *r.* Can.	
130 C1	**Nastapoka Islands** Can.	
120 B3	**Nata** Botswana	
151 E2	**Natal** Brazil	
131 D1	**Natashquan** Can.	
131 D1	**Natashquan** *r.* Can.	
142 B2	**Natchez** U.S.A.	
142 B2	**Natchitoches** U.S.A.	
53 C3	**Nathalia** Austr.	
107 D1	**Nati, Punta** *pt* Spain	
114 C3	**Natitingou** Benin	
151 D3	**Natividade** Brazil	
67 D3	**Natori** Japan	
131 D1	**Natuashish** Can.	
61 B1	**Natuna, Kepulauan** *is* Indon.	
61 B1	**Natuna Besar** *i.* Indon.	
120 A3	**Nauchas** Namibia	
101 F1	**Nauen** Ger.	
88 B2	**Naujoji Akmenė** Lith.	
101 E2	**Naumburg (Saale)** Ger.	
48 F3	**Nauru** *country* S. Pacific Ocean	
145 C2	**Nautla** Mex.	
88 C3	**Navahrudak** Belarus	
106 B2	**Navalmoral de la Mata** Spain	
106 B2	**Navalvillar de Pela** Spain	
97 C2	**Navan** Ireland	
88 C2	**Navapolatsk** Belarus	
83 M2	**Navarin, Mys** *c.* Rus. Fed.	
153 B6	**Navarino, Isla** *i.* Chile	
96 B1	**Naver** *r.* U.K.	
73 B3	**Navi Mumbai** India	
89 D3	**Navlya** Rus. Fed.	
110 C2	**Năvodari** Romania	
77 C2	**Navoiy** Uzbek.	
144 B2	**Navojoa** Mex.	
144 B2	**Navolato** Mex.	
74 A2	**Nawabshah** Pak.	
62 A1	**Nawnghkio** Myanmar	
62 A1	**Nawngleng** Myanmar	
81 C2	**Naxçıvan** Azer.	
111 C3	**Naxos** *i.* Greece	
144 B2	**Nayar** Mex.	
66 D2	**Nayoro** Japan	
62 A2	**Naypyidaw** Myanmar	
80 B2	**Nazareth** Israel	
144 B2	**Nazas** Mex.	
144 B2	**Nazas** *r.* Mex.	
150 A3	**Nazca** Peru	
111 C3	**Nazilli** Turkey	
117 B4	**Nazrēt** Eth.	
79 C2	**Nazwá** Oman	
121 B1	**Nchelenge** Zambia	
122 B1	**Ncojane** Botswana	
120 A1	**N'dalatando** Angola	
118 C2	**Ndélé** C.A.R.	
118 B3	**Ndendé** Gabon	
115 D3	**Ndjamena** Chad	
121 B2	**Ndola** Zambia	
97 C1	**Neagh, Lough** *l.* U.K.	
50 C2	**Neale, Lake** *salt flat* Austr.	
111 B2	**Nea Roda** Greece	
99 B3	**Neath** U.K.	
53 C1	**Nebine Creek** *r.* Austr.	
150 B1	**Neblina, Pico da** *mt.* Brazil	
89 D2	**Nebolchi** Rus. Fed.	
136 C2	**Nebraska** *state* U.S.A.	
137 D2	**Nebraska City** U.S.A.	
108 B3	**Nebrodi, Monti** *mts* Sicily Italy	
153 C4	**Necochea** Arg.	
131 C1	**Nedlouc, Lac** *l.* Can.	
135 D4	**Needles** U.S.A.	
74 B2	**Neemuch** India	
129 E2	**Neepawa** Can.	
87 E3	**Neftekamsk** Rus. Fed.	
82 F2	**Neftyugansk** Rus. Fed.	
120 A1	**Negage** Angola	
117 B4	**Negēlē** Eth.	
150 A2	**Negra, Punta** *pt* Peru	
62 A1	**Negrais, Cape** Myanmar	
153 B5	**Negro** *r.* Arg.	
150 B2	**Negro** *r.* S. America	
152 C4	**Negro** *r.* Uru.	
106 B2	**Negro, Cabo** *c.* Morocco	
64 B2	**Negros** *i.* Phil.	
69 E1	**Nehe** China	
70 A3	**Neijiang** China	
129 D2	**Neilburg** Can.	
150 A1	**Neiva** Col.	
129 E2	**Nejanilini Lake** Can.	
117 B4	**Nek'emtē** Eth.	
89 F2	**Nekrasovskoye** Rus. Fed.	
89 D2	**Nelidovo** Rus. Fed.	
73 B3	**Nellore** India	
128 C3	**Nelson** Can.	
129 E2	**Nelson** *r.* Can.	
54 B2	**Nelson** N.Z.	
52 B3	**Nelson, Cape** Austr.	
53 D2	**Nelson Bay** Austr.	
129 E2	**Nelson House** Can.	
134 E1	**Nelson Reservoir** U.S.A.	
123 D2	**Nelspruit** S. Africa	
114 B3	**Néma** Maur.	
88 B2	**Neman** Rus. Fed.	
104 C2	**Nemours** France	
66 D2	**Nemuro** Japan	
90 B2	**Nemyriv** Ukr.	
99 D2	**Nene** *r.* U.K.	
69 E1	**Nenjiang** China	
137 E3	**Neosho** U.S.A.	
75 C2	**Nepal** *country* Asia	
75 C2	**Nepalganj** Nepal	
135 D3	**Nephi** U.S.A.	
97 B1	**Nephin** *hill* Ireland	
97 B1	**Nephin Beg Range** *hills* Ireland	
131 D2	**Nepisiguit** *r.* Can.	
119 C2	**Nepoko** *r.* Dem. Rep. Congo	
104 C3	**Nérac** France	
53 D1	**Nerang** Austr.	
69 D1	**Nerchinsk** Rus. Fed.	
89 F2	**Nerekhta** Rus. Fed.	
109 C2	**Neretva** *r.* Bos.-Herz./Croatia	
120 B2	**Neriquinha** Angola	
88 B3	**Neris** *r.* Lith.	
89 E2	**Nerl'** *r.* Rus. Fed.	
86 F2	**Nerokhi** Rus. Fed.	
154 C1	**Nerópolis** Brazil	
83 J3	**Neryungri** Rus. Fed.	
92 □C2	**Neskaupstaður** Iceland	
96 C2	**Ness, Loch** *l.* U.K.	

136 D3 **Ness City** U.S.A.
111 B2 **Nestos** r. Greece
100 B1 **Netherlands** country
 Europe
147 D3 **Netherlands Antilles** terr.
 West Indies
127 G2 **Nettilling Lake** Can.
101 F1 **Neubrandenburg** Ger.
105 D2 **Neuchâtel** Switz.
100 C2 **Neuerburg** Ger.
100 B3 **Neufchâteau** Belgium
103 D2 **Neufchâteau** France
104 C2 **Neufchâtel-en-Bray** France
101 D2 **Neuhof** Ger.
102 B1 **Neumünster** Ger.
102 B2 **Neunkirchen** Ger.
153 B4 **Neuquén** Arg.
153 B4 **Neuquén** r. Arg.
101 F1 **Neuruppin** Ger.
100 C2 **Neuss** Ger.
101 D1 **Neustadt am Rübenberge**
 Ger.
101 E3 **Neustadt an der Aisch**
 Ger.
101 F1 **Neustrelitz** Ger.
100 C1 **Neuwied** Ger.
137 E3 **Nevada** U.S.A.
135 C3 **Nevada** state U.S.A.
106 C2 **Nevada, Sierra** mts Spain
135 B2 **Nevada, Sierra** mts U.S.A.
88 C2 **Nevel'** Rus. Fed.
105 C2 **Nevers** France
53 C2 **Nevertire** Austr.
109 C2 **Nevşehir** Bos.-Herz.
87 D4 **Nevinnomyssk** Rus. Fed.
128 B2 **New Aiyansh** Can.
140 B3 **New Albany** U.S.A.
151 C1 **New Amsterdam** Guyana
141 E2 **Newark** NJ U.S.A.
140 C2 **Newark** OH U.S.A.
98 C2 **Newark-on-Trent** U.K.
141 E2 **New Bern** U.S.A.
143 D2 **Newberry** U.S.A.
139 E2 **New Boston** U.S.A.
139 D3 **New Braunfels** U.S.A.
97 C2 **Newbridge** Ireland
48 E3 **New Britain** i. P.N.G.
131 D2 **New Brunswick** prov. Can.
99 C3 **Newbury** U.K.
48 E4 **New Caledonia** terr.
 S. Pacific Ocean
53 D2 **Newcastle** Austr.
123 C2 **Newcastle** S. Africa
97 D1 **Newcastle** U.K.
140 C2 **New Castle** U.S.A.
136 C2 **Newcastle** U.S.A.
98 B2 **Newcastle-under-Lyme**
 U.K.
98 C1 **Newcastle upon Tyne** U.K.
97 C2 **Newcastle West** Ireland
74 B2 **New Delhi** India
128 C3 **New Denver** Can.
53 D2 **New England Range** mts
 Austr.
131 E1 **Newfoundland** i. Can.
131 E1 **Newfoundland and**
 Labrador prov. Can.
131 D2 **New Glasgow** Can.
59 D3 **New Guinea** i. Indon./P.N.G.
141 E2 **New Hampshire** state
 U.S.A.
141 E2 **New Haven** U.S.A.
128 C2 **New Hazelton** Can.
 New Hebrides country
 S. Pacific Ocean see Vanuatu
142 B2 **New Iberia** U.S.A.
48 E3 **New Ireland** i. P.N.G.
141 E3 **New Jersey** state U.S.A.
130 C2 **New Liskeard** Can.

50 A2 **Newman** Austr.
138 D2 **New Mexico** state U.S.A.
142 B3 **New Orleans** U.S.A.
140 C2 **New Philadelphia** U.S.A.
54 B1 **New Plymouth** N.Z.
99 C3 **Newport** England U.K.
99 B3 **Newport** Wales U.K.
142 B1 **Newport** AR U.S.A.
134 B2 **Newport** OR U.S.A.
141 E2 **Newport** RI U.S.A.
141 E2 **Newport** VT U.S.A.
134 C1 **Newport** WA U.S.A.
141 D3 **Newport News** U.S.A.
143 E3 **New Providence** i.
 Bahamas
99 A3 **Newquay** U.K.
142 B2 **New Roads** U.S.A.
97 C2 **New Ross** Ireland
97 C1 **Newry** U.K.
83 K1 **New Siberia Islands**
 Rus. Fed.
52 B2 **New South Wales** state
 Austr.
137 E2 **Newton** IA U.S.A.
137 D3 **Newton** KS U.S.A.
99 B3 **Newton Abbot** U.K.
96 B3 **Newton Stewart** U.K.
97 B2 **Newtown** Ireland
99 B2 **Newtown** U.K.
136 C1 **New Town** U.S.A.
97 C1 **Newtownabbey** U.K.
97 D1 **Newtownards** U.K.
96 C3 **Newton St Boswells** U.K.
97 C1 **Newtownstewart** U.K.
137 E2 **New Ulm** U.S.A.
141 E2 **New York** U.S.A.
141 D2 **New York** state U.S.A.
54 B2 **New Zealand** country
 Oceania
79 C2 **Neyrīz** Iran
76 B3 **Neyshābūr** Iran
145 C3 **Nezahualcóyotl, Presa**
 resr Mex.
61 B3 **Ngabang** Indon.
75 C2 **Ngamring** China
75 C1 **Ngangla Ringco** salt l.
 China
75 C1 **Nganglong Kangri** mts
 China
75 C2 **Ngangzê Co** salt l. China
62 A2 **Ngao** Thai.
118 B2 **Ngaoundéré** Cameroon
54 C1 **Ngaruawahia** N.Z.
62 A2 **Ngathainggyaung**
 Myanmar
118 B3 **Ngo** Congo
63 B2 **Ngok Linh** mt. Vietnam
118 B3 **Ngol Bembo** Nigeria
68 C2 **Ngoring Hu** l. China
115 D3 **Ngourti** Niger
115 D3 **Nguigmi** Niger
59 D2 **Ngulu** atoll Micronesia
115 D3 **Nguru** Nigeria
123 D2 **Ngwelezana** S. Africa
121 C2 **Nhamalabué** Moz.
63 B2 **Nha Trang** Vietnam
52 B3 **Nhill** Austr.
123 D2 **Nhlangano** Swaziland
51 C1 **Nhulunbuy** Austr.
141 D2 **Niagara Falls** Can.
114 C3 **Niamey** Niger
119 C2 **Niangara** Dem. Rep. Congo
114 B3 **Niangay, Lac** l. Mali
60 A1 **Nias** i. Indon.
146 B3 **Nicaragua** country
 Central America
146 B3 **Nicaragua, Lake** Nic.
105 D3 **Nice** France
73 A4 **Nicobar Islands** India
80 B2 **Nicosia** Cyprus

146 B4 **Nicoya, Golfo de** b.
 Costa Rica
88 B2 **Nida** Lith.
103 E1 **Nidzica** Pol.
102 B1 **Niebüll** Ger.
101 D2 **Niederaula** Ger.
118 B2 **Niefang** Equat. Guinea
101 F1 **Niemegk** Ger.
101 D1 **Nienburg (Weser)** Ger.
100 B1 **Nieuwe-Niedorp** Neth.
151 C1 **Nieuw Nickerie** Suriname
122 A3 **Nieuwoudtville** S. Africa
100 A2 **Nieuwpoort** Belgium
80 B2 **Niğde** Turkey
115 C3 **Niger** country Africa
115 C4 **Niger** r. Africa
115 C4 **Niger, Mouths of the**
 Nigeria
115 C3 **Nigeria** country Africa
130 B2 **Nighthawk Lake** Can.
111 B2 **Nigrita** Greece
67 C3 **Niigata** Japan
67 B4 **Niihama** Japan
67 C4 **Nii-jima** i. Japan
67 C3 **Niitsu** Japan
100 B2 **Nijmegen** Neth.
100 C1 **Nijverdal** Neth.
92 J2 **Nikel'** Rus. Fed.
83 M3 **Nikol'skoye** Rus. Fed.
91 C2 **Nikopol'** Ukr.
80 B1 **Niksar** Turkey
79 D2 **Nikshahr** Iran
109 C2 **Nikšić** Serb. and Mont.
116 B1 **Nile** r. Africa
140 B2 **Niles** U.S.A.
105 C3 **Nîmes** France
53 C3 **Nimmitabel** Austr.
117 B4 **Nimule** Sudan
53 C1 **Nindigully** Austr.
73 B4 **Nine Degree Channel**
 India
53 C3 **Ninety Mile Beach** Austr.
54 B1 **Ninety Mile Beach** N.Z.
70 C3 **Ningbo** China
71 B3 **Ningde** China
71 B3 **Ningdu** China
70 B2 **Ningguo** China
71 C3 **Ninghai** China
 Ningjiang China see
 Songyuan
68 C2 **Ningjing Shan** mts China
70 A2 **Ningxia Huizu Zizhiqu**
 aut. reg. China
70 B2 **Ningyang** China
62 B1 **Ninh Binh** Vietnam
63 B2 **Binh Hoa** Vietnam
66 D2 **Ninohe** Japan
137 D2 **Niobrara** r. U.S.A.
114 B3 **Niono** Mali
114 B3 **Nioro** Mali
104 B2 **Niort** France
129 D2 **Nipawin** Can.
130 B2 **Nipigon** Can.
130 B2 **Nipigon, Lake** Can.
131 D1 **Nipishish Lake** Can.
130 C2 **Nipissing, Lake** Can.
135 C3 **Nipton** U.S.A.
151 D3 **Niquelândia** Brazil
73 B3 **Nirmal** India
109 D2 **Niš** Serb. and Mont.
109 D2 **Nišava** r. Serb. and Mont.
108 B3 **Niscemi** Sicily Italy
67 B4 **Nishino-omote** Japan
155 D2 **Niterói** Brazil
96 C3 **Nith** r. U.K.
103 D2 **Nitra** Slovakia
49 H3 **Niue** terr. S. Pacific Ocean
92 H3 **Nivala** Fin.
100 B2 **Nivelles** Belgium
73 B3 **Nizamabad** India

87 E3 **Nizhnekamsk** Rus. Fed.
83 H3 **Nizhnevartovsk** Rus. Fed.
82 G2 **Nizhnevartovsk** Rus. Fed.
89 F3 **Nizhniy Kislyay** Rus. Fed.
87 D3 **Nizhniy Lomov** Rus. Fed.
87 D3 **Nizhniy Novgorod** Rus. Fed.
86 E2 **Nizhniy Odes** Rus. Fed.
86 E3 **Nizhniy Tagil** Rus. Fed.
83 G2 **Nizhnyaya Tunguska** r. Rus. Fed.
91 C1 **Nizhyn** Ukr.
121 D2 **Njazidja** i. Comoros
119 D3 **Njinjo** Tanz.
119 D3 **Njombe** Tanz.
121 C2 **Nkhotakota** Malawi
118 A2 **Nkongsamba** Cameroon
123 C3 **Nkululeko** S. Africa
123 C3 **Nkwenkwezi** S. Africa
67 B4 **Nobeoka** Japan
52 B1 **Noccundra** Austr.
144 A1 **Nogales** Mex.
138 A2 **Nogales** U.S.A.
104 C2 **Nogent-le-Rotrou** France
89 E2 **Noginsk** Rus. Fed.
74 B2 **Nohar** India
100 C3 **Nohfelden** Ger.
104 B2 **Noirmoutier, Île de** i. France
104 B2 **Noirmoutier-en-l'Île** France
67 C4 **Nojima-zaki** c. Japan
74 B2 **Nokha** India
93 H3 **Nokia** Fin.
74 A2 **Nok Kundi** Pak.
118 B2 **Nola** C.A.R.
86 D3 **Nolinsk** Rus. Fed.
123 C3 **Nomonde** S. Africa
123 D2 **Nondweni** S. Africa
62 B2 **Nong Khai** Thai.
52 A2 **Nonning** Austr.
144 B2 **Nonoava** Mex.
65 B2 **Nonsan** S. Korea
63 B2 **Nonthaburi** Thai.
122 B3 **Nonzwakazi** S. Africa
77 C3 **Norak** Tajik.
130 C2 **Noranda** Can.
82 C1 **Nordaustlandet** i. Svalbard
128 C2 **Nordegg** Can.
100 C1 **Norden** Ger.
83 H1 **Nordenshel'da, Arkhipelag** is Rus. Fed.
100 C1 **Norderney** Ger.
100 C1 **Norderney** i. Ger.
101 E1 **Norderstedt** Ger.
93 E3 **Nordfjordeid** Norway
101 E2 **Nordhausen** Ger.
101 D1 **Nordholz** Ger.
100 C1 **Nordhorn** Ger.
Nordkapp c. Norway see North Cape
92 F3 **Nordli** Norway
102 C2 **Nördlingen** Ger.
92 G3 **Nordmaling** Sweden
94 B1 **Norðoyar** i. Faroe Is
97 C2 **Nore** r. Ireland
137 D2 **Norfolk** NE U.S.A.
141 D3 **Norfolk** VA U.S.A.
48 F4 **Norfolk Island** terr. S. Pacific Ocean
93 E3 **Norheimsund** Norway
82 G2 **Noril'sk** Rus. Fed.
75 C2 **Norkyung** China
139 D1 **Norman** U.S.A.
Normandes, Îles is Europe see Channel Islands
51 D1 **Normanton** Austr.
93 G4 **Norrköping** Sweden
93 G4 **Nörtälje** Sweden
50 B3 **Norseman** Austr.
92 G3 **Norsjö** Sweden

98 C1 **Northallerton** U.K.
50 A2 **Northampton** Austr.
99 C2 **Northampton** U.K.
73 D3 **North Andaman** i. India
129 D2 **North Battleford** Can.
130 C2 **North Bay** Can.
130 C1 **North Belcher Islands** Can.
96 C2 **North Berwick** U.K.
92 I1 **North Cape** Norway
54 B1 **North Cape** N.Z.
130 A1 **North Caribou Lake** Can.
143 E1 **North Carolina** state U.S.A.
130 B2 **North Channel** lake channel Can.
96 A3 **North Channel** i. U.K.
128 B3 **North Cowichan** Can.
136 C1 **North Dakota** state U.S.A.
99 C3 **North Downs** hills U.K.
143 E3 **Northeast Providence Channel** Bahamas
101 D2 **Northeim** Ger.
122 A2 **Northern Cape** prov. S. Africa
129 E2 **Northern Indian Lake** Can.
97 C1 **Northern Ireland** prov. U.K.
48 D1 **Northern Mariana Islands** terr. N. Pacific Ocean
50 C1 **Northern Territory** admin. div. Austr.
96 C2 **North Esk** r. U.K.
137 E2 **Northfield** U.S.A.
99 D3 **North Foreland** c. U.K.
54 B1 **North Island** N.Z.
129 E2 **North Knife Lake** Can.
65 B1 **North Korea** country Asia
62 A1 **North Lakhimpur** India
128 B1 **North Nahanni** r. Can.
136 C2 **North Platte** U.S.A.
136 C2 **North Platte** r. U.S.A.
96 C1 **North Ronaldsay** i. U.K.
94 D2 **North Sea** Europe
130 A1 **North Spirit Lake** Can.
53 D1 **North Stradbroke Island** Austr.
54 B1 **North Taranaki Bight** b. N.Z.
130 C1 **North Twin Island** Can.
98 B1 **North Tyne** r. U.K.
96 A2 **North Uist** i. U.K.
131 D2 **Northumberland Strait** Can.
122 C2 **North West** prov. S. Africa
50 A2 **North West Cape** Austr.
143 E3 **Northwest Providence Channel** Bahamas
131 E1 **North West River** Can.
128 B1 **Northwest Territories** admin. div. Can.
98 C1 **North York Moors** moorland U.K.
140 C3 **Norton** U.S.A.
121 C2 **Norton** Zimbabwe
140 C2 **Norwalk** U.S.A.
93 F3 **Norway** country Europe
129 E2 **Norway House** Can.
160 A3 **Norwegian Sea** N. Atlantic Ocean
99 D2 **Norwich** U.K.
141 E2 **Norwich** CT U.S.A.
141 D2 **Norwich** NY U.S.A.
66 D2 **Noshiro** Japan
91 C1 **Nosivka** Ukr.
122 B2 **Nosop** watercourse Africa
86 E2 **Nosovaya** Rus. Fed.
79 C2 **Noṣratābād** Iran
Nossob watercourse Africa see Nosop
103 D1 **Noteć** r. Pol.
93 E4 **Notodden** Norway

67 C3 **Noto-hantō** pen. Japan
131 D2 **Notre Dame, Monts** mts Can.
131 E2 **Notre Dame Bay** Can.
130 C1 **Nottaway** r. Can.
99 C2 **Nottingham** U.K.
114 A2 **Nouâdhibou** Maur.
114 A3 **Nouakchott** Maur.
114 A3 **Nouâmghâr** Maur.
48 F4 **Nouméa** New Caledonia
114 B3 **Nouna** Burkina
154 B2 **Nova Esperança** Brazil
155 D2 **Nova Friburgo** Brazil
109 C1 **Nova Gradiška** Croatia
154 C2 **Nova Granada** Brazil
155 D2 **Nova Iguaçu** Brazil
91 C2 **Nova Kakhovka** Ukr.
155 D1 **Nova Lima** Brazil
154 B2 **Nova Londrina** Brazil
91 C2 **Nova Odesa** Ukr.
150 B1 **Nova Paraíso** Brazil
131 D2 **Nova Scotia** prov. Can.
155 D1 **Nova Venécia** Brazil
83 K1 **Novaya Sibir', Ostrov** i. Rus. Fed.
86 E1 **Novaya Zemlya** is Rus. Fed.
103 D2 **Nové Zámky** Slovakia
91 C1 **Novhorod-Sivers'kyy** Ukr.
110 B2 **Novi Iskŭr** Bulg.
108 A2 **Novi Ligure** Italy
109 D2 **Novi Pazar** Serb. and Mont.
109 C1 **Novi Sad** Serb. and Mont.
87 D3 **Novoanninskiy** Rus. Fed.
150 B2 **Novo Aripuanã** Brazil
91 D2 **Novoazovs'k** Ukr.
91 E2 **Novocherkassk** Rus. Fed.
86 D2 **Novodvinsk** Rus. Fed.
152 C3 **Novo Hamburgo** Brazil
154 C2 **Novo Horizonte** Brazil
90 B1 **Novohrad-Volyns'kyy** Ukr.
103 D2 **Novo Mesto** Slovenia
91 D3 **Novomikhaylovskiy** Rus. Fed.
89 E3 **Novomoskovsk** Rus. Fed.
91 D2 **Novomoskovs'k** Ukr.
91 C2 **Novomyrhorod** Ukr.
91 C1 **Novooleksiyivka** Ukr.
91 C2 **Novopskov** Ukr.
91 D3 **Novorossiysk** Rus. Fed.
88 C2 **Novorzhev** Rus. Fed.
87 E3 **Novosergiyevka** Rus. Fed.
91 D2 **Novoshakhtinsk** Rus. Fed.
82 G3 **Novosibirsk** Rus. Fed.
Novosibirskiye Ostrova is Rus. Fed. see New Siberia Islands
89 E3 **Novosil'** Rus. Fed.
89 D2 **Novosokol'niki** Rus. Fed.
91 C2 **Novotroyits'ke** Ukr.
90 A1 **Novovolyns'k** Ukr.
89 D3 **Novozybkov** Rus. Fed.
103 D2 **Nový Jičín** Czech Rep.
86 E2 **Novyy Bor** Rus. Fed.
91 D1 **Novyy Oskol** Rus. Fed.
86 G2 **Novyy Port** Rus. Fed.
82 G2 **Novyy Urengoy** Rus. Fed.
69 E1 **Novyy Urgal** Rus. Fed.
103 D1 **Nowogard** Pol.
53 D2 **Nowra** Austr.
81 D2 **Now Shahr** Iran
74 B1 **Nowshera** Pak.
103 E2 **Nowy Sącz** Pol.
103 E2 **Nowy Targ** Pol.
87 G2 **Noyabr'sk** Rus. Fed.
105 C2 **Noyon** France

121	C2	**Nsanje** Malawi
118	B3	**Ntandembele**
		Dem. Rep. Congo
119	D3	**Ntungamo** Uganda
79	C2	**Nu'aym** reg. Oman
116	B2	**Nubian Desert** Sudan
150	A3	**Nudo Coropuna** mt. Peru
129	E1	**Nueltin Lake** Can.
153	A5	**Nueva Lubecka** Arg.
145	B3	**Nueva Rosita** Mex.
144	B1	**Nuevo Casas Grandes**
		Mex.
144	B2	**Nuevo Ideal** Mex.
145	C2	**Nuevo Laredo** Mex.
117	C4	**Nugaal** watercourse
		Somalia
105	C2	**Nuits-St-Georges** France
		Nu Jiang r. China see
		Salween
49	G4	**Nuku'alofa** Tonga
49	I3	**Nuku Hiva** i. Fr. Polynesia
76	B2	**Nukus** Uzbek.
50	B3	**Nullagine** Austr.
50	B3	**Nullarbor Plain** Austr.
115	D4	**Numan** Nigeria
67	C3	**Numazu** Japan
93	E3	**Numedal** val. Norway
59	C3	**Numfoor** i. Indon.
53	C3	**Numurkah** Austr.
		Nunap Isua c. Greenland
		see Farewell, Cape
127	G3	**Nunavik** reg. Can.
129	E1	**Nunavut** admin. div. Can.
99	C2	**Nuneaton** U.K.
107	D3	**Nuñomoral** Spain
108	A2	**Nuoro** Sardinia Italy
78	B2	**Nuqrah** Saudi Arabia
101	E3	**Nuremberg** Ger.
52	A2	**Nuriootpa** Austr.
92	I3	**Nurmes** Fin.
		Nürnberg Ger. see
		Nuremberg
62	A1	**Nu Shan** mts China
74	A2	**Nushki** Pak.
127	H2	**Nuuk** Greenland
127	H2	**Nuussuaq** Greenland
127	H2	**Nuussuaq** pen.
		Greenland
78	A2	**Nuwaybi' al Muzayyinah**
		Egypt
122	B3	**Nuweveldberge** mts
		S. Africa
86	F2	**Nyagan'** Rus. Fed.
75	D1	**Nyainqêntanglha Feng**
		mt. China
75	C2	**Nyainqêntanglha Shan**
		mts China
117	A3	**Nyala** Sudan
86	D2	**Nyandoma** Rus. Fed.
118	B3	**Nyanga** r. Gabon
121	C2	**Nyanga** Zimbabwe
121	C1	**Nyasa, Lake** Africa
93	F4	**Nyborg** Denmark
92	I1	**Nyborg** Norway
93	G4	**Nybro** Sweden
119	D3	**Nyeri** Kenya
75	C1	**Nyima** China
68	C3	**Nyingchi** China
103	E2	**Nyíregyháza** Hungary
93	F4	**Nykøbing** Denmark
93	G4	**Nyköping** Sweden
53	C2	**Nymagee** Austr.
93	G4	**Nynäshamn** Sweden
53	C2	**Nyngan** Austr.
88	B3	**Nyoman** r. Belarus/Lith.
105	D3	**Nyons** France
86	E2	**Nyrob** Rus. Fed.
134	C2	**Nyssa** U.S.A.
119	C3	**Nyunzu** Dem. Rep. Congo
91	C2	**Nyzh'n'ohirs'kyy** Ukr.

119	D3	**Nzega** Tanz.
114	B4	**Nzérékoré** Guinea
120	A1	**N'zeto** Angola

O

136	C2	**Oahe, Lake** U.S.A.
124	E5	**O'ahu** i. N. Pacific Ocean
52	B2	**Oakbank** Austr.
142	B2	**Oakdale** U.S.A.
53	D1	**Oakey** Austr.
134	B1	**Oak Harbor** U.S.A.
140	C3	**Oak Hill** U.S.A.
135	B3	**Oakland** U.S.A.
50	B2	**Oakover** r. Austr.
134	B2	**Oakridge** U.S.A.
143	D1	**Oak Ridge** U.S.A.
54	B3	**Oamaru** N.Z.
64	B1	**Oas** Phil.
145	C3	**Oaxaca** Mex.
86	F2	**Ob'** r. Rus. Fed.
118	B2	**Obala** Cameroon
96	B2	**Oban** U.K.
106	B1	**O Barco** Spain
53	C2	**Oberon** Austr.
101	F3	**Oberpfälzer Wald** mts Ger.
101	E3	**Oberviechtach** Ger.
59	C3	**Obi** i. Indon.
151	E2	**Óbidos** Brazil
66	D2	**Obihiro** Japan
69	E1	**Obluch'ye** Rus. Fed.
89	E3	**Obninsk** Rus. Fed.
119	C2	**Obo** C.A.R.
117	C3	**Obock** Djibouti
118	B3	**Obouya** Rus. Fed.
89	E3	**Oboyan'** Rus. Fed.
144	B2	**Obregón, Presa** resr Mex.
109	D2	**Obrenovac** Serb. and Mont.
87	E3	**Obshchiy Syrt** hills
		Rus. Fed.
86	G2	**Obskaya Guba** sea chan.
		Rus. Fed.
114	B4	**Obuasi** Ghana
90	C1	**Obukhiv** Ukr.
86	D2	**Ob"yachevo** Rus. Fed.
143	D3	**Ocala** U.S.A.
144	B2	**Ocampo** Mex.
106	C2	**Ocaña** Spain
150	A1	**Occidental, Cordillera**
		mts Col.
150	A3	**Occidental, Cordillera**
		mts Peru
141	D3	**Ocean City** U.S.A.
128	D3	**Ocean Falls** Can.
135	C4	**Oceanside** U.S.A.
91	C2	**Ochakiv** Ukr.
86	E3	**Ocher** Rus. Fed.
101	E3	**Ochsenfurt** Ger.
143	D2	**Oconee** r. U.S.A.
145	C3	**Ocosingo** Mex.
58	C3	**Ocussi** enclave East Timor
116	B2	**Oda, Jebel** mt. Sudan
66	D2	**Ōdate** Japan
67	C3	**Odawara** Japan
93	E3	**Odda** Norway
106	B2	**Odemira** Port.
111	C3	**Ödemiş** Turkey
93	F4	**Odense** Denmark
101	D2	**Odenwald** reg. Ger.
102	C1	**Oderbucht** b. Ger.
90	C2	**Odesa** Ukr.
139	C2	**Odessa** U.S.A.
114	B4	**Odienné** Côte d'Ivoire
103	D2	**Odra** r. Ger./Pol.
151	D2	**Oeiras** Brazil
100	D2	**Oelde** Ger.
136	C2	**Oelrichs** U.S.A.

101	F2	**Oelsnitz** Ger.
100	B1	**Oenkerk** Neth.
109	C2	**Ofanto** r. Italy
101	D2	**Offenbach am Main** Ger.
102	B2	**Offenburg** Ger.
117	C4	**Ogaden** reg. Eth.
66	C3	**Oga-hantō** pen. Japan
67	C3	**Ōgaki** Japan
136	C2	**Ogallala** U.S.A.
115	C4	**Ogbomosho** Nigeria
134	D2	**Ogden** U.S.A.
141	D2	**Ogdensburg** U.S.A.
126	B2	**Ogilvie** r. Can.
126	B2	**Ogilvie Mountains** Can.
143	D2	**Oglethorpe, Mount** U.S.A.
130	B1	**Ogoki** r. Can.
130	B1	**Ogoki Reservoir** Can.
88	B2	**Ogre** Latvia
109	C1	**Ogulin** Croatia
140	B3	**Ohio** r. U.S.A.
140	C2	**Ohio** state U.S.A.
101	E2	**Ohrdruf** Ger.
109	D2	**Ohrid** Macedonia
151	C1	**Oiapoque** Brazil
142	C2	**Oil City** U.S.A.
100	A3	**Oise** r. France
67	B4	**Ōita** Japan
144	B2	**Ojinaga** Mex.
152	B3	**Ojos del Salado, Nevado**
		mt. Arg./Chile
89	F2	**Oka** r. Rus. Fed.
120	A3	**Okahandja** Namibia
120	A3	**Okakarara** Namibia
128	C3	**Okanagan Falls** Can.
128	C3	**Okanagan Lake** Can.
134	C1	**Okanogan** U.S.A.
134	C1	**Okanogan** r. U.S.A.
74	B1	**Okara** Pak.
120	B2	**Okavango** r.
		Botswana/Namibia
120	B2	**Okavango Delta** swamp
		Botswana
67	C3	**Okaya** Japan
67	B4	**Okayama** Japan
67	C3	**Okazaki** Japan
143	D3	**Okeechobee, Lake** U.S.A.
143	D2	**Okefenokee Swamp** U.S.A.
99	A3	**Okehampton** U.K.
74	A2	**Okha** India
83	K3	**Okha** Rus. Fed.
75	C2	**Okhaldhunga** Nepal
83	K3	**Okhotka** r. Rus. Fed.
83	K3	**Okhotsk** Rus. Fed.
156	C2	**Okhotsk, Sea of**
		Japan/Rus. Fed.
91	C1	**Okhtyrka** Ukr.
69	E3	**Okinawa** i. Japan
67	B3	**Oki-shotō** is Japan
139	D1	**Oklahoma** state U.S.A.
139	D1	**Oklahoma City** U.S.A.
139	D1	**Okmulgee** U.S.A.
78	A2	**Oko, Wadi** watercourse
		Sudan
118	B3	**Okondja** Gabon
128	C2	**Okotoks** Can.
89	D3	**Okovskiy Les** for. Rus. Fed.
118	B3	**Okoyo** Congo
92	H1	**Øksfjord** Norway
62	A2	**Oktwin** Myanmar
86	D2	**Oktyabr'skiy**
		Arkhangel'skaya Oblast'
		Rus. Fed.
83	L3	**Oktyabr'skiy** Kamchatskaya
		Oblast' Rus. Fed.
87	E3	**Oktyabr'skiy** Respublika
		Bashkortostan Rus. Fed.
86	F2	**Oktyabr'skoye** Rus. Fed.
83	H1	**Oktyabr'skoy Revolyutsii,**
		Ostrov i. Rus. Fed.
89	D2	**Okulovka** Rus. Fed.

66 C2 **Okushiri-tō** i. Japan
92 □A3 **Ólafsvík** Iceland
93 G4 **Öland** i. Sweden
52 B2 **Olary** Austr.
153 B4 **Olavarría** Arg.
103 D1 **Oława** Pol.
108 A2 **Olbia** Sardinia Italy
126 B2 **Old Crow** Can.
101 D1 **Oldenburg** Ger.
102 C1 **Oldenburg in Holstein** Ger.
100 C1 **Oldenzaal** Neth.
97 B3 **Old Head of Kinsale** Ireland
128 C2 **Olds** Can.
129 D2 **Old Wives Lake** Can.
141 D2 **Olean** U.S.A.
103 E1 **Olecko** Pol.
83 J2 **Olekminsk** Rus. Fed.
91 C2 **Oleksandriya** Ukr.
86 C2 **Olenegorsk** Rus. Fed.
83 I2 **Olenek** Rus. Fed.
83 I2 **Olenek** r. Rus. Fed.
89 D2 **Olenino** Rus. Fed.
90 B1 **Olevs'k** Ukr.
106 B2 **Olhão** Port.
122 A2 **Olifants** watercourse Namibia
123 D1 **Olifants** S. Africa
123 D1 **Olifants** r. Northern S. Africa
122 A3 **Olifants** r. W. Cape S. Africa
122 B2 **Olifantshoek** S. Africa
154 C2 **Olimpia** Brazil
151 E2 **Olinda** Brazil
123 C1 **Oliphants Drift** S. Africa
107 C2 **Oliva** Spain
155 D2 **Oliveira** Brazil
106 B2 **Olivenza** Spain
152 B3 **Ollagüe** Chile
150 A2 **Olmos** Peru
140 B3 **Olney** U.S.A.
103 D2 **Olomouc** Czech Rep.
64 B1 **Olongapo** Phil.
104 B3 **Oloron-Ste-Marie** France
107 D1 **Olot** Spain
69 D1 **Olovyannaya** Rus. Fed.
100 C2 **Olpe** Ger.
103 E1 **Olsztyn** Pol.
110 B2 **Olt** r. Romania
81 C1 **Oltu** Turkey
111 B3 **Olympia** tourist site Greece
134 B1 **Olympia** U.S.A.
134 B1 **Olympus, Mount** U.S.A.
83 M3 **Olyutorskiy, Mys** c. Rus. Fed.
97 C1 **Omagh** U.K.
137 D2 **Omaha** U.S.A.
79 C2 **Oman** country Asia
79 C2 **Oman, Gulf of** Asia
120 A3 **Omaruru** Namibia
120 B2 **Omatako** watercourse Namibia
116 B3 **Omdurman** Sudan
53 C3 **Omeo** Austr.
145 C3 **Ometepec** Mex.
78 A3 **Om Hajēr** Eritrea
128 B2 **Omineca Mountains** Can.
67 C3 **Ōmiya** Japan
100 C1 **Ommen** Neth.
83 L2 **Omolon** r. Rus. Fed.
100 B3 **Omont** France
82 F3 **Omsk** Rus. Fed.
83 L2 **Omsukchan** Rus. Fed.
110 C1 **Omu, Vârful** mt. Romania
67 A4 **Ōmura** Japan
140 C1 **Onaping Lake** Can.
131 C2 **Onatchiway, L.** Can.
120 A2 **Oncócua** Angola
122 B3 **Onderstedorings** S. Africa
120 A2 **Ondjiva** Angola

86 C2 **Onega** Rus. Fed.
86 C2 **Onega** r. Rus. Fed.
    Onega, Lake l. Rus. Fed. see Onezhskoye Ozero
141 D2 **Oneida Lake** U.S.A.
137 D2 **O'Neill** U.S.A.
141 D2 **Oneonta** U.S.A.
110 C1 **Oneşti** Romania
86 C2 **Onezhskoye Ozero** l. Rus. Fed.
122 B2 **Ongers** watercourse S. Africa
65 B2 **Ongjin** N. Korea
73 C3 **Ongole** India
121 □D3 **Onilahy** r. Madag.
115 C4 **Onitsha** Nigeria
122 A2 **Onseepkans** S. Africa
50 A2 **Onslow** Austr.
143 E2 **Onslow Bay** U.S.A.
130 A1 **Ontario** prov. Can.
134 C2 **Ontario** U.S.A.
141 D2 **Ontario, Lake** Can./U.S.A.
51 C2 **Oodnadatta** Austr.
    Oostende Belgium see Ostend
100 B2 **Oosterhout** Neth.
100 A2 **Oosterschelde** est. Neth.
100 B1 **Oost-Vlieland** Neth.
128 B2 **Ootsa Lake** l. Can.
128 B2 **Ootsa Lake** Can.
118 C3 **Opala** Dem. Rep. Congo
130 C1 **Opataca, Lac** l. Can.
103 D2 **Opava** Czech Rep.
143 C2 **Opelika** U.S.A.
142 B2 **Opelousas** U.S.A.
130 C1 **Opinaca, Réservoir** resr Can.
131 D1 **Opiscotéo, Lac** l. Can.
88 C2 **Opochka** Rus. Fed.
144 A2 **Opodepe** Mex.
103 D1 **Opole** Pol.
106 B1 **Oporto** Port.
54 C1 **Opotiki** N.Z.
93 E3 **Oppdal** Norway
54 B1 **Opunake** N.Z.
120 A2 **Opuwo** Namibia
110 B1 **Oradea** Romania
109 D2 **Orahovac** Serb. and Mont.
114 B1 **Oran** Alg.
152 B3 **Orán** Arg.
65 B1 **Ŏrang** N. Korea
53 C2 **Orange** Austr.
105 C3 **Orange** France
122 A2 **Orange** r. Namibia/S. Africa
139 E2 **Orange** U.S.A.
143 D2 **Orangeburg** U.S.A.
140 C2 **Orangeville** Can.
101 F1 **Oranienburg** Ger.
122 A2 **Oranjemund** Namibia
120 B3 **Orapa** Botswana
110 B1 **Orăştie** Romania
108 B2 **Orbetello** Italy
53 C3 **Orbost** Austr.
50 B1 **Ord, Mount** hill Austr.
106 B1 **Ordes** Spain
70 B2 **Ordos** China
80 B1 **Ordu** Turkey
    Ordzhonikidze Rus. Fed. see Vladikavkaz
91 C2 **Ordzhonikidze** Ukr.
93 G4 **Örebro** Sweden
134 B2 **Oregon** state U.S.A.
134 B1 **Oregon City** U.S.A.
87 C3 **Orekhovo-Zuyevo** Rus. Fed.
89 E2 **Orël** Rus. Fed.
135 D2 **Orem** U.S.A.
111 C3 **Ören** Turkey
87 E3 **Orenburg** Rus. Fed.

54 A3 **Orepuki** N.Z.
93 F4 **Öresund** str. Denmark/Sweden
99 D2 **Orford Ness** hd U.K.
111 C3 **Orhaneli** Turkey
111 C2 **Orhangazi** Turkey
83 I3 **Orhon Gol** r. Mongolia
152 B2 **Oriental, Cordillera** mts Bol.
150 A1 **Oriental, Cordillera** mts Col.
150 A3 **Oriental, Cordillera** mts Peru
107 C2 **Orihuela** Spain
91 D2 **Orikhiv** Ukr.
130 C2 **Orillia** Can.
150 B1 **Orinoco** r. Col./Venez.
150 B1 **Orinoco Delta** Venez.
93 H4 **Orissaare** Estonia
108 A3 **Oristano** Sardinia Italy
93 I3 **Orivesi** l. Fin.
151 C2 **Oriximiná** Brazil
145 C3 **Orizaba** Mex.
145 C3 **Orizaba, Pico de** vol. Mex.
92 E3 **Örkelljunga** Sweden
93 F4 **Örkelljunga** Sweden
92 E3 **Orkla** r. Norway
96 C1 **Orkney Islands** U.K.
154 C2 **Orlândia** Brazil
143 D3 **Orlando** U.S.A.
104 C2 **Orléans** France
74 A2 **Ormara** Pak.
64 B1 **Ormoc** Phil.
99 B2 **Ormskirk** U.K.
92 G3 **Örnsköldsvik** Sweden
114 B3 **Orodara** Burkina
134 C1 **Orofino** U.S.A.
    Oroqen Zizhiqi China see Alihe
64 B2 **Oroquieta** Phil.
108 A2 **Orosei** Sardinia Italy
108 A2 **Orosei, Golfo di** b. Sardinia Italy
103 E2 **Orosháza** Hungary
135 B3 **Oroville** U.S.A.
52 A2 **Orroroo** Austr.
89 D3 **Orsha** Belarus
87 E3 **Orsk** Rus. Fed.
93 E3 **Ørsta** Norway
106 B1 **Ortegal, Cabo** c. Spain
104 B3 **Orthez** France
106 B1 **Ortigueira** Spain
137 D1 **Ortonville** U.S.A.
83 J2 **Orulgan, Khrebet** mts Rus. Fed.
    Orümiyeh, Daryācheh-ye salt l. Iran see Urmia, Lake
152 B2 **Oruro** Bol.
108 B2 **Orvieto** Italy
146 B4 **Osa, Península de** pen. Costa Rica
137 E3 **Osage** r. U.S.A.
67 C4 **Ōsaka** Japan
101 E1 **Oschersleben (Bode)** Ger.
108 A2 **Oschiri** Sardinia Italy
89 E3 **Osetr** r. Rus. Fed.
77 D2 **Osh** Kyrg.
120 A2 **Oshakati** Namibia
130 C2 **Oshawa** Can.
66 C2 **Ō-shima** i. Japan
67 C4 **Ō-shima** i. Japan
140 B2 **Oshkosh** U.S.A.
81 C2 **Oshnoviyeh** Iran
115 C4 **Oshogbo** Nigeria
118 B3 **Oshwe** Dem. Rep. Congo
109 C1 **Osijek** Croatia
128 B2 **Osilinka** r. Can.
108 B2 **Osimo** Italy
123 D2 **Osizweni** S. Africa
137 E2 **Oskaloosa** U.S.A.

Oskarshamn

93 G4 **Oskarshamn** Sweden
89 E3 **Oskol** r. Rus. Fed.
93 F4 **Oslo** Norway
93 F4 **Oslofjorden** *sea chan.*
   Norway
80 B1 **Osmancık** Turkey
111 C2 **Osmanieli** Turkey
80 B2 **Osmaniye** Turkey
88 C2 **Os'mino** Rus. Fed.
100 D1 **Osnabrück** Ger.
153 A5 **Osorno** Chile
106 C1 **Osorno** Spain
128 C3 **Osoyoos** Can.
100 B2 **Oss** Neth.
51 D4 **Ossa, Mount** Austr.
83 L3 **Ossora** Rus. Fed.
89 D2 **Ostashkov** Rus. Fed.
101 D1 **Oste** r. Ger.
100 A2 **Ostend** Belgium
101 E1 **Osterburg (Altmark)** Ger.
93 F3 **Österdalälven** l. Sweden
101 D1 **Osterholz-Scharmbeck**
   Ger.
101 E2 **Osterode am Harz** Ger.
92 F3 **Östersund** Sweden
   Ostfriesische Inseln *is* Ger.
   see **East Frisian Islands**
100 C1 **Ostfriesland** *reg.* Ger.
93 G3 **Östhammar** Sweden
103 D2 **Ostrava** Czech Rep.
103 D1 **Ostróda** Pol.
89 E3 **Ostrogozhsk** Rus. Fed.
103 E1 **Ostrołęka** Pol.
101 F2 **Ostrov** Czech Rep.
88 C2 **Ostrov** Rus. Fed.
103 E1 **Ostrowiec Świętokrzyski**
   Pol.
103 E1 **Ostrów Mazowiecka** Pol.
103 D1 **Ostrów Wielkopolski** Pol.
110 B2 **Osüm** r. Bulg.
67 B4 **Ōsumi-kaikyō** *sea chan.*
   Japan
67 B4 **Ōsumi-shotō** *is* Japan
106 B2 **Osuna** Spain
141 D2 **Oswego** U.S.A.
99 B2 **Oswestry** U.K.
67 C3 **Ōta** Japan
93 E3 **Otta** Norway
54 B3 **Otago Peninsula** N.Z.
67 C3 **Ōtaki** N.Z.
66 D2 **Otaru** Japan
120 A2 **Otavi** Namibia
134 C1 **Othello** U.S.A.
120 A3 **Otjiwarongo** Namibia
117 B3 **Otoro, Jebel** *mt.* Sudan
93 E4 **Otra** r. Norway
109 C2 **Otranto, Strait of**
   Albania/Italy
67 C3 **Ōtsu** Japan
93 E3 **Otta** Norway
130 C2 **Ottawa** Can.
130 C2 **Ottawa** r. Can.
140 B2 **Ottawa** *IL* U.S.A.
137 D3 **Ottawa** *KS* U.S.A.
130 B1 **Otter Rapids** Can.
100 B2 **Ottignies** Belgium
137 E2 **Ottumwa** U.S.A.
150 A2 **Otuzco** Peru
52 B3 **Otway, Cape** Austr.
142 B2 **Ouachita** r. U.S.A.
142 B2 **Ouachita, Lake** U.S.A.
142 B2 **Ouachita Mountains** U.S.A.
118 C2 **Ouadda** C.A.R.
115 D3 **Ouaddaï** *reg.* Chad
114 B3 **Ouagadougou** Burkina
114 B3 **Ouahigouya** Burkina
114 B3 **Oualâta** Maur.
118 C2 **Ouanda-Djallé** C.A.R.
114 B2 **Ouarâne** *reg.* Maur.
115 C1 **Ouargla** Alg.
114 B1 **Ouarzazate** Morocco

100 A2 **Oudenaarde** Belgium
122 B3 **Oudtshoorn** S. Africa
107 C2 **Oued Tlélat** Alg.
104 A2 **Ouessant, Île d'** i. France
118 B2 **Ouesso** Congo
114 B1 **Oujda** Morocco
107 D2 **Ouled Farès** Alg.
92 I2 **Oulu** Fin.
92 I3 **Oulujärvi** l. Fin.
108 A1 **Oulx** Italy
115 E3 **Oum-Chalouba** Chad
115 D3 **Oum-Hadjer** Chad
115 E3 **Ounianga Kébir** Chad
100 B2 **Oupeye** Belgium
106 B1 **Ourense** Spain
154 C2 **Ourinhos** Brazil
155 D2 **Ouro Preto** Brazil
100 B2 **Ourthe** r. Belgium
98 C2 **Ouse** r. U.K.
131 D2 **Outardes** r. Can.
131 D1 **Outardes Quatre,**
   Réservoir *resr* Can.
96 A2 **Outer Hebrides** *is* U.K.
120 A3 **Outjo** Namibia
129 D2 **Outlook** Can.
92 I3 **Outokumpu** Fin.
51 B2 **Ouyen** Austr.
106 B1 **Ovar** Port.
92 H2 **Överkalix** Sweden
135 D3 **Overton** U.S.A.
92 H2 **Övertorneå** Sweden
106 B1 **Oviedo** Spain
93 E3 **Øvre Årdal** Norway
93 F3 **Øvre Rendal** Norway
90 B1 **Ovruch** Ukr.
118 B3 **Owando** Congo
112 B2 **Owase** Japan
137 E2 **Owatonna** U.S.A.
140 B3 **Owensboro** U.S.A.
135 C3 **Owens Lake** U.S.A.
130 B2 **Owen Sound** Can.
115 C4 **Owerri** Nigeria
140 C2 **Owosso** U.S.A.
134 C2 **Owyhee** U.S.A.
134 C2 **Owyhee** r. U.S.A.
54 B2 **Oxford** N.Z.
99 C3 **Oxford** U.K.
142 C2 **Oxford** U.S.A.
129 E2 **Oxford Lake** Can.
52 B2 **Oxley** Austr.
   Ox Mountains *hills* Ireland
   see **Slieve Gamph**
135 C4 **Oxnard** U.S.A.
67 C3 **Oyama** Japan
118 B2 **Oyem** Gabon
129 C2 **Oyen** Can.
105 D2 **Oyonnax** France
64 B2 **Ozamiz** Phil.
142 C2 **Ozark** U.S.A.
137 E3 **Ozark Plateau** U.S.A.
137 E3 **Ozarks, Lake of the** U.S.A.
83 L3 **Ozernovskiy** Rus. Fed.
88 B3 **Ozersk** Rus. Fed.
89 E3 **Ozery** Rus. Fed.
87 D3 **Ozinki** Rus. Fed.

P

127 H2 **Paamiut** Greenland
122 A3 **Paarl** S. Africa
103 D1 **Pabianice** Pol.
75 C2 **Pabna** Bangl.
74 A2 **Pab Range** *mts* Pak.
109 C3 **Pachino** *Sicily* Italy
145 C2 **Pachuca** Mex.
156 **Pacific Ocean**
103 D1 **Paczków** Pol.

60 B2 **Padang** Indon.
60 B1 **Padang Endau** Malaysia
60 B2 **Padangpanjang** Indon.
60 A1 **Padangsidimpuan** Indon.
101 D2 **Paderborn** Ger.
   Padova Italy *see* **Padua**
139 D3 **Padre Island** U.S.A.
52 B3 **Padthaway** Austr.
108 B1 **Padua** Italy
140 B3 **Paducah** *KY* U.S.A.
139 C2 **Paducah** *TX* U.S.A.
65 B1 **Paegam** N. Korea
65 A2 **Paengnyŏng-do** i.
   S. Korea
54 C1 **Paeroa** N.Z.
   Pafos Cyprus *see* **Paphos**
109 C2 **Pag** Croatia
64 B2 **Pagadian** Phil.
60 B2 **Pagai Selatan** i. Indon.
60 B2 **Pagai Utara** i. Indon.
59 D1 **Pagan** i. N. Mariana Is
61 C2 **Pagatan** Indon.
138 A1 **Page** U.S.A.
88 B2 **Pagėgiai** Lith.
136 B3 **Pagosa Springs** U.S.A.
88 C2 **Paide** Estonia
93 I3 **Päijänne** l. Fin.
75 C2 **Paikü Co** l. China
138 A1 **Painted Desert** U.S.A.
96 B3 **Paisley** U.K.
92 H2 **Pajala** Sweden
150 B1 **Pakaraima Mountains**
   Brazil
150 C1 **Pakaraima Mountains**
   Guyana
74 A2 **Pakistan** *country* Asia
62 A1 **Pakokku** Myanmar
88 B2 **Pakruojis** Lith.
103 D2 **Paks** Hungary
130 A1 **Pakwash Lake** Can.
62 B2 **Pakxan** Laos
63 B2 **Pakxé** Laos
115 D4 **Pala** Chad
60 B2 **Palabuhanratu, Teluk** b.
   Indon.
111 C3 **Palaikastro** Greece
111 B3 **Palaiochora** Greece
122 B1 **Palamakoloi** Botswana
107 D1 **Palamós** Spain
83 L3 **Palana** Rus. Fed.
64 B1 **Palanan** Phil.
61 C2 **Palangkaraya** Indon.
74 B2 **Palanpur** India
120 B3 **Palapye** Botswana
83 L2 **Palatka** Rus. Fed.
143 D3 **Palatka** U.S.A.
59 C2 **Palau** *country*
   N. Pacific Ocean
63 A2 **Palaw** Myanmar
64 A2 **Palawan** i. Phil.
93 H4 **Paldiski** Estonia
60 B2 **Palembang** Indon.
106 C1 **Palencia** Spain
145 C3 **Palenque** Mex.
108 B3 **Palermo** *Sicily* Italy
139 D2 **Palestine** U.S.A.
62 A1 **Paletwa** Myanmar
74 B2 **Pali** India
48 E2 **Palikir** Micronesia
111 B3 **Paliouri, Akra** *pt* Greece
100 B3 **Paliseul** Belgium
92 I3 **Paljakka** *hill* Fin.
88 C2 **Palkino** Rus. Fed.
73 B4 **Palk Strait** India/Sri Lanka
54 C2 **Palliser, Cape** N.Z.
49 I3 **Palliser, Îles** *is*
   Fr. Polynesia
106 B2 **Palma del Río** Spain
107 D2 **Palma de Mallorca** Spain

154 B3 **Palmas** Brazil
151 D3 **Palmas** Brazil
114 B4 **Palmas, Cape** Liberia
154 C3 **Palmeira** Brazil
151 D2 **Palmeirais** Brazil
55 P2 **Palmer Land** *reg.* Antarctica
54 C2 **Palmerston North** N.Z.
109 C3 **Palmi** Italy
145 C2 **Palmillas** Mex.
150 A1 **Palmira** Col.
135 C4 **Palm Springs** U.S.A.
49 H2 **Palmyra Atoll** N. Pacific Ocean
117 B3 **Paloich** Sudan
145 C3 **Palomares** Mex.
107 C2 **Palos, Cabo de** *c.* Spain
92 I3 **Paltamo** Fin.
58 B3 **Palu** Indon.
83 M2 **Palyavaam** *r.* Rus. Fed.
104 C3 **Pamiers** France
77 D3 **Pamir** *mts* Asia
143 E1 **Pamlico Sound** *sea chan.* U.S.A.
152 B2 **Pampa Grande** Bol.
153 B4 **Pampas** *reg.* Arg.
150 A1 **Pamplona** Col.
107 C1 **Pamplona** Spain
111 D2 **Pamukova** Turkey
60 B2 **Panaitan** *i.* Indon.
73 B3 **Panaji** India
146 B4 **Panama** *country* Central America
146 C4 **Panama, Gulf of** Panama
146 C4 **Panama Canal** Panama
146 C4 **Panama City** Panama
142 C2 **Panama City** U.S.A.
135 C3 **Panamint Range** *mts* U.S.A.
61 B1 **Panarik** Indon.
64 B1 **Panay** *i.* Phil.
109 D2 **Pančevo** Serb. and Mont.
64 B1 **Pandan** Phil.
75 C2 **Pandaria** India
73 B3 **Pandharpur** India
88 B2 **Panevėžys** Lith.
61 C2 **Pangkalanbuun** Indon.
60 A1 **Pangkalansusu** Indon.
60 B2 **Pangkalpinang** Indon.
123 K2 **Pangnirtung** Can.
86 G2 **Pangody** Rus. Fed.
89 F3 **Panino** Rus. Fed.
74 B2 **Panipat** India
74 A2 **Panjgur** Pak.
65 C1 **Pan Ling** *mts* China
75 C2 **Panna** India
50 A2 **Pannawonica** Austr.
154 B2 **Panorama** Brazil
65 A1 **Panshi** China
145 C2 **Pánuco** Mex.
71 A3 **Panxian** China
62 D1 **Panzhihua** China
109 C3 **Paola** Italy
63 B2 **Paôy Pêt** Cambodia
103 D2 **Pápa** Hungary
54 B1 **Papakura** N.Z.
145 C2 **Papantla** Mex.
49 I4 **Papeete** Fr. Polynesia
100 C1 **Papenburg** Ger.
80 B2 **Paphos** Cyprus
59 D3 **Papua, Gulf of** P.N.G.
59 D3 **Papua New Guinea** *country* Oceania
50 A2 **Parabuirdoo** Austr.
154 C1 **Paracatu** Brazil
155 C1 **Paracatu** *r.* Brazil
52 A2 **Parachilna** Austr.
109 D2 **Paraćin** Serb. and Mont.
155 D1 **Pará de Minas** Brazil
135 B3 **Paradise** U.S.A.

142 B1 **Paragould** U.S.A.
151 C3 **Paraguai** *r.* Brazil
152 C3 **Paraguay** *r.* Arg./Para.
152 C3 **Paraguay** *country* S. America
155 D2 **Paraíba do Sul** *r.* Brazil
154 B1 **Paraíso** Brazil
145 C3 **Paraíso** Mex.
114 C4 **Parakou** Benin
151 C1 **Paramaribo** Suriname
83 L3 **Paramushir, Ostrov** *i.* Rus. Fed.
152 B4 **Paraná** Arg.
154 A3 **Paraná** *r.* S. America
154 C3 **Paranaguá** Brazil
154 B1 **Paranaíba** Brazil
154 B2 **Paranaíba** *r.* Brazil
154 B2 **Paranapanema** *r.* Brazil
154 B2 **Paranapiacaba, Serra** *mts* Brazil
154 B2 **Paranavaí** Brazil
54 B2 **Paraparaumu** N.Z.
155 D2 **Parati** Brazil
154 B1 **Paraúna** Brazil
105 C2 **Paray-le-Monial** France
73 B3 **Parbhani** India
101 E1 **Parchim** Ger.
154 B1 **Pardo** *r.* Bahia Brazil
154 B2 **Pardo** *r.* Mato Grosso do Sul Brazil
154 C2 **Pardo** *r.* São Paulo Brazil
103 D1 **Pardubice** Czech Rep.
150 B3 **Parecis, Serra dos** *hills* Brazil
130 C2 **Parent, Lac** *l.* Can.
58 B3 **Parepare** Indon.
89 D2 **Parfino** Rus. Fed.
111 B3 **Parga** Greece
109 C3 **Parghelia** Italy
147 D3 **Paria, Gulf of** Trin. and Tob./Venez.
150 B1 **Parima, Serra** *mts* Brazil
151 C2 **Parintins** Brazil
104 C2 **Paris** France
142 C1 **Paris** *TN* U.S.A.
139 D2 **Paris** *TX* U.S.A.
93 H3 **Parkano** Fin.
138 A2 **Parker** U.S.A.
140 C3 **Parkersburg** U.S.A.
53 C2 **Parkes** Austr.
140 A1 **Park Falls** U.S.A.
137 D1 **Park Rapids** U.S.A.
108 B2 **Parma** Italy
151 D2 **Parnaíba** Brazil
151 D2 **Parnaíba** *r.* Brazil
111 B3 **Parnassos** *mt.* Greece
54 B2 **Parnassus** N.Z.
111 B3 **Parnon** *mts* Greece
88 B2 **Pärnu** Estonia
65 B1 **P'aro-ho** *i.* S. Korea
52 B2 **Paroo** *watercourse* Austr.
76 C3 **Paropamisus** *mts* Afgh.
111 C3 **Paros** *i.* Greece
144 B2 **Parras** Mex.
126 C2 **Parry, Cape** Can.
126 D1 **Parry Islands** Can.
130 B2 **Parry Sound** Can.
137 D3 **Parsons** U.S.A.
101 D2 **Partenstein** Ger.
104 B2 **Parthenay** France
97 B2 **Partry Mountains** *hills* Ireland
151 C2 **Paru** *r.* Brazil
135 C4 **Pasadena** U.S.A.
62 A2 **Pasawng** Myanmar
142 C2 **Pascagoula** U.S.A.
110 C1 **Paşcani** Romania
134 C1 **Pasco** U.S.A.
102 C1 **Pasewalk** Ger.
129 D2 **Pasfield Lake** Can.

60 B1 **Pasir Putih** Malaysia
74 A2 **Pasni** Pak.
153 A5 **Paso Río Mayo** Arg.
135 B3 **Paso Robles** U.S.A.
155 D2 **Passa Tempo** Brazil
102 C2 **Passau** Ger.
152 C3 **Passo Fundo** Brazil
155 C2 **Passos** Brazil
88 C2 **Pastavy** Belarus
150 A1 **Pastaza** *r.* Peru
150 A1 **Pasto** Col.
61 C2 **Pasuruan** Indon.
88 B2 **Pasvalys** Lith.
153 A6 **Patagonia** *reg.* Arg.
75 C2 **Patan** Nepal
81 C2 **Patea** N.Z.
141 E2 **Paterson** U.S.A.
Pathein Myanmar *see* Bassein
136 B2 **Pathfinder Reservoir** U.S.A.
61 C2 **Pati** Indon.
62 A1 **Patkai Bum** *mts* India/Myanmar
111 C3 **Patmos** *i.* Greece
75 C2 **Patna** India
81 C2 **Patnos** Turkey
154 B3 **Pato Branco** Brazil
152 C4 **Patos, Lagoa dos** *l.* Brazil
155 C1 **Patos de Minas** Brazil
152 B4 **Patquía** Arg.
111 B3 **Patras** Greece
75 C2 **Patratu** India
154 C1 **Patrocínio** Brazil
63 B3 **Pattani** Thai.
63 B2 **Pattaya** Thai.
128 B2 **Pattullo, Mount** Can.
129 D2 **Patuanak** Can.
144 B3 **Pátzcuaro** Mex.
104 B3 **Pau** France
104 B2 **Pauillac** France
62 A1 **Pauk** Myanmar
151 D2 **Paulistana** Brazil
151 E2 **Paulo Afonso** Brazil
123 O2 **Paulpietersburg** S. Africa
139 D1 **Pauls Valley** U.S.A.
62 A2 **Paungde** Myanmar
155 D1 **Pavão** Brazil
108 A1 **Pavia** Italy
88 B2 **Pāvilosta** Latvia
110 C2 **Pavlikeni** Bulg.
77 D1 **Pavlodar** Kazakh.
91 D1 **Pavlohrad** Ukr.
91 E1 **Pavlovsk** Rus. Fed.
91 D2 **Pavlovskaya** Rus. Fed.
60 B2 **Payakumbuh** Indon.
134 C2 **Payette** U.S.A.
134 C2 **Payette** *r.* U.S.A.
86 F2 **Pay-Khoy, Khrebet** *hills* Rus. Fed.
152 C4 **Paysandú** Uru.
81 C1 **Pazar** Turkey
110 B2 **Pazardzhik** Bulg.
111 C3 **Pazarköy** Turkey
108 B1 **Pazin** Croatia
63 A2 **Pe** Myanmar
128 C2 **Peace** *r.* Can.
128 C2 **Peace River** Can.
135 E3 **Peale, Mount** U.S.A.
142 C2 **Pearl** *r.* U.S.A.
139 D3 **Pearsall** U.S.A.
121 C2 **Pebane** Moz.
109 D2 **Peć** Serb. and Mont.
155 D1 **Peçanha** Brazil
86 E2 **Pechora** Rus. Fed.
86 E2 **Pechora** *r.* Rus. Fed.
88 C2 **Pechory** Rus. Fed.
139 C2 **Pecos** U.S.A.
139 C3 **Pecos** *r.* U.S.A.
103 D2 **Pécs** Hungary

155 D1 Pedra Azul Brazil
154 D2 Pedregulho Brazil
151 D2 Pedreiras Brazil
73 C4 Pedro, Point Sri Lanka
151 D2 Pedro Afonso Brazil
154 B1 Pedro Gomes Brazil
152 C3 Pedro Juan Caballero
        Para.

96 C3 Peebles U.K.
143 E2 Pee Dee r. U.S.A.
126 C2 Peel r. Can.
98 A1 Peel Isle of Man
128 C2 Peerless Lake Can.
54 B2 Pegasus Bay N.Z.
101 E3 Pegnitz Ger.
62 A2 Pegu Myanmar
62 A2 Pegu Yoma mts Myanmar
153 B4 Pehuajó Arg.
101 E1 Peine Ger.
88 C2 Peipus, Lake
        Estonia/Rus. Fed.
154 B2 Peixe r. Brazil
61 B2 Pekalongan Indon.
60 B1 Pekan Malaysia
60 B1 Pekanbaru Indon.
        Peking China see Beijing
130 B2 Pelee Island Can.
59 C3 Peleng i. Indon.
92 I2 Pelkosenniemi Fin.
122 A2 Pella S. Africa
59 D3 Pelleluhu Islands P.N.G.
92 H2 Pello Fin.
128 A1 Pelly r. Can.
128 A1 Pelly Mountains Can.
152 C4 Pelotas Brazil
152 C3 Pelotas, Rio das r. Brazil
141 F1 Pemadumcook Lake
        U.S.A.

61 B1 Pemangkat Indon.
60 A1 Pematangsiantar Indon.
121 D2 Pemba Moz.
120 B2 Pemba Zambia
119 D3 Pemba Island Tanz.
128 B2 Pemberton Can.
137 D1 Pembina r. Can.
130 C2 Pembroke Can.
99 A3 Pembroke U.K.
145 C2 Peña Nevada, Cerro mt.
        Mex.

154 B2 Penápolis Brazil
106 B1 Peñaranda de
        Bracamonte Spain
107 C1 Peñarroya mt. Spain
106 B2 Peñarroya-Pueblonuevo
        Spain
106 B1 Peñas, Cabo de c. Spain
153 A5 Penas, Golfo de g. Chile
106 B1 Peña Ubiña mt. Spain
134 C1 Pendleton U.S.A.
128 B2 Pendleton Bay Can.
134 C1 Pend Oreille Lake U.S.A.
74 B3 Penganga r. India
123 D1 Penge S. Africa
70 D2 Penglai China
71 A3 Pengshui China
106 B2 Peniche Port.
98 B1 Penicuik U.K.
108 B2 Penne Italy
98 B1 Pennines hills U.K.
141 D2 Pennsylvania state
        U.S.A.

127 G2 Penny Icecap Can.
141 F2 Penobscot r. U.S.A.
52 B3 Penola Austr.
50 C3 Penong Austr.
49 H3 Penrhyn i. N.Z.
98 B1 Penrith U.K.
142 C2 Pensacola U.S.A.
55 Q1 Pensacola Mountains
        Antarctica

61 C1 Pensiangan Sabah Malaysia
128 C3 Penticton Can.
96 C1 Pentland Firth sea chan.
        U.K.

99 B2 Penygadarr hill U.K.
87 B2 Penza Rus. Fed.
99 A3 Penzance U.K.
140 B2 Peoria U.S.A.
107 C1 Perales del Alfambra
        Spain
51 E2 Percy Isles Austr.
86 F2 Peregrebnoye Rus. Fed.
150 A1 Pereira Col.
154 B2 Pereira Barreto Brazil
90 A2 Peremyshlyany Ukr.
89 E2 Pereslavl'-Zalesskiy
        Rus. Fed.
91 C1 Pereyaslav-
        Khmel'nyts'kyy Ukr.
90 A2 Pergamino Arg.
92 H3 Perhonjoki r. Fin.
152 B3 Perico Arg.
144 B2 Pericos Mex.
104 C2 Périgueux France
147 C4 Perija, Sierra de mts Venez.
153 B6 Perito Moreno Arg.
101 E1 Perleberg Ger.
86 E3 Perm' Rus. Fed.
52 A2 Pernatty Lagoon salt flat
        Austr.
105 C2 Péronne France
145 C3 Perote Mex.
104 C3 Perpignan France
99 A3 Perranporth U.K.
143 D2 Perry FL U.S.A.
143 D2 Perry GA U.S.A.
137 E2 Perry IA U.S.A.
139 C1 Perryton U.S.A.
137 F3 Perryville U.S.A.
99 B2 Pershore U.K.
91 D2 Pershotravens'k Ukr.
        Persian Gulf Asia see
        The Gulf
50 A3 Perth Austr.
96 C2 Perth U.K.
105 D3 Pertuis France
108 A2 Pertusato, Capo c. Corsica
        France
150 A2 Peru country S. America
157 H4 Peru-Chile Trench
        sea feature S. Pacific Ocean
108 B2 Perugia Italy
154 C2 Peruíbe Brazil
100 A2 Péruwelz Belgium
90 C2 Pervomays'k Ukr.
91 C2 Pervomays'ke Ukr.
89 F3 Pervomayskiy Rus. Fed.
91 D2 Pervomays'kyy Ukr.
108 B2 Pesaro Italy
108 B2 Pescara Italy
108 B2 Pescara r. Italy
74 B1 Peshawar Pak.
109 D2 Peshkopi Albania
109 C1 Pesnica Slovenia
89 E2 Pestovo Rus. Fed.
144 B3 Petatlán Mex.
140 B2 Petenwell Lake U.S.A.
52 A2 Peterborough Austr.
130 C2 Peterborough Can.
99 C2 Peterborough U.K.
96 D2 Peterhead U.K.
50 B2 Petermann Ranges mts
        Austr.
129 D2 Peter Pond Lake Can.
128 A2 Petersburg AK U.S.A.
141 D3 Petersburg VA U.S.A.
101 D1 Petershagen Ger.
131 D1 Petit Lac Manicouagan l.
        Can.
131 E1 Petit Mécatina r. Can.

145 D2 Peto Mex.
140 C1 Petoskey U.S.A.
80 B2 Petra tourist site Jordan
66 B2 Petra Velikogo, Zaliv b.
        Rus. Fed.
111 B2 Petrich Bulg.
151 D2 Petrolina Brazil
77 C1 Petropavlovsk Kazakh.
83 L3 Petropavlovsk-
        Kamchatskiy Rus. Fed.
110 B1 Petroşani Romania
89 F3 Petrovskoye Rus. Fed.
86 C2 Petrozavodsk Rus. Fed.
123 C2 Petrusburg S. Africa
123 C2 Petrus Steyn S. Africa
122 B3 Petrusville S. Africa
89 E2 Petushki Rus. Fed.
60 A1 Peureula Indon.
83 M2 Pevek Rus. Fed.
102 B2 Pforzheim Ger.
102 C2 Pfunds Austria
101 D3 Pfungstadt Ger.
123 C2 Phahameng S. Africa
123 D1 Phalaborwa S. Africa
74 B2 Phalodi India
63 B2 Phang Hoei, San Khao
        mts Thai.
63 A3 Phangnga Thai.
62 B1 Phăng Xi Păng mt. Vietnam
63 B2 Phan Rang-Thap Cham
        Vietnam
63 B2 Phan Thiêt Vietnam
63 B3 Phatthalung Thai.
62 A2 Phayao Thai.
129 D2 Phelps Lake Can.
143 C2 Phenix City U.S.A.
63 A2 Phet Buri Thai.
63 B2 Phichit Thai.
141 D3 Philadelphia U.S.A.
136 C2 Philip U.S.A.
100 A2 Philippeville Belgium
100 A2 Philippine Neth.
64 B1 Philippines country Asia
64 B1 Philippine Sea
        N. Pacific Ocean
126 B2 Philip Smith Mountains
        U.S.A.
122 B3 Philipstown S. Africa
53 C3 Phillip Island Austr.
137 D3 Phillipsburg U.S.A.
63 B2 Phitsanulok Thai.
138 A2 Phoenix U.S.A.
49 G3 Phoenix Islands Kiribati
63 B2 Phon Thai.
62 B1 Phôngsali Laos
62 A2 Phrae Thai.
63 A3 Phuket Thai.
63 B2 Phumĭ Sâmraông
        Cambodia
123 C2 Phuthaditjhaba S. Africa
62 A2 Phyu Myanmar
108 A1 Piacenza Italy
110 C1 Piatra Neamţ Romania
151 D2 Piauí r. Brazil
108 B1 Piave r. Italy
117 B4 Pibor r. Sudan
117 B4 Pibor Post Sudan
142 C2 Picayune U.S.A.
152 B3 Pichanal Arg.
144 A2 Pichilingue Mex.
98 C1 Pickering U.K.
130 A1 Pickle Lake Can.
151 D2 Picos Brazil
153 B5 Pico Truncado Arg.
53 D2 Picton Austr.
150 B3 Piedras, Rio de las r. Peru

145 C3 Piedras Negras Guat.
145 B2 Piedras Negras Mex.
93 I3 Pieksämäki Fin.
92 I3 Pielinen l. Fin.
136 C2 Pierre U.S.A.
105 C3 Pierrelatte France
123 D2 Pietermaritzburg S. Africa
110 B1 Pietrosa mt. Romania
128 C2 Pigeon Lake Can.
153 B4 Pigüé Arg.
92 I3 Pihtipudas Fin.
145 C3 Pijijiapan Mex.
136 C3 Pikes Peak U.S.A.
122 A3 Piketberg S. Africa
140 C3 Pikeville U.S.A.
103 D1 Piła Pol.
152 C3 Pilar Arg.
152 C3 Pilar Para.
53 C2 Pilliga Austr.
154 C1 Pilões, Serra dos mts Brazil
150 B3 Pimenta Bueno Brazil
153 C4 Pinamar Arg.
80 C2 Pınarbaşı Turkey
146 B2 Pinar del Río Cuba
103 E1 Pińczów Pol.
151 D2 Pindaré r. Brazil
        Pindos mts Greece see Pindus Mountains
111 B3 Pindus Mountains Greece
142 B2 Pine Bluff U.S.A.
50 C1 Pine Creek Austr.
136 B2 Pinedale U.S.A.
86 D2 Pinega Rus. Fed.
129 D2 Pinehouse Lake Can.
111 B3 Pineios r. Greece
128 C1 Pine Point Can.
136 C2 Pine Ridge U.S.A.
123 D2 Pinetown S. Africa
70 B2 Pingdingshan China
71 A3 Pingguo China
71 B3 Pingjiang China
70 A2 Pingliang China
71 C3 P'ingtung Taiwan
71 A3 Pingxiang Guangxi China
71 B3 Pingxiang Jiangxi China
70 B2 Pingyin China
151 D2 Pinheiro Brazil
101 D1 Pinneberg Ger.
145 C3 Pinotepa Nacional Mex.
88 C3 Pinsk Belarus
135 D3 Pioche U.S.A.
119 C3 Piodi Dem. Rep. Congo
103 E1 Pionki Pol.
103 D1 Piotrków Trybunalski Pol.
137 D2 Pipestone U.S.A.
131 C2 Pipmuacan, Réservoir resr Can.
154 B2 Piquiri r. Brazil
154 C1 Piracanjuba Brazil
154 C2 Piracicaba Brazil
155 D1 Piracicaba r. Brazil
154 C2 Piraçununga Brazil
111 B3 Piraeus Greece
154 C2 Piraí do Sul Brazil
154 C2 Pirajuí Brazil
154 B1 Piranhas Brazil
151 E2 Piranhas r. Brazil
154 C1 Pirapora Brazil
151 D2 Piripiri Brazil
59 C3 Piru Indon.
108 B2 Pisa Italy
152 A2 Pisagua Chile
150 A3 Pisco Peru
102 C2 Písek Czech Rep.
79 D2 Pīshīn Iran
145 D2 Pisté Mex.
108 B2 Pistoia Italy
108 B2 Pistoia Italy

106 C1 Pisuerga r. Spain
134 B2 Pit r. U.S.A.
154 B2 Pitanga Brazil
155 D1 Pitangui Brazil
49 J4 Pitcairn Island terr. S. Pacific Ocean
92 H2 Piteå Sweden
92 H2 Piteälven r. Sweden
110 B2 Pitești Romania
75 C2 Pithoragarh India
96 C2 Pitlochry U.K.
128 B2 Pitt Island Can.
137 E3 Pittsburg U.S.A.
141 D2 Pittsburgh U.S.A.
141 E2 Pittsfield U.S.A.
53 D1 Pittsworth Austr.
155 C2 Piumhi Brazil
150 A2 Piura Peru
90 C2 Pivdennyy Buh r. Ukr.
131 E2 Placentia Can.
135 B3 Placerville U.S.A.
146 C2 Placetas Cuba
139 C2 Plainview U.S.A.
154 C1 Planaltina Brazil
142 B2 Plaquemine U.S.A.
106 B1 Plasencia Spain
153 C4 Plata, Río de la sea chan. Arg./Uru.
147 C4 Plato Col.
137 D2 Platte r. U.S.A.
141 E2 Plattsburgh U.S.A.
101 F1 Plau Ger.
101 F2 Plauen Ger.
101 F1 Plauer See l. Ger.
89 E3 Plavsk Rus. Fed.
129 E2 Playgreen Lake Can.
62 B2 Plây Ku Vietnam
153 B4 Plaza Huincul Arg.
139 D3 Pleasanton U.S.A.
54 B2 Pleasant Point N.Z.
104 C2 Pleaux France
130 B1 Pledger Lake Can.
54 C1 Plenty, Bay of g. N.Z.
136 C1 Plentywood U.S.A.
86 D2 Plesetsk Rus. Fed.
131 C1 Plétipi, Lac l. Can.
104 C2 Plettenberg Ger.
122 B3 Plettenberg Bay S. Africa
110 B2 Pleven Bulg.
109 C2 Pljevlja Serb. and Mont.
109 C2 Ploče Croatia
103 D1 Płock Pol.
109 C2 Pločno mt. Bos.-Herz.
104 B2 Ploemeur France
110 C2 Ploiești Romania
89 F2 Ploskoye Rus. Fed.
104 B2 Plouzané France
110 B2 Plovdiv Bulg.
88 B2 Plungė Lith.
88 C3 Plyeshchanitsy Belarus
147 D3 Plymouth Montserrat
99 A3 Plymouth U.K.
140 B2 Plymouth U.S.A.
88 C2 Plyussa Rus. Fed.
102 C2 Plzeň Czech Rep.
114 B3 Pô Burkina
108 B1 Po r. Italy
77 C2 Pobeda Peak China/Kyrg.
142 B1 Pocahontas U.S.A.
134 D2 Pocatello U.S.A.
90 B1 Pochayiv Ukr.
89 D3 Pochep Rus. Fed.
89 D3 Pochinok Rus. Fed.
145 C3 Pochutla Mex.
141 D3 Pocomoke City U.S.A.
155 C2 Poços de Caldas Brazil
89 D2 Poddor'ye Rus. Fed.
91 D1 Podgorenskiy Rus. Fed.
109 C2 Podgorica Serbia
82 G3 Podgornoye Rus. Fed.

83 H2 Podkamennaya Tunguska r. Rus. Fed.
89 E2 Podol'sk Rus. Fed.
109 D2 Podujevo Serb. and Mont.
122 A2 Pofadder S. Africa
89 D3 Pogar Rus. Fed.
109 D2 Pogradec Albania
65 B2 P'ohang S. Korea
48 E2 Pohnpei i. Micronesia
110 C1 Poiana Mare Romania
118 C3 Poie Dem. Rep. Congo
118 B3 Pointe-Noire Congo
126 D2 Point Lake Can.
140 C3 Point Pleasant U.S.A.
104 C2 Poitiers France
74 B2 Pokaran India
75 C2 Pokhara Nepal
83 J2 Pokrovsk Rus. Fed.
91 D2 Pokrovskoye Rus. Fed.
138 A1 Polacca U.S.A.
106 B1 Pola de Lena Spain
103 D1 Poland country Europe
88 C2 Polatsk Belarus
77 C3 Pol-e Khomri Afgh.
61 C2 Polewali Indon.
118 B2 Poli Cameroon
102 C1 Police Pol.
109 C2 Policoro Italy
105 D2 Poligny France
64 B1 Polillo Islands Phil.
90 B1 Polis'ke Ukr.
103 D1 Polkowice Pol.
109 C3 Pollino, Monte mt. Italy
91 D2 Polohy Ukr.
123 C1 Polokwane S. Africa
90 B1 Polonne Ukr.
134 D1 Polson U.S.A.
91 C2 Poltava Ukr.
66 B2 Poltavka Rus. Fed.
91 D2 Poltavskaya Rus. Fed.
88 C2 Põlva Estonia
111 B2 Polygyros Greece
106 B2 Pombal Port.
102 C1 Pomeranian Bay Pol.
108 B2 Pomezia Italy
92 I2 Pomokaira reg. Fin.
110 C2 Pomorie Bulg.
        Pomorska, Zatoka b. Pol. see Pomeranian Bay
155 D1 Pompéu Brazil
139 D1 Ponca City U.S.A.
147 D3 Ponce Puerto Rico
        Pondicherry India see Puducherry
127 F2 Pond Inlet Can.
106 B1 Ponferrada Spain
117 A4 Pongo watercourse Sudan
123 D2 Pongola r. S. Africa
128 C2 Ponoka Can.
84 D3 Ponta Delgada Azores
154 B3 Ponta Grossa Brazil
154 C1 Pontalina Brazil
105 D2 Pont-à-Mousson France
105 D2 Pontarlier France
142 B2 Pontchartrain, Lake U.S.A.
106 B2 Ponte de Sor Port.
129 D3 Ponteix Can.
150 C3 Pontes-e-Lacerda Brazil
106 B1 Pontevedra Spain
140 B2 Pontiac IL U.S.A.
140 C2 Pontiac MI U.S.A.
61 B2 Pontianak Indon.
104 B2 Pontivy France
151 C1 Pontoetoe Suriname
129 E2 Ponton Can.
99 B3 Pontypool U.K.
108 B2 Ponziane, Isole is Italy
99 C3 Poole U.K.
        Poona India see Pune

52 B2	Pooncarie Austr.	
152 B2	Poopó, Lago de l. Bol.	
150 A1	Popayán Col.	
83 I2	Popigay r. Rus. Fed.	
52 B2	Popiltah Austr.	
129 E2	Poplar r. Can.	
137 E3	Poplar Bluff U.S.A.	
118 B3	Popokabaka	
	Dem. Rep. Congo	
110 C2	Popovo Bulg.	
103 E2	Poprad Slovakia	
151 D3	Porangatu Brazil	
74 A2	Porbandar India	
126 B2	Porcupine r.	
	Can./U.S.A.	
108 B1	Poreč Croatia	
54 B2	Porirua N.Z.	
88 C2	Porkhov Rus. Fed.	
104 B2	Pornic France	
83 K3	Poronaysk Rus. Fed.	
111 B3	Poros Greece	
93 E4	Porsgrunn Norway	
97 C1	Portadown U.K.	
97 D1	Portaferry U.K.	
140 B2	Portage N.Z.	
129 E3	Portage la Prairie Can.	
128 B3	Port Alberni Can.	
106 B2	Portalegre Port.	
139 C2	Portales U.S.A.	
128 A2	Port Alexander U.S.A.	
128 B2	Port Alice U.S.A.	
134 B1	Port Angeles U.S.A.	
51 D4	Port Arthur Austr.	
139 E3	Port Arthur U.S.A.	
96 A3	Port Askaig U.K.	
52 A2	Port Augusta Austr.	
147 C3	Port-au-Prince Haiti	
131 E1	Port aux Choix Can.	
73 D3	Port Blair India	
52 B3	Port Campbell Austr.	
54 B3	Port Chalmers N.Z.	
143 D3	Port Charlotte U.S.A.	
147 C3	Port-de-Paix Haiti	
128 A2	Port Edward Can.	
155 D1	Porteirinha Brazil	
151 C2	Portel Brazil	
130 B2	Port Elgin Can.	
123 C3	Port Elizabeth S. Africa	
96 A3	Port Ellen U.K.	
98 A1	Port Erin Isle of Man	
122 A3	Porterville S. Africa	
135 C3	Porterville U.S.A.	
52 B3	Port Fairy Austr.	
54 C1	Port Fitzroy N.Z.	
118 A3	Port-Gentil Gabon	
115 C4	Port Harcourt Nigeria	
128 B2	Port Hardy Can.	
	Port Harrison Can. see	
	Inukjuak	
131 D3	Port Hawkesbury Can.	
50 A2	Port Hedland Austr.	
99 A2	Porthmadog U.K.	
131 E1	Port Hope Simpson Can.	
140 C2	Port Huron U.S.A.	
106 B2	Portimão Port.	
53 C2	Portland N.S.W. Austr.	
52 B3	Portland Vic. Austr.	
141 E2	Portland ME U.S.A.	
134 B1	Portland OR U.S.A.	
128 A2	Portland Canal inlet Can.	
97 C2	Portlaoise Ireland	
139 D3	Port Lavaca U.S.A.	
52 A2	Port Lincoln Austr.	
114 A4	Port Loko Sierra Leone	
113 K9	Port Louis Mauritius	
53 D2	Port Macquarie Austr.	
128 B2	Port McNeill Can.	
131 D2	Port-Menier Can.	
59 D3	Port Moresby P.N.G.	
122 A2	Port Nolloth S. Africa	
	Port-Nouveau-Québec	
	Can. see Kangiqsualujjuaq	
	Porto Port. see Oporto	
150 B2	Porto Acre Brazil	
152 C4	Porto Alegre Brazil	
151 C3	Porto Artur Brazil	
151 C3	Porto dos Gaúchos Óbidos	
	Brazil	
150 D3	Porto Esperidião Brazil	
108 B2	Portoferraio Italy	
96 A1	Port of Ness U.K.	
151 D2	Porto Franco Brazil	
147 D3	Port of Spain Trin. and Tob.	
108 B1	Portogruaro Italy	
108 B2	Portomaggiore Italy	
154 B2	Porto Mendes Brazil	
152 C3	Porto Murtinho Brazil	
151 D3	Porto Nacional Brazil	
114 C4	Porto-Novo Benin	
154 B2	Porto Primavera, Represa	
	resr Brazil	
151 C2	Porto Santana Brazil	
155 C1	Porto Seguro Brazil	
108 B2	Porto Tolle Italy	
108 A2	Porto Torres Sardinia Italy	
105 D3	Porto-Vecchio Corsica	
	France	
150 B2	Porto Velho Brazil	
150 A2	Portoviejo Ecuador	
52 B3	Port Phillip Bay Austr.	
52 A2	Port Pirie Austr.	
96 A2	Portree U.K.	
128 B3	Port Renfrew Can.	
97 C1	Portrush U.K.	
116 B1	Port Said Egypt	
143 C3	Port St Joe U.S.A.	
123 C3	Port St Johns S. Africa	
123 C3	Port Shepstone S. Africa	
99 C3	Portsmouth U.K.	
141 E2	Portsmouth NH U.S.A.	
140 C3	Portsmouth OH U.S.A.	
141 D3	Portsmouth VA U.S.A.	
97 C1	Portstewart U.K.	
116 B3	Port Sudan Sudan	
142 C3	Port Sulphur U.S.A.	
99 B3	Port Talbot U.K.	
106 B2	Portugal country Europe	
97 B2	Portumna Ireland	
105 C3	Port-Vendres France	
48 F4	Port Vila Vanuatu	
93 I3	Porvoo Fin.	
65 B2	Poryŏng S. Korea	
152 C3	Posadas Arg.	
89 E2	Poshekhon'ye Rus. Fed.	
92 I2	Posio Fin.	
58 C3	Poso Indon.	
151 D3	Posse Brazil	
101 E2	Pößneck Ger.	
139 C2	Post U.S.A.	
	Poste-de-la-Baleine Can.	
	see Kuujjuarapik	
122 B2	Postmasburg S. Africa	
109 C2	Posušje Bos.-Herz.	
139 E1	Poteau U.S.A.	
109 C2	Potenza Italy	
151 D2	Poti r. Brazil	
81 C1	P'ot'i Georgia	
115 D3	Potiskum Nigeria	
141 D3	Potomac, South Branch	
	r. U.S.A.	
152 B2	Potosí Bol.	
64 B1	Pototan Phil.	
138 C3	Potrero del Llano Mex.	
101 F1	Potsdam Ger.	
141 E2	Potsdam U.S.A.	
141 D2	Pottstown U.S.A.	
141 D2	Pottsville U.S.A.	
131 E2	Pouch Cove Can.	
141 E2	Poughkeepsie U.S.A.	
98 B2	Poulton-le-Fylde U.K.	
155 C2	Pouso Alegre Brazil	
63 B2	Poŭthĭsăt Cambodia	
103 D2	Považská Bystrica	
	Slovakia	
109 C2	Povlen mt. Serb. and Mont.	
106 B1	Póvoa de Varzim Port.	
136 B2	Powell U.S.A.	
135 D3	Powell, Lake resr U.S.A.	
128 B3	Powell River Can.	
154 B1	Poxoréu Brazil	
	Poyang China see Boyang	
71 B3	Poyang Hu l. China	
109 D2	Požarevac Serb. and Mont.	
145 C2	Poza Rica Mex.	
109 C1	Požega Croatia	
109 D2	Požega Serb. and Mont.	
79 D2	Pozm Tīāb Iran	
103 D1	Poznań Pol.	
106 C2	Pozoblanco Spain	
106 B2	Pozzuoli Italy	
60 B2	Prabumulih Indon.	
102 C2	Prachatice Czech Rep.	
63 A2	Prachuap Khiri Khan Thai.	
155 E1	Prado Brazil	
102 C1	Prague Czech Rep.	
	Praha Czech Rep. see	
	Prague	
112 C5	Praia Cape Verde	
139 C2	Prairie Dog Town Fork	
	r. U.S.A.	
140 A2	Prairie du Chien U.S.A.	
60 A1	Prapat Indon.	
154 C1	Prata Brazil	
105 E3	Prato Italy	
137 D3	Pratt U.S.A.	
61 C2	Praya Indon.	
63 B2	Preăh Vihéar Cambodia	
89 F2	Prechistoye Rus. Fed.	
129 D2	Preeceville Can.	
88 C2	Preili Latvia	
53 C2	Premer Austr.	
105 C2	Prémery France	
101 F1	Premnitz Ger.	
102 C1	Prenzlau Ger.	
63 A2	Preparis Island Cocos Is	
63 A2	Preparis North Channel	
	Cocos Is	
63 A2	Preparis South Channel	
	Cocos Is	
103 D2	Přerov Czech Rep.	
138 A2	Prescott U.S.A.	
109 D2	Preševo Serb. and Mont.	
152 B3	Presidencia Roque Sáenz	
	Peña Arg.	
151 D2	Presidente Dutra Brazil	
154 B2	Presidente Epitácio Brazil	
154 B2	Presidente Prudente	
	Brazil	
138 C3	Presidio U.S.A.	
103 E2	Prešov Slovakia	
141 F1	Presque Isle U.S.A.	
101 F2	Pressel Ger.	
98 B2	Preston U.K.	
134 D2	Preston U.S.A.	
96 B3	Prestwick U.K.	
155 C1	Preto r. Brazil	
123 C2	Pretoria S. Africa	
111 B3	Preveza Greece	
63 B2	Prey Vêng Cambodia	
109 C2	Priboj Serb. and Mont.	
135 D3	Price U.S.A.	
88 B3	Prienai Lith.	
122 B2	Prieska S. Africa	
103 D2	Prievidza Slovakia	
109 C2	Prijedor Bos.-Herz.	
	Prikaspiyskaya	
	Nizmennost' lowland	
	Kazakh./Rus. Fed. see	
	Caspian Lowland	
109 D2	Prilep Macedonia	

91 D2 **Primorsko-Akhtarsk** Rus. Fed.
129 D2 **Primrose Lake** Can.
129 D2 **Prince Albert** Can.
122 B3 **Prince Albert** S. Africa
126 D2 **Prince Albert Peninsula** Can.
122 B3 **Prince Albert Road** S. Africa
126 C2 **Prince Alfred, Cape** Can.
122 A3 **Prince Alfred Hamlet** S. Africa
127 C3 **Prince Charles Island** Can.
55 E2 **Prince Charles Mountains** Antarctica
131 D2 **Prince Edward Island** prov. Can.
113 I11 **Prince Edward Islands** Indian Ocean
128 B3 **Prince George** Can.
126 E2 **Prince of Wales Island** Can.
128 A2 **Prince of Wales Island** U.S.A.
126 D2 **Prince of Wales Strait** Can.
126 D1 **Prince Patrick Island** Can.
126 E2 **Prince Regent Inlet** sea chan. Can.
128 A2 **Prince Rupert** Can.
51 D1 **Princess Charlotte Bay** Austr.
128 B2 **Princess Royal Island** Can.
128 B3 **Princeton** Can.
134 B2 **Prineville** U.S.A.
90 B1 **Pripet** r. Belarus/Ukr.
90 A1 **Pripet Marshes** Belarus/Ukr.
109 D2 **Priština** Serb. and Mont.
111 F1 **Pritzwalk** Ger.
109 C2 **Privlaka** Croatia
89 F2 **Privolzhsk** Rus. Fed.
109 D2 **Prizren** Serb. and Mont.
151 C1 **Professor van Blommestein Meer** resr Suriname
145 D2 **Progreso** Mex.
81 C1 **Prokhladnyy** Rus. Fed.
109 D2 **Prokuplje** Serb. and Mont.
126 C3 **Prophet** r. Can.
128 B2 **Prophet River** Can.
51 D2 **Proserpine** Austr.
89 E3 **Protvino** Rus. Fed.
110 C2 **Provadiya** Bulg.
141 E2 **Providence** U.S.A.
146 B3 **Providencia, Isla de** i. Caribbean Sea
83 N2 **Provideniya** Rus. Fed.
135 D2 **Provo** U.S.A.
129 C2 **Provost** Can.
154 B3 **Prudentópolis** Brazil
126 B2 **Prudhoe Bay** U.S.A.
100 C2 **Prüm** Ger.
105 D3 **Prunelli-di-Fiumorbo** Corsica France
103 E1 **Pruszków** Pol.
110 C1 **Prut** r. Europe
91 C1 **Pryluky** Ukr.
91 D2 **Prymors'k** Ukr.
139 D1 **Pryor** U.S.A.
Prypyats' r. Belarus see Pripet
103 E2 **Przemyśl** Pol.
111 C3 **Psara** i. Greece
81 C3 **Psebay** Rus. Fed.
91 D3 **Pshekha** r. Rus. Fed.
88 C2 **Pskov** Rus. Fed.
88 C2 **Pskov, Lake** Estonia/Rus. Fed.
111 B2 **Ptolemaïda** Greece

109 C1 **Ptuj** Slovenia
150 A2 **Pucallpa** Peru
71 B3 **Pucheng** China
65 B2 **Puch'ŏn** S. Korea
103 D1 **Puck** Pol.
92 I2 **Pudasjärvi** Fin.
86 C2 **Pudozh** Rus. Fed.
73 B3 **Puducherry** India
145 C3 **Puebla** Mex.
136 C3 **Pueblo** U.S.A.
153 B4 **Puelén** Arg.
106 C2 **Puente-Genil** Spain
153 A5 **Puerto Aisén** Chile
152 B2 **Puerto Alegre** Bol.
145 C3 **Puerto Ángel** Mex.
146 B4 **Puerto Armuelles** Panama
150 B1 **Puerto Ayacucho** Venez.
146 B3 **Puerto Cabezas** Nic.
150 B1 **Puerto Carreño** Col.
153 A5 **Puerto Cisnes** Chile
144 A2 **Puerto Cortés** Mex.
145 C3 **Puerto Escondido** Mex.
152 B2 **Puerto Frey** Bol.
150 B1 **Puerto Inírida** Col.
152 C2 **Puerto Isabel** Bol.
150 A2 **Puerto Leguizamo** Col.
144 A2 **Puerto Libertad** Mex.
146 B3 **Puerto Limón** Costa Rica
106 C2 **Puertollano** Spain
153 B5 **Puerto Madryn** Arg.
150 B3 **Puerto Maldonado** Peru
153 A5 **Puerto Montt** Chile
153 A6 **Puerto Natales** Chile
150 B1 **Puerto Nuevo** Col.
144 A1 **Puerto Peñasco** Mex.
152 C3 **Puerto Pinasco** Para.
147 C3 **Puerto Plata** Dom. Rep.
150 A2 **Puerto Portillo** Peru
64 A2 **Puerto Princesa** Phil.
147 D3 **Puerto Rico** terr. West Indies
158 B3 **Puerto Rico Trench** sea feature Caribbean Sea
146 A3 **Puerto San José** Guat.
153 B6 **Puerto Santa Cruz** Arg.
144 B2 **Puerto Vallarta** Mex.
87 D3 **Pugachev** Rus. Fed.
74 B2 **Pugal** India
54 B2 **Pukaki, Lake** N.Z.
129 D2 **Pukatawagan** Can.
92 I3 **Pukkila** Fin.
134 C1 **Pullman** U.S.A.
64 B1 **Pulog, Mount** Phil.
150 A2 **Puná, Isla** i. Ecuador
54 B2 **Punakaiki** N.Z.
123 D1 **Punda Maria** S. Africa
73 B3 **Pune** India
65 B1 **P'ungsan** N. Korea
121 C2 **Púngoè** r. Moz.
153 B4 **Punta Alta** Arg.
153 A6 **Punta Arenas** Chile
108 A2 **Punta Balestieri** mt. Sardinia Italy
146 B3 **Puntarenas** Costa Rica
150 A1 **Punto Fijo** Venez.
92 I3 **Puolanka** Fin.
82 G2 **Pur** r. Rus. Fed.
75 C3 **Puri** India
100 B1 **Purmerend** Neth.
75 C2 **Purnia** India
75 C2 **Puruliya** India
150 B2 **Purus** r. Peru

61 B2 **Purwakarta** Indon.
65 B1 **Puryŏng** N. Korea
65 B2 **Pusan** S. Korea
88 C2 **Pushkinskiye Gory** Rus. Fed.
88 C2 **Pustoshka** Rus. Fed.
62 A1 **Putao** Myanmar
71 B3 **Putian** China
Puting China see De'an
61 C2 **Puting, Tanjung** pt Indon.
101 F1 **Putlitz** Ger.
58 A2 **Putrajaya** Malaysia
102 C1 **Puttgarden** Ger.
150 A2 **Putumayo** r. Col.
61 C1 **Putusibau** Indon.
91 C1 **Putyvl'** Ukr.
127 F2 **Puvirnituq** Can.
70 B2 **Puyang** China
104 C3 **Puylaurens** France
99 A2 **Pwllheli** U.K.
63 A2 **Pyapon** Myanmar
82 G2 **Pyasina** r. Rus. Fed.
87 D4 **Pyatigorsk** Rus. Fed.
91 C2 **P''yatykhatky** Ukr.
62 A2 **Pyè** Myanmar
88 C3 **Pyetrykaw** Belarus
93 H3 **Pyhäjärvi** l. Fin.
92 I3 **Pyhäjoki** r. Fin.
92 I3 **Pyhäsalmi** Fin.
62 A2 **Pyinmana** Myanmar
65 B2 **Pyŏksŏng** N. Korea
65 B2 **P'yŏnggang** N. Korea
65 B2 **P'yŏngsan** N. Korea
65 B2 **P'yŏngyang** N. Korea
135 C2 **Pyramid Lake** U.S.A.
80 B3 **Pyramids of Giza** tourist site Egypt
107 D1 **Pyrenees** mts Europe
111 B3 **Pyrgos** Greece
91 C1 **Pyryatyn** Ukr.
103 C1 **Pyrzyce** Pol.
88 C2 **Pytalovo** Rus. Fed.
111 B3 **Pyxaria** mt. Greece

Q

Qaanaaq Greenland see Thule
123 C3 **Qacha's Nek** Lesotho
69 D2 **Qagan Nur** China
68 C2 **Qaidam Pendi** basin China
78 B2 **Qal'at Bishah** Saudi Arabia
129 E1 **Qamanirjuaq Lake** Can.
Qamanittuaq Can. see Baker Lake
79 C3 **Qamar, Ghubbat al** b. Yemen
78 B3 **Qam Hadil** Saudi Arabia
77 C3 **Qarshi** Uzbek.
78 B2 **Qaryat al Ulyā** Saudi Arabia
127 H2 **Qasigiannguit** Greenland
79 D2 **Qasr-e Qand** Iran
81 C2 **Qasr-e Shirin** Iran
127 H2 **Qassimiut** Greenland
78 B3 **Qa'tabah** Yemen
79 C2 **Qatar** country Asia
116 A2 **Qattara Depression** Egypt
81 C1 **Qazax** Azer.
81 C1 **Qazımämmäd** Azer.
81 C2 **Qazvin** Iran
127 H2 **Qeqertarsuaq** i. Greenland
127 H2 **Qeqertarsuatsiaat** Greenland
127 H2 **Qeqertarsuup Tunua** b. Greenland
79 C2 **Qeshm** Iran

70 A3 **Qianjiang** Chongqing China
70 B2 **Qianjiang** Hubei China
65 H1 **Qian Shan** mts China
70 C2 **Qidong** China
68 B2 **Qiemo** China
71 A3 **Qijiang** China
68 C2 **Qijiaojing** China
127 G2 **Qikiqtarjuaq** Can.
74 A2 **Qila Ladgasht** Pak.
68 C2 **Qilian Shan** China
127 I2 **Qillak** i. Greenland
70 B3 **Qimen** China
127 G1 **Qimusseriarsuaq** b.
　　Greenland
116 B2 **Qinā** Egypt
70 C2 **Qingdao** China
68 C2 **Qinghai Hu** salt l. China
68 C2 **Qinghai Nanshan** mts
　　China
71 B3 **Qingyuan** Guangdong China
65 A1 **Qingyuan** Liaoning China
　　Qingzang Gaoyuan plat.
　　China see Tibet, Plateau of
70 B2 **Qingzhou** China
70 B2 **Qinhuangdao** China
70 A2 **Qin Ling** mts China
　　Qinting China see Lianhua
70 B2 **Qinyang** China
71 A3 **Qinzhou** China
71 B4 **Qionghai** China
68 C2 **Qionglai Shan** mts China
71 B4 **Qiongshan** China
69 E1 **Qiqihar** China
79 C2 **Qir** Iran
66 B1 **Qitaihe** China
70 B2 **Qixian** China
　　Qogir Feng mt.
　　China/Jammu and Kashmir
　　see K2
81 D2 **Qom** Iran
　　Qomolangma Feng
　　mt. China/Nepal see
　　Everest, Mount
76 B2 **Qo'ng'irot** Uzbek.
　　Qoqek China see Tacheng
77 D2 **Qo'qon** Uzbek.
76 B2 **Qoraqalpog'iston** Kazakh.
100 C1 **Quakenbrück** Ger.
63 B2 **Quang Ngai** Vietnam
63 B2 **Quang Tri** Vietnam
71 B3 **Quanzhou** Fujian China
71 B3 **Quanzhou** Guangxi China
108 A3 **Quartu Sant'Elena** Sardinia
　　Italy
138 A2 **Quartzsite** U.S.A.
81 C1 **Quba** Azer.
53 C3 **Queanbeyan** Austr.
131 C2 **Québec** Can.
130 C1 **Québec** prov. Can.
101 E2 **Quedlinburg** Ger.
128 A2 **Queen Charlotte** Can.
128 A2 **Queen Charlotte Islands**
　　Can.
128 B2 **Queen Charlotte Sound**
　　sea chan. Can.
128 B2 **Queen Charlotte Strait**
　　Can.
126 D1 **Queen Elizabeth Islands**
　　Can.
126 E2 **Queen Maud Gulf** Can.
55 B2 **Queen Maud Land** reg.
　　Antarctica
55 N1 **Queen Maud Mountains**
　　Antarctica
52 B1 **Queensland** state Austr.
51 D4 **Queenstown** Austr.
54 A3 **Queenstown** N.Z.
123 C3 **Queenstown** S. Africa
121 C2 **Quelimane** Moz.
138 B2 **Quemado** U.S.A.

154 B2 **Querência do Norte** Brazil
145 B2 **Querétaro** Mex.
101 E2 **Querfurt** Ger.
128 B2 **Quesnel** Can.
128 B2 **Quesnel Lake** Can.
74 A1 **Quetta** Pak.
64 A2 **Quezon** Phil.
64 B1 **Quezon City** Phil.
120 A2 **Quibala** Angola
150 A1 **Quibdó** Col.
104 B2 **Quiberon** France
104 C3 **Quillan** France
153 C4 **Quilmes** Arg.
73 B4 **Quilon** India
51 C2 **Quilpie** Austr.
153 A4 **Quilpué** Chile
120 A1 **Quimbele** Angola
152 B3 **Quimili** Arg.
104 B2 **Quimper** France
104 B2 **Quimperlé** France
137 E3 **Quincy** IL U.S.A.
141 E2 **Quincy** MA U.S.A.
107 C1 **Quinto** Spain
121 D2 **Quionga** Moz.
53 D2 **Quirindi** Austr.
121 C3 **Quissico** Moz.
120 A2 **Quitapa** Angola
150 A2 **Quito** Ecuador
151 E2 **Quixadá** Brazil
71 A3 **Qujing** China
52 A2 **Quorn** Austr.
79 C2 **Qurayat** Oman
77 C3 **Qürghonteppa** Tajik.
63 B2 **Quy Nhon** Vietnam
71 B3 **Quzhou** China

R

103 D2 **Raab** r. Austria
92 H3 **Raahe** Fin.
100 C1 **Raalte** Neth.
61 C2 **Raas** i. Indon.
61 C2 **Raba** Indon.
114 B1 **Rabat** Morocco
48 E3 **Rabaul** P.N.G.
78 A2 **Rābigh** Saudi Arabia
131 E2 **Race, Cape** Can.
142 B3 **Raceland** U.S.A.
63 B3 **Rach Gia** Vietnam
140 B2 **Racine** U.S.A.
110 C1 **Rădăuţi** Romania
140 B3 **Radcliff** U.S.A.
74 B2 **Radhanpur** India
130 C1 **Radisson** Can.
103 E1 **Radom** Pol.
103 D1 **Radomsko** Pol.
90 B1 **Radomyshl'** Ukr.
109 D2 **Radoviš** Macedonia
88 B2 **Radviliškis** Lith.
78 A2 **Raḍwā, Jabal** mt.
　　Saudi Arabia
90 B1 **Radyvyliv** Ukr.
75 C2 **Rae Bareli** India
128 C1 **Rae-Edzo** Can.
128 C1 **Rae Lakes** Can.
100 C2 **Raeren** Belgium
54 C1 **Raetihi** N.Z.
152 B4 **Rafaela** Arg.
118 C2 **Rafaï** C.A.R.
78 B2 **Rafḥā'** Saudi Arabia
79 C1 **Rafsanjān** Iran
64 B2 **Ragang, Mount** vol. Phil.
109 B3 **Ragusa** Sicily Italy
59 C3 **Raha** Indon.
88 D3 **Rahachow** Belarus
74 B2 **Rahimyar Khan** Pak.

73 B3 **Raichur** India
75 C2 **Raigarh** India
128 C2 **Rainbow Lake** Can.
134 B1 **Rainier, Mount** vol. U.S.A.
130 A2 **Rainy Lake** Can.
129 E3 **Rainy River** Can.
75 C2 **Raipur** India
93 H3 **Raisio** Fin.
73 C3 **Rajahmundry** India
61 C1 **Rajang** r. Sarawak Malaysia
74 B2 **Rajanpur** Pak.
73 B4 **Rajapalaiyam** India
74 B2 **Rajasthan Canal** India
74 B2 **Rajgarh** India
74 B2 **Rajkot** India
74 B2 **Rajpur** India
75 C2 **Rajshahi** Bangl.
54 B2 **Rakaia** r. N.Z.
90 A2 **Rakhiv** Ukr.
91 D1 **Rakitnoye** Rus. Fed.
88 C2 **Rakke** Estonia
88 C2 **Rakvere** Estonia
143 E1 **Raleigh** U.S.A.
48 F2 **Ralik Chain** is Marshall Is
74 B2 **Ramgarh** India
81 C2 **Rāmhormoz** Iran
78 B3 **Ramlat Dahm** des.
　　Saudi Arabia/Yemen
　　Ramlat Rabyānah des.
　　Libya see Rebiana Sand Sea
110 C1 **Râmnicu Sărat** Romania
110 B1 **Râmnicu Vâlcea** Romania
89 E3 **Ramon'** Rus. Fed.
123 C1 **Ramotswa** Botswana
75 B2 **Rampur** India
62 A2 **Ramree Island** Myanmar
98 A1 **Ramsey** Isle of Man
99 D3 **Ramsgate** U.K.
75 C2 **Ranaghat** India
61 C1 **Ranau** Sabah Malaysia
153 A4 **Rancagua** Chile
75 C2 **Ranchi** India
93 F4 **Randers** Denmark
54 B2 **Rangiora** N.Z.
54 C1 **Rangitaiki** r. N.Z.
62 A2 **Rangoon** Myanmar
75 C2 **Rangpur** Bangl.
129 E1 **Rankin Inlet** Can.
53 C2 **Rankin's Springs** Austr.
96 B2 **Rannoch Moor** moorland
　　U.K.
63 A3 **Ranong** Thai.
59 C3 **Ransiki** Indon.
61 C2 **Rantaupanjang** Indon.
60 A1 **Rantauprapat** Indon.
92 I2 **Ranua** Fin.
78 B2 **Ranyah, Wādī** watercourse
　　Saudi Arabia
48 I4 **Rapa** i. Fr. Polynesia
136 C2 **Rapid City** U.S.A.
88 B2 **Rapla** Estonia
74 A2 **Rapur** India
49 H4 **Rarotonga** i. Cook Is
153 B5 **Rasa, Punta** pt Arg.
79 C2 **Ra's al Khaymah** U.A.E.
117 B3 **Ras Dejen** mt. Eth.
88 B2 **Raseiniai** Lith.
81 C2 **Rasht** Iran
74 A2 **Ras Koh** mt. Pak.
88 C2 **Rasony** Belarus
87 D3 **Rasskazovo** Rus. Fed.
79 C2 **Ras Tannūrah**
　　Saudi Arabia
101 C1 **Rastede** Ger.
93 F3 **Rätan** Sweden
74 B2 **Ratangarh** India
63 A2 **Rat Buri** Thai.
62 A1 **Rathedaung** Myanmar
101 F1 **Rathenow** Ger.
97 C1 **Rathlin Island** U.K.

74 B2 **Ratlam** India
73 B3 **Ratnagiri** India
73 C4 **Ratnapura** Sri Lanka
90 A1 **Ratne** Ukr.
138 C1 **Raton** U.S.A.
96 D2 **Rattray Head** U.K.
101 E1 **Ratzeburg** Ger.
92 □B2 **Raufarhöfn** Iceland
54 C1 **Raukumara Range** *mts*
N.Z.
93 H3 **Rauma** Fin.
61 C2 **Raung, Gunung** *vol.* Indon.
75 C2 **Raurkela** India
134 D1 **Ravalli** U.S.A.
81 C2 **Ravänsar** Iran
108 B2 **Ravenna** Italy
102 B2 **Ravensburg** Ger.
74 B1 **Ravi** r. Pak.
74 B1 **Rawalpindi** Pak.
103 D1 **Rawicz** Pol.
50 B3 **Rawlinna** Austr.
136 B2 **Rawlins** U.S.A.
153 B5 **Rawson** Arg.
73 C3 **Rayagada** India
69 E1 **Raychikhinsk** Rus. Fed.
78 B3 **Raydah** Yemen
87 E3 **Rayevskiy** Rus. Fed.
134 B1 **Raymond** U.S.A.
53 D2 **Raymond Terrace** Austr.
139 D3 **Raymondville** U.S.A.
145 C2 **Rayón** Mex.
63 B2 **Rayong** Thai.
78 A2 **Rayyis** Saudi Arabia
104 B2 **Raz, Pointe du** *pt* France
81 C2 **Razãzah, Buhayrat ar**
l. Iraq
110 C2 **Razgrad** Bulg.
110 C2 **Razim, Lacul** *lag.* Romania
110 B2 **Razlog** Bulg.
104 B2 **Ré, Île de** *i.* France
99 C3 **Reading** U.K.
141 D2 **Reading** U.S.A.
115 E2 **Rebiana Sand Sea** *des.*
Libya
66 D1 **Rebun-tõ** *i.* Japan
50 B3 **Recherche, Archipelago
of the** *is* Austr.
89 D3 **Rechytsa** Belarus
151 E2 **Recife** Brazil
123 C3 **Recife, Cape** S. Africa
100 C2 **Recklinghausen** Ger.
152 C3 **Reconquista** Arg.
142 C1 **Red** r. U.S.A.
131 E1 **Red Bay** Can.
135 B2 **Red Bluff** U.S.A.
98 C1 **Redcar** U.K.
129 C2 **Redcliff** Austr.
52 B2 **Red Cliffs** Austr.
128 C2 **Red Deer** Can.
126 D3 **Red Deer** r. Can.
129 D2 **Red Deer Lake** Can.
134 B2 **Redding** U.S.A.
99 C2 **Redditch** U.K.
137 D2 **Redfield** U.S.A.
130 A1 **Red Lake** Can.
137 E1 **Red Lakes** U.S.A.
134 E1 **Red Lodge** U.S.A.
134 B2 **Redmond** U.S.A.
137 D2 **Red Oak** U.S.A.
106 B2 **Redondo** Port.
159 B2 **Red Sea** Africa/Asia
128 B1 **Redstone** r. Can.
100 B1 **Reduzum** Neth.
137 E2 **Red Wing** U.S.A.
137 D2 **Redwood Falls** U.S.A.
97 C2 **Ree, Lough** *l.* Ireland
134 B2 **Reedsport** U.S.A.
54 B2 **Reefton** N.Z.
102 C2 **Regen** Ger.
155 E1 **Regência** Brazil

102 C2 **Regensburg** Ger.
114 C2 **Reggane** Alg.
109 C3 **Reggio di Calabria** Italy
108 B2 **Reggio nell'Emilia** Italy
110 B1 **Reghin** Romania
129 D2 **Regina** Can.
122 A1 **Rehoboth** Namibia
101 F2 **Reichenbach** Ger.
143 E1 **Reidsville** U.S.A.
99 C3 **Reigate** U.K.
105 C2 **Reims** France
101 E1 **Reinbek** Ger.
129 D2 **Reindeer** r. Can.
129 E2 **Reindeer Island** Can.
129 D2 **Reindeer Lake** Can.
92 F2 **Reine** Norway
100 C3 **Reinsfeld** Ger.
123 C2 **Reitz** S. Africa
122 B2 **Reivilo** S. Africa
129 D1 **Reliance** Can.
107 D2 **Relizane** Alg.
79 C2 **Remeshk** Iran
105 D2 **Remiremont** France
100 C2 **Remscheid** Ger.
102 B1 **Rendsburg** Ger.
141 D1 **Renfrew** Can.
60 B2 **Rengat** Indon.
90 B2 **Reni** Ukr.
52 B2 **Renmark** Austr.
100 C2 **Rennerod** Ger.
104 B2 **Rennes** France
129 D1 **Rennie Lake** Can.
108 B2 **Reno** r. Italy
135 C3 **Reno** U.S.A.
70 A3 **Renshou** China
140 B2 **Rensselaer** U.S.A.
75 C2 **Renukut** India
54 B2 **Renwick** N.Z.
58 C2 **Reo** Indon.
136 D3 **Republican** r. U.S.A.
127 F2 **Repulse Bay** Can.
150 A2 **Requena** Peru
107 C2 **Requena** Spain
154 B2 **Reserva** Brazil
152 C3 **Resistencia** Arg.
110 B1 **Reşiţa** Romania
126 E2 **Resolute** Can.
127 G2 **Resolution Island** Can.
105 C2 **Rethel** France
111 B3 **Rethymno** Greece
113 K9 **Réunion** terr. Indian Ocean
107 D1 **Reus** Spain
102 B2 **Reutlingen** Ger.
128 C2 **Revelstoke** Can.
144 A3 **Revillagigedo, Islas** *is* Mex.
128 A2 **Revillagigedo Island** U.S.A.
75 C2 **Rewa** India
134 D2 **Rexburg** U.S.A.
92 □A3 **Reykjanestá** *pt* Iceland
92 □A3 **Reykjavík** Iceland
145 C2 **Reynosa** Mex.
88 C2 **Rēzekne** Latvia
Rhein r. Ger. see Rhine
100 C1 **Rheine** Ger.
101 F1 **Rhin** r. France see Rhine
Rhine r. Europe
100 C2 **Rhine** r. Europe
140 B1 **Rhinelander** U.S.A.
101 F1 **Rhinluch** marsh Ger.
101 F1 **Rhinow** Ger.
141 E2 **Rhode Island** state U.S.A.
111 C3 **Rhodes** Greece
111 C3 **Rhodes** i. Greece
110 B2 **Rhodope Mountains**
Bulg./Greece
105 C3 **Rhône** r. France/Switz.
Rhuthun U.K. see Ruthin
98 B2 **Rhyl** U.K.
154 C1 **Rianápolis** Brazil
60 B1 **Riau, Kepulauan** *is* Indon.

106 B1 **Ribadeo** Spain
106 B1 **Ribadesella** Spain
154 B2 **Ribas do Rio Pardo** Brazil
121 C2 **Ribáuè** Moz.
98 B2 **Ribble** r. U.K.
154 C2 **Ribeira** r. Brazil
154 C2 **Ribeirão Preto** Brazil
104 C2 **Ribérac** France
152 B2 **Riberalta** Bol.
90 B2 **Rîbniţa** Moldova
102 C1 **Ribnitz-Damgarten** Ger.
140 A1 **Rice Lake** U.S.A.
123 D2 **Richards Bay** S. Africa
126 B2 **Richardson Mountains**
Can.
135 D3 **Richfield** U.S.A.
134 C1 **Richland** U.S.A.
140 A2 **Richland Center** U.S.A.
53 D2 **Richmond** N.S.W. Austr.
51 D2 **Richmond** Qld Austr.
54 B2 **Richmond** N.Z.
122 B3 **Richmond** S. Africa
98 C1 **Richmond** U.K.
140 C3 **Richmond** IN U.S.A.
140 C3 **Richmond** KY U.S.A.
141 D3 **Richmond** VA U.S.A.
140 C2 **Rideau Lakes** Can.
135 C3 **Ridgecrest** U.S.A.
102 C1 **Riesa** Ger.
100 D1 **Rieste** Ger.
123 C3 **Riet** r. S. Africa
101 D2 **Rietberg** Ger.
108 B2 **Rieti** Italy
136 B3 **Rifle** U.S.A.
88 B2 **Riga** Latvia
88 B2 **Riga, Gulf of** Estonia/Latvia
79 C2 **Rīgān** Iran
134 D2 **Rigby** U.S.A.
131 E1 **Rigolet** Can.
93 H3 **Riihimäki** Fin.
108 B1 **Rijeka** Croatia
134 C2 **Riley** U.S.A.
78 B2 **Rimah, Wādī al**
watercourse Saudi Arabia
103 E2 **Rimavská Sobota** Slovakia
128 C2 **Rimbey** Can.
108 B2 **Rimini** Italy
131 D2 **Rimouski** Can.
93 F3 **Ringebu** Norway
93 E4 **Ringkøbing** Denmark
92 G2 **Ringvassøya** i. Norway
101 D1 **Rinteln** Ger.
150 A2 **Riobamba** Ecuador
150 B3 **Rio Branco** Brazil
154 B3 **Rio Branco do Sul** Brazil
154 B2 **Rio Brilhante** Brazil
154 C2 **Rio Claro** Brazil
153 B4 **Río Colorado** Arg.
153 B4 **Río Cuarto** Arg.
155 D2 **Rio de Janeiro** Brazil
153 B6 **Río Gallegos** Arg.
153 B6 **Río Grande** Arg.
152 C4 **Rio Grande** Brazil
144 B2 **Río Grande** Mex.
139 D3 **Rio Grande** r. Mex./U.S.A.
139 D3 **Rio Grande City** U.S.A.
150 A1 **Riohacha** Col.
150 A2 **Rioja** Peru
145 D2 **Río Lagartos** Mex.
105 C2 **Riom** France
152 B2 **Río Mulatos** Bol.
154 C3 **Rio Negro** Brazil
155 D1 **Rio Pardo de Minas** Brazil
138 B1 **Rio Rancho** U.S.A.
150 A2 **Río Tigre** Ecuador
154 B1 **Rio Verde** Brazil
145 C2 **Río Verde** Mex.
154 B1 **Rio Verde de Mato Grosso**
Brazil
90 C1 **Ripky** Ukr.

98 C2 **Ripley** U.K.
107 D1 **Ripoll** Spain
98 C1 **Ripon** U.K.
66 D1 **Rishiri-tō** *i.* Japan
93 E4 **Risør** Norway
122 B3 **Ritchie** S. Africa
63 A2 **Ritchie's Archipelago** *is* India
134 C1 **Ritzville** U.S.A.
152 B3 **Rivadavia** Arg.
108 B1 **Riva del Garda** Italy
146 B3 **Rivas** Nic.
152 C4 **Rivera** Uru.
129 D2 **Riverhurst** Can.
52 B2 **Riverina** *reg.* Austr.
122 B3 **Riversdale** S. Africa
135 C4 **Riverside** S. Africa
136 B2 **Riverton** U.S.A.
131 D2 **Riverview** Can.
123 C3 **Rivesaltes** France
131 D2 **Rivière-du-Loup** Can.
90 B1 **Rivne** Ukr.
54 B2 **Riwaka** N.Z.
78 B2 **Riyadh** Saudi Arabia
81 C1 **Rize** Turkey
70 B2 **Rizhao** China
105 C2 **Roanne** France
141 D3 **Roanoke** U.S.A.
143 E1 **Roanoke** *r.* U.S.A.
143 E1 **Roanoke Rapids** U.S.A.
52 A3 **Robe** Austr.
101 F1 **Röbel** Ger.
92 H3 **Robertsfors** Sweden
122 A3 **Robertson** S. Africa
114 A4 **Robertsport** Liberia
131 C2 **Roberval** Can.
50 A2 **Robinson Range** *hills* Austr.
52 B2 **Robinvale** Austr.
129 D2 **Roblin** Can.
128 C2 **Robson, Mount** Can.
108 B3 **Rocca Busambra** *mt.* Sicily Italy
153 C4 **Rocha** Uru.
98 B2 **Rochdale** U.K.
154 B1 **Rochedo** Brazil
100 B2 **Rochefort** Belgium
104 B2 **Rochefort** France
137 E2 **Rochester** *MN* U.S.A.
141 E2 **Rochester** *NH* U.S.A.
141 D2 **Rochester** *NY* U.S.A.
140 B2 **Rockford** U.S.A.
51 E2 **Rockhampton** Austr.
143 D2 **Rock Hill** U.S.A.
50 A3 **Rockingham** Austr.
140 A2 **Rock Island** U.S.A.
136 B1 **Rock Springs** *MT* U.S.A.
139 C3 **Rocksprings** U.S.A.
136 B2 **Rock Springs** *WY* U.S.A.
136 C3 **Rocky Ford** U.S.A.
143 E1 **Rocky Mount** U.S.A.
128 C2 **Rocky Mountain House** Can.
124 G3 **Rocky Mountains** Can./U.S.A.
100 B3 **Rocroi** France
102 C1 **Rødbyhavn** Denmark
131 E1 **Roddickton** Can.
104 C3 **Rodez** France
89 F2 **Rodniki** Rus. Fed.
Rodos Greece *see* Rhodes
Rodos *i.* Greece *see* Rhodes
50 A2 **Roebourne** Austr.
50 B1 **Roebuck Bay** Austr.
123 C1 **Roed** S. Africa
100 B2 **Roermond** Neth.
100 A2 **Roeselare** Belgium
127 F2 **Roes Welcome Sound** *sea chan.* Can.
142 B1 **Rogers** U.S.A.

122 B3 **Roggeveldberge** *esc.* S. Africa
92 G2 **Rognan** Norway
134 B2 **Rogue** *r.* U.S.A.
88 B2 **Roja** Latvia
60 B1 **Rokan** *r.* Indon.
88 C2 **Rokiškis** Lith.
90 B1 **Rokytne** Ukr.
154 B2 **Rolândia** Brazil
137 E3 **Rolla** U.S.A.
51 D2 **Roma** Austr.
123 C2 **Roma** Lesotho
139 D3 **Roma** U.S.A.
Roma Italy *see* Rome
143 E2 **Romain, Cape** U.S.A.
110 C1 **Roman** Romania
59 C3 **Romang, Pulau** *i.* Indon.
110 B1 **Romania** *country* Europe
91 C3 **Roman-Kosh** *mt.* Ukr.
69 D1 **Romanovka** Rus. Fed.
105 D2 **Rombas** France
64 B1 **Romblon** Phil.
108 B2 **Rome** Italy
143 C2 **Rome** *GA* U.S.A.
141 D2 **Rome** *NY* U.S.A.
99 D3 **Romford** U.K.
105 C2 **Romilly-sur-Seine** France
91 C1 **Romny** Ukr.
104 C2 **Romorantin-Lanthenay** France
99 C3 **Romsey** U.K.
96 □ **Ronas Hill** U.K.
151 C3 **Roncador, Serra do** *hills* Brazil
106 B2 **Ronda** Spain
154 B2 **Rondon** Brazil
154 B1 **Rondonópolis** Brazil
74 B1 **Rondu** Jammu and Kashmir
71 A3 **Rong'an** China
129 D2 **Ronge, Lac la** *l.* Can.
71 A3 **Rongjiang** China
62 A1 **Rongklang Range** *mts* Myanmar
Rongmei China *see* Hefeng
93 F4 **Rønne** Denmark
55 P2 **Ronne Ice Shelf** Antarctica
101 D1 **Ronnenberg** Ger.
100 A2 **Ronse** Belgium
75 B2 **Roorkee** India
100 B2 **Roosendaal** Neth.
135 E2 **Roosevelt** U.S.A.
128 B2 **Roosevelt, Mount** Can.
55 K2 **Roosevelt Island** Antarctica
64 B3 **Roquefort** France
150 B1 **Roraima** *state* Guyana
93 F3 **Røros** Norway
153 B4 **Rosario** Arg.
144 A1 **Rosario** *Baja California Norte* Mex.
144 B2 **Rosario** *Sinaloa* Mex.
144 B2 **Rosario** *Sonora* Mex.
151 C3 **Rosário Oeste** Brazil
144 A2 **Rosarito** Mex.
109 C3 **Rosarno** Italy
104 B2 **Roscoff** France
97 C2 **Roscommon** Ireland
97 C2 **Roscrea** Ireland
147 D3 **Roseau** Dominica
137 D1 **Roseau** U.S.A.
134 B2 **Roseburg** U.S.A.
139 D3 **Rosenberg** U.S.A.
101 D1 **Rosengarten** Ger.
102 C2 **Rosenheim** Ger.
129 D2 **Rosetown** Can.
122 A2 **Rosh Pinah** Namibia
110 C2 **Roşiori de Vede** Romania
93 F4 **Roskilde** Denmark
89 D3 **Roslavl'** Rus. Fed.
109 C3 **Rossano** Italy
97 B1 **Rossan Point** Ireland

55 K1 **Ross Ice Shelf** Antarctica
131 D2 **Rossignol, Lake** Can.
128 C3 **Rossland** Can.
97 C2 **Rosslare** Ireland
114 A3 **Rosso** Maur.
105 D3 **Rosso, Capo** *c.* Corsica France
99 B3 **Ross-on-Wye** U.K.
89 D1 **Rossosh'** Rus. Fed.
128 A1 **Ross River** Can.
55 K2 **Ross Sea** Antarctica
92 F2 **Røssvatnet** *l.* Norway
79 C2 **Rostāq** Iran
129 D2 **Rosthern** Can.
102 C1 **Rostock** Ger.
89 E2 **Rostov** Rus. Fed.
91 D2 **Rostov-na-Donu** Rus. Fed.
92 H2 **Rosvik** Sweden
138 C2 **Roswell** U.S.A.
59 D2 **Rota** *i.* N. Mariana Is
59 C3 **Rote** *i.* Indon.
101 D1 **Rotenburg (Wümme)** Ger.
102 C2 **Roth** Ger.
98 C1 **Rothbury** U.K.
98 C2 **Rotherham** U.K.
96 B3 **Rothesay** U.K.
53 C2 **Roto** Austr.
105 D3 **Rotondo, Monte** *mt.* Corsica France
54 C1 **Rotorua** N.Z.
54 C1 **Rotorua, Lake** N.Z.
101 E2 **Rottenbach** Ger.
102 C2 **Rottenmann** Austria
100 B2 **Rotterdam** Neth.
102 B2 **Rottweil** Ger.
49 F3 **Rotuma** *i.* Fiji
105 C1 **Roubaix** France
104 C2 **Rouen** France
Roulers Belgium *see* Roeselare
53 D2 **Round Mountain** Austr.
131 E2 **Round Pond** *l.* Can.
139 D2 **Round Rock** U.S.A.
134 E1 **Roundup** U.S.A.
96 □ **Rousay** *i.* U.K.
130 C2 **Rouyn-Noranda** Can.
92 I2 **Rovaniemi** Fin.
91 D2 **Roven'ki** Rus. Fed.
91 D2 **Roven'ky** Ukr.
108 B1 **Rovereto** Italy
63 B2 **Rôviĕng Tbong** Cambodia
108 B1 **Rovigo** Italy
108 B1 **Rovinj** Croatia
53 C1 **Rowena** Austr.
64 B1 **Roxas** *Mindanao* Phil.
64 A1 **Roxas** *Mindoro* Phil.
64 A1 **Roxas** *Palawan* Phil.
64 B1 **Roxas** *Panay* Phil.
52 A2 **Roxby Downs** Austr.
138 C1 **Roy** U.S.A.
140 B1 **Royale, Isle** *i.* U.S.A.
104 C2 **Royan** France
99 C2 **Royston** U.K.
90 C2 **Rozdil'na** Ukr.
91 C2 **Rozdol'ne** Ukr.
100 B3 **Rozoy-sur-Serre** France
87 D3 **Rtishchevo** Rus. Fed.
54 C1 **Ruapehu, Mount** *vol.* N.Z.
54 A3 **Ruapuke Island** N.Z.
78 B3 **Rub' al Khālī** *des.* Saudi Arabia
91 D2 **Rubizhne** Ukr.
77 E1 **Rubtsovsk** Rus. Fed.
135 C2 **Ruby Mountains** U.S.A.
66 C2 **Rudnaya Pristan'** Rus. Fed.
89 D3 **Rudnya** Rus. Fed.
76 C1 **Rudnyy** Kazakh.
82 E1 **Rudol'fa, Ostrov** *i.* Rus. Fed.
101 E2 **Rudolstadt** Ger.

119 D3	**Rufiji** r. Tanz.	
153 B4	**Rufino** Arg.	
121 D3	**Rufunsa** Zambia	
70 C2	**Rugao** China	
99 C2	**Rugby** U.K.	
136 C1	**Rugby** U.S.A.	
102 C1	**Rügen** i. Ger.	
101 E2	**Ruhla** Ger.	
88 B2	**Ruhnu** i. Estonia	
100 C2	**Ruhr** r. Ger.	
71 C3	**Rui'an** China	
138 B2	**Ruidoso** U.S.A.	
144 B2	**Ruiz** Mex.	
119 D3	**Rukwa, Lake** Tanz.	
96 A2	**Rum** i. U.K.	
109 C1	**Ruma** Serb. and Mont.	
78 B2	**Rumāh** Saudi Arabia	
117 A4	**Rumbek** Sudan	
105 D2	**Rumilly** France	
50 C1	**Rum Jungle** Austr.	
54 B2	**Runanga** N.Z.	
98 B2	**Runcorn** U.K.	
120 A2	**Rundu** Namibia	
68 B2	**Ruoqiang** China	
130 C1	**Rupert** r. Can.	
130 C1	**Rupert Bay** Can.	
121 C2	**Rusape** Zimbabwe	
102 B1	**Ruse** Bulg.	
77 D3	**Rushon** Tajik.	
136 C2	**Rushville** U.S.A.	
53 C3	**Rushworth** Austr.	
129 D2	**Russell** Can.	
54 B1	**Russell** N.Z.	
142 C2	**Russellville** AL U.S.A.	
142 B1	**Russellville** AR U.S.A.	
140 B3	**Russellville** KY U.S.A.	
101 D2	**Rüsselsheim** Ger.	
82 F2	**Russian Federation** country Asia/Europe	
123 C2	**Rustenburg** S. Africa	
142 B2	**Ruston** U.S.A.	
98 B2	**Ruthin** U.K.	
141 E2	**Rutland** U.S.A.	
119 E4	**Ruvuma** r. Moz./Tanz.	
79 C2	**Ruweis** U.A.E.	
77 C1	**Ruzayevka** Kazakh.	
87 D3	**Ruzayevka** Rus. Fed.	
119 C3	**Rwanda** country Africa	
89 E3	**Ryazan'** Rus. Fed.	
89 F3	**Ryazhsk** Rus. Fed.	
86 C2	**Rybachiy, Poluostrov** pen. Rus. Fed.	
89 E2	**Rybinsk** Rus. Fed.	
89 E2	**Rybinskoye Vodokhranilishche** resr Rus. Fed.	
103 D1	**Rybnik** Pol.	
89 E3	**Rybnoye** Rus. Fed.	
99 D3	**Rye** U.K.	
89 D3	**Ryl'sk** Rus. Fed.	
67 C3	**Ryōtsu** Japan	
69 E3	**Ryukyu Islands** Japan	
103 E1	**Rzeszów** Pol.	
89 D2	**Rzhev** Rus. Fed.	

S

79 C2	**Sa'ādatābād** Iran	
101 E2	**Saale** r. Ger.	
101 E2	**Saalfeld** Ger.	
102 B2	**Saarbrücken** Ger.	
88 B2	**Saaremaa** i. Estonia	
92 I2	**Saarenkylä** Fin.	
93 I3	**Saarijärvi** Fin.	
102 B2	**Saarlouis** Ger.	
80 B2	**Sab' Ābār** Syria	
107 D1	**Sabadell** Spain	

61 C1	**Sabah** state Malaysia	
61 C2	**Sabalana** i. Indon.	
155 D1	**Sabará** Brazil	
108 B2	**Sabaudia** Italy	
115 D2	**Sabhā** Libya	
123 D2	**Sabie** r. Moz./S. Africa	
145 B2	**Sabinas** Mex.	
145 B2	**Sabinas Hidalgo** Mex.	
131 D2	**Sable, Cape** Can.	
143 D3	**Sable, Cape** U.S.A.	
131 E2	**Sable Island** Can.	
106 B1	**Sabugal** Port.	
78 B3	**Şabyā** Saudi Arabia	
76 B3	**Sabzevār** Iran	
120 A2	**Sachanga** Angola	
130 A1	**Sachigo Lake** Can.	
65 B3	**Sach'on** S. Korea	
126 C2	**Sachs Harbour** Can.	
135 B3	**Sacramento** U.S.A.	
138 B2	**Sacramento Mountains** U.S.A.	
135 B2	**Sacramento Valley** U.S.A.	
123 C3	**Sada** S. Africa	
107 C1	**Sádaba** Spain	
78 B3	**Şa'dah** Yemen	
62 A1	**Sadiya** India	
67 C3	**Sadoga-shima** i. Japan	
107 D2	**Sa Dragonera** i. Spain	
93 F4	**Säffle** Sweden	
138 B2	**Safford** U.S.A.	
99 D2	**Saffron Walden** U.K.	
114 B1	**Safi** Morocco	
86 D2	**Safonovo** Arkhangel'skaya Oblast' Rus. Fed.	
89 D2	**Safonovo** Smolenskaya Oblast' Rus. Fed.	
78 B2	**Şafrā' as Sark** esc. Saudi Arabia	
75 C2	**Saga** China	
67 B4	**Saga** Japan	
62 A1	**Sagaing** Myanmar	
67 C3	**Sagamihara** Japan	
75 B2	**Sagar** India	
140 C2	**Saginaw** U.S.A.	
140 C2	**Saginaw Bay** U.S.A.	
106 B2	**Sagres** Port.	
146 B2	**Sagua la Grande** Cuba	
141 F1	**Saguenay** r. Can.	
107 C2	**Sagunto** Spain	
76 B2	**Sagyndyk, Mys** pt Kazakh.	
106 B1	**Sahagún** Spain	
114 C3	**Sahara** des. Africa	
	Saharan Atlas mts Alg. see Atlas Saharien	
122 A2	**Saharanpur** India	
75 C2	**Saharsa** India	
114 B3	**Sahel** reg. Africa	
144 B2	**Sahuayo** Mex.	
78 B2	**Sāhūq** reg. Saudi Arabia	
	Saïda Lebanon see Sidon	
75 C2	**Saidpur** Bangl.	
	Saigon Vietnam see Ho Chi Minh City	
62 A1	**Saiha** India	
69 D2	**Saihan Tal** China	
67 B4	**Saiki** Japan	
93 I3	**Saimaa** l. Fin.	
144 B2	**Sain Alto** Mex.	
96 C3	**St Abb's Head** U.K.	
99 B3	**St Albans** U.K.	
99 B3	**St Aldhelm's Head** U.K.	
96 C2	**St Andrews** U.K.	
100 B2	**St Anthonis** Neth.	
131 E1	**St Anthony** Can.	
134 D2	**St Anthony** U.S.A.	
52 B3	**St Arnaud** Austr.	
131 E1	**St-Augustin** Can.	
131 E1	**St-Augustin** r. Can.	
143 D3	**St Augustine** U.S.A.	
99 A3	**St Austell** U.K.	

104 C2	**St-Avertin** France	
98 B1	**St Bees Head** U.K.	
105 D3	**St-Bonnet-en-Champsaur** France	
99 A3	**St Bride's Bay** U.K.	
104 B2	**St-Brieuc** France	
130 C2	**St Catharines** Can.	
99 C3	**St Catherine's Point** U.K.	
137 E3	**St Charles** U.S.A.	
140 C2	**St Clair, Lake** Can./U.S.A.	
105 D2	**St-Claude** France	
137 E1	**St Cloud** U.S.A.	
140 A1	**St Croix** r. U.S.A.	
147 D3	**St Croix** i. Virgin Is (U.S.A.)	
105 C2	**St-Dizier** France	
131 D2	**Ste-Anne-des-Monts** Can.	
105 D2	**St-Égrève** France	
126 B2	**St Elias Mountains** Can.	
131 D1	**Ste-Marguerite** r. Can.	
129 E2	**Sainte Rose du Lac** Can.	
104 B2	**Saintes** France	
105 C2	**St-Étienne** France	
108 A2	**St-Florent** Corsica France	
105 C2	**St-Flour** France	
136 C3	**St Francis** U.S.A.	
105 D2	**St Gallen** Switz.	
104 C3	**St-Gaudens** France	
53 C1	**St George** Austr.	
135 D3	**St George** U.S.A.	
143 D3	**St George Island** U.S.A.	
131 C2	**St-Georges** Can.	
147 D3	**St George's** Grenada	
97 C3	**St George's Channel** Ireland/U.K.	
105 D2	**St Gotthard Pass** Switz.	
113 E8	**St Helena** terr. S. Atlantic Ocean	
122 A3	**St Helena Bay** S. Africa	
122 A3	**St Helena Bay** S. Africa	
98 B2	**St Helens** U.K.	
134 B1	**St Helens, Mount** vol. U.S.A.	
95 C4	**St Helier** Channel Is	
100 B2	**St-Hubert** Belgium	
141 E1	**St-Hyacinthe** Can.	
140 C1	**St Ignace** U.S.A.	
130 B2	**St Ignace Island** Can.	
99 A3	**St Ives** U.K.	
128 A2	**St James, Cape** Can.	
131 C2	**St-Jean, Lac** l. Can.	
104 B2	**St-Jean-d'Angély** France	
104 B2	**St-Jean-de-Monts** France	
130 C2	**St-Jean-sur-Richelieu** Can.	
141 E1	**St-Jérôme** Can.	
134 C1	**St Joe** r. U.S.A.	
131 D2	**Saint John** Can.	
141 F1	**St John** r. U.S.A.	
147 D3	**St John's** Antigua	
131 E2	**St John's** Can.	
138 B2	**St Johns** U.S.A.	
141 E2	**St Johnsbury** U.S.A.	
137 E3	**St Joseph** U.S.A.	
130 A1	**St Joseph, Lake** Can.	
130 B2	**St Joseph Island** Can.	
104 C2	**St-Junien** France	
94 B2	**St Kilda** i. U.K.	
147 D3	**St Kitts and Nevis** country West Indies	
100 A2	**St-Laureins** Belgium	
	St-Laurent, Golfe du g. Can. see St Lawrence, Gulf of	
151 C1	**St-Laurent-du-Maroni** Fr. Guiana	
131 D2	**St Lawrence** inlet Can.	
131 D2	**St Lawrence, Gulf of** Can.	
83 N2	**St Lawrence Island** U.S.A.	
104 B2	**St-Lô** France	
114 A3	**St-Louis** Senegal	
137 E3	**St Louis** U.S.A.	

137 E1	**St Louis** r. U.S.A.	
147 D3	**St Lucia** country	
	West Indies	
123 D2	**St Lucia Estuary** S. Africa	
104 B2	**St-Malo** France	
104 B2	**St-Malo, Golfe de** g. France	
122 A3	**St Martin, Cape** S. Africa	
141 D2	**St Marys** Can.	
130 C2	**St-Maurice** r. Can.	
105 D2	**St Moritz** Switz.	
104 B2	**St-Nazaire** France	
100 B2	**St-Niklaas** Belgium	
104 C1	**St-Omer** France	
129 C2	**St Paul** Can.	
137 E2	**St Paul** U.S.A.	
137 E2	**St Peter** U.S.A.	
95 C4	**St Peter Port** Channel Is	
89 D2	**St Petersburg** Rus. Fed.	
143 D3	**St Petersburg** U.S.A.	
131 E2	**St-Pierre**	
	St Pierre and Miquelon	
131 E2	**St Pierre and Miquelon** terr. N. America	
104 B2	**St-Pierre-d'Oléron** France	
105 C2	**St-Pourçain-sur-Sioule** France	
131 D2	**St Quentin** Can.	
105 C2	**St-Quentin** France	
131 D2	**St-Siméon** Can.	
129 E2	**St Theresa Point** Can.	
130 B2	**St Thomas** Can.	
105 D3	**St-Tropez** France	
105 D3	**St-Tropez, Cap de** c. France	
102 C2	**St Veit an der Glan** Austria	
52 A3	**St Vincent, Gulf** Austr.	
147 D3	**St Vincent and the Grenadines** country	
	West Indies	
100 C2	**St-Vith** Belgium	
129 D2	**St Walburg** Can.	
100 C3	**St Wendel** Ger.	
104 C2	**St-Yrieix-la-Perche** France	
59 D1	**Saipan** i. N. Mariana Is	
152 B2	**Sajama, Nevado** mt. Bol.	
122 B2	**Sak** watercourse S. Africa	
67 C4	**Sakai** Japan	
67 B4	**Sakaide** Japan	
78 B2	**Sakākah** Saudi Arabia	
136 C1	**Sakakawea, Lake** U.S.A.	
111 D2	**Sakarya** r. Turkey	
	Sakarya Turkey see	
	Adapazarı	
66 C3	**Sakata** Japan	
65 B1	**Sakchu** N. Korea	
83 K3	**Sakhalin** i. Rus. Fed.	
123 C2	**Sakhile** S. Africa	
81 C1	**Şäki** Azer.	
88 B3	**Šakiai** Lith.	
69 E3	**Sakishima-shotō** is Japan	
62 B2	**Sakon Nakhon** Thai.	
122 B3	**Sakrivier** S. Africa	
67 D3	**Sakura** Japan	
91 C2	**Saky** Ukr.	
93 G4	**Sala** Sweden	
130 C2	**Salaberry-de-Valleyfield** Can.	
88 B2	**Salacgrīva** Latvia	
109 C2	**Sala Consilina** Italy	
135 C4	**Salada, Laguna** salt l. Mex.	
152 B4	**Salado** r. Arg.	
145 C2	**Salado** r. Mex.	
114 B4	**Salaga** Ghana	
122 B1	**Salajwe** Botswana	
115 D3	**Salal** Chad	
78 A2	**Salālā** Sudan	
79 C3	**Salālah** Oman	
145 B2	**Salamanca** Mex.	
106 B1	**Salamanca** Spain	
106 B1	**Salas** Spain	
63 B2	**Salavan** Laos	
59 C3	**Salawati** i. Indon.	
58 C3	**Salayar** i. Indon.	
104 C2	**Salbris** France	
88 C3	**Šalčininkai** Lith.	
106 C1	**Saldaña** Spain	
122 A3	**Saldanha** S. Africa	
88 B2	**Saldus** Latvia	
53 C3	**Sale** Austr.	
86 F2	**Salekhard** Rus. Fed.	
73 B3	**Salem** India	
137 E3	**Salem** MO U.S.A.	
134 B2	**Salem** OR U.S.A.	
96 B2	**Salen** U.K.	
109 B2	**Salerno** Italy	
98 B2	**Salford** U.K.	
151 E2	**Salgado** r. Brazil	
103 D2	**Salgótarján** Hungary	
151 E2	**Salgueiro** Brazil	
136 B3	**Salida** U.S.A.	
111 C3	**Salihli** Turkey	
88 C3	**Salihorsk** Belarus	
121 C2	**Salima** Malawi	
121 C2	**Salimo** Moz.	
137 D3	**Salina** U.S.A.	
145 C3	**Salina, Isola** i. Italy	
144 B3	**Salina Cruz** Mex.	
155 D1	**Salinas** Brazil	
144 B2	**Salinas** Mex.	
135 B3	**Salinas** U.S.A.	
107 C2	**Salines, Cap de ses** c. Spain	
151 D2	**Salinópolis** Brazil	
99 C3	**Salisbury** U.K.	
141 D3	**Salisbury** MD U.S.A.	
143 D1	**Salisbury** NC U.S.A.	
99 B3	**Salisbury Plain** U.K.	
151 D2	**Salitre** r. Brazil	
92 I2	**Salla** Fin.	
127 F2	**Salluit** Can.	
75 C2	**Sallyana** Nepal	
81 C2	**Salmās** Iran	
134 D1	**Salmon** U.S.A.	
134 C1	**Salmon** r. U.S.A.	
128 C2	**Salmon Arm** Can.	
134 C2	**Salmon River Mountains** U.S.A.	
93 H3	**Salo** Fin.	
87 D4	**Sal'sk** Rus. Fed.	
122 B3	**Salt** watercourse S. Africa	
138 A2	**Salt** r. U.S.A.	
152 B3	**Salta** Arg.	
145 B2	**Saltillo** Mex.	
134 D2	**Salt Lake City** U.S.A.	
154 C2	**Salto** Brazil	
152 C4	**Salto** Uru.	
155 E1	**Salto da Divisa** Brazil	
154 B2	**Salto del Guairá** Para.	
135 C4	**Salton Sea** salt l. U.S.A.	
143 D2	**Saluda** U.S.A.	
108 A2	**Saluzzo** Italy	
151 E3	**Salvador** Brazil	
79 C2	**Salwah** Saudi Arabia	
62 A1	**Salween** r. China	
62 A2	**Salween** r. Myanmar	
81 C2	**Salyan** Azer.	
102 C2	**Salzburg** Austria	
101 E1	**Salzgitter** Ger.	
101 D2	**Salzkotten** Ger.	
101 E1	**Salzwedel** Ger.	
144 B1	**Samalayuca** Mex.	
66 D2	**Samani** Japan	
64 B1	**Samar** i. Phil.	
87 E3	**Samara** Rus. Fed.	
61 C2	**Samarinda** Indon.	
77 C3	**Samarqand** Uzbek.	
81 C2	**Sāmarrā'** Iraq	
81 C1	**Şamaxı** Azer.	
119 C3	**Samba** Dem. Rep. Congo	
61 C1	**Sambaliung** mts Indon.	
75 C2	**Sambalpur** India	
61 C2	**Sambar, Tanjung** pt Indon.	
61 B1	**Sambas** Indon.	
121 □E2	**Sambava** Madag.	
90 A2	**Sambir** Ukr.	
153 C4	**Samborombón, Bahía** b. Arg.	
65 B2	**Samch'ŏk** S. Korea	
81 C2	**Samdi Dag** mt. Turkey	
119 D3	**Same** Tanz.	
78 B2	**Samirah** Saudi Arabia	
65 B1	**Samjiyŏn** N. Korea	
49 G3	**Samoa** country	
	S. Pacific Ocean	
109 C1	**Samobor** Croatia	
111 C3	**Samos** i. Greece	
111 C2	**Samothraki** Greece	
111 C2	**Samothraki** i. Greece	
61 C2	**Sampit** Indon.	
119 C3	**Sampwe** Dem. Rep. Congo	
139 E2	**Sam Rayburn Reservoir** U.S.A.	
80 B1	**Samsun** Turkey	
81 C1	**Samtredia** Georgia	
63 B3	**Samui, Ko** i. Thai.	
63 B2	**Samut Songkhram** Thai.	
114 B3	**San** Mali	
78 B3	**Şan'ā'** Yemen	
118 A2	**Sanaga** r. Cameroon	
81 C2	**Sanandaj** Iran	
146 B3	**San Andrés, Isla de** i. Caribbean Sea	
138 B2	**San Andres Mountains** U.S.A.	
145 C3	**San Andrés Tuxtla** Mex.	
139 C2	**San Angelo** U.S.A.	
135 C4	**San Antonio** U.S.A.	
135 C4	**San Antonio, Mount** U.S.A.	
107 D2	**San Antonio Abad** Spain	
152 B3	**San Antonio de los Cobres** Arg.	
153 B5	**San Antonio Oeste** Arg.	
108 B2	**San Benedetto del Tronto** Italy	
144 A3	**San Benedicto, Isla** i. Mex.	
135 C4	**San Bernardino** U.S.A.	
135 C4	**San Bernardino Mountains** U.S.A.	
143 C3	**San Blas, Cape** U.S.A.	
152 B2	**San Borja** Bol.	
144 B2	**San Buenaventura** Mex.	
64 B1	**San Carlos** Phil.	
147 C4	**San Carlos** Venez.	
153 A5	**San Carlos de Bariloche** Arg.	
147 C4	**San Carlos del Zulia** Venez.	
135 C4	**San Clemente Island** U.S.A.	
104 C2	**Sancoins** France	
152 A1	**San Cristóbal** Venez.	
145 C3	**San Cristóbal de las Casas** Mex.	
146 C2	**Sancti Spíritus** Cuba	
123 D1	**Sand** r. S. Africa	
61 C1	**Sandakan** Sabah Malaysia	
93 E3	**Sandane** Norway	
111 B2	**Sandanski** Bulg.	
96 C1	**Sanday** i. U.K.	
139 C2	**Sanderson** U.S.A.	
150 B3	**Sandia** Peru	
135 C4	**San Diego** U.S.A.	
80 B2	**Sandıklı** Turkey	
93 E4	**Sandnes** Norway	
92 F2	**Sandnessjøen** Norway	
118 C3	**Sandoa** Dem. Rep. Congo	
103 E1	**Sandomierz** Pol.	
89 E2	**Sandovo** Rus. Fed.	

94	B1	Sandoy i. Faroe Is
134	C1	Sandpoint U.S.A.
71	B3	Sandu China
94	B1	Sandur Faroe Is
140	C2	Sandusky U.S.A.
122	A3	Sandveld mts S. Africa
93	F4	Sandvika Norway
93	G3	Sandviken Sweden
131	E1	Sandwich Bay Can.
129	D2	Sandy Bay Can.
51	E2	Sandy Cape Austr.
130	A1	Sandy Lake Can.
130	A1	Sandy Lake Can.
144	A1	San Felipe Baja California Norte Mex.
145	B3	San Felipe Guanajuato Mex.
150	B1	San Felipe Venez.
144	A2	San Fernando Baja California Norte Mex.
145	C2	San Fernando Tamaulipas Mex.
64	B1	San Fernando Luzon Phil.
64	B1	San Fernando Luzon Phil.
106	B2	San Fernando Spain
147	D3	San Fernando Trin. and Tob.
150	B1	San Fernando de Apure Venez.
143	D3	Sanford FL U.S.A.
141	E2	Sanford ME U.S.A.
152	B4	San Francisco Arg.
135	B3	San Francisco U.S.A.
107	D2	San Francisco Javier Spain
74	B3	Sangamner India
83	J2	Sangar Rus. Fed.
108	A3	San Gavino Monreale Sardinia Italy
101	E2	Sangerhausen Ger.
61	C1	Sanggau Indon.
118	B3	Sangha r. Congo
109	C3	San Giovanni in Fiore Italy
64	B2	Sangir i. Indon.
59	C2	Sangir, Kepulauan is Indon.
65	B2	Sangju S. Korea
61	C1	Sangkulirang Indon.
73	B3	Sangli India
118	B2	Sangmélima Cameroon
121	C3	Sango Zimbabwe
136	B3	Sangre de Cristo Range mts U.S.A.
75	C2	Sangsang China
144	A2	San Hipólito, Punta pt Mex.
144	A1	San Ignacio Mex.
130	C1	Sanikiluaq Can.
71	A3	Sanjiang China
135	B3	San Joaquin r. U.S.A.
153	B5	San Jorge, Golfo de g. Arg.
146	B4	San José Costa Rica
64	B1	San Jose Luzon Phil.
64	B1	San Jose Mindoro Phil.
135	B3	San Jose U.S.A.
144	A2	San José, Isla i. Mex.
144	B2	San José de Bavicora Mex.
64	B1	San Jose de Buenavista Phil.
144	A2	San José de Comondú Mex.
144	B2	San José del Cabo Mex.
150	A1	San José del Guaviare Col.
152	B4	San Juan Arg.
146	B3	San Juan r. Costa Rica/Nic.
147	D3	San Juan Puerto Rico
135	D3	San Juan r. U.S.A.
107	D2	San Juan Bautista Spain

145	C3	San Juan Bautista Tuxtepec Mex.
134	B1	San Juan Islands U.S.A.
144	B2	San Juanito Mex.
136	B3	San Juan Mountains U.S.A.
153	B5	San Julián Arg.
75	C2	Sankh r. India
		Sankt-Peterburg Rus. Fed. see St Petersburg
80	B2	Şanlıurfa Turkey
138	B3	San Lorenzo Mex.
106	B2	Sanlúcar de Barrameda Spain
144	B2	San Lucas Mex.
153	B4	San Luis Arg.
145	B2	San Luis de la Paz Mex.
138	A2	San Luisito Mex.
135	B3	San Luis Obispo U.S.A.
145	B2	San Luis Potosí Mex.
144	A1	San Luis Río Colorado Mex.
139	D3	San Marcos U.S.A.
108	B2	San Marino country Europe
108	B2	San Marino San Marino
144	B2	San Martín de Bolaños Mex.
153	A5	San Martín de los Andes Arg.
153	B5	San Matías, Golfo g. Arg.
70	B2	Sanmenxia China
146	B3	San Miguel El Salvador
152	B3	San Miguel de Tucumán Arg.
145	C3	San Miguel Sola de Vega Mex.
71	B3	Sanming China
153	B4	San Nicolás de los Arroyos Arg.
135	C4	San Nicolas Island U.S.A.
123	C2	Sannieshof S. Africa
103	E2	Sanok Pol.
64	B1	San Pablo Phil.
144	B2	San Pablo Balleza Mex.
152	B3	San Pedro Arg.
152	B2	San Pedro Bol.
114	B4	San-Pédro Côte d'Ivoire
144	A2	San Pedro Mex.
138	A2	San Pedro watercourse U.S.A.
106	B2	San Pedro, Sierra de mts Spain
144	B2	San Pedro de las Colonias Mex.
146	B3	San Pedro Sula Hond.
108	A3	San Pietro, Isola di i. Sardinia Italy
144	A1	San Quintín, Cabo c. Mex.
153	B4	San Rafael Arg.
108	A2	San Remo Italy
146	B3	San Salvador El Salvador
152	B3	San Salvador de Jujuy Arg.
109	C2	San Severo Italy
109	C2	Sanski Most Bos.-Herz.
152	B2	Santa Ana Bol.
146	B3	Santa Ana El Salvador
144	A1	Santa Ana Mex.
135	C4	Santa Ana U.S.A.
144	B2	Santa Bárbara Mex.
135	C4	Santa Barbara U.S.A.
154	B2	Santa Bárbara, Serra de hills Brazil
152	B3	Santa Catalina Chile
150	B1	Santa Clara Col.
146	C2	Santa Clara Cuba
135	C4	Santa Clarita U.S.A.
109	C3	Santa Croce, Capo c. Sicily Italy
153	B6	Santa Cruz r. Arg.

152	B2	Santa Cruz Bol.
64	B1	Santa Cruz Phil.
135	B3	Santa Cruz U.S.A.
145	C3	Santa Cruz Barillas Guat.
155	E1	Santa Cruz Cabrália Brazil
107	C2	Santa Cruz de Moya Spain
114	A2	Santa Cruz de Tenerife Canary Is
135	C4	Santa Cruz Island U.S.A.
48	F3	Santa Cruz Islands Solomon Is
152	B4	Santa Fé Arg.
138	B1	Santa Fe U.S.A.
154	B1	Santa Helena de Goiás Brazil
153	B4	Santa Isabel Arg.
154	B1	Santa Luisa, Serra de hills Brazil
152	C3	Santa Maria Brazil
144	B1	Santa María r. Mex.
135	B4	Santa Maria U.S.A.
123	D2	Santa Maria, Cabo de c. Moz.
106	B2	Santa Maria, Cabo de c. Port.
151	D2	Santa Maria das Barreiras Brazil
109	C3	Santa Maria di Leuca, Capo c. Italy
150	A1	Santa Marta Col.
135	C4	Santa Monica U.S.A.
151	D3	Santana Brazil
106	C1	Santander Spain
108	A3	Sant'Antioco Sardinia Italy
108	A3	Sant'Antioco, Isola di i. Sardinia Italy
151	C2	Santarém Brazil
106	B2	Santarém Port.
154	B1	Santa Rita do Araguaia Brazil
153	B4	Santa Rosa Arg.
152	C3	Santa Rosa Brazil
135	B3	Santa Rosa CA U.S.A.
138	C2	Santa Rosa NM U.S.A.
146	B3	Santa Rosa de Copán Hond.
135	B4	Santa Rosa Island U.S.A.
144	A2	Santa Rosalía Mex.
152	C3	Santiago Brazil
153	A4	Santiago Chile
147	C3	Santiago Dom. Rep.
144	B2	Santiago Mex.
146	B4	Santiago Panama
64	B1	Santiago Phil.
106	B1	Santiago de Compostela Spain
144	B2	Santiago Ixcuintla Mex.
144	B2	Santiago Papasquiaro Mex.
107	D1	Sant Jordi, Golf de g. Spain
155	D2	Santo Amaro de Campos Brazil
155	C2	Santo André Brazil
152	C3	Santo Ângelo Brazil
154	B2	Santo Antônio da Platina Brazil
151	E3	Santo Antônio de Jesus Brazil
150	B2	Santo Antônio do Içá Brazil
155	C2	Santo Antônio do Monte Brazil
147	D3	Santo Domingo Dom. Rep.
138	B1	Santo Domingo Pueblo U.S.A.
		Santorini i. Greece see Thira
155	C2	Santos Brazil

152 C3 Santo Tomé Arg.
153 A5 San Valentín, Cerro *mt.* Chile
146 B3 San Vicente El Salvador
144 B1 San Vicente Mex.
150 A3 San Vicente de Cañete Peru
108 B2 San Vincenzo Italy
108 B3 San Vito, Capo *c.* Sicily Italy
71 A4 Sanya China
155 C3 São Bernardo do Campo Brazil
152 C3 São Borja Brazil
154 C2 São Carlos Brazil
151 C3 São Félix *Mato Grosso* Brazil
151 E2 São Félix *Pará* Brazil
155 D2 São Fidélis Brazil
155 D1 São Francisco Brazil
151 E3 São Francisco *r.* Brazil
154 C3 São Francisco, Ilha de *i.* Brazil
154 C3 São Francisco do Sul Brazil
152 C3 São Gabriel Brazil
155 D2 São Gonçalo Brazil
155 C1 São Gotardo Brazil
155 D2 São João da Barra Brazil
155 C3 São João da Boa Vista Brazil
106 B1 São João da Madeira Port.
155 D1 São João do Paraíso Brazil
155 D2 São João Nepomuceno Brazil
154 C2 São Joaquim da Barra Brazil
155 C3 São José do Rio Preto Brazil
155 C3 São José dos Campos Brazil
154 C3 São José dos Pinhais Brazil
155 C2 São Lourenço Brazil
151 D2 São Luís Brazil
154 C2 São Manuel Brazil
154 C1 São Marcos *r.* Brazil
151 D2 São Marcos, Baía de *b.* Brazil
155 E1 São Mateus Brazil
155 C3 São Paulo Brazil
151 D2 São Raimundo Nonato Brazil
155 C1 São Romão Brazil
155 C2 São Sebastião, Ilha do *i.* Brazil
154 C2 São Sebastião do Paraíso Brazil
154 B1 São Simão Brazil
154 B1 São Simão, Barragem de resr Brazil
59 C2 Sao-Siu Indon.
113 F6 São Tomé
     São Tomé and Príncipe
155 D2 São Tomé, Cabo de *c.* Brazil
113 F6 São Tomé and Príncipe country Africa
155 C2 São Vicente Brazil
106 B2 São Vicente, Cabo de *c.* Port.
59 C3 Saparua Indon.
89 F3 Sapozhok Rus. Fed.
66 D2 Sapporo Japan
109 C2 Sapri Italy
81 C2 Saqqez Iran
81 C2 Sarāb Iran
63 B2 Sara Buri Thai.
109 C2 Sarajevo Bos.-Herz.

76 B1 Saraktash Rus. Fed.
141 E2 Saranac Lake U.S.A.
109 D3 Sarandë Albania
64 B2 Sarangani Islands Phil.
87 D3 Saransk Rus. Fed.
87 E3 Sarapul Rus. Fed.
143 D3 Sarasota U.S.A.
90 B2 Sarata Ukr.
136 B2 Saratoga U.S.A.
141 E2 Saratoga Springs U.S.A.
61 C1 Saratok *Sarawak* Malaysia
87 D3 Saratov Rus. Fed.
79 D2 Saravan Iran
61 C1 Sarawak *state* Malaysia
110 C2 Saray Turkey
111 C3 Sarayköy Turkey
79 D2 Sarbāz Iran
74 B2 Sardarshahr India
     Sardegna *i.* Italy *see*
     Sardinia
108 A2 Sardinia *i.* Italy
92 G2 Sarektjåkkå *mt.* Sweden
77 C3 Sar-e Pol Afgh.
158 B3 Sargasso Sea
     Atlantic Ocean
74 B1 Sargodha Pak.
115 D4 Sarh Chad
79 D2 Sarhad *reg.* Iran
81 D2 Sārī Iran
111 C3 Sarigöl Turkey
81 C1 Sarıkamış Turkey
61 C1 Sarikei *Sarawak* Malaysia
51 D2 Sarina Austr.
115 D2 Sarir Tibesti *des.* Libya
65 B2 Sariwŏn N. Korea
111 C2 Sarıyer Turkey
77 D2 Sarkand Kazakh.
111 C2 Sarköy Turkey
59 D3 Sarolangun Indon.
140 C2 Sarnia Can.
90 B1 Sarny Ukr.
60 B2 Sarolangun Indon.
111 B3 Saronikos Kolpos *g.* Greece
111 C2 Saros Körfezi *b.* Turkey
87 D3 Sarova Rus. Fed.
105 D2 Sarrebourg France
106 B1 Sarria Spain
107 C1 Sarrión Spain
105 D3 Sartène *Corsica* France
103 D2 Sárvár Hungary
76 B2 Sarykamyshskoye Ozero salt l. Turkm./Uzbek.
77 D2 Saryozek Kazakh.
77 D2 Saryshagan Kazakh.
82 F3 Sarysu *watercourse* Kazakh.
77 D3 Sary-Tash Kyrg.
75 C2 Sasaram India
67 A4 Sasebo Japan
129 D2 Saskatchewan *prov.* Can.
129 D2 Saskatchewan *r.* Can.
129 D2 Saskatoon Can.
83 I2 Saskylakh Rus. Fed.
123 C2 Sasolburg S. Africa
87 D3 Sasovo Rus. Fed.
114 B4 Sassandra Côte d'Ivoire
108 A2 Sassari *Sardinia* Italy
102 C1 Sassnitz Ger.
114 B3 Satadougou Mali
123 D1 Satara S. Africa
75 C2 Satna India
74 B2 Satpura Range *mts* India
63 B2 Sattahip Thai.
110 B1 Satu Mare Romania
63 B3 Satun Thai.
144 B2 Saucillo Mex.
93 E4 Sauda Norway
92 □B3 Sauðárkrókur Iceland
78 B2 Saudi Arabia country Asia

105 C3 Saugues France
105 C2 Saulieu France
130 B2 Sault Sainte Marie Can.
140 C1 Sault Sainte Marie U.S.A.
77 C1 Saumalkol' Kazakh.
59 C3 Saumlakki Indon.
104 B2 Saumur France
120 B1 Saurimo Angola
109 D2 Sava *r.* Europe
49 G3 Savai'i *i.* Samoa
91 E1 Savala *r.* Rus. Fed.
143 D2 Savannah *GA* U.S.A.
142 C1 Savannah *TN* U.S.A.
143 D2 Savannah *r.* U.S.A.
63 B2 Savannakhét Laos
130 A1 Savant Lake Can.
111 C3 Savaştepe Turkey
89 F2 Savino Rus. Fed.
86 D2 Savinskiy Rus. Fed.
108 A2 Savona Italy
93 I3 Savonlinna Fin.
92 I2 Savukoski Fin.
     Savu Sea Indon. *see*
     Sawu, Laut
74 B2 Sawai Madhopur India
62 A2 Sawankhalok Thai.
136 B3 Sawatch Range *mts* U.S.A.
116 B2 Sawhāj Egypt
53 D2 Sawtell Austr.
59 C3 Sawu, Laut *sea* Indon.
79 C3 Sayhūt Yemen
69 D2 Saynshand Mongolia
141 D2 Sayre U.S.A.
144 B3 Sayula *Jalisco* Mex.
145 C3 Sayula *Veracruz* Mex.
128 B2 Sayward Can.
89 E2 Sazonovo Rus. Fed.
114 B2 Sbaa Alg.
98 B1 Scafell Pike *hill* U.K.
109 C3 Scalea Italy
96 C1 Scapa Flow *inlet* U.K.
130 C2 Scarborough Can.
147 D3 Scarborough Trin. and Tob.
98 C1 Scarborough U.K.
64 A1 Scarborough Shoal *sea feature* Phil.
96 A2 Scarinish U.K.
     Scarpanto *i.* Greece *see*
     Karpathos
105 D2 Schaffhausen Switz.
100 B1 Schagen Neth.
102 C2 Schärding Austria
100 A2 Scharendijke Neth.
101 D1 Scharhörn *sea feature* Ger.
101 D1 Scheeßel Ger.
131 D1 Schefferville Can.
135 D3 Schell Creek Range *mts* U.S.A.
141 E2 Schenectady U.S.A.
101 E3 Scheßlitz Ger.
100 C1 Schiermonnikoog *i.* Neth.
108 B1 Schio Italy
101 F2 Schkeuditz Ger.
101 E1 Schladen Ger.
101 E2 Schleiz Ger.
102 B1 Schleswig Ger.
101 D2 Schloss Holte-Stukenbrock Ger.
101 D2 Schlüchtern Ger.
101 E3 Schlüsselfeld Ger.
101 D2 Schmallenberg Ger.
101 D1 Schneverdingen Ger.
101 E1 Schönebeck (Elbe) Ger.
101 E1 Schöningen Ger.
100 B2 Schoonhoven Neth.
59 D3 Schouten Islands P.N.G.
102 B2 Schwäbische Alb *mts* Ger.
102 C2 Schwandorf Ger.

61 C2 **Schwaner, Pegunungan** mts Indon.
101 C2 **Schwarzenbek** Ger.
101 F2 **Schwarzenberg** Ger.
122 A2 **Schwarzrand** mts Namibia
Schwarzwald mts Ger. see Black Forest
102 D2 **Schwaz** Austria
102 C1 **Schwedt an der Oder** Ger.
101 E2 **Schweinfurt** Ger.
101 E1 **Schwerin** Ger.
101 E1 **Schweriner See** l. Ger.
105 D2 **Schwyz** Switz.
108 B3 **Sciacca** Sicily Italy
95 B4 **Scilly, Isles of** U.K.
140 C3 **Scioto** r. U.S.A.
136 B1 **Scobey** U.S.A.
53 D2 **Scone** Austr.
55 R3 **Scotia Ridge** sea feature S. Atlantic Ocean
158 C8 **Scotia Sea** S. Atlantic Ocean
96 C2 **Scotland** admin. div. U.K.
128 B2 **Scott, Cape** Can.
123 D3 **Scottburgh** S. Africa
136 C3 **Scott City** U.S.A.
136 C2 **Scottsbluff** U.S.A.
142 C2 **Scottsboro** U.S.A.
96 B1 **Scourie** U.K.
141 D2 **Scranton** U.S.A.
98 C2 **Scunthorpe** U.K.
105 E2 **Scuol** Switz.
129 E2 **Seal** r. Can.
122 B3 **Seal, Cape** S. Africa
52 B3 **Sea Lake** Austr.
139 D3 **Sealy** U.S.A.
142 B1 **Searcy** U.S.A.
98 B1 **Seascale** U.K.
134 B1 **Seattle** U.S.A.
141 E2 **Sebago Lake** U.S.A.
144 A2 **Sebastián Vizcaíno, Bahía** b. Mex.
110 B1 **Sebeş** Romania
60 B2 **Sebeşi** i. Indon.
88 C2 **Sebezh** Rus. Fed.
80 B1 **Şebinkarahisar** Turkey
143 D3 **Sebring** U.S.A.
128 B3 **Sechelt** Can.
150 A2 **Sechura** Peru
73 B3 **Secunderabad** India
137 E3 **Sedalia** U.S.A.
105 E2 **Sedan** France
54 B2 **Seddon** N.Z.
138 A2 **Sedona** U.S.A.
101 E2 **Seeburg** Ger.
122 A2 **Seeheim** Namibia
104 C2 **Sées** France
104 E1 **Seesen** Ger.
101 E1 **Seevetal** Ger.
114 A4 **Sefadu** Sierra Leone
123 C1 **Sefare** Botswana
60 B1 **Segamat** Malaysia
86 C2 **Segezha** Rus. Fed.
114 B3 **Ségou** Mali
106 C1 **Segovia** Spain
115 D2 **Séguédine** Niger
114 B4 **Séguéla** Côte d'Ivoire
139 D3 **Seguin** U.S.A.
107 C2 **Segura** r. Spain
106 C2 **Segura, Sierra de** mts Spain
120 B3 **Sehithwa** Botswana
93 H3 **Seinäjoki** Fin.
104 C2 **Seine** r. France
104 B2 **Seine, Baie de** b. France
103 E1 **Sejny** Pol.
60 B2 **Sekayu** Indon.
114 B4 **Sekondi** Ghana
59 C3 **Selaru** i. Indon.

61 C2 **Selatan, Tanjung** pt Indon.
126 A2 **Selawik** U.S.A.
98 C2 **Selby** U.K.
120 B3 **Selebi-Phikwe** Botswana
105 D2 **Sélestat** France
92 □A3 **Selfoss** Iceland
114 A3 **Sélibabi** Maur.
138 A1 **Seligman** U.S.A.
116 A2 **Selima Oasis** Sudan
111 C3 **Selimiye** Turkey
114 B3 **Sélingué, Lac de** l. Mali
89 D2 **Selizharovo** Rus. Fed.
93 E4 **Seljord** Norway
129 E2 **Selkirk** Can.
96 C3 **Selkirk** U.K.
128 C2 **Selkirk Mountains** Can.
142 C2 **Selma** AL U.S.A.
135 C3 **Selma** CA U.S.A.
89 D3 **Sel'tso** Rus. Fed.
150 A2 **Selvas** reg. Brazil
134 C1 **Selway** r. U.S.A.
129 D1 **Selwyn Lake** Can.
128 A1 **Selwyn Mountains** Can.
51 C2 **Selwyn Range** hills Austr.
60 B2 **Semangka, Teluk** b. Indon.
61 C2 **Semarang** Indon.
61 B2 **Sematan** Sarawak Malaysia
118 B2 **Sembé** Congo
81 C2 **Semdinli** Turkey
91 C1 **Semenivka** Ukr.
86 D3 **Semenov** Rus. Fed.
61 C2 **Semeru, Gunung** vol. Indon.
89 E3 **Semiluki** Rus. Fed.
136 B2 **Seminoe Reservoir** U.S.A.
139 C2 **Seminole** U.S.A.
143 D2 **Seminole, Lake** U.S.A.
77 E1 **Semipalatinsk** Kazakh.
61 C1 **Semitau** Indon.
81 D2 **Semnān** Iran
61 C1 **Semporna** Sabah Malaysia
105 C2 **Semur-en-Auxois** France
150 B2 **Sena Madureira** Brazil
120 B2 **Senanga** Zambia
67 B4 **Sendai** Kagoshima Japan
67 D3 **Sendai** Miyagi Japan
114 A3 **Senegal** country Africa
114 A3 **Sénégal** r. Maur./Senegal
102 C1 **Senftenberg** Ger.
119 D3 **Sengerema** Tanz.
151 D3 **Senhor do Bonfim** Brazil
108 B2 **Senigallia** Italy
109 B2 **Senj** Croatia
92 G2 **Senja** i. Norway
122 B2 **Senlac** S. Africa
104 C2 **Senlis** France
63 B2 **Senmonorom** Cambodia
117 B3 **Sennar** Sudan
130 C2 **Senneterre** Can.
123 C3 **Senqu** r. Lesotho
105 C2 **Sens** France
109 D1 **Senta** Serb. and Mont.
128 B2 **Sentinel Peak** Can.
75 B2 **Seoni** India
65 B2 **Seoul** S. Korea
155 D2 **Sepetiba, Baía de** b. Brazil
59 D3 **Sepik** r. P.N.G.
61 C1 **Sepinang** Indon.
131 D1 **Sept-Îles** Can.
59 C3 **Seram** i. Indon.
59 C3 **Seram, Laut** sea Indon.
60 B2 **Serang** Indon.
109 D2 **Serbia** country Europe
76 B3 **Serdar** Turkm.
89 E3 **Serebryanyye Prudy** Rus. Fed.
60 B1 **Seremban** Malaysia
119 D3 **Serengeti Plain** Tanz.
87 D3 **Sergach** Rus. Fed.

89 E2 **Sergiyev Posad** Rus. Fed.
74 A1 **Serhetabat** Turkm.
61 C1 **Seria** Brunei
61 C3 **Serian** Sarawak Malaysia
111 B3 **Serifos** i. Greece
80 B2 **Serik** Turkey
59 C3 **Sermata, Kepulauan** is Indon.
86 F3 **Serov** Rus. Fed.
120 B3 **Serowe** Botswana
106 B2 **Serpa** Port.
89 E3 **Serpukhov** Rus. Fed.
151 D3 **Serra da Mesa, Represa** resr Brazil
154 B1 **Serranópolis** Brazil
100 A3 **Serre** r. France
111 B2 **Serres** Greece
151 E3 **Serrinha** Brazil
155 D1 **Sêrro** Brazil
154 C2 **Sertãozinho** Brazil
61 C2 **Seruyan** r. Indon.
68 C2 **Sêrxü** China
120 A2 **Sesfontein** Namibia
108 B2 **Sessa Aurunca** Italy
108 A2 **Sestri Levante** Italy
105 C3 **Sète** France
155 D1 **Sete Lagoas** Brazil
92 G2 **Setermoen** Norway
93 E4 **Setesdal** val. Norway
115 C1 **Sétif** Alg.
67 B4 **Seto-naikai** sea Japan
114 B1 **Settat** Morocco
98 B1 **Settle** U.K.
106 B2 **Setúbal** Port.
106 B2 **Setúbal, Baía de** b. Port.
130 A1 **Seul, Lac** l. Can.
76 A2 **Sevan, Lake** Armenia
Sevana Lich l. Armenia see Sevan, Lake
91 C3 **Sevastopol'** Ukr.
105 C3 **Sévérac-le-Château** France
130 B1 **Severn** r. Can.
122 B2 **Severn** S. Africa
99 B3 **Severn** r. U.K.
86 D2 **Severnaya Dvina** r. Rus. Fed.
83 H1 **Severnaya Zemlya** is Rus. Fed.
86 D2 **Severnyy** Nenetskiy Avtonomnyy Okrug Rus. Fed.
86 F2 **Severnyy** Respublika Komi Rus. Fed.
86 C2 **Severodvinsk** Rus. Fed.
86 C2 **Severomorsk** Rus. Fed.
91 D3 **Severskaya** Rus. Fed.
135 D3 **Sevier** r. U.S.A.
135 D3 **Sevier Lake** U.S.A.
Sevilla Spain see Seville
106 B2 **Seville** Spain
128 A2 **Sewell Inlet** Can.
128 C2 **Sexsmith** Can.
144 B2 **Sextin** r. Mex.
86 G1 **Seyakha** Rus. Fed.
113 J7 **Seychelles** country Indian Ocean
92 □C2 **Seyðisfjörður** Iceland
91 C1 **Seym** r. Rus. Fed./Ukr.
83 L2 **Seymchan** Rus. Fed.
53 C3 **Seymour** Austr.
140 B3 **Seymour** IN U.S.A.
139 D2 **Seymour** TX U.S.A.
105 C2 **Sézanne** France
111 B3 **Sfakia** Greece
110 C1 **Sfântu Gheorghe** Romania
115 D1 **Sfax** Tunisia
's-Gravenhage Neth. see The Hague
96 A2 **Sgurr Alasdair** hill U.K.
70 A2 **Shaanxi** prov. China

91	D2	Shabel'sk Rus. Fed.
77	D3	Shache China
55	R1	Shackleton Range mts Antarctica
99	B3	Shaftesbury U.K.
75	C2	Shahdol India
77	C3	Shah Fuladi mt. Afgh.
75	B2	Shahjahanpur India
81	D2	Shahr-e Kord Iran
81	D2	Shahrezā Iran
77	C3	Shahrisabz Uzbek.
89	E2	Shakhovskaya Rus. Fed.
91	E2	Shakhty Rus. Fed.
86	D3	Shakhun'ya Rus. Fed.
76	B2	Shakotan-misaki c. Japan
76	B2	Shalkar Kazakh.
68	C2	Shaluli Shan mts China
129	E2	Shamattawa Can.
139	C1	Shamrock U.S.A.
68	C2	Shandan China
70	C2	Shandong prov. China
70	C2	Shandong Bandao pen. China
121	B2	Shangani r. Zimbabwe
70	C2	Shanghai China
70	C2	Shanghai mun. China
71	B3	Shanghang China
70	A2	Shangluo China
71	B3	Shangrao China
70	B2	Shangshui China
70	C2	Shangyu China
69	E1	Shangzhi China
97	B2	Shannon r. Ireland
97	B2	Shannon, Mouth of the Ireland
71	B3	Shantou China
70	B2	Shanxi prov. China
71	B3	Shaoguan China
71	B3	Shaowu China
70	C2	Shaoxing China
71	B3	Shaoyang China
116	C2	Shaqrā' Saudi Arabia
90	B2	Sharhorod Ukr.
79	C2	Sharjah U.A.E.
88	C2	Sharkawshchyna Belarus
50	A2	Shark Bay Austr.
78	A2	Sharm ash Shaykh Egypt
140	C2	Sharon U.S.A.
86	D3	Shar'ya Rus. Fed.
121	B3	Shashe r. Botswana/Zimbabwe
117	B4	Shashemenē Eth.
134	B2	Shasta, Mount vol. U.S.A.
134	B2	Shasta Lake U.S.A.
89	E2	Shatura Rus. Fed.
129	D3	Shaunavon Can.
88	B2	Shawano U.S.A.
131	C2	Shawinigan Can.
139	D1	Shawnee U.S.A.
50	B2	Shay Gap Austr.
89	E3	Shchekino Rus. Fed.
89	E2	Shchelkovo Rus. Fed.
89	E3	Shchigry Rus. Fed.
91	C1	Shchors Ukr.
88	C3	Shchuchyn Belarus
91	D1	Shebekino Rus. Fed.
77	C3	Sheberghān Afgh.
140	B2	Sheboygan U.S.A.
91	D3	Shebsh r. Rus. Fed.
97	C3	Sheelin, Lough l. Ireland
98	C2	Sheffield U.K.
89	E2	Sheksna Rus. Fed.
		Sheksninskoye Vodokhranilishche resr Rus. Fed.
83	M2	Shelagskiy, Mys pt Rus. Fed.
131	D2	Shelburne Can.
134	D1	Shelby U.S.A.
140	B3	Shelbyville IN U.S.A.

142	C1	Shelbyville TN U.S.A.
83	L2	Shelikhova, Zaliv g. Rus. Fed.
129	D2	Shellbrook Can.
134	B1	Shelton U.S.A.
137	D2	Shenandoah U.S.A.
141	D3	Shenandoah r. U.S.A.
141	D3	Shenandoah Mountains U.S.A.
118	A2	Shendam Nigeria
86	D2	Shenkursk Rus. Fed.
65	A1	Shenyang China
71	B3	Shenzhen China
90	B1	Shepetivka Ukr.
53	C3	Shepparton Austr.
99	D3	Sheppey, Isle of i. U.K.
131	D2	Sherbrooke N.S. Can.
131	C2	Sherbrooke Que. Can.
116	B3	Shereiq Sudan
136	B2	Sheridan U.S.A.
139	D2	Sherman U.S.A.
100	B2	's-Hertogenbosch Neth.
96	□	Shetland Islands U.K.
76	B2	Shetpe Kazakh.
		Shevchenko Kazakh. see Aktau
137	D1	Sheyenne r. U.S.A.
79	B3	Shibām Yemen
66	D2	Shibetsu Japan
71	B3	Shicheng China
96	B2	Shiel, Loch l. U.K.
77	E2	Shihezi China
		Shijiao China see Fogang
70	B2	Shijiazhuang China
74	A2	Shikarpur Pak.
67	B4	Shikoku i. Japan
66	D2	Shikotsu-ko l. Japan
86	D2	Shilega Rus. Fed.
75	C2	Shiliguri India
75	D2	Shillong India
89	F3	Shilovo Rus. Fed.
117	C3	Shimbiris mt. Somalia
67	C3	Shimizu Japan
73	B3	Shimoga India
67	B4	Shimonoseki Japan
96	B1	Shin, Loch l. U.K.
67	C3	Shingū Japan
123	D1	Shingwedzi S. Africa
123	D1	Shingwedzi r. S. Africa
119	D3	Shinyanga Tanz.
67	C4	Shiono-misaki c. Japan
138	B1	Shiprock U.S.A.
71	A3	Shiqian China
70	A2	Shiquan China
		Shiquanhe China see Gar
		Shiquan He r. China/Pak. see Indus
67	C3	Shirane-san mt. Japan
81	D3	Shīrāz Iran
66	D2	Shiretoko-misaki c. Japan
66	D2	Shiriya-zaki c. Japan
74	B2	Shiv India
75	B2	Shivpuri India
70	B2	Shiyan China
70	A2	Shizuishan China
67	C4	Shizuoka Japan
89	D3	Shklow Belarus
109	C2	Shkodër Albania
83	H1	Shmidta, Ostrov i. Rus. Fed.
135	C3	Shoshone U.S.A.
135	C3	Shoshone Mountains U.S.A.
123	C1	Shoshong Botswana
91	C1	Shostka Ukr.
70	B2	Shouxian China
138	A2	Show Low U.S.A.
91	C2	Shpola Ukr.
142	B2	Shreveport U.S.A.
99	B2	Shrewsbury U.K.

62	A1	Shuangjiang China
87	E4	Shubarkuduk Kazakh.
116	B1	Shubrā al Khaymah Egypt
89	D2	Shugozero Rus. Fed.
120	B2	Shumba Zimbabwe
110	C2	Shumen Bulg.
88	C2	Shumilina Belarus
89	D3	Shumyachi Rus. Fed.
126	A2	Shungnak U.S.A.
78	B3	Shuqrah Yemen
89	F2	Shushkodom Rus. Fed.
81	C2	Shushtar Iran
128	C2	Shuswap Lake Can.
89	F2	Shuya Rus. Fed.
89	F2	Shuyskoye Rus. Fed.
62	A1	Shwebo Myanmar
62	A1	Shwedwin Myanmar
62	A2	Shwegyin Myanmar
77	C2	Shymkent Kazakh.
91	C2	Shyroke Ukr.
59	C3	Sia Indon.
74	A2	Siahan Range mts Pak.
74	B1	Sialkot Pak.
64	B2	Siargao i. Phil.
88	B2	Šiauliai Lith.
109	C2	Šibenik Croatia
83	I2	Siberia reg. Rus. Fed.
60	A2	Siberut i. Indon.
74	A2	Sibi Pak.
110	B1	Sibiu Romania
60	A1	Sibolga Indon.
62	A1	Sibsagar India
61	C1	Sibu Sarawak Malaysia
118	B2	Sibut C.A.R.
64	B1	Sibuyan i. Phil.
64	B1	Sibuyan Sea Phil.
128	C2	Sicamous Can.
63	A3	Sichon Thai.
70	A2	Sichuan prov. China
70	A3	Sichuan Pendi basin China
105	D3	Sicié, Cap c. France
		Sicilia i. Italy see Sicily
108	B3	Sicilian Channel Italy/Tunisia
108	B3	Sicily i. Italy
150	A3	Sicuani Peru
74	B2	Siddhapur India
111	C3	Sideros, Akra pt Greece
107	D2	Sidi Aïssa Alg.
107	D2	Sidi Ali Alg.
114	B1	Sidi Bel Abbès Alg.
114	A2	Sidi Ifni Morocco
60	A1	Sidikalang Indon.
96	C2	Sidlaw Hills U.K.
99	B3	Sidmouth U.K.
134	B1	Sidney Can.
136	C1	Sidney MT U.S.A.
136	C2	Sidney NE U.S.A.
140	C2	Sidney OH U.S.A.
143	D2	Sidney Lanier, Lake U.S.A.
80	B2	Sidon Lebanon
154	B2	Sidrolândia Brazil
103	E1	Siedlce Pol.
100	C2	Sieg r. Ger.
100	D2	Siegen Ger.
63	B2	Siěmréab Cambodia
108	B2	Siena Italy
103	D1	Sieradz Pol.
106	B1	Sierra de la Cabrera mts Spain
106	C1	Sierra de la Demanda mts Spain
153	B5	Sierra Grande Arg.
114	A4	Sierra Leone country Africa
144	B2	Sierra Mojada Mex.
135	C3	Sierra Vista U.S.A.
105	D2	Sierre Switz.
111	B3	Sifnos i. Greece
107	C2	Sig Alg.

127 H2 Sigguup Nunaa *pen.*
Greenland
103 E2 Sighetu Marmaţiei
Romania
110 B1 Sighişoara Romania
60 A1 Sigli Indon.
92 □B2 Siglufjörður Iceland
102 B2 Sigmaringen Ger.
100 B3 Signy-l'Abbaye France
106 C1 Sigüenza Spain
114 B3 Siguiri Guinea
88 B2 Sigulda Latvia
63 B2 Sihanoukville Cambodia
92 I3 Siilinjärvi Fin.
81 C2 Siirt Turkey
60 B2 Sijunjung Indon.
74 B2 Sikar India
114 B3 Sikasso Mali
137 F3 Sikeston U.S.A.
66 B2 Sikhote-Alin' *mts* Rus. Fed.
111 C3 Sikinos *i.* Greece
144 B2 Sikkim Mex.
75 D2 Silchar India
77 D1 Siletiteniz, Ozero *salt l.*
Kazakh.
75 C2 Sitgarhi Nepal
80 B2 Silifke Turkey
75 C1 Siling Co *salt l.* China
110 C2 Silistra Bulg.
80 A1 Silivri Turkey
93 F3 Siljan *l.* Sweden
93 E4 Silkeborg Denmark
88 C2 Sillamäe Estonia
142 B1 Siloam Springs U.S.A.
123 D2 Silobela S. Africa
88 B2 Šilutė Lith.
81 C2 Silvan Turkey
138 B2 Silver City U.S.A.
136 B3 Silverton U.S.A.
62 B1 Simao China
130 C2 Simãrd, Lac *l.* Can.
111 C3 Simav Turkey
111 C3 Simav Dağları *mts* Turkey
118 C2 Simba Dem. Rep. Congo
141 D2 Simcoe, Lake Can.
60 A1 Simeulue *i.* Indon.
91 C3 Simferopol' Ukr.
110 B1 Simleu Silvaniei Romania
100 C3 Simmern (Hunsrück) Ger.
129 D2 Simonhouse Can.
51 C2 Simpson Desert Austr.
93 F4 Simrishamn Sweden
60 A1 Sinabang Indon.
116 B2 Sinai *pen.* Egypt
71 A3 Sinan China
65 B2 Sinanju N. Korea
62 A1 Sinarum Indon.
150 A1 Sincelejo Col.
111 C3 Sındırgı Turkey
86 E2 Sindor Rus. Fed.
111 C3 Sinekçi Turkey
106 B2 Sines Port.
106 B2 Sines, Cabo de *c.* Port.
75 C2 Singahi India
60 B1 Singapore *country* Asia
61 C2 Singaraja Indon.
119 D3 Singida Tanz.
62 A1 Singkaling Hkamti
Myanmar
61 B2 Singkawang Indon.
60 A1 Singkil Indon.
53 D2 Singleton Austr.
62 A1 Singu Myanmar
108 A2 Siniscola *Sardinia* Italy
109 C2 Sinj Croatia
116 B3 Sinkat Sudan
80 B1 Sinop Turkey
65 B1 Sinp'o N. Korea
61 C1 Sintang Indon.
147 D3 St Maarten *i.* West Indies

139 D3 Sinton U.S.A.
65 A1 Sinüiju N. Korea
103 D2 Siófok Hungary
105 D2 Sion Switz.
137 D2 Sioux Center U.S.A.
137 D2 Sioux City U.S.A.
137 D2 Sioux Falls U.S.A.
130 A1 Sioux Lookout Can.
65 A1 Siping China
129 E2 Sipiwesk Lake Can.
60 A2 Sipura *i.* Indon.
93 E4 Sira *r.* Norway
Siracusa Italy *see* Syracuse
51 C1 Sir Edward Pellew Group
is Austr.
116 B1 Sirhān, Wādī an
watercourse Saudi Arabia
79 C2 Sīrīk Iran
62 B2 Siri Kit Dam Thai.
128 B1 Sir James MacBrien,
Mount Can.
79 C2 Sīrjān Iran
81 C2 Şırnak Turkey
74 B2 Sirohi India
74 B2 Sirsa India
115 D1 Sirte Libya
115 D1 Sirte, Gulf of Libya
88 B2 Širvintos Lith.
145 C2 Sisal Mex.
122 B3 Sishen S. Africa
81 C2 Sisian Armenia
129 D2 Sisipuk Lake Can.
63 B2 Sisŏphŏn Cambodia
105 D3 Sisteron France
75 C2 Sitapur India
123 D2 Siteki Swaziland
128 A2 Sitka U.S.A.
100 B2 Sittard Neth.
62 A2 Sittaung *r.* Myanmar
62 A1 Sittwe Myanmar
61 C2 Situbondo Indon.
80 B2 Sivas Turkey
111 C3 Sivaslı Turkey
80 B2 Siverek Turkey
80 B2 Sivrihisar Turkey
116 A2 Siwah Egypt
74 B1 Siwalik Range *mts*
India/Nepal
105 D3 Six-Fours-les-Plages
France
70 B2 Sixian China
123 C2 Siyabuswa S. Africa
Sjælland *i.* Denmark *see*
Zealand
109 D2 Sjenica Serb. and Mont.
92 G2 Sjøvegan Norway
91 C2 Skadovs'k Ukr.
93 F4 Skagen Denmark
93 E4 Skagerrak *str.*
Denmark/Norway
134 B1 Skagit *r.* U.S.A.
128 A2 Skagway U.S.A.
74 B1 Skardu
Jammu and Kashmir
103 E1 Skarżysko-Kamienna Pol.
103 D2 Skawina Pol.
128 B2 Skeena *r.* Can.
128 B2 Skeena Mountains Can.
98 D2 Skegness U.K.
92 H3 Skellefteå Sweden
92 H3 Skellefteälven *r.* Sweden
97 C2 Skerries Ireland
111 B3 Skiathos *i.* Greece
97 B3 Skibbereen Ireland
92 □B2 Skíðadals-jökull *glacier*
Iceland
98 B1 Skiddaw *hill* U.K.
93 E4 Skien Norway
103 E1 Skierniewice Pol.
115 C1 Skikda Alg.

52 B3 Skipton Austr.
98 B2 Skipton U.K.
93 E4 Skive Denmark
92 H1 Skjervøy Norway
111 B3 Skopelos *i.* Greece
89 E3 Skopin Rus. Fed.
109 D2 Skopje Macedonia
93 F4 Skövde Sweden
141 F2 Skowhegan U.S.A.
88 B2 Skrunda Latvia
128 A1 Skukum, Mount Can.
123 D1 Skukuza S. Africa
88 B2 Skuodas Lith.
98 A2 Skye *i.* U.K.
111 B3 Skyros Greece
111 B3 Skyros *i.* Greece
93 F4 Slagelse Denmark
97 C2 Slaney *r.* Ireland
88 C2 Slantsy Rus. Fed.
109 C1 Slatina Croatia
110 B2 Slatina Romania
129 C1 Slave *r.* Can.
114 C4 Slave Coast Africa
128 C2 Slave Lake Can.
82 G3 Slavgorod Rus. Fed.
109 C1 Slavonski Brod Croatia
90 B1 Slavuta Ukr.
90 C1 Slavutych Ukr.
91 D2 Slavyansk-na-Kubani
Rus. Fed.
89 D3 Slawharad Belarus
103 D1 Sławno Pol.
97 A2 Slea Head Ireland
130 C1 Sleeper Islands Can.
97 D1 Slieve Donard *hill* U.K.
97 B1 Slieve Gamph *hills* Ireland
97 B1 Sligo Ireland
97 B1 Sligo Bay Ireland
93 G4 Slite Sweden
110 C2 Sliven Bulg.
110 C2 Slobozia Romania
128 C3 Slocan Can.
88 C3 Slonim Belarus
100 B1 Sloten Neth.
99 C3 Slough U.K.
103 D2 Slovakia *country* Europe
108 B1 Slovenia *country* Europe
91 D2 Slov'yans'k Ukr.
90 B1 Sluch *r.* Ukr.
103 D1 Słupsk Pol.
88 C3 Slutsk Belarus
97 A2 Slyne Head Ireland
131 D1 Smallwood Reservoir Can.
88 C3 Smalyavichy Belarus
88 C3 Smarhon' Belarus
129 D2 Smeaton Can.
109 D2 Smederevo
Serb. and Mont.
109 D2 Smederevska Palanka
Serb. and Mont.
91 C2 Smila Ukr.
88 C2 Smiltene Latvia
128 B2 Smithers Can.
143 E1 Smithfield U.S.A.
141 D3 Smith Mountain Lake
U.S.A.
130 C2 Smiths Falls Can.
137 D3 Smoky Hills U.S.A.
92 E3 Smøla *i.* Norway
89 D3 Smolensk Rus. Fed.
110 B2 Smolyan Bulg.
130 B2 Smooth Rock Falls Can.
Smyrna Turkey *see* İzmir
92 □B3 Snæfell *mt.* Iceland
98 A1 Snaefell *hill* Isle of Man
132 B2 Snake *r.* U.S.A.
134 D2 Snake River Plain U.S.A.
100 B1 Sneek Neth.
97 B3 Sneem Ireland
122 B3 Sneeuberge *mts* S. Africa

108	B1	Snežnik *mt.* Slovenia
91	C2	Snihurivka Ukr.
93	E3	Snøhetta *mt.* Norway
129	D1	Snowbird Lake Can.
98	A2	Snowdon *mt.* U.K.
		Snowdon Can. *see*
		Łutselk'e
129	C3	Snowdrift *r.* Can.
138	A2	Snowflake U.S.A.
129	D2	Snow Lake Can.
52	A2	Snowtown Austr.
53	C3	Snowy *r.* Austr.
53	C3	Snowy Mountains Austr.
139	C2	Snyder U.S.A.
121	□D2	Soalala Madag.
117	B4	Sobat *r.* Sudan
89	F2	Sobinka Rus. Fed.
151		Sobradinho, Barragem de *resr* Brazil
151	D2	Sobral Brazil
87	C4	Sochi Rus. Fed.
65	B2	Sŏch'ŏn S. Korea
49	H4	Society Islands Fr. Polynesia
150	A1	Socorro Col.
138	B2	Socorro U.S.A.
144	A3	Socorro, Isla *i.* Mex.
56	F6	Socotra *i.* Yemen
63	B3	Soc Trăng Vietnam
106	C2	Socuéllamos Spain
92	I2	Sodankylä Fin.
134	D2	Soda Springs U.S.A.
93	G3	Söderhamn Sweden
93	G3	Södertälje Sweden
116	A3	Sodiri Sudan
117	B4	Sodo Eth.
93	G3	Södra Kvarken *str.* Fin./Sweden
100	D3	Soest Ger.
110	B2	Sofia Bulg.
		Sofiya Bulg. *see* Sofia
68	C2	Sog China
93	E3	Sognefjorden *inlet* Norway
111	D2	Söğüt Turkey
100	B2	Soignies Belgium
105	C2	Soissons France
90	A1	Sokal' Ukr.
111	C3	Söke Turkey
81	C1	Sokhumi Georgia
114	C4	Sokodé Togo
89	F2	Sokol Rus. Fed.
101	F2	Sokolov Czech Rep.
115	C3	Sokoto Nigeria
115	C3	Sokoto *r.* Nigeria
90	B2	Sokyryany Ukr.
73	B3	Solapur India
135	B3	Soledad U.S.A.
89	F2	Soligalich Rus. Fed.
99	C2	Solihull U.K.
86	E3	Solikamsk Rus. Fed.
87	E3	Sol'-Iletsk Rus. Fed.
100	C2	Solingen Ger.
92	G3	Sollefteå Sweden
93	G4	Sollentuna Sweden
101	D2	Solling *hills* Ger.
89	E2	Solnechnogorsk Rus. Fed.
60	B2	Solok Indon.
48	E3	Solomon Islands *country* S. Pacific Ocean
48	E3	Solomon Sea S. Pacific Ocean
105	D2	Solothurn Switz.
101	D1	Soltau Ger.
89	D2	Sol'tsy Rus. Fed.
96	C3	Solway Firth *est.* U.K.
120	B2	Solwezi Zambia
111	C3	Soma Turkey
117	C4	Somalia *country* Africa
120	B1	Sombo Angola
109	C1	Sombor Serb. and Mont.
144	B2	Sombrerete Mex.
140	C3	Somerset U.S.A.
123	C3	Somerset East S. Africa
126	E2	Somerset Island Can.
122	A3	Somerset West S. Africa
101	E2	Sömmerda Ger.
75	C2	Son *r.* India
93	E4	Sønderborg Denmark
101	E2	Sondershausen Ger.
		Søndre Strømfjord *inlet* Greenland *see* Kangerlussuaq
63	B2	Sông Ba *r.* Vietnam
62	B1	Sông Da, Hồ *resr* Vietnam
119	D4	Songea Tanz.
65	B1	Sŏnggan N. Korea
65	B1	Songhua *r.* resr China
65	B1	Sŏngjin N. Korea *see* Kimch'aek
63	B3	Songkhla Thai.
65	B2	Sŏngnam S. Korea
65	B2	Songnim N. Korea
120	A1	Songo Angola
121	C2	Songo Moz.
69	E1	Songyuan China
		Sonid Youqi China *see* Saihan Tal
89	E2	Sonkovo Rus. Fed.
62	B1	Sơn La Vietnam
74	A2	Sonmiani Pak.
101	E2	Sonneberg Ger.
138	A2	Sonoita Mex.
144	A2	Sonora *r.* Mex.
135	B3	Sonora *CA* U.S.A.
139	C2	Sonora *TX* U.S.A.
117	A4	Sopo *watercourse* Sudan
103	D2	Sopron Hungary
108	B2	Sora Italy
130	C2	Sorel Can.
51	D4	Sorell Austr.
106	C1	Soria Spain
76	B2	Sor Mertvyy Kultuk *dry lake* Kazakh.
90	B2	Soroca Moldova
154	C2	Sorocaba Brazil
87	E3	Sorochinsk Rus. Fed.
59	D2	Sorol *atoll* Micronesia
59	C3	Sorong Indon.
119	D2	Soroti Uganda
92	H1	Sørøya *i.* Norway
92	G2	Sorsele Sweden
64	B1	Sorsogon Phil.
86	C2	Sortavala Rus. Fed.
92	G2	Sortland Norway
65	B2	Sŏsan S. Korea
123	C2	Soshanguve S. Africa
89	E3	Sosna *r.* Rus. Fed.
153	B4	Sosneado *mt.* Arg.
86	E2	Sosnogorsk Rus. Fed.
86	D2	Sosnovka Rus. Fed.
88	C2	Sosnovyy Bor Rus. Fed.
103	D1	Sosnowiec Pol.
91	D2	Sosyka *r.* Rus. Fed.
145	C2	Soto la Marina Mex.
118	B2	Souanké Congo
104	C3	Souillac France
		Sŏul S. Korea *see* Seoul
104	B2	Soulac-sur-Mer France
104	B3	Soulom France
		Soûr Lebanon *see* Tyre
107	D2	Sour el Ghozlane Alg.
129	D3	Souris *Man.* Can.
131	D2	Souris *P.E.I.* Can.
129	E3	Souris *r.* Can.
151	E2	Sousa Brazil
115	D1	Sousse Tunisia
104	B3	Soustons France
122	B3	South Africa, Republic of *country* Africa
99	C3	Southampton U.K.
127	F2	Southampton Island Can.
73	D3	South Andaman *i.* India
52	A1	South Australia *state* Austr.
130	B2	South Baymouth Can.
140	B2	South Bend U.S.A.
143	D2	South Carolina *state* U.S.A.
156	B4	South China Sea N. Pacific Ocean
136	C2	South Dakota *state* U.S.A.
99	C3	South Downs *hills* U.K.
129	D2	Southend Can.
99	D3	Southend-on-Sea U.K.
54	B2	Southern Alps *mts* N.Z.
50	A3	Southern Cross Austr.
129	E2	Southern Indian Lake Can.
159		Southern Ocean
143	E1	Southern Pines U.S.A.
96	B3	Southern Uplands *hills* U.K.
149	F6	South Georgia and South Sandwich Islands *terr.* S. Atlantic Ocean
96	A2	South Harris *pen.* U.K.
129	E1	South Henik Lake Can.
54	B2	South Island N.Z.
65	B2	South Korea *country* Asia
135	B3	South Lake Tahoe U.S.A.
55	Q4	South Orkney Islands S. Atlantic Ocean
136	C2	South Platte *r.* U.S.A.
98	B2	Southport U.K.
143	E2	Southport U.S.A.
96	C1	South Ronaldsay *i.* U.K.
123	D3	South Sand Bluff *pt* S. Africa
129	D2	South Saskatchewan *r.* Can.
129	E2	South Seal *r.* Can.
55	P3	South Shetland Islands Antarctica
98	C1	South Shields U.K.
54	B1	South Taranaki Bight *b.* N.Z.
130	C1	South Twin Island Can.
96	A2	South Uist *i.* U.K.
53	D2	South West Rocks Austr.
99	D2	Southwold U.K.
109	C3	Soverato Italy
88	B2	Sovetsk Rus. Fed.
86	F2	Sovetskiy Rus. Fed.
91	C2	Sovyets'kyy Ukr.
123	C2	Soweto S. Africa
66	D1	Sōya-misaki *c.* Japan
90	C1	Sozh *r.* Europe
110	C2	Sozopol Bulg.
106	C1	Spain *country* Europe
99	C2	Spalding U.K.
135	D2	Spanish Fork U.S.A.
97	B2	Spanish Point Ireland
108	B3	Sparagio, Monte *mt.* Sicily Italy
135	C3	Sparks U.S.A.
140	A2	Sparta U.S.A.
143	D2	Spartanburg U.S.A.
111	B3	Sparti Greece
109	C3	Spartivento, Capo *c.* Italy
89	D3	Spas-Demensk Rus. Fed.
89	F2	Spas-Klepiki Rus. Fed.
66	B2	Spassk-Dal'niy Rus. Fed.
89	F3	Spassk-Ryazanskiy Rus. Fed.
111	B3	Spatha, Akra *pt* Greece
136	C2	Spearfish U.S.A.
139	C1	Spearman U.S.A.
137	D2	Spencer U.S.A.
52	A2	Spencer Gulf *est.* Austr.
98	C1	Spennymoor U.K.
54	B2	Spenser Mountains N.Z.
101	D3	Spessart *reg.* Ger.
96	C2	Spey *r.* U.K.

102 B2 Speyer Ger.
100 C1 Spiekeroog *i.* Ger.
100 B2 Spijkenisse Neth.
128 C2 Spirit River Can.
103 E2 Spišská Nová Ves Slovakia
82 C1 Spitsbergen *i.* Svalbard
102 C2 Spittal an der Drau Austria
109 C4 Split Croatia
129 E2 Split Lake Can.
129 E2 Split Lake Can.
134 C1 Spokane U.S.A.
140 A1 Spooner U.S.A.
102 C1 Spree *r.* Ger.
122 A2 Springbok S. Africa
131 E2 Springdale Can.
142 B1 Springdale U.S.A.
101 D1 Springe Ger.
138 C1 Springer U.S.A.
138 B2 Springerville U.S.A.
136 C3 Springfield *CO* U.S.A.
140 B3 Springfield *IL* U.S.A.
141 E2 Springfield *MA* U.S.A.
137 E3 Springfield *MO* U.S.A.
140 C3 Springfield *OH* U.S.A.
134 B2 Springfield *OR* U.S.A.
123 C3 Springfontein S. Africa
131 D2 Springhill Can.
143 D3 Spring Hill U.S.A.
54 B2 Springs Junction N.Z.
98 D2 Spurn Head U.K.
128 B3 Squamish Can.
109 C3 Squillace, Golfo di *g.* Italy
109 C2 Srebrenica Bos.-Herz.
110 C2 Sredets Bulg.
83 L3 Sredinnyy Khrebet *mts* Rus. Fed.
83 L2 Srednekolymsk Rus. Fed.
Sredne-Russkaya Vozvyshennost' *hills* Rus. Fed. *see* Central Russian Upland
Sredne-Sibirskoye Ploskogor'ye *plat.* Rus. Fed. *see* Central Siberian Plateau
110 B2 Srednogorie Bulg.
69 D1 Sretensk Rus. Fed.
61 C1 Sri Aman *Sarawak* Malaysia
73 B4 Sri Jayewardenepura Kotte Sri Lanka
73 C3 Srikakulam India
73 C4 Sri Lanka *country* Asia
74 B1 Srinagar Jammu and Kashmir
73 B3 Srivardhan India
101 D1 Stade Ger.
101 D1 Stadensen Ger.
100 C1 Stadskanaal Neth.
101 D2 Stadtallendorf Ger.
101 D1 Stadthagen Ger.
101 E2 Stadtfelstein Ger.
99 B2 Stafford U.K.
99 C3 Staines U.K.
91 D2 Stakhanov Ukr.
Stalingrad Rus. Fed. *see* Volgograd
103 E1 Stalowa Wola Pol.
99 C2 Stamford U.K.
141 E2 Stamford *CT* U.S.A.
139 D2 Stamford *TX* U.S.A.
122 A1 Stampriet Namibia
92 F2 Stamsund Norway
123 C2 Standerton S. Africa
99 A3 Standish U.K.
123 D2 Stanger S. Africa
53 C6 Stanley Falkland Is
136 C1 Stanley U.S.A.
83 I3 Stanovoye Nagor'ye *mts* Rus. Fed.

83 J3 Stanovoy Khrebet *mts* Rus. Fed.
53 D1 Stanthorpe Austr.
103 E1 Starachowice Pol.
Stara Planina *mts* Bulg./Serb. and Mont. *see* Balkan Mountains
89 D2 Staraya Russa Rus. Fed.
89 D2 Staraya Toropa Rus. Fed.
110 C2 Stara Zagora Bulg.
103 D1 Stargard Szczeciński Pol.
142 C2 Starkville U.S.A.
91 D2 Starobil's'k Ukr.
89 D3 Starodub Rus. Fed.
103 D1 Starogard Gdański Pol.
90 B2 Starokostyantyniv Ukr.
91 D2 Starominskaya Rus. Fed.
91 D2 Staroshcherbinovskaya Rus. Fed.
91 D2 Starotitarovskaya Rus. Fed.
89 F3 Staroyur'yevo Rus. Fed.
99 B3 Start Point U.K.
88 C3 Starya Darohi Belarus
89 E3 Staryy Oskol Rus. Fed.
101 E2 Staßfurt Ger.
141 D2 State College U.S.A.
143 D2 Statesboro U.S.A.
143 D1 Statesville U.S.A.
93 E4 Stavanger Norway
87 D4 Stavropol' Rus. Fed.
87 D4 Stavropol'skaya Vozvyshennost' *hills* Rus. Fed.
52 B3 Stawell Austr.
123 C2 Steadville S. Africa
136 B2 Steamboat Springs U.S.A.
101 E2 Stedten Ger.
128 C2 Steen River Can.
134 C2 Steens Mountain U.S.A.
100 C1 Steenwijk Neth.
126 D2 Stefansson Island Can.
101 E3 Steigerwald *mts* Ger.
128 B2 Steinbach Can.
100 C1 Steinfurt Ger.
120 A3 Steinhausen Namibia
92 F3 Steinkjer Norway
122 A2 Steinkopf S. Africa
122 B2 Stella S. Africa
105 D2 Stenay France
101 E1 Stendal Ger.
Stepanakert Azer. *see* Xankändi
131 E2 Stephenville Can.
139 D2 Stephenville U.S.A.
122 B3 Sterling S. Africa
136 C2 Sterling *CO* U.S.A.
140 B2 Sterling *IL* U.S.A.
87 E3 Sterlitamak Rus. Fed.
101 E1 Sternberg Ger.
128 C2 Stettler Can.
140 C2 Steubenville U.S.A.
99 C3 Stevenage U.K.
129 E2 Stevenson Lake Can.
126 C2 Stevens Village U.S.A.
128 B2 Stewart Can.
126 B2 Stewart *r.* Can.
54 A3 Stewart Island N.Z.
127 F2 Stewart Lake Can.
102 C2 Steyr Austria
123 B3 Steytlerville S. Africa
128 A2 Stikine *r.* Can.
128 A2 Stikine Plateau Can.
122 B3 Stilbaai S. Africa
139 D1 Stillwater U.S.A.
109 D2 Štip Macedonia
96 C2 Stirling U.K.
92 F3 Stjørdalshalsen Norway
103 D2 Stockerau Austria
93 G4 Stockholm Sweden

98 B2 Stockport U.K.
135 B3 Stockton U.S.A.
98 C1 Stockton-on-Tees U.K.
63 B2 Stœng Trêng Cambodia
96 B1 Stoer, Point of U.K.
98 B2 Stoke-on-Trent U.K.
109 D2 Stol *mt.* Serb. and Mont.
109 C2 Stolac Bos.-Herz.
100 C2 Stolberg (Rheinland) Ger.
88 C3 Stolin Belarus
101 F2 Stollberg Ger.
101 D1 Stolzenau Ger.
96 C2 Stonehaven U.K.
129 E2 Stonewall Can.
129 D2 Stony Rapids Can.
92 G2 Storavan *l.* Sweden
Store Bælt *sea chan.* Denmark *see* Great Belt
92 F3 Støren Norway
92 F2 Storforshei Norway
126 D2 Storkerson Peninsula Can.
137 D2 Storm Lake U.S.A.
93 E3 Stornosa *mt.* Norway
96 A1 Stornoway U.K.
86 E2 Storozhevsk Rus. Fed.
90 B2 Storozhynets' Ukr.
92 F3 Storsjön *l.* Sweden
92 H2 Storslett Norway
92 G3 Storuman Sweden
99 C3 Stour *r.* England U.K.
99 C3 Stour *r.* England U.K.
99 C3 Stour *r.* England U.K.
130 A1 Stout Lake Can.
88 C3 Stowbtsy Belarus
97 C1 Strabane U.K.
102 C2 Strakonice Czech Rep.
102 C1 Stralsund Ger.
122 A3 Strand S. Africa
93 E3 Stranda Norway
97 D1 Strangford Lough *inlet* U.K.
96 B3 Stranraer U.K.
105 D2 Strasbourg France
140 C2 Stratford Can.
54 B1 Stratford N.Z.
139 C1 Stratford U.S.A.
99 C2 Stratford-upon-Avon U.K.
128 C2 Strathmore Can.
96 C2 Strathspey *val.* U.K.
102 C2 Straubing Ger.
51 C3 Streaky Bay Austr.
110 B2 Streator U.S.A.
110 B2 Strehaia Romania
111 B2 Strimonas *r.* Greece
153 B5 Stroeder Arg.
101 D1 Ströhen Ger.
109 C3 Stromboli, Isola *i.* Italy
96 C1 Stromness U.K.
92 G3 Strömsund Sweden
96 C1 Stronsay *i.* U.K.
53 D2 Stroud Austr.
99 B3 Stroud U.K.
100 C1 Strücklingen (Saterland) Ger.
109 D2 Struga Macedonia
88 C2 Strugi-Krasnyye Rus. Fed.
122 B3 Struis Bay S. Africa
109 D2 Strumica Macedonia
122 B2 Strydenburg S. Africa
90 A2 Stryy Ukr.
128 B2 Stuart Lake Can.
130 A1 Stull Lake Can.
83 H3 Stupino Rus. Fed.
140 B2 Sturgeon Bay U.S.A.
130 C2 Sturgeon Falls Can.
130 A2 Sturgeon Lake Can.
140 B2 Sturgis *MI* U.S.A.
136 C2 Sturgis *SD* U.S.A.
50 B1 Sturt Creek *watercourse* Austr.

Sturt Stony Desert

242

52	B1	Sturt Stony Desert Austr.
123	C3	Stutterheim S. Africa
102	B2	Stuttgart Ger.
142	B2	Stuttgart U.S.A.
92	□A2	Stykkishólmur Iceland
90	B1	Styr r. Belarus/Ukr.
155	D1	Suaçuí Grande r. Brazil
116	B3	Suakin Sudan
78	A3	Suara, Mount Eritrea
110	C1	Suceava Romania
97	B2	Suck r. Ireland
152	B2	Sucre Bol.
154	B2	Sucuriú r. Brazil
89	E2	Suda Rus. Fed.
91	C3	Sudak Ukr.
117	A3	Sudan country Africa
130	B2	Sudbury Can.
117	A4	Sudd swamp Sudan
89	F2	Sudislavl' Rus. Fed.
89	F2	Sudogda Rus. Fed.
94	B1	Suðuroy i. Faroe Is
107	C2	Sueca Spain
116	B2	Suez Egypt
116	B2	Suez, Gulf of Egypt
80	B2	Suez Canal Egypt
141	D3	Suffolk U.S.A.
79	C2	Şuḩār Oman
69	D1	Sühbaatar Mongolia
101	E2	Suhl Ger.
109	C1	Suhopolje Croatia
70	B2	Suide China
66	B2	Suifenhe China
69	E1	Suihua China
70	A2	Suining China
70	B2	Suiping China
70	B2	Suiyang China
70	B2	Suizhou China
74	B2	Sujangarh India
74	B1	Sujanpur India
74	A2	Sujawal Pak.
60	B2	Sukabumi Indon.
61	B2	Sukadana Indon.
61	C2	Sukaraja Indon.
89	E3	Sukhinichi Rus. Fed.
89	F2	Sukhona r. Rus. Fed.
62	A2	Sukhothai Thai.
74	A2	Sukkur Pak.
89	E2	Sukromny Rus. Fed.
59	C3	Sula, Kepulauan is Indon.
74	A1	Sulaiman Range mts Pak.
		Sulawesi i. Indon. see Celebes
150	A2	Sullana Peru
137	E3	Sullivan U.S.A.
139	D2	Sulphur Springs U.S.A.
64	B2	Sulu Archipelago is Phil.
64	A2	Sulu Sea N. Pacific Ocean
101	E3	Sulzbach-Rosenberg Ger.
79	C2	Sumāil Oman
		Sumatera i. Indon. see Sumatra
60	A1	Sumatra i. Indon.
58	C3	Sumba i. Indon.
61	C2	Sumbawa i. Indon.
61	C2	Sumbawabesar Indon.
119	D3	Sumbawanga Tanz.
120	A2	Sumbe Angola
96	□	Sumburgh U.K.
96	□	Sumburgh Head U.K.
61	C2	Sumenep Indon.
67	D4	Sumisu-jima i. Japan
131	D2	Summerside Can.
140	C3	Summersville U.S.A.
128	B2	Summit Lake Can.
103	D2	Šumperk Czech Rep.
81	C1	Sumqayıt Azer.
143	D2	Sumter U.S.A.
91	C1	Sumy Ukr.
75	D2	Sunamganj Bangl.

65	B2	Sunan N. Korea
79	C2	Şunaynah Oman
52	B3	Sunbury Austr.
141	D2	Sunbury U.S.A.
65	B2	Sunch'ŏn N. Korea
65	B3	Sunch'ŏn S. Korea
123	C2	Sun City S. Africa
60	B2	Sunda, Selat str. Indon.
136	C2	Sundance U.S.A.
75	C2	Sundarbans reg. Bangl./India
98	C1	Sunderland U.K.
128	C2	Sundre Can.
93	G3	Sundsvall Sweden
123	D2	Sundumbili S. Africa
60	B2	Sungailiat Indon.
60	B2	Sungaipenuh Indon.
60	B1	Sungai Petani Malaysia
80	B1	Sungurlu Turkey
93	E3	Sunndalsøra Norway
134	C1	Sunnyside U.S.A.
135	B3	Sunnyvale U.S.A.
83	I2	Suntar Rus. Fed.
74	A2	Suntsar Pak.
114	B4	Sunyani Ghana
82	D2	Suoyarvi Rus. Fed.
138	A2	Superior AZ U.S.A.
137	D2	Superior NE U.S.A.
140	A1	Superior WI U.S.A.
140	B1	Superior, Lake Can./U.S.A.
89	D3	Suponevo Rus. Fed.
81	C2	Sūq ash Shuyūkh Iraq
70	B2	Suqian China
78	A2	Sūq Suwayq Saudi Arabia
79	C2	Şūr Oman
74	A2	Şurab Pak.
61	C2	Surabaya Indon.
61	C2	Surakarta Indon.
74	B2	Surat India
74	B2	Suratgarh India
63	A3	Surat Thani Thai.
89	D3	Surazh Rus. Fed.
109	D2	Surdulica Serb. and Mont.
74	B2	Surendranagar India
82	F2	Surgut Rus. Fed.
64	B2	Surigao Phil.
63	B2	Surin Thai.
151	C1	Suriname country S. America
		Surt Libya see Sirte
		Surt, Khalīj g. Libya see Sirte, Gulf of
60	B2	Surulangun Indon.
89	F2	Susanino Rus. Fed.
135	B2	Susanville U.S.A.
80	B1	Suşehri Turkey
131	D2	Sussex Can.
101	D1	Süstedt Ger.
100	C1	Sustrum Ger.
83	K2	Susuman Rus. Fed.
111	C3	Susurluk Turkey
75	B1	Sutak Jammu and Kashmir
122	B3	Sutherland S. Africa
99	C2	Sutton Coldfield U.K.
66	D2	Suttsu Japan
49	F4	Suva Fiji
89	E3	Suvorov Rus. Fed.
103	E1	Suwałki Pol.
63	B2	Suwannaphum Thai.
143	D3	Suwannee r. U.S.A.
		Suways, Qanāt as canal Egypt see Suez Canal
65	B2	Suwŏn S. Korea
79	C2	Sūzā Iran
89	F2	Suzdal' Rus. Fed.
70	B2	Suzhou Anhui China
70	C2	Suzhou Jiangsu China
67	C3	Suzu Japan
67	C3	Suzu-misaki pt Japan

82	B1	Svalbard terr. Arctic Ocean
91	D2	Svatove Ukr.
63	B2	Svay Riêng Cambodia
93	F3	Sveg Sweden
88	C2	Švenčionys Lith.
93	F4	Svendborg Denmark
		Sverdlovsk Rus. Fed. see Yekaterinburg
109	D2	Sveti Nikole Macedonia
88	B3	Svetlogorsk Rus. Fed.
88	B3	Svetlyy Rus. Fed.
93	I3	Svetogorsk Rus. Fed.
110	C2	Svilengrad Bulg.
110	B2	Svinecea Mare, Vârful mt. Romania
110	C2	Svishtov Bulg.
103	D2	Svitavy Czech Rep.
91	C2	Svitlovods'k Ukr.
69	E1	Svobodnyy Rus. Fed.
92	F2	Svolvær Norway
88	C3	Svyetlahorsk Belarus
143	D2	Swainsboro U.S.A.
120	A3	Swakopmund Namibia
52	B3	Swan Hill Austr.
128	C2	Swan Hills Can.
129	D2	Swan Lake Can.
129	D2	Swan River Can.
53	D2	Swansea Austr.
99	B3	Swansea U.K.
123	C3	Swartruggens S. Africa
		Swatow China see Shantou
123	D2	Swaziland country Africa
93	G3	Sweden country Europe
139	C2	Sweetwater U.S.A.
136	B2	Sweetwater r. U.S.A.
122	B3	Swellendam S. Africa
103	D1	Świdnica Pol.
103	D1	Świdwin Pol.
103	D1	Świebodzin Pol.
103	D1	Świecie Pol.
129	D2	Swift Current Can.
97	C1	Swilly, Lough inlet Ireland
99	C3	Swindon U.K.
102	C1	Świnoujście Pol.
105	D2	Switzerland country Europe
97	C2	Swords Ireland
88	C3	Syanno Belarus
89	D2	Sychevka Rus. Fed.
53	D2	Sydney Austr.
131	D2	Sydney Can.
131	D2	Sydney Mines Can.
91	D2	Syeverodonets'k Ukr.
86	E2	Syktyvkar Rus. Fed.
142	C2	Sylacauga U.S.A.
75	D2	Sylhet Bangl.
102	B1	Sylt i. Ger.
111	C3	Symi i. Greece
91	D2	Synel'nykove Ukr.
109	C3	Syracuse Sicily Italy
136	C3	Syracuse KS U.S.A.
141	D2	Syracuse NY U.S.A.
77	C2	Syrdar'ya r. Asia
80	B2	Syria country Asia
80	B2	Syrian Desert Asia
111	B3	Syros i. Greece
87	D3	Syzran' Rus. Fed.
102	C1	Szczecin Pol.
103	D1	Szczecinek Pol.
103	E1	Szczytno Pol.
103	E2	Szeged Hungary
103	D2	Székesfehérvár Hungary
103	D2	Szekszárd Hungary
103	E2	Szentes Hungary
103	D2	Szentgotthárd Hungary
103	D2	Szigetvár Hungary
103	E2	Szolnok Hungary
103	D2	Szombathely Hungary

T

78 B2 **Tābah** Saudi Arabia
76 B3 **Tabas** Iran
81 D3 **Tabas, Kūh-e** *mt.* Iran
150 D2 **Tabatinga** Brazil
114 B2 **Tabelbala** Alg.
129 C3 **Taber** Can.
102 C2 **Tábor** Czech Rep.
119 D3 **Tabora** Tanz.
114 B4 **Tabou** Côte d'Ivoire
81 C1 **Tabrīz** Iran
78 A2 **Tabūk** Saudi Arabia
77 E2 **Tacheng** China
102 C2 **Tachov** Czech Rep.
64 B1 **Tacloban** Phil.
150 A3 **Tacna** Peru
134 B1 **Tacoma** U.S.A.
152 C4 **Tacuarembó** Uru.
138 B3 **Tacupeto** Mex.
117 C3 **Tadjourah** Djibouti
80 B2 **Tadmur** Syria
129 E2 **Tadoule Lake** Can.
65 B3 **Taegu** S. Korea
65 B3 **Taejōn** S. Korea
65 B3 **Taejōng** S. Korea
65 B2 **T'aepaek** S. Korea
69 E1 **Ta'erqi** China
107 C1 **Tafalla** Spain
152 B3 **Tafí Viejo** Arg.
79 D2 **Taftān, Kūh-e** *mt.* Iran
91 D2 **Taganrog** Rus. Fed.
91 D2 **Taganrog, Gulf of** Rus. Fed./Ukr.
62 A1 **Tagaung** Myanmar
64 B1 **Tagaytay City** Phil.
64 B1 **Tagbilaran** Phil.
64 B2 **Tagudin** Phil.
64 B2 **Tagum** Phil.
106 B2 **Tagus** *r.* Port./Spain
60 B1 **Tahan, Gunung** *mt.* Malaysia
115 C2 **Tahat, Mont** *mt.* Alg.
69 E1 **Tahe** China
49 I4 **Tahiti** *i.* Fr. Polynesia
139 E1 **Tahlequah** U.S.A.
135 B3 **Tahoe, Lake** U.S.A.
135 B3 **Tahoe City** U.S.A.
126 D2 **Tahoe Lake** Can.
115 C3 **Tahoua** Niger
79 C2 **Tahrūd** Iran
128 B3 **Tahsis** Can.
70 B2 **Tai'an** China
    Taibus Qi China see Baochang
71 C3 **T'aichung** Taiwan
54 C1 **Taihape** N.Z.
70 C2 **Tai Hu** *l.* China
52 A3 **Tailem Bend** Austr.
71 C3 **T'ainan** Taiwan
155 D1 **Taiobeiras** Brazil
71 C3 **T'aipei** Taiwan
60 B1 **Taiping** Malaysia
71 B3 **Taishan** China
153 A5 **Taitao, Península de** *pen.* Chile
71 C3 **T'aitung** Taiwan
92 I2 **Taivalkoski** Fin.
91 H2 **Taivaskero** *hill* Fin.
71 C3 **Taiwan** *country* Asia
71 B3 **Taiwan Strait** China/Taiwan
70 B2 **Taiyuan** China
71 C3 **Taizhou** *Jiangsu* China
71 C3 **Taizhou** *Zhejiang* China
78 B3 **Ta'izz** Yemen
77 D3 **Tajikistan** *country* Asia
75 D2 **Taj Mahal** *tourist site* India
    Tajo *r.* Port. see Tagus

58 A1 **Tak** Thai.
54 B2 **Takaka** N.Z.
54 B4 **Takamatsu** Japan
67 C3 **Takaoka** Japan
54 B1 **Takapuna** N.Z.
67 C3 **Takasaki** Japan
122 B1 **Takatokwane** Botswana
67 C3 **Takayama** Japan
67 C3 **Takefu** Japan
60 A1 **Takengon** Indon.
63 B2 **Takêv** Cambodia
63 B2 **Ta Khmau** Cambodia
66 D2 **Takikawa** Japan
128 B2 **Takla Lake** Can.
128 B2 **Takla Landing** Can.
77 E3 **Taklimakan Desert** China
    Taklimakan Shamo *des.* China see Taklimakan Desert
128 A2 **Taku** *r.* Can./U.S.A.
63 A3 **Takua Pa** Thai.
115 C4 **Takum** Nigeria
88 C3 **Talachyn** Belarus
74 B1 **Talagang** Pak.
150 A2 **Talara** Peru
59 C2 **Talaud, Kepulauan** *is* Indon.
106 C2 **Talavera de la Reina** Spain
153 A4 **Talca** Chile
153 A4 **Talcahuano** Chile
89 E2 **Taldom** Rus. Fed.
77 D2 **Taldykorgan** Kazakh.
59 C3 **Taliabu** *i.* Indon.
64 B1 **Talisay** Phil.
61 C2 **Taliwang** Indon.
81 C2 **Tall 'Afar** Iraq
143 D2 **Tallahassee** U.S.A.
88 B2 **Tallinn** Estonia
142 B2 **Tallulah** U.S.A.
104 B2 **Talmont-St-Hilaire** France
90 C2 **Tal'ne** Ukr.
117 B3 **Talodi** Sudan
91 E1 **Talovaya** Rus. Fed.
126 E2 **Taloyoak** Can.
88 B2 **Talsi** Latvia
152 A3 **Taltal** Chile
129 C1 **Taltson** *r.* Can.
60 A1 **Talu** Indon.
53 C1 **Talwood** Austr.
114 B4 **Tamale** Ghana
115 C2 **Tamanrasset** Alg.
99 A3 **Tamar** *r.* U.K.
145 C2 **Tamazunchale** Mex.
114 A3 **Tambacounda** Senegal
61 B1 **Tambelan, Kepulauan** *is* Indon.
91 E1 **Tambov** Rus. Fed.
145 C2 **Tamiahua, Laguna de** *lag.* Mex.
143 D3 **Tampa** U.S.A.
143 D3 **Tampa Bay** U.S.A.
93 H3 **Tampere** Fin.
145 C2 **Tampico** Mex.
69 D1 **Tamsagbulag** Mongolia
102 C2 **Tamsweg** Austria
53 D2 **Tamworth** Austr.
99 C2 **Tamworth** U.K.
119 E3 **Tana** *r.* Kenya
117 B3 **Tana, Lake** Eth.
67 C4 **Tanabe** Japan
92 I1 **Tana Bru** Norway
61 C2 **Tanahgrogot** Indon.
58 C3 **Tanahjampea** *i.* Indon.
51 C1 **Tanami Desert** Austr.
126 A2 **Tanana** U.S.A.
108 A1 **Tanaro** *r.* Italy
65 B1 **Tanch'ŏn** N. Korea
64 B2 **Tandag** Phil.
110 C1 **Ţăndărei** Romania
153 C4 **Tandil** Arg.
74 A2 **Tando Adam** Pak.

74 A2 **Tando Muhammmad Khan** Pak.
114 B2 **Tanezrouft** *reg.* Alg./Mali
119 D3 **Tanga** Tanz.
119 C3 **Tanganyika, Lake** Africa
114 B1 **Tanger** Morocco
101 E1 **Tangermünde** Ger.
75 C1 **Tanggula Shan** *mts* China
    Tangier Morocco see Tanger
75 C1 **Tangra Yumco** *salt l.* China
70 B2 **Tangshan** China
68 C2 **Taniantaweng Shan** *mts* China
59 C3 **Tanimbar, Kepulauan** *is* Indon.
64 B2 **Tanjay** Phil.
60 A1 **Tanjungbalai** Indon.
61 B2 **Tanjungpandan** Indon.
60 B1 **Tanjungpinang** Indon.
61 C1 **Tanjungredeb** Indon.
61 C1 **Tanjungselor** Indon.
74 B1 **Tank** Pak.
115 C3 **Tanout** Niger
75 C2 **Tansen** Nepal
116 B1 **Ţanţā** Egypt
119 D3 **Tanzania** *country* Africa
69 E1 **Taonan** China
138 B1 **Taos** U.S.A.
114 B2 **Taoudenni** Mali
88 C2 **Tapa** Estonia
145 C3 **Tapachula** Mex.
151 C2 **Tapajós** *r.* Brazil
60 A1 **Tapaktuan** Indon.
145 C3 **Tapanatepec** Mex.
150 B2 **Tapauá** Brazil
114 B4 **Tapeta** Liberia
74 B2 **Tapi** *r.* India
141 D3 **Tappahannock** U.S.A.
150 B2 **Tapurucuara** Brazil
154 A1 **Taquari** *r.* Brazil
154 B1 **Taquari, Serra do** *hills* Brazil
154 C2 **Taquaritinga** Brazil
115 D4 **Taraba** *r.* Nigeria
    Ṭarābulus Libya see Tripoli
61 C1 **Tarakan** Indon.
88 A3 **Taran, Mys** *pt* Rus. Fed.
54 B1 **Taranaki, Mount** *vol.* N.Z.
106 C1 **Tarancón** Spain
109 C2 **Taranto** Italy
109 C2 **Taranto, Golfo di** *g.* Italy
150 A2 **Tarapoto** Peru
91 E2 **Tarasovskiy** Rus. Fed.
150 A2 **Tarauacá** Brazil
150 B2 **Tarauacá** *r.* Brazil
48 F2 **Tarawa** *i.* Kiribati
77 D2 **Taraz** Kazakh.
107 C1 **Tarazona** Spain
77 E2 **Tarbagatay, Khrebet** *mts* Kazakh.
96 C2 **Tarbert** *Scotland* U.K.
96 B3 **Tarbert** *Scotland* U.K.
104 C3 **Tarbes** France
96 B2 **Tarbet** U.K.
51 C3 **Tarcoola** Austr.
53 D2 **Taree** Austr.
110 C2 **Târgoviște** Romania
110 B1 **Târgu Jiu** Romania
110 B1 **Târgu Mureș** Romania
110 C1 **Târgu Neamţ** Romania
79 C2 **Tarīf** U.A.E.
152 B3 **Tarija** Bol.
78 B3 **Tarim** Yemen
77 E2 **Tarim Basin** China
77 E2 **Tarim He** *r.* China
    Tarim Pendi *basin* China see Tarim Basin
59 C3 **Taritatu** *r.* Indon.
82 G2 **Tarko-Sale** Rus. Fed.

114 B4 **Tarkwa** Ghana
64 B1 **Tarlac** Phil.
92 G2 **Tärnaby** Sweden
77 C3 **Tarnak** r. Afgh.
110 B1 **Târnăveni** Romania
103 E1 **Tarnobrzeg** Pol.
103 E1 **Tarnów** Pol.
114 B1 **Taroudannt** Morocco
108 B2 **Tarquinia** Italy
107 D1 **Tarragona** Spain
107 D1 **Tàrrega** Spain
111 D1 **Tarsus** Turkey
152 B3 **Tartagal** Arg.
104 B3 **Tartas** France
88 C2 **Tartu** Estonia
80 B2 **Ţarţūs** Syria
155 D1 **Tarumirim** Brazil
89 E3 **Tarusa** Rus. Fed.
108 B1 **Tarvisio** Italy
81 D3 **Tashk, Daryācheh-ye** l. Iran
   Tashkent Uzbek. see
   Toshkent
131 D1 **Tasiujaq** Can.
77 E2 **Taskesken** Kazakh.
54 B3 **Tasman Bay** N.Z.
51 D4 **Tasmania** state Austr.
54 B2 **Tasman Mountains** N.Z.
156 D8 **Tasman Sea**
   S. Pacific Ocean
115 C3 **Tassili du Hoggar** plat. Alg.
115 C2 **Tassili n'Ajjer** plat. Alg.
103 D2 **Tatabánya** Hungary
90 B2 **Tatarbunary** Ukr.
83 K3 **Tatarskiy Proliv** str.
   Rus. Fed.
67 C4 **Tateyama** Japan
128 C1 **Tathlina Lake** Can.
78 B3 **Tathlith** Saudi Arabia
78 B2 **Tathlīth, Wādī** watercourse
   Saudi Arabia
53 C1 **Tathra** Austr.
62 A1 **Tatkon** Myanmar
128 B2 **Tatla Lake** Can.
103 D2 **Tatry** mts Pol./Slovakia
74 A2 **Tatta** Pak.
154 C2 **Tatuí** Brazil
139 C2 **Tatum** U.S.A.
81 C2 **Tatvan** Turkey
151 D2 **Taua** Brazil
155 C2 **Taubaté** Brazil
101 D3 **Tauberbischofsheim** Ger.
54 C1 **Taumarunui** N.Z.
62 A1 **Taunggyi** Myanmar
62 A2 **Taung-ngu** Myanmar
62 A2 **Taungup** Myanmar
99 B3 **Taunton** U.K.
100 C0 **Taunus** hills Ger.
54 C1 **Taupo** N.Z.
54 C1 **Taupo, Lake** N.Z.
88 B2 **Tauragė** Lith.
54 C1 **Tauranga** N.Z.
111 D3 **Taurus Mountains** Turkey
111 F3 **Tavas** Turkey
86 F3 **Tavda** Rus. Fed.
106 B2 **Tavira** Port.
99 A3 **Tavistock** U.K.
63 A2 **Tavoy** Myanmar
111 C3 **Tavşanlı** Turkey
99 A3 **Taw** r. U.K.
140 C2 **Tawas City** U.S.A.
61 C1 **Tawau** Sabah Malaysia
64 A2 **Tawitawi** i. Phil.
145 C3 **Taxco** Mex.
77 D3 **Taxiatosh** Uzbek.
77 D3 **Taxkorgan** China
96 C2 **Tay** r. U.K.
96 C2 **Tay, Firth of** est. U.K.
96 B2 **Tay, Loch** l. U.K.
128 B2 **Taylor** Can.
139 D2 **Taylor** U.S.A.

140 B3 **Taylorville** U.S.A.
78 A2 **Taymā'** Saudi Arabia
83 H2 **Taymura** r. Rus. Fed.
83 H2 **Taymyr, Ozero** l. Rus. Fed.
   Taymyr, Poluostrov pen.
   Rus. Fed. see **Taymyr**
   Peninsula
83 G2 **Taymyr Peninsula**
   Rus. Fed.
63 B2 **Tây Ninh** Vietnam
64 A1 **Taytay** Phil.
82 G2 **Taz** r. Rus. Fed.
114 B1 **Taza** Morocco
129 D2 **Tazin Lake** Can.
86 G2 **Tazovskaya Guba**
   sea chan. Rus. Fed.
81 C1 **T'bilisi** Georgia
81 C1 **Tbilisskaya** Rus. Fed.
118 B3 **Tchibanga** Gabon
118 B2 **Tcholliré** Cameroon
103 D1 **Tczew** Pol.
144 B2 **Teacapán** Mex.
54 A3 **Te Anau** N.Z.
54 A3 **Te Anau, Lake** N.Z.
145 C3 **Teapa** Mex.
54 C1 **Te Awamutu** N.Z.
115 C1 **Tébessa** Alg.
60 A1 **Tebingtinggi** Sumatera
   Indon.
60 B2 **Tebingtinggi** Sumatera
   Indon.
114 B4 **Techiman** Ghana
144 B3 **Tecomán** Mex.
144 B2 **Tecoripa** Mex.
145 B3 **Tecpan** Mex.
144 B2 **Tecuala** Mex.
110 C1 **Tecuci** Romania
68 C1 **Teeli** Rus. Fed.
98 C1 **Tees** r. U.K.
111 C3 **Tefenni** Turkey
61 B2 **Tegal** Indon.
146 B3 **Tegucigalpa** Hond.
115 C3 **Teguidda-n-Tessoumt**
   Niger
114 B4 **Téhini** Côte d'Ivoire
81 D2 **Tehrān** Iran
145 C3 **Tehuacán** Mex.
145 C3 **Tehuantepec, Gulf of** Mex.
145 C3 **Tehuantepec, Istmo de**
   isth. Mex.
99 A2 **Teifi** r. U.K.
76 C3 **Tejen** Turkm.
76 C3 **Tejen** r. Turkm.
   Tejo r. Spain see **Tagus**
145 B3 **Tejupilco** Mex.
54 B2 **Tekapo, Lake** N.Z.
145 D2 **Tekax** Mex.
116 B3 **Tekezē Wenz** r. Eritrea/Eth.
111 C2 **Tekirdağ** Turkey
54 C1 **Te Kuiti** N.Z.
75 C2 **Tel** r. India
81 C1 **T'elavi** Georgia
80 B2 **Tel Aviv-Yafo** Israel
145 D2 **Telchac Puerto** Mex.
128 A2 **Telegraph Creek** Can.
154 B2 **Telêmaco Borba** Brazil
99 B2 **Telford** U.K.
60 A2 **Telo** Indon.
86 E2 **Tel'pos-Iz, Gora** mt.
   Rus. Fed.
88 B2 **Telšiai** Lith.
61 B2 **Telukbatang** Indon.
60 A1 **Telukdalam** Indon.
60 B1 **Teluk Intan** Malaysia
130 C2 **Temagami Lake** Can.
61 C2 **Temanggung** Indon.
58 B3 **Temba** S. Africa
60 B2 **Tembilahan** Indon.
120 A1 **Tembo Aluma** Angola
99 B2 **Teme** r. U.K.

60 B1 **Temerluh** Malaysia
77 D1 **Temirtau** Kazakh.
53 C2 **Temora** Austr.
139 D2 **Temple** U.S.A.
97 C2 **Templemore** Ireland
145 C2 **Tempoal** Mex.
91 D2 **Temryuk** Rus. Fed.
153 A4 **Temuco** Chile
54 B2 **Temuka** N.Z.
145 C2 **Tenabo** Mex.
73 C3 **Tenali** India
63 A2 **Tenasserim** Myanmar
99 A3 **Tenby** U.K.
117 C3 **Tendaho** Eth.
105 D3 **Tende** France
108 A2 **Tende, Col de** pass
   France/Italy
73 D4 **Ten Degree Channel** India
67 D3 **Tendō** Japan
114 B3 **Ténenkou** Mali
115 D2 **Ténéré du Tafassâsset**
   des. Niger
114 A2 **Tenerife** i. Canary Is
107 D2 **Ténès** Alg.
61 C2 **Tengah, Kepulauan** is
   Indon.
62 A1 **Tengchong** China
61 C2 **Tenggarong** Indon.
70 A2 **Tengger Shamo** des. China
71 B3 **Tengxian** China
119 C4 **Tenke** Dem. Rep. Congo
114 B3 **Tenkodogo** Burkina
51 C1 **Tennant Creek** Austr.
142 C1 **Tennessee** r. U.S.A.
142 C1 **Tennessee** state U.S.A.
145 C3 **Tenosique** Mex.
53 D1 **Tenterfield** Austr.
154 B2 **Teodoro Sampaio** Brazil
155 D1 **Teófilo Otôni** Brazil
145 C3 **Teopisca** Mex.
144 B2 **Tepache** Mex.
54 B1 **Te Paki** N.Z.
144 B3 **Tepalcatepec** Mex.
144 B2 **Tepatitlán** Mex.
109 D2 **Tepelenë** Albania
144 B2 **Tepic** Mex.
102 C1 **Teplice** Czech Rep.
89 F2 **Teploye** Rus. Fed.
144 B2 **Tequila** Mex.
108 B2 **Teramo** Italy
89 E3 **Terbuny** Rus. Fed.
90 B2 **Terebovlya** Ukr.
87 D4 **Terek** r. Rus. Fed.
151 D2 **Teresina** Brazil
155 D2 **Teresópolis** Brazil
63 A3 **Teressa Island** India
80 B1 **Terme** Turkey
108 B3 **Termini Imerese** Sicily Italy
145 C3 **Términos, Laguna de**
   lag. Mex.
77 C3 **Termiz** Uzbek.
109 B2 **Termoli** Italy
59 C2 **Ternate** Indon.
100 A2 **Terneuzen** Neth.
108 B2 **Terni** Italy
90 B2 **Ternopil'** Ukr.
128 B2 **Terrace** Can.
130 B2 **Terrace Bay** Can.
122 B2 **Terra Firma** S. Africa
140 B3 **Terre Haute** U.S.A.
131 E2 **Terrenceville** Can.
100 B1 **Terschelling** i. Neth.
108 A3 **Tertenia** Sardinia Italy
107 C1 **Teruel** Spain
92 H2 **Tervola** Fin.
109 C2 **Tešanj** Bos.-Herz.
116 B3 **Teseney** Eritrea
66 D2 **Teshio-gawa** r. Japan
128 A1 **Teslin** Can.

128 A1 Teslin Lake Can.
154 B1 Tesouro Brazil
115 C3 Tessaoua Niger
121 C2 Tete Moz.
90 C1 Teteriv r. Ukr.
101 F1 Teterow Ger.
90 B2 Tetiyiv Ukr.
114 B1 Tétouan Morocco
109 D2 Tetovo Macedonia
152 B3 Teuco r. Arg.
144 B2 Teul de González Ortega Mex.
101 D1 Teutoburger Wald hills Ger.
Tevere r. Italy see Tiber
54 A3 Teviot N.Z.
51 E2 Tewantin Austr.
54 C2 Te Wharau N.Z.
139 E2 Texarkana U.S.A.
53 D1 Texas Austr.
139 D2 Texas state U.S.A.
139 E3 Texas City U.S.A.
100 B1 Texel i. Neth.
139 D2 Texoma, Lake U.S.A.
123 C2 Teyateyaneng Lesotho
89 F2 Teykovo Rus. Fed.
89 F2 Teza r. Rus. Fed.
75 D2 Tezpur India
62 A1 Tezu India
129 E1 Tha-anne r. Can.
123 C2 Thabana-Ntlenyana mt. Lesotho
123 C2 Thaba Putsoa mt. Lesotho
123 C1 Thabazimbi S. Africa
123 C2 Thabong S. Africa
63 A2 Thagyettaw Myanmar
62 B1 Thai Binh Vietnam
63 B2 Thailand country Asia
63 B2 Thailand, Gulf of Asia
62 B1 Thai Nguyên Vietnam
62 B2 Thakèk Laos
63 A3 Thalang Thai.
74 B1 Thal Desert Pak.
101 E2 Thale (Harz) Ger.
62 B2 Tha Li Thai.
123 C1 Thamaga Botswana
116 C3 Thamar, Jabal mt. Yemen
79 C3 Thamarit Oman
130 B2 Thames r. Can.
54 C1 Thames N.Z.
99 D3 Thames est. U.K.
99 D3 Thames r. U.K.
63 A2 Thanbyuzayat Myanmar
62 A2 Thandwè Myanmar
62 B2 Thanh Hoa Vietnam
73 B3 Thanjavur India
63 A2 Thanlyin Myanmar
74 A2 Thano Bula Khan Pak.
62 B1 Than Uyên Vietnam
74 A2 Thar Desert India/Pak.
52 B1 Thargomindah Austr.
81 C2 Tharthār, Buḩayrat ath l. Iraq
111 B3 Thasos i. Greece
62 B1 Thât Khê Vietnam
62 A2 Thaton Myanmar
62 A1 Thaungdut Myanmar
62 A2 Thayawadi Myanmar
62 A2 Thayetmyo Myanmar
62 A1 Thazi Myanmar
146 C2 The Bahamas country West Indies
98 B1 The Cheviot hill U.K.
134 B1 The Dalles U.S.A.
99 C2 The Fens reg. U.K.
114 A3 The Gambia country Africa
The Great Oasis Egypt see Khārijah, Wāḩāt al
79 C2 The Gulf Asia
100 B1 The Hague Neth.
129 E1 Thelon r. Can.

101 E2 Themar Ger.
96 A1 The Minch sea chan. U.K.
150 B2 Theodore Roosevelt r. Brazil
129 D2 The Pas Can.
111 B2 Thermaïkos Kolpos g. Greece
136 B2 Thermopolis U.S.A.
53 C3 The Rock Austr.
130 B2 Thessalon Can.
111 B2 Thessaloniki Greece
99 D2 Thetford U.K.
131 C2 Thetford Mines Can.
62 A1 The Triangle mts Myanmar
131 D1 Thévenet, Lac l. Can.
99 D2 The Wash b. U.K.
139 D2 The Woodlands U.S.A.
142 B3 Thibodaux U.S.A.
129 E2 Thicket Portage Can.
137 D1 Thief River Falls U.S.A.
105 C2 Thiers France
119 D3 Thika Kenya
73 B4 Thiladhunmathi Atoll Maldives
75 C2 Thimphu Bhutan
105 D2 Thionville France
111 C3 Thira i. Greece
98 C1 Thirsk U.K.
Thiruvananthapuram India see Trivandrum
93 E4 Thisted Denmark
129 E1 Thlewiaza r. Can.
62 A2 Thoen Thai.
123 D1 Thohoyandou S. Africa
101 E1 Thomasburg Ger.
97 C2 Thomastown Ireland
143 D2 Thomasville U.S.A.
100 C2 Thommen Belgium
129 E2 Thompson Can.
128 E3 Thompson r. U.S.A.
134 C1 Thompson Falls U.S.A.
128 B2 Thompson Sound Can.
96 C3 Thornhill U.K.
55 C2 Thorshavnheiane reg. Antarctica
104 B2 Thouars France
128 C2 Three Hills Can.
63 A2 Three Pagodas Pass Myanmar/Thai.
114 B4 Three Points, Cape Ghana
63 B2 Thu Dâu Môt Vietnam
100 B2 Thuin Belgium
127 G1 Thule Greenland
121 B3 Thuli Zimbabwe
130 B2 Thunder Bay Can.
63 A3 Thung Song Thai.
101 E2 Thüringer Becken reg. Ger.
101 E2 Thüringer Wald mts Ger.
97 C2 Thurles Ireland
96 C1 Thurso U.K.
96 C1 Thurso r. U.K.
151 D2 Tianguá Brazil
70 B2 Tianjin China
70 B2 Tianjin mun. China
71 A3 Tianlin China
70 B2 Tianmen China
70 A2 Tianshui China
154 B2 Tibagi r. Brazil
118 B2 Tibati Cameroon
108 B2 Tiber r. Italy
Tiberias, Lake Israel see Galilee, Sea of
115 D2 Tibesti mts Chad
Tibet aut. reg. China see Xizang Zizhiqu
Tibet, Plateau of China
68 B2 Tibet, Plateau of China
52 B1 Tibooburra Austr.
144 A2 Tiburón, Isla i. Mex.
114 B3 Tîchît Maur.
114 A2 Tichla Western Sahara

145 D2 Ticul Mex.
114 A3 Tidjikja Maur.
100 B1 Tiel Neth.
65 A1 Tieling China
100 A2 Tielt Belgium
100 B2 Tienen Belgium
68 B2 Tien Shan mts China/Kyrg.
Tientsin China see Tianjin
93 G3 Tierp Sweden
145 C2 Tierra Blanca Mex.
145 C3 Tierra Colorada Mex.
153 B6 Tierra del Fuego, Isla Grande de i. Arg./Chile
154 C2 Tietê Brazil
Tiflis Georgia see T'bilisi
143 D2 Tifton U.S.A.
90 B2 Tighina Moldova
131 D2 Tignish Can.
150 A2 Tigre r. Ecuador/Peru
81 C2 Tigris r. Asia
145 C2 Tihuatlán Mex.
144 A1 Tijuana Mex.
91 E2 Tikhoretsk Rus. Fed.
89 D2 Tikhvin Rus. Fed.
89 D2 Tikhvinskaya Gryada ridge Rus. Fed.
54 C1 Tikokino N.Z.
81 C2 Tikrīt Iraq
83 J2 Tiksi Rus. Fed.
100 B2 Tilburg Neth.
152 B3 Tilcara Arg.
52 B1 Tilcha Austr.
114 C3 Tillabéri Niger
134 B1 Tillamook U.S.A.
73 C3 Tillanchong Island India
111 C3 Tilos i. Greece
52 B2 Tilpa Austr.
86 F2 Til'tim Rus. Fed.
89 E3 Tim Rus. Fed.
86 D2 Timanskiy Kryazh ridge Rus. Fed.
54 B2 Timaru N.Z.
91 D2 Timashevsk Rus. Fed.
114 B3 Timbedgha Maur.
50 C1 Timber Creek Austr.
114 B3 Timbuktu Mali
114 C2 Timimoun Alg.
110 B1 Timiş r. Romania
110 B1 Timişoara Romania
130 B2 Timmins Can.
89 E2 Timokhino Rus. Fed.
151 D2 Timon Brazil
59 C3 Timor i. Indon.
58 C3 Timor Sea Austr./Indon.
93 G3 Timrå Sweden
114 B2 Tindouf Alg.
75 C2 Tingri China
93 F4 Tingsryd Sweden
59 D2 Tinian i. N. Mariana Is
152 B3 Tinogasta Arg.
111 C3 Tinos Greece
111 C3 Tinos i. Greece
115 C2 Tinrhert, Plateau du Alg.
62 A1 Tinsukia India
107 D2 Tipasa Alg.
97 B2 Tipperary Ireland
109 C2 Tirana Albania
Tiranë Albania see Tirana
108 B1 Tirano Italy
90 B2 Tiraspol Moldova
111 C3 Tire Turkey
96 A2 Tiree i. U.K.
74 B1 Tirich Mir mt. Pak.
73 B3 Tiruchchirappalli India
73 B4 Tirunelveli India
73 B3 Tirupati India
73 B3 Tiruppattur India
73 B3 Tiruppur India
109 D1 Tisa r. Europe
129 D2 Tisdale Can.

107	D2	**Tissemsilt** Alg.
152	B2	**Titicaca, Lake** Bol./Peru
75	C2	**Titlagarh** India
73	D1	**Titu** Romania
143	D3	**Titusville** U.S.A.
99	B3	**Tivaro** Turk.
108	B2	**Tivoli** Italy
79	C2	**Tiwi** Oman
145	D2	**Tizimín** Mex.
107	D2	**Tizi Ouzou** Alg.
114	B2	**Tiznit** Morocco
145	C3	**Tlacotalpán** Mex.
144	B2	**Tlahualilo** Mex.
145	C3	**Tlapa** Mex.
145	C3	**Tlaxcala** Mex.
145	C3	**Tlaxiaco** Mex.
114	B1	**Tlemcen** Alg.
123	C1	**Tlokweng** Botswana
128	B2	**Toad River** Can.
121	□D2	**Toamasina** Madag.
60	A1	**Toba, Danau** *l.* Indon.
74	A1	**Toba and Kakar Ranges** *mts* Pak.
147	D3	**Tobago** *i.* Trin. and Tob.
59	C3	**Tobelo** Indon.
130	B2	**Tobermory** Can.
96	A2	**Tobermory** U.K.
129	D2	**Tobin Lake** Can.
58	C2	**Toboali** Indon.
76	C1	**Tobol** *r.* Kazakh./Rus. Fed.
86	F3	**Tobol'sk** Rus. Fed.
151	E2	**Tocantinópolis** Brazil
151	D2	**Tocantins** *r.* Brazil
143	D2	**Toccoa** U.S.A.
108	A1	**Toce** *r.* Italy
152	A3	**Tocopilla** Chile
53	C3	**Tocumwal** Austr.
144	A2	**Todos Santos** Mex.
128	B3	**Tofino** Can.
96	□1	**Toft** U.K.
49	G4	**Tofua** *i.* Tonga
59	C3	**Togian, Kepulauan** *is* Indon.
114	C4	**Togo** *country* Africa
74	B2	**Tohana** India
126	B2	**Tok** U.S.A.
116	B3	**Tokar** Sudan
69	E3	**Tokara-rettō** *is* Japan
91	E1	**Tokarevka** Rus. Fed.
49	G3	**Tokelau** *terr.* S. Pacific Ocean
91	D2	**Tokmak** Ukr.
77	D2	**Tokmok** Kyrg.
54	C1	**Tokoroa** N.Z.
68	B2	**Toksun** China
67	B4	**Tokushima** Japan
67	C3	**Tōkyō** Japan
121	□D3	**Tôlañaro** Madag.
154	B2	**Toledo** Brazil
106	C2	**Toledo** Spain
140	C2	**Toledo** U.S.A.
106	C2	**Toledo, Montes de** *mts* Spain
142	B2	**Toledo Bend Reservoir** U.S.A.
121	□D3	**Toliara** Madag.
58	C2	**Tolitoli** Indon.
108	B1	**Tolmezzo** Italy
104	B3	**Tolosa** Spain
145	C3	**Toluca** Mex.
87	D3	**Tol'yatti** Rus. Fed.
140	A2	**Tomah** U.S.A.
66	D2	**Tomakomai** Japan
106	B2	**Tomar** Port.
103	E1	**Tomaszów Lubelski** Pol.
103	E1	**Tomaszów Mazowiecki** Pol.
144	B3	**Tomatlán** Mex.
142	C2	**Tombigbee** *r.* U.S.A.
155	□3	**Tombos** Brazil

		Tombouctou Mali *see* Timbuktu
120	A2	**Tombua** Angola
123	C1	**Tom Burke** S. Africa
53	C2	**Tomingley** Austr.
58	C3	**Tomini, Teluk** *g.* Indon.
109	C2	**Tomislavgrad** Bos.-Herz.
50	A2	**Tom Price** Austr.
82	G3	**Tomsk** Rus. Fed.
93	F4	**Tomtabacken** *hill* Sweden
145	C3	**Tonalá** Mex.
150	B2	**Tonantins** Brazil
59	C2	**Tondano** Indon.
49	G4	**Tonga** *country* S. Pacific Ocean
49	G4	**Tongatapu Group** *is* Tonga
71	B3	**Tongcheng** China
70	A2	**Tongchuan** China
62	B1	**Tonghai** China
65	B1	**Tonghua** China
65	B1	**Tongjosŏn-man** *b.* N. Korea
62	B1	**Tongking, Gulf of** China/Vietnam
69	E2	**Tongliao** China
70	B2	**Tongling** China
52	B2	**Tongo** Austr.
71	A3	**Tongren** China
70	B2	**Tongtian He** *r.* China *see* Yangtze
96	B1	**Tongue** U.K.
65	B3	**T'ongyŏng** S. Korea
69	E2	**Tongyu** China
65	A1	**Tongyuanpu** China
74	B2	**Tonk** India
63	B2	**Tonle Sap** *l.* Cambodia
135	C3	**Tonopah** U.S.A.
93	F4	**Tønsberg** Norway
135	D2	**Tooele** U.S.A.
52	B3	**Tooleybuc** Austr.
53	D1	**Toowoomba** Austr.
137	D3	**Topeka** U.S.A.
144	B2	**Topia** Mex.
144	B2	**Topolobampo** Mex.
86	C2	**Topozero, Ozero** *l.* Rus. Fed.
134	B1	**Toppenish** U.S.A.
111	C3	**Torbalı** Turkey
76	B3	**Torbat-e Heydariyeh** Iran
76	C3	**Torbat-e Jām** Iran
106	C1	**Tordesillas** Spain
107	C1	**Tordesilos** Spain
107	D1	**Torelló** Spain
101	F2	**Torgau** Ger.
100	A2	**Torhout** Belgium
		Torino Italy *see* Turin
154	B1	**Torixoréu** Brazil
106	B1	**Tormes** *r.* Spain
92	H2	**Torneälven** *r.* Sweden
127	G3	**Torngat Mountains** Can.
92	H2	**Tornio** Fin.
106	B1	**Toro** Spain
130	C2	**Toronto** Can.
119	D2	**Tororo** Uganda
		Toros Dağları *mts* Turkey *see* Taurus Mountains
99	B3	**Torquay** U.K.
106	B2	**Torrão** Port.
106	B1	**Torre** *mt.* Port.
107	D1	**Torreblanca** Spain
106	B1	**Torrecerredo** *mt.* Spain
106	B1	**Torre de Moncorvo** Port.
106	C1	**Torrelavega** Spain
106	C2	**Torremolinos** Spain
52	A2	**Torrens, Lake** *salt flat* Austr.

107	C2	**Torrent** Spain
144	B2	**Torreón** Mex.
106	B2	**Torres Novas** Port.
106	B2	**Torres Vedras** Port.
107	C2	**Torrevieja** Spain
96	B2	**Torridon** U.K.
106	C2	**Torrijos** Spain
141	E2	**Torrington** *CT* U.S.A.
136	C2	**Torrington** *WY* U.S.A.
107	D1	**Torroella de Montgrí** Spain
94	B1	**Tórshavn** Faroe Is
108	A3	**Tortolì** *Sardinia* Italy
107	D1	**Tortosa** Spain
103	D1	**Toruń** Pol.
97	B1	**Tory Island** Ireland
89	D2	**Tosno** Rus. Fed.
152	B3	**Tostado** Arg.
101	D1	**Tostedt** Ger.
80	B1	**Tosya** Turkey
86	D3	**Tot'ma** Rus. Fed.
67	B3	**Tottori** Japan
114	B4	**Touba** Côte d'Ivoire
114	B1	**Toubkal, Jbel** *mt.* Morocco
114	B3	**Tougan** Burkina
115	C1	**Touggourt** Alg.
104	C2	**Toul** France
71	C3	**Touliu** Taiwan
105	D3	**Toulon** France
104	C3	**Toulouse** France
100	A2	**Tournai** Belgium
105	C2	**Tournus** France
151	E2	**Touros** Brazil
104	C2	**Tours** France
115	D2	**Tousside, Pic** *mt.* Chad
122	B3	**Touwsrivier** S. Africa
66	D2	**Towada** Japan
134	D1	**Townsend** U.S.A.
51	D1	**Townsville** Austr.
77	E2	**Toxkan He** *r.* China
66	D2	**Tōya-ko** *l.* Japan
67	C3	**Toyama** Japan
67	C3	**Toyota** Japan
115	C1	**Tozeur** Tunisia
81	C1	**Tqvarch'eli** Georgia
		Trâblous Lebanon *see* Tripoli
80	B1	**Trabzon** Turkey
106	B2	**Trafalgar, Cabo** *c.* Spain
128	C3	**Trail** Can.
88	B3	**Trakai** Lith.
97	B2	**Tralee** Ireland
97	C2	**Tramore** Ireland
63	A3	**Trang** Thai.
59	C3	**Trangan** *i.* Indon.
55	I2	**Transantarctic Mountains** Antarctica
110	B1	**Transylvanian Alps** *mts* Romania
108	B3	**Trapani** *Sicily* Italy
53	C3	**Traralgon** Austr.
63	B2	**Trat** Thai.
102	C2	**Traunstein** Ger.
140	B2	**Traverse City** U.S.A.
103	D2	**Třebíč** Czech Rep.
109	C2	**Trebinje** Bos.-Herz.
103	E2	**Trebišov** Slovakia
109	C1	**Trebnje** Slovenia
153	C4	**Treinta y Tres** Uru.
153	B5	**Trelew** Arg.
93	F4	**Trelleborg** Sweden
130	C2	**Tremblant, Mont** *hill* Can.
109	C2	**Tremiti, Isole** *is* Italy
134	D2	**Tremonton** U.S.A.
107	D1	**Tremp** Spain
103	D2	**Trenčín** Slovakia

153 B4 **Trenque Lauquén** Arg.
98 C2 **Trent** r. U.K.
108 B1 **Trento** Italy
141 D2 **Trenton** Can.
137 E2 **Trenton** MO U.S.A.
141 E2 **Trenton** NJ U.S.A.
131 E2 **Trepassey** Can.
153 B4 **Tres Arroyos** Arg.
155 C2 **Três Corações** Brazil
154 B2 **Três Lagoas** Brazil
153 A5 **Tres Lagos** Arg.
155 C1 **Três Marias, Represa** resr
      Brazil
155 C2 **Três Pontas** Brazil
153 B5 **Tres Puntas, Cabo** c. Arg.
155 D2 **Três Rios** Brazil
101 F1 **Treuenbrietzen** Ger.
108 A1 **Treviglio** Italy
108 B1 **Treviso** Italy
99 A3 **Trevose Head** U.K.
109 C3 **Tricase** Italy
73 B3 **Trichur** India
53 C2 **Trida** Austr.
100 C3 **Trier** Ger.
108 B1 **Trieste** Italy
108 B1 **Triglav** mt. Slovenia
59 D3 **Trikora, Puncak** mt. Indon.
97 C2 **Trim** Ireland
73 C4 **Trincomalee** Sri Lanka
154 C1 **Trindade** Brazil
152 B2 **Trinidad** Bol.
147 D3 **Trinidad** i. Trin. and Tob.
136 C3 **Trinidad** U.S.A.
147 D3 **Trinidad and Tobago**
      country West Indies
131 E2 **Trinity Bay** Can.
111 B3 **Tripoli** Greece
80 B2 **Tripoli** Lebanon
115 D1 **Tripoli** Libya
113 D10 **Tristan da Cunha** i.
      S. Atlantic Ocean
73 B4 **Trivandrum** India
108 B2 **Trivento** Italy
103 D2 **Trnava** Slovakia
109 C2 **Trogir** Croatia
109 C2 **Troia** Italy
100 C2 **Troisdorf** Ger.
131 C2 **Trois-Rivières** Can.
86 E2 **Troitsko-Pechorsk**
      Rus. Fed.
151 C2 **Trombetas** r. Brazil
123 C3 **Trompsburg** S. Africa
92 G2 **Tromsø** Norway
92 F3 **Trondheim** Norway
128 C2 **Trout Lake** Can.
128 B1 **Trout Lake** N.W.T. Can.
130 A1 **Trout Lake** Ont. Can.
99 B3 **Trowbridge** U.K.
142 C2 **Troy** AL U.S.A.
141 E2 **Troy** NY U.S.A.
105 C2 **Troyes** France
109 D2 **Trstenik** Serb. and Mont.
89 D3 **Trubchevsk** Rus. Fed.
106 B1 **Truchas** Spain
79 C2 **Trucial Coast** U.A.E.
146 B3 **Trujillo** Hond.
150 A2 **Trujillo** Peru
106 B2 **Trujillo** Spain
147 C4 **Trujillo** Venez.
142 B1 **Trumann** U.S.A.
131 D2 **Truro** Can.
99 A3 **Truro** U.K.
138 B2 **Truth or Consequences**
      U.S.A.
103 D1 **Trutnov** Czech Rep.
93 F3 **Trysil** Norway
103 D1 **Trzebiatów** Pol.
68 B1 **Tsagaannuur** Mongolia
121 □D2 **Tsaratanana, Massif du**
      mts Madag.

110 C2 **Tsarevo** Bulg.
122 A2 **Tses** Namibia
122 B1 **Tsetseng** Botswana
68 C1 **Tsetserleg** Mongolia
122 B2 **Tshabong** Botswana
122 B1 **Tshane** Botswana
91 D2 **Tshchikskoye**
      Vodokhranilishche resr
      Rus. Fed.
118 B3 **Tshela** Dem. Rep. Congo
118 C3 **Tshikapa** Dem. Rep. Congo
118 C3 **Tshikapa** r. Dem. Rep. Congo
123 D1 **Tshipise** S. Africa
118 C3 **Tshitanzu** Dem. Rep. Congo
118 C3 **Tshuapa** r. Dem. Rep. Congo
      Tshwane S. Africa see
      Pretoria
87 D4 **Tsimlyanskoye**
      Vodokhranilishche resr
      Rus. Fed.
      Tsingtao China see
      Qingdao
      Tsining China see Jining
121 □D2 **Tsiroanomandidy** Madag.
123 C3 **Tsomo** S. Africa
67 C4 **Tsu** Japan
67 D3 **Tsuchiura** Japan
66 D2 **Tsugarū-kaikyō** str. Japan
120 A2 **Tsumeb** Namibia
122 A1 **Tsumis Park** Namibia
120 B2 **Tsumkwe** Namibia
67 C3 **Tsuruga** Japan
66 C3 **Tsuruoka** Japan
67 A4 **Tsushima** is Japan
      Tsushima-kaikyō str.
      Japan/S. Korea see
      Korea Strait
67 B3 **Tsuyama** Japan
123 C2 **Tswelelang** S. Africa
91 C2 **Tsyurupyns'k** Ukr.
      Tthenaagoo Can. see
      Nahanni Butte
59 C3 **Tual** Indon.
97 B2 **Tuam** Ireland
49 I3 **Tuamotu Archipelago** is
      Fr. Polynesia
91 D3 **Tuapse** Rus. Fed.
54 A3 **Tuatapere** N.Z.
96 A1 **Tuath, Loch a'** b. U.K.
138 A1 **Tuba City** U.S.A.
61 C2 **Tuban** Indon.
152 D3 **Tubarão** Brazil
102 B2 **Tübingen** Ger.
115 E1 **Tubruq** Libya
49 I4 **Tubuai** i. Fr. Polynesia
49 H4 **Tubuai Islands**
      N. Pacific Ocean
144 A1 **Tubutama** Mex.
152 C2 **Tucavaca** Bol.
128 B1 **Tuchitua** Can.
138 A2 **Tucson** U.S.A.
139 C1 **Tucumcari** U.S.A.
150 B1 **Tucupita** Venez.
151 D2 **Tucuruí** Brazil
151 D2 **Tucuruí, Represa** resr
      Brazil
107 C1 **Tudela** Spain
106 B1 **Tuela** r. Port.
62 A1 **Tuensang** India
123 D2 **Tugela** r. S. Africa
64 B1 **Tuguegarao** Phil.
106 B1 **Tui** Spain
59 C3 **Tukangbesi, Kepulauan** is
      Indon.
126 C2 **Tuktoyaktuk** Can.
88 B2 **Tukums** Latvia
145 C2 **Tula** Mex.
89 E3 **Tula** Rus. Fed.
145 C2 **Tulancingo** Mex.
135 C3 **Tulare** U.S.A.

138 B2 **Tularosa** U.S.A.
110 C1 **Tulcea** Romania
90 B2 **Tul'chyn** Ukr.
129 E1 **Tulemalu Lake** Can.
139 C2 **Tulia** U.S.A.
142 C1 **Tullahoma** U.S.A.
97 C2 **Tullamore** Ireland
104 C2 **Tulle** France
51 D1 **Tully** Austr.
139 D1 **Tulsa** U.S.A.
150 A1 **Tumaco** Col.
123 C2 **Tumahole** S. Africa
93 G4 **Tumba** Sweden
118 B3 **Tumba, Lac** l.
      Dem. Rep. Congo
53 C3 **Tumbarumba** Austr.
150 A2 **Tumbes** Peru
128 B2 **Tumbler Ridge** Can.
52 A2 **Tumby Bay** Austr.
65 B1 **Tumen** China
150 B1 **Tumereng** Guyana
74 A2 **Tumindao** i. Phil.
74 A2 **Tump** Pak.
151 C1 **Tumucumaque, Serra** hills
      Brazil
53 C3 **Tumut** Austr.
99 D3 **Tunbridge Wells, Royal**
      U.K.
80 B2 **Tunceli** Turkey
53 D2 **Tuncurry** Austr.
119 D4 **Tunduru** Tanz.
110 C2 **Tundzha** r. Bulg.
128 B1 **Tungsten** Can.
115 D1 **Tunis** Tunisia
115 C1 **Tunisia** country Africa
150 A1 **Tunja** Col.
92 F3 **Tunnsjøen** l. Norway
      Tunxi China see Huangshan
154 B2 **Tupã** Brazil
154 C1 **Tupaciguara** Brazil
142 C2 **Tupelo** U.S.A.
152 B3 **Tupiza** Bol.
83 H2 **Tura** Rus. Fed.
86 F3 **Tura** r. Rus. Fed.
78 B2 **Turabah** Saudi Arabia
83 J3 **Turana, Khrebet** mts
      Rus. Fed.
54 C1 **Turangi** N.Z.
76 B2 **Turan Lowland** Asia
78 A1 **Turayf** Saudi Arabia
88 B2 **Turba** Estonia
74 A2 **Turbat** Pak.
150 A1 **Turbo** Col.
110 B1 **Turda** Romania
      Turfan China see Turpan
76 C2 **Turgay** Kazakh.
111 C3 **Turgutlu** Turkey
80 B1 **Turhal** Turkey
106 C2 **Turia** r. Spain
108 A1 **Turin** Italy
86 F3 **Turinsk** Rus. Fed.
90 A1 **Turiys'k** Ukr.
119 D2 **Turkana, Lake** salt l.
      Eth./Kenya
77 C2 **Turkestan** Kazakh.
80 B2 **Turkey** country Asia
76 C3 **Türkmenabat** Turkm.
76 B2 **Türkmenbaşy** Turkm.
76 B2 **Turkmenistan** country Asia
147 C2 **Turks and Caicos Islands**
      terr. West Indies
93 H3 **Turku** Fin.
135 B3 **Turlock** U.S.A.
54 C2 **Turnagain, Cape** N.Z.
100 B2 **Turnhout** Belgium
129 D2 **Turnor Lake** Can.
110 B2 **Turnu Măgurele** Romania
68 B2 **Turpan** China
77 D2 **Turugart Pass** China/Kyrg.
142 C2 **Tuscaloosa** U.S.A.

142 C2 **Tuskegee** U.S.A.
73 B4 **Tuticorin** India
120 B3 **Tutume** Botswana
49 F3 **Tuvalu** *country*
S. Pacific Ocean
78 B2 **Tuwayq, Jabal** *hills*
Saudi Arabia
78 B2 **Tuwayq, Jabal** *mts*
Saudi Arabia
78 A2 **Tuwwal** Saudi Arabia
144 B2 **Tuxpan** *Nayarit* Mex.
145 C2 **Tuxpan** *Veracruz* Mex.
145 C3 **Tuxtla Gutiérrez** Mex.
62 B1 **Tuyên Quang** Vietnam
63 B2 **Tuy Hoa** Vietnam
80 B2 **Tuz, Lake** *salt l.* Turkey
Tuz Gölü *salt l.* Turkey *see*
Tuz, Lake
81 C2 **Tuz Khurmātū** Iraq
109 C2 **Tuzla** Bos.-Herz.
91 E2 **Tuzlov** *r.* Rus. Fed.
89 E2 **Tver'** Rus. Fed.
98 B1 **Tweed** *r.* U.K.
122 A2 **Twee Rivier** Namibia
135 C4 **Twentynine Palms** U.S.A.
131 E2 **Twillingate** Can.
134 D2 **Twin Falls** U.S.A.
137 E1 **Two Harbors** U.S.A.
129 C2 **Two Hills** Can.
139 D2 **Tyler** U.S.A.
83 J3 **Tynda** Rus. Fed.
93 F4 **Tynset** Norway
80 B2 **Tyre** Lebanon
111 B3 **Tyrnavos** Greece
52 B3 **Tyrrell, Lake** *dry lake* Austr.
108 B2 **Tyrrhenian Sea** France/Italy
76 B2 **Tyub-Karagan, Mys** *pt*
Kazakh.
87 E3 **Tyul'gan** Rus. Fed.
86 F3 **Tyumen'** Rus. Fed.
83 J2 **Tyung** *r.* Rus. Fed.
99 A3 **Tywi** *r.* U.K.
123 D1 **Tzaneen** S. Africa

U

120 B2 **Uamanda** Angola
150 B2 **Uaupés** Brazil
155 D2 **Ubá** Brazil
155 D1 **Ubaí** Brazil
151 E3 **Ubaitaba** Brazil
118 B3 **Ubangi** *r.* C.A.R./
Dem. Rep. Congo
67 B4 **Ube** Japan
106 C2 **Úbeda** Spain
154 C1 **Uberaba** Brazil
154 C1 **Uberlândia** Brazil
123 D2 **Ubombo** S. Africa
63 B2 **Ubon Ratchathani** Thai.
119 C3 **Ubundu** Dem. Rep. Congo
150 A2 **Ucayali** *r.* Peru
74 B2 **Uch** Pak.
77 E2 **Ucharal** Kazakh.
66 D2 **Uchiura-wan** *b.* Japan
83 J3 **Uchur** *r.* Rus. Fed.
128 B3 **Ucluelet** Can.
52 D2 **Udaipur** India
91 C1 **Uday** *r.* Ukr.
93 F4 **Uddevalla** Sweden
92 G2 **Uddjaure** *l.* Sweden
100 B2 **Uden** Neth.
74 B1 **Udhampur**
Jammu and Kashmir
108 B1 **Udine** Italy
89 E2 **Udomlya** Rus. Fed.
62 B2 **Udon Thani** Thai.
73 B3 **Udupi** India

83 K3 **Udyl', Ozero** *l.* Rus. Fed.
67 C3 **Ueda** Japan
58 C3 **Uekuli** Indon.
118 C2 **Uele** *r.* Dem. Rep. Congo
101 E1 **Uelzen** Ger.
119 C2 **Uere** *r.* Dem. Rep. Congo
87 B2 **Ufa** Rus. Fed.
119 D3 **Ugalla** *r.* Tanz.
119 D2 **Uganda** *country* Africa
89 E2 **Uglich** Rus. Fed.
89 D2 **Uglovka** Rus. Fed.
89 D3 **Ugra** Rus. Fed.
103 D2 **Uherské Hradiště**
Czech Rep.
101 E2 **Uichteritz** Ger.
96 A2 **Uig** U.K.
120 A1 **Uíge** Angola
65 B2 **Uijŏngbu** S. Korea
135 D2 **Uinta Mountains** U.S.A.
120 A3 **Uis Mine** Namibia
65 B2 **Ŭisŏng** S. Korea
123 C3 **Uitenhage** S. Africa
100 C1 **Uithuizen** Neth.
74 B2 **Ujjain** India
89 F3 **Ukholovo** Rus. Fed.
62 A1 **Ukhrul** India
86 F2 **Ukhta** Rus. Fed.
135 B3 **Ukiah** U.S.A.
127 H2 **Ukkusissat** Greenland
88 B2 **Ukmergė** Lith.
90 C2 **Ukraine** *country* Europe
Ulaanbaatar Mongolia *see*
Ulan Bator
68 C1 **Ulaangom** Mongolia
69 D1 **Ulan Bator** Mongolia
Ulanhad China *see* Chifeng
69 E1 **Ulanhot** China
87 D4 **Ulan-Khol** Rus. Fed.
69 D1 **Ulan-Ude** Rus. Fed.
75 D1 **Ulan Ul Hu** *l.* China
65 B2 **Ulchin** S. Korea
Uleåborg Fin. *see* Oulu
88 C2 **Ülenurme** Estonia
73 B3 **Ulhasnagar** India
69 D1 **Uliastai** China
68 C1 **Uliastay** Mongolia
59 D2 **Ulithi** *atoll* Micronesia
53 D3 **Ulladulla** Austr.
96 B2 **Ullapool** U.K.
98 B1 **Ullswater** *l.* U.K.
65 C2 **Ullŭng-do** *i.* S. Korea
102 B2 **Ulm** Ger.
65 B2 **Ulsan** S. Korea
96 □ **Ulsta** U.K.
97 C1 **Ulster** *reg.* Ireland/U.K.
52 B3 **Ultima** Austr.
111 C3 **Ulubey** Turkey
111 C2 **Uludağ** *mt.* Turkey
123 D2 **Ulundi** S. Africa
77 E2 **Ulungur Hu** *l.* China
50 C2 **Uluru** *hill* Austr.
98 B1 **Ulverston** U.K.
87 D3 **Ul'yanovsk** Rus. Fed.
136 C3 **Ulysses** U.S.A.
90 C2 **Uman'** Ukr.
86 C2 **Umba** Rus. Fed.
59 D3 **Umboi** *i.* P.N.G.
92 H3 **Umeå** Sweden
92 H3 **Umeälven** *r.* Sweden
127 I2 **Umiivip Kangertiva** *inlet*
Greenland
126 D2 **Umingmaktok** Can.
123 D2 **Umlazi** S. Africa
117 A3 **Umm Keddada** Sudan
78 A2 **Umm Lajj** Saudi Arabia
117 B3 **Umm Ruwaba** Sudan
115 E1 **Umm Sa'ad** Libya
134 B2 **Umpqua** *r.* U.S.A.
120 A2 **Umpulo** Angola
123 C3 **Umtata** S. Africa

154 B2 **Umuarama** Brazil
109 C1 **Una** *r.* Bos.-Herz./Croatia
155 E1 **Una** Brazil
154 C1 **Unaí** Brazil
78 B2 **'Unayzah** Saudi Arabia
136 C1 **Underwood** U.S.A.
89 D3 **Unecha** Rus. Fed.
53 C2 **Ungarie** Austr.
52 A2 **Ungarra** Austr.
127 G2 **Ungava, Péninsule d'**
pen. Can.
127 G3 **Ungava Bay** Can.
65 C1 **Unggi** N. Korea
90 B2 **Ungheni** Moldova
Unguja *i.* Tanz. *see*
Zanzibar Island
154 B3 **União da Vitória** Brazil
150 B3 **Unini** *r.* Brazil
142 C1 **Union City** U.S.A.
122 B3 **Uniondale** S. Africa
141 D3 **Uniontown** U.S.A.
79 C2 **United Arab Emirates**
country Asia
95 C3 **United Kingdom** *country*
Europe
132 D3 **United States of America**
country N. America
129 D2 **Unity** Can.
96 □ **Unst** *i.* U.K.
101 E2 **Unstrut** *r.* Ger.
89 E3 **Upa** *r.* Rus. Fed.
119 C3 **Upemba, Lac** *l.*
Dem. Rep. Congo
122 B2 **Upington** S. Africa
134 B2 **Upper Alkali Lake** U.S.A.
128 C2 **Upper Arrow Lake** Can.
134 B2 **Upper Klamath Lake**
U.S.A.
128 B1 **Upper Liard** Can.
97 C1 **Upper Lough Erne** *l.* U.K.
93 G4 **Uppsala** Sweden
78 B2 **'Uqlat as Suqūr**
Saudi Arabia
Urad Qianqi China *see*
Xishanzui
76 B2 **Ural** *r.* Kazakh./Rus. Fed.
53 D2 **Uralla** Austr.
87 E3 **Ural Mountains** Rus. Fed.
76 B1 **Ural'sk** Kazakh.
Ural'skiy Khrebet *mts* Rus.
Fed. *see* Ural Mountains
119 D3 **Urambo** Tanz.
53 C3 **Urana** Austr.
129 D2 **Uranium City** Can.
86 F2 **Uray** Rus. Fed.
98 C1 **Ure** *r.* U.K.
86 D3 **Uren'** Rus. Fed.
144 A2 **Ures** Mex.
76 C2 **Urganch** Uzbek.
100 B1 **Urk** Neth.
111 C3 **Urla** Turkey
81 C2 **Urmia, Lake** *salt l.* Iran
109 D2 **Uroševac** Serb. and Mont.
144 B2 **Uruáchic** Mex.
151 D3 **Uruaçu** Brazil
144 B3 **Uruapan** Mex.
150 A3 **Urubamba** *r.* Peru
151 C2 **Urucara** Brazil
151 D2 **Uruçuí** Brazil
151 C2 **Urucurituba** Brazil
152 C3 **Uruguaiana** Brazil
153 C4 **Uruguay** *country* S. America
Urümchi China *see* Ürümqi
68 B2 **Ürümqi** China
53 D2 **Urunga** Austr.
59 D3 **Urville, Tanjung d'** *pt*
Indon.
110 C2 **Urziceni** Romania
67 B4 **Usa** Japan
82 E2 **Usa** *r.* Rus. Fed.

111 C3 **Uşak** Turkey
82 G1 **Ushakova, Ostrov** i.
　　Rus. Fed.
77 D2 **Ushtobe** Kazakh.
153 B6 **Ushuaia** Arg.
86 E2 **Usinsk** Rus. Fed.
88 C3 **Uskhodni** Belarus
89 E3 **Usman'** Rus. Fed.
86 D2 **Usogorsk** Rus. Fed.
104 C2 **Ussel** France
82 C2 **Ussuriysk** Rus. Fed.
108 B3 **Ustica, Isola di** i. *Sicily* Italy
83 H3 **Ust'-Ilimsk** Rus. Fed.
86 E2 **Ust'-Ilych** Rus. Fed.
103 D1 **Ustka** Pol.
83 L3 **Ust'-Kamchatsk** Rus. Fed.
77 E2 **Ust'-Kamenogorsk** Kazakh.
86 F2 **Ust'-Kara** Rus. Fed.
86 E2 **Ust'-Kulom** Rus. Fed.
83 I3 **Ust'-Kut** Rus. Fed.
91 D2 **Ust'-Labinsk** Rus. Fed.
88 C2 **Ust'-Luga** Rus. Fed.
86 E2 **Ust'-Nem** Rus. Fed.
83 K2 **Ust'-Nera** Rus. Fed.
83 K2 **Ust'-Omchug** Rus. Fed.
83 H3 **Ust'-Ordynskiy** Rus. Fed.
86 E2 **Ust'-Tsil'ma** Rus. Fed.
86 D2 **Ust'-Ura** Rus. Fed.
76 B2 **Ustyurt Plateau**
　　Kazakh./Uzbek.
89 E2 **Ustyuzhna** Rus. Fed.
86 D2 **Usvyaty** Rus. Fed.
135 D3 **Utah** *state* U.S.A.
135 D2 **Utah Lake** U.S.A.
93 I4 **Utena** Lith.
141 D2 **Utica** U.S.A.
107 C2 **Utiel** Spain
128 C2 **Utikuma Lake** Can.
100 B1 **Utrecht** Neth.
106 B2 **Utrera** Spain
92 I2 **Utsjoki** Fin.
67 C3 **Utsunomiya** Japan
87 D4 **Utta** Rus. Fed.
62 B2 **Uttaradit** Thai.
　　Uummannaq Greenland *see*
　　　Dundas
127 H2 **Uummannaq Fjord** *inlet*
　　　Greenland
93 H3 **Uusikaupunki** Fin.
119 D3 **Uvalde** U.S.A.
119 D3 **Uvinza** Tanz.
68 C1 **Uvs Nuur** *salt l.* Mongolia
84 B2 **Uwajima** Japan
78 A2 **'Uwayrid, Harrat al**
　　　lava field Saudi Arabia
116 A2 **Uweinat, Jebel** *mt.* Sudan
83 H3 **Uyar** Rus. Fed.
115 C4 **Uyo** Nigeria
152 B3 **Uyuni, Salar de** *salt flat*
　　　Bol.
76 C2 **Uzbekistan** *country* Asia
104 C2 **Uzerche** France
105 C3 **Uzès** France
90 C1 **Uzh** r. Ukr.
90 A2 **Uzhhorod** Ukr.
109 C2 **Užice** Serb. and Mont.
89 E3 **Uzlovaya** Rus. Fed.
111 C3 **Üzümlü** Turkey
111 C2 **Uzunköprü** Turkey

V

123 B2 **Vaal** r. S. Africa
123 C2 **Vaal Dam** S. Africa
123 C1 **Vaalwater** S. Africa
92 H3 **Vaasa** Fin.
103 D2 **Vác** Hungary

152 C3 **Vacaria** Brazil
154 B2 **Vacaria, Serra** *hills* Brazil
135 B3 **Vacaville** U.S.A.
74 B2 **Vadodara** India
92 I1 **Vadsø** Norway
105 D2 **Vaduz** Liechtenstein
94 B1 **Vágar** i. Faroe Is
94 B1 **Vágur** Faroe Is
103 D2 **Váh** r. Slovakia
49 F3 **Vaiaku** Tuvalu
88 B2 **Vaida** Estonia
136 B3 **Vail** U.S.A.
79 C2 **Vakīlābād** Iran
108 B1 **Valdagno** Italy
89 D2 **Valday** Rus. Fed.
89 D2 **Valdayskaya**
　　　Vozvyshennost' *hills*
　　　Rus. Fed.
106 B2 **Valdecañas, Embalse de**
　　　resr Spain
93 G4 **Valdemarsvik** Sweden
106 C2 **Valdepeñas** Spain
153 B5 **Valdés, Península** *pen.*
　　　Arg.
153 A4 **Valdivia** Chile
130 C2 **Val-d'Or** Can.
143 D2 **Valdosta** U.S.A.
128 C2 **Valemount** Can.
105 C3 **Valence** France
107 C2 **Valencia** Spain
150 B1 **Valencia** Venez.
107 D2 **Valencia, Golfo de** g.
　　　Spain
100 A2 **Valenciennes** France
136 C2 **Valentine** U.S.A.
64 B1 **Valenzuela** Phil.
150 A1 **Valera** Venez.
109 C2 **Valjevo** Serb. and Mont.
88 C2 **Valka** Latvia
93 H3 **Valkeakoski** Fin.
100 B2 **Valkenswaard** Neth.
91 D2 **Valky** Ukr.
55 D2 **Valkyrie Dome** *ice feature*
　　　Antarctica
145 D2 **Valladolid** Mex.
106 C1 **Valladolid** Spain
93 E4 **Valle** Norway
145 C2 **Vallecillos** Mex.
150 B1 **Valle de la Pascua** Venez.
150 A1 **Valledupar** Col.
145 C2 **Valle Hermoso** Mex.
135 B3 **Vallejo** U.S.A.
152 A3 **Vallenar** Chile
85 H5 **Valletta** Malta
137 D1 **Valley City** U.S.A.
134 B1 **Valley Falls** U.S.A.
128 C2 **Valleyview** Can.
107 D1 **Valls** Spain
129 D3 **Val Marie** Can.
88 C2 **Valmiera** Latvia
88 C3 **Valozhyn** Belarus
154 B2 **Valparaíso** Brazil
153 A4 **Valparaíso** Chile
105 C3 **Valréas** France
59 D3 **Vals, Tanjung** c. Indon.
74 B2 **Valsad** India
122 B2 **Valspan** S. Africa
91 D1 **Valuyki** Rus. Fed.
106 B2 **Valverde del Camino** Spain
81 C2 **Van** Turkey
81 C2 **Van, Lake** *salt l.* Turkey
141 F1 **Van Buren** U.S.A.
128 B3 **Vancouver** Can.
134 B1 **Vancouver** U.S.A.
128 B3 **Vancouver Island** Can.
140 B3 **Vandalia** U.S.A.
123 C2 **Vanderbijlpark** S. Africa
128 B2 **Vanderhoof** Can.
88 C2 **Vändra** Estonia
93 F4 **Vänern** l. Sweden

93 F4 **Vänersborg** Sweden
121 □D3 **Vangaindrano** Madag.
　　　Van Gölü *salt l.* Turkey *see*
　　　Van, Lake
138 C2 **Van Horn** U.S.A.
59 D3 **Vanimo** P.N.G.
83 K3 **Vanino** Rus. Fed.
81 C2 **Van, Lake** *salt l.* Turkey
104 B2 **Vannes** France
59 D3 **Van Rees, Pegunungan**
　　　mts Indon.
122 A3 **Vanrhynsdorp** S. Africa
93 H3 **Vantaa** Fin.
49 F4 **Vanua Levu** i. Fiji
48 E3 **Vanuatu** *country*
　　　S. Pacific Ocean
140 C2 **Van Wert** U.S.A.
122 B3 **Vanwyksvlei** S. Africa
122 B2 **Van Zylsrus** S. Africa
75 C2 **Varanasi** India
92 I1 **Varangerfjorden** *sea chan.*
　　　Norway
92 I1 **Varangerhalvøya** *pen.*
　　　Norway
109 C1 **Varaždin** Croatia
93 F4 **Varberg** Sweden
109 D2 **Vardar** r. Macedonia
93 E4 **Varde** Denmark
92 J1 **Vardø** Norway
100 C1 **Varel** Ger.
88 B3 **Varėna** Lith.
108 A1 **Varese** Italy
155 C2 **Varginha** Brazil
93 I3 **Varkaus** Fin.
110 C2 **Varna** Bulg.
93 F4 **Värnamo** Sweden
155 D1 **Várzea da Palma** Brazil
86 C2 **Varzino** Rus. Fed.
　　　Vasa Fin. *see* Vaasa
88 C2 **Vasknarva** Estonia
110 C1 **Vaslui** Romania
93 G4 **Västerås** Sweden
93 G3 **Västerdalälven** r. Sweden
88 A2 **Västerhaninge** Sweden
93 G4 **Västervik** Sweden
108 B2 **Vasto** Italy
90 C1 **Vasyl'kiv** Ukr.
104 C2 **Vatan** France
108 B2 **Vatican City** Europe
92 □B3 **Vatnajökull** *ice cap* Iceland
110 C1 **Vatra Dornei** Romania
93 F4 **Vättern** l. Sweden
138 B2 **Vaughn** U.S.A.
105 C3 **Vauvert** France
49 G4 **Vava'u Group** is Tonga
88 B3 **Vawkavysk** Belarus
93 F4 **Växjö** Sweden
86 E1 **Vaygach, Ostrov** i.
　　　Rus. Fed.
101 D1 **Vechta** Ger.
110 C1 **Vedea** r. Romania
100 C1 **Veendam** Neth.
100 B1 **Veenendaal** Neth.
129 C2 **Vegreville** Can.
106 B2 **Vejer de la Frontera** Spain
93 E4 **Vejle** Denmark
109 D2 **Velbŭzhdki Prokhod** *pass*
　　　Macedonia
100 B1 **Veldhoven** Neth.
109 B2 **Velebit** *mts* Croatia
100 C2 **Velen** Ger.
109 C1 **Velenje** Slovenia
109 D2 **Veles** Macedonia
106 C2 **Vélez-Málaga** Spain
155 D1 **Velhas** r. Brazil
109 D2 **Velika Plana** Serb. and Mont.
88 C2 **Velikaya** r. Rus. Fed.
89 D2 **Velikiye Luki** Rus. Fed.
89 D2 **Velikiy Novgorod** Rus. Fed.
86 D2 **Velikiy Ustyug** Rus. Fed.

Veliko Tŭrnovo

110 C2 Veliko Tŭrnovo Bulg.
108 B2 Veli Lošinj Croatia
89 D2 Velizh Rus. Fed.
101 F1 Vel'sk Rus. Fed.
91 D1 Velykyy Burluk Ukr.
108 B2 Venafro Italy
154 C2 Venceslau Bráz Brazil
104 C2 Vendôme France
89 E3 Venev Rus. Fed.
Venezia Italy see Venice
150 B1 Venezuela country S. America
150 A1 Venezuela, Golfo de g. Venez.
108 B1 Venice Italy
143 D3 Venice U.S.A.
108 B1 Venice, Gulf of Europe
100 B2 Venlo Neth.
100 B2 Venray Neth.
88 B2 Venta r. Latvia/Lith.
88 B2 Venta Lith.
123 C3 Venterstad S. Africa
99 C3 Ventnor U.K.
88 B2 Ventspils Latvia
135 C4 Ventura U.S.A.
139 C3 Venustiano Carranza, Presa resr Mex.
107 C2 Vera Spain
145 C3 Veracruz Mex.
74 B2 Veraval India
108 A1 Verbania Italy
108 A1 Vercelli Italy
105 D3 Vercors reg. France
92 F3 Verdalsøra Norway
154 B1 Verde r. Goiás Brazil
154 B2 Verde r. Mato Grosso do Sul Brazil
144 B2 Verde r. Mex.
138 A2 Verde r. U.S.A.
155 D2 Verde Grande r. Brazil
101 D1 Verden (Aller) Ger.
154 B1 Verdinho, Serra do mts Brazil
108 A2 Verdon r. France
105 D2 Verdun France
123 C2 Vereeniging S. Africa
106 B1 Verín Spain
91 D3 Verkhnebakanskiy Rus. Fed.
92 J2 Verkhnetulomskiy Rus. Fed.
91 E1 Verkhniy Mamon Rus. Fed.
89 E3 Verkhov'ye Rus. Fed.
90 A2 Verkhovyna Ukr.
83 J2 Verkhoyanskiy Khrebet mts Rus. Fed.
129 C2 Vermilion Can.
137 D2 Vermilion U.S.A.
130 A2 Vermilion Bay Can.
141 E2 Vermont state U.S.A.
135 E2 Vernal U.S.A.
128 C2 Vernon Can.
139 D2 Vernon U.S.A.
143 D3 Vero Beach U.S.A.
111 B2 Veroia Greece
108 B1 Verona Italy
104 C2 Versailles France
104 B2 Vertou France
123 D2 Verulam S. Africa
100 B2 Verviers Belgium
105 C2 Vervins France
105 D3 Vescovato Corsica France
87 E3 Veselaya, Gora mt. Rus. Fed.
91 C2 Vesele Ukr.
105 D2 Vesoul France
92 F2 Vesterålen is Norway
92 F2 Vestfjorden sea chan. Norway

94 B1 Vestmanna Faroe Is
93 E3 Vestnes Norway
108 B2 Vesuvius vol. Italy
89 E2 Ves'yegonsk Rus. Fed.
93 G4 Vetlanda Sweden
86 D3 Vetluga Rus. Fed.
100 A2 Veurne Belgium
105 D2 Vevey Switz.
91 D1 Veydelevka Rus. Fed.
80 B1 Vezirköprü Turkey
151 D2 Viana Brazil
106 B1 Viana do Castelo Port.
Viangchan Laos see Vientiane
62 B1 Viangphoukha Laos
154 C1 Viangópolis Brazil
108 B2 Viareggio Italy
93 E4 Viborg Denmark
109 C3 Vibo Valentia Italy
107 D1 Vic Spain
144 A1 Vicente Guerrero Mex.
108 B1 Vicenza Italy
105 C2 Vichy France
142 B2 Vicksburg U.S.A.
155 D2 Viçosa Brazil
52 A3 Victor Harbor Austr.
50 C1 Victoria r. Austr.
52 B3 Victoria state Austr.
128 B3 Victoria Can.
153 A4 Victoria Chile
113 K7 Victoria Seychelles
139 D3 Victoria U.S.A.
119 D3 Victoria, Lake Africa
52 B2 Victoria, Lake Austr.
62 A1 Victoria, Mount Myanmar
59 D3 Victoria, Mount P.N.G.
120 B2 Victoria Falls Zambia/Zimbabwe
126 D2 Victoria Island Can.
50 C1 Victoria River Downs Austr.
122 B3 Victoria West S. Africa
135 C4 Victorville U.S.A.
110 C2 Videle Romania
92 □A2 Víðidalsá Iceland
153 B5 Viedma Arg.
153 A5 Viedma, Lago l. Arg.
100 B2 Vielsalm Belgium
101 E2 Vienenburg Ger.
103 D2 Vienna Austria
104 C2 Vienne France
104 C2 Vienne r. France
62 B2 Vientiane Laos
100 C2 Viersen Ger.
104 C2 Vierzon France
62 B2 Viesca Mex.
109 C2 Vieste Italy
62 B2 Vietnam country Asia
62 B1 Viêt Tri Vietnam
64 B1 Vigan Phil.
108 A1 Vigevano Italy
106 B1 Vigo Spain
73 C3 Vijayawada India
92 □B3 Vík Iceland
129 C2 Viking Can.
106 B2 Vila Franca de Xira Port.
106 B1 Vilagarcía de Arousa Spain
106 B1 Vilalba Spain
106 B1 Vila Nova de Gaia Port.
107 D1 Vilanova i la Geltrú Spain
106 B1 Vila Real Port.
106 B1 Vilar Formoso Port.
155 D2 Vila Velha Brazil
150 A3 Vilcabamba, Cordillera mts Peru
92 G3 Vilhelmina Sweden
150 B3 Vilhena Brazil
88 C2 Viljandi Estonia
88 B3 Vilkaviškis Lith.

83 H1 Vil'kitskogo, Proliv str. Rus. Fed.
144 B1 Villa Ahumada Mex.
106 B1 Villablino Spain
102 C2 Villach Austria
144 B2 Villa de Cos Mex.
152 B4 Villa Dolores Arg.
145 C3 Villa Flores Mex.
145 C2 Villagrán Mex.
145 C3 Villahermosa Mex.
144 A2 Villa Insurgentes Mex.
152 B4 Villa María Arg.
152 B3 Villa Montes Bol.
144 B2 Villanueva Mex.
106 B2 Villanueva de la Serena Spain
106 C2 Villanueva de los Infantes Spain
152 C3 Villa Ocampo Arg.
108 A3 Villaputzu Sardinia Italy
152 C3 Villarrica Para.
106 C2 Villarrobledo Spain
152 B3 Villa Unión Arg.
144 B2 Villa Unión Durango Mex.
144 B2 Villa Unión Sinaloa Mex.
150 A1 Villavicencio Col.
152 B3 Villazon Bol.
107 C2 Villena Spain
104 C3 Villeneuve-sur-Lot France
142 B2 Ville Platte U.S.A.
105 C2 Villeurbanne France
102 B2 Villingen Ger.
88 C3 Vilnius Lith.
91 C2 Vil'nohirs'k Ukr.
91 D2 Vil'nyans'k Ukr.
100 B2 Vilvoorde Belgium
88 C3 Vilyeyka Belarus
83 J2 Vilyuy r. Rus. Fed.
93 G4 Vimmerby Sweden
153 A4 Viña del Mar Chile
107 D1 Vinaròs Spain
140 B3 Vincennes U.S.A.
55 G3 Vincennes Bay Antarctica
141 D3 Vineland U.S.A.
62 B2 Vinh Vietnam
63 B2 Vinh Long Vietnam
139 D1 Vinita U.S.A.
90 B2 Vinnytsya Ukr.
55 O2 Vinson Massif mt. Antarctica
93 E3 Vinstra Norway
108 B1 Vipiteno Italy
64 B1 Virac Phil.
129 D3 Virden Can.
104 B2 Vire France
120 A2 Virei Angola
155 D1 Virgem da Lapa Brazil
138 A1 Virgin r. U.S.A.
123 C2 Virginia S. Africa
137 E1 Virginia U.S.A.
141 D3 Virginia state U.S.A.
141 D3 Virginia Beach U.S.A.
135 C3 Virginia City U.S.A.
147 D3 Virgin Islands (U.K.) terr. West Indies
147 D3 Virgin Islands (U.S.A.) terr. West Indies
63 B2 Viróchey Cambodia
109 C1 Virovitica Croatia
100 B3 Virton Belgium
88 B2 Virtsu Estonia
109 C2 Vis i. Croatia
88 C2 Visaginas Lith.
135 C3 Visalia U.S.A.
74 B2 Visavadar India
64 B1 Visayan Sea Phil.
93 G4 Visby Sweden
126 D2 Viscount Melville Sound sea chan. Can.
151 D2 Viseu Brazil

106 B1 Viseu Port.
73 C3 Vishakhapatnam India
88 C2 Viški Latvia
109 C2 Visoko Bos.-Herz.
103 D1 Vistula r. Pol.
108 B2 Viterbo Italy
49 F4 Viti Levu i. Fiji
83 I3 Vitim r. Rus. Fed.
155 D2 Vitória Brazil
151 D3 Vitória da Conquista
   Brazil
106 C1 Vitoria-Gasteiz Spain
104 B2 Vitré France
105 C2 Vitry-le-François France
89 D2 Vitsyebsk Belarus
105 D2 Vittel France
108 B3 Vittoria Sicily Italy
108 B1 Vittorio Veneto Italy
91 B1 Viveiro Spain
144 A2 Vizcaíno, Sierra mts Mex.
110 C2 Vize Turkey
73 C3 Vizianagaram India
100 B2 Vlaardingen Neth.
87 D4 Vladikavkaz Rus. Fed.
89 F2 Vladimir Rus. Fed.
66 B2 Vladivostok Rus. Fed.
109 D2 Vlasotince Serb. and Mont.
100 B1 Vlieland i. Neth.
100 A2 Vlissingen Neth.
109 C2 Vlorë Albania
102 C2 Vöcklabruck Austria
101 D2 Vogelsberg hills Ger.
119 D3 Voi Kenya
105 D2 Voiron France
131 D1 Voisey Bay Can.
109 C1 Vojvodina prov.
   Serb. and Mont.
92 J3 Voknavolok Rus. Fed.
   Volcano Bay Japan see
   Uchiura-wan
89 E1 Volga Rus. Fed.
89 F2 Volga r. Rus. Fed.
87 D4 Volgodonsk Rus. Fed.
87 D4 Volgograd Rus. Fed.
89 D2 Volkhov Rus. Fed.
89 D1 Volkhov r. Rus. Fed.
101 E2 Volkstedt Ger.
91 D2 Volnovakha Ukr.
90 B2 Volochys'k Ukr.
91 D2 Volodars'ke Ukr.
90 B1 Volodars'ka-Volyns'kyy Ukr.
90 B1 Volodymyrets' Ukr.
90 A1 Volodymyr-Volyns'kyy Ukr.
89 E2 Vologda Rus. Fed.
89 E2 Volokolamsk Rus. Fed.
91 D1 Volokonovka Rus. Fed.
111 B3 Volos Greece
88 C2 Volosovo Rus. Fed.
89 D2 Volot Rus. Fed.
89 E3 Volovo Rus. Fed.
87 D3 Vol'sk Rus. Fed.
114 C4 Volta, Lake resr Ghana
155 D2 Volta Redonda Brazil
87 D4 Volzhskiy Rus. Fed.
92 □C2 Vopnafjörður Iceland
89 E2 Voranava Belarus
86 F2 Vorkuta Rus. Fed.
88 D1 Vormsi i. Estonia
89 E3 Voronezh Rus. Fed.
91 E1 Voronezh r. Rus. Fed.
91 C2 Vorontsovka Rus. Fed.
91 C2 Vorskla r. Ukr.
88 C2 Võrtsjärv l. Estonia
88 D2 Võru Estonia
122 B3 Vosburg S. Africa
105 D2 Vosges mts France
89 E2 Voskresensk Rus. Fed.
93 E3 Voss Norway
83 H3 Vostochnyy Sayan mts
   Rus. Fed.

86 E3 Votkinsk Rus. Fed.
154 C2 Votuporanga Brazil
100 B3 Vouziers France
92 J2 Voynitsa Rus. Fed.
91 C2 Voznesens'k Ukr.
93 E4 Vrådal Norway
66 B2 Vrangel' Rus. Fed.
   Vrangelya, Ostrov i.
   Rus. Fed. see Wrangel Island
109 D2 Vranje Serb. and Mont.
110 C2 Vratnik pass Bulg.
110 B2 Vratsa Bulg.
109 C1 Vrbas r. Bos.-Herz.
109 C1 Vrbas Serb. and Mont.
122 A3 Vredenburg S. Africa
122 A3 Vredendal S. Africa
100 B3 Vresse Belgium
109 D1 Vršac Serb. and Mont.
122 B2 Vryburg S. Africa
123 D2 Vryheid S. Africa
89 D1 Vsevolozhsk Rus. Fed.
109 D2 Vučitrn Serb. and Mont.
109 C1 Vukovar Croatia
86 E2 Vuktyl' Rus. Fed.
123 C2 Vukuzakhe S. Africa
109 B3 Vulcano, Isola i. Italy
74 B2 Vung Tau Vietnam
74 B2 Vyara India
89 D2 Vyatka r. Rus. Fed. see Kirov
93 I3 Vyaz'ma Rus. Fed.
88 C2 Vyborg Rus. Fed.
88 C2 Vyerkhnyadzvinsk Belarus
87 D3 Vyksa Rus. Fed.
90 B2 Vylkove Ukr.
90 A2 Vynohradiv Ukr.
89 D2 Vypolzovo Rus. Fed.
89 D2 Vyritsa Rus. Fed.
91 D2 Vyselki Rus. Fed.
90 C1 Vyshhorod Ukr.
89 D2 Vyshniy-Volochek
   Rus. Fed.
103 D2 Vyškov Czech Rep.
86 C2 Vytegra Rus. Fed.

W

114 B3 Wa Ghana
100 B2 Waal r. Neth.
100 B2 Waalwijk Neth.
128 C2 Wabasca r. Can.
128 C2 Wabasca-Desmarais Can.
140 B3 Wabash r. U.S.A.
117 C4 Wabē Gestro r. Eth.
117 C4 Wabē Shebelē Wenz r. Eth.
129 E2 Wabowden Can.
143 D3 Waccasassa Bay U.S.A.
101 D2 Wächtersbach Ger.
139 D2 Waco U.S.A.
74 A2 Wad Pak.
115 D2 Waddān Libya
100 B1 Waddeneilanden is Neth.
100 B1 Waddenzee sea chan. Neth.
128 C2 Waddington, Mount Can.
100 B1 Waddinxveen Neth.
129 D2 Wadena Can.
137 D1 Wadena U.S.A.
116 B2 Wadi Halfa Sudan
116 B3 Wad Medani Sudan
70 C2 Wafangdian China
100 B2 Wageningen Neth.
127 F2 Wager Bay Can.
53 C2 Wagga Wagga Austr.
137 D2 Wahoo U.S.A.
137 D1 Wahpeton U.S.A.
54 B2 Waiau r. N.Z.
59 C3 Waigeo i. Indon.
58 B3 Waikabubak Indon.

52 A2 Waikerie Austr.
54 B2 Waimate N.Z.
75 B3 Wainganga r. India
58 C3 Waingapu Indon.
129 C2 Wainwright Can.
54 C1 Waiouru N.Z.
54 B2 Waipara N.Z.
54 C1 Waipawa N.Z.
54 B2 Wairau r. N.Z.
54 C1 Wairoa N.Z.
54 B2 Waitaki r. N.Z.
54 B1 Waitara N.Z.
54 B1 Waiuku N.Z.
119 E2 Wajir Kenya
67 C3 Wakasa-wan b. Japan
54 A3 Wakatipu, Lake N.Z.
129 D2 Wakaw Can.
67 C4 Wakayama Japan
136 D3 WaKeeney U.S.A.
54 B2 Wakefield N.Z.
98 C2 Wakefield U.K.
48 F1 Wake Island
   N. Pacific Ocean
66 D1 Wakkanai Japan
123 D2 Wakkerstroom S. Africa
103 D1 Wałbrzych Pol.
53 D2 Walcha Austr.
100 C1 Walchum Ger.
103 D1 Wałcz Pol.
99 B2 Wales admin. div. U.K.
53 C2 Walgett Austr.
119 C3 Walikale Dem. Rep. Congo
135 C3 Walker Lake U.S.A.
52 A2 Wallaroo Austr.
98 B2 Wallasey U.K.
134 C1 Walla Walla U.S.A.
101 D3 Walldürn Ger.
53 C2 Wallendbeen Austr.
49 G3 Wallis and Futuna Islands
   terr. S. Pacific Ocean
96 □ Walls U.K.
98 B1 Walney, Isle of i. U.K.
99 C2 Walsall U.K.
136 C3 Walsenburg U.S.A.
101 D1 Walsrode Ger.
143 D2 Walterboro U.S.A.
120 A3 Walvis Bay Namibia
119 C3 Wamba Dem. Rep. Congo
52 B1 Wanaaring Austr.
54 A2 Wanaka N.Z.
54 A2 Wanaka, Lake N.Z.
130 B2 Wanapitei Lake Can.
154 B3 Wanda Arg.
66 B1 Wanda Shan mts China
62 A1 Wanding China
54 C1 Wanganui N.Z.
53 C3 Wangaratta Austr.
65 B1 Wangqing China
62 A1 Wan Hsa-la Myanmar
71 B4 Wanning China
100 B2 Wanroij Neth.
99 C3 Wantage U.K.
70 A2 Wanxian China
70 A2 Wanyuan China
73 B3 Warangal India
101 D2 Warburg Ger.
50 B2 Warburton Austr.
52 A1 Warburton watercourse
   Austr.
75 B2 Wardha India
96 C1 Ward Hill U.K.
128 B2 Ware Can.
101 F1 Waren Ger.
100 C2 Warendorf Ger.
53 D1 Warialda Austr.
122 A2 Warmbad Namibia
135 C3 Warm Springs U.S.A.
134 C2 Warner Lakes U.S.A.
143 D2 Warner Robins U.S.A.
152 B2 Warnes Bol.

Warracknabeal Austr. 52 B3
Warrego r. Austr. 53 C2
Warren Austr. 53 C2
Warren AR U.S.A. 142 B2
Warren OH U.S.A. 140 C2
Warren PA U.S.A. 141 D2
Warrenpoint U.K. 97 C1
Warrensburg U.S.A. 137 E3
Warrenton S. Africa 122 B2
Warri Nigeria 115 C4
Warrington U.K. 98 B2
Warrnambool Austr. 52 B3
Warsaw Pol. 103 E1
Warszawa Pol. see Warsaw
Warta r. Pol. 103 C1
Warwick Austr. 53 D1
Warwick U.K. 99 C2
Wasco U.S.A. 135 C3
Washburn U.S.A. 136 C1
Washington DC U.S.A. 141 D3
Washington IA U.S.A. 137 E2
Washington IN U.S.A. 140 B3
Washington MO U.S.A. 137 E3
Washington NC U.S.A. 143 E1
Washington PA U.S.A. 140 C2
Washington state U.S.A. 134 B1
Washington, Mount U.S.A. 141 E2
Washington Court House U.S.A. 140 C3
Washuk Pak. 74 A2
Waskaganish Can. 130 C1
Waskaiowaka Lake Can. 129 E2
Wasser Namibia 122 A2
Waswanipi, Lac l. Can. 130 C2
Watampone Indon. 58 C3
Waterbury U.S.A. 141 E2
Waterbury Lake Can. 129 D2
Waterford Ireland 97 C2
Waterford Harbour Ireland 97 C2
Waterloo U.S.A. 137 E2
Waterpoort S. Africa 123 C1
Watertown NY U.S.A. 141 D2
Watertown SD U.S.A. 137 D2
Watertown WI U.S.A. 140 B2
Waterville U.S.A. 141 F2
Watford U.K. 99 C3
Watford City U.S.A. 136 C1
Wathaman r. Can. 129 D2
Watonga U.S.A. 139 D1
Watrous Can. 129 D2
Watsa Dem. Rep. Congo 119 C2
Watseka U.S.A. 140 B2
Watsi Kengo Dem. Rep. Congo 118 C3
Watson Lake Can. 128 B1
Watsonville U.S.A. 135 B3
Watubela, Kepulauan is Indon. 59 C3
Wau P.N.G. 59 D3
Wau Sudan 117 A4
Wauchope Austr. 53 D2
Waukegan U.S.A. 140 B2
Waurika U.S.A. 139 D2
Wausau U.S.A. 140 B2
Waveney r. U.K. 99 D2
Waverly U.S.A. 137 E2
Waycross U.S.A. 143 D2
Wayne U.S.A. 137 D2
Waynesboro GA U.S.A. 143 D2
Waynesboro VA U.S.A. 141 D3
Waynesville U.S.A. 143 D1
Wazirabad Pak. 74 B1
Wear r. U.K. 98 C1
Weatherford U.S.A. 139 D2
Weaverville U.S.A. 134 B2
Webequie Can. 130 B1
Webi Shabeelle r. Somalia 117 C4
Webster U.S.A. 137 D1
Webster City U.S.A. 137 E2
Weddell Sea Antarctica 55 Q2

Weert Neth. 100 B2
Wee Waa Austr. 53 C2
Wegberg Ger. 100 C2
Węgorzewo Pol. 103 E1
Weiden in der Oberpfalz Ger. 101 F3
Weifang China 70 B2
Weihai China 70 C2
Weilmoringle Austr. 53 C1
Weimar Ger. 101 E2
Weinan China 70 A2
Weipa Austr. 51 D1
Weir r. Austr. 53 C1
Weirton U.S.A. 140 C2
Weishan China 62 B1
Weißenfels Ger. 101 E2
Weißkugel mt. Austria/Italy 102 C2
Wejherowo Pol. 103 D1
Wekweetì Can. 128 C1
Welch U.S.A. 140 C3
Weldiya Eth. 117 B3
Welkom S. Africa 123 C2
Welland r. U.K. 99 C2
Wellesley Islands Austr. 51 C1
Wellington Austr. 53 C2
Wellington N.Z. 54 B2
Wellington S. Africa 122 A3
Wellington U.K. 99 B3
Wellington, Isla i. Chile 153 A5
Wellington, Lake Austr. 53 C3
Wells U.K. 128 B2
Wells, Lake salt flat Austr. 50 B2
Wells U.S.A. 134 D2
Wellsford N.Z. 54 B1
Wells-next-the-Sea U.K. 98 D2
Wels Austria 102 C2
Welshpool U.K. 99 B2
Wembesi S. Africa 123 C2
Wemindji Can. 130 C1
Wenatchee U.S.A. 134 B1
Wenchang China 71 B4
Wenchi Ghana 114 B4
Wendeng China 70 C2
Wendisch Evern Ger. 101 E1
Wendo Eth. 117 B4
Wendover U.S.A. 134 D2
Wengyuan China 71 B3
Wenling China 71 C3
Wenshan China 71 A3
Wentworth Austr. 52 B2
Wenzhou China 71 C3
Wepener S. Africa 123 C2
Werda Botswana 122 B2
Werdau Ger. 101 F2
Werder Ger. 101 F1
Wernberg-Köblitz Ger. 101 F3
Wernigerode Ger. 101 E2
Werra r. Ger. 101 D2
Werris Creek Austr. 53 D2
Wertheim Ger. 101 D3
Wesel Ger. 100 C2
Wesendorf Ger. 101 E1
Weser r. Ger. 101 D1
Weser sea chan. Ger. 101 D1
Wessel, Cape Austr. 51 C1
Wessel Islands Austr. 51 C1
Wesselton S. Africa 123 C2
West Bank terr. Asia 80 B2
West Bend U.S.A. 140 B2
West Bromwich U.K. 99 C2
Westburg Ger. 100 C2
Westburg Ger. 100 C1
Westerholt Ger. 100 C1
Western Australia state Austr. 50 B2
Western Cape prov. S. Africa 122 B3
Western Desert Egypt see Aş Şaḩrā' al Gharbīyah
Western Ghats mts India 73 B3

Western Sahara terr. Africa 114 A2
Westerschelde est. Neth. 100 A2
Westerstede Ger. 100 C1
Westerwald hills Ger. 100 C2
West Falkland i. Falkland Is 153 B6
West Frankfort U.S.A. 140 B3
West Indies N. America 147 D2
West Loch Roag b. U.K. 96 A1
Westlock Can. 128 C2
Westmalle Belgium 100 B2
West Memphis U.S.A. 142 B1
Weston U.S.A. 140 C3
Weston-super-Mare U.K. 99 B3
West Palm Beach U.S.A. 143 D3
West Plains U.S.A. 137 E3
West Point U.S.A. 137 E3
Westport N.Z. 54 B2
Westport Ireland 97 B2
Westray Can. 129 D2
Westray i. U.K. 96 C1
West-Terschelling Neth. 100 B1
West Town Ireland 97 B1
West Virginia state U.S.A. 140 C3
West Wyalong Austr. 53 C2
West Yellowstone U.S.A. 134 D2
Wetar i. Indon. 59 C3
Wetaskiwin Can. 128 C2
Wetzlar Ger. 101 D2
Wewak P.N.G. 59 D3
Wexford Ireland 97 C2
Weyakwin Can. 129 D2
Weyburn Can. 129 D3
Weyhe Ger. 101 D1
Weymouth U.K. 99 B3
Whakatane N.Z. 54 C1
Whale Cove Can. 129 E1
Whalsay i. U.K. 96 □
Whangarei N.Z. 54 B1
Wharfe r. U.K. 98 C2
Wharton U.S.A. 139 D3
Wha Ti Can. 128 C1
Wheatland U.S.A. 136 B2
Wheeler Peak NM U.S.A. 138 B1
Wheeler Peak NV U.S.A. 135 D3
Wheeling U.S.A. 140 C2
Whernside hill U.K. 98 B1
Whistler Can. 128 B2
Whitby U.K. 98 C1
White r. U.S.A. 142 B2
White, Lake salt flat Austr. 50 B2
White Bay Can. 131 E2
White Butte mt. U.S.A. 136 C1
White Cliffs Austr. 52 B2
Whitecourt Can. 128 C2
Whitefish U.S.A. 134 D1
Whitehaven U.K. 98 B1
Whitehead U.K. 97 D1
Whitehorse Can. 128 A1
White Lake U.S.A. 142 B3
White Mountain Peak U.S.A. 135 C3
White Nile r. Sudan/Uganda 116 B3
White Sea Rus. Fed. 86 C2
White Sulphur Springs U.S.A. 134 D1
Whiteville U.S.A. 143 E2
White Volta watercourse Burkina/Ghana 114 B3
Whitewater Baldy mt. U.S.A. 138 B2
Whitewater Lake Can. 130 B1
Whitewood Can. 129 D2
Whithorn U.K. 96 B3
Whitianga N.Z. 54 C1
Whitney, Mount U.S.A. 135 C3
Whitsunday Island Austr. 51 D2
Whyalla Austr. 52 A2
Wichelen Belgium 100 A2
Wichita U.S.A. 137 D3
Wichita Falls U.S.A. 139 D2

96 C1 **Wick** U.K.
138 A2 **Wickenburg** U.S.A.
97 C2 **Wicklow** Ireland
97 C2 **Wicklow Head** Ireland
97 C2 **Wicklow Mountains** Ireland
98 B2 **Widnes** U.K.
101 D1 **Wiehengebirge** *hills* Ger.
100 C2 **Wiehl** Ger.
103 D1 **Wieluń** Pol.
Wien Austria *see* Vienna
103 D2 **Wiener Neustadt** Austria
100 B1 **Wieringerwerf** Neth.
100 D2 **Wiesbaden** Ger.
100 C1 **Wiesmoor** Ger.
103 D1 **Wieżyca** *hill* Pol.
99 C3 **Wight, Isle of** *i.* U.K.
96 B3 **Wigtown** U.K.
100 B2 **Wijchen** Neth.
52 B2 **Wilcannia** Austr.
123 C3 **Wild Coast** S. Africa
123 C2 **Wilge** *r.* S. Africa
100 D1 **Wilhelmshaven** Ger.
141 D2 **Wilkes-Barre** U.S.A.
55 H3 **Wilkes Land** *reg.* Antarctica
129 D2 **Wilkie** Can.
138 B2 **Willcox** U.S.A.
100 B2 **Willebroek** Belgium
147 D3 **Willemstad** Neth. Antilles
52 B3 **William, Mount** Austr.
52 A1 **William Creek** Austr.
138 A1 **Williams** U.S.A.
141 D3 **Williamsburg** U.S.A.
128 B2 **Williams Lake** Can.
140 C3 **Williamson** U.S.A.
141 D2 **Williamsport** U.S.A.
143 E1 **Williamston** U.S.A.
136 C1 **Williston** S. Africa
136 C1 **Williston** U.S.A.
128 B2 **Williston Lake** Can.
135 B3 **Willits** U.S.A.
137 D1 **Willmar** U.S.A.
122 B3 **Willowmore** S. Africa
123 C3 **Willowvale** S. Africa
50 B2 **Wills, Lake** *salt flat* Austr.
52 A3 **Willunga** Austr.
52 A2 **Wilmington** Austr.
141 D3 **Wilmington** *DE* U.S.A.
143 E2 **Wilmington** *NC* U.S.A.
100 D2 **Wilnsdorf** Ger.
143 E1 **Wilson** U.S.A.
53 C3 **Wilson's Promontory** *pen.* Austr.
100 B3 **Wiltz** Lux.
50 B2 **Wiluna** Austr.
99 C3 **Winchester** U.K.
140 C3 **Winchester** *KY* U.S.A.
141 D3 **Winchester** *VA* U.S.A.
98 B1 **Windermere** *l.* U.K.
120 A3 **Windhoek** Namibia
137 D2 **Windom** U.S.A.
51 D2 **Windorah** Austr.
136 B2 **Wind River Range** *mts* U.S.A.
53 D2 **Windsor** Austr.
130 B2 **Windsor** Can.
147 D3 **Windward Islands** Caribbean Sea
147 C3 **Windward Passage** Cuba/Haiti
137 D3 **Winfield** U.S.A.
100 A2 **Wingene** Belgium
53 D2 **Wingham** Austr.
130 B1 **Winisk** Can.
130 B1 **Winisk** *r.* Can.
130 B1 **Winisk Lake** Can.
62 A2 **Winkana** Myanmar
129 E3 **Winkler** Can.
114 B4 **Winneba** Ghana
140 B2 **Winnebago, Lake** U.S.A.
134 C2 **Winnemucca** U.S.A.

136 C2 **Winner** U.S.A.
142 B2 **Winnfield** U.S.A.
137 E1 **Winnibigoshish, Lake** U.S.A.
129 E3 **Winnipeg** Can.
129 E2 **Winnipeg** *r.* Can.
129 E2 **Winnipeg, Lake** Can.
129 D2 **Winnipegosis, Lake** Can.
141 E2 **Winnipesaukee, Lake** U.S.A.
142 B2 **Winnsboro** U.S.A.
137 E2 **Winona** *MN* U.S.A.
142 C2 **Winona** *MS* U.S.A.
100 C1 **Winschoten** Neth.
101 D1 **Winsen (Aller)** Ger.
101 E1 **Winsen (Luhe)** Ger.
138 A1 **Winslow** U.S.A.
143 D1 **Winston-Salem** U.S.A.
101 D2 **Winterberg** Ger.
143 D3 **Winter Haven** U.S.A.
100 C2 **Winterswijk** Neth.
105 D2 **Winterthur** Switz.
51 D2 **Winton** Austr.
54 A3 **Winton** N.Z.
52 A2 **Wirrabara** Austr.
99 D2 **Wisbech** U.K.
140 A2 **Wisconsin** *r.* U.S.A.
140 B2 **Wisconsin** *state* U.S.A.
140 B2 **Wisconsin Rapids** U.S.A.
Wisła *r.* Pol. *see* Vistula
101 E1 **Wismar** Ger.
123 C2 **Witbank** S. Africa
98 D2 **Withernsea** U.K.
100 B1 **Witmarsum** Neth.
99 C3 **Witney** U.K.
123 D2 **Witrivier** S. Africa
101 E1 **Wittenberge** Ger.
101 E1 **Wittenburg** Ger.
101 E1 **Wittingen** Ger.
100 C3 **Wittlich** Ger.
100 C1 **Wittmund** Ger.
101 F1 **Wittstock** Ger.
120 A3 **Witvlei** Namibia
101 D2 **Witzenhausen** Ger.
103 D1 **Władysławowo** Pol.
103 D1 **Włocławek** Pol.
53 C3 **Wodonga** Austr.
59 C3 **Wokam** *i.* Indon.
99 C3 **Woking** U.K.
101 F2 **Wolfen** Ger.
101 E1 **Wolfenbüttel** Ger.
101 E1 **Wolfhagen** Ger.
136 B1 **Wolf Point** U.S.A.
101 E1 **Wolfsburg** Ger.
100 C1 **Wolfstein** Ger.
131 D2 **Wolfville** Can.
102 C1 **Wolgast** Ger.
102 C1 **Wolin** Pol.
129 D2 **Wollaston Lake** Can.
129 D2 **Wollaston Lake** Can.
126 D2 **Wollaston Peninsula** Can.
53 D2 **Wollongong** Austr.
101 E2 **Wolmirstedt** Ger.
101 E1 **Wolmirsleben** Ger.
100 C1 **Wolvega** Neth.
99 B3 **Wolverhampton** U.K.
65 B2 **Wŏnju** S. Korea
128 B2 **Wonowon** Can.
65 B2 **Wŏnsan** N. Korea
52 A3 **Wonthaggi** Austr.
52 A2 **Woocalla** Austr.
51 C1 **Woodah, Isle** *i.* Austr.
99 D2 **Woodbridge** U.K.
136 B3 **Woodland Park** U.S.A.
50 C2 **Woodroffe, Mount** Austr.
51 C1 **Woods, Lake** *salt flat* Austr.
129 E3 **Woods, Lake of the** Can./U.S.A.
53 C3 **Woods Point** Austr.
131 D2 **Woodstock** *N.B.* Can.

140 C2 **Woodstock** *Ont.* Can.
54 C2 **Woodville** N.Z.
139 D1 **Woodward** U.S.A.
53 D2 **Woolgoolga** Austr.
52 A2 **Woomera** Austr.
140 C2 **Wooster** U.S.A.
122 A3 **Worcester** S. Africa
99 B2 **Worcester** U.K.
141 E2 **Worcester** U.S.A.
102 C2 **Wörgl** Austria
98 B1 **Workington** U.K.
98 C2 **Worksop** U.K.
136 B2 **Worland** U.S.A.
101 D3 **Worms** Ger.
99 C3 **Worthing** U.K.
137 D2 **Worthington** U.S.A.
58 C3 **Wotu** Indon.
59 C3 **Wowoni** *i.* Indon.
83 N2 **Wrangel Island** Rus. Fed.
128 A2 **Wrangell** U.S.A.
96 B1 **Wrath, Cape** U.K.
136 C2 **Wray** U.S.A.
122 A2 **Wreck Point** S. Africa
98 B2 **Wrexham** U.K.
136 B2 **Wright** U.S.A.
63 A2 **Wrightmyo** India
128 B1 **Wrigley** Can.
103 D1 **Wrocław** Pol.
103 D1 **Wrzésnia** Pol.
70 B2 **Wu'an** China
70 A2 **Wudu** China
70 A2 **Wuhai** China
70 B2 **Wuhan** China
70 B2 **Wuhu** China
Wujin China *see* Changzhou
115 C4 **Wukari** Nigeria
62 B1 **Wuliang Shan** *mts* China
59 C3 **Wuliaru** *i.* Indon.
62 B1 **Wumeng Shan** *mts* China
130 B1 **Wunnummin Lake** Can.
101 F2 **Wunsiedel** Ger.
101 D1 **Wunstorf** Ger.
62 A1 **Wuntho** Myanmar
100 C2 **Wuppertal** Ger.
122 A3 **Wuppertal** S. Africa
101 E2 **Wurzbach** Ger.
101 D3 **Würzburg** Ger.
101 F2 **Wurzen** Ger.
68 C2 **Wuwei** China
70 A2 **Wuxi** *Chongqing* China
70 C2 **Wuxi** *Jiangsu* China
Wuxing China *see* Huzhou
71 A3 **Wuxuan** China
Wuyang China *see* Zhenyuan
69 E1 **Wuyiling** China
71 B3 **Wuyishan** China
71 B3 **Wuyi Shan** *mts* China
70 A1 **Wuyuan** China
71 A4 **Wuzhishan** China
70 A2 **Wuzhong** China
71 B3 **Wuzhou** China
53 C2 **Wyangala Reservoir** Austr.
52 B3 **Wycheproof** Austr.
99 B3 **Wye** *r.* U.K.
50 B1 **Wyndham** Austr.
142 B1 **Wynne** U.S.A.
129 D2 **Wynyard** Can.
136 B2 **Wyoming** *state* U.S.A.
103 E1 **Wyszków** Pol.
140 C3 **Wytheville** U.S.A.

X

117 D3 **Xaafuun** Somalia
62 B2 **Xaignabouli** Laos
121 C3 **Xai-Xai** Moz.
70 A1 **Xamba** China

Xam Nua

62 B1	**Xam Nua** Laos	
120 A2	**Xangongo** Angola	
81 C2	**Xankändi** Azer.	
111 B2	**Xanthi** Greece	
150 B3	**Xapuri** Brazil	
107 C2	**Xàtiva** Spain	
	Xiaguan China *see* **Dali**	
71 B3	**Xiamen** China	
70 A2	**Xi'an** China	
70 A3	**Xianfeng** China	
70 B2	**Xiangfan** China	
62 A1	**Xianggelila** China	
	Xiangjiang China *see*	
	Huichang	
62 B2	**Xiangkhoang** Laos	
71 B3	**Xiangtan** China	
	Xiangyang China *see*	
	Xiangfan	
70 B2	**Xiantao** China	
70 A2	**Xianyang** China	
70 B2	**Xiaogan** China	
69 E1	**Xiao Hinggan Ling** *mts* China	
70 C2	**Xiaoshan** China	
62 B1	**Xichang** China	
145 C2	**Xicohténcatl** Mex.	
70 A2	**Xifeng** *Gansu* China	
71 A3	**Xifeng** *Guizhou* China	
75 C2	**Xigazê** China	
83 I4	**Xilinhot** China	
70 B2	**Xincai** China	
68 C2	**Xinghai** China	
70 B2	**Xinghua** China	
71 B3	**Xingning** China	
70 A2	**Xingping** China	
70 B2	**Xingtai** China	
151 C2	**Xingu** *r.* Brazil	
71 A3	**Xingyi** China	
71 B3	**Xinhua** China	
68 C2	**Xining** China	
75 C1	**Xinjiang Uygur Zizhiqu**	
	aut. reg. China	
	Xinjing China *see* **Jingxi**	
65 A1	**Xinmin** China	
71 B3	**Xinning** China	
70 B2	**Xintai** China	
70 B2	**Xinxiang** China	
70 B2	**Xinyang** China	
71 B3	**Xinyu** China	
70 B2	**Xinzhou** *Shanxi* China	
106 B1	**Xinzo de Limia** Spain	
	Xiongshan China *see* **Zhenghe**	
68 C2	**Xiqing Shan** *mts* China	
151 D3	**Xique Xique** Brazil	
70 A1	**Xishanzui** China	
71 A3	**Xiushan** China	
71 B3	**Xiuying** China	
70 B2	**Xixia** China	
75 C1	**Xizang Zizhiqu** *aut. reg.* China	
76 B2	**Xo'jayli** Uzbek.	
70 B2	**Xuancheng** China	
71 A3	**Xuanwei** China	
70 B2	**Xuchang** China	
	Xucheng China *see* **Xuwen**	
117 C4	**Xuddur** Somalia	
	Xujiang China *see*	
	Guangchang	
71 B3	**Xun Jiang** *r.* China	
71 B3	**Xunwu** China	
71 B3	**Xuwen** China	
71 A3	**Xuyong** China	
	Xuzhou China *see* **Tongshan**	

Y

117 B4	**Yabëlo** Eth.	
69 D1	**Yablonovyy Khrebet** *mts*	
	Rus. Fed.	

143 D1	**Yadkin** *r.* U.S.A.	
75 C2	**Yadong** China	
89 E2	**Yagnitsa** Rus. Fed.	
118 B1	**Yagoua** Cameroon	
128 C3	**Yahk** Can.	
144 B2	**Yahualica** Mex.	
80 B2	**Yahyalı** Turkey	
67 C4	**Yaizu** Japan	
134 B1	**Yakima** U.S.A.	
114 B3	**Yako** Burkina	
66 D2	**Yakumo** Japan	
126 B3	**Yakutat** U.S.A.	
83 J2	**Yakutsk** Rus. Fed.	
91 D2	**Yakymivka** Ukr.	
63 B3	**Yala** Thai.	
53 C3	**Yallourn** Austr.	
111 C2	**Yalova** Turkey	
91 C3	**Yalta** Ukr.	
65 A1	**Yalu Jiang** *r.*	
	N. Korea	
67 D3	**Yamagata** Japan	
67 B4	**Yamaguchi** Japan	
	Yamal, Poluostrov *pen.*	
	Rus. Fed. *see*	
	Yamal Peninsula	
86 F1	**Yamal Peninsula** Rus. Fed.	
53 D1	**Yamba** Austr.	
117 A4	**Yambio** Sudan	
110 C2	**Yambol** Bulg.	
86 G2	**Yamburg** Rus. Fed.	
62 A1	**Yamethin** Myanmar	
114 B4	**Yamoussoukro**	
	Côte d'Ivoire	
90 B2	**Yampil'** Ukr.	
75 C2	**Yamuna** *r.* India	
75 D2	**Yamzho Yumco** *l.* China	
83 K2	**Yana** *r.* Rus. Fed.	
70 A2	**Yan'an** China	
150 A3	**Yanaoca** Peru	
78 A2	**Yanbu' al Baḥr**	
	Saudi Arabia	
70 C2	**Yancheng** China	
50 A3	**Yanchep** Austr.	
70 B2	**Yangcheng** China	
71 B3	**Yangchun** China	
65 B3	**Yangdok** N. Korea	
71 B3	**Yangjiang** China	
	Yangôn Myanmar *see*	
	Rangoon	
70 B2	**Yangquan** China	
71 B3	**Yangshuo** China	
70 C3	**Yangtze** *r.* China	
69 E2	**Yangtze, Mouth of the**	
	China	
70 B2	**Yangzhou** China	
65 B1	**Yanji** China	
137 D2	**Yankton** U.S.A.	
83 K2	**Yano-Indigirskaya**	
	Nizmennost' *lowland*	
	Rus. Fed.	
83 K2	**Yanskiy Zaliv** *g.* Rus. Fed.	
53 C1	**Yantabulla** Austr.	
70 C2	**Yantai** China	
118 B2	**Yaoundé** Cameroon	
59 D2	**Yap** *i.* Micronesia	
59 D3	**Yapen** *i.* Indon.	
59 D3	**Yapen, Selat** *sea chan.*	
	Indon.	
144 A2	**Yaqui** *r.* Mex.	
51 A2	**Yaraka** Austr.	
86 D3	**Yaransk** Rus. Fed.	
48 F3	**Yare** *r.* U.K.	
78 B3	**Yarîm** Yemen	
77 D3	**Yarkant He** *r.* China	
75 D2	**Yarlung Zangbo** *r.* China	
131 D2	**Yarmouth** Can.	
86 F2	**Yarongo** Rus. Fed.	
89 E2	**Yaroslavl'** Rus. Fed.	
66 D2	**Yaroslavsky** Rus. Fed.	
53 C3	**Yarram** Austr.	

89 D2	**Yartsevo** Rus. Fed.	
89 E3	**Yasnogorsk** Rus. Fed.	
63 B2	**Yasothon** Thai.	
53 C2	**Yass** Austr.	
111 C3	**Yatağan** Turkey	
129 E1	**Yathkyed Lake** Can.	
67 B4	**Yatsushiro** Japan	
150 B2	**Yavari** *r.* Brazil/Peru	
75 B2	**Yavatmal** India	
90 A2	**Yavoriv** Ukr.	
67 B4	**Yawatahama** Japan	
81 D2	**Yazd** Iran	
142 B2	**Yazoo City** U.S.A.	
111 B3	**Ydra** *i.* Greece	
63 A2	**Ye** Myanmar	
77 D3	**Yecheng** China	
144 B2	**Yécora** Mex.	
89 E3	**Yefremov** Rus. Fed.	
89 E2	**Yegor'yevsk** Rus. Fed.	
117 B4	**Yei** Sudan	
86 F3	**Yekaterinburg** Rus. Fed.	
89 E3	**Yelets** Rus. Fed.	
114 A3	**Yélimané** Mali	
96 □	**Yell** *i.* U.K.	
128 C1	**Yellowknife** Can.	
70 B2	**Yellow River** *r.* China	
69 E2	**Yellow Sea**	
	N. Pacific Ocean	
136 C1	**Yellowstone** *r.* U.S.A.	
136 A2	**Yellowstone Lake** U.S.A.	
88 C3	**Yel'sk** Belarus	
78 B3	**Yemen** *country* Asia	
86 E2	**Yemva** Rus. Fed.	
91 D2	**Yenakiyeve** Ukr.	
62 A1	**Yenangyaung** Myanmar	
62 B1	**Yên Bai** Vietnam	
114 B4	**Yendi** Ghana	
111 C3	**Yenice** Turkey	
111 C3	**Yenifoça** Turkey	
68 C1	**Yenisey** *r.* Rus. Fed.	
53 C2	**Yeoval** Austr.	
99 B3	**Yeovil** U.K.	
51 E2	**Yeppoon** Austr.	
83 I2	**Yerbogachen** Rus. Fed.	
81 C1	**Yerevan** Armenia	
77 D1	**Yereymentau** Kazakh.	
87 D3	**Yershov** Rus. Fed.	
65 B2	**Yesan** S. Korea	
77 C1	**Yesil'** Kazakh.	
111 C3	**Yeşilova** Turkey	
99 A3	**Yes Tor** *hill* U.K.	
53 D1	**Yetman** Austr.	
62 A1	**Ye-U** Myanmar	
104 B2	**Yeu, Île d'** *i.* France	
91 C2	**Yevpatoriya** Ukr.	
91 D2	**Yeysk** Rus. Fed.	
88 C2	**Yezyaryshcha** Belarus	
71 A3	**Yibin** China	
70 B2	**Yichang** China	
69 E1	**Yichun** *Heilong.* China	
71 B3	**Yichun** *Jiangxi* China	
110 C2	**Yıldız Dağları** *mts* Turkey	
80 B2	**Yıldızeli** Turkey	
70 A2	**Yinchuan** China	
65 B1	**Yingchengzi** China	
71 B3	**Yingde** China	
70 C1	**Yingkou** China	
70 B2	**Yingshan** *Hubei* China	
70 A2	**Yingshan** *Sichuan* China	
71 B3	**Yingtan** China	
77 E2	**Yining** China	
117 B4	**Yirga Alem** Eth.	
70 B2	**Yishui** China	
68 C2	**Yiwu** China	
71 B3	**Yiyang** China	
71 A3	**Yizhou** China	
92 I2	**Yli-Kitka** *l.* Fin.	
92 H2	**Ylitornio** Fin.	
92 H3	**Ylivieska** Fin.	
61 C2	**Yogyakarta** Indon.	

118 B2 **Yoko** Cameroon
67 C3 **Yokohama** Japan
115 D4 **Yola** Nigeria
67 D3 **Yonezawa** Japan
71 B3 **Yong'an** China
71 B3 **Yongchun** China
70 A2 **Yongdeng** China
65 B2 **Yŏngdŏk** S. Korea
71 C3 **Yongkang** China
62 B1 **Yongsheng** China
71 B3 **Yongzhou** China
150 A1 **Yopal** Col.
50 A3 **York** Austr.
98 C2 **York** U.K.
137 D2 **York** *NE* U.S.A.
141 D1 **York** *PA* U.S.A.
51 D1 **York, Cape** Austr.
52 A3 **Yorke Peninsula** Austr.
52 A3 **Yorketown** Austr.
98 C2 **Yorkshire Wolds** *hills* U.K.
129 D2 **Yorkton** Can.
87 D3 **Yoshkar-Ola** Rus. Fed.
97 C3 **Youghal** Ireland
53 C2 **Young** Austr.
52 A3 **Younghusband Peninsula**
      Austr.
140 C2 **Youngstown** U.S.A.
114 B3 **Youvarou** Mali
77 E2 **Youyi Feng** *mt.*
      China/Rus. Fed.
80 B2 **Yozgat** Turkey
134 B2 **Yreka** U.S.A.
      Yr Wyddfa *mt.* U.K. *see*
      Snowdon
105 C2 **Yssingeaux** France
93 F4 **Ystad** Sweden
      Ysyk-Köl Kyrg. *see* Balykchy
92 □A3 **Ytri-Rangá** *r.* Iceland
92 C2 **Ysyk-Köl** *salt l.* Kyrg.
72 B1 **Yuanjiang** China
62 B1 **Yuan Jiang** *r.* China
62 B1 **Yuanmou** China
135 B3 **Yuba City** U.S.A.
66 D2 **Yūbari** Japan
146 B2 **Yucatán** *pen.* Mex.
146 B2 **Yucatan Channel**
      Cuba/Mex.
50 C2 **Yuendumu** Austr.
71 B3 **Yueyang** China
86 F2 **Yugorsk** Rus. Fed.
      Yugoslavia *country* Europe
      see Bosnia-Herzegovina,
      Croatia, Macedonia,
      Montenegro, Serbia,
      Slovenia
83 L2 **Yukagirskoye**
      Ploskogor'ye *plat.*
      Rus. Fed.
126 A2 **Yukon** *r.* Can./U.S.A.
128 A1 **Yukon Territory** *admin. div.*
      Can.
71 B3 **Yulin** *Guangxi* China
70 A2 **Yulin** *Shaanxi* China
62 B1 **Yulong Xueshan** *mt.* China
138 A2 **Yuma** *AZ* U.S.A.
136 C2 **Yuma** *CO* U.S.A.
68 C2 **Yumen** China
80 B2 **Yunak** Turkey
71 B3 **Yuncheng** China
71 B3 **Yunfu** China
62 B1 **Yunnan** *prov.* China
52 A2 **Yunta** Austr.
70 B2 **Yunyang** China
150 A2 **Yurimaguas** Peru
77 E3 **Yurungkax He** *r.* China
71 C3 **Yü Shan** *mt.* Taiwan
68 C2 **Yushu** China
      Yushuwan China *see*
      Huaihua
81 C1 **Yusufeli** Turkey

77 E3 **Yutian** China
62 B1 **Yuxi** China
66 D2 **Yuzhno-Kuril'sk** Rus. Fed.
83 K3 **Yuzhno-Sakhalinsk**
      Rus. Fed.
91 C2 **Yuzhnoukrayinsk** Ukr.
69 D2 **Yuzhou** China
104 C2 **Yvetot** France

Z

100 B1 **Zaandam** Neth.
69 D1 **Zabaykal'sk** Rus. Fed.
78 B3 **Zabid** Yemen
76 C3 **Zābol** Iran
79 D2 **Zāboli** Iran
144 B3 **Zacapa** Mex.
144 B2 **Zacatecas** Mex.
145 C3 **Zacatepec** Mex.
145 C3 **Zacatlán** Mex.
111 B3 **Zacharo** Greece
144 B2 **Zacoalco** Mex.
145 C3 **Zacualtipán** Mex.
109 C2 **Zadar** Croatia
63 A3 **Zadetkyi Kyun** *i.* Myanmar
89 E3 **Zadonsk** Rus. Fed.
106 B2 **Zafra** Spain
109 C1 **Zagreb** Croatia
      Zagros, Kūhhā-ye *mts* Iran
      see Zagros Mountains
81 C2 **Zagros Mountains** Iran
79 D2 **Zāhedān** Iran
80 B2 **Zahlé** Lebanon
78 B3 **Zahrān** Saudi Arabia
      Zaire *country* Africa *see*
      Congo, Democratic
      Republic of the
109 D2 **Zaječar** Serb. and Mont.
89 E3 **Zakharovo** Rus. Fed.
81 C2 **Zākhō** Iraq
111 B3 **Zakynthos** Greece
111 B3 **Zakynthos** *i.* Greece
103 D2 **Zalaegerszeg** Hungary
110 B1 **Zalău** Romania
78 B2 **Zalim** Saudi Arabia
117 A3 **Zalingei** Sudan
78 A2 **Zalmā, Jabal az** *mt.*
      Saudi Arabia
128 C2 **Zama City** Can.
121 C2 **Zambeze** *r.* Moz.
120 B2 **Zambezi** *r.* Africa
120 B2 **Zambezi** Zambia
120 B2 **Zambia** *country* Africa
64 B2 **Zamboanga** Phil.
64 B2 **Zamboanga Peninsula**
      Phil.
106 B1 **Zamora** Spain
144 B3 **Zamora de Hidalgo** Mex.
103 E1 **Zamość** Pol.
71 C3 **Zandè** China
100 B2 **Zandvliet** Belgium
140 C3 **Zanesville** U.S.A.
81 C2 **Zanjān** Iran
75 B1 **Zanskar Mountains** India
      Zante *i.* Greece *see*
      Zakynthos
119 D3 **Zanzibar** Tanz.
119 D3 **Zanzibar Island** Tanz.
89 E3 **Zaokskiy** Rus. Fed.
115 C2 **Zaouiatallaz** Alg.
70 B2 **Zaozhuang** China
89 D2 **Zapadnaya Dvina** *r.* Europe
89 D2 **Zapadnaya Dvina**
      Rus. Fed.
68 B1 **Zapadnyy Sayan** *reg.*
      Rus. Fed.
139 D3 **Zapata** U.S.A.

92 J2 **Zapolyarnyy** Rus. Fed.
91 D2 **Zaporizhzhya** Ukr.
101 E2 **Zappendorf** Ger.
80 B2 **Zara** Turkey
145 B2 **Zaragoza** Mex.
107 C1 **Zaragoza** Spain
76 B3 **Zarand** Iran
76 C3 **Zaranj** Afgh.
88 C2 **Zarasai** Lith.
89 E3 **Zaraysk** Rus. Fed.
150 A1 **Zaraza** Venez.
115 C3 **Zaria** Nigeria
90 B1 **Zarichne** Ukr.
81 D3 **Zarqān** Iran
66 B2 **Zarubino** Rus. Fed.
103 D1 **Żary** Pol.
115 D1 **Zarzis** Tunisia
123 C3 **Zastron** S. Africa
69 E1 **Zavitinsk** Rus. Fed.
103 D1 **Zawiercie** Pol.
77 E2 **Zaysan** Lake Kazakh.
      Zaysan, Ozero *l.* Kazakh.
      see Zaysan, Lake
90 B1 **Zdolbuniv** Ukr.
93 F4 **Zealand** *i.* Denmark
100 A2 **Zeebrugge** Belgium
123 C2 **Zeerust** S. Africa
50 C2 **Zeil, Mount** Austr.
101 F2 **Zeitz** Ger.
88 B3 **Zelenogradsk** Rus. Fed.
82 E1 **Zemlya Aleksandry** *i.*
      Rus. Fed.
82 F1 **Zemlya Vil'cheka** *i.*
      Rus. Fed.
107 D2 **Zemmora** Alg.
145 C3 **Zempoaltépetl, Nudo de**
      mt. Mex.
65 B1 **Zengfeng Shan** *mt.* China
105 D2 **Zermatt** Switz.
91 E2 **Zernograd** Rus. Fed.
100 C1 **Zeulenroda** Ger.
101 D1 **Zeven** Ger.
100 C2 **Zevenaar** Neth.
83 J3 **Zeya** Rus. Fed.
79 C2 **Zeydābād** Iran
83 J3 **Zeyskoye Vodokhranilishche**
      resr Rus. Fed.
103 D1 **Zgierz** Pol.
88 B3 **Zhabinka** Belarus
76 A2 **Zhalpaktal** Kazakh.
77 C1 **Zhaltyr** Kazakh.
76 B2 **Zhanaozen** Kazakh.
      Zhangde China *see* Anyang
71 B3 **Zhangjiajie** China
70 B3 **Zhangjiakou** China
71 B3 **Zhangping** China
71 A3 **Zhangshu** China
68 C2 **Zhangye** China
71 B3 **Zhangzhou** China
87 D4 **Zhanibek** Kazakh.
71 B3 **Zhanjiang** China
71 B3 **Zhao'an** China
71 B3 **Zhaoqing** China
71 A3 **Zhaotong** China
75 C1 **Zhari Namco** *salt l.* China
77 E2 **Zharkent** Kazakh.
89 D2 **Zharkovskiy** Rus. Fed.
77 E2 **Zharma** Kazakh.
90 C2 **Zhashkiv** Ukr.
71 C3 **Zhejiang** *prov.* China
82 F1 **Zhelaniya, Mys** *c.*
      Rus. Fed.
89 E3 **Zheleznogorsk** Rus. Fed.
70 A2 **Zhenba** China
71 A3 **Zheng'an** China
71 B3 **Zhenghe** China
70 B2 **Zhengzhou** China
71 A3 **Zhenyuan** China
91 E1 **Zherdevka** Rus. Fed.
86 D2 **Zheshart** Rus. Fed.

77 C2 **Zhezkazgan**
Karagandinskaya Oblast'
Kazakh.
77 C2 **Zhezkazgan**
Karagandinskaya Oblast'
Kazakh.
83 J2 **Zhigansk** Rus. Fed.
Zhi Qu *r.* China *see* **Yangtze**
76 C1 **Zhitikara** Kazakh.
88 D3 **Zhlobin** Belarus
90 B2 **Zhmerynka** Ukr.
74 A1 **Zhob** Pak.
83 L1 **Zhokhova, Ostrov** *i.*
Rus. Fed.
75 C2 **Zhongba** China
Zhonghe China *see* **Xiushan**
70 A2 **Zhongning** China
71 B3 **Zhongshan** China
Zhongshan China *see*
Lupanshui
70 A2 **Zhongwei** China
Zhongxin China *see*
Xianggelila
70 B2 **Zhoukou** China
70 C2 **Zhoushan** China
91 C2 **Zhovti Vody** Ukr.
65 A2 **Zhuanghe** China
70 B2 **Zhucheng** China
89 D3 **Zhukovka** Rus. Fed.
89 E2 **Zhukovskiy** Rus. Fed.
70 B2 **Zhumadian** China
Zhuoyang China *see*
Suiping
71 B3 **Zhuzhou** *Hunan* China
71 B3 **Zhuzhou** *Hunan* China
90 A2 **Zhydachiv** Ukr.

88 C3 **Zhytkavichy** Belarus
90 B1 **Zhytomyr** Ukr.
103 D2 **Žiar nad Hronom**
Slovakia
70 B2 **Zibo** China
103 D1 **Zielona Góra** Pol.
62 A1 **Zigaing** Myanmar
71 A3 **Zigong** China
114 A3 **Ziguinchor** Senegal
144 B3 **Zihuatanejo** Mex.
103 D2 **Žilina** Slovakia
83 H3 **Zima** Rus. Fed.
144 B2 **Zimapán** Mex.
121 B2 **Zimbabwe** *country*
Africa
114 A4 **Zimmi** Sierra Leone
110 C2 **Zimnicea** Romania
115 C3 **Zinder** Niger
78 B3 **Zinjibär** Yemen
103 D2 **Zirc** Hungary
62 A1 **Ziro** India
79 C2 **Zïr Rüd** Iran
103 D2 **Zistersdorf** Austria
145 B3 **Zitácuaro** Mex.
103 C1 **Zittau** Ger.
87 E3 **Zlatoust** Rus. Fed.
103 D2 **Zlín** Czech Rep.
89 D3 **Zlynka** Rus. Fed.
89 E3 **Zmiyevka** Rus. Fed.
91 D2 **Zmiyiv** Ukr.
89 E3 **Znamenka** *Orlovskaya*
Oblast' Rus. Fed.
91 E1 **Znamenka** *Tambovskaya*
Oblast' Rus. Fed.
91 C2 **Znam"yanka** Ukr.
103 D2 **Znojmo** Czech Rep.

91 D1 **Zolochiv** *Kharkivs'ka Oblast'*
Ukr.
90 A2 **Zolochiv** *L'vivs'ka Oblast'*
Ukr.
91 C2 **Zolotonosha** Ukr.
89 E3 **Zolotukhino** Rus. Fed.
121 C2 **Zomba** Malawi
80 B1 **Zonguldak** Turkey
105 D3 **Zonza** *Corsica* France
114 B4 **Zorzor** Liberia
115 D2 **Zouar** Chad
114 A2 **Zouérat** Maur.
109 D1 **Zrenjanin** Serb. and Mont.
89 D2 **Zubtsov** Rus. Fed.
105 D2 **Zug** Switz.
81 C1 **Zugdidi** Georgia
106 B2 **Zújar** *r.* Spain
100 C2 **Zülpich** Ger.
121 C2 **Zumbo** Moz.
145 C3 **Zumpango** Mex.
138 B1 **Zuni Mountains** U.S.A.
71 A3 **Zunyi** China
109 C1 **Županja** Croatia
105 D2 **Zürich** Switz.
100 C1 **Zutphen** Neth.
115 D1 **Zuwärah** Libya
90 C2 **Zvenyhorodka** Ukr.
121 C3 **Zvishavane** Zimbabwe
103 D2 **Zvolen** Slovakia
109 C2 **Zvornik** Bos.-Herz.
123 C3 **Zwelitsha** S. Africa
103 D2 **Zwettl** Austria
101 F2 **Zwickau** Ger.
100 C1 **Zwolle** Neth.
83 L2 **Zyryanka** Rus. Fed.